The International Retirement Directory

Editors

David & Daniel Creffield

M

Millfield Publishing – England

Colin Miller
Director of Publishing

First published 2010

Copyright © Millfield Publishing 2010

Millfield Publishing, Brighton Media Centre
15-17 Middle Street,
Brighton, Sussex BN15 1AL, United Kingdom
Tel +44 (0) 1273 648909
Fax +44 (0) 1273 201379
info@internationalretirement.co.uk
www.internationalretirement.co.uk

British Library Cataloguing in Publication Data.
A CIP record for this book is available from the
British Library.
ISBN 978-0-9561935-0-6

Design & layout: Graphic Traffic

Printed and bound in England
by Newman Thompson

Acknowledgements

The authors are indebted to the many contributors to this book who, by sharing their own experiences, give our readers the opportunity to sample life in countries in many corners of the world before, they too, make a life-changing decision about their own retirement.

Why not share your story?

Have you already retired abroad? Or are you planning to do so? Sharing your experiences will help readers with their own decisions about where to retire abroad and what to expect.

Your story could be published in the next edition of the International Retirement Directory.

Interested? Send us a brief synopsis by post to the address on the opposite page or by email to: editor@internationalretirement.co.uk

Contents

Country profiles

Join the queue soon or risk being the last one to leave

One in 12 British pensioners now lives abroad and one in five will be doing so by 2050

What is that we Brits don't like about living here? Whatever it is, it's driving us to move abroad at the extraordinary rate of almost 200,000 a year, about half of whom are retirees.

If you believe the endless reports and surveys that are churned out on the subject by all kinds of institutions and companies for all sorts of reasons, most of us would prefer nothing more than being somewhere else – almost anywhere else.

While many retirees may be perfectly happy to settle for a couple of weeks holiday on the Med once or twice a year, you're reading this because the thought of retiring somewhere sunny with a leisurely pace of life figures often in your daytime dreams.

You want to be among the tens of thousands of

Britons who turn their retirement years into a new life of adventure, allowing the sun to warm your bones, tan your skin and nourish your social life.

You would like to be somewhere more exotic than the UK, probably in a community of like-minded people and preferably where your money goes further.

Over a million Britons already draw their state pension overseas and the number is set to increase enormously.

According to 'Brits Abroad', a report by the independent think tank IPPR (the Institute for Public Policy Research), more than 3.3 million British pensioners – one in five – will be living overseas by 2050 and a government report published in March, 2010 found that 42 per cent of people aged over 55 said

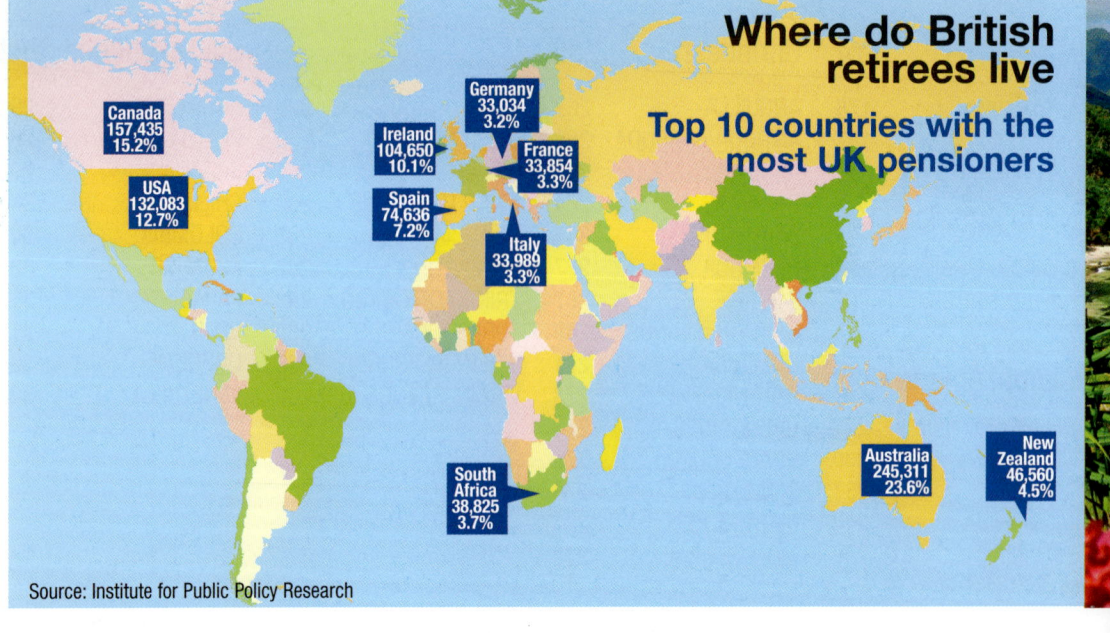

Where do British retirees live

Top 10 countries with the most UK pensioners

Canada 157,435 15.2%

Ireland 104,650 10.1%

Germany 33,034 3.2%

France 33,854 3.3%

USA 132,083 12.7%

Spain 74,636 7.2%

Italy 33,989 3.3%

South Africa 38,825 3.7%

Australia 245,311 23.6%

New Zealand 46,560 4.5%

Source: Institute for Public Policy Research

British pensioners abroad – a forecast

Britons of pensionable age	2010	2020	2030	2040	2050
	12,218,000	12,544,000	15,057,000	16,806,000	17,512,000
Briton of pensionable age overseas	1,196,000	1,516,000	2,166,000	2,805,000	3,325,000
% British pensioners overseas	9.8%	12.1%	14.4%	16.7%	19%

Source: Institute for Public Policy Research

they were thinking of relocating overseas with 38 per cent considering doing so within the next five years.

The chart on the opposite page tells the story of the numbers who live abroad.

But what about the reasons?

Why we want to go

If we wait long enough global warming might address our No. 1 complaint about life in Britain – the weather. It's this factor that appears at the top of most people's list when giving reasons for wanting to retire overseas.

Global warming might help. The 'best guess' is that it could raise average temperatures by up to 5°C but, one, that isn't very much and, two, most of us don't have enough time left to see the benefits since that forecast is for the end of the century!

There's another worrying aspect of global warming; it will, according to some scientists, flood dozens of the world's major cities, including London, by the end of the century. They say vast areas of the country, including the whole of Norfolk, could disappear under the sea. The threat comes from melting ice sheets in

Greenland and Antarctica, which could cause sea levels to rise by up to 20ft by 2100.

This would exacerbate another of our problems: overcrowding.

The population density of England has overtaken that of Holland to become the highest in Europe (not counting Malta which has 1,274 people per square km). The figure for England is 395 and in Britain overall it's 253.

This overcrowding is not helped by immigration levels – another reason high on the list of reasons retirees give for wishing to leave.

Ironically, while we might find the UK dull, overcrowded and with lousy weather, our country is a magnet to would-be immigrants from all over the world.

According to the Office of National Statistics, Britain admitted about four million immigrants between 2000-2008. By 2050, according to the UN, the UK population will have risen from 61 million to 72 million, almost entirely through immigration. Our own government forecasts that the 70 million mark will be reached by 2028.

Where we want to go

Some 112 countries are estimated to have British populations of more than 1,000. The largest groups of British retirees live in Australia, Canada, the USA, Ireland, Spain and New Zealand but this is not a modern picture of migration and the statistics are distorted by the many thousands of Britons who moved to the 'old' colonies decades ago and never bothered to give up their UK citizenship.

Today's retirees seeking a haven abroad are most likely to look first at the Mediterranean – Spain, Portugal, Italy, Greece and Cyprus being the favourites.

These countries have their obvious merits – you can flit back and forth relatively inexpensively, being the main one – but property bargains are harder to find and the cost of living is sometimes more than it is here, making life increasingly expensive for those on a pension.

Mediterranean winters may be milder but if you've ever taken a winter holiday on the Costas or the Greek islands you will know it can be pretty miserable.

The 'old' colonies

Australia, New Zealand Canada and the USA may welcome our young, skilled workers, but these 'old' colonies create the most barriers to retiree immigration from the UK. Money is the key that will open the door. And you need plenty of it.

Another disadvantage is the cost of long haul flights if you want to come 'home' from time or receive visits from friends and relatives you have left behind.

All four countries have a visa of one sort or another to admit affluent retirees.

Australia has an 'Investor Retirement Visa'. To live in a 'high-growth urban area', you'll need to invest AUS$750,000 (about £422,000) and have an income of at least AUS$65,000 (£36,000) a year on top.

It gets cheaper if you opt for a low-growth area. These visas allow you to live out your days there as long as the level of income and investment remain but do not lead to Australian permanent residence or citizenship.

New Zealand offers two investor categories; under the 'Investor Plus' category you must 'nominate' (that means bring in) funds/assets equivalent to at least NZ$10 million – not far short of £5 million.

There is no maximum age.

The second option is much cheaper – you need about £1 million - but you must be no older than 65.

There are two options under **Canada's** Business Immigration Program: The Entrepreneur program and the Investor Immigration program.

For the first you require net assets worth $300,000 (about £180,000) and you must have 'the ability and intention' to establish or purchase a business with an investment of at least $125,000 (£76,000) and one that will create jobs for one to three Canadians.

You get this back after five years but with no interest.

Under the Investor Program you have to prove you have successfully operated a business outside Canada and have a net worth of C$800,000 (£487,000) and make an investment of half that amount in an approved fund (fixed deposit) for a five-year period.

As far as **America** is concerned you can spend up to 90 days per visit without a visa or up to 180 days with a B-2 visa. This, the so-called 'snowbird' visa, is usually issued for 10 years and allows a stay of six months at a time.

The E2 visa is a non-immigrant visa allowing investors to live in the US with their family members (spouses and unmarried children under 21). E-2 visas are generally issued for four or five years, with extensions of the same period.

However, these are 'non-immigrant' visas and renewal cannot be taken for granted. The level of investment is flexible but needs to be around $150,000-$400,000 (£96,000-256,000) depending on location.

A better bet – since it leads to a Green Card and permanent residence – is the EB-5 category created in 1990 with the aim of attracting foreign capital and creating jobs for American workers. Ten thousand are available a year and just over 4,000 were issued in 2009.

EB-5 applicants have to invest $1 million in a new commercial enterprise that employs 10 people although the investment level is reduced to $500,000 if the new enterprise is in an area of high unemployment.

The investor applies for a temporary Green Card, valid for two years, and if after that period the investment is still in the business the investor receives a permanent Green Card.

Further afield

While southern Europe and the 'old' colonies may be the most popular choice, today's retirees are being successfully wooed by dozens of countries around the world that offer visas to 'affluent' Western retirees, often with an enticing package of benefits.

With their warm seas and year-round sunshine, these far-flung tropical and sub-tropical countries are becoming increasingly popular with the more adventurous. They include countries from **Malaysia** to **Mexico**, **Belize** to **Bolivia** and **Panama** to the **Philippines.**

Panama's Pensionado programme is considered one of the best in the world and offers 'seniors' income tax exemption, a 20-year property tax holiday and discounts on everything from cinema tickets to doctor visits.

All Panama requires is proof of a minimum income of US$1,000 per month plus an additional US$200pm for each dependent.

Here are some other examples:

- Thailand wants you to have £14,000 in the bank and an annual income equivalent to at least £14,000.
- For Malaysia it's assets worth a minimum of £66,000 and a pension income of £1,900 a month.
- If Peru appeals you need evidence of a permanent income of at least US$1,000 a month and US$500 for each dependent.

Healthcare

If you are of retirement age – or heading that way – access to healthcare in the retirement country of your choice will be important to you. In some EU countries, the healthcare system may not cover all the costs or provide all the services you would normally expect from the NHS.

Just as important for you to know is that once you have retired abroad – and informed the UK authorities that you have done so – you lose automatic right to NHS healthcare. This applies if you have moved abroad for a period longer than three months.

If you retire within Europe, the European Health Insurance Card (EHIC) allows you to access state-provided healthcare in all the European Economic Area (EEA) countries and Switzerland at a reduced cost or sometimes free of charge.

You can apply for the card at www.direct.gov.uk/en/Dio11

To access healthcare services within the EEA you must obtain form E121 that entitles you to health-care cover at the same level as a pensioner of the host country. Remember, you can only use the E121 if you are of pensionable age.

You can obtain form E121 from the DWP when you inform them of your plans to move abroad. The E121 is only valid once it has been registered with the scheme in the country you are moving to.

There is comprehensive explanation at: www.ageconcern.org.uk (Age Concern is now Age UK) or you can download a useful document at: www.firststopcareadvice.org.uk

There is also a detailed country-by-country summary at: www.nhs.uk/NHSEngland/Healthcareabroad/Pages/EEAcountries.aspx

It is important to remember that each member country's health system is different and might not include all the things you would expect to get free of charge from the NHS, dentistry for example.

In some countries you may have to make a patient contribution to the cost of your care. In others you may have to pay all charges up front and claim back the charges later so it's important to keep your receipts.

Outside Europe

The following countries have reciprocal healthcare arrangements with the UK which normally gives you access to some level of treatment.

Anguila	Kazakhstan
Armenia	Kyrgyzstan
Australia	Macedonia
Azerbaijan	Moldova
Barbados	Montserrat
Belarus	New Zealand
Bosnia/Herzegovina	Russia
British Virgin Islands	St Helena
Channel Islands	Serbia & Montenegro
Croatia	Tajikistan
Falkland Islands	Turkmenistan
Georgia	Turks & Caicos Isles
Gibraltar	Uzbekistan
Isle of Man	Ukraine

Find out more at: www.nhs.uk/NHSEngland/Healthcareabroad

If your retirement destination is a country that is outside these arrangements you obviously need to take out private healthcare which, depending on your choice of country, can cost an arm or a leg – or both, and the older you are, the more expensive it becomes.

While the quality of healthcare in the USA may be the highest you can find anywhere, it is no good if you don't have the money to pay for it. And routine medical costs are frighteningly high.

How much?

Examples: A visit to the doctor: $100. An overnight hospital stay: $600.

Fidelity Brokerage Services LLC estimates that an average 65-year-old in the USA should budget for at least $645 monthly or $7,740 annually in healthcare expenses.

And be warned: When you take out insurance, undeclared, pre-existing conditions are the biggest single reason for claims being rejected.

Some insurers will accept people of any age while others have an age limit. Over the age of 50, premiums rocket.

Language

This is certainly something you need to think about – not if you move to Australia, New Zealand, Canada and the USA – but if the Med's your choice you will really need to learn the language. Do so and you'll adapt more quickly, get greater respect and integrate more easily into the local community. However, many people never bother and are perfectly content to socialise within their own community.

If you're not up to learning a language and want to be somewhere hot, there are still plenty of options. In the Far East, Malaysia and the Philippines are English speaking and, even in Indonesia and Thailand, English is fairly widely spoken.

You won't have any communication problems in the **Caribbean**, or in countries such as **Egypt** and, in Central America, **Belize**, **Panama**, **Costa Rica** and **Mexico**.

You'll find it harder though in South America where it makes sense to learn some basic Spanish – or Portuguese in the case of Brazil. While English is generally understood in the main towns and cities, you'll find it harder to get by in rural areas.

Another major consideration is travel times and costs. How often would you want to return to the UK? A home somewhere on the Mediterranean will guarantee you plenty of visitors from home but you won't see many if you move to Malaysia or Mexico.

Can you afford it?

Money is, of course, a consideration. If you're rich you can retire to just about anywhere you care to. If, like most of us, you have to consider financial constraints you need to do some research or get advice. Or both.

Tax laws vary from country to country and there are many traps for the unwary. In Spain and France, for example, there is a tax on your worldwide assets.

You must research these topics carefully or pay experts to assess your position regarding income tax, inheritance tax, wealth or capital gains tax.

Obtaining non-resident status will normally mean you will be exempt from paying UK tax on any income paid outside the UK but your visits home should not average 91 days or more in a tax year.

Proceed with caution

We can't find comparable figures for the UK, but in the USA, although individuals aged 60 or older make up just 15 per cent of population, they account for 30 per cent of fraud victims.

Those in this age group are targeted for obvious reasons: as they edge into retirement they are more likely to have substantial funds and the need to find a safe and profitable haven for them.

The oldest rip-offs remain the most popular – Ponzi and pyramid schemes and 'high-return, risk free' investments – but property, and overseas property in particular, is another minefield for the unwary.

We've all seen the horror stories: developers go bust or disappear leaving you with a half-built apartment

... or nothing; you may often have to wait months – sometimes years – before the title deeds turn up and you can't sell without them.

Will the quality of work match the specs? It often doesn't. What you see isn't always what you get.

All too often, the developer runs short of money and the promised communal facilities – pool, tennis courts, etc. – don't materialise.

It seems extraordinary but many people buy property abroad not only without ever having seen it, but sometimes without even having ever visited the country.

There's nothing wrong with buying off-plan properties – this form of investment can be incredibly profitable – but your due diligence needs to be very thorough.

Do your homework

The first question: Is it too good to be true?

Don't allow yourself to be herded into a presentation where you are urged to 'sign now or miss the opportunity of a lifetime'. These presentations are often accompanied by glossy brochures with a smiling 'Mr and Mrs G. from Walthamstow', pictured outside their Spanish villa.

In any case, buying off-plan will often cost you more than buying a similar resale property

In the UK we are used to – and comfortable with – our high street solicitor taking care of the tedious searches relating to property purchase: all that stuff about drainage, access rights, subsidence, land title registry and so forth.

Abroad it's not so safe. Don't, for example, rely on the lawyer recommended by the agent. He may be

perfectly OK but ... and, of course, your property purchase will not be covered by UK legislation.

When you're in touch with agents you don't know be wary of 0800 numbers and accommodation addresses, both commonly used by overseas agents to make you believe they are based in the UK.

Then there's the taxman

Apart from the crooks trying to part you from your money there are perfectly legitimate organisations, which want to share it. Chief among them is the taxman. Domicile is the key word here and it is particularly relevant to inheritance tax rather than income and capital gains tax.

If you are not domiciled in the UK your personal income from dividends, capital gains and interest paid outside is not normally taxable unless you transfer those funds to the UK.

Inheritance tax is a different kettle of fish.

You will see in some of the country sections in this book that some have no inheritance tax; property companies where this is the case will, quite fairly, be quick to draw your attention to the fact.

However, that does not mean the UK taxman will not want to get his hands on your money via the IHT laws.

It is very important to understand this business of domicile since, no matter where in the world you live, the Inland Revenue will do its best to classify you as being domiciled in the UK which means that when you die, your entire estate could become liable to inheritance tax rates of up to 40 per cent.

UK inheritance tax will still apply to an overseas property if you were domiciled in the UK in the previous three tax years, or if you were resident in 17 of the previous 20 tax years.

Editor's Note – currency conversion

In just a few months the pound has lost about a third of its value against the euro and a fifth against the US dollar.

For those planning to buy a property abroad, the decline of sterling against other currencies can be a painful experience. On the purchase of a £300,000 property in Spain, for example, a few short months meant the buyer had to stump up an additional £20,000.

Conversely, the weakness of the pound has been a benefit for those selling an overseas property.

Because of this volatility and in order to be as faithful to the original figure as possible, we have

retained prices and costs in their original form – US dollars, euros or pounds – relying on readers' willingness to make their own conversions where necessary. The exception is where we have tried to give readers a quick 'at-a-glance' idea of prices.

For those saving to buy an overseas property one option is for buyers to protect themselves from currency fluctuations by opening euro or dollar denominated accounts – or both.

This can, of course, work for or against you but the advantage is that you can convert currencies between accounts when exchange rates are most favourable.

Meet our contributors
Europe

Barbara & Art Skinner

With 50 flights a week from the UK in the summer, **Croatia** is an ideal retirement destination for those who want to keep a foot in each country.

The writer of our Croatia country section, estate agent **Aleksandra Kallay** manages to do that. What's great about Croatia? "Laid-back, friendly, good food – great sea-food – sun, crystal clear waters, beautiful islands and wild natural landscapes," says Aleksandra.

George Bernard Shaw, enchanted by the Croatian capital, shared this view. It was, he said, "the pearl of the Adriatic", adding, "those who seek paradise on earth should come to Dubrovnik."

David Greenwood who wrote our section on **Cyprus** retired there with his wife Margaret in 2001. Two other contributors describe their lives there.

Malcolm and **Jean Goulding** sensibly chose a large three-bedroom villa when they retired to Cyprus in 2007 to ensure there was going to be enough space for visits from their five children and six grandchildren. They chose Cyprus after briefly considering Portugal.

Karon and **Barry Leese** beat the Gouldings by about a year, taking early retirement and moving to nearby Paphos in 2006. Apart from the bureaucracy which "can drive you mad, we love living by the sea in a country where the sun shines nearly all year and where we can enjoy a quieter and calmer way of life."

David Seymour wrote our main section on **France** and begins his section by asking – and answering – the question: "What is it about France that casts a spell on us? Is it the rich history, culture and cuisine or the exquisitely beautiful French countryside where you can step back in time to a less stressful era?"

Answering a similar question, **Sharon Colback**, one of two other contributors to the section, paints a blissful picture of life in rural France: "It offers the luxury of space, peace and a stress-free, unhurried pace of life ...

"Throughout the year we have fetes and festivals, music and storytelling and feasting for any reason – or none."

Brian and **Carol McDermott** chose the other end of France when they retired early to Brittany's Cote d'Armor region. Too early, they decided and opened a cattery instead.

Italy, with its rich cultural history, wonderful cuisine, music and art, is the choice of large numbers of retirees, not only from northern Europe but also from North America and elsewhere.

Our two writers, **Barbara Skinner** and **Valerie Schneider**, are both American.

Valerie, former travel professional and now a freelance writer, "cappuccino drinker and tour guide," moved to Italy in 2006. Barbara may describes herself as "a realist,

Colin Davies

Cameron Deggin

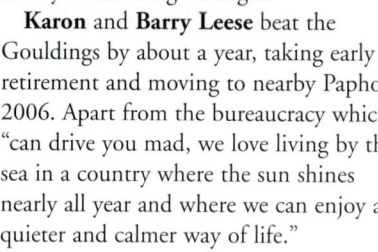

Sharon Colback

Aleksandra Kallay

Karon and Barry Leese

Kevin Galea Pace

Malcolm and Jean Goulding

Valerie Schneider

Alan and Lesley Woodward

Brian and Carol McDermott

Violet King

Rhona Hutchinson

not a dreamer" but it was to find a dream that led her and her husband Art to move from Kentucky to Umbria in 2002.

Maltese Australian **Kevin Galea Pace**, who wrote our section on **Malta**, moved with his family to Melbourne as a child. Now he's back in Malta – "a friendly, laid-back island in the middle of the Mediterranean, where the sea is clear and the climate mild and warm."

The content for our **Portugal** section is courtesy of **Simon Pownall's** Expatsportugal.com, an entertaining and useful resource for those thinking of moving to Portugal. **Corinne Frieden**, a contributor to the website, and her husband have lived in Portugal for four years. By the time you read this, they will have left and Cori's diary makes rather sad reading.

She explains what has finally driven them away.

Sail about 700 miles west of Portugal and – if your sextant is accurate – you might be lucky enough to hit the **Azores**, a group of nine islands located in the Atlantic and an autonomous region of Portugal.

That's what Britons **Alan** and **Lesley Woodward** did after a decade of round-the-world sailing adventures. They liked what they saw, eventually returning to the islands to make their home there.

We have three contributors to the **Spain** section: **Rhona Hutchinson**, who was responsible for the main section, **Violet King** and **Colin Davies**.

Born and brought up in Argentina, Rhona has worked with leading estate agents in London and Spain where she has lived for about 20 years.

Violet, who retired to the Costa Blanca in 1999 with husband Philip, says: "There is so much wonderful to say about life here but the explosion of newcomers has played a big part in things becoming chaotic at times."

Colin, a writer who lives in the north-west of Spain finds time to "enjoy the relaxing, fun-oriented life that Spain offers".

We include the Canary Islands in the Spain section, the winter destination of choice of millions of sun-starved snowbirds from northern Europe. Our section on the Canary Islands comes from the www.spanish-living.com website.

Why should retirees consider **Turkey?** "Simple," says **Cameron Deggin** of this increasingly popular destination, "sunshine, natural beauty, friendly people and a low cost of living."

Meet our contributors

Melanie Benna and family

Middle East & Africa

Cheryl Thomas

Born and raised in South Wales, **Cheryl Thomas** moved to Birmingham when she was 18 and had a 33-year career in the leisure industry. She first visited **Cape Verde** in 2005 to investigate the investment potential of the islands.

Follow-up visits convinced Cheryl not to return to her day job in the UK and eventually she followed her own advice to make her home there.

Our section on **Egypt** was put together with help from **Ian Marsh** of Think-Egypt who advises the Egyptian Government on "residential tourism" – a term it uses to turn tourists into property buyers.

Another valuable contribution is provided by **Graham** and **Pauline Warren**, who sold up in Britain in 2004, crammed their possessions into two suitcases and retired to Luxor where they share their small villa with four dogs and their cat Molly.

Melanie Benna, originally from Nottinghamshire, swapped life in a three-bedroomed terrace house in Ramsgate for a seven-bedroomed villa in **Tunisia**. A glamourous mother of six, Melanie and her husband run a property business there and are well placed to advise retirees on life and property purchase.

Don't presume **Diane Niemiec** leads a frivolous lifestyle in the **UAE** capital of **Abu Dhabi** just because she confesses to indulging herself in the standard expat lifestyle activities of 'sunbathing, drinking coffee and shopping' since Diane, originally from West Yorkshire, also occupies much of her time doing voluntary work with runaway maids who have been abused by their employers.

Diane Niemiec

Ian Marsh

Graham and Pauline Warren

Asia & the Far East

The **Far East** holds considerable allure for retirees. Developers and real estate companies in Thailand, Malaysia, the Philippines and Indonesia have grown rich on the dreams of Western retirees to live in these exotic countries.

Those in Goa would like to do the same; with its sleepy towns and perfect beaches, this Indian state should be an idyllic retirement location, but it gets a pretty bad press when it comes to the treatment of foreign residents.

Our section on **Goa** was provided with help from **Tony Clack** and **Hugh Taylor** who run the interesting and useful website www.laterlife.com

Goa comes in for a lot of stick from a variety of sources on the Internet and from a British couple, **Martin Smith** and his wife **Sue**, who have left Goa with bitter memories. Their story starts: "Goodbye Goa – it's a shame it had to end this way."

Two writers are responsible for our section on **Indonesia**: American **Danielle Surkatty,** who runs a website for foreigners living there, and Briton **Rachel Lovelock** who has lived in Bali since 1998 and is the author of numerous magazine and newspaper articles on Bali and Indonesia.

Danielle's advice: "Make friends with the local people, learn the language, acknowledge the dangers, take care on the roads, accept the things you can't change, embrace the challenges."

Hugh Taylor

Nancy & Roger Lindley

Vicky Gray

Margaret and Gordon Penny

Australasia

Rachel Lovelock

Neil & Jorva Hamilton

Kevin Butters

Bob Holland

Danielle Surkatty

You would expect a an ex-copper to have an eye for detail and the man responsible for the comprehensive section on **Malaysia** is **Bob Holland** who retired to Penang with his wife **Elena** in 1997 after serving as a police officer in Hong Kong for 20 years.

His contribution is seasoned by another retiree, **Neil Hamilton** who says Malaysia has four huge pluses as a retirement destination, the first being "it's summer every day of the year."

Neil adds: "Since retiring here I have never worn a tie, only once a jacket and no more than 20 times socks inside my shoes. You don't spend much money on clothes!"

About 1,000 miles up the road in northern **Thailand** is Chiang Mai, and – if you pop into the Chiang Mai Expats Club – you might bump into **Nancy** and **Roger Lindle** who moved there after selling their plant nursery in Michigan.

This American couple visited Chiang Mai in late 2006 to "practice" living as retirees, as Nancy puts it. They enjoyed the experience and four years later finds them still happily living in Thailand's northern capital.

Another contributor, **Kevin Butters**, had an interesting route to retirement in Thailand. He visited the Far East frequently to source products for in the family's horticultural wholesale business in the East Midlands.

"My personal passions are my lovely Thai wife Rose, baby daughter Coco and spicy Thai food, so Chiang Mai is the perfect location for us to live and is a great retirement option for those seeking affordable yet comfortable living, without compromising on natural beauty, entertainment and great food."

Who better to ask to write about retirement in **Australia** than the couple who wrote the book? **'Where to Retire In Australia'** by **Jill** and **Owen Weeks** has sold thousands of copies in Australia and around the world.

The Weeks have visited over 200 locations around Australia to come up with the best Australia has to offer.

Their book – summarised for our readers – provides tons of practical advice covering recreation, real estate, climate, shopping, dining, transport, retirement villages, pet ownership and more.

Vicky Gray emigrated to **Australia** in 2006 with her husband and three children. She is the author of **Didgeridoos and Didgeridon'ts,** writes for magazines in Australia and New Zealand and runs a blog at **www.australiauncovered.com**.

Gordon and **Margaret Penny**, who provided our section on **New Zealand**, also travelled extensively around the country before deciding on Auckland for their retirement. They moved there from London in 2002.

Gordon, a retired publishing executive, says: "We had a wide circle of friends in the UK so the decision to sell up and move here was not an easy one to make. However, seven years down the line we have no regrets."

Jill & Owen Weeks

Helen Owen

Vinnie Apicella

Mauricio Jaimes

The Americas

Mexico vies with Panama as the retirement destination of choice for Americans. **Julia Taylor**, author of '**Mexico: The Trick is Living Here**,' moved there in 2001 and says Mexicans will welcome you into their community with open arms.

Canadian **Pamela Dayka** had a bad start to retirement in **Belize**: mugged, burgled, seriously injured in a car accident – her love of the country was severely tested.

"I love Belize but it is not without its challenges for us foreigners," she writes.

Robert Holloway chose **Costa Rica** for his retirement for the low cost of living, the climate and quality of life.

He sums up its appeal thus: "… a marvellous subtropical climate, the beaches are absolute beauties, great deep-sea fishing, plenty of championship-designed golf courses with unparalleled scenery."

Forget everything you thought you knew about **Nicaragua**, writes **Vinnie Apicella**, travel writer, property investor and native Nicaraguan.

"Today's Nicaragua is a country with plentiful natural beauty framed by a coastal paradise that is being embraced by adventurous investors and adventure seekers alike."

Adventure is writ large on the resumé of **Helen Owen**, our **Panama** writer. Originally from Cambridge, Helen worked in Paris for six years, moved to Istanbul, then to Panama and now lives in the USA.

"…not that my life has been about new adventures or anything," she jokes.

Matt Ridgway

Julia Taylor

Robert Holloway

Andrew Bartlett

Bolivia may not be on your shortlist but first hear what our contributor there has to say.

"Bolivia has a lot to offer…a very low cost of living, an unspoiled natural environment, friendly people and a range of climates to suit virtually every taste," writes **Shannon Roxborough**.

Briton **Matt Ridgway** has lived and worked in **Chile** since 2003. Apart from its other merits – excellent and cheap wine, for example – Matt says Chile's police force is renowned for its honesty and incorruptibility and is one of the lowest risk countries in the world.

Forget the past too when you consider **Colombia** – once famed for its gun-toting guerrillas and drug cartel shoot-outs.

While remote parts of the south and east are controlled by rebels, "today you will find stunning landscapes, beautiful beaches, warm and friendly people," reports **Mauricio Jaimes**.

Briton, **Andrew Bartlett**, is our man in the **USA** He is a Florida-based relocation and property specialist providing independent advice and briefings to clients on relocation and retirement to the USA .

Caribbean

Feona Gray and **James Henderson**, responsible for our section on the Caribbean, have lived and worked there for more than 20 years.

Together they run the website **definitiveCaribbean.com**, an unrivalled insider guide with detailed information on everything from which island to choose to what to eat.

Let us help you find your new life abroad

The International Retirement Directory

David & Daniel Creffield

Why, Where and How to retire abroad

Simply return this questionnaire and we will arrange for you to receive information from companies that can help you make that move

Free Reader Service

Please complete and post to:
Millfield Publishing,
Brighton Media Centre, 15-17 Middle Street, Brighton, Sussex BN1 1AL, UK.
Or you can fax it to: +44 (0) 1273 201379; or email to: info@internationalretirement.co.uk;
or visit www.internationalretirement.co.uk where you can complete the questionnaire on-line

Your contact details:

Name

Address

Tel. no.

Email address

Your age:
Under ❏ 40
❏ 41-50
❏ 51-60
❏ 60+

Are you: ❏ married
❏ single
❏ living with partner

Which country/countries are you interested in moving to?

Reason/s for moving:
❏ Employment
❏ Setting up/investing in a business
❏ Repatriation
❏ Retirement

I would like to receive information from companies that specialise in the following areas:
❏ Emigration services
❏ Property sales (destination country)
❏ Property rentals (destination country)
❏ Rental management (in the UK)
❏ Property sales (in the UK)
❏ Equity release
❏ Currency exchange
❏ Legal services (destination country)
❏ Legal services (in the UK)
❏ Tax and pensions
❏ Offshore banking
❏ Private healthcare
❏ Language courses
❏ Shipping and packing
❏ Shipping pets

Property
Do you intend to buy ❏ or rent ❏
Type of property required (ie house with pool, villa, apartment, golf property, number of bedrooms) - please specify

Price range:
❏ Up to £50,000
❏ £51-100,000
❏ £101-150,000
❏ £151-250,000
❏ £251-400,000
❏ £401-600,000
❏ £601-900,000
❏ £901+

I am planning to buy ❏ rent ❏
as:
❏ Second home/holiday home
❏ Permanent home
❏ Investment
❏ Other

When are you planning to relocate?

Will you need a mortgage:
yes ❏ no ❏

Here's the quick answer

For easy reference all amounts in this section are quoted in £sterling

This is a 'snapshot' view of entry requirements for all the countries covered in the International Retirement Directory. You will find fuller details in each country section. All the figures have been converted into sterling to enable easy comparison.

ARGENTINA
A monthly income of £500.

AUSTRALIA
No family there? You need a minimum annual income of £28,000 – and a lump sum of 10 times that amount.

AZORES
No problem – the Azores are an autonomous region of Portugal.

BALEARICS
No problem. The islands are a province of Spain.

BELIZE
£1,250 a month gets you in under the Qualified Retired Persons Incentive law. You need to be 45 years or older.

BOLIVIA
Permanent residence available to retirees and their families with unspecified but "adequate" means of support. Citizenship can be obtained by donation of £6,250-15,500, the larger sum covering the main applicant, spouse and dependent children under 18.

BRAZIL
The minimum required for a Permanent Resident Visa is a monthly income of £1,250 for the applicant and two legal dependants.

CANADA
There's a 10-year waiting list for parents and grandparents under the family reunification visa classification. You can jump the queue if you're worth £444,000 and be willing to lend half of it to the Canadian Government – interest free! Options: Investor/ Entrepreneur programmes which require candidates to commit £166,000-444,000.

CANARY ISLANDS
Straightforward. It's another autonomous region of Spain.

CAPE VERDE
To obtain residency you need evidence of a monthly pension or income of 130,000 Cape Verdean escudos (about $1,500).

CARIBBEAN
It's all to do with money – and plenty of it, in fees, investment or property ownership – which opens the door to most Caribbean islands but different rules apply to most of the islands. See country sections.

CHILE
One of the easiest countries in which to obtain residency with various classes of permanent residence. A Temporary Residence Visa takes about two months to obtain and costs £220. An application for a Rentista or Retiree Visa can be made by post once you arrive and requires you to prove unspecified but adequate funds.

COLOMBIA
To obtain a permanent visa as a retiree you need a monthly guaranteed income of 10 times the Colombian minimum monthly wage. The bottom line is that you need about £14,000 a year to qualify.
An alternative is the Investor's Visa for which there is a requirement for a minimum deposit of £66,000 with the Banco de la Republica.

COSTA RICA
One of the cheapest. You can obtain a retiree Pensionado Visa if you can prove an income of £625 a month from a source outside Costa Rica.

CROATIA
No visa is required for a stay of up to 90 days but red tape is worst here than most places. First a Temporary Residence Permit and loads of documents are required, all translated into Croatian by certified translator and legalised at the Croatian Embassy at £11 for the first page, and £5 per page for all other pages. An 'apostille'* must be attached to each relevant document.

CYPRUS
Cyprus does not require EU citizens to have residence permits. Residential status is established after living there for 185 days a year.

ECUADOR
The Pensioner 10-I Visa is available for those who receive a guaranteed monthly income of £500, plus £66 for each dependant. An alternative is the Investment Visa, under which the applicant has to purchase real estate worth £15,625 (£330 more for each dependant).

EGYPT
Three-month tourist visa on arrival, then you must apply for either a three-year Temporary Residence Permit or a five-year Residence Permit, a formality if you own property in Egypt.

FRANCE
Few formalities for EU citizens.

GREECE
The Residence Permit has been replaced by the Registration Certificate but a new document available to EU nationals is the Permanent Residence Certificate (Engrafo Monimis Diamonis) which is optional.

INDIA (GOA)
A visa for a six-month stay is relatively easy to obtain but there are tough laws on foreigners buying property and a five-year residential visa is notoriously difficult to obtain and renew.

INDONESIA
To obtain a Temporary Stay Permit, renewable annually, you must be at least 55 years old and be able to prove an income of at least £940 a month. After five years you can apply for a permanent permit (KITAP).

ITALY
Few formalities for EU citizens.

* An 'apostille certificate' authenticates the signature of the public official who has signed a document and deems it to be a legal entity.

MALAYSIA

Applicants aged 50 and above must have a pension income of £2,000 a month and £100,000 in liquid assets. Other requirements include a medical report and medical insurance but exemptions may be given in the case of age or medical condition.

MALTA

'Economically self-sufficient' EU nationals can move to Malta providing they have sufficient resources not to become a burden on the state. Current requirements are capital of at least £12,000 or a weekly income of £77 or, in the case of a married couple, capital of £20,000 or a weekly income of £80.

MEXICO

The Rentista Visa (FM3 visa) is for foreign nationals who live off the income from savings and investments or any legal income from abroad. The minimum monthly income is £720 per head of family plus £340 for each dependant.

NEW ZEALAND

New Zealand has no such thing as a retirement visa. There are two visas which allow in those over 55: the Investor Visa – you need £608,000 to invest and there is an upper age limit of 65 – or the Family Visa but candidates must still meet health, character and (fairly low) minimum income requirements.

NICARAGUA

Nicaragua offers a package of incentives to encourage foreign retirees. The minimum age is 45. Applicants must prove a "stable, permanent income generated abroad" of not less than £250 a month and £66 for each family member.

PANAMA

Panama offers a mass of incentives and discounts on everything from travel to restaurant meals, doctors' bills and cinema tickets. You need an income of at least £625 a month and £155 for each dependent.

PARAGUAY

You need a health certificate, an 'economic solvency statement' showing a deposit in a bank in Paraguay of at least £3,125 and a deed showing you have bought a property in Paraguay.

PERU

£625 a month will get you permanent residence plus £310 for each dependent.

PHILIPPINES

The Special Resident Retiree's Visa (SRRV) is a non-immigrant visa with multiple entry/indefinite stay privileges and comes with a number of services, privileges and benefits.
The visa requires financial deposts of £50,000 for those aged 35-49 years old and £33,000 for those aged 50 years and over.

PORTUGAL

EU nationals can stay in Portugal for up to three months without having to comply with any formalities. To remain longer you must apply for a Registration Certificate which is valid for five years and requires you to show you have sufficient funds to support yourself.

SOUTH AFRICA

You need to prove a monthly income of at least about £1,500 from a pension, an annuity or other assets. Initially you apply for a Temporary Residence Permit which allows multiple re-entry.
You can then apply for a Retired Person Permit which has to be renewed every four years.

SPAIN

The same as in Portugal. After three months EU citizens must register in person at the Foreigners' Office (Oficina de Extranjeros) in their province of residence or at designated police and obtain a Registration Certificate.

THAILAND

You need the "O-A" (Long Stay) visa which has to be renewed annually. You have to be 50 or over and apply inperson at Thai Embassy. You need a bank statement showing you have assets of £14,000 and an annually income equivalent to about £14,000.

TUNISIA

Big on bureaucracy and it's a long-winded process to get a Carte de Sejour. Some foreign residents don't bother and simply leave the country every three months.
The police issue a Temporary Carte de Sejour and you may have to make several return visits and wait several weeks (or even months). Loads of documents required and everything has to be translated into Arabic or French – or both. You also need evidence of adequate means of support.

TURKEY

You get a 30-day visitor visa on entry and can then apply for a residence permits at the Alien's Branch of local police (you can apply from abroad – it takes up to eight weeks). You will also need evidence to prove adequate (unspecified) retirement income.

UAE

A 30-day visitor visa is granted on arrival. Property purchase normally entitles the buyer and immediate family to residence visas, normally issued for three years. Applicants for residency visas must pass medical and security checks.

URUGUAY

Any foreigner with temporary immigration status can apply for permanent residence. Change in status must be by written request to the immigration authority and you need evidence of a monthly income of £940.

USA

There's no retirement visa that allows permanent residence but you can legally spend up to 90 days per visit without a visa or up to 180 days with a B-2 'snowbird' visa. Then there's the (non-immigrant) E-2 visa that enables investors to live in the USA. The investment level is £95,000-250,000. The downside of the E-2 is that it has a 'non-immigrant' status and lapses if you dispose of the investment.
Best bet is the EB5 which requires an investment of £310,000 and, although not a retirement visa as such, is as good as since it leads to a Green Card.

VENEZUELA

A monthly (attested) income of £750 (plus £330 for each accompanying family member) will get you a 'Visitors with Fixed Income' visa.

Mediterranean lifestyle at bargain basement prices

Why Croatia?

Ask any Croatian to describe their country and they will say things like "laid-back, friendly, good food – great sea-food – sun, crystal clear waters, beautiful islands, and wild natural landscapes."

Ask any non-Croatian visitor and they are likely to say "all of the above."

"The Mediterranean as it once was …" that's how the Croatian National Tourist Board describes Croatia.

Croatia borders Hungary to the north, Slovenia to the west, Serbia to the east and Bosnia/Herzegovina to the south. With Italy only 27km from the Croatian border, the canals of Venice are less than three hours away and Vienna is about four hours by car.

The coastal climate is Mediterranean with an average of 2,600 hours of sunshine a year. The Adriatic is one of the sunniest coastlines in Europe where the sea temperature can reach 27°C during summer. Inland there is more of a continental climate with hot summers and cold winters.

Croatia's capital Zagreb boasts more museums per square mile than any other city in the world. Culture lovers the world over also enjoy its art galleries, theatres, concert halls and festivals. Croatia is also home to some of the most breathtaking scenic views.

The Plitvice Lakes National Park, located between Zagreb and Zadar, is Croatia's leading tourist destination. Added to the UNESCO World Heritage list in 1979 it features 16 lakes separated by mountains and connected by a network of waterfalls.

Istria

Often referred to as Croatia's Tuscany, this heart-shaped peninsula in the north-west of the country is characterised by its rolling valleys and culturally rich hill-top villages and towns – always a favourite with holiday-makers.

Typical of Istria is the town of Rovinj, known for its romantic allure, a perfect lovers' paradise.

The Kvarner Gulf

Located in the north-west of Croatia, and adjacent to the Istrian peninsula, the Kvarner Gulf is easily accessible from all Mediterranean and mid-European countries. It stretches from the Opatija Riviera in the northwest to the island of Pag in the south and encompasses the islands of Krk, Cres, Losinj and Rab. The Kvarner region truly belongs to the sunny Mediterranean. Snowfall is extremely rare.

ABOUT THE WRITER: Aleksandra Kallay was born in Zagreb and now lives in the UK. After an international career working for several blue chip companies Aleksandra set up Croatian Villas For Sale following her own frustrating experience of trying to buy a property in Croatia. Her company focuses exclusively on the requirements of property buyers and through partner agencies in Croatia is able to provide a personal service to buyers throughout the property buying process.

FACTFILE

Capital: Zagreb **Population:** 4.5 million
Area: 56,689sq km **Language:** Croatian;
English is widely spoken in tourist areas.
Climate: Mainly Mediterranean with mild
winters and warm, sunny and sometimes
very hot summers. In the mountains winter
temperatures are sub-zero with plenty of
snow. Temperatures on the coast are in the
range 10°C in winter to 30°C in the summer.
Time difference: GMT +1
Entry requirements: You can stay in
Croatia for 90 days without a visa.
Retirement/residence visa: See: The rules
for getting in.
Electricity: 220-240V/50Hz, 2-point plugs.
Money: Kuna. ATMs are widely available.
Major debit/credit cards and travellers
cheques are usually accepted.

Public holidays 2010

Jan 1	New Year's Day
Jan 6	Epiphany
Apr 2 & 5	Easter
May 1	Labour Day
June 3	Corpus Christi
June 22	Anti-Fascist Resistance Day
June 25	National Day
Aug 5	Victory Day
Oct 8	Independence Day
Nov 1	All Saint's Day
Dec 25-26	Christmas

Opening hours:
Shops: 8am-8pm, 8am-3pm, Sat (later in
summer when many shops also open on
Sundays).
Banks: 7am-7pm, Mon-Fri; 7am-1pm, Sat
Offices: 8.30 am to 4.30pm

Water: Tap water is drinkable.
Tipping: A few coins or 10-15 per cent for
exceptional service.
Medical/Healthcare: There are no
particular risks or health concerns
associated with living in or visiting Croatia.
The standard of healthcare is reasonable.
Visiting foreigners are entitled to free basic
emergency first aid at state hospitals.
Citizens of countries with which Croatia has
reciprocal healthcare agreement have free
state healthcare.
Pets: You need proof of rabies vaccination
issued within 15 days prior to date of arrival
and an International Health Certificate from
a veterinarian.

CROATIA CONTACT DIRECTORY

Embassies/Government
Croatian Embassy in London
http://uk.mfa.hr
UK Embassy in Croatia
http://ukincroatia.fco.gov.uk/en

Travel & Health Advice
Foreign Office travel advice
www.fco.gov.uk/travel
www.nhs.uk/Healthcareabroad
www.masta.org

About Croatia
www.about-croatia.com
www.mycroatia.com
www.worldtravelguide.net
http://croatiaonline.blogspot.com
http://uk.mfa.hr/?mh=43&mv=170
www.alertnet.org/db/cp/croatia.htm

General & Expat
www.expatfocus.com
www.britishexpat.com
www.transitionsabroad.com

Media
Croatia news online
www.croatiaexclusive.com
www.croatiantimes.com
www.findcroatia.com
www.nacional.hr/en
www.hic.hr/english

Property
www.croatianvillasforsale.co.uk
www.sunshineestates.net
www.europeanproperty.com/sales/hr
www.croatianhomes4sale.com

www.adriaticpropertyservices.com
www.savills.co.uk
www.korculainfo.com

Travel & Tourism
www.croatiatraveller.com
www.find-croatia.com
www.croatia-travel-guide.net
www.travel-2-croatia.com
Tourist Office
www.croatia.hr/English

Getting There
By air
British Airways: www.british-airways.com
Easyjet: www.easyjet.com
Croatia Airlines: www.croatiaairlines.hr
Air France: www.airfrance.com
Alitalia: www.alitalia.it
KLM: www.klm.com
By train
Inter Rail: www.interrailnet.com
Eurail: www.eurail.com

Getting Around
Air: Croatia Airlines connects major cities in

Croatia but distances are comparatively
short so other options are preferable.
Train: Croatia's rail network connects all
major Croatian cities, except Dubrovnik.
There is a (relatively) high-speed train
between Zagreb and Split, which has cut
travel time from the capital to the coast to
about six hours.
Bus: A reliable and efficient way to travel
within Croatia. Most long-distance buses
have reclining seats and air-conditioning.
Ferry: Ferries, hydrofoils and catamarans
leave from the coastal towns of Croatia to
the islands and there are some inter-island
ferry services (cut back in winter months).
Driving: Driving in Croatia can be
amazingly convenient or utterly nerve-
wracking, according to the website
www.croatiatraveller.com. Your UK licence
is valid for up to six months from date of
entry. International Driving Licences are not
recognised.
Road conditions are of a fairly good
standard. You must have a fluorescent vest
for emergencies and wear this when
changing a tyre, for example.

Split ferry

THE RULES FOR GETTING IN

No visa is required for a stay of up to 90 days. For longer stays you need to apply at the nearest Croatian Embassy for a temporary residence permit which is granted for one year. This must be renewed annually at a police station in Croatia.

You need a certificate confirming you have no criminal convictions; proof of health insurance; proof of assured accommodation (a tenancy agreement or a deed of ownership, for example); and some kind of proof of adequate funds such as a bank statement.

Then there's the usual bureaucratic stuff – worst here than most places: original or notarised copies of birth and marriage certificates (all translated into Croatian by a certified translator and legalised at the Croatian Embassy at €12 for the first page, and €6 per page for all other pages. To back this up an 'apostille' must be attached to each relevant document.

[An apostille certificate authenticates the signature of the public official who has signed a document you hold and deems the document to be a legal entity.]

Applications take 8-12 weeks.

Gorski Kotar

Half-way between Zagreb and the Adriatic coast, Gorski Kotar – "the green heart of Croatia" – features centuries-old lush forests, imposing mountain peaks, meandering emerald green rivers, gentle rolling valleys, crystal clear lakes and rich wildlife.

During the winter Gorski Kotar is a winter sports resort with skiers enjoying the crisp air and pure white snow. During the spring and summer other outdoor pursuits take over and you can choose from a wide range of activities from rafting and mountain biking through to fishing and hunting.

Dalmatia and its islands

Zadar, Split, Sibenik: A popular area for sailing and from here there are ferries to the outlying islands. The old town of Zadar is squeezed into a narrow peninsula partially enclosed by its medieval walls.

Other attractions include an old Roman forum and a 9th century church and the amazing Morske Orgulje in which organ music is created by nature through underwater pipes. Kornati islands national park includes 147 uninhabited islands and islets and

FOR LARGER MAP

is a sailor's paradise.

Hvar & Korcula: Two romantic islands which can compete with the best that the Amalfi coast has to offer. Hvar, which lays claims to be the sunniest place in Europe with 2,724 hours of sunshine a year, is trendier and has quite a nightlife.

Korcula is beautiful with thousands of years of cultural tradition.

Dubrovnik and surroundings: George Bernard Shaw, who described Dubrovnik as "the pearl of the Adriatic", was enchanted by this beautiful city, about which he said: "Those who seek paradise on earth should come to Dubrovnik …"

The surrounding towns and villages have wonderful beaches and scenery and are a favourite with visitors worldwide.

Cost of living

The cost of living in Croatia is approximately 30 per cent lower than the UK. Housing costs are the chief contributor to the lower cost followed by transport. Food shopping bills are similar although eating out is about half the price of that in the UK; a good meal out including starter, main course and dessert can be found for about €15.

A good hairdresser will charge less than half UK prices, while a Croatian dentist will charge about 40 per cent of the price a UK dentist would charge.

Is it safe?

Croatia has a low crime rate and violent crime is rare.

How much tax will I pay?

There is no tax on pensions or investment income received from abroad. There is no inheritance tax and no capital gains from the sale of property once you have owned it for three years.

There is a Real Estate Transfer Tax (RETT), similar to UK Stamp Duty, of five per cent.

Is Coatian property a good investment?

The level of price increase for properties on the Adriatic coast is explained by the fact that the most sought after houses and apartments, in quality locations, were mainly bought by non-Croatians, for

whom a quality property on the Adriatic represents a good investment owing to Croatia's expected entry into the EU by 2011.

According to CentarNekretnina.net, the largest Croatian property portal, prices of properties in the north are about 25 per cent cheaper than the middle and Southern Adriatic. This excludes property prices in Zagreb.

Property purchase

The main issue with buying property is to establish whether the property has a "clean" title. The property market has only really existed in its current form for the last 10 years. Prior to that time records were not as rigorously kept as they are now. Properties would be handed down from generation to generation and as a result a particular property could well have ended up being co-owned by several members of the same family. It is imperative that the precise ownership of the property being purchased is established.

You can buy property either as an individual or by setting up a Croatian company. If you want to let your property you have to buy through a company. Each route has its advantages and disadvantages.

If you keep the property for at least three years before selling, you will not be liable for Capital Gains Tax if you buy it as an individual. In addition, as of February 2009, EU citizens do not need to apply for permission to own a property.

The advantages of buying through a company are that non-EU citizens no longer need to apply for Ministry of Justice permission to own a property – a process that can take up to 24 months, though usually 6-12 months; it is quicker to get registered title deeds in the Land Registry; and, if buying a new build from a developer, you can subsequently reclaim the PDV (Value Added Tax).

Where's best to live?

The southern Croatian areas of Dubrovnik and Split have the largest concentration of expats if you feel the need to have fellow countrymen close by, although property prices here are the highest outside of Zagreb.

For sun and the sea, the coastal areas of Istria, Kvarner and Dalmatia are preferable. Inland, Istria and Gorski Kotar are recommended for peaceful living surrounded by beautiful countryside.

Interested in owning your own farm or vineyard? Then the areas around Karlovac and Zagorje, north of Zagreb, are the best bet. Properties in these regions can be significantly cheaper to buy although they may be more remote from major conurbations. However, wherever you may end up in Croatia, you are only an hour away from a major city.

1 bed apartment
Fully furnished second floor apartment in Pula, Istria with view of Medulin bay.Open plan living room, mezzanine area, balcony.
Price: €109,950

More info:
www.croatianvillasforsale.co.uk
Croatian Villas For Sale Ltd
Tel: +44 (0) 7817 294 110
Email: info@croatianvillasforsale.co.uk

CYPRUS HIGH COMMISSION
13 St James's Square
London SW1Y 4LB
Tel: 020 7321 4100
Fax: 020 7321 4164/5
E-mail: cyphclondon@dial.pipex.com

Cyprus's wonderful, sun-filled climate, stunningly varied scenery, excellent infrastructure, relatively low cost of living and friendly, hospitable people are some of the advantages that have rendered the island a favourite venue for retirees and expatriates.

Following its accession to the European Union, Cyprus is rapidly developing into one of the most popular destinations for Britons, with respect to retirement and ranks third in popularity after Spain and Portugal.

Cyprus enjoys very strong ties with the UK, making a Briton's transition to the Cypriot way of life immeasurably easier. English is spoken throughout the island and British influence is still obvious. In addition to its wonderful beaches and delicious cuisine, Cyprus life also enjoys an exceptionally low crime rate and a reliable public health system. The cost of medical treatment in government hospitals is also very low. People wishing to consult private doctors will find a large selection of competent doctors, specialists, and surgeons practicing on the island. Cyprus also offers golf courses and spas for those who want to make the most of the island.

In addition, Cyprus benefits from an extremely resilient banking system, which closely resembles the British one, as well as many duty free shopping benefits for its residents.

It is also a popular destination for active retirees due to the fact that there are a number of double taxation treaties in place, enabling them to receive private and public pensions and investment income in Cyprus, free of withholding tax. UK citizens may also take advantage of the Double Taxation Treaty existing between the UK and Cyprus.

Leaving behind the stresses and responsibilities of your working life, Cyprus represents the ideal setting to relax and enjoy the fruits of your labour. Catering for all tastes and lifestyles, and with so much to see and experience, Cyprus can guarantee that there will never be a dull moment in this new phase of your life.

Alexandros N. Zenon
High Commissioner

Friendly people, great food, 300 days of sunshine – a retirement location that is hard to match

Why Cyprus?

In the 21st century Cyprus has been the favoured destination of tens of thousands of British people. The weather is a major factor in deciding to retire here but a lot of expatriates find it too hot in August when the temperature can exceed 40°C. In the winter, houses can be cold principally because they are designed to keep their occupants cool in the long hot summers.

While the climate is often given as the first reason for living here there are other reasons too. Cyprus is accessible from the UK with many flights daily between most major UK airports and Paphos and Larnaca. The flight takes between four and five hours.

The pace of living is much slower than in the UK making it ideal for those who want a relaxing retirement away from the hassle of the British way of life. The fact that the overwhelming majority of the population speak English is a major attraction.

Cyprus has some stunning scenery including the unspoiled Akamas Peninsula, the Paphos Forest and the Troodos Mountains that includes Olympus which is higher than any British mountain.

The Mediterranean is warm enough to swim in for nine months a year and some hardy souls go in at Christmas too. Agia Napa in the east and Coral Bay in the west are among many beautiful beaches. It is not

unknown for people to ski in the mountains and swim in the sea on the same day.

For those whose lives have revolved around the M25 or M62, taking the motorway between Paphos to Limassol is a dream because it is often deserted and there are never any traffic jams.

It is said in Cyprus amongst expatriates that there is a phenomenon called 'The Cyprus Stone.' The reference is to the fact that even those not prone to putting on weight tend to do so when they come to live here because eating out is a lot less expensive.

Restaurateurs are extremely friendly and hospitable and Greek Cypriot food is generally excellent and portions are generous. Tavernas are nearly all family owned and the service matches the food.

Singing and dancing are very popular and many restaurants have live shows. Live opera is staged in the open at Paphos Harbour every September with famous international performers.

Cypriots are generally welcoming. Family ties are very strong with what British people might call old-fashioned values such as respect for parents and for authority being normal.

Most of the population are Christian and members of the Greek Orthodox Church. Although church attendance is in decline probably a larger proportion of

ABOUT THE WRITER In a career that included spells living in Barbados and Sri Lanka, **David Greenwood**, now aged 67, worked in the bus industry from 1960 until his retirement to Cyprus with his wife Margaret in 2001. For several years David served as secretary of his local community association in Cyprus and accumulated a vast knowledge of island life and property purchase. If you are considering Cyprus as a retirement destination and would like to see the full version of a property purchase advisory David wrote for association members, you can email David at davidaxiothea@cytanet.com.cy

FACTFILE

Capital: Nicosia **Population:** 796,740
Area: 9,251 sq km **Language:** Greek
(official). English is widely spoken.
Climate: Mediterranean climate with short,
mild winters and long dry summers with
over 300 days of sunshine. Summer
temperatures average 35°C but frequently
exceeds 40°C. In the winter the average
temperature is around 16°C.
Entry requirements: No visa required for
stays of up to 90 days
Retirement/residence visa: Residential
status is established after a person has
resided in Cyprus for 185 days a year or
more. Cyprus does not require EU citizens to
have residence permits and they can
acquire property without any restrictions.
See: The rules for getting in and 'Moving
Within the EU' – page xx
Time difference: Time: GMT +2
Electricity: 240V AC, 50 HZ, 3-pin plugs
Money: Euro. ATMs are plentiful.
Credit/debit cards and travellers cheques
are widely accepted throughout Cyprus.

Public holidays 2010

Jan 1	New Year's Day
Jan 6	Epiphany
Feb 15	Green Monday
March 25	Greek Independence Day
April 1	Greek Cypriot National Day
April 2	Greek Orthodox Good Friday
April 5	Greek Orthodox Easter Monday
May 1	Labour Day
May 24	Pentecost (Kataklysmos)
Aug 15	Assumption
Oct 1	Cyprus Independence Day
Oct 28	Greek National Day (Ochi Day)
Dec 24-26	Christmas

Opening hours
Banks: 08.30am-1pm (later on Mondays)
(Some banks open later in tourist areas)
Shops: 9am-1pm, 2.30pm-8.30pm (Mon,
Tues, Thurs)
9am-2pm (Wed)
9am-1pm, 2.30pm-9.30pm (Fri)
9am-5pm (Sat)
(Shops close earlier in winter)
Offices: 8am-1pm, 3pm-6pm

Water: Tap water is safe to drink.
Tipping: If a service charge is not included,
a tip of 10-15 per cent is expected. Taxi
drivers expect 10 per cent.
Medical/Healthcare: There are no
compulsory vaccinations. Some authorities
recommended tetanus vaccinations.
Healthcare in Cyprus is good and
inexpensive. EU residents should be treated
on the same basis as a resident.
Pets: To get in without quarantine, pets
must be microchipped, vaccinated against
rabies and issued with an EU Pet Passport.

CYPRUS CONTACT DIRECTORY

Embassies/Government
British Embassy
http://ukincyprus.fco.gov.uk
Cyprus High Commission in London
www.mfa.gov.cy/mfa/highcom/highcom_lond
on.nsf/DMLindex_en/DMLindex_en

Travel & Health Advice
Foreign Office travel advice
www.fco.gov.uk/travel
www.nhs.uk/Healthcareabroad
www.masta.org

About Cyprus
www.cyprusedirectory.com
www.cyprusabc.com
www.cyprus.gov.cy
(click on 'English')
www.earth.org/travel-guide/Cyprus
www.sol-agency.com/cyprus

General & Expat
www.cypruswebsites.com
www.ukgovabusesexpats.co.uk
www.expatforum.com
www.expatfocus.com
www.britishexpat.com
www.transitionsabroad.com

Travel & Tourism
www.visitcyprus.com
www.cyprus-travel-secrets.com
www.discovercyprus.com
www.agta.co.uk
(Association of Greek-Cypriot Travel Agents)

English Language Media
http://bfbs-radio.com/index.php
(British Forces Broadcasting Service)
www.cybc.com.cy
Cyprus Broadcasting Service
(some English programmes, both radio and TV)
Newspapers
Cyprus Mail, daily (www.cyprus-mail.com)
Cyprus Weekly, Fridays
(www.cyprusweekly.com.cy)
Financial Mirror, weekly
(www.financialmirror.com)
Intouch magazine, monthly lifestyle
magazine (www.intouchcyprus.com)

Property
Quality Group
www.qualitydevelopments.com
www.CyprusEstateAgents.com/
(lists leading estate agents)
Barton Wyatt International

Tel (UK): 01344 843 000
www.bw-international.com
G & P Lazarou & Associates Real Estate
Agencies Ltd.
www.gp-lazarou.com
Antonis Loizou & Associates
www.aloizou.com.cy
Genesis Real Estate
www.genesisrealestates.com
FSB Properties
www.fsbproperties.com/cyprops.php

Getting There
British Airways www.BritishAirways.com
Cyprus Airways www.cyprusairways.com
Easyjet www.easyjet.com
Thomas Cook www.thomascook.com

Getting Around
Bus: The public bus network is cheap and
efficient connecting all parts of the island
but are infrequent and virtually non-existent
on Sunday. Shared taxis operate on the
main routes.
Driving: Car hire is reasonable and by far
the best option and often the only way to
reach the more remote parts of the island.
Driving is on the left.

Cypriots attend church than do UK citizens and Cypriots' personal standards and values are based on their faith. Winter temperatures compare favourably with the UK but it can get cold and snow, though rare except on the mountains, is not unknown. Generally it is hot and dry for seven or eight months of the year.

Little England?

It is amazing how many people come to live in Cyprus and expect to find England with sun. The culture of Cyprus is predominantly Greek and if you wish to live here it is you who will have to change your attitude.

Most expatriates in Cyprus would agree that life is far more laid back. You shouldn't be in a hurry to achieve things. Because Cyprus was once a British colony many people believe that it is like Britain. Yes,

we drive on the left and most Cypriots speak English but, while the legal system purports to be the same as the English one, it is not.

Cost of living

Seven or eight years ago it was much cheaper to live in Cyprus than in the UK. Today the costs are now similar primarily because of the fall in the value of sterling.

Certainly there are now many items which may be dearer than in the UK, nevertheless, most would agree that it is still less expensive to live here. Eating out remains much cheaper, income tax is much lower, council tax can be as low as €110 a year and petrol costs less.

White goods, furniture, electrical goods and computers are more expensive and British people planning to move here would be well advised to buy in the UK before they leave.

Cleaning, gardening, odd jobs, plumbing and electrical jobs cost less and it is easier to secure someone to perform them. Property prices are lower in Cyprus than they are in London and the Home Counties but not, for example than East Yorkshire.

Is it safe?

While crime is much lower than in the UK and its absence is a major attraction for expatriates, crime here is on the increase. However, the chances of your property being broken into are remote. Many people still go out and leave doors and windows open though this is not advisable.

While crimes such as mugging and violence against the person are virtually unheard of, there is gang crime which is generally confined to the cities.

Pegeia villas
A pair of villas with sea and mountain views ccupying a prime position on the side of a picturesque valley. 3 bedrooms, 2 bathrooms, private pool and extensive terracing off the living area and roof with panoramic views to the sea and hills
Price: €300,000
More info: www.fitzgeraldcyprus.com Tel (UK): 44(0)845 688 8380
Email: contact@FitzgeraldCyprus.com

Limassol centre
Located in the heart of Limassol, the apartments of St. George Residences offer 1, 2 and 3-bedroom apartments with spacious living areas and large verandas. All properties come with covered parking and storage rooms.
Price: €222,000-449,000
More info: Cybarco www.cybarco.com
Tel (UK): 208 371 9700 Email: london@cybarco.com

QUALITY GROUP

THE ART OF BUILDING

LET
YOUR
NEW
LIFE
START
HERE

With an extensive portfolio, Quality Group is one of the most respected property developers in Cyprus and the Mediterranean.

14 United Nations Street, 6042 Larnaca, CY
Tel.: +357 24 821855, Fax: +357 24 662922
email: sales@qualitydevelopments.com
www.qualitydevelopments.com

for 40-50 per cent of a property's overall cost.

With the present over-supply of properties for sale prices are expected to fall in the short-term.

Where's best to live?

The Republic of Cyprus is divided into the districts of Nicosia, Famagusta, Larnaca, Limassol and Paphos.

Although many expatriates live in coastal locations in Larnaca and Limassol Districts and others in the mountains, the largest expatriate communities are to be found in the Paphos District where some villages have almost become towns and where British expatriates are in the majority.

Property purchase

Many people are told that the legal system in Cyprus is similar to that in the UK and that therefore they have the same legal guarantees as they would have there. Similar statements appear in some developers' brochures. This is very misleading and should be treated with extreme caution.

Most significantly the Cyprus legal system does not give the legal remedies or safeguards that are standard in some other countries. There are many pitfalls into which an unsuspecting purchaser may fall. Many lawyers are too closely associated with developers to represent purchasers properly, effectively and honestly. It is strongly advised that a lawyer from another town be used.

There are now British lawyers practising in Cyprus who do not have a close relationship with developers. Additionally, it is necessary to ensure that the lawyer you appoint is experienced in conveyancing.

A good independent lawyer is essential. Some developers tell prospective clients that they do not need a lawyer as they will complete all the necessary

How much tax will I pay?

Cyprus has an extremely favourable tax regime for foreign residents. Levels of income tax are lower than they are in the UK although no one can guarantee that this will always be the case. Retired residents from overseas are taxed on their pensions at the rate of five per cent above €3,417 a year, whether it is a state, company or personal pension.

There is 0 per cent tax on investment income (i.e. dividends and interest) brought into Cyprus. There is no inheritance tax. When title deeds are issued a Property Transfer Tax of 3-8 per cent is levied.

Is Cyprus property a good investment?

In early 2010 the average price per house in Cyprus was €2,000sq m and €1,865sq m for an apartment, according to the first-ever quarterly Cyprus Property Price Index (PPI).

In March 2010, Lakis Tofarides, chairman of the Cyprus Land and Building Developers Association, blamed high property prices on the cost of land which has rocketed over the last 10 years and now accounts

Aphrodite Hills
17km east of Paphos, Aphrodite Hills is a leisure, golf and real estate development tied in with the five-star InterContinental hotel. 1,2 and 3 bedroom apartments are centred around a village square, with restaurants and bars, near a nature trail, beach and horse riding. Price: €270,000-700,000.
More info: Barton Wyatt International
www.bw-international.com Tel: (UK) 01344 843000

Peyia lifestyle
The Acropolis Panorama Lifestyle Club offers fully-furnished studios and 1, 2 or 3 bed apartments with indoor and outdoor swimming pools, a clubhouse, restaurant, bar, gym, sauna, steam room, mini-market and a treatment room with a qualified nurse. The development overlooks the south-east coast and is close to a planned new marina. Freehold or a long-term lease. Price: €167,544-770,288.
More info: www.acropolispanorama.com
Tel: (UK) 01889 565806
Email: David@univac.com

We live here

Karon and Barry Leese decided to bring their retirement to Cyprus forward. They have no regrets but the move was not without problems.

We had been to Paphos on holiday and were drawn to retiring there. Cyprus is a lovely country where the people are friendly and there is the added attraction of English being widely spoken.

Other attractions: they drive on the same side of the road as we do in the UK and as a resident of Cyprus Barry would only pay five per cent tax.

Our move was accelerated because I had two cardiac arrests and had to have an ICD (implanted cardiac defibrillator) fitted.

Barry took early retirement from work and we moved to Cyprus in August 2006. This was naive of us because if you are not of pensionable age in Cyprus you are required to take out private medical insurance.

That was not the only hitch. We had had estimates from three removal firms and chose the one that we felt offered more of a personal touch. The vans came and loaded our goods, itemising everything and giving us copies of all the paperwork. Three weeks later we flew out to take delivery of our container.

What they didn't give us was a contact telephone number in Cyprus and when we arrived we had no way of getting in touch with the company. We were about to fly home when we received a phone call from Limassol telling us that the company had gone into liquidation and its assets had been frozen.

Dozens of phone calls later we were told our container was in Limasol being held by customs and could not be released until we paid everyone involved what they were due. We ended up having to pay another €2,200. We chose to move into the villa two months before the completion date. The villa was ready but what the developer forgot to tell us was that if we moved in before the completion date then we wouldn't have any electricity.

We brought a second hand generator which broke down more than it worked, and a gas barbecue so that we could cook outside and boil water in the middle of the night when we couldn't sleep because of the noisy generator.

The developer kept telling us that everything was an 'extra' and we had to pay cash for these. We never got an exact amount of what things were costing but one of these 'extras' was a storage area under the house. When we got the bill for these extras it was around €4,800 more than we had anticipated.

Since we moved here we have had to find another €24,000 extra to pay for things that we hadn't anticipated.

More problems

In our contract for the house we have a road and footpath. However, there is no completion date for them and two years on we are still waiting.

We had thought that we could have a telephone land line and Internet straight away but hadn't realised that we were in a village area where it would be at least a year before it was possible for Internet and then at a very costly price because it would only be available by satellite.

We won't be able to have a land line until the road is completed so today we still manage with mobile phones making it expensive to keep in touch with relatives and friends.

We never considered language was going to be a problem as English is so widely spoken but when dealing with government officials you have to speak the language or have an interpreter.

The bureaucracy here can drive you mad. Adjusting to culture change is hard and in a strange country it is easy to become disillusioned and to feel vulnerable.

We've encountered many problems and still continue to have problems today, especially with medical issues, but we have no regrets about leaving the UK. We love living by the sea in a country where the sun shines nearly all year and where we can enjoy a more quiet and calmer way of life.

If we were in the UK we would still have a mortgage and I would need to work full time. We may not be rich but we do have a beautiful home in a beautiful country.

formalities so producing a considerable cost saving. This is very poor advice.

Developers

Developers are in business to make money and must not be blamed if they pursue this objective. They may wine and dine you, take you to their homes for meals and even invite you to their daughter's wedding. Do not be fooled; these may be methods that have proved successful and you will be paying for them.

Take advice from those who have purchased properties in Cyprus and know the mistakes that can be made. While it is obvious sense to inspect a property before deciding whether to buy, do not be fooled into allowing the developer to take you to see people who have already bought properties from the company. These 'satisfied customers' may be phonies, paid for playing this role.

If you intend to purchase a property from a developer ensure that the specifications, extras, etc are included in the purchase price.

Before you sign a contract to buy a property you must ensure that the land on which it is to be built does not have a mortgage attached to it.

It's your responsibility

There is a legal requirement that your contract must be registered with the Lands Registry within a specified, short timescale. Your lawyer may do this on your behalf but ultimately it is your responsibility.

Unlike many other countries there is no cooling off period in Cyprus so once you sign a contract you are legally committed. Even if the contract specifies that the deposit is refundable you may not get it or, if you do, it could take many years.

If the vendor has told you that he will provide water, electricity, telephones, roads, pavements, sewerage, landscaping, etc., he is under no obligation to do so unless they are specified in the contract.

The best advice that can be given is to buy a property with title deeds available upon purchase. This is more likely but not necessarily so where the property is a re-sale. There are thousands of re-sale properties available and they offer an alternative to buying from a developer, a much safer bet than buying without title deeds.

Beware of developers who tell you that you will have 'beneficial ownership' because this concept has little meaning in law.

Contact David directly to see the full version of his property advisory:

Email davidaxiothea@cytanet.com.cy

With 14 new courses golf goes crazy

With an average of 330 days of sunshine a year Cyprus is a popular destination for those seeking year-round golf on lush green fairways.

But with a limited number of courses golfers have faced frustration in the past. No longer! The government has approved plans for the creation of 14 new courses and some of them are already taking shape.

The new courses will bring the total on the island to 17. Many of the new clubs will cater for non-golfing partners or family members with facilities such as tennis and spas.

Aphrodite Hills, regarded as one of the most luxurious and exclusive resorts in the Eastern Mediterranean, combines sophisticated golf and recreation facilities with up-market properties to match. These include a 5-star hotel, a health club and spa and a tennis academy.

On offer at Aphrodite Hills is a variety of villas, apartments, bungalows and terraced villas. The setting overlooks the Mediterranean.

YOUR DAILY LINK WITH THE WORLD

We live here

With expectations of regular visits from their five children, Malcolm and Jean Goulding from Macclesfield chose a large home when they retired to Cyprus in 2007

Both in their early 70s they chose a generous-sized three-bedroom villa to ensure there was going to be enough space for visits from their five children and six grandchildren who come to visit at different times of the year.

"We see more of the family now than we did in the UK," jokes Malcolm.

When they're not busy with visits from friends and family the couple's time is taken up with their own hobbies and interests. Jean is an active member of the local church group, Malcolm is learning Greek.

They chose Cyprus after briefly considering Portugal; it was pretty much a no-brainer for Malcolm. Fifty years earlier as a young soldier he had been based in Limassol and fallen for the island then.

The couple's retirement choice was a villa development in the picturesque village of Argaka in the foothills of the Paphos forest, only a few metres from some of Cyprus' best beaches with views of the surrounding forest land and the Mediterannean.

Close by is the town of Polis Chrysochous and the Tsada golf course.

The villa has broadband access so the couple can keep in touch with home and access their favourite TV programmes from the UK.

They bought the property through one of the island's largest property companies, Aristo Developers, which offers a wide range of properties in Cyprus and Greece.

More info

Prices at Argaka Village range from €133,600 for apartments to €367,800 for villas.
Tel: 0800 082 0601
www.aristodevelopers.com

---

7 bedrooms, Vavatsina

Five minutes from the village centre and 10 minutes to Lefkara village with hotels, swimming pools, restaurants, bars and super-markets. 30

minutes from the sea. 7 large bedrooms, 3-car garage, fully furnished. Large garden. **More info:** www.ebuypc.co.uk Email: property@ebuypc.co.uk Tel (UK): 01414160115

Larnaca apartments

Ria Court 39 in Larnaca is close to a broad range of local amenities – 10 minutes drive from the sea, shopping centre and airport. Consisting of 12 2-bedroom apartments and two 3-bedroom apartments on the top (4th) floor. Private parking and storage rooms. Completion, December, 2010.
Price: €145,000-240,000
More info: www.livadiotis.com Tel: +357 24 828 000
Email: info@livadiotis.com

French allure that beckons thousands of new retirees every year

Why France?

What is it about France that casts a spell on us? Is it the rich history, culture and cuisine or the exquisitely beautiful French countryside where you can step back in time to a less stressful era?

France offers wonderful food: for breakfast, crisp baguettes, croissants and batons fresh from the boulangerie, ready to smother in rich butter and confiture to accompany your aromatic café au lait or espresso.

Later in the day indulge in some hors d'œuvre, côtes d'agneau, canard a l'orange, quails, sparrows or pâté de foie gras. Haute cuisine? Nouvelle cuisine? The choice is yours.

Not to your fancy? – then try that favourite venue of all holidaymakers, the French pavement café, and watch the world go by as you sip your aperitif.

Once you've tired of lazing by the boulevards, visit an art gallery to see the work of Monet, Renoir, Degas, Toulouse-Lautrec, Cézanne, Gauguin and Matisse or, in Paris, check out the flea markets of the Left Bank or dawdle in the Gothic cathedrals of Notre Dame, Rennes, Chartres or the abbey church of Saint Denis.

France and Britain have always had somewhat of a love-hate relationship but when Lord Lansdowne and Paul Cambon, the French Ambassador, signed the Entente Cordiale 100 years ago it is unlikely they could have anticipated that this 'friendly understanding' would not only resolve certain international political disputes but might lead to the long love affair we have with the French lifestyle.

Of course, friendship grows with mutual understanding and, especially in more remote areas, you will find that being able to speak the language, or even just knowing the most important phrases, will take you a long way and make life much easier.

Thousands of Britons move to France every year and while France is only a short hop across the Channel, there is a world of difference between the two countries and lifestyles – enough of a difference to make thousands start a new life in 'La Douce France'.

There is a very good reason why France has always held the top spot as the world's most visited country: it has everything anyone would need in a vacation and as a retirement destination.

The cost of living, especially in the countryside areas, is usually lower than the United Kingdom.

The south tempts many with its Mediterranean climate of mild winters and warm summers. Others opt for the less pricey and less crowded parts of the country, such as the south-west, where property represents some of the best bargains available.

Nowhere is served better than France by the budget airlines and getting around in France is a pleasure compared to the UK.

The French autoroutes branch out from Paris like the spokes of a wheel, allowing you to drive in comfort to all parts of the country. However, you should

ABOUT THE WRITER: David Seymour left the UK eight years ago and runs a small marketing boutique in south-west France **James [www.seymour-james.com]**. If you would like to see the stunning renovation he carried out on his own property go to: **http://www.seymour-james.com/french-property-renovation/ruin.htm**

remember that the autoroutes are toll roads and should you decide to drive from Paris to the Cote d'Azur on the A6 or A7 Rhone valley route, you will pay as much in tolls as you will in petrol.

If you prefer a more leisurely drive, pottering through little towns and villages, the 'N' designated roads are toll free.

The French railway system is one of the best in the world, with high speed, clean trains running to all parts of the country. The TGV rail system provides super-fast trains to carry you to all urban centres.

Is it safe?
France has a significantly lower crime rate than Britain.

How much tax will I pay?
Unless your retirement income exceeds €70,000 you will be better off in France. Residents are liable for tax on their worldwide income, so a pension being drawn in another country needs to be declared in France.

There is a property tax (taxe foncières) and a residence tax (taxe d'habitation). If you rent you only pay the taxe d'habitation; if you are an owner-occupier you pay both.

Property tax varies from region to region and urban taxes are usually higher than rural rates.

Profits on the sale of property are subject to capital gains tax but are exempt if it is your principal residence. Also exempt are costs and expenses associated with the purchase and sale and, after five years of ownership, there is a 10 per cent allowance for each subsequent year of ownership. After 15 years ownership any profit on sale is tax free.

Is French property a good investment?
A French home, whether it is an apartment, villa, cottage, townhouse or chateau, is virtually guaranteed to make you a profit. It will probably make you a considerable profit over a longer term and, although no one can exactly predict the future market, even in less prosperous times, it is highly unlikely that you'll lose money by investing in French property.

Watermill
Dating from the 16th Century and reached by a 200m lane, the house has been completely renovated. Large sitting room with veranda overlooking the river, large kitchen and 3 bedrooms, all en-suite. Property has terraced gardens, 4 bridges and a small island.
Price: €834,750
More info: www.pavilionsofsplendourinternational.com
Email: diana@pavilionsofsplendourinternational.com

Cannes apartment
Situated in the private Parc Fiorentina with beautiful gardens and a swimming pool, Les Aquarelles is a tranquil, stylish haven in the heart of Cannes. Private terrace and garden which leads to communal gardens and pool.
Floor area of 83sq m with 3 bedrooms. In addition there is a large dry cellar for storage and a secure garage. Fully furnished and equipped with electrical appliances: dishwasher, oven, hob, fridge freezer, washing machine. Master bedroom with ensuite.
Price: €650,000
More info: www.lesaquarelles.com
Tel (owner): 01702 580697   Email chezhutch@btinternet.com

FACTFILE

Capital: Paris   **Population:** 62 million

Area: 545,630 sq km   **Language:** French

Climate: Temperate in the north with cool winters and mild summers. Mediterranean in the south with hot summers and mild winters. Mountainous regions cooler with heavy snow in winter.

Time difference: GMT +1 hour

Entry requirements: EU member, no visa required.

Retirement/residence: EU citizens have the right to live in France without a visa.

Electricity: 220V 50Hz

Money: Euro. ATMs are widely available. Credit/debit cards and traveller's cheques are accepted in most shops and hotels.

Public holidays 2010

Jan 1	New Year's Day	July 14	Bastille Day
Apr 13	Easter Monday	Aug 15	Assumption
May 1	Labour Day	Nov 1	All Saints' Day
May 8	1945 Victory Day	Nov 11	Remembrance Day
June 1	Whit Monday	Dec 25	Christmas Day
May 21	Ascension		

Opening hours

Shops: 9am or 10am to 7pm or 8pm in towns and cities. In rural areas shops usually close for lunch. Small grocery shops and bakers usually open very early and close around 7-8pm.

Banks: 10am-5pm, Mon-Fri in major cities; 10am-1pm and 3-5pm elsewhere.

Offices: Varies considerably but 8.30am-5.30pm or 9.30am-6.30pm is usual.

Water: Tap water is OK unless labelled 'non-potable'.

Tipping: France is a tipping society. Taxi drivers expect 10-15 per cent, hairdressers 10 per cent and small tips for cloakroom attendants, tour guides and drivers. Restaurants include tax and a 15 per cent service charge. A small additional tip is usual.

Medical/healthcare

Healthcare in France is rated as the best in the world by the World Health Organisation. No special precautions/vaccinations are necessary. The European Health Insurance Card will allow you to have your medical fees reimbursed. See page xx.

Pets: To get in without quarantine, pets must be microchipped, vaccinated against rabies and issued with an EU Pet Passport.

After an increase of about four per cent in 2007, house prices were around 10 per cent lower at the end of 2008 compared with 2007, according to FNAIM, the national association of estate agents.

There are, however, large variations between regions and towns, most noticeably in Cannes where apartment prices dropped by 13.2 per cent. In other towns – Limoges, Meaux and Angers among them – prices increased over the year by about six per cent.

On a regional basis prices fell dramatically in Charentes and Champagne.

FNAIM forecasts that prices will continue to decrease throughout 2010 and 2011.

Normandy cottage

Tastefully restored 2-bedroom cottage in a hamlet in the heart of the Cotentin peninsular, near to the market town of La Haye du Puits and close to beaches and ports. Terraced garden of 850sq m. The house is south facing and has a superb sun trap terrace across the front which is ideal for those lazy summer evenings with a glass of wine and BBQ. Price: €160,775

More info: www.frenchestateagents.co.uk Tel (UK): 08700115151

Country retreat

Part mediaeval farmhouse and two barns in the peaceful, hilly countryside of the South Aveyron. Modern comfort with authentic French charm. Four double bedrooms, three bath/shower rooms. 1/3 acre garden. Glorious views.

Price: €295,000

More info: Sharon Colback, Tel: 00 33 5 65 99 7645
Email: sharon.colback@wanadoo.fr

Where's best to live?

The Mediterranean Côte d'Azur and French Riviera, for long the playgrounds of European aristocrats and the mega-rich, are among the most scenic areas in Europe.

Less glamorous, but more bracing is the French Atlantic coast near Biarritz, Bayonne, and further down in the Camargue, home of wild horses and French gypsies, or the French Basque country.

Aquitaine

Most regions enjoy good food and wine as a part of daily life but Aquitaine benefits from truly great food and wine – perhaps the best that France has to offer. And, of course, Bordeaux is the major wine-producing area, known the world over.

Famous for fabulous beaches and superb wine, Aquitaine was named by the Romans who were extremely pleased to find so many rivers flowing through the land.

Home to more than a million people, Gironde is the largest of the 'departments' in Aquitaine. It has more than 3,200km of rivers and 112km of fine coastline.

Bordeaux, nestled in the heart of the Gironde, with a population of just over half a million, is probably better known for its neoclassical architecture and spacious, well kept town centre.

Bordeaux also boasts wide boulevards and well tended parks. An air of the 18th century pervades the streets, a feeling which appears to have been effortlessly cultivated.

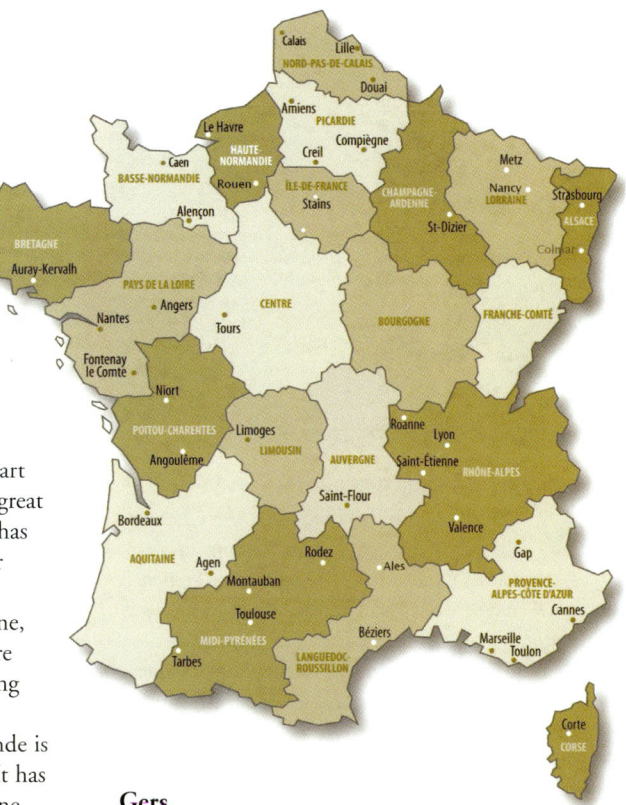

Gers

Little known to many, the area known as the Gers lies deep in the south west and is part of the Midi-Pyrenees region. It sits just to the west of the university town of Toulouse and is named after the river Gers that has its source in the foothills of the Pyrenees.

Due to the proximity of Spain, the strong influence of Spanish culture is evident throughout this area.

Vineyard homes

French developer Garrigae Resorts has opened a 20-acre vineyard development and spa, 'Les Jardins de St Benoît', of 171 townhouses and villas inspired by the traditional architecture of the Languedoc region. Owners enjoy a share in the ownership of the on-site vineyard and olive grove and can choose to integrate with the local community by participating in the traditions of wine-making and olive pressing.
Prices: €205,000 for a 1-bedroom townhouse, rising to €635,000 for a-5 bedroom villa. All prices include furniture.
More info: www.garrigae.com Tel (from UK): 0871 218 2103
Email: jbranch@garrigae.com

8 bedrooms in Brittany

Spacious house 2 minutes from the shops and a few minutes from the beach and the harbour of Locquirec in Brittany. Recently renovated, the house has 8 bedrooms and 2 stone outbuildings. Area is popular for holidaying and for water sports.
Price: €445,200
More info: www.frenchestateagents.co.uk
Tel (UK): 08700115151

I Live Here

After a career as an international financial journalist, Sharon Colback bought an old farmhouse and spent eight years turning it into a des res where she gives creative writing courses. Now it's time for another challenge she says.

What springs to mind when you think of France? The Eiffel Tower and the Champs-Elysees? Champagne? Or perhaps more basic – a bottle of wine, a baguette and some French cheese. Or maybe you think of Provence with its fields of lavender, its vines and its rather worn image of groups of jolly workers seated at wooden tables under trees, enjoying a glass of wine and a huge feast of bread and sausage.

But there are other, less familiar, scenes in the unspoiled French countryside where life goes on in the same calm way it has for centuries, but with modern comfort thrown in. Take where I live, in the Aveyron. This hilly, sparsely populated area where the clocks on the village churches still chime, day and night, is little known even to the French from other parts of the country.

It offers the luxury of space, peace and a stress-free, unhurried pace of life that has all but disappeared from the larger centres of Europe.

The Aveyron is in south-west France to the north-east of Toulouse. Here, farmers raise sheep to provide milk for the many producers of Roquefort cheese – the 'King of Cheese and the Cheese of Kings' as they like to refer to it here.

This is an area of old stone houses, of fortified villages and of tumbling rivers like the Tarn, the Dourdou and the Aveyron which cut steep-sided valleys through the densely forested hills.

The Aveyron was once a poor area, turned in on itself. Until the invention of the bicycle and later the car, families married amongst themselves, provided their own entertainment and rarely strayed further away than walking distance from their village.

They gathered together for communal feasts, for story telling throughout the long, cold winter evenings and to bake bread in the village oven.

These traditions continue. In my village and those all around, throughout the year we have fetes and festivals, music and storytelling and feasting for any reason – or none. At some of the feasts, the village wood oven is still lit and we enjoy bread baked in a way which hasn't changed for centuries.

Throughout the summer, in the neighbouring village of Coupiac, we meet at the night market each Monday. Local snail farmers, pancake makers, butchers barbecueing brochettes and wine merchants ring the parking lot beneath the towering Chateau.

In the middle are long trestle tables seating 50 people. We buy our food and wine and take it to eat amongst our friends and neighbours. There is always music or dancing to accompany the meal and some, dressed in Mediaeval costume, go on to perform in the tableau which wakes the Chateau from its sleep.

The small produce market takes place in Coupiac every Wednesday morning throughout the summer. There, our pretty, plump poultry farmer sells her chickens, quail and guinea fowl, the young woman cheesemaker brings fresh new cheeses, made of sheep and goats' milk, Fred, our village baker, provides fouace, a typical Aveyronaise sweet bread, and flaune, a spongy cheesecake made of sheeps' milk cheese, while Annie, arms akimbo, blocks the end of the road with her stall laden with jams of every imaginable kind. We buy, we greet each other with a kiss on each cheek and, in the custom of the Aveyron, a third for luck, we chat, then we gather at the bar for an apero of pastis or kir.

A bistro too

Living in the countryside of south-west France has many advantages over life in the more familiar, densely populated areas. Pollution? What's that? Sunshine? We can guarantee a lot, although there are cool days which come almost as a relief after a long run of heat.

The food, too, comes straight off the farm and we have our own village bistro and grocery store, our baker and our village school.

You do not need to speak French to enjoy life here but it certainly helps. The French are very open these days to communicating with residents who don't, but it is much more fun if you can chat easily with the hardware shop owner, the handyman or the builder.

If you need the familiar comfort of a group of English people, getting together regularly at the bar to speak English and advise each other on the nearest stockist of baked beans, this is not the place to come. But if you yearn for an authentic taste of La France Profonde, your search has ended here.

Property in the Gers tends to reflect this influx of Spanish culture. The rolling countryside is lush and green and forts and castles adorn the hilltops.

Historically, Gers was part of Gascony and was one of the original 83 departments created during the French Revolution. Gers is mainly an agricultural region, producing a variety of cereals, poultry and well known gastronomic specialities including 'fois gras'.

Les Pyrenees

The stunning scenery is beautiful throughout all four seasons. In winter, snow is guaranteed and there are many ski slopes to choose from. Summer brings a different kind of tourism, mainly campers, hikers and mountain climbers.

While autumn is a grey, wet and depressing season in much of northern Europe, in the Pyrenees it is another beautiful period of transformation when the forests change their colours and the first snows start to fall on the mountains.

Although a very quiet and secluded area, the Pyrenees is easily accessible by road and air. On both the western and eastern side of the mountains there are the main traffic arteries linking France with Spain and there is a motorway running along the northern edge of the mountains linking Biarritz and Bordeaux with Montpellier and Perpignan via Toulouse.

From the UK there are direct flights to Biarritz, Carcassonne, Pau, Perpignan and Toulouse.

Property in the Pyrenees is much more affordable than similar mountain properties in Switzerland.

Biarritz

Biarritz has a beautiful long coastline of wide, sandy beaches, which attracts many tourists, both French and international, during its long, warm summers. The city is located between the sea and the Pyrenees. This spectacular mountain range, which forms a natural border between France and Spain, has great ski slopes for lovers of winter sports.

While the snow is never far away, winters are mild and pleasant. Biarritz is easily accessible by road, rail and air. Its international airport has direct flights to destinations in the UK.

Dordogne

The Dordogne, created during the French Revolution in 1790 from the former province of Perigord, is one of the most beautiful and historic areas in France.

If you love architecture and enjoy living in an area where medieval architecture is a part of life, then look no further. Property in the Dordogne comes in all shapes and sizes but because of the size of the area and its past you are far more likely to find an older property awaiting your renovation skills.

The area is steeped in history and this is reflected in the stunning architecture prevalent throughout the whole of the region. This area has more than a thousand castles including Castelnaud-la-Chapelle, Beynac, Biron and Bourdeilles.

The north-east of the Dordogne is full of lush rolling hills, forests and even prairies. It is often referred to as 'Le Perigord Vert'. The Limestone plateaux in the centre of the region are referred to as 'le Perigord Blanc'.

Whilst these regions have a great deal to offer tourists and residents alike, southeast Dordogne is probably the most popular part of the area with many prehistoric sites, caves and castles. This is the ideal place to appreciate some of France's most stunning mediaeval architecture.

We Live Here

Life in Brittany is the cat's whiskers

When, in their 50s, Brian and Carol McDermott decided to retire to Brittany, little did they know that it would be the start of a whole new career. The energetic couple were probably not really cut out for early retirement anyway and deliberately chose a lively area of Brittany's Cote d'Armor region for their new home.

Within months they had spotted a niche in the market which led to the making of many new friends, a useful income and retirement being postponed for a further five years.

The couple had lived in various parts of Britain and when retirement approached, the long-service policeman and his wife drew up a short list of places they might make their home.

Brian, originally from Oban, and Carol from Kent, liked the gorgeous countryside, old fashioned values and peace and quiet of Oban, but it didn't have much to offer socially or for shopping.

Of all the places they considered, only Brittany seemed to fulfil all their needs: affordable, safe, picturesque, well serviced with shops, restaurants and plenty of things to do and a health service second to none.

They made the move from the Midlands to an attractive modern house in St Goueno, 45 minutes from the beach, and immersed themselves into their new life, joining clubs, taking French lessons and exploring the area.

Their chosen village hosts a very large motorsport hill climb each year with around 100 entrants competing. An audience of several thousand spectators gathers to watch and when the local mayor found out about Brian's police background he was enlisted as a marshal to help ensure public safety.

Brian quickly become more involved helping British drivers with their registrations and with translation work related to the event.

Meanwhile – as she made friends in the local community – Carol realised that there was a lack of high quality, professional care for the cats of owners returning to the UK to visit friends and family.

A few catteries existed, but they often did not adhere to the very high standards owners expected. In their usual thorough way, Brian and Carol researched the requirements and set about building their own cattery which was completed in 2004.

Ready to retire ... again

The business is busy all year round with a loyal clientele of both British and French clients.

The local people were delighted at their success and have been very supportive of the enterprise.

Today, seven years after their original attempt to retire, Brian and Carol are ready to have another go, but are very keen that the work they have invested in their cattery does not go to waste.

Forward bookings for the cattery are very healthy and the couple are keen for it to continue.

Brian and Carol plan to stay in the area, in the same village if possible, but to do some travelling.

"In a way we've been the victims of our own success," says Brian.

More info:
Interested in taking over? The cattery and the McDermott's 4 bedroom, 2 bathroom house is on the market for €246,100.

Brian and Carol are happy to answer any questions on how the business operates and are even prepared to give very serious potential buyers a chance to 'try before they buy' with a two-day stay at the property.

More info:
www.lasaudecattery.com
Tel (0033) 0296 344726
email: mcdermott@orange.fr

Embassies/Government
French Embassy in London
www.ambafrance-uk.org

British Embassy in France
http://ukinfrance.fco.gov.uk

Travel & Health Advice
Foreign Office travel advice
www.fco.gov.uk/travel
www.nhs.uk/Healthcareabroad
www.masta.org

About France
www.frenchentree.com
www.france-pub.com
www.readyforfrance.com
www.understandfrance.org
www.livingfrance.com
www.readyforfrance.com
www.readyforfrance.com
http://melbelin.com/AllThingsFrench.html
www.francethisway.co

General & Expat
www.expatfocus.com
www.britishexpats.com
www.britishexpat.com
www.transitionsabroad.com
www.readyforfrance.com/taxes
www.suite101.com
www.newlifeinfrance.co.uk

English Language Media
English-language newspapers and magazines are widely available at news-stands in cities and major towns, especially in tourist areas.
International Herald Tribune
www.thefrenchpaper.com
Monthly print publication
Riviera Times: www.rivieratimes.com
French Property News:
www.french-property-news.com
Online publications
Go Go Paris:www.gogoparis.com
ParisVoice: http://parisvoice.com
Irish Eyes: www.irisheyes.fr
TV
Sky channels are available of as well as English-language programmes via CNN, and BBC World. Canal+ and Arte show some English-language films. It is also possible to access UK-based free-to-air (FTA) programming and other channels with a free-to-view (FTV) card installed).

Property
www.bw-international.com
www.frenchestateagents.com
www.french-property.com
www.seymour-james.com
www.property-loire-atlantic.com
www.garrigae.com

www.savills.co.uk
www.francepropertyshop.com
www.leggettimmobilier.com
www.frenchhouses.co.uk/
www.cotedazurestates.com
www.dordognepropertyagency.com
www.creme-de-languedoc.com
www.breton-homes.com

Travel & Tourism
www.francetourism.com
www.dordogne-on-line.info
www.france.com
www.streetwise-france.com
www.franceguide.com
www.whytraveltofrance.com
http://gofrance.about.co
www.franceonecall.com
www.francethisway.com
www.thisfrenchlife.com
Regional info
Ardennes: www.ardennes.com
Auvergne: www.auvergne-tourisme.info
Loire Valley: www.visaloire.com
Haute-marne: www.tourisme-hautemarne.com
Jura: www.jura-tourism.com
Limousin: www.tourismelimousin.com
Midi-pyrenees:
www.tourisme-midi-pyrenees.org
Pyrenees Orientalles: www.cdt-66.com
Riviera Cote D'Azur: www.guideriviera.com
Somme: www.somme-tourisme.com
Loir Valley: www.vallee-du-loir.com

Getting There
Air
Budget airlines such as Ryanair and Easyjet fly to most regional airports: Provence, Normandy, Brittany, the French Riviera and the South West. All of these airlines have online booking facilities.
Bus
Eurolines is the largest operator of scheduled coach services, offering regular services to Avignon, Bordeaux, Grenoble, Marseilles, Nantes, Paris (up to four services daily), Perpignan, St Malo, Strasbourg, Toulouse and Tours. Connections are available to Eurolines via National Express.
Eurolines UK: www.eurolines.co.uk
National Express: www.nationalexpress.com
Train
Eurostar's ultra modern, high-speed service to travels from London St Pancras International or Ebbsfleet International in Kent direct to Paris, Brussels or Lille. Eurostar also offers direct services to Disneyland Paris and to the French Alps. Certain services also serve Ashford International in Kent and Calais-Fréthun.
More info

www.eurostar.com
Rail Europe Travel Centre
www.raileurope.co.uk
International Rail
www.internationalrail.com
www.tgv.com
Boat
There are numerous option to reach France by ferry.
Brittany Ferrieswww.brittanyferries.com
Condor Ferrieswww.condorferries.co.uk
HD Ferries www.hdferries.co.uk
LD Lines & Transmanche Ferries
www.transmancheferries.com
www.ldlines.co.uk
Norfolkline www.norfolkline.com
P&O Ferries www.poferries.com
SeaFrance www.seafrance.com
SpeedFerries
www.speedferries.com
By car
French autoroutes are excellent but driving from the ferry ports to the south of France coast will cost you around £100 in petrol and almost as much in tolls. [See: Driving]

Getting Around
Within France most towns have metro or tram systems and a comprehensive bus network.
In Paris the metro is by far the quickest and most practical way of getting about. Numerous connections with the RER (Regional express network) and the SNCF railway stations allow easy travel to the suburbs.
Train: Practical, fast and comfortable, the train is one of the best ways of getting about in France. The rail network is very developed (especially from Paris) and connects every town by either TGV or TER (regional express trains).
Bus: Efficient services in major cities and towns but services in rural areas can be few and far between.
Driving: French autoroutes branch out from Paris like the spokes of a wheel, allowing you to drive in comfort to all parts of the country on the Autoroutes. Remember they are toll roads, and if you drive from Paris to the Cote d'Azur on the A6 or A7 Rhone valley route, for example, you will pay as much in tolls as you will in petrol.
The alternative is a more leisurely drive, pottering through towns and villages on the N designated roads which are toll free. It is compulsory for all vehicles to carry a warning triangle, a florescent jacket, spare bulbs, first aid kit and a fire extinguisher.
For driving times/distances:
english.controleradar.org
Driving is on the right.

Ministry of Tourism
Greek National Tourism Organisation
www.visitgreece.gr

Greece is a country with much to experience. It boasts natural scenery with rare beauty on the mainland, azure seawaters and magnificent beaches in the innumerable islands, and plenty of archaeological monuments everywhere. It continues dynamically into its modern history with its rich historical past of culture, art, poetry, theater, philosophy, and Olympic ideals.

Its history and culture is famous all over the world. The Acropolis in Athens, the "Sacred Rock", with such monuments as the Parthenon, Propylaea, Erechtheion, and the temple of Nike, is an architectural jewel that still crowns Greece as the "cradle of Western civilization". A day-trip away from Athens are the beautiful temple of Poseidon, ancient God of the Sea at Cape Sounio; the ancient Panhellenic sanctuary of Delphi, which the ancient Greeks believed to be the "omphalos of the world"; and the timeless experience of ancient Greek drama in the well-preserved ancient theater of Epidaurus.

Greece is also one of the richest countries in the world in terms of natural spas. Thermal and mineral springs appear at 850 different geographical locations, some of which are the medicinal springs of Edipsos, the springs at Thermopiles, the thermal baths at Kyllini, the sulphur at Kaiafas etc.

Greek gastronomy stimulates all five senses and satisfies the most demanding tastes with its ingredients combining tradition with modern concepts. Anyone traveling around the country "tastes" the uniqueness – in the virgin olive oil and the fruits of the olive groves. Honey, mastic, saffron, olives, ouzo, and tsipouro are all products of Greece with a unique aroma and taste.

Greece is an ideal tourist destination that caters to all modern forms of tourism in their most attractive and qualitative version. It is a special tourist experience all year-round, either for city breaks or business, for sea and sun or culture and education, for supports and ecotourism or religious and pilgrimage tourism, or for the beneficial action of health and wellness and spa therapy.

Greece invites you to live your own unique experience.

Homer's ancient land offers modern delights for retirees

Why Greece?

Beautiful scenic Greece has an abundance of fine beaches, rugged mountains, bustling towns and cultural attractions. Southern Greece and the islands enjoy a warm Mediterranean climate with long hot summers and short winters.

The famous Greek hospitality and the community spirit is alive and much in evidence throughout the country. The Greeks have a love of food, wine, music and dancing, with whole towns and villages celebrating major festivals.

The rich cultural past of Greece is never far from the present: traces of the Minoan civilization, evidence of Roman and Turkish occupations remain throughout the country; the archaeological sites, Byzantine churches and monasteries, Venetian architecture, even minarets and mosques.

Athens is the gateway to Greece and boasts a new modern airport, with daily flights to and from major European destinations throughout the year. Easyjet and Aegean Airlines offer budget airfares to and from the UK and local domestic airlines serve all the major islands. In the summer months charter flights fly directly between the UK and many Greek Islands.

Greece is a popular retirement destination and many Brits and others have chosen to retire here. After exploring mainland Greece I first arrived in Crete in 1984 and fell under the island's spell immediately. It's such a beautiful and diverse place.

Crete and the other tourist resorts in Greece are swamped by visitors in the summer months but October sees the last charter flights going back to the UK and Europe and from November to March Greece returns to its old rhythms of life. While hotels in the towns stay open during the winter months, hotels, tavernas, cafes and bars all close down in the resorts.

Nightlife changes from the summer scene of beach bars and outdoor tavernas to trendy indoor town cafés and restaurants, and cosy village cafeneons and tavernas with wood-burning stoves or open fireplaces.

Greeks turn to their fields and collect their orange harvests. Weekends are often spent away from the towns as people head for their 'horio' (village) to gather their olives, or to visit relatives.

The island towns are still very much alive and busy in the winter as the locals go about their daily business. On the roads there are numerous pick-up trucks loaded with olives, firewood or livestock as well as the usual traffic but with hardly a hire-car in sight.

ABOUT THE WRITER: Carol Palioudakis is the author of the book "**Living in Crete – A Guide to Living, Working, Retiring & Buying Property in Crete**". She also runs the website: www.livingincrete.net, a comprehensive resource for those moving to Crete and Greece. Carol moved there in 1986 and lives in Chania, Crete with her Cretan husband and two children.

FACTFILE

Capital: Athens

Population: 11.1 million

Area: 131,957sq km

Language: Greek. English is the predominant second language

Climate: Mediterranean; mild, wet winter and hot, dry summer.

Time differece: GMT+ 2.

Entry requirements: EU member, no visa required.

Retirement/residence: Very straightforward for EU nationals. The residence permit has been replaced by the registration certificate and EU nationals staying longer than three months must hold this certificate which will be open dated with no need for it to be renewed.However, a new document available to EU nationals is the permanent residence certificate (Engrafo Monimis Diamonis) which is optional, but can be applied for by anyone who wants it for their own reasons provided they can show that they have been a permanent resident of Greece for five years.

In districts outside Athens application should be made to the nearest police station.

Electricity: 220V 50 Hz. You may require an adapter for the round two-pin sockets in use in Greece.

Money: Euro. ATMs are widely available. Credit/debit cards and travellers cheque are accepted in most shops and hotels.

Public holidays: 2010

Jan 1	New Year's Day
Jan 6	Epiphany or 12th Night
March	10 Shrove Mon or Ash
March 25	Independence Day
April 17	Orthodox Good Friday
April 20	Orthodox Easter Monday
May 1	Labour Day
June 16	Orthodox Whit Monday
Aug 15	Assumption Day
Oct 28	Ochi Day ('No' Day)
Dec 25	Christmas Day
Dec 26	Boxing Day

Opening hours

Banks: 8.30-2pm (1.30pm on Fridays)

Offices: 8am-1pm

Shops: 9am-2pm and 5pm-8pm

Water: Tap water in Athens and the major cities is drinkable. Bottled water is advisable in remote areas and in most of the islands.

Tipping: a 13 per cent service charge is added to restaurant bills. It is customary to leave a little extra if the service was satisfactory. Taxi drivers do not expect tips but toilet attendants do.

Medical/Healthcare: EU pensioners who take up residence in Greece can obtain form E121 from their Department of Health for free treatment in the Greek public health system. Those who remain UK residents may obtain an EHIC health card for free treatment in Greece. Greek public hospitals are well equipped but sometimes overcrowded.

Pets: Your pet must be micro-chipped and registered, and must have had a rabies vaccination within the previous 30 days. Animals travelling within the EU are required to have PET passport.

Greek culture is unique and can take a little getting used to, while the laid-back lifestyle is not without its frustrations. Bureaucracy, for example, seems to have been refined into an art form and often requires endless patience.

Much of the Greek culture revolves around the Greek Orthodox Church which is instrumental in daily life and cultural traditions; 97 per cent of the population is Greek Orthodox. Religious holidays are rigidly observed; some are designated as national holidays and others are celebrated with colourful festivals.

In Greece there is a contrast between town and village life. Many villages still retain the 'old' way of life – men in the cafeneons sipping Greek coffee and raki while women gather outside their homes, crocheting and gossiping together.

PROPERTY

Renovated cottage

Traditional stone property of 109sq m in a quiet hillside street with sea and mountain views in the unspoilt village of Kirianna, Crete, 14km east of Rethymnon and 10 minutes from the nearest beach. Renovated in 2004 and sold fully furnished. 2 bedrooms (1 en-suite). Can sleep up to 6 people. Many traditional features.

Price: €92,500 Ref: CADM

More info: www.apropertyingreece.com

Tel (UK): 020 8302 6616

Email: sales@apropertyingreece.com

Cost of living

The real cost of living in Greece is higher than many imagine. Since the introduction of the euro in 2002, costs have risen steeply.

However, a pensioner contributing to the expatforum.com website as recently as January 2010, wrote: "We left the UK in May last year. As pensioners we simply could not afford to stay there without working.

"Who wants to work by choice beyond 65. So here we are in Rhodes, in a 100-year-old house in a fantastic village paying €280 a month in rent. Our phone/broadband for two months is €70. Our electric bills in summer were around €40 for two months. A monthly

shop at Carrefour is €110-150 with small top-ups in the village in between.

"We don't have need of a car full time so we just rent for one or two days a month. Two days in winter costs €30. In summer its €50. So here we are living the good life. In the UK we were working to live. Here we are working and living.

"The crime rate here is low. We go to bed at night and leave our doors open. Even in winter the weather is fantastic.

"So go for it. You wont regret moving to Greece."

While property costs and rents are still relatively low, the cost of living has spiralled and those living in Greece on a fixed income are feeling the pinch as the

Peloponnese

Traditional 2-storey stone village property of 126sq m approx 20km from the beaches of Kalamata, sleeps 6. Renovated in 2000 and located in the village of Katsaros, prefecture of Messinia, South Peloponnese. Property enjoys lovely views from the upper level.

Mature garden of 200sq m. A further plot of 4,000sq m for agricultural purposes could be purchased for €10,000. Telephone, electricity and water supplies are all connected. Ref: PPSG Price €80,000

More info: www.apropertyingreece.com
Tel (UK): 0208 302 6616

Western Crete

Snobby Homes in the area around the picturesque fishing village of Kolimbari in western Crete, on small developments, within walking distance of everyday amenities. These detached homes, with 2 or 3 double bedrooms, include a spacious and private walled courtyard garden large enough for a swimming pool with space left over for sun terraces and a vegetable garden.

Prices: Range from €130,000 inclusive of all taxes and legal fees
More info: www.snobbyhomes.co.uk
Snobby Homes
Tel (UK): 0871 900 8690

pound drops against the euro.

Savings can be made at the large supermarket chains such as Carrefour and Lidl by buying their own brand goods. Buy local fresh fruit and vegetables only when they are in season. Shop at the local farmers market, the laiki.

Eating out in Greece is still fairly cheap, particularly away from the main tourist areas and local 'in' places. Village tavernas usually offer the best value.

Is it safe?

Greece is generally a safe, law-abiding and friendly country with an extremely low crime rate – one of the lowest in the world. There are occasional reports of handbag snatching in Athens but in rural areas particularly many Greeks still leave their front doors unlocked and their car keys in the ignition.

How much tax will I pay?

One of the first things you should do when you move to Greece or buy property is register for a tax number (AFM – pronounced aa-fee-mee). An AFM number is required to buy a car or motorcycle and to rent or buy property.

The local Tax Office (Eforia) is the place to do this. An accountant or lawyer can obtain one for you or you can apply in person. You'll need your passport, birth and marriage certificates (if married) and photocopies of all three documents.

Once registered, you are required to submit a yearly tax return regardless of income, even if it is a nil return. Property owners must also file an annual property declaration. Income tax is only payable on income arising in Greece. In order to avoid paying income tax on money transferred from abroad – to buy property,

land, a car or boat for example – you must obtain a 'pink slip' from your Greek bank which proves where the money originated and that tax has already been paid.

Property tax: Property holdings are subject to a real estate tax calculated on the basis of location, age, etc. of the property ('objective value') which are subject to revision every one or two years.

The tax applies at a rate 0.1 per cent or one euro per square metre of the home, whichever is the highest. Land that is located outside of the village is exempt from the tax.

Is Greek property a good investment?

Between 1994-2005, property prices in Greece increased by an average of 175 per cent. Here in Crete estate agents have reported 30-40 per cent annual price rises in the past for properties near the sea.

Today property inflation is below 3.2 per cent. Greece is a slow market and there are bargains away from the tourist spots.

There is a strong demand for property in places like Crete and Corfu. Northern Europeans love the long, hot summers and wonderful beaches. Prices in Crete are still low compared to Spain, France and Italy.

If you are thinking of moving to Greece you may already have an idea of which area you will choose to live. However you have probably only visited in the summer and you may find that an attractive village near a small resort but far from town becomes much less attractive in the winter months when everything in the nearby resort is closed down.

Before you buy a home it is well worth renting in the area you are considering to get a feel for the area and the people. How far are the nearest shops and tavernas

for year-round living? What about accessibility of the property – steep tracks, steps, etc?

Where's best to live?

Popular retiree destinations include
Kalymnos: Part of the Dodecanese islands, the Paliki peninsula of Kefalonia (around Lixouri). Out of the way, enjoying magnificent sea views, there are many beaches with tavernas to pick from.
Kefalonia: For some of the most colourful sunsets you have ever seen.
Crete. The largest of all the Greek islands with a year-round population of 630,000. Crete boasts an amazing combination of rugged mountains and scenic beaches, all within reach of major towns.
In and around Chania to the west is popular with retirees, as is the area around Rethymnon in central Crete and Agios Nikolaos and Sitia in the east.
Corfu – Acharavi, Sidari, Kalimari
Paros – has a thriving art community of expatriates as well as Greeks. This out-of-the-main-stream island town is relatively quiet even in high season yet never more than a 30 minute drive (1 hour by bus) from anywhere else on the island.

Mountain views
1 bedroom renovated apartment of 43sq m in a 200-year-old building in the village of Pinokohori, approx 10km from Lefkas Town. Stunning sea and mountain views and within easy reach of several sandy beaches and other mountain beauty spots.
Less than 1km away is the larger village of Lazarta which has several shops. Apartment comes with a fitted kitchen with washing machine, microwave, fridge and a newly-fitted shower/WC.
Price €50,000 Ref: LPJK
More info: www.apropertyingreece.com

Corfu villa
Luxury villa 5km from Corfu Town. Large landscaped gardens, up to 8 bedrooms, 5 bathrooms, large swimming pool. Price: €840,000
More info: www.corfu-house-for-sale.com
Email: enquiries@corfu-house-for-sale.com
UK+07710 542 799 Greece +30 6942 907 747

GREECE CONTACT DIRECTORY

Embassies/Government
Greek Embassy in London
www.greekembassy.org.uk

British Embassy in Greece
http://ukingreece.fco.gov.uk/en

Travel & Health Advice
Foreign Office travel advice
www.fco.gov.uk/travel
www.nhs.uk/Healthcareabroad
www.masta.org

About Greece
http://en.wikipedia.org/wiki/Greece
www.in2greece.com/
http://www.soulis.com/greece1.html A

General & Expat
www.livingincrete.net
www.expatfocus.com
www.britishexpat.com
www.transitionsabroad.com

Media (English)
Athens News
Also online at www.athensnews.gr

Athens Plus weekly
Also online at www.ekathimerini.com
ERT (http://www.ert.gr)
Current news in Greek and English.

Property
www.property-in-greece.co
www.agreekproperty.com
www.cretanresidences.com/site/
www.creteproperty.gr
www.newland-realestate.gr
http://www.corfuproperty.gr
http://ipg.franglo.com/classifieds
www.sunshineestates.net
www.greekproperty.gr
www.cretan-resorts.gr
www.giakoumakis.gr

Travel & Tourism
http://www.gnto.gr/?langID=2
www.greektravel.com
www.athensinfoguide.com/
www.tours2greece.info
www.greekisland.co.uk
www.mykonos-greece.biz
www.santorini-greece.biz
www.harrys-athens-greece-guide.com
http://www.gtp.gr/

Getting There
Air:Athens and other Greek destinations
are served by numerous holiday charter
operators and scheduled carriers
including:
British Airwayswww.britishairways.com
Air France www.airfrance.co.uk
Olympic Airwayswww.olympic-airways.gr
Aegean Airlineswww.aegeanair.com
Easyjet www.easyjet.com
The advantage of using Olympic or Aegean
is discounted connections to smaller
domestic airports.
By bus and train
Eurolines – it's a four-day journey
By train to Italy (Ancona, Bari or Brindisi)
and then by ferry.

Getting Around
Greece has a comprehensive, cheap and
reliable public transport network of buses
and trains that reaches even the smallest
villages. There are extensive ferry and
flight connections from Athens to islands in
the Adriatic and the Aegean.
Driving is on the right.

Art, culture, cuisine – here's where to find La Dolce Vita

Why Italy?

Italy has been popular among Britons since the days of the Grand Tour. It has an incredibly rich cultural history spanning many centuries and is the birthplace of some of the world's greatest artists and is home to many of its finest art treasures.

One of the oldest civilizations in the world, Italy has Venice and the Rialto bridge, opera, Pompeii and the Colosseum. It is the birthplace and home of many renowned artists and composers including Botticelli, Leonardo da Vinci, Michelangelo, Tintoretto, Caravaggio, Verdi and Puccini.

Visit Florence to see Michelangelo's 'David' and original paintings by Botticelli, Leonardo, Raphael and countless others, many contained in beautiful churches.

Throughout the country museums, monuments and cathedrals celebrate and commemorate its religious,

cultural and artistic traditions.

From the sunny southern slopes of the Alps to the lush orange groves of Sicily, Italy offers enormous variety in its natural scenery and, with 5,310 miles of coastline, an unlimited choice of beaches.

Because a good part of Italy grew up as a collection of independent city-states, customs and food vary greatly from region to region. This rich history is preserved in the colourful folk festivals that take place in all of Italy's regions throughout the year.

Italy is also a very family-oriented society and one which is famed for its cuisine. It remains a country of great cultural sophistication and is now a centre of the worldwide fashion industry.

Italy offers a good quality of life at relatively low cost and a relaxed lifestyle. Generally speaking Italians are friendly and outgoing. Property is still a bargain in many rural areas, especially older properties needing renovation.

No wonder then that Italy is the retirement choice of large numbers of retirees, not only from northern Europe but from North America and elsewhere.

The down side: foreign residents often complain about the inefficiencies and slowness of service, the poor plumbing and the horrendous traffic congestion in the cities. There is a high rate of petty crime such as pick-pocketing and house burglaries, although the violent crime rate is low.

How easy is it to obtain residential status?

Those planning to move to Italy must register with the local police authority (Questura), fill in forms declaring they plan to stay, and obtain a residence permit (permesso di soggiorno).

Apart from the usual bureaucracy you need evidence

FACTFILE

Capital: Rome
Population: 58m
Area: 301,225sq km
Language: Italian, with French and German in some regions.
Climate: Temperate Mediterranean climate, with warm summers and cool winters in the north and hot summers and mild winters in the south.
Entry requirements: EU member, no visa required.
Permanent residence: EU citizens have the right to take up residence.
Time difference: GMT +1
Electricity: 230V/50Hz
Money: Euro. ATMs widely available. Credit/debit cards and travellers cheques are widely accepted but less so in rural areas.
Public holidays 2010

Jan 1	New Year's Day	Aug 15	Assumption
Jan 6	Epiphany	Nov 1	All Saints' Day
April 5	Easter Monday	Dec 8	Immac Conception
April 25	Liberation Day	Dec 25	Christmas Day
May 1	Labour Day	Dec 26	St Stephen's Day
June 2	Republic Day		

Opening hours
Shops: 9am-1pm/4.30-7.30pm , Mon-Sat
Banks: 8.30am-1.30pm/2.45-4.15pm , Mon-Fri
Offices: 8.30am-1pm/3-6pm, Mon-Fri
Water: Considered safe but is sometimes heavily chlorinated.
Tipping: Service is almost always included in restaurants and there is often also a cover charge. Tips can be rounded up by a few euros. Taxi drivers don't expect but appreciate a tip.
Medical/Healthcare: No special precautions/vaccinations are necessary. The European Health Insurance Card will allow you to have your medical fees reimbursed. See page xx.
Pets: To get in without quarantine, pets must be microchipped, vaccinated against rabies and issued with an EU Pet Passport.

that you have sufficient money to support yourself.

A residence certificate is necessary to obtain customs clearance, to open a bank account, to purchase property.

Is it safe?

Petty theft – stealing from parked cars, pick-pocketing and purse snatching – is common at train stations and crowded tourist sites. So too is distraction theft, often by children – one throws liquid over your coat, another helps you clean up while a third steals your wallet or purse. Rome is probably the worst place for such thefts and also for vehicle break-ins.

How much tax will I pay?

If you are registered as a resident (residenza anagrafica), you are automatically liable for income tax on your worldwide income. The Imposta sul Reddito delle

Persone Fisiche (IRPEF) is a tax on personal income derived from any source. However, Italy has neither wealth tax nor inheritance tax.

Everyone must have a tax code number (codice fiscale) which is required for almost all paperwork: opening a bank account, signing official contracts (including with utility companies), starting a job, buying and registering a car.

You have to take your passport to the provincial tax office and your codice fiscale will be issued to you.

Is Italian property a good investment?

Between 1997 and 2007 house prices rose by almost 100 per cent. Buying a property involves three stages:
- Proposta irrevocabile d'acquisto (reservation offer).
- Contratto preliminare di vendita (preliminary contract).
- Atto di vendita (deed of sale).

When the Proposta irrevocabile d'acquisto is signed you pay a small deposit and the property is taken off the market, usually for two weeks, while your solicitor makes all the necessary searches. Once signed by both parties the reservation offer becomes legally binding.

The preliminary contract sets detailed terms and conditions of the sale and requires the payment of a non-returnable deposit of 10 per cent. The balance of the purchase price must be paid once the deed of sale, drafted by the notary, has been signed by all parties,

Where's best to live?

Food, culture or cosmopolitan life? Or all three? City, town or country? Florence, Rome, Tuscany or Umbria? North or south?

You may think that Italy's more industrial north would not be the first choice of retirees and property buyers, but according to a report by the Italian daily Il Sole 24 Ore, it's the north of the country that's best.

Not only did the northeast city of Trento score the highest points in its annual survey but the north also took second and third place with Bolzano and Aosta respectively.

The survey compares Italy's 103 provincial capitals according to six basic measuring sticks: living standards, business and work conditions, law and order, health and environmental services, population and leisure time.

The survey also took into account what residents thought about where they live. Agrigento in Sicily was found to be the worst city, a position held last year by Catania, also in Sicily.

The bottom ten cities – all in the south – were Caserta, Palermo, Vibo Valentia, Caltanissetta, Reggio

Lake Como villas

These new villas are on hills close to Gera Lario and all amenities and with spectacular views of Lake Como. Built on 2 levels with terraces and gardens, the villas have 2 bedrooms, 2 bathrooms, a living room and kitchen. Ref: 2061 Domaso
Prices from €243.000
More info: Casa Travella Ltd. www.casatravella.com
Tel: 01322-660988

Stone built house in Tuscany

This traditional stone built house with oak beams, terracotta floor tiles and a cellar is in the small village of Casentino, 30 minutes north of Arezzo in Tuscany. Florence is one hour away. On the first floor are two double bedrooms and a sitting room with views over the Pratomagno hills. The second floor has 2 double bedrooms and another room which could also be used as a bedroom. The village has a bar, small general store and a restaurant.
Price: €250,000
More info: Cluttons Italy www.cluttonsitaly.com

Mastering the time warp

Valerie Schneider is an American writer, who, with her husband, Bryan lived in New Mexico for 20 years before trading the high desert for the medieval hill towns of Italy. She is a regular contributor to the Slow Travel website: www.slowtrav.com

September arrived with a bang. Literally. I heard the familiar clatter of metal door shutters being noisily rolled upward, signaling officially the end of August. The neighborhood shops were again open for business after the limpid weeks of staring at drab grey gates plastered with ferie signs. And not a moment too soon, either.

August can be brutal. Not because of the heat - July is actually hotter – but because it is The Month of the Screeching Halt. What is one to do when all of one's favorite coffee bars are 'chiuso' and one cannot get a decent espresso? In Italy?!

The umbrella-bedecked outdoor tables in the piazza that are so festively inviting do not seem to serve up a cup of caffe quite as well as our beloved baristas can do. My butcher, fruit vendor, pizzaiuolo

and herbalist had all likewise deserted me. Even one of the local parish priests had locked up and left town, but then I guess most of his flock had fled for greener pastures so why not?

Their September mass re-entry was such a relief I nearly broke out into a rousing rendition of the Hallelulah Chorus.

As anyone who has ever traveled here can attest Italy operates on a time frame all her own. The unique rhythm that makes up an Italian day was one of the things that drew us in.

We quickly adopted the afternoon riposo into our routine and decided that our own frenetically-paced nation could take some lessons from our adopted country. Who doesn't benefit from a little afternoon rest, after all? Rising refreshed and going out into the piazza for a caffe is a treasured ritual.

Likewise the late afternoon passeggiata, when the entire town goes out for a stroll and a little face time with their neighbours.

It is fascinating to see the day unfold like a tidal movement. Mornings are bustling with activity, but if you happen to walk through the piazza at 3pm or 8.30pm you may think you've arrived in a ghost town, so deserted are these public spaces while the residents are tucked away at home eating.

After 9pm, out they emerge like fireflies to flit around the streets for a post-dinner walk and gelato while the kids run off excess energy. The timeless cadence of these unchanging activities is alluring and comforting, and we love it. But there is more than rhythm to understand and adapt to here.

It has taken a year but I think we may have gotten the hang of Standard Operating Italian Time. Each town has its own personalised variation on the theme but the song goes a little something like this: Museums are closed on Monday. No exceptions. Everything is closed on Sunday except pasticcerias, a handful of bars, and the pasta fresca shops. On Monday the pasta shops are closed to make up for being open on Sunday.

The post office closest to us slams its doors shut for the day at 1pm, while the main post office remains open all day, though service is no better even during lunch time when there are no customers. Go figure that one out.

From quirky to surreal

Here in our town, Monday mornings also mark a halt to retail operations; every clothing store, shoe store, phone store, and general store in the centro storico is closed until 4 or 4.30pm.

Sometimes the hours can be downright quirky, though. For instance, a nearby bank opens from 8.25am until 1.25pm, shuts down for lunch, then reopens from 2.40pm and closes at 4.10pm. Now, I ask you ... would knocking it back to nice, half-hour increments really be so bad? A friend in the States who is a banker would love this work schedule.

Quirky can turn to surreal when a holiday is involved, as I discovered this past spring when I tried to visit the Contemporary Art Museum. I lay before you the calendar: Easter was Sunday. In Italy, Monday is also a holiday, and everyone took advantage of it to create a long weekend. Tuesday would be the start of the work week, right? Hold that thought.

On Wednesday I tried to visit our contemporary art museum. The hours are posted on a bronze plaque, and I happen to know from previous trial-and-error that Monday is a normal closure. Now remember, folks, I went on Wednesday. Naturally, the gate was locked. I looked closer at the sign which said, "Closed Mondays and days after holidays." Tuesday wasn't a holiday, but it was the day after a holiday, meaning the museum would have been closed Tuesday. But because so many people take long-weekend mini-vacations to include Monday, they figure Tuesday is their travel-back-home day, and consider that a holiday as well. Still with me?

A lesson in patience

Monday – holiday. Tuesday – not a true holiday, but everyone counts it to be one. Wednesday – the day after the non-holiday meant that the museum was closed. Yeah. The weird thing is, that it is starting to make perfect sense to me.

Bureaucracy has its own time zone altogether that is better understood by watching the Twilight Zone. Even Standard Italian Operating Time holds no sway over Bureaucracy Time and no predictability or pattern can ever be attempted to be imposed upon it. The only thing one can do when dealing with Bureaucracy Time is to get down on one's knees and pray for patience. Lots of it.

Yes, it took a while but we've distinguished the pattern in all this. It's a rite of passage, like learning that *preservativi* does not mean chemical preservatives, and that stating you like a delicacy or liqueur is a blatant request for more. Maybe it's all about rhythm after all. But look at the time. It's 4:30pm, riposo is over, and there is a barista expecting me.

Calabria, Taranto, Catanzaro , Catania, Foggia, Benevento and Agrigento.

These are some of the favourites of property buyers and retirees:

Tuscany: Has the art cities of Florence, Lucca and Siena, exquisite countryside with hilltowns, wineries and excellent restaurants, the famous Chianti wine region between Florence and Siena, mountains in the north and the Mediterranean coast to the west.

Popular towns include Arezzo – voted in another survey as one of the best places to live in Italy – Montepulciano and Pienza. With cheap properties to renovate, warm weather and renowned food and wine, Tuscany has long been a favourite of British retirees but, over the years, retirement to 'Chiantishire', where ordinary properties change hands for upwards of €500,000, has become beyond the means of all but the rich.

Trentino: Adjacent to Italy's north-eastern border with Austria, this is the place for winter sports enthusiasts with popular ski resorts, alpine meadows and waterfalls and medieval towns set among snow-capped peaks. German is the most common language.

Molise: 'Undiscovered' and the least densely populated region in Italy where the local economy depends on subsistence agriculture. However it is yet to find much favour with English-speaking residents.

Veneto: One of Italy's major wine producing regions with familiar names such as Soave and Pinot Grigio. The towns of Veneto are **Padua** (elegant and prosperous; **Treviso:** (great atmosphere, friendly people; **Belluno** (on the edge of the Dolomites and adjacent to the Belluno National Park) and **Soave**

We live here

'A realist, not a dreamer' is how American Barbara Skinner describes herself. But it was to find a dream that led Barbara and her husband Art to move from Kentucky to Umbria in 2002. You can find the full story of their Italian adventure at: www.artnbarb.com

We had no interest in Italy. None. Nada. Then Frank, my son, was stationed near Naples for two years, so we decided to go. Our first trip was in September, 2000. We took an organised tour with our good friends Sherry and Dave. We had a fantastic time, and the four of us talked of returning.

For Art and me that opportunity would come in January, 2001 when NWA offered tickets with frequent flier miles. In March we went again – a three-week trip planned with my daughter Angela, her husband Duffy, and our grandson Nicholas. We were going to have a family reunion of sorts.

Art and I spent a week in Umbria and then went to Sorrento for a few days, Later we all met up in Formia, where Frank and Shannon lived. We then went to Rome with Angela, Duffy and Nicholas. The saga of losing my purse and all three passports deserves a story all its own but personally, I would just as soon forget the whole incident!

Chocolate in Perugia

At this point we've been to Italy three times in less than eight months. And we are now wondering, when will we get there again? How can we wait? We have one week of vacation scheduled for October and, as if heavenly ordained, that turns out to be the same week as the Chocolate Festival in Perugia! So we go.

Next we return in May 2002, for a two-week visit, one week in Florence, one week in Umbria.

Then we began thinking: Could we live in Italy? How would we do it? Could we afford it? After all, retiring to Italy is not something for people like us. People with just an average amount of money, little savings, and no language skills.

And slowly, we start to get the idea, maybe we can do this. Expats tell us we have enough monthly income from Art's retirement. They even say we could probably afford a house.

We scour the web, finding page after page of real estate agencies. Most of the places we see are way too expensive for us, but most people seem to think that with some luck and patience we can afford a house.

We make lots of helpful contacts, and decide that we will take our November vacation time to return to Italy to search for the perfect town. We think we know what we want … to be in a town, not isolated. If we were in a town, we could get to know our neighbours and our Italian would come much faster.

We would want a town that was large enough to have the basics, such as a grocery, bakery, newsstand, butchers etc; just large enough so that we didn't have to get in the car every time we ran out of bread or needed a few things for dinner. And just small enough so that we could become a part of the community.

Armed with a good map and lots of notes, we spent every day driving, driving, driving. We looked at Spina … too small. Marsciano … too large. Deruta … just not right. And so it went. Every day, new cities on the map, new suggestions, new ideas.

Eventually we decide to see a house Art had found online. It was in a town called San Venanzo, it looked fairly modern, and it was within our price range.

Although Art is impressed with many things about the house, I remain sceptical. It is definitely not my dream house. The town is cute … not too small, not too large and it does have a gelateria and a bakery.

Art likes it because it is not just modern, but also because it is not falling down. No chipping plaster. No uneven floors. Central heating. Gas mains. Lots of windows and cross ventilation.

I remain unmoved. The house has no charm. It does have a small yard (a plus), but it's all in shade so no tomato plants in the summer (a minus).

The yard backs up to a park which adds to the

privacy (a plus) but the only access to the yard is from the outside (a minus). It does have a garage, which is a big plus. There are kitchens all over the place … one is in the garage. Rooms are a nice size.

We walk through the town, down the main street. In addition to the shops already mentioned, there is a flower shop, a post office, a gas station, a hardware store, a news-stand, a butcher shop, two small grocery stores, several bars, even a hotel. Oh, and the volcano museum which we would not discover until later.

The fairly tale goes on hold

The second visit has improved my opinion and Art has made some valid points about the house but I am still waiting for it to say something to me. Anything. It says nothing, maybe just because I don't understand Italian.

I know that I could live here, but do I want to live here? I have to decide. Do I want to live in a fairy tale, which I probably can't afford, or do I want to live in San Venanzo? And slowly I do decide: it's better to live in San Venanzo for real than to wait for the fairy tale. If I wait for the fairy tale it may never come and all that time will have been wasted.

And so we bought the house in San Venanzo.
Postscript: Although we love Umbria and our life here we have a wanderlust that makes us ready to move on to our next adventure. We're in no hurry to sell, but when the right person comes along we do plan to return to the States.

(walled town famous for its wine and castle; and **Chioggia** (great fish market and excellent seafood restaurants).
Sicily: Good weather, beaches, food and friendly people, laid-back attitude and slow to get things done.
Calabria: One of the most beautiful parts of the country. Excellent climate, countryside and beaches.
Lombardy: Home of the major Italian lakes: Maggiore, Varese, lseo, Como and the northern part of Lake Garda.
Valle D'aosta: The last Italian region before you enter the Mont Blanc tunnel through the Alps. Plenty of mountain activities and ski resorts and, in summer, glorious hiking/walking and wildlife spotting.
Lazio: Lazio is the region around Rome, once a major port of call on the Grand Tour. Today, the region is depopulated and rather run down but it offers a variety of extraordinary landscapes of long uncrowded beaches, pine groves, mountains and lakes, hills and plains with its rich historical, artistic and cultural heritage.
Campania: Campania has Vesuvius, the Amalfi Coast and the Sorrento Peninsula, with wonderful beaches and fisherman's villages. Offshore there are islands surrounded by crystal clear water. They include Ischia with the greatest number of thermal spas in the world, and Capri.

This coast has familiar names such as Positano, the setting of the "summer" Dolce Vita in the 1960s, Ravello, a place loved by Greta Garbo and Richard Wagner. The most famous islands are Ischia, which has one of the greatest number of thermal spas in the world with its three stacks and timeless charm.

ITALY CONTACT DIRECTORY

Embassies/Government
UK Embassy in Italy
http://ukinitaly.fco.gov.uk/en
Italian Embassy in London
www.amblondra.esteri.it/Ambasciata_Londra

Travel & Health Advice
Foreign Office travel advice
www.fco.gov.uk/travel
www.nhs.uk/Healthcareabroad
www.masta.org

About Italy
www.italyheaven.co.uk
http://madaboutitaly.com
www.abcitaly.com
www.guardian.co.uk/travel/italy+travelwebsites
www.state.gov/r/pa/ei/bgn/4033.htm
www.lifeinitaly.com

General & Expat
www.expatfocus.com
www.britishexpat.com
www.transitionsabroad.com

English Language Media
Apart from the international newspapers and
magazine, Italy is particularly well-served by
print and on-line publications devoted to
regions, culture, etc. This is a selection.
Italy Italy Magazine
www.italyitalymagazine.com
The Americanwww.theamericanmag.com
www.informer.it
www.wantedinrome.com
www.einnews.com/italy
www.romepost.it
www.valleylife.it
www.italymag.co.uk
www.easymilano.it/eng
www.theromanforum.com
www.luccagrapevine.com
www.theflorentine.net

Property
www.cluttonsitaly.com
www.casatravella.com
www.italymag.co.uk
www.tuscanyrealestate.co.uk
www.realpointitaly.com
www.homesinitaly.co.uk
www.viviun.com

Travel & Tourism
www.enit.it
www.justitaly.org/
http://italy.co.uk/
www.tourist-attraction.co.uk
http://travel.mapsofworld.com/italy
www.travel.it
http://goitaly.about.com

Getting There
There are scheduled flights to Italy from
Gatwick, Heathrow, Manchester and
Edinburgh with BA, Alitalia and BMI.
Ryanair and Easyjet flying to various
destinations in Italy and there are other
budget options.
Easyjet: www.easyjet.com
Ryanair: www.ryanair.org.uk
British Airways: www.britishairways.com
Air France: www.airfrance.co.uk
Olympic Airways: www.olympic-airways.gr
Aegean Airlines: www.aegeanair.com
Lufthansa: www.lufthansa.com
bmi: flybmi.com
KLM: KLM.com

Getting Around
Public transport in and between cities is
cheap and efficient with a wide choice of
buses, trams, trains and underground trains
(Catania, Milan, Naples, Rome and Turin).
Tickets must be stamped before boarding
trains, underground trains and buses.
Motorway tolls, high parking charges and
petrol costs make driving expensive.
Domestic flights are expensive.
By air: There are over 30 regional airports
served by Alitalia and domestic services
including:
Air Dolomiti: www.airdolomiti.it/en/
Air One: www.flyairone.it
Meridiana: www.meridiana.it
Volare: www.buy.volareweb.com
Blue Panorama Airline   :
www.blu-express.com

Train: Train travel is quick, relatively
inexpensive and offers stunning views.
Intercity and Intercity Plus trains run the
length of Italy, stopping at the large cities.
More info: www.italiarail.com
Bus: Bus tickets are often not sold on board
and need to be purchased at tobacconists
and newsstands. Long-distance buses are
available only on a few routes.
www.senabus.it: Rome and Milan to Siena
www.sadem.it: Turin to Milan, Val d'Aosta
www.sitabus.it: Florence to Siena
www.marinobus.it: various routes
www.autostradale.it: Milan and resorts
Driving: You can use your UK licence for up
to a year after you arrive after which you
should exchange it for an Italian one –
patente di guida.
Drink driving laws are tougher than in the
UK (50mg per 100ml of blood).
Roads are good and there is an extensive
network of motorways. Tolls are high. In the
north driving conditions can be dangerous
in winter. Cities are often very congested.
Ferry: There is a highly-developed network
of ferries and hydrofoils operated by private
companies. Car ferries connect the major
islands of Sardinia and Sicily with the
mainland ports of Genoa, Livorno, La
Spezia, Civitavecchia, Fiumicino, Naples,
Genoa and Palermo.
Mainland towns nearest to them have
services to the Tremiti islands, the Bay of
Naples islands and the Pontine islands.
Frequencies are drastically reduced in the
winter. Some stop altogether.

via dei Colli

Real Estate and Property Services Agency

And now the time has come to harvest! Your precious investment in your ultimate dream only deserves the best you can get!

Via dei Colli Real Estate Agency operates in the most scenic part of Italy: Umbria, well known for its dreamy landscapes, affordable living standard and friendly atmosphere.

Founded early 2004, our agency has since then supported many foreigners among whom a lot from the UK to find, in some cases even construct, maintain and rent out their beautiful home in Italy. We are a small team of highly qualified internationally oriented professionals who believe in a personal and direct relationship with our clients.

We are specialized as well in offering you the most beautiful holiday homes for rent, also at attractive rates for longer periods during off season periods. You will find special places where one immediately feels at home!

Be most welcome for first meeting us at **www.viadeicolli.com**

Via dei Colli Real Estate and Property Services Agency
Piazza Italia 9 - 06100 - Perugia - Italy
Tel. (+39) 075.966.11.42 - info@viadeicolli.com

MALTA HIGH COMMISIONER
Malta House
36-38 Piccadilly
London W1J OLE
Tel: 020 7292 4800
Fax: 020 7734 1831

THE HIGH COMMISIONER

Welcome to Malta

I am delighted to have this opportunity to welcome you to the Malta section of the International Retirement Directory.

Malta welcomes retirees and other property buyers from many parts of Europe and has had a long and special association with Britain and British people.

A scheme for foreigners to take up residence in Malta came into effect as long ago as 1988. Offering an attractive tax structure, among other advantages, it is of particular interest to those nationals with a relatively high income, who are subject to a high tax rate in their present country of residence.

At the very heart of the Mediterranean, the Maltese islands boast 7,000 years of history in which cultures and languages blended to create a unique land and people. This can be seen from our Megalithic Temples, Phoenician pottery, Punic inscriptions, Roman mosaic floors and thermal baths to Pagan, Jewish and Christian catacombs, Byzantine basilicas and Arab tombstones.

The people of Malta are very welcoming with the result that non-Maltese residents have made their homes throughout Malta in towns, villages and even the smallest hamlets. They are readily welcomed and accepted by the local people, most of whom speak good English, and it is easy for them to become actively involved in a wide range of social, sporting and cultural activities.

The British Residents' Association (BRA) has been long established and fosters friendly and harmonious relations between its members and the people of the Maltese Islands.

Newcomers to Malta will find the cost of living is significantly cheaper than other major European cities with groceries, clothing, furniture and utility services all very reasonably priced. Domestic staff can also be found at relatively low hourly rates.

Malta has reciprocal medical care agreements with other EU countries and is blessed with excellent medical facilities, including well-equipped state and privately owned hospitals run by highly qualified doctors and staff. Every permanent resident has the right to free medical treatment at public hospitals and clinics. English, the second official language in Malta, is widely spoken and correspondence with public authorities is usually bilingual.

The crime rate is low and all areas are safe to walk or drive around at night.

The climate is typically Mediterranean, with hot, dry summers, warm and sporadically wet autumns and short, mild winters. The weather usually shows signs of warming up in April, heralding in a long spell of hot, dry weather. It rarely rains from April to August.

We look forward to welcoming you to our beautiful country.

Tiny island that exerts a big pull

Why Malta?

A British colony for 200 years, the Republic of Malta is a friendly, laid-back island in the middle of the Mediterranean where the sea is clear and the climate mild and warm.

Approximately 93km south of Sicily and 350km north of Africa, it is part of an archipelago consisting of five islands: Malta, Gozo, Comino, Comminotto and Filfla. Malta is the largest of these, the other two inhabited isles being Gozo and Comino.

Surrounded on three sides by the Mediterranean, the city of Valletta is one of Europe's finest historic attractions where sumptuous palaces, theatres, gardens and churches recall the heyday of the Knights of St John. The Knights were founded in Jerusalem in the 11th century as a multi-national Christian medical order, providing assistance to pilgrims.

The Holy Roman Emperor granted the Knights the Maltese archipelago in 1530. Valletta was constructed as a fortified town to deter the Ottomans. It was designed from scratch in an early example of a gridiron street plan. In time the city grew more lavish, with stunning Baroque design embodied in the homes and places of worship of the Knights.

Evidence of its rich history still remains in numerous baroque churches and other historic buildings and sites, including the impressive bastions around the harbour built by the knights.

Remarkably Valletta has hardly been altered since the Order left and is now one of the world's best-conserved cities. UNESCO recognised it as such in 1980, granting it World Heritage Status.

Tourism and financial services are the two most influential sectors of the economy and English is widely spoken and understood.

Maltese people are friendly, cheerful, opinionated and very family-orientated. They show great respect to their parents and the elderly and adore children – their own and everyone else's.

The cost of living is comparatively low. Property costs are rising, but are still relatively inexpensive by international standards. Education and health systems are very good and compare well with those of mainland Europe.

Malta is easily accessible – within two to four hours flying time from most European countries and there are daily flights to most European capitals and international hubs.

The nightlife is lively and there are annual arts and music festivals throughout the year offering a blend of local and international cultural events, entertainment, exhibitions and traditional seasonal events such as carnival just before Easter and summer

ABOUT THE WRITER Sports mad **Kevin Galea Pace** is an Aussie whose roots are in Malta. As a child Kevin moved with his family from Malta to Melbourne where he studied in various international schools before starting his career in the insurance industry. Father of three Kevin, aged 42, is a director of a number of financial services firms in Malta including **First Retirement Planning Ltd**, and runs www.retiremalta.com which offers relocation advice to retirees moving to Malta

FACTFILE

Capital: Valletta
Population: 401,880
Area: 316 sq km
Language: Maltese and English
Climate: Typical Mediterranean. Rainy season Sept-May. Nov-Feb are the wettest months. It rarely rains from mid May to mid-Sept.
Time difference: GMT+1
Entry requirements: Visas are not required for stays up to three months.
Electricity: 240 Volts, 50Hz. UK-style three-pin square plugs
Money: Euro. ATMs are widely available. Credit/Debit cards/Traveller's Cheques accepted in most shops and hotels.

Public holidays 2010

Jan 1	New Year's Day
Feb 10	Feast of St Paul's Shipwreck
March19	St Joseph's Day
March 31	Freedom Day
Apr 2	Good Friday
May 1	Labour Day
June 7	Commemoration of 1919 Riot
June 29	Feast of St Peter and St Paul
Aug 14	Assumption Day
Sept 8	Our Lady of Victories
Sept 21	Independence Day
Dec 8	Immaculate Conception
Dec 13	Republic Day
Dec 25	Christmas Day

Opening hours
Banks: 8.30am-2pm (Mon-Thurs), 8.30am-3.30pm (Fri), Offices: 8.30am-5.30pm Shops: 9am-1pm and 4pm-7pm in commercial centres, much later in tourist areas during summer.
Water: Tap water is safe, but most people use bottled for drinking.
Tipping: 5-10 per cent is customary.
Medical/healthcare: First class medical care is available. EU citizens are eligible to receive free medical treatment from government-funded hospitals and clinics.
Pets: Must have a veterinary health certificate issued immediately prior to travel, stating that it is healthy and has been vaccinated against rabies within six months.

MALTA CONTACT DIRECTORY

Embassies/Government
Malta High Commission in UK
www.foreign.gov.mt
British Embassy in Malta
http://ukinmalta.fco.gov.uk/en
Malta Government www.gov.mt
Malta Immigration
www.foreign.gov.mt/Library/Citizenship]

Travel & Health Advice
Foreign Office travel advice
www.fco.gov.uk/travel
www.nhs.uk/Healthcareabroad
www.masta.org

About Malta
www.allmalta.com
www.searchmalta.com
www.di-ve.com
www.searchmalta.com
www.101malta.com

General & Expat
http://britishresidentsinmalta.org
www.expatfocus.com
www.britishexpat.com
www.transitionsabroad.com

English Language Media
Malta Today (weekly)
www.maltatoday.com.mt
www.independent.com.mt
Malta Business Week
www.maltabusinessweekly.com
MaltaStarhttp://www.maltastar.com
www.one.com.mt   bilingual TV channel

Property
Tigne Point www.tignepoint.com
www.belair-malta.com
www.barongroupmalta.com
www.dhalia.com
www.franksalt.com.mt
www.saragrech.com.mt
www.fairwise.com.mt

Travel & Tourism
http://mta-news.info
www.visitmalta.com
www.gozochannel.com

Getting There
www.britishairways.com
www.airmalta.com
www.easyjet.com
http://flybmi.com
www.justtheflight.co.uk
www.mymalta.co.uk
www.cheapflights.co.u
www.emiratestours.co.uk
www.airfrance.netflights.com

Getting Around
Bus: Malta has an excellent, cheap and extensive bus network. Since buses carry a number, rather than the name of their destination, you need to know the routes. Most buses start their routes from the Valletta Bus Terminus just outside the entrance to the City.
Taxis: All taxis are fitted with meters, which drivers prefer not to use. It is advisable to agree the fare in advance.
Driving: There is a speed limit of 80km/hr on highways and 50km/hr in urban areas. Car hire is readily available. Maltese drivers tend to be excitable and competitive so driving can be somewhat stressful. Driving is on the left.

fiestas. The feast celebrations are truly unique in Malta. There is at least one feast a week in the summer.

Malta joined the European Union in 2004 and is still a member of the Commonwealth.

Is it safe?

Yes. There is very little serious crime and a low incidence of muggings and other street crime.

How easy is it to obtain residential status?

Relatively simple for EU nationals though, unlike other EU nations, Malta imposes certain financial constraints. EU nationals must show they have

adequate funds to support themselves and must be covered by sickness insurance. The minimum is capital of at least €14,000 or a weekly income of €84.95 or, in the case of a married couple, capital of €23,300 or a weekly income of €93.10.

Permanent residence can be obtained once the EU national (and his/her family members) has lived in Malta for a continuous period of five years.

[See: www.foreign.gov.mt/Library/Citizenship]

Family members of qualifying EU nationals have the right to join them in Malta.

There is an annual minimum cost of maintaining a Maltese residence permit composed of a minimum annual property rental of €4,400 and a minimum

Tigne Point, Malta

Set in landscaped gardens in Malta's most prestigious location, surrounded on 3 sides by the sea, apartments and penthouses at Tigne Point offer spectacular views of the Mediterranean or Valletta harbour.

Development include pedestrianised piazza, a shoreline pool, walkways and sports facilities. Debenhams and other major stores also due to open shortly.

Price: 2-bedroom apartments starting from €400,000 and stunning penthouses from €1,450,000

More info: Tigne Point
www.tignepoint.com + 356 2065 5510

Malta) and are subject to the minimum tax liability of €4,400 referred to above. Various exemptions cover household and personal belongings, including the purchase of a car.

There is no death duty by that name but the heirs of a deceased property owner have to pay seven per cent tax on the value of of an inherited property.

If a permanent resident sells his Maltese residence within three years the profit made from the sale is taxed as a capital gain at the rate of 35 per cent. Profit on a sale after three years is tax free. There is a five per cent stamp-duty on the transfer of property.

Used household and personal effects may be imported free of duty if imported within six months of taking up residence.

Is Malta property a good investment?

Property values have grown by about 10 per cent annually, increasing as the island has become more popular with foreign buyers, attracted by cheap flights among other things.

The rules on property purchase are relatively straightforward but non-resident purchasers must obtain an AIP Permit from the Ministry of Finance which sets a minimum price of €85,000 for apartments and €145,000 for other properties. These limits are revised annually.

Mortgages are available to non-residents but the Central Bank of Malta will require a banker's guarantee from your home bank.

You can let your house or apartment once you own it but only on property worth in excess of about €115,000 which must also have access to a swimming pool. The property must be registered with the Hotel

income tax liability of €4,400.

Applicants for permanent residence also need to show they are of good character (via a police good conduct certificate and professional references).

How much tax will I pay?

Permanent residence permit holders pay income tax at a flat rate of 15 per cent on all income from local or foreign sources (but not on income not remitted to

and Catering Establishments Board and rental income is taxed at 15 per cent.

Where's best to live?

Malta and Gozo boast of a good selection of luxury accommodation in developments that are referred to as Special Feature Properties.

Frank Salt Real Estate [www.franksalt.com] explains: "These refer to a cluster of apartments, maisonettes and penthouses built with a common theme on an extensive piece of land, often enhanced by their location, amenities and finishes.

"Situated all across the island, people interested in purchasing a property can choose from a selection of waterfront and marina developments, such as Portomaso, St Angelo Mansions (Cottonera Marina) and shortly Tigne Point. Those who are more interested in the countryside and country views can go for Madliena Village and Verdala Mansions."

Sliema and St Julian's, considered to be Malta's fashionable and commercial districts, boast the largest selection of such developments, including Portomaso, Pendergardens, Tigne Point and Fort Cambridge.

"All four enjoy lovely seaviews and encompass luxury finishes and an array of amenities, including shopping areas, health and fitness facilities, massive communal and private pools, underground parking, and so on," says Frank Salt Real Estate.

The neighbouring town of Gzira hosts Metropolis and Savoy Gardens.

Selmun Village is situated in the northern part of Malta, in Mellieha and is only a five minutes drive from Malta's top sandy beaches.

Gozo also has its own flagship development – Fort Chambray, situated on the edge of the Ta' Cenc cliffs, overlooking views of Malta and Comino, as well as Mgarr Harbour. Smaller developments may be found at lower prices in other areas and villages around Malta and Gozo.

Seafront property

Maltese beaches – and the roads to them – become quite crowded in summer, particularly at the weekend. Nevertheless seafront and seaview properties carry a premium.

Ghadira Bay in Mellieha is the most popular of the beaches. Ghajn Tuffieha and Golden Bay are adjacent bays on the west part of the island near the village of Mgarr. The former has one of the island's largest hotels – the five-star Radisson Golden Sands – the latter is unspoilt with golden sand and clear waters. Gnejna is another beautiful bay in the same area.

Paradise Bay, one of the most picturesque beaches on the island and popular with a younger crowd, is nestled in a more secluded place in the north of Malta, close to the ferry terminal for Gozo.

If you don't have to live near the beach, the older and greener villages are nearer to the centre of the island, places such as Gharghur, Zebbug, Rabat and Siggiewi where you can find a choice of converted houses of character.

Renting

Rental prices vary between locations, with the highest being found in the Sliema and St. Julian's areas, and lower cost accommodation available in Msida, Bugibba and the island of Gozo.

MINISTÉRIO DA ECONOMIA E DA INOVAÇÃO

GABINETE DO SECRETÁRIO DE ESTADO DO TURISMO

THE INTERNATIONAL RETIREMENT DIRECTORY

Portugal is one of the top destinations for Britons looking to move abroad due to its fantastic climate and excellent standard of living. If you're searching for a place that will offer you excellent value for money, cost of living, a healthy lifestyle and plenty of activities to do and culture to enjoy, Portugal could be the perfect choice. Portugal is an intriguing destination for expatriates with beautiful landscapes, incredible weather and, of course, the Portuguese people – who have a long established reputation for being very warm and welcoming.

With one of the highest number of sunshine hours per year in Europe, Portugal could be the perfect destination for you, whether you wish to make a new life in the beautiful mountains in the north of the country or somewhere along its magnificent western or southern coastlines.

In Lisbon and Porto, Portugal boasts two cities of major cultural and historical importance. Lisbon, the capital, is a lively, exciting city with plenty going on to keep you occupied and active. In addition, there are a number of other towns and cities that would appeal to those looking for an urban home, such as Braga or Coimbra. The archipelagos of Madeira and the Azores on the other hand are wonderful island locations with some spectacular scenery that will also tempt overseas investors and property buyers.

Along Portugal's coast, especially the Algarve region, or just north of Lisbon, you'll find sophisticated beach resorts and golf complexes, and in more rural areas you'll discover a countryside still relatively undiscovered by tourism. Away from the coast, the countryside is geographically diverse and home to mountains and plains, national parks, lakes, olive groves and rivers.

Portuguese gastronomy is also not to be overlooked and, as expected from a country with a vast coastline, fresh seafood plays a major part in our cuisine. Our wines too are of exceptional quality. Port and Madeira wines are already famous, but there are many table wines for you to discover.

Whatever lifestyle you are looking to achieve you'll soon discover plenty of opportunities to fulfil your expectations. From a sophisticated life in a vibrant European city to experiencing life that has changed little over the last century, Portugal can offer you both.

Accept my invitation and come and discover Portugal – a small, friendly and diverse country.

Bernardo Trindade
Secretary of State for Tourism of Portugal

Hot summers, mild winters, fine wines – what more do you need?

Why Portugal?

In addition to second home owners, an estimated 5,000 British retirees live in Portugal. The appeal? Winters are generally mild, summers hot, while spring and autumn are warm with strong winds and frequent rainfall. The north has colder and wetter winters; central regions have a mixture of Atlantic and Mediterranean climates, mild winters and hot and dry summers; the south has a very dry climate with mild winters and very hot summers

Far less affected by mass tourism than its neighbours, Portugal has a slower pace of life, hospitable people who are welcoming to outsiders, stunning coastlines, beautiful uncrowded beaches, excellent food and wines.

The most popular areas for retirees are the Algarve, the Silver Coast (Costa Prata) and Central Portugal (Beiras). The Algarve offers superb beaches, sporting activities, quaint fishing ports and intimate bars, restaurants and cafés for delicious local cuisine. The Silver Coast has become a magnet for British retirees, particularly in the areas around Óbidos and Nazaré.

In the Beiras region ancient towns, villages, spa towns, Roman ruins, castles, monasteries and convents remain as evidence of its vast cultural and historical past. But there are also sandy white beaches, pine forests and wildlife reserves providing a wealth of flora and fauna.

Cost of living

The Algarve and Lisbon may be expensive but otherwise Portugal is relatively cheap. Cars and imported consumer goods are taxed and expensive. The cost of domestic fuel is high, as are international and regional telephone calls. Grocery bills can amount to more than is expected though local produce, such as olive oil, fruit, vegetables and wine, is relatively cheap.

Accommodation is expensive, particularly in and around Lisbon, Oporto and Funchal. Long-term rentals in the Algarve are difficult to find and, if available, are often very expensive.

Public transport fares are reasonable in comparison with those in Britain and it is still possible for a family of four to eat out for little more than €70. The cost of private dental and medical treatment is high.

How easy is it to obtain residential status?

You can stay in Portugal for a maximum of three months without having to comply with any formalities. If you intend to remain you just go the your local town hall and apply for a Registration Certificate which will be valid for five years from the date of issue or for your period of intended residence (if less than five years).

You will be required to show your British passport and make a declaration to the effect that you fulfil the conditions of residence, one of which is that you have sufficient funds to support yourself and your family.

Is it safe?

Crime is comparatively low in Portugal but pick-pocketing, handbag snatching and theft from cars are increasingly common in major tourist areas.

www.expatsportugal.com: This section was put together with help and information from expatsportugal.com, an entertaining and useful resource for English-speaking expats who live in, or are thinking of moving there.

FACTFILE

Capital: Lisbon
Population: 10,707,924
Area: 92391sq km
Language: Portuguese
Climate: Regional variations influenced by relief, latitude and proximity to the sea. Mainly mild winters, especially in the Algarve. In the north and central regions the winters are colder. Summers are hot and dry, especially in inland areas.
Time difference: GMT + 1
Entry requirements: European Union citizens can enter and remain in Portugal for three months without any formalities.
Electricity: 220v 50 cycles. Sockets are two pin round.
Money: Euro. ATMSs are widely available. Credit and debit cards and traveller's cheques are accepted in most shops and hotels.
Public holidays: 2010

Jan 1	New Year's Day	Aug 15	Assumption
Feb 24	Mardi Gras	Oct 5	Republic Day
April 10-13	Easter	Nov 1	All Saints' Day
Apr 25	Freedom Day	Dec 1	Restoration of Ind. Day
May 1	Labour Day	Dec 8	Immaculate Conception
June10	Portugal Day	Dec 25	Christmas Day
June 11	Corpus Christi		

Opening hours
Banks: 8.30am-3pm Mon-Fri.
Offices: 9am-12:30pm and 2pm-5pm, Mon-Fri
Shops: 9/10am-7pm, Mon-Fri. Some close for lunch 1-3 pm.
Water: Use bottled. According to the European Commission, half of Portugal's water suppy zones does not comply with EU standards.
Tipping: Restaurants include a service charge though it is customary to leave an additional tip of about 5-10 per cent. Tip taxi drivers 5-10 per cent.
Medical/healthcare: EU citizens are entitled to any non-hospital care in any other member state without prior authorisation and to be reimbursed by their own system. For those who are planning to permanently move to Portugal and live as European Union residents, there is free basic healthcare; this includes doctor appointments and medication.
Pets: An animal arriving from another EU country must be accompanied by a health certificate translated into Portuguese.

How much tax will I pay?

Residents are liable to Portuguese tax. Non-residents who own property are liable for property tax and property transfer tax. You need to apply for a taxpayer's number from your local tax office which is also necessary to open a bank account, enter into a long-term rental agreement and to purchase property.

Property prices

Property prices, which rose by about four per cent in

Monte Rei Golf Club
Apartments, villas and plots of land are for sale at this development based around two 18-hole golf courses in eastern Algarve.
Prices: €1-2 million
More info: www.bw-international.com
Tel: 00 34 959 399 982

Villa Sol Resort
Apartments and land plots for sale on the Villa Sol Spa & Golf Resort with a 27-hole golf course, tennis courts, swimming pools, spa, 6 restaurants and 2 bars.
Apartments face the new marina of Olhão, part of the Ria Formosa nature reserve, 10 minutes from Faro Airport. Olhão is famed for its lively outdoor market.
Prices: €225,000-1 million
More info: Barton Wyatt www.bw-international.com
Tel (UK): 01344 843 000

2008 and dipped by about the same amount the following year, are expected to pick up by the end of 2010.

Property purchase

Buying a property in Portugal has potential pitfalls. The legal and other procedures are different to those in the UK, so it pays to do all the necessary research in advance.

In order to purchase property in Portugal you will need a fiscal number which is obtainable from the nearest tax office.

You will need a proof of identity (your residency card, identity card or passport) and an address in Portugal so that the tax office can send your fiscal card (Cartão de Contribuinte). If you do not have a Portuguese address you can use that of a solicitor or a friend.

When you have chosen a property and have agreed a price, you will sign a Promissory contract (Promessa de Compra e Venda) with the owner. This states that you promise to buy the property and the owner promises to sell it at an agreed price and within an agreed timescale.

You then pay a deposit (normally 10 per cent of the purchase price) and agree on a date to complete the purchase. If you withdraw from the purchase you will lose your deposit and if the owner fails to keep their side of the bargain, they must repay you twice the amount of your deposit. It is highly recommended that you employ a Portuguese solicitor to handle the contract.

Purchase tax

You must pay the purchase tax (IMT) before you complete the sale. IMT is on a sliding scale based on the value of the property. The rates differ for permanent

residence and non-permanent occupation. The following rates are for permanent residence.

Purchase Price	% of Purchase Price	Adjustment (reduce by)
Up to €89,700	0	0
€89,700-122,700	2%	€1,794.00
€122,700-167,300	5%	€5,475.00
€167,300-278,800	7%	€8,821.06
€278,800-557,500	8%	€11,608.95
over €557,500	single flat rate of 6%	

You can see more details at:
www.apemip.pt/DOCs/Tab_IMT_2009.pdf

If the property is to be your main residence you will normally be able to claim exception of the local

Quintas de Óbidos
Located on Portugal's Silver Coast, 80km from Lisbon, Quintas de Óbidos is a development of 79 luxurious villas in 16 different styles, each in 1.3 acres of private gardens. The villas have an average of 8,500sq ft (800 m2) of living space.
Onsite facilities include an equestrian centre and a country club, restaurant and spa, swimming pools, tennis courts and sports pitch. There is a golf course 300m from the entrance of the resort.
Prices: €1.5-1.9m
More info: www.qdo.pt Tel: + (00) 351 22 606 15 40

Quinta do Vale villas
No two villas amongst the 66 will be alike at this Quinta do Vale development in eastern Algarve, promise the developers. Occupying plots of up to 1,700sq m, each property has 3 en-suite bedrooms, a basement areas for a gym or home cinema, garaging for 2 cars and landscaped gardens with a pool – and all with views across the 18-hole golf course.
Prices start from €1.2 million.
More info: www.titan-algarve.com
Tel: 00 34 959 399 982 UK Freephone 0800 358 7969
Email info@titan-algarve.com

council tax (IMI) for up to the first six years, depending on the value of the property

| Up to €150,000 | 6 years exception |
| Up to €225,000 euros | 3 years exception |

Where's best to live?

Algarve: The Algarve is the country's major tourist resort. Year round sunshine, glorious beaches and low prices make this a great holiday destination. The southern coastal region offers long stretches of fine sandy beaches broken up by rugged cliffs and grottoes. In the northern area the Espinhaco de Cao, Monchique and Caldeiral mountain ranges shelter the coastline from strong winds.

One of Portugal's most luxuriant and charming areas, it is wreathed in fig trees, orange groves and almond trees.

The Algarve also provides a wealth of activities including aquatic sports, golf, tennis and horse-riding, as well as numerous fishing ports, beaches, restaurants, cafés and quaint bars where you can sample delicious local cuisine.

Faro, the capital of the Algarve, is an attractive town with a wealth of restaurants, cafés, bars and clubs as well as a beautiful old theatre, offering a full programme of dance, music and drama. Along the coast from Faro you will come to Albufeira, passing a glorious coastline, terrific beaches and around 20 golf courses. Albufeira is one of the most popular tourist destinations.

Tavira, a picturesque little town 30km east of Faro is a maze of old streets and 37 churches overlooked by the castle ruins. Fishing boats bob on the water and a traditional market is held daily. A quiet relaxing little place, there are bars and restaurants in which to savour the delicious local fish.

Traditionally the first port of call for the English buyer, the Algarve offers plenty of choice with many villas and apartments for sale. It's a great area for golfers.

The Silver Coast (Costa Prata) is beginning to attract more British buyers, particularly in the areas around Óbidos and Nazaré. Nazaré, a favourite holiday destination, has a stunning beach, typical fishermen houses and steep cliffs over a bright blue sea.

Other popular towns are Alcobaça, Figueira da Foz, the largest resort in the region, and Aveiro, famous for its lagoon, and once an important fishing port.

The Beiras region is one of tremendous contrasts combining ancient and modern, seaside and mountains, forests and plains.

It is geographically divided into three areas: alto,

Near Albufeira
Just completed, this villa with seaviews. West of Albufeira within walking distance to beaches and the new marina and a short drive to Salgados Golf Club. Built and finished to a very high standard with underfloor heating, air-conditioning, double glazing, central vacuum system and solar panels. Landscaped gardens and large balconies and terraces and a cascade swimming pool. Price: €1.7m
More info: www.holprop.com

Casa da Casal
Central Portugal , 2 bedrooms, 2 living rooms, kitchen all recently decorated, various store rooms and outbuildings, ready to move into, Price: €25,000
More info: www.portuguesepropertyatportugueseprices.com

boasting over 700 species of trees. This monastic centre dates back to the 6th Century and now houses the magnificent Buçaco Hotel, once a palace built by Dom Carlos.

Other areas

Alentejo: Unspoilt countryside, rural traditions, fishing ports, renaissance towns and medieval villages, fertile plains in the south to the granite hills that border Spain in the north-east.

Lisbon: Settled by the Phoenicians almost 3,000 years ago, the entire city was rebuilt after the devastating earthquake of 1755. Lisbon is now one of Europe's most exciting and beautiful cities, with breathtaking architecture, world-class museums, a lively cultural scene, terrific restaurants and tree-lined avenues graced by art nouveau buildings.

Portalegre: Located to the north of the Alentejo, with Spain to the east and within easy reach of Crato, Castelo de Vide, Marvão and the Serra de S. Mamede.

Porto: Portugal's second largest city, bustling but small enough to be an enjoyable place to live. The Douro river runs down into Porto from Spain and past the wine lodges (caves) on the riverfront at Vila Nova de Gaia.

Minho borders on to Galicia in northern Spain, and there are many similarities in both culture and language. Minho, one of the lushest areas in Portugal, with a climate and landscape similar to northern Europe, produces the popular 'green wine' (young wine) vinho verde.

baixa, and litoral; upper, lower and coastal.

Here ancient towns, villages, spa towns, Roman ruins, castles, monasteries and convents remain as evidence of its vast cultural and historical past but there are also white sandy beaches, pine forests, and wildlife reserves providing a wealth of flora and fauna.

Property in this area has been increasing in value over the last five years as more and more Brits discover the area's attractions and good value. However, it is still possible to find a stone ruin for little money, or new build villas at low cost.

Buçaco is an ancient forest 28km north of Coimbra

We Live Here
(…but not for much longer)

Corinne Frieden and her husband have lived in Portugal for four years but, for a variety of reasons, will not be staying. That's not to say that everything Corinne has to say about Portugal is negative…

These are among the 'Snippets 'n' Stuff' Corinne has posted on the website: www.expatsportugal.com

On the move and settling in …

December 19: The journey was shockingly easy. We left last Monday at 4.40pm, stopped overnight halfway across France. We were planning on stopping overnight again but when we got to Portugal the few hotels we did see looked like they probably would not take dogs so we just drove on and arrived in Cascais at about 2am on Wednesday.

We spent the night on the floor with no lights and no water. By Wednesday evening the agent had managed to get us hooked up to water, albeit by a plastic hosepipe to the house next door (the house was empty as luck would have it).

The removal guys arrived Wednesday evening and unloaded our bed … heaven!

By Friday night we finally had the house to ourselves. Spent Saturday cleaning, washing, cutting the grass (a week before Christmas, how strange was that?) and walking the dog … life goes on with a big smile on my face.

A few minor hitches still to iron out, like not having a letterbox. We were told we were No. 1 but it seems it might be 145. The numbering system makes absolutely no sense (another Portuguese quirk it seems) so no use looking what number next door has.

No dustbin … what's the deal with that? We have to take the trash to big bins placed around the streets which are emptied every day. Strange thing is though, I never see anyone else actually using the bins so they must go out after dark.

Even most importantly, no TV aerial, dish or cable. Even though I enjoy them, I can only take watching those Friends videos one more time. But who cares when you can look out to the sea in the sunshine? I'm loving the area – sea, mountains, forests, blue skies … Awesome! The place just has a magical feel to it that I was not expecting.

December 22: We've got a post box … and a number, or I should say two numbers. We are Lote 1 and also No. 45. Next-door-but-one is 67 and the other side is 17a. That's in a street of seven houses!

It's a dog's life

February 10: The Portuguese are just so friendly but I met an old lady who was somewhat less enamoured with me because I had my dog off the lead. The sight of it sent her dog into a crazed squealing frenzy.

The old lady emerged from her house none to pleased at what could possibly have caused her dog's reaction. I used two of the seven Portuguese words I have learned so far to tell her that my dog was 'nao mau' (not bad).

She was kind enough to give me a new Portuguese word to add to my vocabulary: 'estupido'. I didn't need the dictionary for that one.

On shopping and food

Feb 13: I have to start this with a small confession. We like baked beans. I know it can be hardly classed as a Portuguese delicacy and that when in Rome one should eat bull steaks and gladiator chops or even those nasty looking dried out slabs of fish that look like they were a fur rug in a past life.

But, like I said, we do like our baked beans. I discover I can actually buy baked beans (not Heinz but you can't have it all) at our little local corner shop. How did they know we were coming? So yesterday while shopping at Conforama I decided to ease my guilt and buy a Portuguese brand. No problem spotting them on the shelf as they have a big picture on the label.

So last night was to be our Baked Beans on Toast Night. Nothing like pushing out all the boats on a Saturday night is there? Even let my husband in on the treat although he is not normally allowed beans for reasons I won't go into here.

The bread was in the toaster, the table was set and so I turned to opening my two tins of baked beans.

What the …? Looks like anaemic kidney beans floating in a clear globby liquid. Where's the tomato sauce? I run for the translator. It seems I've bought 'Beans White'.

I search the cupboards and come up triumphantly with a bottle of ketchup. I heat the beans, squeeze over the ketchup and we swallow our punishment quietly.

What can a woman do when she has hungry mouths to feed?

"A lot better," is my daughter's surly answer.

Tomorrow I'll pick up a pepperoni pizza at Lidl.

PORTUGAL CONTACT DIRECTORY

Embassies/Government
Embassy of Portugal
portugal.embassyhomepage.com

British Embassy in Portugal
ukinportugal.fco.gov.uk/en

Travel & Health Advice
Foreign Office travel advice
www.fco.gov.uk/travel
www.nhs.uk/Healthcareabroad
www.masta.org

About Portugal
www.visitportugal.com
www.state.gov/r/pa/ei/bgn/3208.htm
http://iportugaltravel.com
http://portugal-info.net
http://madeiraislanddirect.com
www.madeiraisland.com
http://lisbon.angloinfo.com
www.portugalvirtual.pt

General & Expat
Expatfocus.com
www.expatworld.net
www.justlanded.com
www.expatexchange.com
www.expatica.com

English Language Media
Euro-Weekly News
www.euroweeklynews.com Published in
Spain with Algarve and Lisbon editions.
The Portugal Newswww.the-news.net
Portugal's largest circulation English-
language newspaper.
The Resident www.algarveresident.com
English-language weekly newspaper

To pick up English-language free-to-air

programmes, you need a satellite reception
system capable of picking up the Astra-1
satellite cluster.
The Astra 2 system allows you to see ITV,
BBC 1 and BBC 2 programmes, although a
large dish is required.

Property
Barton Wyatt
www.abpropertymarketing.co.uk
Titan Algarvewww.titan-algarve.com
Chavetejo Estate Agents
www.chavetejo.com
Villas Luzwww.eastalgarve-properties.com
Mackenzie Real Estatewww.mackenzie-
realestate.com
Cerro Novo Real Estate Agency
www.cerronovo.com
Inside Villaswww.inside-villas.com
Casas do Barlavento
www.casasdobarlavento.com
Algarve Homeswww.algarvehomes.com
Luz Bay Real Estatewww.luz-bay.com
Protealvor www.protealvor.com

Travel & Tourism
www.visitportugal.com
www.portugaloffice.org.uk
www.madeira-web.com
www.justportugal.org

Getting There
www.thomascook.co
www.aerlingus.com
www.bmibaby.com
www.ba.com
www.easyjet.com
www.flybe.com
www.jet2.com
www.flymonarch.com
www.ryanair.com
www.sata.pt

www.tap-airportugal.co.uk
www.flythomascook.com
www.airfrance.com
lwww.iberia.com
www.klm.com

Getting Around
Internal travel is cheap and efficient.
Since distances are short, train and bus
are usually the better option.
Air: The national carrier, TAP Air Portugal,
has regular domestic flights between
Porto, Lisbon, Faro, Madeira and the
Azores.
Train: An extensive rail network serves
almost every town and connects the
different areas of Portugal. There are
Express trains from Lisbon through
Coimbra to Oporto (Alfa trains). First and
second class are available except for
local and suburban trains.
Train info:www.cp.pt,
Bus: In towns and cities most bus and
tram services operate on a flat fare basis.
Express or ordinary coaches link main
cities and towns. There is an extensive
network of privately run companies.
Taxi: Taxis are all metered. If you go
outside the city limits taxis charge per
kilometre and are entitled to charge for
the return fare.
Driving: Portugal has one of the highest
rates of road accidents and fatalities in
Europe. Driving can be hazardous due to
poor lighting on narrow, uneven roads
and poorly marked road works. You can
use a UK-issued driver's licence until it
expires. If you move to Portugal there are
sensible reasons to obtain a Portuguese-
issued licence.
Driving is on the right.

Atlantic paradise is Europe's best-kept secret

Why the Azores?

On a line between Lisbon and New York, surrounded by the Atlantic Ocean, the Azores was first settled in the 15th century and today still has a population of less than a quarter of a million, spread among the nine islands.

Average temperatures range between 13-14° C during the winter and 22-23°C during the summer, with sea temperatures slightly higher. Summer highs of 30°C and winter lows (especially on higher ground) of 10°C are possible.

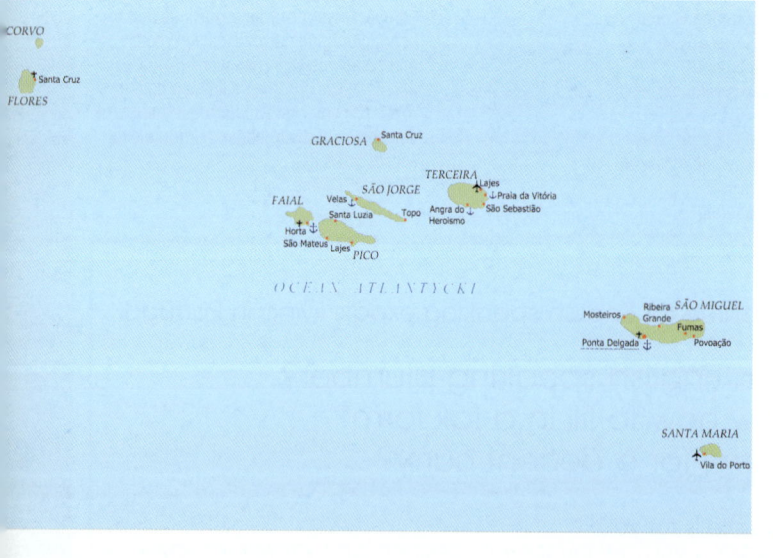

The archipelago is split into three groups. Faial and Pico, along with Terceira, Sao Jorge and Graciosa, form the Central Group. The western group is comprised of Flores and Corvo, whilst the eastern group has Sao Miguel and Santa Maria. The groups are spread over a large area so while you can take a passenger ferry between islands within a group you you need to fly between groups.

The Azores is a multi-national, multi-cultural society with nationals from throughout Europe living on Faial, as well as South Africans, Canadians, Americans, Ukranians and Russians.

The Azores is for those who are attracted to a quieter and slower lifestyle and who enjoy lush gardens and exquisite views.

The port of Horta – the main town on Faial – is an important stop-over for transatlantic yachts with more than 1,000 visiting boats a year joining the many local boats and yachts moored in the two modern marinas.

For walkers the islands are a paradise – you can wander the many tracks and trails at will, or follow the marked trails. The most popular walks on Faial are the crater rim, which offers a complete 360° view of the island as you walk and the Capelinhos eruption site, the

ABOUT THE WRITERS: This article is based on material from the websites of **Alan and Lesley Woodward**, a British couple who settled in the Azores in 2002 after a decade of round-the-world sailing adventures. They run an estate agency, Azores Properties [**www.azoresproperties.com**] and a holiday accommodation business [**www.azoreshigh.com**]. Turn over to read their full story.

dramatic moonscape that produced a new piece of Faial in 1957.

Nature and maritime life are the key attractions of the islands; whale and dolphin watching trips have replaced the traditional whaling industry as a way to make a living from the sea. Boats leave the marina daily for whale watching, swimming with dolphins, sport fishing, line fishing, diving and sailing, or you can just take a cruise along the scenic coastline.

On all the islands there are a number of excellent hotels, pensions and B&B establishments, many of which operate year round. There is also plenty of self-catering accommodation.

Cost of living
The average food bill is around 20 per cent less than the UK. An espresso coffee at the local café costs 50 cents and the cake or sandwich to go with it rarely more than a euro.

House insurance for a modest house is around 200 euros and a small family car will cost about 175 euros to insure. The islands' mild climate means you need to spend less on heating and warm clothes.

Is it safe?
There is very little crime in the Azores.

How much tax will I pay?
[See Main Portugal Section]

Is property a good investment?
On Faial you can buy a piece of land for building for €50,000 -70,000. The building costs for a new house are around €700 per sq m. If you buy an existing house in need of renovation you can pay anything from about €65,000 depending on the condition, size and location. Good quality modern villas start at around €190,000.

Where's best to live?
Take your pick: the eastern group includes Santa Maria and São Miguel; the central group includes Terceira, Graciosa, São Jorge, Pico and Faial; and the western group includes Flores and Corvo. The minimum distance between two islands is 6km (Pico and Faial) and the maximum distance – approximately 600km – divide Santa Maria and Corvo.

FACTFILE

Capital: Ponta Delgada   **Population:** 244,000
Area: 2,333 sq km
Language: Portuguese. The second language is English and is widely spoken in the main towns, but not in the countryside.
Climate: The Azores has a mild maritime climate controlled by the high pressure area, known as the "Azores High", and the warm Gulf Stream. Temperatures vary between 13-14°C during the winter and 22°-23°C during the summer, frequently climbing to the high 20s and low 30s in July and August.
Sea temperatures vary from between 14-15°C in winter and 22-23°C in the height of the summer.
   Rain falls throughout the year, however in summer the showers are brief but sometimes very heavy. There is an average of 78 per cent humidity.
Enty requirements: European Union citizens can enter and remain in the Azores for three months without any formalities.
Retirement/residence visa: See Main Portugal section
Electricity: 220V/50 Hz.
Money: Euro. ATMs are available in all towns and some villages. Credit/debit cards and travellers cheques are accepted in larger shops and restaurants but travellers cheques carry high transaction charges.
Public holidays: Basically the same as Portugal but the Azores also has numerous festivals.
Water: Tap water is perfectly OK to drink.
Tipping: 5-10 per cent in restaurants and for taxis.
Medical/healthcare: There are no special health requirements for visitors. There are modern hospitals in Ponta Delgada, Faial, Angra and Horta and health centres on each island. Treatment is free for most European nationals on production of your passport.
Pets: Pets must have a Pet Passport, health certificate and rabies vaccination certificate.

The most popular islands for property purchasers are:

Faial which lies in the central group of the Azores. The circular road around the island is 54km. The population is around 15,000 with half this number living in the main town of Horta.

The facilities available on Faial have dramatically improved since Portugal joined the EU and most daily requirements are readily available via supermarkets, a fresh food market and a good fish market with locally caught stock, plus a wide selection of specialist stores.

The tourist attractions of Faial include breathtaking scenery, a caldeira (crater), a huge variety of walking routes, beaches and black sand beaches and swimming places at various points. The plant life is very varied and prolific and in the summer months blue hydrangeas abound as hedgerows all over the island (Faial is also known as Ilha Azul).

There is a cinema and theatre, restaurants, clubs and sporting facilities with a municipal indoor swimming pool.

Pico Island, named for its imposing mountain, (the highest in Portugal at 2351 metres) is one of the most beautiful and underrated islands of the Azores. Only second to S. Miguel in size the 'Mountain Island' stands majestically in the middle of the Azorean central group, at about 4.5 nautical miles from Faial Island and 11 miles from S. Jorge Island.

Pico Island history was built on the legacy of its whale hunting and winery traditions. The famous Pico wines and the UNESCO world patrimony designated vineyards, as well as wooden boat building, are contemporary fixtures of Pico.

Volcanic eruptions ended 300 years ago. Pico is considered a dormant volcano adding to the mystique

of the island and serving as a magnet for scientists.

The Pico Island landscape is a mixture of lava rock and exotic vegetation in an ever-changing scenery that envelops this scarcely populated island.

Pico has the best swimming holes in the Azores and every so often an occasional sand beach appears. It is also the ideal island to trek, hike, jog, walk, bird watch, whale and dolphin watch, swim, fish, ride bikes and moto-quad bikes. Speleology is also a favourite pastime of Pico and its visitors.

Flores: This westernmost island of the Azores is stunningly beautiful, a veritable Garden of Eden with lakes, rivers, waterfalls and a spectacular rocky coast.

Only 4,000 people live there, spread between the main towns and villages, giving the island a peaceful, serene atmosphere and allowing you to wander and enjoy it without seeing another soul for hours.

The typography of the island is extremely rugged, marked by high elevations with cliffs descending gently at some points and sharply at others and terminating in valleys and lakes amidst extensive areas of natural vegetation.

Among the main tourist attractions in Flores are the seven beautiful lakes formed in the craters of the extinct volcanoes there.

Of the two existing municipalities on the island, the municipality of Lajes has a population of 1,500 inhabitants and is the second smallest municipality in Portugal.

We Live Here

Alan and Lesley Woodward ran a bar in the Canaries, sailed the Caribbean for four years before settling in the Azores

Alan Woodward, an apprenticed toolmaker from Birmingham back in the early '90s, met Lesley as they sat on a harbour wall in Tenerife in 1993.

Both were experienced sailors. Through the Duke of Edinburgh's Award Scheme, Alan had sailed across the Atlantic in the Tall Ships race. Lesley had qualified with a RYA Ocean Yachtmaster certificate, which enabled her to work as a yacht captain.

The last five years of her "normal" life, as Lesley puts it, were as an operator in the control room of Dorset Fire Brigade.

"I left that in 1990 to go sailing and haven't had a 'proper' job since!"

With their shared interests and adventurous spirit, the couple hit it off immediately. They joined forces, sailed around the Canaries and ended up running the 'Aloha Bar – English Bar and Restaurant' in Gran Canaria.

"After two years running that successfully we had topped up our cruising fund, refurbished our 10m yacht and set sail for the Azores for the summer. We loved it as a cruising ground, but had no thoughts of settling at that time."

The couple headed for the Caribbean and spent the next four years there, working in the yachting industry and crossing the Atlantic many times on yacht deliveries, each time stopping in Horta.

"We fell in love with the islands and bought a ruin in 2000, returning to restore it in 2001. Our B&B business was opened in 2002."

Helping out guests interested in buying property on the island led them to start their own property business, Azores Properties. They gave up the B&B to run the property agency full time and a holiday rental business.

Their property agency, Azores Properties [www.azoresproperties.com] is run with local businessmen José Mendonça and Luis Vieira da Silva both Azorean Portuguese who have lived on Faial all their lives.

Lesley's holiday rental business, Azores High [www.azoreshigh.com] offers a range of self-catering accommodation.

PROPERTY

Caminho do grotto, Salão

Quiet location on a minor road, with spectacular sea views and within walking distance of the local shop, cafés, school and garage and a few minutes from the port and swimming area.

The house has two floors with a living room, 2 bedrooms, kitchen and bathroom on the upper floor with workshop/utility area below which could be converted to further living accommodation. 2 garages and a study/office outside with garden and small orchard.
Price: €70,000 euros
More info: azoresproperties.com

Maçapês, Cedros

Settled into the hillside, on a quiet no-through road with Atlantic views. A few minutes walk to all the village amenities – shop, café, bank, church, school, etc.
2 bedrooms, bathroom, open-plan kitchen/diner/sitting room.

Furnished. Workshop, dog pound, pigsty and orchard and piece of uncultivated land.
Price: €57,000
More info: azoresproperties.com
Tel: +351 292949018
Email: azoresproperties@sapo.pt

The British armada: a million of us now call Spain home

Why Spain?

Spain absorbs far more immigrants than any other European country – over four million in the past decade alone. Most are economic migrants – from Africa, South America and Eastern Europe but the figure includes about 350,000 permanent residents from Britain – many of them retirees. An additional, and estimated three-quarters of a million Britons own property in Spain and spend a significant part of the year there.

The figure may be much higher. There is no requirement for expatriate Britons to register with the British embassy whose staff say the real figure may be as much as three times higher than official estimates. The Costa del Sol alone has a shifting British population of up to 300,000 and this doesn't include tourists.

The provinces of Alicante, Málaga and Murcia account for well over half of all British residents. What has traditionally drawn them to Spain – along with hundreds of thousands of other northern Europeans – has been the attraction of warm, sunny weather, an abundance of kindred spirits, cheap property and low cost of living, an outdoor way of life, cheap flights and welcoming locals.

Most of these reasons still apply. Others don't. Property prices are no longer cheap and many Spaniards resent the fact that the invasion of foreign property buyers has pushed prices beyond the means of their young people.

History and culture

However, the appeal remains. Spain is a spectacular and richly varied country soaked in history and culture. The north is covered in rolling green hills while the south boasts exotic northern African landscapes and architecture. Its miles of sandy beaches and beautiful landscapes are world famous as are its bullfights, flamenco dancers and delicious food and wine.

The country was originally divided into separate regions, which include Andalucía, Aragon, Asturias, Basque Country, the Balearic Islands, the Canary Islands, Cantabria, Castilla La Mancha, Castilla León, Catalonia, Extremadura, Galicia, La Rioja, Madrid, Murcia, Navarra and Valencia. These autonomous regions remain diverse in their language, culture, cuisine and art.

The Spanish lifestyle is as varied and rich as the landscapes of the country. For those who enjoy a livelier pace of life, living in larger towns or cities may be preferable, while those who want a quieter time may head for peaceful areas on the coast or inland. The Spanish are generous, hospitable and fun-loving

ABOUT THE WRITER: Rhona Hutchinson is fluent in Spanish and has worked with leading estate agents in both London and Spain, where she has lived for some 20 years and from where she runs www.integratedrelocationspain.com, which advises companies and individuals on all aspects of relocation and property purchase, and www.retirementspain.com which specialises in relocating the over 55s

FACTFILE

Capital: Madrid   **Population:** 40.5 million
Area: 504,782sq km
Language: Castilian Spanish (official) 74 per cent, Catalan 17 per cent, Galician 7 per cent, Basque 2 per cent, are official regionally.
Climate: Temperate; clear, hot summers in interior, more moderate and cloudy along coast; cloudy, cold winters in interior, partly cloudy and cool along coast.
Entry requirements: EU member, no visa required.
Permanent residence: EU citizens have the right to take up residence.
Time difference: GMT+1
Money: Euro. ATMs are widely available. Credit/debit cars and travellers cheques are accepted in most shops and hotels.
Electricity: 220v
Public holidays 2010

Jan 1	New Year's Day	Aug 15	Assumption
Jan 6	Epiphany	Oct 12	National Day
March 19	San Joske	Nov 1	All Saints' Day
April 1	Maundy Thursday	Nov 1	All Saints' Day
April 2	Good Friday	Dec 6	Constitution Day
May 1	Labour Day	Dec 8	Imm. Conception
Dec 25	Christmas Day		

Opening hours
Shops: 9:30am-2pm, 5pm to 8pm, Mon-Sat
Banks: 8am-2pm Mon-Fri, some open 9am-1pm Sat.
Offices: 9am-5-6pm Mon-Fri
Water: OK in larger towns, bottled is best in more remote areas.
Tipping: Tipping is not common in Spain other than by tourists
Medical/healthcare: Spain's state healthcare system is regarded as one of the best in the EU. The European Health Insurance Card will allow you to have your medical fees reimbursed. See page xx.
Pets: To get in without quarantine, pets must be microchipped, vaccinated against rabies and issued with an EU Pet Passport.

people who enjoy the outdoors and the sun.

The Spanish mañana, or 'do it tomorrow' attitude, continues to prevail but this is dying out, as is the siesta culture. In fact, most shops, businesses and restaurants stay open later than in the UK, and it is common for things to kick off when the sun goes down, especially in the summer. Bars and nightclubs often stay open well after the new day has dawned.

How easy is it to obtain residential status?

Britons and other EU nationals do not require a visa to enter Spain but EU citizens planning to reside in Spain for more than three months are required to register in person at the Foreigners' Office (Oficina de Extranjeros) in their province of residence or at designated police stations.

PROPERTY

Andalucia apartments

Finished to the last detail, these five elegant apartmentshave been renovated by a British couple in Andalucia,. They have luxury kitchens complete with appliances and lighting. The apartments are either 2 or 3 bedrooms, each with 2 bathrooms. Community areas include a swimming pool and sun terraces. The annual community charge of €300 is fixed for five years.

Mortgages and furniture packages can be arranged.

Price range: €327,000-€365,000
More info: Steve Breckon, Surmarly Promociones
Tel: +34 956 410 808 Mob: +34 657 640 591
www.surmarly.com

La Zagaleta, Andalucia

La Zagaleta is a gated nature reserve occupying 900 hectares of wild Andalucian countryside with views of the Mediterranean, Gibraltar and North Africa. La Zagaleta offers a country club lifestyle with two 18-hole golf courses, private fishing lakes, a riding club, heliport and on-site services from banking to catering. Prices: Homes are priced from €4 million for 5 bedrooms with full indoor spa and heated swimming pool.
More info: Bolt Property Group
www.boltpropertygroup.com

You will be issued a certificate stating your name, address, nationality, identity number and date of registration. The certificate serves as confirmation that the registration obligation has been fulfilled.

Is it safe?

On the whole, yes; Spain's crime rate is among the lowest in Europe, third only to Portugal and Ireland. However, it shouldn't be forgotten that there is an ongoing threat from terrorism in Spain. The Basque terrorist organisation ETA announced a ceasefire in 2006 but retracted it in June 2007.

The Spanish respect law and order, although 'minor' laws (such as illegal parking and making too much noise) are usually ignored. In most villages, especially away from the tourist areas, crime is almost unknown.

Like other countries, major cities have the highest crime rates with Alicante, Barcelona, Madrid, Malaga, Seville and Valencia the worst.

How much tax will I pay?

If you are resident of Spain (i.e. spend more than 183 days there a year) you will pay tax on your worldwide income at a rate of up to 43 per cent. Savings and capital gains are taxed at a single flat tax rate of 18 per cent. Personal and family allowances are taxed at a zero rate.

While as a Spanish resident you have to declare income earned outside Spain, in practice it is difficult for the Spanish tax authorities to find out about such income. Britain has an agreement with Spain to avoid double taxation. Apply for certificate E101 to declare your tax paying status in Spain which negates your tax obligations in the UK. Capital gains tax has been reduced from 35 per cent to 18 per cent. Wealth tax has been abolished.

Property purchase

Two-bedroom bungalows in a coastal area, with services and amenities nearby, start from around €140,000 for something half decent, while detached villas start at around €265,000. It is important to seek advice on property purchase.

As in all countries, prices vary from area to area. The big cities are expensive, as are the more popular coastal areas such as Marbella or Sitges. Here you can expect London prices for everyday living and some of the most expensive property in Spain. If your pension is limited, then going a little way inland will reduce living costs substantially.

Mortgages are available up to the age of 75 in Spain and depending whether the land is urban or rustic, will determine the percentage amounts you can borrow. Normally you could borrow up to 70 per cent of the cost of the property, paying one per cent above

Villa Villamarchante, Costa del Azahar
Villas with up to 8 bedrooms, staff and guest accommodation, spa and gymnasium, indoor swimming pool, cinema, games room with bar and option for a bowling alley at La Zagaleta, a nature reserve on 900 hectares of Andalucian countryside, with views of the Mediterranean, Gibraltar and Africa, has two 18-hole golf courses, private fishing lakes, a riding club, heliport and full on-site services.
Prices: From €4 million
More info: Bolt Property Group
www.boltpropertygroup.com

Rancho Verde, Malaga
Country chalet of 230sq m on 2 floors with 5 bedrooms and 1 bathroom on a fenced plot of 4,000sq m between the towns of Villamarchante and Cheste.
Price: €300,000
More info: International Homes (Yorks)
www.international-homes-yorks.co.uk

I live here

Colin Davies, 62, lives in Galicia in the very north west of Spain spending his time enjoying the relaxing, fun-oriented life that Spain offers and writing for his websites www.colindavies.net and www.colindavies.blog-spot.com

After retiring early from a business career in the UK, I came to Galicia eight years ago because my then wife had lived here during a previous marriage.

I liked it sufficiently to decide to retire here after our divorce and, in due course, I bought a property overlooking the city of Pontevedra. This is part of the northern third of the country called 'Green Spain', where the cooler, wetter weather provides a countryside as verdant and as beautiful as anything in the UK and Ireland.

Still largely unknown by the British, it is very popular with those Spaniards seeking a summer holiday away from the heat of Madrid and the south. Some Brits may be familiar with Galicia as the home of the Cathedral of Santiago de Compostela, the end point of the 1,000-year-old Pilgrimage of St James.

Like much of Spain, a great deal of Galicia is mountainous and most of the population lives along or near the stupendous coast, in the major cities of Vigo, Pontevedra, Santiago, Ferrol and La Coruña. Vigo is the largest fishing port in Spain and La Coruña is, of course, the resting place of Sir John Moore, who died during the retreat from the French in the Peninsular War of 1808.

The region is famous for its wide variety of excellent seafood and its fine wines, particularly those of the

Albariño grape, currently in vogue around the world.

Like every region in Spain, it likes to see itself as different from everywhere else. And, like Catalunia and the Basque Country, it has its own language – Gallego which resembles a mixture of Spanish and Portuguese. Life, however, is essentially Spanish and there is an enormous range of gastronomic and cultural fiestas.

Weather-wise, Galicia resembles Britain more than it does southern Spain. Plentiful rainfall means it's definitely not the retirement destination for those needing several hours of sun a day.

Restoration opportunities

Although summers are appreciably better than those of the UK, Galicia's attractions lie rather more in the magnificence of its indented coastline and the natural beauty of its heavily-forested interior.

Property prices are lower than elsewhere in Spain, particularly up in the mountains where there are still plenty of old granite farmhouses to restore and large plots of land.

While the property crash and the fall-off of demand from Brits because of the low pound have led to a slide in prices, Galicians are renowned for their stubbornness and, if they don't need to sell, owners may well try to hold out for the asking price. A good local intermediary is always a sound idea – a lawyer rather than the agent who's on a commission.

If you're thinking of retiring to Galicia you should know that few people speak English here and there are no expatriate communities to join. There are now quite a few British families around the inland cities of Lugo and Ourense but there are none of the expat-oriented facilities of Spain's well-developed coasts.

Essentially you have to join Spanish society and it's crucial to speak some Spanish. If, like the majority of Brits, you opt for the rural delights of the regions close to the cities of Lugo or Ourense, you may have to acquire more than a smattering of Gallego as well.

the base rate. Mortgages are expensive in Spain, as you need to pay a mortgage tax of around 1.5 per cent on top of the bank's opening charge of 1-2 per cent.

Some of the UK banks operating in Spain offer equity release on your UK home allowing you to fund a Spanish home purchase using the equity available in your UK property, an obvious advantage if retirement in Spain falls short of your expectations. The main disadvantage with this scheme is that it is expensive to arrange and you may not be able to raise all that you need.

Cost of living
In general terms a euro will buy you what a pound sterling does in the UK. As for a budget, it is possible to live off €1,200 a month for a retired couple (with no rental or mortgage costs), whereas €1,600 would be more comfortable and allow for some flights back home, and €2,000 per month or above will make retirement in Spain easy.

Money and banking
It is possible to have your pensions and income paid directly into your Spanish bank account. However it is important to set everything up correctly in order to minimise bank transfer charges, Spanish reception fees and to ensure that the best exchange rate is always achieved. Doing this properly will save you thousands of euros a year.

Britain's refusal to adopt the euro means complications for the UK pensioner which are not experienced by his northern European counterparts

when retiring to Spain.

While in the last five years sterling has operated within a fairly broad band of €1.15 to €1.50 to the pound, historically the fluctuations have been much higher so you need to consider a "what if" scenario: if my pension income were to drop due to the adverse exchange rate, then what would be the implications for me?

Where's best to live?
Which communities in Spain are right for you? It is important to do your research, visit different areas at different times of year, use local specialists to point out areas that correspond to your desired lifestyle criteria. Do not be over-influenced by the property itself, as in time you will be unhappy in your dream house if the area does not live up to your lifestyle requirements.

In general terms, Valencia and areas south have

Golf apartment, Gazules del Sol
2 and 3 bedroom apartments and penthouses all over 100sq m with sea, garden and mountain views. Gated community with four communal swimming pools, spa with indoor heated pool, gymnasium, sauna and jacuzzi, at the heart of Benahavís' 'golf valley', a 10-minute drive from Puerto Banús and the Costa del Sol. Air-conditioning, electric blinds, Bang & Olufsen surround-sound system. Kitchens with Siemens appliances, lifts to all floors.
Price: Reduced from €351,278 to €200,781.
More info: GEM Established
www.gemestablished.com. Tel: 00 34 952 799 286 (in Spain)
(UK Freephone) 0800 036 0068

El Convento, Andalucia
16th century monastic house, 12km from the village of El Burgo in the heart of the Sierra de las Nieves and set in approximately 70,000sq m of olive groves and mixed pine forest with two ruined hermitages for renovation. Kitchen, living and dining area, 4 bedrooms, private internal patio, garden, yoga exercise suite. Price includes a fifth share of the old church. Various outbuildings.
Price €495,000
More info: Pavilions of Splendour International
www.pavilionsofsplendourinternational.com

Email:
diana@pavilionsofsplendourinternational.com

We live here

Violet King, 69, moved to the Costa Blanca from Hainault, Essex, with her husband, Philip, 73, in 1999 after the couple retired, he as a psychologist with Mind and Violet as a motivational counsellor.

There are many wonderful things to say about life here but the explosion of newcomers to the Costa Blanca has played a big part in things becoming chaotic at times.

Even the authorities are overwhelmed. We have turned up at offices only to be told we're in the wrong place and sent somewhere else to find we're still in the wrong place. It can be a little wearing as the system changes at the drop of a hat.

Bureaucracy and a system that is constantly changing makes life a bit tricky when you are dealing with a language you don't understand. No complaints really …after nine years we are getting there.

It's the same with getting around. New roads, shopping centres and roundabouts suddenly appear and if you haven't visited a particular area for a few weeks you can become very confused.

Healthcare here can be excellent, but again, it isn't easy when you don't speak the language and an interpreter is needed when you visit health centres, town halls and police stations. After 10 years our Spanish is still not very good.

Driving in Spain is good most of the time as so many of the roads are new but the quality of driving leaves something to be desired. Roundabouts and traffic lights are often ignored and pedestrians step off the kerb

without looking. Locals park across street corners and in the weirdest places but no one seems to care.

What we love here is the lower cost of living, clean air and better quality of life. Once you get away from the coast it is very relaxed and Spanish … as you would expect.

Until recently eating out was incredibly reasonable and even now it is still a lot cheaper than the UK. There are masses of eating places, Chinese and Indian leading the way.

There are plenty of entertainment options and sport and leisure facilities.

Property prices have definitely gone down here and there's supposedly a glut of property.

Some resentment

We live just outside Torrevieja on the Costa Blanca. At one time the only trades here were farming and fishing. The huge growth of neighbouring areas has made things tricky for the Spaniards and although the money and investment that comes in as a result is appreciated, understandably there tends to be a little resentment with some expats expecting things to be done the UK way.

I started two non-smoking social clubs here but resigned from both eventually as I wanted to concentrate on my writing and counselling.

We go home two or three times a year and our children – three daughters and six grandchildren come to visit.

Violet trained as a motivational counsellor and now runs the website: www.freewebs.com/makechanges which helps people to take control of their lives by making the right choices.

She also writes articles for several monthly magazines in the English-speaking community and her book, "Change Your Life … Do It Today" was published in 2006.

clement winters, Marbella has the best winter climate of all and Murcia/Almeria regions have the most sun.

Bear in mind that vast areas of Spain have cold and often wet winters. The best places for milder winters are the Costa Blanca, Costa Calida, Costa Almeria, Costa Tropical and Costa del Sol. As a rule of thumb, if lemons or avocados are grown then the winter climate is a mild one.

Spain usually has 10 lovely months a year and then two – July and August – when it is so hot it is often a good idea to let your house and go visit friends and family back home. Particularly hot summer temperatures are found in Seville, Cordoba, Madrid, Jerez, Huelva, Murcia capital, Albacete, Toledo, Extremadura and all of Almeria. If you don't like the heat, then avoid these communities.

Ideal climates include Costa Blanca North, Costa Calida and Costa del Sol – i.e., the coastal areas of Alicante up to Valencia – and Murcia and Nerja to Gibraltar. Anywhere in the lee of a northerly wind is often advantageous in winter e.g., Moraira.

Coastal or Inland?

Arguments for the coast are that it is more developed, has a more clement climate, a breeze in the summer, a warming sea in the winter, a higher concentration of expats, lovely beaches, good infrastructure, roads, hospitals, main cities and railways.

Arguments against the coast are that the resorts are often deserted in winter leaving you rattling around in a ghost town, property prices are high, development has often been unregulated leading to concrete jungles, the cost of living is higher, you cannot move during the summer due to road and beach congestion and restaurants are packed and there is a proliferation of

Atalaya Fairways, near Marbella
Atalaya Fairways is a luxury golf development of 16 3-storey villas 15 minutes from Marbella. The community overlooks the second of Atalaya's two 18-hole golf courses with views across to the Mediterranean and North Africa. Remote-control wooden doors to substantial basement and garaging for 3 cars and additional open-plan space, lift to upper floors. Large sitting room/dining area, kitchen with Siemens appliances, 2 en-suite bedrooms. Top floor has 2 or 3 additional en-suite bedrooms and master suite with dressing room and spacious terrace.
Bathrooms have under-floor heating, hydro-massage tub in the master bathrooms, pre-installation for home cinema and integral music system, remote video control system for alarm, lighting, air-conditioning, garden irrigation and other household conveniences. Outside there are landscaped gardens and a swimming pool with underwater lighting.
Prices: Start at €885,000
More info: Contemporary Villas   www.contemporary-villas.com
Email: info@contemporary-villas.com
Tel: 00 34 952 799 200 (in Spain) UK 0845 094 1168

EWN: THE most comprehensive and definitive FREE English newspaper in Europe. Providing existing and future expatriates with unprecedented access to essential information.

- **Find** a property from established estate agents
- **Source** jobs and businesses for sale
- **Learn** how to navigate the Spanish system
- **Delve** deep into expatriate topics
- **Get** expert financial and legal advice
- **Research** news in the area you are moving to

Euro Weekly News is the most established free English language newspaper in the whole of Europe with five different editions and a circulation of 360,000 copies every month to over 2,500 distribution points every week on mainland Spain and the island of Mallorca. Each edition contains local, national and international news, a full TV and satellite guide, plus financial information including stocks and shares listings. Where free newspapers differ here in Spain from those back 'home' is that there is no English yellow pages here; there is no directory enquiries that can find you a plumber in your area. Adverts provide the same service (if not more important) to the expatriate community as the news articles, weekly columns, and TV pages do.

The EWN Media Group offers access to the latest useful information BEFORE you arrive via our website that contains a free virtual newspaper so you can familiarise yourself with your chosen area before you retire there.

EWN - Connecting expatriate retirees with local business owners, local service providers and local retailers with a unique and professional platform.

Europe's No.1 Free Local Weekly Newspaper
www.euroweeklynews.com

(although the heat and the cold tend to be dry in nature and as such more tolerable and kinder to the joints). People are simpler, less sophisticated and often ignorant to Anglo Saxon ways.

However, if you go too far inland you will find the winters can be very cold, often wet and bad for arthritis. Summers can be dry and unbearably hot.

Depending on how mountainous the area and also where the prevailing winds come from, you are often best to be between a half and one hour's drive away from the coast. There are exceptions to this rule.

high-rise apartments and a general lack of green spaces.

Arguments for inland include that it is a more authentic Spain, a better all-year-round environment for daily living, with cheaper property, quieter roads, spectacular scenery, cheaper cost of living and a calmer pace of life.

Arguments against inland include the fact that there is less expat infrastructure, you really need to speak Spanish and it can be very hot in the summer

Surveys have shown that the five most popular coastal destinations – chosen on the basis of climate, infrastructure, healthcare provision and expat/local mix – are Javea/Moraira, Estepona, Roquetas del Mar, Guardamar and Nerja while the most popular inland areas are Ronda, Caravaca de la Cruz, Jalon, La Nucia and Antequera. A strong alternative is the relatively unspoilt Atlantic coastline with sandy beaches between Gibraltar and the Portuguese border.

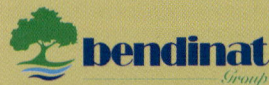

Mark Stucklin's Spanish property Insight

If you're considering Spain as a retirement destination you should subscribe to Mark Stucklin's free Spanish Property Insight [www.spanishpropertyinsight.com]

Mark, who provided the chart below on Spanish property prices, writes a regular Spanish property column in the Sunday Times and is the author of 'Need to Know: Buying Property in Spain' published by Collins.

The following notes summarise an advisory on his website:

- Always do your own research before you buy and learn how the conveyancing process works in Spain.
- Approach the purchase in a structured and organised way and keep your wits about you.
- Start by creating a clear, written brief of your property requirements.
- Hire an independent, competent Spanish lawyer and never use the in-house lawyer of an estate agent or developer.
- Never sign a contract or pay a deposit before carrying out an appropriate due diligence and getting the all-clear from your lawyer.
- When buying off-plan always make sure that a building licence has been granted by the town hall.
- Retain a healthy sense of scepticism about the claims people make when trying to sell you property especially in regard to off-plan investments.
- Never allow yourself to be pressurised into a decision.
- Make sure you understand your fiscal obligations once you have purchased property in Spain.

Spanish property price data for selected regions

Region I Province	Latest price €/m2	Quarterly change	Annual change	Decade change
Madrid	2.706	-2.6%	-9.9%	152%
Barcelona	2.663	-2.8%	-3.5%	146%
Cataluna	2.366	-2.8%	-3.7%	158%
Baleares	2.261	-5.5%	-6.1%	167%
Malaga	2.097	-4.7%	-10.7%	241%
Girona	2.087	-2.5%	-4.5%	197%
Cadiz	1.881	-1.8%	-1.6%	236%
Cantabria	1.877	-4.1%	-7.8%	142%
Tarragona	1.831	-3.3%	-6.2%	217%
Sevilla	1.748	-2.2%	-2.4%	217%
Las Palmas	1.747	-3.2%	-8.5%	108%
Andalucia	1.698	-2.4%	-5,7%	199%
Canarias	1.688	-2.6%	-7.9%	110%
Huelva	1.671	-0.4%	-6.4%	193%
Asturias	1.655	-5.6%	-6.8%	123%
Pontevedra	1.621	-2.4%	-7.7%	147%
Tenerife	1.613	-2.3%	-7.6%	113%
Castellon	1.604	-2.9%	-6.9%	177%
Alicante	1.580	-5.8%	-9.2%	160%
Comunidad Valenciana	1.572	-3.5%	-6.7%	165%
Valencia	1.561	-2.0%	-4.5%	170%
Almeria	1.544	-3.6%	-8.1%	187%
Region de Murcia	1.476	-3.1%	-8.5%	200%
Galicia	1.476	-2.3%	-6.1%	123%
Granada	1.455	-1.9%	-4.4%	166%
Cordoba	1.444	-3.0%	-6.9%	179%
Extremadura	1.015	-1.1%	-1.1%	130%
Teruel	965	-5.1%	-8.1%	94%
ESPANA	1.958	-3.0%	-6.8%	151%

www.spanishpropertyinsight.com   source: Mm. viveznda

Average Spanish property prices fell by 6.8 per cent in the first quarter of the year, compared to the same time last year, according to official figures just out from the Ministry of Housing. This is the first time since the Spanish property market downturn began that the official figures look even vaguely realistic.

On a quarterly basis, Spanish house prices fell by 3 per cent in the first three months of the year, compared to a fall of 2.4 per cent in the final quarter of 2008.

For the annual figures, there were big differences between regions, with prices falling by 10.7 per cent in Malaga province, home to the Costa del Sol, but by just -1.1 per cent in Extremadura.

With the exception of Malaga province, the biggest falls were to be found in 'real Spain', well away from the coasts where foreigners tend to buy. Prices fell by 14.6 per cent in Toledo (Castilla La Mancha), 12.3 per cent in Salamanca (Castilla Leon), and 11.9 per cent in Guadalajara (Castilla La Mancha).

SPAIN CONTACT DIRECTORY

Embassies/government
British Embassy
www.ukinspain.com
Spanish Embassy in London
www.conspalon.org

About Spain
www.retirementspain.com
www.euroresidentes.com
www.thinkspain.com
www.spanishindex.com
www.aboutspain.net
www.hotcosta.com
www.spanish-fiestas.com
www.integratedrelocationspain.com
www.idealspain.com
Barcelona: www.bcn.es/english
Madrid: www.gomadrid.com
Sevilla: www.andalucia.com
Alicante: www.alicante-city-insiders-guide.com

General & Expat
www.expatfocus.co,
www.retirementspain.com
www.thisisspain.info
www.expatexchange.com
www.costablancaexpats.net
www.spainexpat.com
www.expatica.com
www.seg-social.es
www.spainexpat.com

English Language Media
Euro Weekly News
ww.euroweeklynews.com
www.spainview.com/media4.html
www.theolivepress.es
www.thinkspain.com
Sur in Englishwww.surinenglish.com
Majorca Daily Bulletin
www.majorcadailybulletin.es
Inland Traderhttp://www.inlandtrader.net
The Costa Newswww.costa-news.com
Essential Magazine (Marbella)
www.essentialmagazine.com
The Paper (Tenerife)www.thepaper.net
Baleares Magazinewww.baleares.com
www.webexpressguide.com/costadelsol
There are many more and the Expatriate
Café (www.expatriatecafe.com) lists 13
more English titles.

Travel & Tourism
www.spain.info
(Spanish Tourist Office)
www.spanish-fiestas.com
www.toptravelsites.com
www.searchiberia.com
www.in-spain.info
www.tienda.com/links.htm
www.travelinginspain.com

Airlines from UK
www.easyjet.com
www.ryanair.com
www.bmibaby.com
www.flybmi.com
www.flyglobespan.com
www.jet2.com
www.spanair.com
www.flymonarch.com
www.air-scotland.com
www.aerlingus.com

Property
Spanish Property Insight
www.spanishpropertyinsight.com
Portocolom www.bendinat.com
Tel: 0034 971405000
Email: info@bendinat.com
Sanyres Senior Resorts
www.sanyresresorts.es
www.euroresidencias.com/uk
www.propertyinspain.net
www.kei-retirement.co.uk
Villas www.contemporary-villas.com
www.taylorwoodrow.es
www.gemestablished.com.
www.pavilionsofsplendourinternational.com
www.boltpropertygroup.comwww.vivaestates.com
www.inspain.tv
www.fbeas.com
(website of the Federation of British Estate
Agents in Spain)

Sun-blessed Balearics – holiday home of the rich and famous

Why the Balearic Islands?

The Balearic Islands are just over two hours flying time from the UK. They lie in the western Mediterranean off the east coast of mainland Spain. The best known and most visited of the four main islands are Mallorca (Majorca) and Ibiza which are two of Europe's top holiday spots.

Ibiza is world renowned for its sizzling nightlife whilst Mallorca is all things to all people – princes and poets are drawn to the island along with pop idols and package holidaymakers.

Menorca is popular with those who want sunshine and breathtaking scenery without the crowds and fast pace of top resorts such as Mallorca's manic Magaluf. Homebuyers and holidaymakers seeking total tranquility head for the beautiful unspoilt island of Formentera,

which is a mecca for nature lovers (and naturists) from all over Europe.

The Cabrera National Park, to the south of Mallorca, is an archipelago of 19 small islands which are part of the Balearics but only day trips are allowed and even an overnight stay in a private boat requires a permit.

Together the islands form one of Spain's 17 autonomous communities. Different versions of the Catalan language predominate on all of the islands though English is widely spoken in the resort areas.

Mallorca, Ibiza and Menorca all have international airports and numerous low cost airlines offer cheap flights from the UK and other European destinations (flying time from London is under 2.5 hours).

Formentera is reached by ferry from Ibiza Town – the journey takes between 35 minutes and an hour depending on whether you take the fast or standard ferry. There are regular ferries between all the four main islands and day excursions from Mallorca around the Cabrera marine reserve.

It's a common misconception that Ibiza is only for round-the-clock razzlers. It certainly boasts some of the world's biggest and best nightclubs but they're largely confined to the two main resorts of Ibiza Town and San Antonio.

There are plenty of relaxed resort areas and the northern end of the island is a delight to explore with its lush, green countryside, rugged cliffs and hidden coves.

Similarly, Mallorca offers both action-packed seaside resorts along with wild, mountainous areas, traditional villages untainted by tourism and remote beaches only accessible by boat or on foot. Magaluf, in the south-

FACTFILE/ CONTACT INFO

The Balearics is an autonomous region of Spain and general information (entry requirements, residence, holidays, currency, credit cards, etc) also applies in the Balearics. Please consult the main Spain section.

Capital: Palma   **Population:** 880,000

Area: 5,040sq km Language: Catalan and Castilian

Climate: Mediterranean with mild, dry winters.

Water: Bottled is better.

Medical/Healthcare: The main risks are sunburn and hangovers. No vaccinations are required. Healthcare is on the same terms as Spanish nationals.

Getting There

Iberia: www.iberiaairlines.co.uk

British Airways: www.ba.com

Easyjet: www.easyjet.com

Ryanair: www.ryanair.com

Monarch: www.flymonarch.com

Thomson Airways: www.thomson.co.uk

Air Europa: www.aireuropa.com

Air France: www.airfrance.co.uk

Getting Around: Flights and ferries between the four main islands are efficient but expensive.

Train: On Mallorca narrow-gauge trains run from Palma to Soller several times daily and less frequently to Inca. There are no railways on the other islands.

Bus: There are extensive bus services throughout the islands.

Ferry: There are extensive ferry services throughout the islands.

west corner of the island, is the main magnet for British package holidaymakers and has become notorious for attracting the most hardened revellers.

Meanwhile neighbouring Palma, the cosmopolitan capital of the Balearics, lures millionaires and movie moguls to its sumptuous five-star hotels. Elsewhere on the island, serenity seekers spend their holidays in converted castles, medieval monasteries and rural farmhouses which seem a million miles away from Magaluf.

Menorca's attractions include more than 100 beaches, a wealth of historic sites to explore, some of the finest seafood restaurants in the archipelago and a good range of family-orientated sports and leisure facilities.

Formentera has lovely unspoilt beaches and good quality restaurants serving up traditional local fare.

PROPERTY

Villa in Pollensa

Previously used as a cattle ranch, the house is at the end of a cul de sac providing peace and privacy. 3 double rooms, one en suite. Huge dining room facing a terrace and outside garden, modern fully-equipped kitchen. Extensive garden with barbecue, pool, shower and utility room and covered parking for 2 cars.

Price: POA

More info: www.solmallorca.com

Tel: +34 971 53 50 45

Apartment with pool

2 bedroom , 2 bathroom apartment in Pollentia Mar, an urban area of Puerto de Pollena, Mallorca, 50m from the beach and the famous Voramar seaside promenade. Communal area with swimming pool. Parking spaces and lifts.

Price: €288,000

More info:

www.spanishhotproperties.com

Property market

Expect to pay at least 50 per cent – and probably more like 100 per cent – more for a property in the Balearics than you would for the equivalent property on the Spanish mainland.

The capital, Palma, is a cosmopolitan melting pot. Buy a home here and you'll be rubbing shoulders with the rich and famous. Pay the right price and your neighbours could be Michael Douglas, Richard Branson, Claudia Schiffer or Sir Andrew Lloyd Webber. They all have homes in Majorca.

British buyers account for about 30 per cent of the market. If you've got plenty of money the chap to talk to is Matthias Kühn whose estate agency Kühn & Partner dominates the high-end side of the market with no less than 21 branches on Mallorca and Ibiza.

[www.kuhn-partner.com]

If you have the right financial credentials Matthias will whiz you around in the company jet or helicopter to look at properties in the many millions.

Kühn's closest competitor is Engel & Volkers who have 20 offices on the islands [www.engelvoelkers.com].

Other agencies include:
- www.balearicestateagents.co.uk
- www.novipropertymallorca.com
- www.balearicresidence.com
- www.homefindermallorca.com
- www.buyinibiza.com
- www.realhomesmallorca.com
- www.puertopollensa.ws
- www.meridianainmo.com

Country home, Majorca

Estate of 21,000sq m in the Mondragó nature park with fabulous panoramic views, minutes from Porto Petro and its beautiful beaches. 3 bedrooms, 3 bathrooms, living room with high ceilings, library (can be used as an extra bedroom) and an open gallery on the first floor.
Central heating, alternative solar and wind energy, stables and outbuildings. Pine, almond and fruit trees including lemons, mandarins, oranges, figs, apricots and grapes.
Price: €890.000
More info: www.mallorca-property-exclusive.com
Email: irene.portopetro@gmail.com

Villa Los Arcos, Ibiza

Villa of 375sq m on 1,800sq m plot on first line above 2 beaches. 6 bedrooms with dressing rooms, 4 bathrooms. Quiet residential area. Large lounge. Large dining area. Large modern kitchen. Covered terraces. Fully air-conditioned.
Recreational terrace with bar. Pool with sunbathing terrace and pergolas. Electric gates, garage, landscaped gardens.
Price: €2.3 million
More info: www.ibizavillasforsale.com
Please quote reference : PI126
UK: 0044 (0)1480 434290
Email: ibiza@gatehouseinternational.co.uk

Seven islands to choose from in the 'land of eternal spring'

Why the Canaries?

Seven large islands, eight airports, 41 marinas, 17 golf courses, four national parks and approximately 12 million visitors per year…phew!

The Romans dubbed them the 'Fortunate Islands' when they stumbled upon these hidden treasures off the west coast of Africa more than 2000 years ago.

And the Canary Islands are fortunate indeed – blessed with a near perfect climate and magnificent landscapes which make them a magnet for millions of 21st Century foreign "invaders" each year.

Despite their proximity to Africa, the islands together form one of the 17 autonomous communities of Spain. But unlike the costas of mainland Spain, the Canaries enjoy pleasantly warm temperatures throughout the year making them a favourite holiday destination for winter and summer sun seekers alike.

The sub-tropical climate of the islands (which are more or less on the same latitude as Orlando in Florida) is tempered by the cooling trade winds and the warm waters of the Gulf Stream. The result is a "land of eternal spring" where the temperature range is 18-24°C and the sea is a pleasure to swim in at any time of the year.

The islands offer a huge range of natural and man-made attractions: there are vast volcanic craters, spectacular black beaches, ancient forests and crystal clear waters inhabited by whales and dolphins. The quieter islands are a paradise for nature lovers whilst the most popular islands provide action-packed resort areas with every conceivable form of facility and entertainment for foreign visitors.

The archipelago consists of five main holiday islands – Tenerife, Lanzarote, Gran Canaria, Fuerteventura and La Palma – along with the two small islands of Gomera and Hierro and several tiny uninhabited islands.

Tenerife is the biggest and busiest of all the islands and is the one with the broadest appeal. The island offers everything from bustling beachfront resorts and family fun centres to ancient pyramids and Spain's highest mountain.

Gran Canaria, to the south east of Tenerife, is at the heart of the archipelago and another island which appeals both to party people and those who prefer to enjoy Canarian culture and quiet country villages.

The island boasts one of the most riotous resorts in the Canaries – Playa del Ingles which is a mecca for gays, travellers and round-the-clock revellers.

The capital, Las Palmas, has a different feel altogether with its distinctly Canarian character, historic buildings and museums. Elsewhere on the island you'll find snow capped mountains, traditional villages virtually untouched by tourism, a desert landscape and tropical fruit plantations.

Fuerteventura and Lanzarote lie at the eastern edge of the island group, closest to Africa. Fuerteventura has some of the longest and best beaches in the Canaries and attracts watersports enthusiasts and those wanting a relaxing "sun and sea" holiday rather than foam party aficionados.

Lanzarote is home to some of the most mind-blowing landscapes in the world with its weird petrified lava formations, volcanic craters and underground cave systems.

The most westerly islands – La Palma, Gomera and El Hierro – are lusher, greener and more unspoilt than

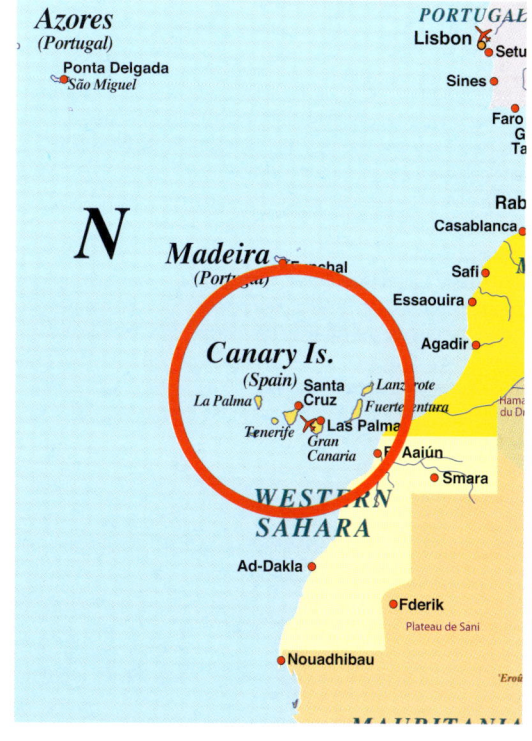

the bigger islands. They're the haunts of artists, walkers and nature lovers who prefer to steer clear of resorts geared to the package holiday market.

It's a common misconception that the Canaries are named after the songbirds which inhabit the islands. In fact the reverse is true and the birds take their name from the islands which were home to packs of wild dogs in ancient times.

The Spanish Canarias comes from the Latin word meaning "of the dogs".

Roque del Conde villa

Detached villa in the popular area of Roque del Conde in Torviscas Alto. 3 double bedrooms, 2 bathrooms, spacious lounge/dining area leading onto terrace, garden and private swimming pool. Apartment with a separate entrance, a workshop and a large garage.
Price: €990,000   Ref: LAV 08-170
More info: www.sunway-tenerife.com
Tel: (0034) 922 790 021 or UK 0871 711 5079

El Cotillo apartment

El Cotillo on Fuerteventura has miles of white sandy coves and conditions that are ideal for wind-surfing and kite surfing. 1 bedroom apartments come with white goods included – fridge freezer washing machine and oven/hob/extractor fan; bedroom with fitted wardrobes, marble floors and non-slip flooring on the balcony.
Price: €90,000
More info: www.thinkspain.com Property Ref: 781016

FACTFILE

The Canary Islands are an autonomous region of Spain and general information (entry requirements, residence, holidays, currency, credit cards, etc) also applies in the Canaries. Please consult the main Spain section.

Capital: Shared by Las Palmas and Santa Cruz
Population: 2 million   **Area:** 7,242sq km
Language: Spanish
Climate: Mild sub-tropical climate throughout the year with an average temperature of 19-22°C. Temperatures and rainfall differ between the islands; the closer to the African coast, the warmer and drier.
Enty requirements: No visa required
Permanent residence: EU citizens have the right to take up residence.
Electricity: 220 V 50 Hz
Time Difference: GMT -1 hour
Water: Bottled is better.
Medical/Healthcare: No vaccinations are required. Healthcare is on the same terms as Spanish nationals.

CONTACT INFO

About the Canary Islands
www.bestofthecanaries.com
www.canarias24.com
www.canaryforum.com
www.gran-canaria-info.com
http://grancanaria.ca
http://savic.com/canarias
www.turismodecanarias.com
/en/islas/gran-canaria

Property
www.engelvoelkers.com
www.cactusconsulting.com
www.LanzaroteInvestments.com
www.horizonpropertygroup.com
www.lanzarote-properties.com
www.lanzabusiness.com
www.optimaestate.com
www.canaryislandsproperty.es
www.etenerife.com
www.casaquest.com

Travel & Tourism
Website: www.canarias.es
www.canaryislandstouristguide.com
www.turismodecanarias.com
www.canaries-live.com
www.lonelyplanet.com/canary-islands

Getting There
There are numerous charter flights. All seven islands have airports, with international flights only to and from the 'big three' (Tenerife, Gran Canaria and Lanzarote).
Thomas Cook: ThomasCook.com
Iberia: www.iberiaairlines.co.uk
British Airways: www.ba.com
Easyjet: www.easyjet.com
Monarch: www.flymonarch.com
Ryanair: www.ryanair.com
Thomson Airways: www.thomson.co.uk
Aer Lingus: www.aerlingus.com
Air France: www.airfrance.co.uk
Ferry: There is a weekly ferry from Cádiz on the Spanish mainland to Las Palmas and on to Tenerife.

Property market

It's not easy to get a realistic view of the property market in the Canaries. Naturally enough – with few exceptions – every estate agent out there says you're a mug if you don't buy now.

A more realistic view is you're a mug if you *do* buy now unless substantial discounts are on offer.

Reporting generally about the Spanish construction sector, Euroconstruct, a construction sector forecast group comprised of 19 European research institutes, forecasts that the Spanish construction sector will bottom in 2010.

In March, 2009, Tinsa, a leading Spanish property valuer published figures showing that residential property values in the Balearic Islands and Canary Islands fell by 8.3 per cent in the preceding 12months.

It said: "It is also interesting to note that the Spanish Islands were the last area to experience deflating property values, but May 2008 was the time when most property prices started falling."

"… we conclude the Spanish Islands … are fairing better than elsewhere in Spain."

Engel & Volkers [www.engelvoelkers.com] is one realtor prepared to tell it like it is and this is what E&V says:

Lanzarote: The boom years started to tail off in 2005 but new developments continued apace.

In 2006 values increased at 10-20 per cent but levelled out towards the end of last year becoming a buyers market.

The average price for an apartment is around €180,000 rising to €580,000 for a villa.

In its 2008 report E&V says of Las Palmas: "Last year, the market started to slow down slightly (around two per cent) in the island's capital, where the average price of an apartment costs approximately €450,000 up to €1 million for a villa."

The most requested properties are penthouses followed by townhouses and villas, according to E&V. Good plots of land are also in demand with an average price of €2,000 per sq metre. The most requested areas are Las Canteras, Mesa y López, Triana/Vegueta, Cuidad Jardín, Tafira and Santa Brígida

We Live Here

Widowed pensioner Pat Hume developed a taste for living abroad after visits to the Far East where her daughter Julie was living. These adventures eventually led Pat to retirement in Tenerife.

There are as many reasons for moving to Tenerife and stories behind doing so, as there are expat residents on the island. This is my story about how we came to live in Tenerife.

Julie was a pretty uncomplicated child until she turned 15 when her adventurous spirit began to show itself. By the time she was 18 she was living and working in Hong Kong.

While she was in Hong Kong I went over at least once a year. I found the pace of life there very fast and I was usually in need of a holiday by the time I got home to Scotland. In 1997 she moved to Thailand and I had a couple of wonderful holidays there.

It was there I first seriously entertained the notion of retiring abroad.

My partner and I first came to Tenerife for a niece's wedding. My niece is Belgian (but that's another story) and her husband is Canarian or, to be more exact, Tenerifian. They now have a lovely little girl called Ornella.

Not long afterwards another niece, Connie, got hitched here. She and her husband run the Happy Days tennis club in Costa Del Silencio.

My partner and I came over for the weddings and both thought what a beautiful place Tenerife was.

We wondered what it would be like to retire here.

I put the blame for us even thinking of pulling up sticks firmly at the door of my adventurous daughter.

If she had not shown us just what could be done with some determination we would not be here.

We immediately fell in love with the island and its microclimates. The plan to come here to retire took quite a time to develop. We came back over every opportunity we had: Christmases, New Years and Easters.

In the year before we moved here I was in Tenerife very nearly more than I was in Scotland.

Connie helped us find a small apartment in a nice complex and we bought a studio in Costa del Silencio in the south of the island in 1997. In August, 1999 we took the plunge, selling our assets in Scotland and moving permanently to Tenerife.

No regrets

Don and I have been here for a few years now and don't regret the decision. We love the weather for, although the seasons change, a winter's day here can be as warm as a summer's day in Scotland. The sun and heat suits us.

Our life is quite laid back; nothing is done in a rush. We seem to have got to know more people in a few months than we did in a lifetime in Scotland. Perhaps it's the climate that puts people in a friendlier frame of mind.

Since moving into the studio, Don has made considerable changes and we now have a bedroom – albeit a small one. When the opportunity arose, we also bought a second apartment to let to holidaymakers or for family when they visit.

My wandering daughter also surprised us by showing up for a holiday. While here – and to everyone's astonishment – she fell pregnant. After 20 years in Asia, where it seems she had given up hope of ever hearing the patter of tiny feet (and I had long stopped thinking of her presenting me with any grandkids), she ended up expecting a baby here after being on the island less than three months.

Perhaps there's something in the water, because five years on and two babies later she is still here.

The fact that my daughter and her partner have settled here to raise their children is a delightful bonus.

I miss my son and his family but visit them once a year. He also comes out to Tenerife regularly. We are after all, only four hours away from the UK.

More info: *This article first appeared on www.etenerife.com, a website with a mass of information for residents and might-be residents.*

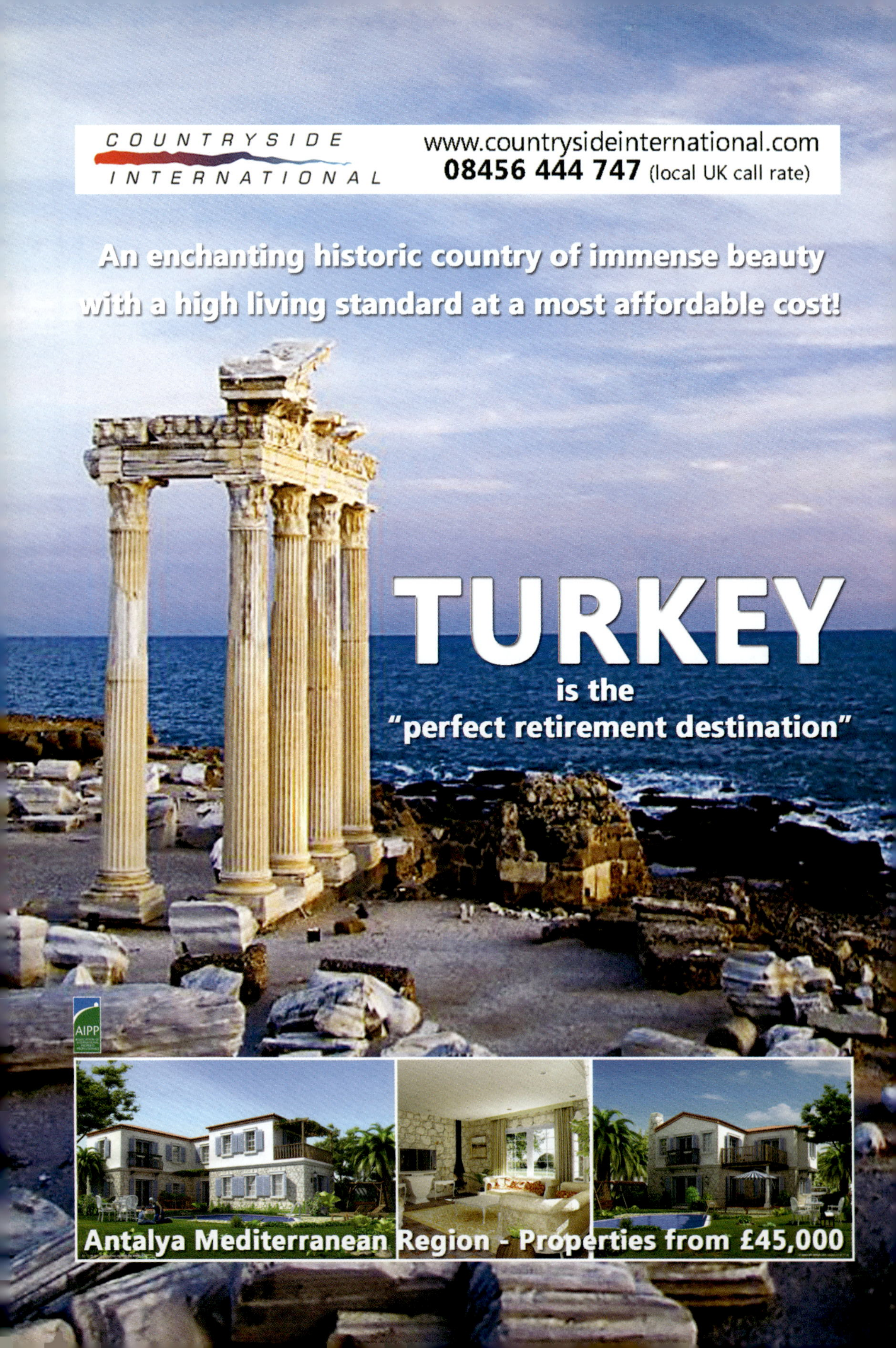
COUNTRYSIDE INTERNATIONAL
www.countrysideinternational.com
08456 444 747 (local UK call rate)
An enchanting historic country of immense beauty with a high living standard at a most affordable cost!
TURKEY
is the
"perfect retirement destination"
AIPP
Antalya Mediterranean Region - Properties from £45,000

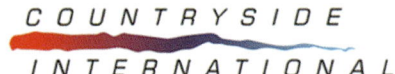

Rich culture in the land where East meets West

Why Turkey?

Sunshine, natural beauty, friendly people and a low cost of living puts Turkey high on the list of desirable places for retirement. Although it borders the volatile Middle East, it is a modern, secular state with a healthy combination of ancient tradition, democracy and a contemporary outlook.

Turkey's population is 99 per cent Muslim but most Turks are far more moderate in their beliefs than their Islamic neighbours.

Turkey's position straddling two continents gives its culture a unique blend of eastern and western tradition. Bordered by Georgia, Bulgaria, Greece, Armenia, Azerbaijan, Iran, Iraq and Syria, Turkey has a rich history, countless historic and archaeological sites and thousands of miles of beautiful and varied landscape. The Mediterranean coastline offers stunning Greco-Roman cities including Pergamom and Ephesus. Istanbul boasts ancient Roman aqueducts, Byzantine churches and Ottoman mosques and palaces.

The tourism industry and foreign property market are concentrated in the west of the country as well as the main cities such as Istanbul, Izmir, Adana, Antalya and Bursa.

Turkey is split into seven regions, each with its own distinct climate, landscape and traditions. The first four are named according to their adjacent seas (the Black Sea, the Marmara, the Aegean and the Mediterranean Regions); the other three in relation to their location in the whole of Anatolia (Central, Eastern and South East Anatolia Regions).

Turkey has been home to 20 fascinating civilizations, spanning over 10,000 years of history, and many of her ancient secrets have still to be uncovered. Fascinating sites include statues of gods and goddesses, temples, theatres, agoras, churches, mosques and palaces.

The regions

Aegean: Arguably the most beautiful of Turkey's coastlines, the Aegean Region is perhaps best known

ABOUT THE WRITER: With his partner **Naim Pektas**, **Cameron Deggin** (pictured) runs **www.propertyturkeyforsale.com**. Cameron, who is responsible for sales and marketing, is a chartered certified accountant and experienced financial analyst. The business is based in London with other offices in Amsterdam, Berlin and Copenhagen.

FACTFILE

Capital: Ankara   **Population:** 73 million
Area: 780,000 sq km   **Language:** Turkish
Climate: Temperate; hot, dry summers with mild, wet winters; harsher in interior.
Entry requirements: No visa required for visits of up to four months.
Permanent residence: Relatively straightforward. Once there, applications for residence permits can be made to the Alien's Branch of local police departments. Alternatively applications can be made before leaving Britain. You will need evidence to prove adequate (unspecified) retirement income and your retirement status, which may need to be notarised.
Electricity: 220 volts AC
Money: Turkish lira. ATMs are widely available. Credit/debit cards and traveller's cheques are widely accepted.
Public holidays 2010

Jan 1	New Year's Day
April 23	National Sovereignty and Children's Day
May 1	May Day (Istanbul only)
May 19	Atatürk and Youth Sports Day
Aug 30	Victory Day
Sept 9-12	Ramazan Bayrami
Oct 28-29	Republic Day
Nov 16-19	Kurban Bayrami.

Opening hours
Shops: 9.30am-7pm (later in tourist areas)
Banks: 8.30-12am; 1:30pm-5.30pm (Mon-Fri)
Offices: 9-12am and 1pm-5.30pm (Mon-Fri)
Water: Mains water is chlorinated but bottled water is safest.
Tipping: Small tips are appreciated generally but more (10-15%) in luxury establishments.
Medical/healthcare: Turkey has a three-tier health system with state hospitals and health centres funded by the equivalent of National Insurance. There are privately run clinics and hospitals which generally have some English-speaking staff.
There is no health agreement between Turkey and the UK so private health insurance is necessary.
Pets: You will need a certificate of health, rabies vaccination, an export certificate and pet identification card.

for its turquoise sea and ancient sites, including two of the Seven Wonders of the Ancient World: the Temple of Artemis at Ephesus and King Mausolus' Tomb in Bodrum.

Istanbul: Straddles both Europe and Asia and the two continents are separated by the Bosphorus, the Sea of Marmara and the Dardanelles.

Mediterranean: Stretching from the south of the Taurus Mountains, Turkey's Mediterranean coast is awash with sandy beaches, beautiful scenery, secluded coves and fascinating ancient sites, including the amazing Aspendos Theatre. The region also boasts an enviable climate of long, hot summers and mild winters.

South-East Region: High mountain ranges, plunging valleys, expansive plains and vast lakes, east and south-east Turkey is a region of contrast and colours. Adorned with the unique architectural samples of Turkish culture, attractions include the impressive Ishak Pasa Palace and the imposing Mount Ararat, thought to be the landing point of Noah's Ark.

Black Sea Region: Among the most fertile regions of the country, the Black Sea area is famed for verdant plateaux, traditional villages with a way of life unchanged for generations and fields of tea, hazelnuts, tobacco and corn.

Central Anatolia: Home to Ankara, Turkey's capital and political centre, and Konya, the country's spiritual heart, as well as the expansive natural wonder that is the region of Cappadocia.

Is it safe?

The crime rate in Turkey is very low compared to Britain and other western European countries. Violent crime is particularly rare. Burglary and car crime are

also less common and almost entirely confined to the larger cities and towns.

How much tax will I pay?
Your UK pension is not taxed in Turkey. Otherwise there are no special tax provisions for expatriates who, once they remain in Turkey for more than six months a year, are classed as residents and are taxed on their worldwide income. Non-residents only pay taxes on their Turkish source income.

Capital gains tax (although classed as income tax) is payable on property sold within a five-year-period following its acquisition. The tax is based on the difference between the selling price and the inflation-adjusted acquisition price if the inflation exceeds 10 per cent. TL7,600 (£3,200) of the gain attained from a sale is exempt from income tax.

Annual real estate tax (similar to UK council tax) of one per cent is paid on residential property, two per cent in major metropolitan areas.

On the transfer of ownership both buyer and seller pay a sale-and-acquisition levy of 1.5 per cent, based on the declared value of the property.

There is also an inheritance and succession tax: one per cent on the first TL160,000 (£67,500), three per cent on the next TL350,000 (£148,000) and five per cent on the next TL760,000 (£320,000).

Is Turkish property a good investment?
The stability of Turkey's economy and high growth rates in recent years have attracted significant foreign interest in its property, which is regarded as excellent investment value.

Turkish lira deposit accounts are currently paying around 11 per cent (net) annual interest on bank deposits. It is very easy to deposit and withdraw with no restrictions.

A wide range of property is available in areas that offer unspoilt coastlines, a low cost of living, high quality of life, a friendly and welcoming local population and a modern infrastructure.

Property in Istanbul begins from around £45,000 for a two-bedroom apartment so prices are still good value compared to those in Western Europe with significantly lower building costs.

The demand for residential property is extremely high, with the market requiring at least 700,000 new homes yearly. Over the next ten years residential

Quiet bay in Bodrum
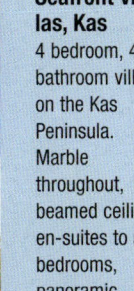
A development of 13 detached and 6 semi-detached villas 5 minutes walk to the beach in a quiet bay known for the crystal clear sea. Local amenities include seafood restaurants, a pharmacy, bakery, mini-supermarket, as well as a windsurfing and water sports school. Prices: From £175,330
More info
www.internationalpropertyagents.co.uk Tel (UK): 01706 216333

Seafront villas, Kas

4 bedroom, 4 bathroom villas on the Kas Peninsula. Marble throughout, beamed ceilings, en-suites to all bedrooms, panoramic windows and large terraces.
Price: £450,000
More info Place Overseas www.propertyturkeyforsale.com/ Tel (UK): 020 8371 0059

building development is expected to move further into the suburbs, further increasing prices.

Turkish lira bank deposit accounts are currently paying 12 per cent (net) annual interest. It is very easy to deposit ands withdraw.

Purchasing costs

The following illustrates the approximate cost of purchasing a £100,000 property in Turkey.

Purchase Tax	£3,000	Buyer's Fee	£3,000
Solicitor's Fee	£750	Notary Fee	£300
Gas & electricity	£200	Military tax	£900
		Total	£8,150

Communal charges for your Turkey property (if applicable) will vary according to the size and value of the property. A guideline figure for a 2/3 bedroom apartment would be £400-600 a year and would include pool and garden maintenance, exterior repair and decoration and building insurance.

Where's best to live?

Overseas property buyers tend to look in three main areas, Istanbul, the Aegean coast and the Mediterranean coast. South and south-western regions of Turkey have some of the best coastlines in Europe. Trendy western and traditional Turkish lifestyles combine to offer the best of both worlds. With low property prices and high build quality standards, the property market in Turkey is often compared with the fledgling Spanish property market of the 1970s.

The property hotspots are:

Bodrum Peninsula: The bustling town of Bodrum, with its grand castle, stands on the site of an old Roman town and it is located within a highly protected conservation area. No buildings higher than two storeys are permitted. The town itelf is very modern and upmarket with two new marinas and a new international airport.

There are many smaller resorts along the coast and Bodrum is rapidly becoming a property hotspot among Turkish celebrities, although so far, the area remains unspoilt by commercialisation.

House prices are expensive compared to the rest of Turkey, with prices having risen by 40-50 per cent in recent years. However, a luxury two-bedroom villa with swimming pool and sea view can still be bought for £55,000 and a four-bedroom property for around £150,000.

Dalaman: One of the few coastal areas that is still relatively undeveloped and unspoilt. The town is several miles inland and remains predominantly Turkish, with basic English spoken in most of the cafés and restaurants. Tourism is relatively new, hence prices are lower than in the resort towns and villages.

The Turkish government has now designated the town a main tourist area, making Dalaman an ideal location for property investment. With plans for a new marina and golf course it is rapidly becoming a popular location for European property investors.

Antalya, Belek & Kemer: With a population that has risen by approximately 400 per cent in the last 20 years, Antalya is the fastest-growing city in Turkey and has become one of the country's most popular holiday destinations. Perched on top of a limestone plateau, this stunning area is lush with banana plantations, citrus fruit orchards, palm groves and pine forests. The hub of the city centres on the old harbour within the ancient Roman walls. The marina is a lively area packed with cafés, bars and restaurants.

Prices rose by an average of 30 per cent last year. In

the sea from special platforms, while in Kas the small, pebbled beaches are often overcrowded.

All top-of-the-range homes have sea views in Kalkan and Kas in contrast to the majority of Turkish resorts where the seafront is a designated tourist area and given over to large hotel complexes. Property prices in Kalkan are booming and have increased by 100 per cent in recent years. Now the most expensive location on the Turkish property market, it is still a very popular investment area among British buyers.

The limited amount of land available is pushing prices up even further, with sales averaging £200,000. In Kas prices have soared by 30 per cent recently and demand for property in this chic harbour town shows no sign of waning.

Fethiye: Picturesque market town very popular with British tourists. Fethiye stands on the site of the ancient city of Telmessos.

The local beaches are superb but very busy during the summer, while the surrounding mountains are clad with lush, green pine trees. Dalaman International Airport is 45 minutes drive away.

Property prices have risen 20-25 per cent over the last year. A two-bedroom, newly built property costs around £85,000-105,000, a four-bedroom villa with private pool and a good sized garden £155,000, and smaller villas with communal pool around £120,000.

Istanbul: The capital of empires, the meeting point of cultures and the unique sample of peace between religions with the mosques, churches, and synagogues; this is a fascinating living city with its legends, palaces, music, art, cuisine and landscape.

Istanbul is Turkey's largest city even though it is not the capital. It sits right on the point where Europe meets Asia and has straddled both continents for centuries, initially as Byzantium and then as Constantinople.

Home to an official population of around 12 million, with some estimates as high as 16 million, Istanbul is the powerhouse of the Turkish economy.

Prices of apartments start from £50,000.

Antalya region, a two-bedroom semi-detached luxury house can be bought for £45,000-50,000. A new top-of-the-range three bedroom apartment with sea views can be picked up for £90,000.

In Kemer, brand new luxury four-bedroom maisonettes with private gardens and swimming pool are available for £135,000. Keen golfers can buy a brand new three or four bedroom villa with pool and sea views, located close to Belek's international golf courses, for around £150,000.

Altinkum & Didyma: The main attraction in Didyma is the ancient ruin of the oracular sanctuary of Apollo. A shrine has stood on this site since the 8th century BC.

Just 5km to the south lies the busy resort of Altinkum. Up until a couple of years ago, Altinkum was a small town, but it is fast gaining in popularity, particularly among British package holidaymakers. The length of its golden sandy beach is jam-packed with cafés, hotels, and with restaurants offering rather dubious 'English' cuisine.

It has only recently become possible to buy property in Altinkum and although relatively cheap properties are easy to come by now, prices are booming to meet the demand. Some homes have risen in value by as much as 50 per cent in the last year. A top-notch, three-bedroom semi-detached property in Altinkum costs around £85,000, while a decent sized two-bedroom apartment is £45,000.

Kalkan & Kas: Despite the developments that have turned Kalkan & Kas into popular, modern tourist resorts, both have retained much of their original fishing village charm. Neither town has much by way of a beach. In Kalkan, swimmers usually have to enter

TURKEY CONTACT DIRECTORY

Embassies/Government
Turkish Embassy in UK
www.londra.be.mfa.gov.tr/default.aspx

British Embassy in Turkey
http://ukinturkey.fco.gov.uk

Travel & Health Advice
Foreign Office travel advice
www.fco.gov.uk/travel
www.nhs.uk/Healthcareabroad
www.masta.org

About Turkey
ww.turkeycentral.com
www.turkuaz-guide.net
www.welcometurkey.net
www.turkishculture.org
www.adiyamanli.org
www.kusadasi.com
www.marmarisinfo.com

General & Expat
www.expatfocus.com
www.mymerhaba.com
www.turkishliving.com
www.britishexpat.com
www.transitionsabroad.com

English Language Media
Turkish Daily News Online
www.hurriyet.com.tr/english
English version of Turkish Daily News
Turkey Post www.turkeypost.com/
Voiceswww.voicesnewspaper.com
English-language weekly in Altinkum
Bodrum Bulletinwww.bodrumbulletin.com
Free fortnightly
Fethiye Timeswww.fethiyetimes.org.uk
For expats living in the Fethiye are
Milliyet News Onlinewww.milliyet.com.tr
English version of a daily Turkish newspaper
The Bodrum Observer

www.bodrumobserver.com
Bbi-monthly on the local and national news
Turkish Radio & TVwww.trt.net.tr
Some English language broadcasts
Satellite TV is readily available

Property
www.countrysideinternational.com
www.spotblue.co.uk
www.propertyturkeyforsale.com
www.turkishpropertypeople.co.uk
www.turkeypropertyinvestments.com
www.turkishpropertypeople.co.uk
www.nirvanainternational.com
www.seasidepropertiesturkey.com
www.kayaestate.com
www.kusadasihomes.com
www.marehla.com
www.efesestate.com
www.tulipproperties.com
www.adoproperties.com/en
www.turkishsweethomes.com
www.jadeestateagent.com
www.taureanproperties.co.uk
www.turkeypropertyforsale.com

Travel & Tourism
www.goturkey.com
www.turkiye-online.com
www.twarp.com
www.turkishodyssey.com
www.Welcometurkey.net
www.allaboutturkey.com

Getting There
British Airways: www.BritishAirways.com
Turkish Airlines: www.thy.com
Air France: www.airfrance.co.uk
Olympic Airways: www.olympic-airways.gr
KLM: www.klm.com
Lufthansa: www.lufthansa.com
SAS: www.flysas.com/en/uk
Thomas Cook: www.flyThomasCook.com

EasyJet: easyJet.com

Getting Around
Air: Turkish Airlines: www.thy.com provides
the widest network of domestic flights.
Onur Air: www.onurair.com.tr
Anadolu Jet: www.anadolujet.com
IzAir: www.izair.com/Tr
Pegasus Air: www.pegasusairlines.com
Sun Express: www.sunexpress.com.tr
Train: Turkey's rail network was mostly built
by the Germans which might account for its
efficiency. The Istanbul-Ankara train travels
at up to 95mph and will get you there in
five hours. By 2010 the journey time will be
reduced to just three hours.
Other services, many with sleeping
carriages, may not be quite so impressive
but the service is more than adequate and
more comfortable than going by bus.
There are international services from
Istanbul to Bucharest, Budapest, Vienna,
Paris, London.
Bus: Buses are modern and reasonably
comfortable. There are several operators
serving every corner of the country.
Ferry: Istanbul/Sea of Marmara: High-speed
catamarans and car ferries operate from
Istanbul to Yalova, Bandirma and other
towns around the Sea of Marmara.
Black Sea: There is a weekly ferry service
along the Black Sea coast in summer, from
Istanbul to Sinop, Samsun, Trabzon and
Rize, returning via the same ports.
There is also an overnight service between
Istanbul and Izmir during the summer.
Driving: Driving standards are poor. Red
lights and stop signs are routinely ignored.
Traffic in the major cities, especially Istanbul
and Ankara, is chaotic. You need to drive
very defensively and exercise extreme
caution while driving at night.
Driving is on the right.

Summer all year round in this tropical Garden of Eden off the African coast

Why Cape Verde?

Deserted beaches, year-round sunshine, friendly people, great seafood and a unique blend of African and Portuguese cultures. What's not to like about this sprinkling of volcanic islands at the crossroad of three continents?

About 600km off the coast of Senegal, the islands were uninhabited when they were discovered by the Portuguese in the mid-15th Century. They became the centre of the slave trade in the Atlantic and the population today are the descendants of both the Portuguese colonisers and African slaves.

The official language is Portuguese but the real natives speak Creole – a mix of Portuguese, a bit of English and various African languages.

There are direct flights from London (Gatwick), Birmingham and Manchester.

Cape Verde is misnamed. Even those among us who are not sharp on languages can translate the name. Cape Verde means Green Cape. It is not green. It is mainly dry, barren and consists mainly of brown hills and volcanic rocks.

Some greenery can be found on the banana and sugar cane estates in the few fertile valleys but the name was probably derived from the green lichen that grows on the rocks or maybe the early Portuguese thought the name would give their descendent estate agents a better chance of selling property.

One downside is the wind. The islands are windy most of the year, fierce at times, the hot, dry east winds blowing in from the African continent.

There are also social problems exacerbated by chronic poverty, large unplanned families and unmarried mothers and high levels of emigration of adult men. (There are more Cape Verdeans living abroad than there are in the islands themselves).

The compensations

Despite the general poverty, Cape Verdeans are generous and hospitable. There are huge deserted beaches, great fishing and diving, sailing and windsurfing, interesting and challenging walking.

The islands are divided into two groups: windward and leeward. The first group consists of Santo Antão – the greenest island, with spectacular views and great walks – S.Vicente, Santa Luzia, S.Nicolau, Sal, Boavista, and the second, more to the south, of the islands of Maio, Santiago, Fogo and Brava.

The climate is tropical and dry. It's like an English summer all year round but rainfall is very low and water is scarce (some swimming pools are fed with salt water) and golf courses are pretty threadbare.

However, large sums are being invested to improve golf with six new courses designed by such golf worthies as Ernie Els, Nick Faldo and Jack Nicklaus. The new courses are part of developments that include hotels, apartments, spas and marinas. The first of these resorts opened at the end of last year.

To combat the water shortage there are an increasing number of desalination plants.

Information on Cape Verde is culled from **www.expatscapeverde.com** and **www.capeverdetips.co.uk,** the two websites of Cheryl Thomas who moved to Sol after a long career in the leisure industry. Cape Verde's beaches, year-round sunshine, friendly people, great seafood and a unique blend of African and Portuguese cultures combine to offer a perfect retirement destination, she says.

FACTFILE

Capital: Praia   **Population:** 430,000
Area: 4,033sq km **Language:** Portuguese (official) and Creole (some islands have their own dialect).
Climate: Tropical. Warm and dry all year. Temperatures are in a range of 24-30°C throughout the year. The rainy season, such as it is, usually lasts from August until October. The windiest period, when dry hot, dust-carrying winds blow in from the Sahara, is from October to June.
Time difference: GMT +1
Entry requirements: All foreign visitors require a visa. It is possible to apply on arrival but you may have to queue in the heat for upto two hours.
Retirement/residence visa: You need a provable income of about £1,000 a month. [See: The rules for getting in]

Electricity: 220V 50 Hz, round 2-pin plug.
Money: Cape Verde escudo. The euro is generally accepted on the main islands but not the US$ or UK£. ATMs are generally available.
Public holidays 2010

Jan 1	New Year's Day
Jan 20	Heroes' Day
Feb 16	Carnival
Feb 17	Ash Wednesday
May 1	Labour Day
May 19	Municipal Day
July 5	Independence Day
Aug 15	Assumption
Sept 12	National Day
Nov 1	All Saints' Day
Dec 25	Christmas Day

Opening hours
Banks: 8am-3pm, Mon-Fri

Offices: 8.30am-4.30/5pm
Shops: 8/8.30am-12/12.30pm and 2/2.30-6-6.30pm. Shops are mainly closed on Sundays and public holidays.
Water: Drink bottled or boiled water.
Tipping: 10 per cent
Medical/Healthcare: There are no compulsory vaccinations but typhoid, hepatitis A and diphtheria are recommended and precautions against malaria should be taken. Medical facilities are limited and some medicines are unavailable. There are hospitals in Praia and Mindelo, with smaller medical facilities on other islands. Health insurance is essential.
Pets: A veterinarian health certificate is required. Dogs also require a rabies inoculation certificate.
There is one vet in Santa Maria, Sal Island.

CAPE VERDE CONTACT DIRECTORY

Embassies/Government
There is no Cape Verde embassy in the UK and no British embassy in Cape Verde but there is an Honorary Consul:
Email: canutoantoniorc@yahoo.com
Email: isabelspencer5@yahoo.com.br

Cape Verde Government: www.governo.cv
Mainly in Portuguese with efforts to translate some parts and not particularly helpful regarding immigration and residency matters. Here's an example: "With the abolition of the slaves' trade and the constant deterioration of the climatic conditions, Cape Verde entered in decadence and it started to live with base in a poor economy, of subsistence."

About Cape Verde
www.caboverde.com
www.capeverdetips.co.uk
www.capeverdebureau.com
http://virtualcapeverde.net
www.capeverdepropertynews.org
http://international.assetz.co.uk/palm-view/
http://allafrica.com/capeverde/
www.caboverde24.com/
www.travelblog.org/Africa/Cape-Verde
www.caboverde24.com
www.thinkcapeverde.com

General & Expats
www.expatscapeverde.com
www.expat-blog.com/en/destination/africa/cape-verde/www.expat-blog.com/en/destination/africa/cape-verde/
www.expatfocus.com
www.britishexpat.com
www.transitionsabroad.com

English Language Media
www.asemana.cv

Property
www.capeverdepropertynews.org
www.capeverdeproperty.co.uk
www.capeverdepropertynews.org
www.capeverdeportal.com
www.property-abroad.com/cape-verde
www.cottonbay-sal.com
www.sambaladevelopments.com
www.noscasacv.com
www.capeverdepropertyworld.com

Travel
www.caboverde.com
(where you can click through for info on all the different islands)
www.capeverdetravel.co.uk
www.travelguide2capeverde.co.uk
www.capeverdeexperience.co.uk
www.destination-capeverde.co.uk
www.capeverdetips.co.uk
www.capeverdeportal.com
www.pontabicuda.com

Getting There
There are direct flights to Sal with Thomson from Gatwick, Manchester and Birmingham. Return flights can be had from about €360, although occasionally as low as €220. There are currently three international airports in Cape Verde: On the islands of Santiago, Sal and Boavista. A fourth is due to open on Sao Vicente.
School holiday periods are always more expensive. All-inclusive package holidays sometimes make this the cheaper option.
Thomsonfly: http://flights.thomson.co.uk

TAP (via Lisbon): www.flytap.com
TACV (via Lisbon): www.tacv.cv
www.travelrepublic.co.uk

Getting around
Flying is best and in the range 15-45 mins.
By air: Inter-Island flights are with TACV: www.tacv.cv or Cabo Verde Express: www.caboverdeexpress.com
TACV serves all the islands except Brava.
Ferry: There are regular ferry services between most of the inhabited islands.
Bus: Public transport is by aluguers – vans or minibuses which operate on a fixed route. You can hop on or off as you like.
Taxi: Taxis are readily available in the larger towns and resort areas. Agree the fare in advance.
Driving: Road conditions and driving standards are pretty good but narrow, winding mountain roads need to be taken with care.
Car hire is readily available but is quite expensive. An international licence is required. Driving is on the right.

THE RULES FOR GETTING IN

There's the usual red tape procedures – you must get a police certificate issued in the last two months prior to submitting your residency application; photocopies of identification documents, marriage and birth certificate, etc; you need to sign a declaration that you will respect the laws and customs and assume your medical and health expenses. All this stuff has to be translated into Portuguese.

The bottom line is that you need evidence of a monthly pension or income of about €1,200. The permanent residency authorisation covers your spouse, children under 18 and "other dependent members of the petitioner's immediate family".

Benefits include the right to import tax-free a vehicle for personal use every three years, tax-free import of personal use and furniture, TVs, computer equipment, etc. every five years and tax exemption on the purchase of property.

Cost of living

It is best to bring your branded and electrical goods with you as you may find that some goods are sub-European standard. Chinese (lojas) stores in the villages, towns and cities sell cheap imported Chinese goods.

Is it safe?

What little crime there is in Cape Verde consists mainly of petty theft and occasional robbery.

How much tax will I pay?

Typical property acquisition costs, including notary fees, are about six per cent of the purchase price including a transfer tax of three per cent. There is an annual property tax of three per cent on the registered value paid in two instalments.

Capital gains tax becomes payable when a property is sold for more than 130 per cent of the purchase price.

The gain above this amount is taxed at three per cent for capital gains and 20 per cent for income tax.

There is inheritance tax of three per cent.

Property owners also pay tax of 20 per cent on letting income less various allowances for maintenance, service charges, legal costs, agents and accountants' fees.

Is Cape Verde property a good investment?

Foreign tourist numbers are increasing by over 20 per cent a year and expected to pass one million arrivals by 2015. While property prices are bound to

Vila Jardins do Oceano
Development of 40 beachfront villas on the island of Santiago, due to open this year, which has direct flights from Paris and Lisbon and is the location of Cape Verde's first golf course. White sand and facilities include tennis courts, a bar, restaurant and swimming pool. Prices from €299,999 for a 2 bedroom villa 60m from the beach.
More info: GEM Estatesinfo@gem-estates.com
www.gem-estates.com Tel: UK Freephone 0800 036 0068, Ireland Freephone 1800 211 462 Spain 00 34 952 799 286

Murdeira Beach Club, Sal
2-bedroom apartments from €148,179, 3-bedroom semi-detached villas from €247,069 and 5-bedroom townhouses from €573,293.
Properties are based around a 75-berth marina.
More info: Experience International
www.experience-international.com. Tel: +44 (0)207 321 5858

increase over time they are already fairly high, a fact that has to be taken into consideration with the expense of getting there – €320 upwards – considerably more than popular destinations along the Mediterranean.

Propertyshowrooms.com offers a detailed analysis of the property market.

Where's best to live?

Sal
Sal is the most developed of the Cape Verde islands and one of the four major gateways to Cape Verde.

The flattest island of the archipelago, it has miles of white sandy beaches, numerous water sports including kite surfing, sailing, wind surfing and scuba diving. Hiking and cycling are popular. There is an abundance of restaurants offering fresh seafood – tuna, lobster and swordfish – some with live Cape Verdean music.

Sao Vicente
For those who like a lively nightlife, this is also the cultural and cosmopolitan island of the archipelago. Mindelo, the capital, has a colony of artists and musicians. Cape Verde's biggest carnival is held here and the annual music festival held for three days in August has become an international music event.

Life revolves around Mindelo's town square and the labyrinth of streets leading off it. Popular with British buyers, Sao Vicente even has a cricket team.

Santiago
The largest of the Cape Verde islands and one of the greenest, it is also home to Praia, the Cape Verde capital, a city of 105,000 people (about a quarter of the islands' total population). Santiago, with its international airport, is also the largest 'gateway' island and the most African. A maze of streets full of bars and restaurants, it is noisy, crowded and bustling with African markets and music.

There is increasing criminality in Praia: muggings, bag-snatching but even more serious violent crime.

Boa Vista
This is the most eastern island of the archipelago with 55km of white sandy beaches including the 16km Santa Monica beach. The island is covered with sand dunes, which give it a lunar landscape.

Great seafood is on offer including dishes made with limpets and crab and fish soup.

Supposedly this is one of the biggest shipping cemeteries in the world and the more adventurous can dive here in the hope of finding treasure ships lost in the transatlantic trade with the New World.

Otherwise there is a variety of water sports on offer and a good but low key nightlife.

Fogo
The volcanic peak of Pico de Fogo is one of the most distinctive landmarks in Cape Verde. You can climb to the peak and be rewarded with a fantastic view into the crater. Hiring a horse is a less tiring alternative.

Fogo has dramatic landscape, small farms, forests, coffee plantations and orchards. The capital, Sao Filipe, a world heritage town, is built on a cliff and boasts old colonial architecture and pretty squares. Fogo is the most volcanically active of all the islands.

The crater with its black volcanic moonscape and contorted lava flows has two small villages, vineyards, farms growing exotic fruit and a French restaurant.

Sao Nicolau
This is a mainly barren island with rocky peaks, but – in the central massif – there is stunning, mountainous scenery, banana and coffee farms cobbled paths and terraced fields stretching up into the mountainside.

The island has black sand beaches and is a haven for fishermen and hikers.

Ribeira Brava, one of the quietest and prettiest towns in the archipelago, has colonial architecture and fertile gardens. Over the centuries it has suffered grievously from desertification. Here, miles of cobbled tracks link abandoned farmhouses and villages.

Maio
Isolated, flat, its white sand beaches mainly deserted apart from sea turtles that lay their eggs there, Maio is not very easy to reach and is largely ignored by tourists. In the north of the island there is a large

I live here

Keith Bruford worked as an electrician in the UK – 13 years at ITV's studios in Birmingham. He retired to Cape Verde at the age of 62 and will eventually be joined by his wife, Annette, when she retires as a teacher.

Having played a lot of sport in the UK I have plenty of wear and tear on my joints which ached a lot back in England. Here on Sal the sun is my doctor and I feel great. I can't wait for the golf course to be built on the island. I miss my golf and here I can blame the wind for my wayward shots.

It is easier if you speak Portuguese here as most people don't speak English.

I first saw the opportunity to buy a property on Cape Verde islands in 2006. I had been looking on the Internet for somewhere with an all-year-round warm climate and Cape Verde fitted the bill.

I visited Sao Vicente in 2008 and looked at plans for a detached bungalow in Calhau but it was going to be a while before it would be completed. I decided to take a look at Sal Island, which is more touristy, had a number of developments and the advantageof direct flights from the UK. The airport is just a short distance away from where I live although there is not a problem with noise.

I bought a one-bed apartment in a complex up at Murdeira on the west coast of the island. It's very quiet, some properties are empty so there aren't many people about. There's a bar, restaurant, swimming pool and some wonderful sea views but not much to do at night. I do my shopping in the capital, Espargos, as it's cheaper than Santa Maria.

I am quite happy here but would prefer it if there were more English speakers. However, if I feel the need I just walk up to the main road and hop on an aluger, a local minibus, pay my 100 escudos (one euro) and pop into Santa Maria to have a drink or meal and sometimes meet up with the other British expats.

A bistro too

In the evenings I play my music or watch football on TV. I want to help coach young local footballers but this hasn't happen yet.

When I'm in the UK I long to return to Sal. England has a lot of good things going for it, but the weather isn't one of them. I am also a smoker and the rules over where you can or cannot smoke have not yet hit these islands.

I come out here mostly on my own and stay for as long as I can. My wife joins me in the school holidays and we just relax around our apartment and the pool and take things easy. Last summer we spoiled ourselves and stayed a week in a lovely hotel along Santa Maria beach which my wife

lagoon surrounded by lush vegetation.

The capital, Vila de Maio, with its colonial buildings, offers delicious fresh seafood in basic restaurants and the opportunity to chat to locals. Maio is also known by the name of Vila do Porto Inglês (Town of the English Port) due to the presence of English vessels in the 17th and 18th Centuries.

Santa Antao

What it lacks in the way of beaches it makes up in greenery which has earned it the label 'Island of the flowers'. Said by some to be the most interesting island on earth, with an incredible variety of landscapes, from patches of jungles to treeless mountains.

Centuries old mule tracks lead down from the altoplano to the green valleys of the northern coastline, crossing pinewood and subtropical forests and steep terraced meadows where farmers grow sugar cane, maize and manioc.

Brava

Thanks to its microclimate Brava is a floral paradise – or at least it is at the top of the mountain where the island's main town, Nova Sintra, is perched. Here there are colourful markets, quaint streets and picturesque old houses.

The smallest inhabited island in the archipelago, Brava is also one of its most mountainous and the southern most point in Cape Verde.

There is a series of small bays along the coast: Furna, Anciao, Faja d'Agua and Sorno.

With deep gorges and dramatic peaks Brava has more than its fair share of what little rainfall there is in Cape Verde which gives it a humid climate and abundant greenery: lobelia and hibiscus, bougainvillea and jasmine grow in profusion.

Fishing and agriculture are mainstays of the island's economy.

A SPECIAL WELCOME TO EGYPT

I'm delighted that Egypt now welcomes millions of visitors from all over the world. Our country attracts people for so many different reasons whether it is our fantastic history and Pharaonic treasures, the beautiful sea and coastline of our Red Sea Riviera, the magic of a Nile cruise, our capital city Cairo and the buzzing cities of Luxor, Alexandria and Aswan: to all of you who visit, I bid you a warm welcome to Egypt.

And I won't be alone with my welcome as Egyptians are hospitable, friendly people who enjoy engaging with visitors. Maybe it is because of the sunshine but when you visit, you'll notice that life goes on at a gentler pace than you may be used to.

We now have a wonderful choice of accommodation including eco-lodges, desert camps, historic city hotels and hotels by the sea in the 3-5 star category offering international luxury brands with top spas and sporting facilities. A Nile cruise is something which, in my opinion, everyone should try to do once. The memories and experiences of our antiquities in ancient Thebes (Luxor) and the sheer wonder you will see as you cruise along the mighty Nile will truly stay with you forever.

Visitors who are short of time are now coming for long weekends and short breaks thanks to improved flight schedules and golfers are finding that our 18 hole championship courses near Cairo and in Red Sea Riviera resorts are equal to those in Europe. Diving in the Egyptian waters needs no introduction and people come back again and again for our incredibly turquoise sea, corals and fish the colours of one million rainbows. Conservation is important to us and the Egyptian Government is carefully controlling development which could affect marine habitats.

But what about visitors who have plenty of time ? We are seeing people from Great Britain buying homes in Egypt and coming to retire here.

The pace of life is relaxed, our infrastructure is improving all the time with an excellent road and domestic air network and there's a high standard of living for those who make Egypt their home.

Enjoy your time in Egypt !

H.E. Hatem Seif EL Nasr
Egyptian Ambassador to London

History and the heat combine to lure retirees

Why Egypt

Almost 11 million tourists a year visit Egypt. The ambition of tourism officials is to increase numbers by a million a year, adding 15,000 hotel rooms and creating 200,000 jobs in tourism every year.

That's half the story. The other is Egypt's invitation to overseas residents to buy a home and share what it expects to be a prolonged period of growth.

Here are some of the reasons why you should consider Egypt:

History: From the pyramids, to the Sphinx, the ancient town of Luxor and the Valley of the Kings – Egypt has an astonishing two-thirds of the world's ancient monuments.

The climate: Hot, sunny weather – too hot at times – clear blue skies, little rain.

A **surging economy** with foreign direct investment up six-fold since 2003 and GDP growing by seven per cent a year.

For the price of a bedsit in Western Europe you can still buy a three-bedroom holiday home in Egypt. In fact, you can buy a one-bedroom flat here for the price of a mid-range car in Europe.

Egypt is exotic with big appeal to European visitors: over a million from Britain last year, just under a million from Russia and Germany and three-quarters of a million from Italy.

For those planning for the future and thinking of letting until their retirement, these numbers offer a huge potential catchment of customers within a few hours flying time from Europe.

There's no capital gains tax, no inheritance tax and no restriction on repatriation of funds when you sell.

The cost of living is low. Although Cairo has gone from 97th city to 93rd on the global cost of living report produced annually by Mercer Human Resource Consulting, Cairo is still way, way down on the list on which London is fifth.

Cheap flights: There is an increasing number of charter flights from the UK to Egypt's popular holiday destinations and direct scheduled flights with a number of European carriers as well as Egyptair.

Shop around and you can find direct charter flights to Egypt from £240 return. A one-week package holiday, including flights and accommodation, can be obtained from £200 or so and there are bargains between November and March. The flight time from the UK is about five hours.

The peak tourist season runs from November through February when prices for both flights and hotels can go up by as much as 30 per cent.

The majority of people avoid Egypt from May to September since it is too hot for most. Spring and autumn are considered the best times to go.

ABOUT THE WRITER: Ian Marsh is chairman of Think Egypt – an organisation that specialises in the research and development of residential tourism in Egypt. Its primary function is to work with the Egyptian government, major developers and international agents, to turn tourists to the country into property owners whether for investment, as holiday homes, or for permanent residence

FACTFILE

Capital: Cairo **Population**: 72 million
Area: 1,001,450sq km
Language: Egyptian Arabic but English is widely spoken.
Climate: A mild winter November to April and a hot summer May to October. Nights are cool.
Time difference: GMT+2 (GMT +3 from last Friday in April to last Thursday in Sept)
Entry requirements: UK citizens can obtain a visa obtainable on arrival, cost £10, for stays of up to one month.
Electricity: 220V AC 50Hz. Round-pronged plugs. If you are coming from the UK, you will need an adaptor.
Money: Egyptian Pound (EGP 1 = 100 Piastres). Credit Cards/Travellers Cheques are widely accepted. It's safer to use banks and exchange offices although a higher rate can often be found on the streets.

Public Holidays 2010

Jan 7	Coptic Christmas Day	Sept 10-13	End of Ramadan
Feb 26	Birth of the Prophet	Sept 11	Coptic New Year
April 28	Sham el-Nassim	Oct 6	Armed Forces Day
May 1	Labour Day	Nov 16-17	Grand Feast
July 23	National Day	December 7	Islamic New Year

Opening hours
Bank: 0830-1400 Sun-Thur
Offices: 0900-1500 Sat-Thur
Shops: 0900- late
Water: Use only bottled variety.
Tipping: Service charges normally added to restaurant & hotel bills but additional tips of around 5% are customary. Tip taxi drivers 10%.
Medical/healthcare: Vaccinations not required but recommended – typhoid (10 days before travel); hepatitis A (2 weeks before travel); diphtheria (3 months before travel).
English is widely spoken so communicating with doctors, dentists and chemists is straightforward. European medicines are generally quite expensive but there is always a much cheaper Egyptian equivalent.

Tourism Minister, Zoheir Garranah, believes his country will double tourist arrivals within six years. Ambitious maybe, but the independent World Travel and Tourism Council (WTTC) agrees with him and estimates that Egypt will see international arrivals increase to 13 million annually and transform the country into one of the world's most popular tourism hotspots by 2011.

A key part of the strategy to achieve this is to encourage foreign direct investment in property development – resorts, hotels and holiday homes and to pile money into the infrastructure.

Royal Oasis Resort
1 and 2 bed apartments at the Royal Oasis Resort in the centre of Naama Bay, 10 minutes from Sharm El Sheikh International airport. The apartments are bright, airy and spacious, designed and developed with European taste in mind. The kitchen is fully fitted with integral fridge and microwave oven included in the price. Air-conditioning is also included.
Prices: from £65,000
More info: www.egyptpropertyforsale.com

Golden Park Resort
A five star residential development midway between Hurghada and Sahl Hasheesh on the Red Sea. It offers a range of studios and condominium apartments, townhouses, villas and even six bed 'palaces', all with the latest home appliances including entertainment equipment and contemporary furnishings.
Prices from: $69,000.
More info: www.goldenparkegypt.com Tel Egyptian Property Partners: +44 (0) 121 288 1231

THE RULES FOR GETTING IN

Obtaining a three-year Temporary Residence Permit or a five Year Residence Permit is a formality if you own property in Egypt.

Early days

So is this the opportunity to get in on the ground floor of a rapidly developing market? We believe it is.

While individual buyers and investors may be moving only hesitantly into the Egyptian market, the big players are not. And where the big fish lead, the small fry will quickly follow.

The projects currently moving from drawing board to sites on the Mediterranean coast and the Red Sea are mind-boggling in their dimensions; forget millions of dollars – these schemes are measured only in billions. The biggest of these massive projects are composed of hotels, golf courses, shopping entertainment malls and thousands of villas and apartments.

Is it safe?

Where is nowadays? While safety is an issue and most Western governments issue warnings to their citizens to take extreme care when they travel to Egypt, all stop short of advising their nationals to avoid the country altogether. About a million Brits visit Egypt every year – all but a few with no problems – so the risk is low.

Advice: Steer clear of demonstrations and be vigilant in all public places, particularly those frequented by foreigners.

How much tax will I pay?

There is no capital gains tax, no inheritance tax and no restriction on repatriation of funds when you sell your property.

Is Egyptian property a good investment?

Property prices have increased 15-20 per cent annually for the last three years.

Where's best to live?

The major destinations are:

The **north-west coast** for azure seas, miles of silver sands and **Alexandria**, the ancient centre of the world, as well as for seafood and history.

Ain Sohkna for Egyptian residents and expats alike to enjoy a lazy weekend away from the hustle and bustle of the Cairo.

Sharm el Sheikh for a resort with everything the holiday-maker could need in terms of leisure, entertainment, world class hotels and the best scuba.

Hurghada and the surrounding areas for established resorts that offer 365 days of sunshine.

Marsalam for sailors with a superb new resort and marina and infrastructure that has everything to offer.

Luxor and **Aswan** are home to the major tourist attractions.

For the metropolitan buyer **Cairo** offers an opera house, the pyramids, culture and history.

Golfers should consider **Soma Bay (Hurghada)**, **Sharm el Sheikh, Cairo** (seven golf courses), **Alexandria, El Gouna (Hurghada)** and **Luxor**.

Is buying property easy?

Since the rules are different, a good and properly qualified lawyer is essential for property transactions. Don't rely on the vendor or his solicitor/agent for advice. Ask around.

Soma Bay

Soma Bay on the Red Sea Riviera, 45km from Hurghada International Airport, is a 10m sq m self-contained community surrounded on all sides by the sea, and renowned for its bays, sandy beaches, coral reefs, a PGA golf course as well as a world class thalasso-therapy centre.

Soma Bay has some of the best dive sites in the Red Sea and a fully-equipped dive centre, wind-surfing, sailing, and kitesurfing.

The Cascades Golf Villas – detached or semi-detached – have views of golf courses, lakes, the Red Sea and mountains.

Bay Villas on the south side of the peninsula with uninterrupted views of the bay and the Red Sea overlook and have access to one of the most beautiful beaches on the Red Sea. Facing a sheltered bay, they range from two to five bedrooms. Land areas start from approximately 1,350sq ft.

More info: www.somabay.com
Email: info@somabay.com

We live here

Graham and Pauline Warren sold up in East Anglia and arrived in Luxor in September 2004, their remaining possessions crammed into two suitcases. They have a small, one floor, villa on the outskirts of Luxor and share it with four dogs, a cat and three kittens. Graham tells their story.

Why Egypt? This is what we were so frequently asked when we told friends and family that we were leaving England. To us, the obvious answer was "why not?" With sunshine all year round, a lush green environment and, most importantly, people who are welcoming and friendly, how misguided were their reservations.

What could be better than taking the ferry across the Nile from Luxor Temple, walk in the Theban Hills that encompass the Valley of the Kings, the Valley of the Queens, Queen Hatshepsut's temple?

Stop for a tea with one of the welcoming locals and on your way back home walk through the souk to buy really fresh, great tasting, organically-grown produce.

Egypt is very welcoming to foreigners who want to live here and a trip to the passport office in Cairo or Luxor will get you a visa to stay in the country for a year and costs about £10.

There are many Europeans living in and around Luxor. Some stay here all year but many split their time between Luxor and Europe and there are always tourists from home to chat with as well as the locals

so there is no need to ever feel lonely.

There are many places to eat out as you would expect in any tourist resort and eating out is cheap. A local Stella beer costs typically £2-£2.20 a bottle in a five star hotel and 60p-£1.10 in the restaurants and bars around Luxor.

A spaghetti bolognaise might cost £1-1.50 and a good steak with a nice sauce, vegetables and chips £3-4.

On the East bank of Luxor, where the main town is, there are many flats available to rent or buy. The Fayruze area is extremely popular as it tends to be quieter than most areas. Prices are extremely cheap by European standards. A two-bedroom unfurnished flat in Fayruze will sell for around £15,000.

We started with a two bedroom flat on the first floor in Fayruze and sold it and bought another nearby that was double the size which we sold when our villa was ready.

PROPERTY

El Gouna

One of the Red Sea's sought-after locations for property. It offers a wide range of accommodation and facilities including a golf course and marina.

Lying 22km north of Hurghada International Airport, it is within easy reach of Europe's capitals.

There are two marinas, an 18-hole golf course and a European-standard hospital. A diver's paradise, El Goun also offers a wide variety of other water-based activities.

Nearby Kafr El Gouna is a lively downtown area with shopping arcades, bazaars, an art village, a big selection of restaurants, bars, cafes and discotheques.

Pyramisa

This 5-star resort at Sal Hasheesh on the Red Sea Riviera, 14km from Hurghada international airport has on-site facilities including gym, sauna, steam rooms, restaurants, bars, tennis, squash, diving centre and children's playground.

Bedroom suites and studios are sold freehold with turnkey options to include full furniture packages, satellite TV, air conditioning, stylish bathrooms and terraces with outstanding sea views across the Red Sea.

The hotel has a huge 4,000 sq m outdoor swimming pool with waterslides and an exclusive stretch of sandy beach.

Prices: Studios from £59,500, 2 bed apts from £103,600
More info: www.pyramisaegypt.com
email: nazab@pyramisaegypt.com

EGYPT CONTACT DIRECTORY

Embassies/government
Egyptian Embassy in London
www.egyptian-embassy.org.uk
British Embassy in egypt
www.britishembassy.gov.uk/egypt

Travel & health advice
Foreign Office travel advice
www.fco.gov.uk/travel
www.nhs.uk/healthcareabroad
wwww.masta.org

About Egypt
www.egyptinsight.com
www.beesker.com/ancient-egypt.asp
www.sphinx-egyptexpat.blogspot.com
www.cia.gov/library/publications/the-world-factbook
www.virtualegypt.com
www.lexicorient.com
www.egyptiantouch.com

General & expat
www.expatfocus.com
www.expatfinder.com
www.britishexpat.com
www.transitionsabroad.com
www.cairohash.com
www.transitionsabroad.com

Media (English)
Egyptian Mail (daily)
Daily Star (daily)
Al-Ahram weekly
www.weekly.ahram.org.eg/
www.cairotimes.com/
www.weekly.ahram.org.eg/
www.cairolive.co
www.egypttoday.com

Property
Universal-properties.info
www.egyptianpropertypartners.com
www.think-egypt.com
WWW.egyptianbritishltd.com
www.egyptianexperience.co.uk
www.redseaproperties.net
www.ancientsandsresort.com
www.sinairealestate.com
www.concordservice.com

Travel & tourism
Egypt tourist office www.egypt.travel
www.touregypt.net
www.egyptforall.com - for handicapped
travellers.

Getting there
Airlines serving Egypt
www.britishairways.com
www.egyptair.com
www.firstchoice.co.uk

www.flythomascook.com
www.flybmi.com
www.easyjet.com
www.thomson.co.uk
www.aerlingus.com
www.elgouna.com/
www.thebestofegypt.co.uk

Charter & budget
www.charterflights.co.uk
www.ebookers.com
www.bargainholidays.com
www.cheapflights.co.uk
www.justtheflight.co.uk
www.lastminute.com
www.goredsea.com

Fare range: £240 (low season) - £450 (high
season) although Egyptair has low season
flights for as low as £170 to Sharm-el-
Sheikh, Hurghada and Luxor. High seasons
(Christmas/New Year, Easter, July/August.)
The flight time from the UK is about five
hours.

Getting about
Travelling on foot is hazardous in the cities.
Drivers don't give way to pedestrians and
many areas don't have pavements or
pedestrian crossings.

Train: Book ahead if possible. Tickets are
cheap so it's worth getting a local travel
agent to get your tickets to avoid the long
queues and hassle at the station. Travel

either first or second class.
Info from:
www.seat61.com/egypt.htm
www.egyptrail.gov.eg
www.sleepingtrains.com
Bus: There is an extensive and cheap
long-distance bus network operated by
private companies from Cairo and
Alexandria to most parts of Egypt. Air-
conditioned buses cost more but are highly
recommended. Book seats in advance
whenever possible.
Taxis: Generally safe and cheap. Find out
the fare in advance and tell the driver what
you're prepared to pay when you get in to
avoid arguments when you arrive. For a
little extra your driver will double up as a
guide, particularly if you have hired him for
the day – costing £15-25. Sharing is
common. Forget meters. They either don't
work or are not used. The exception is a
new line of air-conditioned yellow taxis
introduced in Cairo. They can be hailed on
the street, hired from a rank or (in Cairo)
tel. 16516.
Boat: There is a ferry service between the
red sea resorts of Hurghada and Sharm el
Sheikh.
Air: Egyptair's domestic air network covers
most major towns: Luxor, Aswan, Abu
Simbel, Hurghada, Sharm el Sheikh,
Alexandria, Marsa Matruh and Kharga
Oasis.
Driving: Driving is on the right.
International driving permit required.

Is this rainbow nation the 'fairest in all the world'

Why South Africa?

South Africa has a lot of appeal as a retirement destination: it is one of the world's most beautiful countries with a high standard of living and quality of life; a comfortable climate, stunning scenery and wildlife, a thriving and a modern infrastructure and cheap property where you can buy a four-bedroom house with a pool for £100,000. Over 50 per cent of foreign buyers are British.

Famed for its gold and diamond mines, South Africa has a fascinating history. The 'rainbow nation' also has an incredibly diverse culture. An estimated half a million tourists from the UK alone travel there every year.

Cape Town, rated as one of the most beautiful cities in the world, is the No. 1 choice of overseas retirees and they have a choice of havens in coastal, mountainous, vineyard or grassland regions.

South Africans are sports mad and there are hundreds of golf courses and other outdoor sports opportunities and facilities.

Cost of living

In its 2009 annual cost of living survey Mercer placed Johannesburg the least expensive city in a ranking of 143 cities across six continents.

The website www.insidesa.com quotes these prices:
- Meal out for two including a nice bottle of wine £10.50
- Daily rate for a maid £7
- Packet of cigarettes £1.13
- Pint of lager £1
- 3-4 bedroom house, with swimming pool £140,000 (depending upon area)

Is it safe?

Crime is a big problem in South Africa. Robbery and murder rates are among some of the highest in the world.

How much tax will I pay?

Overseas pensions are not liable for tax.

Inheritance Tax was abolished when Capital Gains Tax was introduced in 2001. However, at the time of

FACTFILE

Capital: Pretoria **Population:** 49m
Area: 1,219,090sq km
Language: English, Afrikaans and many indigenous languages including Zulu, Xhosa, Ndebele.
Climate: South Africa lies within the southern temperate zone. Generally the winter months are April-August with summer Sept-March. Cape Town and the southernmost part of Western Cape have a Mediterranean-type climate, mild and changeable in winter when most rainfall occurs. The Durban and Kwa-Zulu-Natal coastline has a sub-tropical climate. The western coastal belt is a winter rain area. Along the Cape south coast winter months are April-August with summer Sept-March. Rain falls in both seasons.
Time difference: GMt +2
Entry requirements: British passport holders (along with those from most Western European countries, Japan, and USA) can stay for up to 90 days without a visa. Visitors may be asked for proof of adequate funds.
Retirement/residence visa: The retired person's visa makes moving there relatively simple. [See: The rules for getting in]
Electricity: 220/230V/50 Hz.
Currency: South African Rand. ATMs available in main centres. Credit cards/debit cars/travellers' cheques widely accepted.
Public holidays (2010)

Jan 1	New Year's Day	June 16	Youth Day
March 21	Human Rights Day	Aug 9	Women's Day
March 22	Public Holiday	Sept 24	Heritage Day
April 2	Good Friday	Dec 16	Day of Reconciliation
April 5	Family Day	Dec 25	Christmas Day
April 27	Freedom Day	Dec 26	Day of Goodwill
May 1	Worker's Day	Dec 27	Public Holiday

Opening hours
Banks: 8.30/9am-3.30/4pm (Mon-Fri); 8.30-11.30am/12 (Sat)
Offices: 8.30/9am-5pm (Mon-Fri)
Shops: 9am-5/6pm (Mon-Sat) 10am-4pm (Sun - urban areas)
Water: Tap water is OK to drink but bottled water is recommended in rural areas.
Tipping: Universally practiced in South Africa. Norms are 10-15 per cent in restaurants and bars, small tips for parking and petrol pump attendants, porters at train stations and airports, taxi drivers, tour guides and hairdressers.
Medical/Healthcare: Medical facilities are of a high standard, particularly in urban areas. State-run hospitals are over-stretched and overcrowded so private health insurance is essential.
No vaccinations required unless arriving from a country where yellow fever is present, but typhoid and hepatitis A vaccinations are recommended. South Africa has one of the highest rates of HIV in the world.
Pets: Pet entry is strict and requires an import permit, microchip identification and an international health certificate issued by a veterinarian. Dogs require blood tests within 30 days of entry. With the exception of the UK, Australia and New Zealand, animals must be vaccinated against rabies not less than 30 days and not more than a year before arrival.

death the owner of the property is deemed to have disposed of it and CGT becomes due.

The expenses incurred in improving a property, and other costs, can be deducted from the capital gain.

Municipal taxes are charged for the maintenance of local services and vary from province to province.

Is South Africa property a good investment?

After at least a year or more of falling house prices values appear to be stabilising, even increasing slightly, according to some sources. South Africa's Standard Bank believes prices are at the bottom of the market

THE RULES FOR GETTING IN

You need to prove a monthly income of at least about £1,500 from a pension, an annuity or other assets. Initially you apply for a Temporary Residence Permit which allows multiple re-entry. You can then apply for a Retired Person Permit which has to be renewed every four years.

Prospects of a successful application are improved by owning of a property in South Africa and proof of medical insurance.

Applications for Retired Person Permits must apply at the nearest South African high commission, embassy or consular mission to where you live.

In addition to birth and marriage certificates you need a police clearance certificate, medical and radiological reports and proof of income.

The fee is £35.

More info: www.southafricahouse.com

and should pick up from next year.

Knight Frank's Global House Price Index indicated that prices dipped by 1.4 per cent in the second quarter of 2009, down by 0.4 per cent less than in the first quarter.

Whether prices have bottomed out or not, buyers from almost anywhere in a Western country will find bargains abound.

According to Lew Geffen, chairman of Sotheby's International Realty SA, the price of a one-bedroom apartment in London, could buy a three-bed beachfront property in the Sea Point area of Cape Town.

Where's best to live?

Western Cape: Sir Francis Drake described it as "the fairest Cape in all the circumference of the World". Situated at the foot of Table Mountain, Cape Town is, without doubt, one of the most beautiful cities in the world, offering outstanding interest and variety.

Blending the old with the new, it has a relaxed, almost continental atmosphere that will charm even the most sophisticated jet-setter.

East of Cape Town are the famous winelands, around the towns of Stellenbosch and Paarl. The old estate houses are built in the attractive Cape Dutch style and there are plenty of opportunities for sampling the vintages.

To the east of Cape Town, set along a rugged

Eastern Cape
Immaculate, spacious and secure home in East London, Eastern Cape. Lounge, dining room, 3 bedrooms, 2 bathrooms, kitchen, pool, double carport and 2 helpers' rooms. Excellent condition.
House size 238sqm, lands size 1,138sqm.
Price: £178,000
More info:
www.periwinkleproperties.co.za
Tel: +27(0) 43 735 4543
Email:
info@periwinkleproperties.co.za

coastline, are a number of quaint fishing villages and picturesque resorts.

Further into the interior is Namaqualand, a semi-desert area until the rains of June or July turn the arid countryside into a spectacular floral display in August or September.

East of Cape Town is the Garden Route through forests, lakes, golden beaches, mountains and semi-arid expanses. This enchanting area stretches along the South Cape Coast from the town of Heidelberg, eastwards to the Tsitsitkamma Forest and Storms River.

Riverdale, Still Bay, Albertina, Mossel Bay, George, Wilderness, Knysna and Plettenberg Bay are some of the main towns.

Eastern Cape: A province steeped in history as well as blessed with beautiful beaches and rugged mountain scenery. This is the birthplace of Nelson Mandela and is the melting pot of three cultures, Xhosa, British and Afrikaner.

The country's longest and most magnificent coastline runs from the rugged Tsistikamma Forest area through the famed surfing spots of Jeffreys Bay to the golden beaches of the Sunshine Coast and the Wild Coast.

The coast is dotted with relaxing holiday resorts. Many comprise only a cluster of houses and shops but boast sports facilities such as bowling greens and tennis courts. There are also some excellent spots for fishermen.

Inland are the wooded Amatola Mountains, a paradise for hikers, climbers and trout fishermen, as well as the brooding Karoo Desert.

This region includes the major seaport of Port Elizabeth, known as "The Friendly City". There are also two national parks and several private reserves.

Northern Cape: The rugged regions of the Northern

Cape appeal to those seeking broad horizons and peace and quiet. It is an area of outstanding natural beauty and contains the Kalahari Gemsbok National Park, set in the rolling dunes of the Kalahari Desert.

The region has only one major town, Upington, the jumping-off point for the Kalahari, the Augrabies Falls and Fish River Canyon; and one city, Kimberley, dubbed the 'City of Diamonds' whose 'Big Hole' bears testament to the diamond-rush days of the last century.

Free State: This landlocked province between the Vaal

beauty, has a network of nature trails and provides the opportunity to see a variety of antelope and birdlife.

Capital of the Free State is Bloemfontein, known as the 'City of Roses'

Kwazulu-Natal: One of South Africa's smallest provinces encompassing the territory known as Zululand towards the north. In this region are a number of important wildlife conservation areas, including the award-winning Hluhluwe/Umfolozi public game reserve, where the white rhino was saved from extinction, and the coral reefs and water wonderland of the St Lucia estuary and Lake St. Lucia.

To the west are the soaring peaks of the Drakensberg Mountains.

The province is also known for its Anglo-Zulu and Anglo-Boer battlefield sites. At its heart is the city of Pietermaritzburg which, with its "olde worlde" dignity, is affectionately referred to as "The Last Outpost of the British Empire".

The Midlands region boasts excellent country hotels, white water rafting on the Tugela River, trout fishing and wonderful scenery.

KwaZulu-Natal's sub-tropical climate makes it the year-round haunt of sunbathers, swimmers and watersports enthusiasts. Cities and towns, such as Umhlanga Rocks, have well-developed resort areas and Durban, with its "golden mile" of modern hotels and restaurants, has been dubbed South Africa's "Sunshine Playground"

Mpumalanga is a sportsman's paradise. There are golf courses in some of the province's most scenic areas. Hang-gliding, micro-lighting and para-gliding are popular and hiking is available throughout the province including the world-renowned Kruger

River in the north and the Orange River in the south is an area of wide, open spaces – an immense rolling prairie, chequered with farmsteads and windmills.

One of South Africa's major rivers, the Vaal, flows through the province and there are attractive holiday resorts near two of the river's largest dams.

The mountains of the eastern highlands harbour romantic hideaways and rugged hiking trails. The Golden Gate National Park in the north-east, with its spectacular sandstone formations, an area of scenic

Garden Route home
4 bedroom home in a gated estate in the popular coastal Westford suburb of Knysna, in the heart of the South African Garden Route in the Western Cape. Enjoys the best of views of the Knysna Lagoon and River just 7 minutes from the town centre yet set in a tranquil estate away from the hurly-burly of the tourist crowds. It also has a 1-bedroom self-contained flat with lounge and kitchenette and a separate entrance.
Price: £315,000
Ref. 10306
More info: Choice Knysna Property
http://choiceknysna.co.za Email: bstrain@pixie.co.za
Tel: Tel: +27 (0)44 382 6230

National Park. Large dams provide the opportunity for watersports whilst dams and streams in the high country attract trout anglers.

In past times gold diggers, transport-riders and big game hunters roamed the area and have left behind a fascinating history. The area known as the Lowveld is the haunt of big game. West of the Kruger National Park there are a number of private game reserves, each with their own distinct character.

Gautemg is the commercial heart of South Africa containing the important cities of Johannesburg and Pretoria. Despite the urbanisation of the Johannesburg region, opportunities for getting back to nature abound.

There are game farms, hiking trails, dams, lakes and rivers for watersports and fishing and picnic spots are plentiful. The Vaal River area is a particularly popular recreational area.

The province is described as "The Heartbeat of Africa". Johannesburg, known as the "City of Gold" or Egoli, is the commercial powerhouse of South Africa.

Pretoria, about 30 miles north of Johannesburg and the country's administrative capital, is known as

'Jacaranda City' after the purple-blossomed trees.

It is a fascinating melting pot of different cultures. Outside the city are bushveld game farms as well as more than 100 nature reserves and bird sanctuaries.

Limpopo Province (formally Northern Province) is a vast region with a culturally rich and diverse people.

The Southern Region is famous for its many hot spring resorts, the Nylsvlei wetland and the unspoilt mountains and flowing streams of the Waterberg. Wildlife in the game reserves is abundant and the scenery ranges from rolling hills to mighty cliffs of stark red rock.

To the east lies the immense wildlife heritage of the Kruger National Park.

In the centre is the vibrant capital city of Pietersburg - the industrial and commercial heart of the Great North. Here gold was first mined and smelted in the 19th century.

Sweeping across from the northwest – and flowing along the northern border – is the Limpopo River Valley, a vast, natural area with cultures that date back to the Iron Age.

North-West: Home to the Batswana people and Sun City, a fabulous resort complex which includes The Palace at the Lost City, Africa's most extravagant hotel.

Sun City and the Lost City attract top international entertainers, provide exceptional sporting facilities, including two championship golf courses, and feature casinos, excellent restaurants and nightclubs. The province boasts some excellent game reserves such as the 60,000-hectare Pilanesberg National Park, adjoining Sun City.

The province also includes Stellaland in the Vryburg area, described as the "Texas of South Africa", where large cattle farms and game ranches are to be found.

SOUTH AFRICA CONTACT DIRECTORY

Embassies/Government
South Africa High Commission
www.southafricahouse.com
British High Commission in South Africa
ukinsouthafrica.fco.gov.uk

Travel & Health Advice
Foreign Office travel advice
www.fco.gov.uk/travel
www.nhs.uk/Healthcareabroad
www.masta.org

About South Africa
www.southafrica.info
www.info.gov.za
www.africaguide.com
www.southafrica.net
www.southafrica.info
www.mysouthafrica.tv
www.cape-town.info
www.aboutcapetown.com
www.joburg.org.za
www.durban.kzn.org.za
www.mediaclubsouthafrica.com
www.home-bru.com
(cost of living info)

General & Expat
www.xpat.co.za
www.expatfocus.com
www.britishexpat.com
www.expatforum.com

Media (English)
There are over 20 daily newspapers, most
published in English and 4 terrestrial TV
channels. The South African Broadcasting
Corporation (SABC) is the state-owned
public broadcaster. There are 2 independent
television broadcasters.
Satellite services include Multichoice, M-
Net, and DStv, a digital satellite television
network with over 55 local and international
channels.

Property
www.capewaterfrontestates.co.za
HomeNet (South Africa)
www.pamgolding.co.za
www.acutts.co.za
www.real-estate-south-africa.com
www.bw-international.com
www.susandeacon.co.za
www.chproperties.co.za
www.viviun.com
www.calitzdorp.co.za
www.homenet.co.za
www.alecmassel.co.za
www.finecountry.co.za
www.homeguide.co.za
www.wildnetafrica.com
www.topcoastal.co.za

Travel & Tourism
www.southafrica.net
www.southafrica.to
http://www.africaguide.com
www.sa-venues.com
www.traveldex.co.za
www.southafricatravel.com

Getting There
South African Airways: www.flysaa.com
British Airways: www.british-airways.com
KLM: KLM.com
Virgin:www.virgin-atlantic.com

Getting Around
Air
South African Airways: www.saairlink.co.za
South African Express: www.flysax.com
Kulula Air: www.kulula.com
1time: www.1time.aero
www.flymango.com
Airlink: www.saairlink.co.za
Train
Extensive services in Gauteng, Western
Cape, KwaZulu-Natal and Eastern Cape. The
Blue Train travels 1,600km trip between
Pretoria and Cape Town and is one of the
most luxurious train journeys in the world.
Bus
A number of operators operate an inter-city
coach service. Among them: Translux,
Greyhound, Baz Bus, Intercape Mainliner,
Luxury Inter-City Transport and Intercape
Mainliner.
Driving
The road infrastructure is excellent. Foreign
driving licences are valid in South Africa for
up to 6 months, but must be printed in
English. Many of the roads between major
centres are toll roads.
In cities drive with your doors locked and
windows up, especially when stopped at
traffic lights. Night driving is also not
advised
Traffic drives on the left.

Plettenberg Bay
3-bedroom house in the
Robberg area of
Plettenberg Bay. 10
minutes walk to the beach.
Open plan lounge/dining
room and deluxe kitchen
with bachelor flat with
private entrance or use as
study/office.
Double garage, back
garden with Wendy hut.
Safe environment.
Price: £145,000
More info:
www.pabotha.co.za
Email: info@pabotha.co.za

A welcome Message
from H.E. Hamida Mrabet Labidi,
Ambassador of Tunisia

Lying directly south of Italy's Sardinia, Tunisia has 1,300km of coastline to enjoy thanks to a sharp right-angle turn on its Mediterranean-facing shoreline. The sandy beaches front an impressive infrastructure of luxurious hotels, modern international airports, chic boutiques and jet-set marinas whilst the barren south has long-been the chosen setting for blockbusting films including Star Wars, Raiders of the Lost Ark, Monty Python's Life of Brian and Minghella's The English Patient. Providing a taste of the Mediterranean, a glimpse of Africa and an enchanting insight into Middle Eastern life, Tunisia is also an intriguing mix of cultures and landscape.

These assets, together with its strategic location, have propelled the nation on to the global stage and helped attract an increasing number of tourists who are set to reach 7 million by the end of 2008. This steadily developing tourism is the result of socio-political stability, a prerequisite for a harmonious development of the tourism sector.

While retaining this traditional beach holiday market, however, Tunisia is looking to diversify its tourist mix, focusing especially on attracting higher-spending visitors and opening up to a new breed of travellers by promoting the country's 3000 year-old-heritage; sports, golf, spa and adventure packages; eco-tourism and winter tourism. The importance of cruises should rise as well, with the opening up of several new routes from Tunis to airports in Africa and Europe.

As tourism becomes more important, leisure facilities are springing up at a significant rate, particularly around the honeypot resorts of Hammamet and Monastir, and Tunisia now boasts six golf courses, two of which have 27-holes, international diving centres and plenty of yachting clubs. Investment is pouring into the sector, a nod to the country's future potential. Two significant projects currently underway, Mediterranean Gate "Century City" and "Tunis Sports City", two investments of 25 billion USD and 5 billion USD respectively, will bring further golf courses and marinas, world-class sporting academies, Olympic grade facilities, business and leisure hubs as well as thousands of residential units and hotel beds.

Yours faithfully

Endless hot summers and just a hop from Europe

Why Tunisia?

There are many plus points to living in Tunisia. Less than three hours flying time from the UK, it has beautiful beaches, cultural and historical attractions and hot, sunny summers that seem to last forever.

Sandwiched between Algeria and Libya, Tunisia is the northernmost African state and was a French colony until 1956. The official language is Arabic and French is the official second language.

Most Tunisians speak French fluently as well as English which is the official third language and is taught in primary schools from aged 10. (French is taught from aged 8.)

In the "Happy Planet Index" published by the British think-tank New Economics Foundation, Tunisia is ranked 29th out of 143 countries in the world. (The UK was 74th).

Healthcare is on a par with Europe. Many people come to Tunisia to have dental work done or for plastic

surgery; both are very popular. If you live here you must have healthcare insurance in case

you need to have major surgery or other expensive treatment. A normal visit or consultation at the doctors or dentist is very cheap compared to the UK.

Tunisia is largely a secular country but the official religion is Islam and even if people do not fully practise the religion, most of its values are still upheld.

Is it safe?

There is little violent crime in Tunisia but you should watch out for petty criminals such as pickpockets, particularly in crowded market places.

How much tax will I pay?

Income tax: Individuals are subject to income tax only on income arising in Tunisia.

Inheritance tax: Basic 2.5 per cent but rising (up to 35 per cent) depending on the relationship of the heir to the deceased - the closer the relationship, the lesser the tax.

Property Taxes & Costs

Transfer Tax

Buying a new property from a developer   1%

Buying a resale   6% (5% + 1%)

Solicitor's fees   1-3%

Import tax: Holders of temporary resident permits

ABOUT THE WRITER: Melanie Benna, originally from Nottinghamshire, lives in Beni Khiar with her husband Adel, an accountant, who lived in the UK for nearly 20 years but was born and brought up in Tunisia. Apart from bringing up six children Melanie and her husband run a property business, The Tunisian House [**www.thetunisianhouse.co.uk**] - the only British registered estate agency operating in Tunisia - and Melanie also has a very useful website, **www.nomarmiteintunisia.co.uk**, for those interested in moving to or buying property in Tunisia.

FACTFILE

Capital: Tunis

Population: 10,043,000

Area: 164,000sq km

Language: Arabic (official) and French. English is widely spoken.

Climate: Typical Mediterranean with hot summers and mild wet winters.

Time difference: GMT +1

Entry requirements: EU nationals do not require a visa for stays of up to three months (four months for US nationals).

Retirement/residence visa

After three months you must apply for a carte sejour (residence permit). [see: The rules for getting in]

Electricity: 230V, 50Hz. Round pin plugs.

Money: Dinar. There are ATM machines in larger towns and tourist areas. Credit cards and travellers cheques are accepted in larger towns and tourist areas.

Public holidays: 2010

Jan 1	New Year's Day	July 25	Republic Day
Feb 26	Prophet's Birthday	Aug 13	Women's Day
March 20	Independence Day	Sept 11	End of Ramadan
March 21	Youth Day	Nov 7	New Era Day
April 9	Martyrs' Day	Nov 16	Feast of Sacrifice
May 1	Labour Day	Dec 7	Islamic New Year

Opening hours

Banks: 7.30-11am and 2-4.15pm (Mon-Fri)

Offices: 8.30am-1pm and 3pm-6pm (Mon-Fri); 8.30am-1pm (Sat)

Shops: 8am-12p and 4pm-7pm

Water: Stick to bottled variety.

Tipping: Tunisians are not big tippers but restaurant staff in tourist areas and taxi drivers will expect a 10 per cent tip.

Medical/Healthcare: Tunisia has a developed healthcare system and standards are equivalent to those in Europe. Private healthcare is recommended. Prices are reasonable.

Pets: Pets require a certificate of health from veterinary authorities in the country of departure stating it has no contagious diseases.

can import personal belongings, furniture, etc. up to the value of 15,000 dinar (£6,800) and a car (max. three years old) free of duty. Personal possessions must be imported within two years from the date of a temporary residential permit being granted.

Is Tunisian property a good investment?

Property prices rose by nearly 15 per cent in the summer of 2008 but are still low compared to the rest of Europe, Morocco and the Middle East.

Since we moved here there has been an explosion of interest in investing in Tunisian property and prices have risen dramatically.

However, they remain lower than most countries considered by UK expats such as Morocco, France or

PROPERTY

Near town and beach

Spacious 4/6 bedroom family home in the popular Nabeul area a short walk to town and the beach. Roof terrace, tiled yard with additional 3 room studio apartment.

Ground floor: Large lounge/diner, reception room/bedroom, cloakroom with shower, fitted kitchen.1st floor: 4 double bedrooms, bathroom, French doors to terrace. 2nd floor: Large utility room.

Price: £121,400 Ref: TH.VNa.05

More info: www.thetunisianhouse.co.uk

Tel (Tunisia): +216 25225205 Email: thetunisianhouse@yahoo.co.uk

Long-term rental

Furnished apartment with 3 double bedrooms in Meriem, Hammamet South, a lovely neighbourhood, close to the Cultural Centre. Large lounge diner, kitchenette, downstairs shower and upstairs bathroom, outdoor pool, 5 minute's walk from the beach and tourist area.

More info: Contact owner for long-term rental rates. Ref: HA02

Email: erb@planet.tn Tel: +216 98226034/+216 22308556

Italy and building, rather than buying, means that for the cost you can end up with a magnificent property, considerably larger and more luxurious than you would find in the UK for the same price.

Add tourism growth edging up to five per cent a year and economic growth at nearly six per cent this year (2009) making property analysts believe property is an excellent investment.

Many Tunisian workers abroad are hurrying to invest in their home country as well as Middle Eastern developers who are pouring money into Tunisia in huge investments in the capital, Tunis, and other places such as Hergla, near to Sousse.

In a recent article Property Mall ranked Tunisia among the top global investment destinations for property for long-term gains.

Where's best to live?

Beni Khiar, where we live, has a wonderfully cheap vegetable and fruit market from around Saturday midday to Sunday afternoon, joined by the main market with a variety of stalls on a Sunday. It has a working port, so fish lovers are in their element here.

Nearby **Maamoura** is still very undeveloped and excellent for getting away from it all. Even further along the coast, travelling through stunning countryside, lies **Korba**, with its pristine, white sandy beaches and home to the magnificent (and my all time favourite) hotel the Africa Jade.

The area around **Nabeul** and **Hammamet** is sometimes called the Garden Resort of Tunisia and travelling just a little further away from the main seaside resorts, it is not hard to see why.

Nabeul is the capital of the Cap Bon and is often described by many as "The Jewel in the Crown." It is a

THE RULES FOR GETTING IN

To reside permanently in Tunisia you need a Carte de Sejour which can be a long-winded process. Some foreign residents don't bother and simply leave the country every three months. You can apply for a Carte de Sejour at the local police station.

You need the usual mass of paperwork: copies of relevant pages from your passport, evidence of adequate means of support (a bank statement would normally suffice), documents to prove you are either renting or buying property – title deeds or rental contract, either in Arabic or French or both – which have been officially registered.

The police station will usually issue a Temporary Carte de Sejour and you may have to make several return visits and wait several weeks (or even months) for your permanent card. A temporary card is only valid for a month so until the permanent card is issued you will have to keep going back.

The Carte de Sejour is valid for a year after the date that you applied for it and you must renew it before it expires.

popular and cosmopolitan market town, with many shops and amenities, all surrounded by the picturesque countryside, historical sites and attractive beaches of the region.

Hammamet, like Nabeul, is a very lively town, with plenty of hotels and restaurants although one British resident complains that the one supermarket is very small with limited stock.

Compensation for those lucky enough to live in Hammamet with its tree-lined boulevards, 12th century kasbah, medina and miles of sandy beaches, is you could be living in one of the most beautiful places on earth.

Korbous is in a dramatic setting where the air is pure and the place so quiet and traffic-free you could hear a pin drop.

To get there one must drive along rugged mountainside roads with breathtaking views. This is a spa town where you can bathe in hot thermal springs, which gush from the mountainsides or swim in the clear, blue waters of the sea, or picnic on the cliffs taking in your stunning surroundings.

Monastir, famous for its beautiful beach and marina, was used as a location for films such as Life of Brian and Life of Christ. It's easy to reach from neighbouring Sousse; a louage from the main louage station will take you there in around 10 minutes for a few dinars.

Port el Kantaoui is stunningly beautiful. You will be bowled over by the beauty of the modern marina

We live here

In 2005 Melanie Benna and her husband Adel swapped life in their three-bedroomed terrace house in Ramsgage for a seven-bedroomed, two bathroom villa in Beni Khiar, Tunisia.

Beni Khiar is a small town about three miles from Nabeul. It has one main street and many small, winding alleyways where you will see carpets being woven in the traditional way.

We built our villa on what was farmland which means that we have fig, olive, orange and pomegranate trees in our garden and a wonderful view of open countryside stretching all the way down to the sea.

Although we started building the villa in 2005, this was done at our leisure while we lived in the basement as the work was carried out. It is now virtually complete.

The cost of the land and building the house, including sculptured, domed ceilings has amounted to less than the price of purchasing a tiny flat in the UK.

Food is so cheap here we think nothing of buying a kilo of shark or tuna every day. Fruit and vegetables are found in abundance and a box of plum tomatoes is about the same price as a single tomato in Britain.

I have found Tunisia very easy to live in and I hardly speak a word of the language. Most people here are excellent at languages and even in the smallest and remotest of towns there will be at least one person who will pop up and speak to you in English.

Those of us who paid a little bit of attention in our French lessons at school will find that the few words we remember, coupled with a lot of gestures and hand movements, will suffice in most situations.

Although Beni Khiar is becoming home to quite a few Brits, we are still somewhat of a rarity which means becoming a bit of a minor celebrity.

A visit to the school or shops often means fighting your way through the crowds of schoolchildren, all anxious to practise their English on you, or elderly ladies dashing out of their homes to stare in amazement.

Our estate agency is located near Nabeul and we offer properties or land in and around this area, especially in the town of Beni Khiar, as well as Hammamet and the Sousse/Port el Kantaoui/Hergla area.

We have some stunning seafront off-plan developments between Port el Kantaoui and Hergla. We also help with designing and building villas and are doing this at the moment for a couple of our customers.

We keep in touch with all of our customers as many are now living near us and we are beginning to form quite a little community!

with its Moorish architectural style while wandering around on a warm, summer, evening, looking at the boats and yachts.

Many British expats live in the Sousse area and hold a regular Thursday morning meet up in nearby Port el Kantaoui.

I never tire of visiting this lovely little marina with its cobbled walkways, whitewashed homes, trees, flowers and fountains lying beside the picturesque boats and yachts bobbing up and down on the sparkling waters.

There are two 18-hole golf courses here and if golf's not your thing, there's the Aqua Palace Water Park, quad biking and a family funfair. Those who have chosen to make their home in Port El Kantaoui delight in spending many a pleasant summer night in the lively atmosphere on the terraces of the cafe bars and restaurants lining the water's edge.

So popular with the British, everywhere you go English can be heard spoken, as tourists flock to this little gem. Even the waiters, shop and stall sellers or guys offering one of the many available boat rides will shout after you in English first instead of the customary French.

For those seeking traditional Tunisia, without a mass influx of tourism, and keen to get to know the culture of the 'real' Tunisia, then look no further than **Hergla**.

Hergla is simply stunning. Whitewashed houses, covered in bougainvillea, quaint little streets and alleyways, winding their way down to the sparkling, clear, blue Mediterranean sea, and cliff top walks through lush, mature gardens.

Hergla's main streets are lined with pots, bursting with plants and flowers. Fresh fish, straight from the sea, can be purchased from the port in the mornings.

But the thing that hits you most about Hergla is the peace, the calm, the solitude and the serenity. Feel all your troubles melt away as you enjoy refreshments at one of the picturesque little coffee shops, overlooking the sea or cliff top gardens.

How long will Hergla be allowed to remain like this? Work is to start soon on a new Port El Kantaoui style marina just a bit further along from the old fishing port. Sounds great as long as they leave sweet and lovely Hergla, the old town, just as it is, allowing tourists and us expats out here to continue enjoying our relaxing, day trips to the picture-postcard resort.

Bizerte is another stunning town located in the far North of Tunisia. Its port and waterways have sometimes led it to be called the "Venice of Tunisia."

Tunis itself, the capital city, has tree-lined avenues, and an endless maze of streets in its medina. There are some beautiful areas such as Sidi Bou Said and Carthage although property prices in these places are extortionate as they are World Heritage sites.

Areas in the capital that expats choose to live are near to Les Berges du Lac, where both the British and American embassies are situated, as well as the American International School, or Gammarth and La Marsa which are seaside towns and near to the French International School.

Gammarth, La Marsa, Carthage and Sidi Bou Said are breathtaking areas with stunningly expensive and luxurious villas

Tabarka is a town in the north of Tunisia and is a mountainous region surrounded by a rocky coastline and towering forests. The annual jazz festival is held there. 35 miles from its coast are **La Galite islands**, home to a colony of monk seals in its nature reserve, and where, if you enjoy diving, there is a well preserved shipwreck.

TUNISIA CONTACT DIRECTORY

Embassies/Government

UK Embassy in Tunisia
http://ukintunisia.fco.gov.uk/en

Tunisian Embassy in London
29 Princes Gate, London, SW7 1QG
Phone: +44 171 584 8117
Fax: +44 171 225 2884
No website but the tourist Office website
[www.tunisia.com] has info on visas.

Travel & Health Advice

Foreign Office travel advice
www.fco.gov.uk/travel
www.nhs.uk/Healthcareabroad
www.masta.org

About Tunisia

www.cometotunisia.co.uk
www.tunisia.com
www.investintunisia.com
www.africaguide.com/country/tunisia

General & Expat

www.nomarmiteintunisia.co.uk
www.expatfocus.com
www.britishexpat.com
www.transitionsabroad.com

English Language Media

www.tunisiamedia.com
www.tunisiaonlinenews.com
(Tunisian news in English)
All government official websites are now
being translated into English in addition to
French and Arabic.
Satellite television is cheap and readily
available. The main satellite stations are
Arabsat, Nilesat, Hotbird and Astra.
For those who simply cannot do without
British TV, a slingbox will enable you to keep
up with all the latest soaps etc.
Generally prices for broadband are a lot
cheaper than in the UK.
There are internet cafes in most towns.

Property

www.thetunisianhouse.co.uk
www.europeanproperty.com/sales/tn
www.follaproperties.com
www.sunshineestates.net

Travel & Tourism

www.tourismtunisia.com
www.cometotunisia.co.uk
www.tunisia.com

Getting There

Flying time to Tunis from London is around
2 1/2 hours. Tunisia has six international
airports: Djerba, Monastir, Sfax, Tabarka,
Tozeur, Tunis.
Tunisair and British Airways operate several
flights a week from Heathrow and Gatwick
to Tunis respectively.
Nouvelair operates a weekly flight every
Sunday from Gatwick to Monastir.
Charter flights usually fly to Monastir from
regional airports (Birmingham, Glasgow,
Belfast etc) all over the UK & Ireland.
There are more adventurous ways of
getting to Tunisia. For example, you can
travel by Eurostar, changing at Lille onto a
direct TGV to Marseille, overnighting there
and taking a cruise ferry in the morning or
lunchtime and arriving in Tunis the
following morning.

By air

All major European airlines have flights to
Tunisia including:
British Airways: www.britishairways.com
KLM: www.klm.com
Tunisian carriers are:
Nouvelair: www.nouvelair.com
Tunisair: www.tunisair.com
Charter flights are available from many UK
cities including Aberdeen, Belfast,
Birmingham, Edinburgh, Glasgow, Leeds,
London, Manchester, Newcastle,
Southampton and Teesside.

By train & ferry

You can get to Tunis by ferry from Italy,
France and Spain. Journey times are 16-24
hours.
www.southernferries.co.uk
www.traghettiweb.it/en
www.sncm.fr
www.ctn.com.tn.
www.gnv.it.

Getting Around

By air: Tunisair operates regular domestic
flights from Tunis to Djerba, Sfax and
Tozeur.

Train: Trains are comfortable, modern and
air-conditioned and are the best way to
travel between Tunis, Sousse, El Jem, Sfax
and Gabès. There are other routes including
a branch line from Sousse to Monastir and
Mahdia.

Bus: Local services are good value and the
network covers most of the country.

Taxis: Louage taxis are shared taxis
operating along the main routes and
serving the function of buses. They can be
hailed anywhere along the route. The price
is fixed and comparable to the cost of a
local bus.
They are Ideal for a long journey. They will
only leave when all of the seats are full.
There are stations in every town.

Driving: Defensive driving is a must in
Tunisia Roads are fairly good but driving is
chaotic and sometimes dangerous with a
high accident rate especially at night.
Traffic signs and signals are ignored and
bicycles and mopeds often have no lights.
Driving is on the right.

Emirates are not as dry as you may think

Why the UAE?

For those considering the United Arab Emirates as a retirement destination, this usually means Dubai or Abu Dhabi although the UAE is composed also of Sharjah, Ajman, Umm Al Qaiwain, Ras Al Khaimah and Fujairah. Sharjah is a cheaper possibility but is completely dry – alcoholically speaking.

Dubai is the most Westernised of the emirates but, in this respect, Abu Dhabi is quickly catching up. Known until independence in 1971 from the UK as the Trucial States, the UAE is ruled by a Supreme Council of Rulers composed of one emir from each emirate although each functions with considerable autonomy.

The population of the UAE is around five million and only about 20 per cent of the population are native Emiratis. There are about 100,000 Britons and tens of thousands of other western expatriates and a huge army of Third World workers: 1.75 million from India, 1.25 million from Pakistan, and 500,000 Bangladeshis. Other Asian communities, including China, the Philippines, Thailand, Korea, Afghanistan and Iran account for another million.

There is a legal – but often overlooked – requirement to have a licence to buy alcohol which is widely available at restaurants and bars in Dubai and in the tourist hotels of the other emirates except Sharjah.

Beach clubs are a popular escape for western expatriates in both Dubai and Abu Dhabi. These are not the simple beach bars/restaurants you might find, for example, in the Caribbean or Goa. In addition to sophisticated dining, they provide an array of leisure and sporting facilities.

There are beach clubs at many of the major hotels such as the Hilton, Sheraton, Intercontinental, Meridien and Shangri-la. As the number of expatriate residents has grown, annual memberships of beach clubs can now cost as much as $10,000 per family.

Although the dry, sub-tropical climate is uncomfortably hot during the summer months, for around eight months of the year it is extremely pleasant. Efficient irrigation systems keep these cities amazingly lush and green all year round and there are many beautifully maintained parks and gardens.

Despite their cosmopolitan nature, Dubai and Abu Dhabi still retain their Arabic heritage and culture. There are some lifestyle restrictions relating to Islamic laws and traditions and, during Ramadan, there is a ban on eating and drinking in public during daylight hours.

ABOUT THE WRITER: Originally from West Yorkshire, **Diane Niemiec** says she and her husband, **Graham**, have learned to adapt to the Muslim way of life since they moved to Abu Dhabi in 2002.

An occasional freelance writer, Diane occupies her time doing voluntary work with runaway maids who have been abused by their employer, working with local women's' groups, as well as "sunbathing, drinking coffee, shopping - all the stuff expat women here fill their time with."

FACTFILE

Capital: Abu Dhabi **Population:** 5m

Area: 83,600sq km

Language: Arabic. English is widely understood .

Climate: The best time to be in the UAE is Oct-May although the weather is still very hot (up to 35ºC) in Oct. June-Sept are even hotter, especially the July-Aug period (high 40s) with 100 per cent humidity. Daytime temperatures are ideal in Nov, Dec, Jan and Feb (around 24C) the evenings are cooler (13C). Most rainfall occurs in Dec-March, with brief heavy downpours. Hotels, restaurants and shops are air-conditioned as are taxis and buses.

Time difference: GMT +4

Entry requirements: UK citizens, other EU nationals and those from the USA, Canada, Australia, New Zealand, can get a visa on arrival.

Retirement/residence visa: The UAE introduced a new system of residence visas for property owners last year. A multi-entry visa, still commonly (but wrongly) referred to as a residence visa, is valid for six months at a time and permits multiple entry. [See: The Rules for Getting in]

Electricity: 220 V/50Hz

Money: Emirati dirham (Dh or AED), divided into 100 fils. ATMs are located at many local banks. Credit cards/debit cars/travellers cheques are generally accepted except at smaller retailers and restaurants.

Public holidays (2010)

Jan 1	New Year's Day	Nov 17	Eid al-Adha
Feb 26	Birth of the Prophet	Dec 2	National Day
July 9	Leilat al-Meiraj	Dec 7	Al-Hijra
Sept 11	Eid al-Fitr	Dec 16	Ashoura

Opening hours

Banks: 8am-1pm Sat-Thurs

Offices: Government offices 7.30am-2.30pm (closed Fri and Sat). Private offices keep longer hours with a extended mid-day break. Shops: 9am-1 pm, 4-9pm although many shops in Dubai and Abu Dhabi stay open all day. Shopping malls are usually open 10am-10pm, sometimes later and some supermarkets are open for 24 hours. Most shops close for Friday prayers from 11.30am-1.30pm.

Water: Use bottled water.

Tipping: Service charges are usually added (16 per cent in Abu Dhabi, 10 per cent in Dubai). If not included, add 10 per cent. Taxi drivers do not expect a tip but supermarket baggers and carriers and windscreen washers at petrol stations expect a few coins.

Medical/Healthcare: No special immunisations are required. While 'free' treatment is available at government hospitals and at the Dubai Medical Center, this is only for emergency treatment. Everything else needs to be paid for or covered by insurance.

Pets: Since most people live in apartments, large dogs are not ideal pets to bring to the UAE. Documents required: Import permit, rabies vaccination certificate and a health certificate with the name, age, breed, colour and sex of the animal stating that it is rabies-free and in a healthy condition to travel. All pets must be microchipped and the number must appear on all documentation.

Traditional souks, mosques and merchant's houses sit fairly comfortably alongside ultra-modern skyscrapers, shopping malls, hotels and office blocks. Along the creek, sailing dhows – now motor-powered – are moored and water-taxis ferry passengers from one bank to other at all hours of day and night. City life, sandy beaches and the desert are all within easy reach.

Cost of living

In the last few years the cost of living in Dubai has increased rapidly and Abu Dhabi is catching up. In its March, 2009 survey of cost of living in cities around the world, Mercer HR Consulting placed Dubai and Abu Dhabi at 20th (52nd in 2008) and 26th (65th) respectively.

There may be no tax, amazingly low fuel prices for your (tax-free) car and cheap utility prices, but property prices have doubled in the past five years and rental property is pricey, accounting for at least 50 per cent of most residents' cost of living.

Expect to pay £800-1,200 for a one-bedroom flat or studio and you can add £400-500 a month per bedroom, slightly less in Abu Dhabi.

A look at www.gnads4u.com/properties will give you a rough idea of rental prices in the region.

A good source of current property information are the Time Out websites: www.timeoutabudhabi.com and at www.timeoutabudhabi.com

Landlords or their agents will want a year's rent up-front usually in the form of post-dated cheques, as well as a hefty security deposit.

Locally produced foods are relatively cheap but most grocery items are imported and therefore fairly expensive. You need to budget about £600 a month for food per person.

The price of designer label fashion items may make your wife's eyes sparkle, but you can't eat them. Local clothing and footwear is reasonable and electrical goods – imported from China or Taiwan – are much cheaper.

Wines and spirits are not permitted unless you have a licence; prices are about the same as in the UK. Utility prices are subsidised throughout the UAE and are about nearly 40 per cent cheaper.

There's good cost of living info at: www.dubaifaqs.com

Dubai

The second largest of the seven states and its main port and commercial centre, Dubai has developed into a truly cosmopolitan city, with over three-quarters of its

population being expatriates from around the world who generally enjoy an excellent standard of living.

Dubai is entertaining, exciting, liberal and stable and, with its beaches, beach clubs, bars, restaurants, golf clubs and other leisure facilities, modern malls and traditional souks, it has become popular among those retirees who can afford it.

The city has built its wealth mainly on its role as an international trading centre and it is less dependent on oil revenue than the other Emirates.

Dubai has implemented vast construction projects, the best known being Burj Al Arab ("Tower of the Arabs") – the world's tallest building used exclusively as a hotel – which stands on an artificial island 280m from Jumeirah beach, as well as the Palm Islands development with its hotels, villas, apartments, shopping malls, entertainment facilities, a marine park and around 75 miles of new beaches.

Dubai is also a shopper's paradise, with imported goods from around the world available in its shopping malls, souks and gold stores.

The city is very family-friendly, with playgrounds in virtually very shopping mall, restaurants, that welcome children and a wealth of family-oriented festivals and activities. In contrast with some of its neighbours, there are fewer restrictions in Dubai on what women are allowed to wear. They should, however, dress

I live here

UAE's capital is ready to say 'marhaba' to an increasing number of tourists, writes Di Miller

A frequent greeting you'll hear in the Gulf is 'Marhaba' which means 'welcome' in Arabic. The fascination of Abu Dhabi for me is a simple one: wander through the back streets where the perfume shops, gold shops, crafts and spices all mingle together; visit the clothing shops with material from all over the world made up into exotic gowns for local women.

Try the local foods – 'fatayer' (pastries made with cheese, tomatoes, honey and chicken) or shwarma (chicken or lamb roasted on a spit and served in pitta bread); meander along to the shisha cafes where you can sit with locals smoking hubbly bubbly (fruit flavoured tobacco through a water pipe) or try mint tea – good for the digestive system!

Abu Dhabi is one of the seven emirates, which make up United Arab Emirates. It is the largest emirate, the capital and the one with the oil. Dubai, the second emirate is better known due to its tourism industry.

The Arabian Gulf coast has many offshore islands, coral reefs and salt-flats, which make for a spectacular landscape.

You can drink too!

It would take a year to try out all the restaurants in Abu Dhabi and certainly, the range of food reflects the cosmopolitan nature of the place: Sri Lankan, Indian, Chinese, Moroccan, Arabic, French, Arabic, you name it, we have it here.

Prices also vary, from cheap Arabic restaurants where you can enjoy a simple meal and pay next to nothing, to the pricier hotels serving gourmet food. As a bonus you can drink alcohol since, unlike Saudi Arabia, the Emiratis are more flexible in their understanding of our drinking culture.

Hotels, from three-star cheaper Arabic style to the five-star plus, are here – the Sheraton, Le Meridien and the Millennium, to name a few. Yes they are grand and their prices reflect this.

Recently some of the older hotels, including the Gulf Hotel and Khalidia Palace hotel, have been pulled down or refurbished to prepare for a new influx of tourists. The Abu Dhabi of five years ago has undergone a radical change and is gearing up for the tourism industry.

Abu Dhabi is an island and the largest part is desert. On an evening, people stroll up and down the Corniche (promenade) where you can just sit and relax under huge white canopies as the sun sets, or for the more energetic, rollerblade up and down.

The newly-upgraded Corniche, with its play areas for children, is a big improvement on the old Corniche which was looking shabby, so a thumbs up to the Government.

Weather-wise we are blessed with a warm breeze from the Arabian Gulf. The winter months – cool but pleasant, with temperatures ranging from 10°C plus is definitely the best time to visit.

Hot, but bearable

As we move into spring, the temperature heats up, and humidity kicks in, but still it is bearable (20°C plus). However, come June we have the fierce heat and humidity which lasts through the following months, a time when most residents choose to take a long summer break elsewhere.

Most sports can be found here – from jet skiing, windsurfing, skiing, sailing (the latter at private marinas such as Abu Dhabi International Marine Club), golf, of which we presently have three courses, all of a high standard and in beautifully landscaped grounds.

When you have finished your round at the golf and equestrian centre, you can slip up to the racecourse and admire the Arab stallions as the international jockeys prepare for a race.

If that hasn't enticed you, the desert activities might: Take a guide into the desert with jeeps and 4x4s and experience dune bashing (like roller-coasting and just as scary) or drive through wadis (dried up river beds). If you're not that adventurous you can just sit under the stars, with Arabic food, listen to the music and watch the belly dancing.

Hospitality here is the best in the world and you will be assured that a warm 'marhaba' awaits on these Arabian shores.

modestly – no shoulders or knees showing – but enforcement is fairly lax. Women can drive and there is much less segregation in public life of men and women.

While public drunkenness is frowned upon, alcohol is widely available in hotels and restaurantsl.

Abu Dhabi

The capital of the UAE and the largest of the emirates, this gleaming city was a small fishing and pearling village just 40 years ago.

Today it is one of the richest, safest tourist destinations in the world with many attractions ranging from Bronze Age archaeological sites to large zoological parks and museums.

The riches of the city can be seen in the towering skyscrapers, modern shopping malls and luxury hotels. Although less lively than Dubai, here you can shop till you drop in air-conditioned plazas, stroll in tree-lined avenues and landscaped parks and gardens and play golf on green fairways that were once deserts.

Abu Dhabi's corniche, a park-lined boulevard skirting the city and one of the picturesque sights in Abu Dhabi, is where tourists and local residents can stroll, cycle or rollerblade alongside the seashore. Many of the attractions of are located in Al Ain, an oasis that is home to the UAE's largest museum and the Al Ain Zoo.

Off the coast directly across from the Corniche and a 10-minute boat ride is the man-made Lulu Island, a commercial and residential area of over 1,000 acres. Opened in 2007, it offers leisure and recreational activities and stunning coastal panoramas.

Lulu Island has marinas, water parks, botanical gardens, scores of restaurants and cafés, amusement parks and horse and camel riding centres. South of Lulu Island are white palm-fringed sandy beaches.

The downside

Along with the rapid increase in population and property prices comes increased traffic congestion and pollution throughout the UAE.

The cost of living in Dubai has gone up so much that many choose to live in neighbouring Sharjah. Public transportation is not yet practical so you have to plan on having at least one car for yourself and another car for your spouse. Sharjah, however, is no longer a cheap option and the traffic is so bad that the '20 minute' commute can take up to two hours.

Censorship in the emirates is widely practised – not only the self-imposed censorship of local publications but also of imported overseas newspapers and magazines. It's not unusual to find photographs or text blacked out in your favourite magazine.

There is also heavy government censorship of videos, DVDs, CDs and books. The Internet is also censored with blocks on many websites

Driving habits are atrocious and Dubai has one of the highest road death tolls in the world. Westerners may find the roads chaotic, but most quickly adapt. Penalties for driving offences are stiff and there is zero tolerance for drinking and driving.

Is it safe?

Very. The UAE has an extremely low crime rate but this is a region where there is always a risk of terrorist activity and caution is advised at all times.

How much tax will I pay?

There is no income tax, investment income tax, wealth tax, capital gains tax, inheritance and gift tax, property tax, stamp duty, transfer tax or VAT. Some emirates charge tax on certain luxury products.

Is UAE property a good investment?
In the wake of the global economic meltdown property values have tumbled and – unless you are brave or foolish – this is a definite wait-and-see market. A large number of projects have been delayed or cancelled and, with around 22,500 residential units completed in Dubai in 2009, and even more coming on-stream, there is over-supply.

A recent report by financial services firm UBS predicts that property prices in Dubai could drop a further 30 per cent over the next 18 months as the sector absorbs new supply coming online coupled with damaged investor confidence in the market.

In both Dubai and Abu Dhabi you will generally be asked to pay a year's rent up-front, usually with post-dated cheques, and a refundable deposit.

There is a large choice among compounds of villas and apartments, most with facilities including swimming pools, gyms and tennis courts. Many of the recently opened luxury apartment complexes also have health clubs. Most properties are let unfurnished.

In Abu Dhabi the annual rent of a smaller, 1- and 2-bedroom, apartment is in the £20,000-40,000 range, upwards of £30,000 for a large unfurnished apartment and £30,000-50,000 for a 3-bedroom villa, depending on quality, location and facilities.

Utility costs are normally additional. There may be maintenance charges for communal facilities and municipality tax, usually 10 per cent of the rent. Rents cannot be increased during the contract period, normally one year, and there is a limit of five per cent per cent on the amount of any increase if you renew.

Where's best to live?
In Dubai popular residential areas include **Emirates Hills, The Springs** and **Dubai Marina** near Dubai Internet City and the Emirates Golf Club. The latter is composed of 70 towers with 20,000 apartments, hotels and offices. There are 700 berths for boat owners.

The Palm Islands – Jumeirah, Jebel Ali and **Deira** – with villas, residential towers and theme parks. Here the developer, Nakheel, has created the world's three largest man-made islands. Another giant developer, Emaar, has created a number of new residential projects inland from the Marina, including **The Greens, The Springs, The Meadows, The Lakes, Arabian Ranches**

and **Emirates Hills** with all the leisure facilities the names imply. Emaar has already handed over 13,000 homes.

Apart from being home to the world's tallest building, **The Burj Dubai** has hundreds of apartments and offices, the world's largest shopping mall, restaurants and recreation facilities.

The Corniche is a popular expat neighbourhood but is becoming expensive as it is central, by the sea, with larger apartments, four bedrooms, four bathrooms, maid's room, massive living areas and maybe a balcony. Underground parking is a plus.

There is an excellent and detailed overview of the Abu Dhabi's suburbs at www.timeoutabudhabi.com summarised here:

Al Bateen – a quiet, family area, with a marina is with its sports club, restaurant and nightclub.

Khalidiya A – A vibrant area where "the multinational population has grouped together into a thriving expat community … awash with takeaways" and easy access to the central hub of the city. More and more expats are living here, as property is considerably cheaper. It's a 45-minute drive in to the centre.

Khalifa City 'A' – quiet and peaceful but "the nightlife is non-existent."

Al Markaziyah – Essentially 'downtown', a high-rise city, with 17-storey apartment blocks rising above shops and stores with "umpteen miscellaneous streets packed with local flavour, and shopkeepers selling everything from holy water to carpets."

Mohammed Bin Zayed City –"… pretty desolate. If the UAE had tumbleweed, this is where it would blow across the streets. That said, it's coming on apace, and current inhabitants tend to think they got in early on something special."

Muroor – Built-up residential villas and townhouses, nice community feel and just a 10-minute drive from the city centre. "Offers the convenience of inner-city living without having to actually live there," says timeoutabudhabi.com

Al Raha Gardens – A "vibrant waterfront community" screams the brochure. Residents say it's developing into a reasonably quiet area" with easy access to the airport and the heart of the city.

Al Rowdah/Karama/Al Dhafra – Low-rise houses and compounds make up the majority of the area... ideal for those in search of quiet suburbs within the city limits, but … "there is little to do in the area".

Tourist Club Area – home to the usual array of tower block apartments and low-rise flats. "The location is a peach, with Abu Dhabi Mall just a short walk from most areas. It also boasts plenty of shops, a cinema and a host of restaurants and cafés," says at www.timeoutabudhabi.com which adds: "The traffic is also a nightmare".

The TimeOutabudhabi website also looks in detail at new developments where non-nationals are permitted to buy on 99-year leases.

UAE CONTACT DIRECTORY

Embassies/Government
UK Embassy, Abu Dhabi
www.britishembassy.gov.uk/uae
UAE Embassy, London
www.uaeembassyuk.net/
Ministry of Information and Culture in the UAE with news, events and general informationwww.uaeinteract.com
Department of Naturalisation and Residency Dubai www.dubaifaqs.com/dnrd.php

Travel & Health Advice
Foreign Office travel advice
www.fco.gov.uk/travel
www.nhs.uk/Healthcareabroad
www.masta.org

About the UAE
www.emirates.org
http://albawaba.com/en/countries/UAE
www.grapeshisha.com
www.dcb.ae
ww.abudhabi.ms
www.eyeofdubai.com
www.hello-dubai.co
Arab Net: www.arab.net
http://aethoughts.blogspot.com
www.arab.de/arabinfo/uae.htm
www.cia.gov/library/publications/the-world-factbook/geos/ae.html

General & Expat
www.expatfocus.com
www.dubai-livethedream.com
www.justlanded.com/english/Dubai
www.costoflivingdubai.net
www.dubaifaqs.com
www.expatforum.com
http://abudhabiliving.blogspot.com
www.thatsdubai.com
www.mymoveabudhabi.com
www.expatwoman.com/Dubai
www.expatgossip.com/
http://dubailime.com/

Media
Gulf News   www.gulfnews.com
www.arabianbusiness.com
www.timeoutdubai.com
AME Info   www.ameinfo.com
Online version of the daily newspaper
www.dubaiforums.com
www.arabianbusiness.com
www.khaleejtimes.ae

Property
Better Homeswww.bhomes.com
LLJ Propertywww.lljproperty.com
Damacwww.damacproperties.com
Al-Futtaim Real Estate
www.afrealestate.com
Asteco's
http://web.asteco.com/eng/default.asp
Landmark Propertieswww.landmark-dubai.com
Future View Real Estate
www.futureviewproperty.com
www.homesdubai.com
The Specialistswww.dubaiuae.com
Oryx Real Estatewww.oryxrealestate.com
ZTEC Propertieswww.aztecproperties.ae
Silver Lake Propertywww.silverlakeuae.com
Union Properties   www.up.ae

Travel & Tourism
www.uaeinteract.com
www.visitabudhabi.ae
www.dubai-information-site.com
www.dubaitourism.ae

Getting There
Emirates: www.emirates.com
Air Arabia: www.airarabia.com
Gulf Air: www.gulfairco.com
British Airways: www.britishairways.com
Cathay Pacific: www.cathaypacific.com
KLM: www.klm.com
Qatar Airways: www.qatarairways.com

Getting Around
Air
The main UAE hub is Dubai airport and Abu Dhabi has the next best international connections. Air Arabia has set up a hub at Sharjah airport.
Etihad Airways: www.etihadairways.com
Emirates: www.emirates.com
Serves the UAE's six international airports at Abu Dhabi, Al Ain, Dubai, Sharjah, Ra's al-Khaimah and Fujairah.
Train
There are no rail services.
Bus
Comfortable and frequent intercity bus services serve all major destinations.
Taxis
Plentiful and inexpensive.
Driving
The UAE has a network of first-class roads connecting all parts of Dubai and surrounding areas and a multi-lane highway to Abu Dhabi. However, while the roads are fine, those arriving from Western countries may find them chaotic and the driving is suicidal. The UAE has the third-highest death rate from traffic accidents in the world (behind Saudi and Oman) and it is necessary to drive defensively. The UAE is home to approximately 180 different nationalities, all of who bring with them the worst habits from their own country.
All of the leading car-hire companies are represented.
A driving license from your home country normally allows you to acquire a local driving license. Otherwise you need an International Driving Permit.
Zero tolerance exists for drinking and driving and even a rude hand gesture can land you in court.
Driving is on the right.

This is India with a Portuguese flavour

Why Goa?

The 65 miles of gorgeous Goan coastline were 'discovered' by the hippies of the 1960s. Attracted by superb golden beaches, the dropouts flocked to this idyllic winter paradise where fish, rice and alcohol were cheap, and a palm-thatched hut could be rented for peanuts.

Following the hippy pioneers, developers built resort hotels that catered for much wealthier visitors. Finally, charter flights arrived, to establish Goa as an international gateway into the Indian sub-continent. Holidaymakers who can afford £500-1,000 for a two-week holiday can be on a Goan beach tomorrow in a non-stop overnight flight.

Located 400km south of Mumbai, long stretches of golden beach are backed by a lush green countryside.

Goa has three seasons: summer, monsoon and winter. The best tourist months are November to March, bone dry and comfortably warm. April until mid-June becomes extremely hot, then the monsoon takes over until mid-October, with over two metres of rainfall.

Goa is about the size of Cornwall with a population of 1.2 million, 60 per cent Hindu and 37 per cent Catholic. The national sport is football – unlike the rest of cricket-mad India.

Panaji is the main shopping centre, but traditional markets at Margao and Mapusa are more fun.

In Mapusa the daily market activity peaks on Friday into a big tourist attraction. It's a good place to buy local crafts and souvenirs, as well as gold and silver jewellery, spices, ready-made garments, nuts and liquors and enjoy the hustle and bustle.

Occupied by the Portuguese in 1510, Goa became the capital of all Portuguese territories in India. The 16th and 17th Centuries were the age of 'Golden Goa', the greatest trading centre of the Far East, handling luxury products of China, Persia and India: silks, spices and carpets.

For 100 years the Portuguese kept their trading monopoly until the Dutch and then the English gained a hold in other areas of India. Bypassed for the next few centuries, Goa slumbered in a backwater until Portugal's colonial rule ended in 1961.

Goa's airport still has a vintage Portuguese appearance. Standing half an hour for immigration rituals, visitors begin to get the message that the pace of life is rather more sedate than elsewhere.

In contrast to the great tourist cities and teeming populations elsewhere in India, the largest town and capital of Goa is Panaji with 60,000 people. Most of the remaining 1.2 million inhabitants live in villages. Their houses are built of red stone or brick with several rooms and a veranda dripping with flowers. It

ABOUT THE CONTRIBUTOR: This section was put together with the help of **Hugh Taylor**, an award-winning travel writer, broadcaster and photographer. Hugh edits the travel and holidays section of www.laterlife.com, a web site founded 10 years ago by Tony Clack who says its aim is "to help everyone enjoy and make the most of retirement".

could be southern Portugal, planted among the coconut groves.

Whichever beach resort you choose, rural India is only a short walk away. A drive through the tranquil countryside is beautiful everywhere.

All along the coast is a lush belt of coconut groves, with spacious bungalows in the shade. Rice paddies are planted with green vegetables and beans after the grain is harvested. Bullock carts take produce to market while cattle wander in leisured style across the road, heedless of scooters, which steer around them.

The inland hills are a breathtaking feature of Goa. Winding country roads pass terraced fields and a myriad of fruit trees. A major cash income comes from cashews, which yield their nut harvest in April. Cashew fruit also keeps people happy with a local firewater called fenny, distilled from the fermented juice and pulp, and selling for under a pound a bottle. Toddy is tapped from coconut trees, to yield a similar source of alcohol with the delicate flavour of meths.

Local plants and trees produce black pepper, coriander, saffron, cloves, cinnamon, cumin and tamarind. Tropical fruits and stubby little bananas are plentiful as are the local pineapples.

The best eating in Goa is seafood, cooked in many styles. Along the beaches shack restaurants serve lobster, tiger prawns, squid, oysters, mussels, crabs, shark, mullet, pomfret, grouper and mackerel sold at less than one-third of the cost in hotels and more formal restaurants.

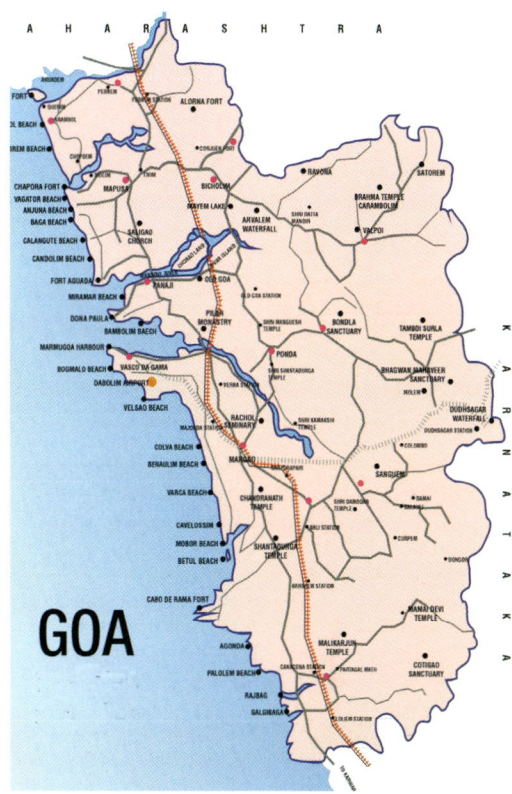

There's no such thing as a crowded beach. The sands are powder-fine, often several hundred yards deep from the shoreline to the palm trees. Colva Beach is the second longest in India.

Very little is left of the hippy scene of 30 years ago, though a few veterans base themselves at Anjuna Beach where an ultra-simple room costs only a few pounds. A weekly craft market is held there, but hippy vendors are greatly outnumbered by Kashmiris and Tibetans.

All the beach resorts are low profile. By local rules, new buildings are set well back from the shoreline, and nothing is taller than a palm tree. Architectural styles must conform to local patterns with sloping roofs and red tiles.

Nobody goes to Goa for the nightlife, except for an occasional rave, which causes local indignation for the 'noise pollution'. Otherwise, a folk-dance performance at the principal hotels is about the wildest it gets.

Goan music and dancing combine a rich cultural mixture of Hindu and Portuguese. The most-favoured musical instrument is the guitar. Many dances and costumes have come from Portugal and popular tunes are sung in Portuguese or in the Goan mother tongue.

FACTFILE

Capital: Panaji

Commercial capital: Margao

Population: 13.4m

Area: 3702sq.km.

Language: English (official) and Goa's own language, Konkani, predominate. Marathi, Hindi and Portuguese are also spoken.

Climate: Tropical with a June to September monsoon with heavy rainfall (300-400cms). Outside this period the humidity is relatively low with an average daily temperature of 27°C (85°F). The coolest months are November to February.

Time difference: GMT +5.30

Entry requirements: Visa required

Retirement/residence visa: A visa for a six-month stay is relatively easy to obtain. [See: The Rules for Getting in]

Electricity: 230 V 50 Hz

Money: Rupees. ATMs are increasingly available. Credit cards are accepted in most major tourist centres but not in smaller hotels and restaurants. Travellers cheques are widely accepted as are US and UK banknotes.

Public holidays 2010

Jan 26	Republic Day	Sept 16	Ganesh Chaturthi (2)
March 16	Gudi Padva	Oct 2	Gandhi's birthday
April 2	Good Friday	Oct 17	Vijaya Dashami
April 14	Birth of Dr Ambedkar	Nov 5	Diwali
May 1	May Day	Nov 17	Id-Ul-Zuha
Aug 15	Independence Day	Dec 3	St Françis Xavier Day
Sept 10	Id ul Fitr	Dec 19	Liberation Day
Sept 11	Ganesh Chaturthi	Dec 25	Christmas Day

Opening hours

Banks: 10am-2/3pm (Mon-Fri)   Offices: 10am-6pm (Mon-Fri)
Shops: 9am-1pm, 3.30/4-8pm Street markets are open all hours.

Water: Stick to bottled or boiled water. Avoid ice in drinks.

Tipping: 10 per cent at restaurants; a few coins if service is already charged. Taxi drivers appreciate but do not usually expect a tip unless hired by the day. Staff at beach shacks are happy with some loose change.

Medical/Healthcare

Health facilities are good in the cities and chemists and hospitals are available in larger towns and villages. Most doctors speak English. Hospitals vary in standard but in the event of illness it's best to seek treatment in one of the many private clinics.

There is no legal requirement for entry to Goa, but meningitis, typhoid and hepatitis A jabs are recommended.

Pets: Pets must be micro-chipped and dogs must have a rabies certificate.

At Christmas there are serenades of guitars, mandolins and violins, with the singing of popular carols and the Portuguese love songs called fados. This is India, Portuguese flavour!

How much tax will I pay?

Tax evasion is widespread in India. According to some reports, there are only 30 million taxpayers in a country of over one billion people.

All residents are taxable for all their income, including income from outside India. Non-residents are taxable only for the income received in India. 'Not Ordinarily' residents are taxable in relation to income received in India. Senior citizens (over 65) get some special tax breaks. For example, the Basic Exemption Limit is increased to about $4,875 for senior citizens and a number of deductions are available that may be excluded from your income for tax purposes.

Is Goan property a good investment?

An estimated 3,000 Britons own property in Goa and around 5,000 units of property have been sold to foreign buyers since the introduction of the Foreign Exchange Management Act which stipulates that non-residents cannot buy real estate until they have been resident in Goa for 182 days in any one given financial year.

According to The Goa Properties Company [www.goa-properties.co.uk], property price growth has been 25 per cent a year for the last two years with an estimate of capital growth over the next five years of 15-25 per cent.

The company warns that property purchase in India is complex – so maybe better to rent.

If you buy property with foreign currency the amount you eventually take out is not allowed to exceed the amount paid for the property.

The sale of properties held for three years or more attracts a tax rate of 22.6 per cent. Short Term Capital Gains for properties held for less than three

---

THE RULES FOR GETTING IN

A visa for a six-month stay is relatively easy to obtain. However, stringent laws and numerous legal processes and formalities apply to foreigners buying property and foreigners entering India on a visa valid for more than 180 days or six months have to register with the Foreigners Registration Officer in the local jurisdiction within 14 days of arrival.

Foreigners must stay in Goa for at least 180 days on any type of visa prior to buying property. Before the purchase can take place the foreigner must leave India and apply for

permission from the Reserve Bank of India for a five-year residential visa which, from all accounts, is notoriously difficult to obtain and even more difficult to renew.

It is only after this permission that the process of purchasing a property can begin. All transactions have to be ratified and channelled through the RBI.

There is considerable political agitation against too many foreigners settling down in Goa as well as official steps to deprive foreign owners who used loopholes to obtain property.

The bottom line is that renting seems to be much the better option.

The other side of paradise

With its sleepy towns and perfect beaches it may seem an idyllic retirement location, but Goa – and India – gets some pretty bad press when it comes to the treatment of foreign residents.

Polluted water, beaches spoilt by piles of plastic rubbish, high road fatalities and crime, corrupt police, soaring crime figures. It doesn't stop there. Goan men will hassle your wife or girlfriend and, if you buy a property, you run a serious risk of losing it with no compensation.

This is the other side of life in Goa.

About 400 – mainly British – victims have fallen foul of supposed violations of FEMA, the Foreign Exchange Management Act, which came into force in 2000.

Dozens of British owners have already had their properties seized. Hundreds of others 'own' properties which they can live in – but cannot sell or formally register as their own.

Vikram Varma, a local solicitor who is risking his livelihood by representing about 20 of those whose property is at risk, says the Goan government is applying a new interpretation to an old law which effectively excludes foreigners from buying property.

The UK's Foreign Office has raised its concerns with the Indian authorities. "We have made clear to the state authorities in Goa that we would be extremely concerned if there were to be any question of property acquired legally by British nationals being expropriated through the retrospective application of any new legislation," says the FO.

"We have also raised this as a matter of concern with the Indian government in Delhi. We will continue to pursue this issue with the Indian authorities both in Goa and in Delhi.

"… we have revised the travel advice on the Foreign & Commonwealth Office website to make clear to British nationals the potential problems they could face."

The Reserve Bank of India has a FAQ on the foreign ownership of property at: www.rbi.org.in

This is the interpretation of rules according to the Goa Chamber of Commerce:

"A foreign national of non-Indian origin, resident outside India cannot purchase any immovable property in India but he/she may take residential accommodation on lease provided the period of lease does not exceed five years.

"A foreign national who is 'a person resident in India' can purchase immovable property in India but the person concerned would have to obtain the approvals, and fulfil the requirements if any, prescribed by other authorities, such as the concerned State Government, etc."

Under FEMA, "a person resident in India" is defined as a person residing in India for more than 182 days during the course of the preceding financial year (April-March).

Expat websites are full of disaster stories relating to property purchase in Goa.

Now we can't sell

Here's one from the website of The Huddersfield Examiner (www.examiner.co.uk): "We 'purchased' our property in 2006 and opened a business on the advice of a local advocate, with the intention of letting the property while we were not there, mainly during the rainy season, until we retired.

"We were quite prepared to pay tax and anything else required. To date the utilities are still not in our name and we do not have the deeds either as the builder is refusing to part with them.

"Even if we did have the deeds we could not register them because the registry is closed to foreigners and has been for some time. We can't 'sell' the properties we have paid for because we don't have the deeds.

"We have not been permitted to obtain a business visa, another so-called 'requirement of ownership', therefore we cannot open a business bank account. Without a business bank account we cannot have the accounts audited and pay taxes.

"Do you see how it goes? I have many friends on other developments in the same situation and some who have sold up and retired, only to find they do not own the property and may not get a lease or visa extended.

"In most other countries we would at least get compensation but that is not on offer either. The Goan government are hell bent in driving out 'Johnny foreigner' both buyer and holidaymaker alike, whilst still taking our money through UK sharks, oops sorry representatives. "

The Indian 'e-paper', DNA Read The World [www.dnaindia.com] dishes out some uncomfortable truths in a report. So too does a BBC report by Karen Pirie: 'Threat to expat homes in Goa'.

Both are recommended reading for anyone considering buying in Goa.

The DNA item starts: "They helped build 'Brand Goa', fell in love with it and decided to stay on forever. But it seems that they have worn out their welcome.

"Foreigners who helped make Goa what it is today are no longer welcome to stay. 'Spend your Euros and return home', is the clear message that is being sent out to the expatriates – especially the predominant British population.

"This message also extends to the French, German and Italian populace, among others, who have made Goa their home ..."

Karen Pirie's report, "Trouble in Paradise", broadcast last year on the BBC Radio programme Face The Facts [http://news.bbc.co.uk/1/hi/business/7507766.stm], highlighted the cases of Britons who have lost their properties.

It quotes Anupam Kishore, joint secretary of the Goan government's finance department, as saying that property buyers should have taken proper advice from the right authorities and that those found in breach of the law could have their properties confiscated.

GOA CONTACT DIRECTORY

Embassies/government
High Commission of India in London
www.hcilondon.net
Email: 114343.3045@compuserve.com,
British High Commission in India
http://ukinindia.fco.gov.uk/en
Email: postmaster.NEDEL@fco.gov.uk
Goan State Government
http://goagovt.nic.in

Travel & Health Advice
Foreign Office travel advice
www.fco.gov.uk/travel
www.nhs.uk/Healthcareabroad
www.masta.org

About Goa
www.indiamike.com
www.liveindia.com/goa
www.goablog.org

General & Expat
www.expatfocus.com
www.britishexpat.com
www.transitionsabroad.com

English Language Media
There's no shortage of English-language publications in Goa. All of India's English language national newspapers are available and Goa has its own newspapers: the Navhind Times, The Herald, originally published in Portuguese, and the Gomantak Times. In addition there's Goa Today, the Goa Messenger and the Goan Observer. Satellite channels are received through cable in most parts of Goa. TV channels available include MTV, ESPN, Fox, BBC, CNN, AXN, Star World, Star News, and several others.

EstateAgents
www.lifestylehomesgoa.com
www.goa-properties.co.uk
www.goapropertysales.co.uk
www.acronindia.com
www.axiomestates.com
www.goaholidayhomes.com
http://www.homesgoa.com
www.realtygoa.com
www.hotpropertiesgoa.com

Travel & Tourism
www.goa-tourism.com
www.goainfosearch.com
http://goatourism.gov.in
southgoa.nic.in/tourism.htm
www.goahub.com
www.goatravelinfo.com
www.tourismofgoa.com
www.goa.world-guides.com
www.virtualtourist.com/travel/Asia/India/Goa

Getting There
Flights to Goa are mainly charters
Thomson Holidays: www.thomson.co.uk
British Airways: www.justtheflight.co.uk
Avro: www.avro.co.uk
http://holidays.monarch.co.uk/destinations/goa
www.tvl4u.com/Goa

Getting Around
Train: The South Central Railway runs from Mormugao due east through Margao to Karnataka. The Konkan Railway starts from Mumbai and goes to to Mangalore (in Karnataka) through Goa from north to south.
Bus: Plentiful, cheap and crowded.
Taxis: All kinds: motorcycles, autorickshaws and regular taxis. Agree the fare in advance.
Boat: There is hydrofoil service from Mumbai to Goa (8 hours) and there are ferry services (foot and car) across the several rivers that run into the sea near Panjim.
Driving: Driving yourself (by motorboke, jeep or car) is the best and most adventurous way to get around. The police are likely to tap you for 'baksheesh' if you don't have the right paperwork. Supposedly you are permitted to drive for a week using your own country licence.
Driving is on the left.

We lived here
By Martin and Sue Smith

Goodbye Goa; it's a shame it had to end this way. My wife and I started a small business in Goa about 12 years ago. In those days, everyone we spoke to (Western and Goan) could not believe that we wanted to leave the comfort of the UK and start afresh in Goa. At the time, we thought we would be here for the rest of our lives. Sadly we are leaving for the last time at the end of May. [This article was written in 2008].

During our time here we have seen many changes, some good, some bad, some hard to understand. Our business was a small hotel with a restaurant and bar. We had some money invested abroad so being overly prosperous was not essential for us to survive. As a result, both our accommodation and restaurant prices were modest.

We paid our taxes in full (much to the dismay of our accountant), kept all of our obligatory paperwork up-to-date and tried to get on with the local residents. Over time, we became prosperous owing to repeat customers, both in dining and accommodation. As result, we feel that we have had a positive impact on both local and state prosperity.

But over the last 18 months, the 'Foreigner go home' campaign waged in the media and by local politicians has grown from something that was mildly amusing in the early days to a monster of epic proportions.

This season, all the powers-that-be seem to have been hell-bent on destroying the Goa tourist industry.

The late issuing of shack licences, the ban on music even when there are no complaints from people living nearby, the difficulty in obtaining visas, the forcible removal of sun-beds while tourists are laying on them, the dumping of refuse in the streets and on the beaches, a higher number of deaths in the sea than ever before, accusing all tourists of being drug users/dealers or, amazingly, importers, calling regular visitors to Goa the "dregs of the tourism industry", taxi drivers trying to increase their fares to a minimum of Rs700, even for a trip of a kilometre or less...

The Foreigners Registration Office has even asked my wife and I why we do not charge more for our rooms: "Is it because you get money from drugs?" This, even after 10 years of being a law-abiding resident of Goa!

We are getting out before next season turns into a major disaster. Fortunately, we have been able to sell the whole business to a couple from Delhi, unlike some foreigners who put their business property in their personal names and now cannot sell.

We would like to say farewell to all the friends and acquaintances we have in India and Goa in particular.

To all those who want the foreigners out, we hope you are happy with the reduction in tourism next season. Unfortunately, it will not be the politicians who go hungry but all the businessmen and women who depend on the tourist industry.

It should be interesting to see Delhi's reaction to this situation when foreign exchange inflow drops drastically in the next 12 months. Whatever it is, it will be too little too late.

This article first appeared in The Herald, Goa popular English language daily [http://oheraldo.in]

Rich culture in the land of 583 languages and 17,000 islands

Why Indonesia?

Indonesians are warm and welcoming, in spite of the prevailing poverty and corruption in what is the fourth most populous nation in the world. The cost of living is low as long as you're willing to live like a local. Most working expats live in Jakarta where there is a wide range of leisure and recreation activities available, including clubs, bars, restaurants and sports facilities.

Many expatriate homes have their own swimming pool and housing complexes and apartments often have a communal pool and other facilities such as a fitness centre and tennis courts.

There are also family-oriented sports clubs such as the International Sports Club of Indonesia, a long established club located beside a small lake on the southwest outskirts of the city with soccer, rugby, cricket, hockey, basketball, tennis, squash, badminton and sailing on the lake. There are over 40 golf courses in and around Jakarta and, with very reasonable charges, making Jakarta a golfer's paradise.

Many shopping centres and malls in Jakarta have food courts, restaurants and indoor recreation facilities and multiplex cinemas showing the latest movies not too long after their international release.

There are excellent art galleries and museums, regular cultural performances including ballet, theatre, symphony orchestras and choirs, chamber music and the traditional Indonesian puppetry.

English is spoken in large cities and tourist destinations but less so in rural areas.

The last decade has seen enormous growth of hypermarkets and supermarkets throughout the larger cities and shoppers have a wide choice of pleasant, hygienic surroundings in which to shop as well as a myriad of choices from vegetable sellers, traditional markets to mom and pop grocery stores.

Geography

Indonesia is the largest archipelago in the world, straddling the equator between the Indian Ocean and the Pacific. Its tropical climate is mostly equatorial, with temperatures between 16-35°C. It is vast, with over 17,000 islands providing 108,000km of beaches and more than 400 volcanoes, of which 130 are active.

About 6,000 islands are inhabited, with Java accounting for more than half the nation's population.

Regions include the island of New Guinea, Sumatra, Borneo, Java, Celebes, the historic Spice Islands, Papua, Komodo and West Timor. Much of this territory is a paradise for the adventurer and more sedate holidaymaker alike, including jungles, mighty rivers,

ABOUT THE WRITER: Danielle Surkatty, an American web developer and writer who has lived in Indonesia for over 17 years, is chief editor and director of content for **www.expat.or.id**, an award-winning website for foreigners planning to live, or already living, in Indonesia. The 12+ year old website was a natural follow-up for Danielle and colleague Gene Sugandy's book publishing efforts for the American Women's Association in Jakarta.

tropical rainforests, mountains and swamps.

There are some 300 ethnic groups in Indonesia, a result of both the country's unique geography and history. The majority are of Malay extraction with the remainder of Chinese, Indian and Arabian ancestry.

Is it safe?

Yes. Most expats who have lived in the country for any amount of time agree that the crime rates in Jakarta are substantially lower than most Western cities. But just as in any major city anywhere in the world, there are areas of Jakarta that may not be safe at night.

There are various scams, ranging from people seeking access to homes claiming they have been sent to "check for termites" and crime targeted at drivers or people in taxis. Incidents of petty thefts and pick-pocketing on the streets are not unusual. But overall, crime is rare.

How much tax will I pay?

Even on a retirement visa you will be liable for Indonesian personal income tax, at a rate of 35 per cent for incomes over about £13,000 a year.

Credit is given for income tax paid overseas, subject to double taxation agreements in place. You may also receive credit for tax taken on interest income for local bank accounts and time deposits and other interest earning methods that are taxed.

Since income from overseas investment can be

FACTFILE

Capital: Jakarta   **Population:** 245,000,000

Area: 1,919,440sq km

Language: Bahasa Indonesia (official) and numerous regional languages.

Climate: Hot and humid all year, especially along coastal areas. Inland highlands are cooler. Heavy monsoon rains Dec-March, often causing damage and making local travel difficult. Dry season April-Oct.

Time difference: GMT +7

Entry requirements: A visa is not required for stays of up to 30 days.

Retirement/Residence Visa: Relatively easy although the financial requirement, at £11,700 a year, is high compared to other countries' conditions. Applicants need to be 55 or older. [See: The rules for getting in]

Electricity: 220V/50Hz

Money: Rupiah. Credit/debit cards and travellers cheques are accepted in main towns and resort areas.

Public holidays 2010

Jan 1	New Year's Day	July 9	Prophet's Ascension
Feb 14/15	Chinese New Year	Aug 17	Independence Day
Feb 26	Prophet's birth	Sept 10	End of Ramadan
March 16	Hindu New Year	Nov 17	Feast of Sacrifice
Apr 2	Good Friday	Dec 7	Islamic New Year
May 13	Ascension Day	Dec 25	Christmas Day
May 28	Buddha's Birthday	Dec 26	Boxing Day

Opening hours

Offices: 8/9am-4/5pm

Banks: 8am-3pm Mon-Fri

Shops: 9am-9pm daily (large stores)

Water: Drink bottled water or boil tap water

Tipping: 10 per cent to taxi drivers and in restaurants

Medical/Healthcare: By Western standards, healthcare in Indonesia is inexpensive. There are several hospitals and clinics in Jakarta offering international standard facilities although many expatriates still prefer to go to Singapore for operations and major medical problems.

In rural areas the standard of care given by most medical facilities is not up to international standards and not all drugs are available. Service providers do not routinely accept a guarantee of payment from an overseas insurance or medical assistance company so it is necessary to have sufficient funds in cash to meet the expenses. Few medical service providers take credit cards.

Travellers and foreign residents should carry or have rapid access to sufficient funds to pay the emergency and initial medical costs. There are no reciprocal medical arrangements between the government of Indonesia and other countries.

Recommended immunisations: hepatitis A, hepatitis B, typhoid, rabies (depending on location), adult polio booster, Japanese B encephalitis in certain areas, malaria prophylaxis.

Pets: You need a letter of permission from Indonesia's Ministry of Agriculture: Up. Direktorat Jenderal Peternakan

Jl. Harsono RM No. 3-Ragunan-Jakarta 12550 Indonesia.

The pet's name, breed, age, colour must be given. Documents must include a health certificate from a veterinarian and a rabies vaccination certificate.

THE RULES FOR GETTING IN

To obtain a Temporary Stay Permit you must be at least 55 years old and produce evidence (pension company or bank) to show an income of at least US$1,500 a month.

This should include a 'statement letter' indicating your financial ability to rent accommodation costing at least US$500 a month in Jakarta or US$300 a month outside Jakarta.

Numerous other documents need to be produced including a statement of intent to employ an Indonesian maid and/or driver.

The Temporary Stay Permit, renewable annually, can be extended five times without having to leave the country. Each extension is valid for one year.

After five years you can apply for a permanent stay permit (KITAP)

More info: www.indonesianembassy.org.u

taxed, it is best to consult an accountant and financial consultant to determine how these new regulations will affect any current and future investment strategies.

Is Indonesian property a good investment?

Low interest rates and robust consumer spending has led to tremendous economic growth in Indonesia, with real estate leading the way. Residential units, commercial buildings and industrialised plants have all spread rapidly across the nation.

For many years Indonesia decreed that only citizens could own land in the country. In the late '90s this changed and foreigners can purchase apartments if the building has a 'strata' title status. This enables the foreigner to own the apartment or office space but not the land on which it stands.

PROPERTY

High floor, Jakarta

New condo in Jakarta Utara on the 18th floor with panoramic views. 2 bedroom, 1 bathroom, furnished with air-con. Underground parking for 1 car. Amenities include swimming pool with waterfall, function room, sauna and steam room, gym/fitness centre, table tennis, minimart.

Rent: Annual rent £4,000

More info: www.muamat.com
Email SanDjunTjin@gmail.com

Caddies at one of the over 40 golf courses in the Jakarta area

Foreigners can also own land indirectly if they enter an agreement with an Indonesian, by which the Indonesian is the 'legal owner' while the foreigner is the 'rightful owner' of the land. However, if the Indonesian 'owner' changes their mind, you will not have any legal title to the land. Clearly this route is inadvisable.

Strata title

Ownership of apartments is possible through strata title deeds. The law states that foreigners can purchase an apartment or condominium as long as it is not a part of a government-subsidised housing development.

However, foreigners can only hold land-use deeds, which creates difficulties and unclear ownership issues.

One way for foreigners to purchase property is to sign a Convertible Lease Agreement, but the title is still held in the name of the developer or property management firm. This lease agreement is for a definite period.

If you're considering buying a condominium through this type of agreement, investigate the property management company thoroughly and use a bona fide lawyer.

Where's best to live?

There is so little support for expats outside the major population centres – very few people speak English – so we tend not to see retirees far from those areas.

Above all other locations is Bali. Most people come for a visit and think it would be wonderful to stay forever. Other locations tend to be mountain towns – Bogor (near Jakarta), Bandung, Malang (near Surabaya), and pretty much all of Bali.

Most working expatriates live in or around Jakarta but some retirees also choose to live in or near the capital. Before deciding where to live it is important to get a feel for the city's many neighbourhoods. In Central Jakarta, the district of Menteng is one of the oldest and most prestigious neighbourhoods and the site of many diplomatic residences. Rents are high but some pavilions (apartment over a garage/small guest house) are available for reasonable rates.

Just west and east of Jl. Rasuna Said there are substantial planned housing developments favoured by expats. The neighbourhood is well planned with tree-lined streets and lots of space for parking.

Town house
House of 250sq m in Semarang Timur. 3 bedrooms, 3 bathrooms, garage for 2 cars. Price: £70,000
More info: indonesia.ljhooker.com

Large house near Kuta
Kuta, a south-coast fishing village with a white sand beach, is the main tourist area of Bali. The house is 10 minutes to the airport, 15 minutes to Kuta, Price: £90,000
More info: property.baliwww.com

I live here

Briton Rachel Lovelock, a freelance writer who has lived in Bali since 1998, is the author of over 1,000 magazine and newspaper articles on Bali and Indonesia.

Breaking away from the stressful city life and escaping to a sunny tropical island sounds like an idyllic fantasy. Most people acknowledge that it's just a fantasy and would never pursue the idea.

Many of Bali's visitors say they love the place but couldn't live here. Others, however, claim that they feel a strong affinity with the island: "As soon as I arrived, I just knew that I wanted to stay"…"I felt very strongly that I was meant to be here"…"Immediately I got off the plane, I felt as though I had come home".

If you're really considering the possibility of living here, you'll have probably already spoken to some, or many, of the Westerners who already do. You'll have probably heard some mixed reports; most expats will have had many similar experiences.

Just try it!

You will have heard some incredible, heart-warming, magical stories; you might have been told about the great business possibilities – or the numerous business initiatives that have failed. You'll have heard some scary stories and some horror stories. You'll never really know what living in Bali is like until you try it. A two or three month holiday or a series of one-month stays might help, but nothing can prepare you for the real thing!

The truth is that Bali is not entirely the paradise that people imagine; it's stressful – but in a different way from the West. Don't expect things to run smoothly. It is expensive – sure you can buy street food for as little as Rp 5,000 (40p); but visas, imported commodities, education, and medical attention are all expensive requirements.

Paradise is hot, wet, dangerous, exciting, challenging, scary and wonderful. You can fulfil your dreams here or you can drown in a treacherous sea.

If you make this momentous decision as part of a couple or a family, you can help and support each other, but if you don't share the same passion for the place it won't work. If you come here on your own, you will only have yourself to consider, initially, but during those difficult early days you'll have a lot of challenges to face alone.

If you've never lived in Asia before the first six months will be a culture shock. You won't think of it as culture shock, you might think you're coping well, but you'll wonder why your emotions are so intensified. Why do you feel so happy, joyful, tearful, angry, frustrated and scared?

Don't fight the system

If you're financially comfortable, you can make things easier by employing someone to help you deal with the complicated necessities of living here, but isolate yourself too much from the reality of everyday life in Bali and you might find that you're not learning the essential lessons. Moreover, you will be ill equipped to cope with some of the challenges you are presented with.

If you attempt to fight the system you will just stress yourself out; there's no point in getting angry with every taxi driver who says he hasn't got any change, or the supermarket check-out girl who gives you candies instead of coins.

The frustrations of living in Bali and attempting to conduct business here are enough to try the patience of a saint. Why is everything so complicated? Why isn't it possible to pay the bills by direct debit? Why does so much incoming post go astray? Why don't things work properly? Why is everybody always late? Why are there so many power-cuts? Why is the traffic so terrifying?

Make friends with the local people, learn the language, acknowledge the dangers, take care on the roads, accept the things you can't change, embrace the challenges, explore the island and the culture, and be open to the intense spiritual energy here. Bali is full of magic and wonder, if you truly want to be here you will find a way to make it work. There are a lot of lessons to be learned on the way, but if you have a passion for Bali, the joy and rewards of living here are immeasurable.

Good luck!

In South Jakarta, Kebayoran Baru is an attractive neighbourhood with large homes and wide, tree-lined streets. The Permata Hijau/Simprug communities consist of spacious avenues boasting a good infrastructure and green surroundings. Nearby shopping is available in Permata Hijau and Plaza Senayan.

Pondok Indah's stately mansions line the major thoroughfare of Jl. Metro Pondok Indah, just south of the Pondok Indah Mall. Just south of Pondok Indah is Lebak Bulus with very nice housing complexes with good access via the outer ring road to all parts of Jakarta.

Kemang boasts beautiful homes tucked down alleys and narrow streets. In East Jakarta, Kelapa Gading is another well-planned community favoured by many expats.

Hillside villa
New condo in Jakarta Utara on the 18th floor with panoramic views. 2 bedroom ,1 bathroom, furnished with air-con. Underground parking for 1 car. Amenities include swimming pool with waterfall, function room, sauna and steam room, gym/fitness centre, table tennis, minimart.
Rent: Annual rent £4,000
More info: www.balihomevilla.com info@balihomevilla.com

Bali property
Hidden away in a quiet residential area, this villa development, with view to rice fields, is only minutes to popular tourist area and beach. Price: £96,000
More info: www.propertiindonesiaku.com

INDONESIA CONTACT DIRECTORY

Embassies/Government
Indonesia Embassy in London
www.indonesianembassy.org.uk/
British Embassy in Jakarta
http://ukinindonesia.fco.gov.uk/en

Travel & Health Advice
Foreign Office travel advice
www.fco.gov.uk/travel
www.smartraveller.gov.au/zw-cgi/view/advice/Indonesia
www.nhs.uk/Healthcareabroad
www.masta.org

About Indonesia
www.expat.or.id
www.worldbank.org/id
http://livinginindonesia.info
www.guardian.co.uk/world/indonesia
www.baliguide.com
www.geographia.com/indonesia
www.indonesiamatters.com
news.bbc.co.uk/1/hi/world/asia-pacific/country_profiles

General & Expat
www.expat.or.id
www.expat.com.my
www.expatfocus.com
www.britishexpat.com

English Language Media
The Jakarta Post
www.thejakartapost.com
www.pbs.org/newshour/bb/asia/indonesia
Inside Indonesia
www.insideindonesia.org
TV: http://tritv.net/
Limited English language radio and TV but satellite/cable available from various suppliers.

Property
www.colliers.com/Markets/Indonesia
www.ciptanuansa.com
www.the-ascott.com
www.plazaresidences.co.id
http://bpibali.com
www.binamega.com
www.kemangclubvillas.com
www.procon.co.id
www.arkadiaapartment.com
www.AstonMarinaAncol.com
www.summerville-apartment.com
http://balirealestate.net
www.exotiqrealestate.com
www.balilandexplorer.com

Travel & Tourism
www.my-indonesia.info
www.tourismindonesia.com
http://iguide.travel/Indonesia
www.lonelyplanet.com/indonesia
www.indonesia.com

Getting There
British Airways www.british-airways.com
Emirates: Emirates.com/uk
KLM: KLM.com
Singapore Airlines: www.singaporeair.com
Lufthansa: www.lufthansa.com
Far Eastern carriers offering connecting flights through their hub cities include Singapore Airlines, Royal Brunei, Thai Airways, Malaysia Airlines, and Cathay Pacific.
After a number of fatal crashes in Indonesia, two years ago the EU imposed a ban on the Indonesian airline Garuda. It operates a service via other carriers including Malaysia Airlines.
Garuda Indonesia: www.garuda-indonesia.com

Getting Around
Air: Indonesia has a good internal air system linking most of the larger towns to Jakarta. Domestic operators include:
Garuda Indonesia: www.garuda-indonesia.com
Batavia Air: www.batavia-air.co.id
Lion Air: www.lionair.co.id
Mandala Air: www.mandalaair.com
AirAsia: www.airasia.com
Merpati Nusantara Airlines: www.merpati.co.id

Train: The train operator (www.infoka.kereta-api.com) offers three classes of travel with first-class only on limited routes. There is some air-conditioned accommodation.
In Sumatra, trains connect Belawan, Medan and Tanjong Balai/Rantu Prapet (2/3 trains daily) in the north, and Palembang and Panjang (3 trains daily) in the south. An extensive rail network runs throughout Java, the best being a modern, air-conditioned service between Jakarta and Surabaya twice a day.
There is a regular service between Jakarta and Bandung and twice-daily trains on to Surabaya.

Bus: Jakarta has a comprehensive network of buses, some air-conditioned. All buses have set routes and set fares. Travel within other towns and cities is best served by a variety of taxi services (see below).
Long distance bus travel is usually hot, crowded and uncomfortable but cheap and fairly efficient. Express buses are more comfortable. Better still are luxury buses with reclining seats that need to be booked in advance.

Ferry: The National Indonesia Shipping Company operates a large network of ferries and ships connecting Indonesia's thousands of islands with fast boats on a small number of routes. Main ports: Padang Bai and Benoa (Bali), Tanjung Priok (Jakarta), Belawan (Medan) and Sekupang (Batam).

Taxis: Taxis, motorbike taxis, bicycle rickshaws (the latter are banned in Jakarta) are all widely available in cities and towns. The bajaj, Indonesia's version of Thailand's tuk-tuk, is the most popular form of getting around. The bajaj seats two passengers comfortably and up to five passengers uncomfortably. The drivers are not allowed to go out of their area or onto many main roads, so routes may be a bit circuitous.
Ojek are motorcycle taxis that congregate at T-junctions and smaller roads not serviced by bus routes. Fare determination on all these forms of transport is by bargaining.

Driving: There are relatively good roads in Java, Bali and Sumatra; significantly worse on most other islands. During the rainy season floods are common and many roads in Sumatra, Kalimantan and Sulawesi are flooded. The standard of driving is poor. It's a cheap and safer option to hire a driver. An International Driving Permit is required.
Driving is on the left.

Playboy pensioners find heaven in a tropical paradise

Why Malaysia?

As long as you are comfortable in the heat, the lifestyle of expatriate retirees in Malaysia is an enviable one. With temperatures ranging from 32°C during the day to 22°C at night, Malaysia is a tropical paradise of friendly people, wonderful food, beautiful beaches, cool hill stations, historic towns, a dynamic capital and the world's oldest rainforests.

The ticket to this lush retirement paradise is Malaysia's MM2H scheme which allows retirees with sufficient, but relatively modest funds to take up residence.

Several thousand Britons have settled here under MM2H. Most are completely retired while a few have received special dispensation to work part-time in specialised IT fields and others work offshore as consultants.

Malaysia's low cost of living allows retirees to enjoy what the country offers, on pensions that go much further than in the UK, an advantage that permits – at around £100 a month – the employment of either a full time or part time maid, giving these playboy pensioners far more time to enjoy the multiple benefits of living in this tropical paradise.

In today's Malaysia, most towns have large shopping malls stocked with produce from all over the world so expatriate retirees are not denied a plentiful supply of those favourite items which, in earlier decades, often led to suitcases being filled with one or two year's supply of 'vital' necessities such as Marmite and Paxo Stuffing.

Another worry of the expatriate family of earlier years was the absence of top quality healthcare. This has now changed to such an extent that foreigners are visiting Malaysia as health tourists.

While the expatriate rubber planters of earlier years suffered feelings of isolation, as news and contact with home was often seriously delayed, the internet allows residents in Malaysia – eight hours ahead of GMT – to trade their stocks and shares and to read the UK morning papers before they drop on doormats back home, and via email and SKYPE, correspondence and contact with friends and family is instantaneous.

Malaysia also offers English language newspapers, English radio and satellite TV with over 30 English-language channels.

Seasoned expatriates – mostly from other parts of Southeast Asia or the Middle East – moving to Malaysia for the first time, tend to continue their gregarious lifestyle without any culture shock and immediately fit into an existing group, often meeting old friends from earlier years.

New expatriates sometimes suffer from culture shock and can take time to settle in. These feelings are

ABOUT THE WRITER: Sandhurst graduate **Bob Holland**, 62, retired to Penang with his Hong Kong Chinese wife Elena in 1997 after serving for 20 years as a police officer in Hong Kong, the final 12 years in the then colony's bomb squad, which he commanded. He offers a mentoring service for those interested in retiring to Malaysia [see page 160].

Ready to retire? Why not make Malaysia your second home? The country offers an enviable modern infrastructure, benefitting from impressive transport links and medical facilities. With all the amenities and facilities you find at home, Westerners will easily feel at ease. As one of the most politically stable countries in the world, Malaysia also offers safety and security to its population. Aside from the infrastructure, the country also boasts a wide and varied culture; Malays make up around 57% of the population with Chinese, Indians and other ethnic groups making up the rest and, despite the diversity, English remains widely spoken throughout the country. This melting pot of nationalities ensures Malaysia is a very welcoming country to expatriates. With all of these reasons to move to Malaysia and a tropical climate with warm weather year round to boot, what are you waiting for?

To help ease the process of relocation, the Malaysian government has introduced a programme to assist foreign nationals wanting to retire in Malaysia, Malaysia My Second Home (MM2H). The programme entitles participants to a social visit pass and multiple-entry visa from the Malaysian Immigration Department which is valid for ten years, and is renewable thereafter. Both documents give MM2H participants the freedom to come and go whenever they wish. Other incentives include the ability to purchase a house and a car as well as tax exemption on pensions and foreign income brought into the country. If you would like to find out more please visit the website at www.mm2h.gov.my.

We look forward to welcoming you to Malaysia – whether it be for a day or a lifetime. Our smiles are genuine; our hearts glad to see you. Make 2010 your year to visit Malaysia! We know you'll be glad you did.

Ministry Of Tourism, Malaysia

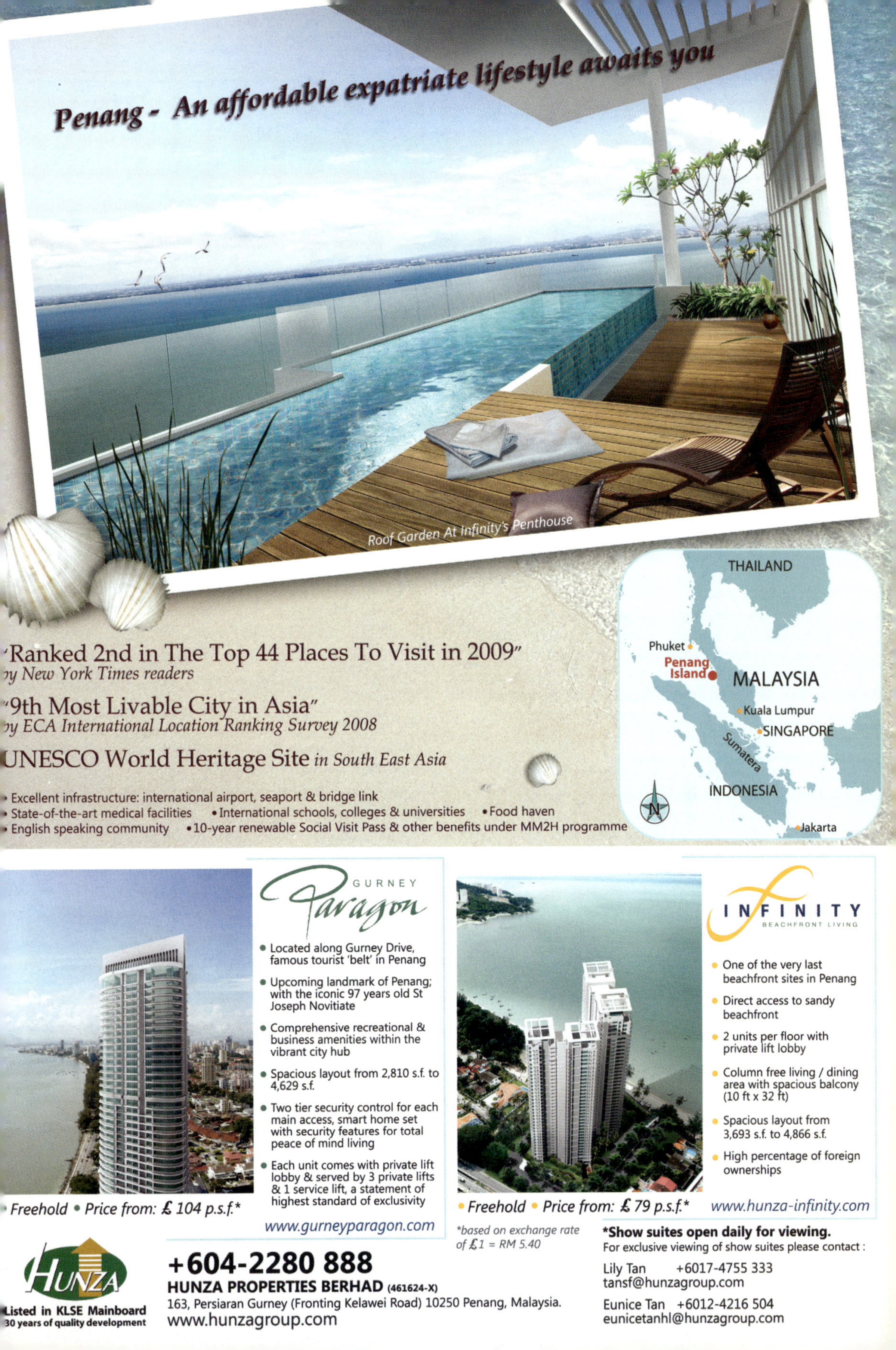

Penang - An affordable expatriate lifestyle awaits you
Roof Garden At Infinity's Penthouse
THAILAND
Phuket
Penang Island
MALAYSIA
Kuala Lumpur
SINGAPORE
Sumatera
INDONESIA
Jakarta
N
"Ranked 2nd in The Top 44 Places To Visit in 2009"
by New York Times readers
"9th Most Livable City in Asia"
by ECA International Location Ranking Survey 2008
UNESCO World Heritage Site in South East Asia
• Excellent infrastructure: international airport, seaport & bridge link
• State-of-the-art medical facilities • International schools, colleges & universities • Food haven
• English speaking community • 10-year renewable Social Visit Pass & other benefits under MM2H programme
GURNEY Paragon
• Located along Gurney Drive, famous tourist 'belt' in Penang
• Upcoming landmark of Penang; with the iconic 97 years old St Joseph Novitiate
• Comprehensive recreational & business amenities within the vibrant city hub
• Spacious layout from 2,810 s.f. to 4,629 s.f.
• Two tier security control for each main access, smart home set with security features for total peace of mind living
• Each unit comes with private lift lobby & served by 3 private lifts & 1 service lift, a statement of highest standard of exclusivity
• Freehold • Price from: £ 104 p.s.f.*
www.gurneyparagon.com
INFINITY
BEACHFRONT LIVING
• One of the very last beachfront sites in Penang
• Direct access to sandy beachfront
• 2 units per floor with private lift lobby
• Column free living / dining area with spacious balcony (10 ft x 32 ft)
• Spacious layout from 3,693 s.f. to 4,866 s.f.
• High percentage of foreign ownerships
• Freehold • Price from: £ 79 p.s.f.*
www.hunza-infinity.com
*based on exchange rate of £1 = RM 5.40
*Show suites open daily for viewing.
For exclusive viewing of show suites please contact :
Lily Tan +6017-4755 333
tansf@hunzagroup.com
Eunice Tan +6012-4216 504
eunicetanhl@hunzagroup.com
HUNZA
Listed in KLSE Mainboard
30 years of quality development
+604-2280 888
HUNZA PROPERTIES BERHAD (461624-X)
163, Persiaran Gurney (Fronting Kelawei Road) 10250 Penang, Malaysia.
www.hunzagroup.com

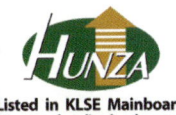

FACTFILE

Capital: Kuala Lumpur   **Population:** 4,821,286
Area: 329,758sq km
Language: Bahasa Malaysia is the national language although English is widely spoken. Since ethnic Chinese represent almost a quarter of the Malaysian population, Mandarin, Cantonese and Hokkien are also widely spoken.
Climate: Seven degrees north of the Equator, Malaysia has a warm and humid climate throughout the year with cooler temperatures in the hill stations. Rainfall averages 220cm a year.
Time difference: GMT +8
Entry requirements: No visa is required for a stay not exceeding three months for most EU nationals including Britons.
Retirement/Residence Visa: All applicants must have a pension income of £2,000 a month. In addition, those under 50 require assets of £100,000 and those aged 50 and above must have about £70,000 in assets.
See: The Rules for Getting In
Electricity: UK standard 220-240 volts with 3-prong plug. No adaptors are necessary.
Money: The ringitt. Best exchange rates are from street money changers. ATMs are available in most cities. Credit cards are widely accepted in hotels and shops.

Public holidays 2010

Jan 1	New Year's Day	Aug 31	National Day
Feb 1	Fed Territory Day	Sept 10	End of Ramadan
Feb 14	Chinese New Year	Nov 5	Diwali
Feb 26	Prophet Birth	Nov 16/17	Feast of the Sacrifice
April 28	Birth of Buddha	Dec 7	Islamic New Year
May 1	Labour Day	Dec 25	Christmas Day
June 5	King's Birthday		

Opening hours
Banks: 9.30am-4pm, Mon-Fri, 9.30am-11.30am, Sat
Offices: 9am-6pm, Mon-Fri
Shops: 9am-5pm but much later in market areas and Chinatown.
Water: Tap water is safe to drink but bottled water is recommended.
Tipping: A 10 per cent service charge is usually added onto restaurant bills as well as a five per cent government tax. If a service charge is not included 10-15 per cent per cent is the norm.
Medical/Healthcare: Health services in Malaysia are both world class and economical. No immunisations are required but it is recommended that injections for typhoid, polio, tetanus, and hepatitis A are up to date. Malaria tablets may be advisable for deep jungle treks in Borneo. General standards of cleanliness and hygiene are high.
Pets: Dogs and cats from the UK are not subjected to quarantine provided they are healthy and all the documents are in order. These include an import licence from the Director General of Veterinary Services, Malaysia. Certain dog breeds are banned.
More info: Malaysian Veterinary Department
http://agrolink.moa.my/jph

quickly banished when they join 'the club' – finding there kindred spirits and a relaxed, friendly lifestyle. Both the two large expatriate centres of the capital, Kuala Lumpur (KL), and Penang, have a wide variety of clubs, and even smaller towns have one or two.

Most clubs here have reciprocal arrangements with other clubs around the world and so club members in the UK who are thinking of retiring here should check their club's affiliations. There is also an extremely active International Woman's Association.

In Penang there are several groupings of expatriates based on where they previously lived or worked. I belong to two lunch groups made up of ex-Hong Kong expats. Each group meets once a month in different

PROPERTY

Golden Palm Tree Water Villa, Sepang (Right)
Luxurious 2 and 3 bed water villas set on stilts above the sea include amenities such as swimming pool, gym, spa and library. Price: From £102,400
More info: Experience International
Tel: +44 (0)207 321 5858
www.experience-international.com

THE RULES FOR GETTING IN

With recent refinements to its MM2H (Malaysia My Second Home) programme, Malaysia now has the most liberal of criteria for its retirement visa. About 1,500 Britons (out of a total of around 15,000 MM2H settlers) have set up home in Malaysia under the programme.

MM2H, launched by the government to attract foreigners to live and invest in Malaysia in 2002, replaced the 'Silver Hair Program' started in 1996. Applicants must be financially capable of supporting themselves but, as part of the liberalisation, can now bring in unmarried children aged under 21 and are also permitted to work part-time (no more than 20 hours a week in approved sectors). Other incentives include the purchase or import of a car free of import duty, excise duty and sales tax and tax exemption on pension funds remitted into Malaysia.

Applicants aged under 50 must provide proof of liquid assets worth a minimum of £100,000 and a pension income of £2,000 a month.

Those aged 50 and above must have the same monthly income and about £70,000 in liquid assets.

New applicants who have purchased properties worth at least £195,000 qualify to place a lower fixed deposit amount.

After a period of one year, new settlers can withdraw up to £30,000 for approved expenses relating to house purchase, education for children in Malaysia and medical purposes.

Other requirements for candidates and dependents include a medical report and medical insurance coverage (exemptions may be given for participants who face difficulty in obtaining medical insurance due to their age or medical condition).

More info: www.mm2h.gov.my/

venues. Neither is exclusively expatriate, as both include several locals who have also worked in Hong Kong.

An advantage of this sort of grouping is that it not only acts as a broad-based social group but also allows for the transfer of relevant information and forms a safety net of friends who can often help and give advice in times of trouble as well as welcoming and mentoring new arrivals.

Most retirees here plan to stay indefinitely, just returning to the UK on 'home leave' once in a while to see friends and family. Some retain a home in the UK or elsewhere. If the average length of visit over the previous four years is less than 90 days per annum, with no visit exceeding 182 days, then the expatriate can maintain the

Sea-Tropics Village, Sepang

2 and 3 bedroom villas designed with a blend of Maldivian Polynesian architecture. Landscaped gardens and views of the Malaysian coast.
Price: From £111,531
More info
Experience International
Tel: +44 (0)207 321 5858
www.experience-international.com

Nexus Residence, Karambunai

Adjacent to the 5-star Nexus Resort Hotel in Sabah on the island of Borneo, 25 minutes from the Kota Kinabalu International Airport. Buyers here will have use of hotel facilities including spa and golf club membership. All villas are fully furnished and have a balcony or courtyard, jacuzzi, steam-bath or lap pool.
Price: 1 bed from £125,000, 2 bed from £160,000.
More info: www.propertyfrontiers.com Tel: 01865 202700

We live here

Former Hong Kong policeman Bob Holland and his wife Elena decided to retire to Penang

Flying into Penang from the north-east, we look down on the scattering of rugged islands that stud the jade-green sea. My wife, Elena, says that the scene reminds her of the opening page of a fairy tale. The geological freaks below us – technically limestone karsts – are like giant teeth stuck in a bowl of green jelly.

The extraordinary scenery, perhaps the most beautiful in Malaysia, was chosen as a location for the James Bond film The Man with the Golden Gun for good reason: it lends itself to flights of fancy.

As the plane makes its final approach we see white sand beaches and brilliant blue sea by the landing strip. They whet our thirsts for hot sunshine, fresh breezes and the taste of coconut juice. We've been away too long.

It's about 30 miles from the airport in the north to our house on a lush, 75-acre compound called Fisherman Way with its coconut palms and exotic plants and flowers.

The 30 cottages in Fisherman Way are owned or rented mostly by expats of various nationalities, and several (including ourselves) are former residents of Hong Kong. A retired teacher from Dulwich College owns the place next door. A few people work – there's a diving instructor and a couple of hotel executives – but we're mostly retirees.

We are fortunate to rent one of the few beachfront properties in the compound. The rent we pay is slightly less than we get for our flat in Brighton. Eventually we might sell the flat and buy here. The stunning location of the three-bed bungalow offers views across the sea towards distant islands. We have a million-dollar view for a thousand bucks a month.

We spend more time than we should sitting on our terrace marvelling at the endlessly changing colours and textures of the sea and sky and watching the passing boats – sailboats, luxury yachts and fishing boats.

Secluded but conveniently located, Fisherman Way is half a mile from local markets (good for a huge variety of tropical fruit and vegetables, as well as delicious and inexpensive takeaway dinners). There's a 7-Eleven, two cash machines, a pharmacy, a bakery, laundries, hairdressing salons, a couple of internet cafes, a photo-processing shop, a post office and a police station.

There are also a growing number of good restaurants nearby and several lively bars popular with expats. My local, the Islander, boasts tables for pool and table tennis. There's Victoria Bitter from Australia. My drinking mates include yachties, a handful of hacks, hotel employees and retired airline pilots.

Another social meeting place is a beach just 10 minutes away where I go for a swim a couple of times a week and to watch the sunset. I drive down a narrow road thick with lush green vegetation and palm trees on both sides. Here there is a wide range of restaurants, shops and traditional houses.

Apart from the absence of Marmite and good bookshops there are, of course, some real drawbacks to this tropical lifestyle. For anyone who can't survive without horseracing, hunting, live music, art films and exhibitions, draught English beer, crisp winter weather and log fires, this is not the place to be.

tax advantages of being a Malaysian tax resident.

A few retirees spend up to six months a year in the UK but they have to be very careful about how they arrange their tax affairs.

Many people wonder how retirees can fill their day, especially if the normal work of running a home has been reduced by having domestic help. The answer is that in Malaysia it feels as though there are never enough hours in the day for all the activities available.

Due to the constant warm weather, sport forms an important part of the social scene here for the entire year. Most clubs have sporting facilities with squash for younger retirees and racquetball, badminton and tennis for the not so young.

Sailing and golf are also popular and both KL and Penang are endowed with many reasonably priced golf courses. Scuba diving is excellent on both the east coast and on the islands off East Malaysia, home of several of the world's top dive sites.

Hill walking is popular as are morning exercises in the parks where tai chi and other routines are followed in the cool of the early morning.

Travel within Malaysia is another popular pastime since the country offers a great variety of attractions from hill stations to coastal resorts. For travel further afield, budget airlines give easy access to the rest of Asia and Australia.

Singapore and Thailand are both an easy drive away and it is simple to take one's car to either. For more adventurous drivers there is a 4 x 4 off road club that arranges expeditions throughout the region as well as jungle expeditions within Malaysia. There is also a thriving vintage car club which arranges rallies in both Malaysia and Singapore.

Even the simple daily routines here take on an added charm, from breakfasting on fresh tropical fruits on a balcony overlooking the sea, to dawn walks up Penang Hill or through the Botanical Gardens.

After breakfast, a round of golf followed by lunch at the club with friends, or a sail, then – after an afternoon nap – it's down to the Eastern and Oriental (E&O) Hotel for drinks on the seafront terrace, overlooking the Channel between Penang and mainland Malaysia, followed by an international buffet dinner in Sarkies.

Cost of living

To give you an idea of the cost of living here, the golf, with lunch, then drinks and dinner will set you back about £30 per person.

Utility charges in Malaysia are lower than in the UK and with temperatures never dropping below 22°C at night, there is no need for central heating, but air-conditioning is normally considered essential, at least for the bedrooms. Even if air-conditioning is

Luxury living on the Penang waterfront
Hunza Properties' Infinity project on the Penang waterfront offers luxury living on Tanjung Bungah, one of the island's most exclusive neighbourhoods, with views across the Straits of Malacca.
These huge condos (320-400sq m) have balconies to match, spacious private lobbies, master bedrooms with their own balconies and walk-in dressing areas.
Close to Georgetown, the ferry terminal and Penang Bridge, Infinity has a range of resort-style amenities and is within easy reach of 5 golf clubs and 7 private medical centres.
Facilities include swimming and wading pools, pool deck, jacuzzi, barbeque pits, children's playground and playroom, cabanas, gymnasium, steam bath and business centre.
Price: A typical apartment costs £325,000.
More info: Hunza Properties (North) Sdn Bhd
www.hunza-infinity.com

used regularly the total electricity bill should not exceed £625 a year and many families only use half that amount.

There is no piped natural gas but a large cylinder of LP gas is less than £3 including delivery, usually within four hours but often within 30 minutes. Telephone land lines cost £4.20 a month and local calls are the equivalent of three cents a minute. There is an option for unlimited local calls within Malaysia for £12 per month, and SKYPE is easy to set up for free international calls. The cheapest international calls are via call cards and an £5 card enables just under four hours of call time to the UK.

Water and sewage combined charges average less than £3.24 a month. Local domestic help is readily available for £2.25 an hour and hiring a maid for just a few hours a day to do the washing, ironing and cleaning is sufficient for most retirees.

A full-time live-in Indonesian maid can be hired for about £100 per month compared to £180 for an English-speaking maid from the Philippines. Most larger properties contain separate maid's quarters.

Public transport is much cheaper than in the UK. Cars, however, are significantly more expensive, although foreigners coming in on the MM2H scheme are entitled to buy or import one car, tax and duty free, making it considerably cheaper than in the UK.

Running costs – petrol, road tax and insurance – is also much cheaper.

Imported cigarettes cost less than £1.60 a packet – local brands even less. While premium imported spirits are about £14 a bottle, locally bottled gin, vodka, rum, brandy and whisky are available for less than £5 per bottle. Much of one's supply can be obtained totally duty free at Langkawi Island, a short ferry ride from Penang.

Wine is available from £3.60 per bottle upwards – a long way upwards, alas – as the percentage duty increases with the value of the wine.

Eating out is one of the great joys of Malaysia and costs range from less than a £1 per person for a casual – but delicious – snack at one of the hawker stalls, to £5 for a delightful dinner in a small restaurant or club.

A sumptuous buffet – wine and beer included – in a premier hotel such as the Eastern and Oriental on the harbour front in Penang, will set you back less than £13 per person. Food of every variety and flavour is available in Penang, a melting pot of culinary styles.

Shopping for food and general household products is generally cheaper than in the UK and there are several international chains such as Tesco's, Carrefour, Welcome and Cold Storage.

Local markets are good value, especially for vegetables

which are offered for sale only hours after being picked. There is an abundant choice of fresh fruit, both local and imported and in the wet markets the fish and poultry are killed and prepared to order. The price of most basic ingredients is controlled by the government, so inflation remains low.

Join the club

An additional expense in Malaysia is club membership. The majority of expatriates who retire to Malaysia join at least one club as membership forms a pleasant part of the social fabric of retired life.

Malaysia is a land blessed with many golf clubs and around both KL and Penang there are at least half a dozen. Green fees are in the $10-26 range, inclusive of buggy. Caddies cost £3 upwards.

In general terms, whatever the disposable income, a retiree to Malaysia can guarantee a lifestyle far better than that available in the UK with the same funds. Money in Malaysia really does go a lot further.

Is it safe?

Violent crime involving expatriates is uncommon and Malaysia is considered a safe country in which to live. However, street crime – pick-pocketing, bag slashing, and bag snatching – has risen steadily in recent years and there have been increasing reports of muggings and violent robberies especially in Kuala Lumpur and Johor Bahru.

How much tax will I pay?

Malaysia has a tax regime that is most welcoming to foreigners. The general overriding principle is that neither a long term visitor nor a retiree coming here under the MM2H scheme would normally pay Malaysian income tax.

However, after living in Malaysia for 182 days in the first tax year and for 90 days in each subsequent

We live here

After a working life as a globe-trotting expatriate, Neil Hamilton and his wife Jorva, both 65, have retired to Penang.

Malaysia has four huge pluses as a retirement destination. It's summer every day of the year, life moves at a pace that savours existence, not working to death, it does not cost an arm and a leg to feed or clothe oneself and, with only one language, English, one can happily exist and interact sufficiently well with a broad enough section of society to be absorbed into the community as a whole.

After a working life spent mostly in Asia and Australasia, some in the USA, and a horrifying six months commuting to work on the London underground, when retirement arrived, warmth, the sea, a beach and peace and quiet were high on our list of priorities.

We knew Penang from holiday trips with our family when based in Hong Kong in the '70s. We paid a visit, liked it, bought a place, and have lived here for six years.

Penang's population is ethnic Chinese, Indian, and Malay. Outdoor eating is common. The variety of food is such that many local people never eat at home. And I mean never! My breakfast when I go out, which is most of the time, varies from Western – sausage, egg, hash browns, and toast – to Chinese – chicken porridge/Cha Siu Bao – to Malay – noodles or roti – accompanied by a large cup of local coffee made with condensed milk. It costs less than five ringgit ($1.50).

The advantage of heat, other than the obvious plus of not feeling cold, is the effect it has on one's wardrobe which shrinks to almost nothing. My daily garb is sandals, shorts and a polo shirt. Going out in the evening: long pants and a batik shirt.

Since retiring here I have never worn a tie, only once a jacket and no more than 20 times socks inside my shoes. You don't spend much money on clothes.

I sail, play tennis and squash, the occasional game of darts. I walk in the jungle with binoculars stalking a staggering variety of birds and butterflies. If I played golf I would have a large selection of inexpensive courses to choose from, but I don't.

There isn't time. We have a gym and swimming pool as part of our apartment complex, This is usual. Security is good, petrol is cheap, books are plentiful, TV is English, with all UK sports.

Only one piece of advice: when you drive here forget that your car has a horn. Just relax. It's what the locals do. That, and smile a lot.

tax year, a retiree becomes and remains resident for tax purposes, which is actually beneficial in several ways.

Everyone should be tax resident somewhere and where better than a tax friendly country, outside of the EU and its onerous regulations? Put simply, for a foreigner no tax is charged on any income derived outside of Malaysia. Interest on any number of fixed deposits of RM100,000 (£20,000) or less, held in a Malaysian registered bank is also tax free.

There is no inheritance or capital gains tax on any assets including property. There is no VAT, but there is a Government Sales Tax (GST) of five per cent on hotel and restaurant bills and on professional bills.

Possessions imported for personal use when retiring to Malaysia are exempt from tax.

Once the retiree has been out of the UK for the prescribed period, then offshore investments become free of UK tax and are not taxed in Malaysia. Several retirees have calculated that their living expenses within Malaysia are far less than their tax savings making it, in effect, cost free to live here.

Is Malaysia property a good investment?

Property prices are well below those in the UK, with, for example, a three-bedroomed apartment in a condominium in Penang available from just £44.000. In addition to the savings in buying a property, the 'assessment' (equivalent of council tax) is much less.

Land on Penang Island is limited and even more so within the popular areas of George Town, so landed property is noticeably more expensive to buy but due to the rating system, cheaper to rent, than are condominium apartments of equal size.

In the long term, homes with gardens have tended to appreciate, while the value of apartments tends to fluctuate according to supply and demand.

Under the MM2H scheme there is no requirement to purchase property and to do so foreigners require both Federal and State permission.

Property prices

Three bedroomed condos of 130sq m in "Mount Pleasure" on a hill overlooking the north coast of Penang are currently on sale for £43,000-48,000. (Rent for one of these apartments, furnished to a holiday let standard, would be about £255 per month.)

These apartments need some renovation, an easy and cheap matter in Malaysia. Local hand-made and fitted kitchen cabinets are cheaper than MFI flat packs! A good condominium apartment of about 260sq m with four bedrooms and four bathrooms and can be purchased for about £160,000. (Rental £870-1,000 pm)

There is, however, a large premium on beachside properties. A five bedroom, five bathroom condominium of 540sq m with beachside frontage would cost up to £255,000. (Rental £1,100-1,350 per month.)

Within the range £45,000-160,000 there is a very large selection of properties currently available but above this price level the range is quite restricted. UK buyers should be aware that properties bought from a developer will often have no light fittings and no fitted furniture unless included in the purchase agreement.

Where's best to live?

It is generally accepted that immigrants are happiest if they settle in an area that offers the safety net of an expatriate community and this narrows down the choice considerably.

There are two large expatriate communities in Malaysia, one in KL and the other in Penang, the latter composed mainly of retirees under the MM2H scheme.

Within Penang there are areas which are more suitable than others for an expatriate to live and probably the most popular location to either buy or rent is the north coastal belt between the beach at Batu Ferringhi and the Eastern and Oriental hotel in George Town.

However, the most common advice to retirees, given by those who have lived here for several years, is not to buy at first, but to rent.

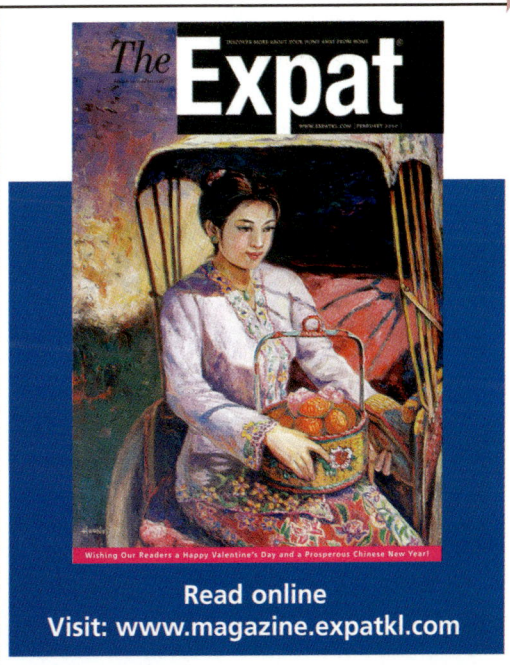

MALAYSIA CONTACT DIRECTORY

Embassies/Government
UK High Commission in Kuala Lumpur
Embassies/Government
http://ukinmalaysia.fco.gov.uk
Malaysian High Commission in London
http://www.kln.gov.my/perwakilan/london

Travel & Health Advice
Foreign Office travel advice
www.fco.gov.uk/travel
www.nhs.uk/Healthcareabroad
www.masta.org

About Malaysia
www.mycen.com.my
www.topsitesasia.co
www.searchenginecolossus.com/Malaysia.htm
www.geographia.com/malaysia

General & Expat
www.expat.com.my
www.expatfocus.com
www.britishexpat.com
www.expat.com.my/xorgs.htm
www.expatkl.com is a useful expat site
covering all aspects of life in Malaysia
www.mm2h.com offers info and insights into
the Malaysia, My Second Home programme

English Language Media
Malaysia has four English dailies:
New Straits Times (daily) /www.nst.com.my
The Star (daily)http://thestar.com.my
Business Times (daily) www.btimes.com.my
The Malay Mail (daily) www.mmail.com.my
Radio-Television Malaysia (RTM) operates
radio and TV with a limited English-language
service. www.rtm.gov.my
Malaysiakini (www.malaysiakini.com) is an
English-language online news service
The Expat (monthly) free lifestyle magazine
for expats and MM2Hers living in Malaysia

Property
Hunza Group
http://www.hunzagroup.com
www.malaysiapropertyblog.com
Fullhouse
http://www.fullhouse.com.my
Malaysia Real Estate and Property Agent
http://www.metrohomes.com
Kuala Lumpur Real Estate Search
http://www.kualalumpurproperty.com
Pen Properties
www.penangproperties.com
VPC Alliance (Malaysia) Sdn. Bhd.
http://www.vpc.com.my
Homesearch
http://www.homesearch.com.my
Carey Real Estate
www.careypenang.com
Malaysia Property Directories
http://www.hartanah.net
Malaysia real estate
http://www.realestate2u.com.my
Malaysia Real Estate Network
http://www.realestate.net.my/
www.propnet.com.my

Travel & Tourism
www.tourismmalaysia.gov.my
www.virtualmalaysia.co
www.backpackingmalaysia.com
http://travelmalaysiaguide.com
www.all-malaysia-hotels.com
www.tourismpenang.gov.my

Getting There
Malaysian Airlines
www.malaysiaairlines.com
British Airways
www.british-airways.com
Emirates: Emirates.com/uk
Lufthansa: www.lufthansa.com
KLM: KLM.com

Getting Around
Malaysia has an excellent public transport
system and good roads. The main
transportation hub is from Kuala Lumpur.
Air: Internal air travel is by Air Asia, Berjaya
Air and Transmile Air.
Train: Slower than by bus but comfortable
and cheap. The Eastern and Oriental
Express travels the 2,000km route from
Bangkok to Singapore via Kuala Lumpur. An
intracity light rail transit (LRT) system
connects major parts of Kuala Lumpur and
there is a monorail connecting Kuala
Lumpur's major attractions.
Bus: Several companies operate air-
conditioned coach services throughout
Malaysia covering all destinations.
Boat: Peninsular Malaysia and East Malaysia
are easily accessible via sea ports.
Driving: A UK driving licence can be used
in Malaysia for three months. Driving is on
the left.

Tax-free

Affordable properties

Great food

Low cost of living

Apartments with great views

Living

Slow pace of life

Excellent healthcare

Fantastic weather

Everyone speaks English!

Welcome to Penang, Malaysia

Visit Penang or have a look at our website and find out why many foreigners choose to retire here.

Stay in Penang with the long term Malaysia My Second Home (MM2H) visa.

Have no worries ! We will help you from visa application, settling down to telling you which plumber is reliable and good.

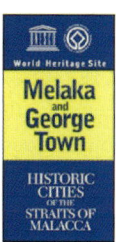

World Heritage Site

Melaka and George Town

HISTORIC CITIES OF THE STRAITS OF MALACCA

Penang

MALAYSIA

has it all !

Pasuguan ng Pilipinas *Embassy of the Philippines*

London

Dear Readers

Greetings from the Philippine Embassy in London.
I wish to take this opportunity to tell you about my beautiful country – the Philippines, Asia's best kept secret and a paradise for retirees and expatriates alike.

The Philippines, with its more than 7,100 islands made famous among tourists for its splendid sunsets, white-sand beaches, world's finest scuba diving sites and weird land formations, is possibly the most welcoming country in Asia.

Our country is a melting pot of cultures where everyone is readily greeted with a genuine smile and warm hospitality. With our cheerful disposition and accommodating culture, coupled with the widespread use of the English language, the Philippines is increasingly becoming a retirement haven for a growing number of foreign nationals.

The Philippines caters to practically everyone's tastes.

For those approaching retirement age and those retiring either full-time or part-time, the Philippines makes a top destination for various reasons:

First, our temperate climate affords one to relax under the warm balm of the sun all-year-round with a fringe benefit of escaping the high cost of winter bills.

Second, the Philippines boasts world-class package developments and professional healthcare comparable to those in the developed economies sans the exorbitant price. There now exists a number of retirement villages across the country where top-class medical facilities are on everyone's doorstep and medical professionals just a phone call away.

Apart from medical care the Philippines offers a life-changing approach to health and wellness with its wide selection of health spas and massage and beauty clinics that provide a variety of special treatments catering to every individual's needs.

Third, one can live in the Philippines in a luxurious lifestyle at an affordable cost where every pound or dollar stretches a mile.

For the more adventurous types the country's mountain terrains, rolling hills and mysterious rock formations provide a good outlet for expending one's energy. For those with more conservative tastes, strolling along white-sand beaches, bird and whale watching, golfing, fishing and spelunking offer an intoxicating alternative.

Romantic types can find enjoyment walking along our lush and verdant landscapes that stretch along our archipelago's coastlines. For the culturally inclined, our historic cities, ancient forts, museums housing our centuries-old heritage and colourful year-round festivals provide a respite from the hectic city lifestyle and a treat to the discriminating cultural palate.

There are still a hundred more reasons why the Philippines is the place to live. But I leave it to you to discover for yourselves why you would choose the Philippines for your retirement destination. You do not have to live on a shoestring budget existence when there is a paradise that awaits you in the Philippines.

Edgardo. B. Espiritu
Ambassador

Land of 7,107 islands ... and a few more when the tide goes out

Why the Philippines?

First the people. In spite of much poverty, Filipinos are charming, courteous and fun-loving. Most speak English. Throughout the islands, frequent fiestas are celebrated and foreigners are always made especially welcome.

Next there's the weather: The Philippines is tropical with hot, humid weather all year round, although a little cooler between November and February and rainy from July to October. Temperatures are in the range of 25-35°C.

The cost of living and leisure is one of the lowest in the world. Transportation, communication, housing and recreation, both in the countryside and in the cities, are very affordable as are medical services – so much so that the Philippines is a favoured destination for medical tourists.

No wonder then that about 2,500 foreigners a year take advantage of the Philippines' Special Resident Retiree's Visa (SRRV).

But there's more. The Philippines has long, white sand beaches, an immense variety of marine life and a tropical party lifestyle. With over 7,000 islands, and a coastline twice the length of that of the United States, the Philippines might one day become Asia's holiday capital.

It is also home to Boracay, whose 4km white beach has been hailed as the "finest beach in the world."

The famous jeepney is the most popular mode of transport. It's cheap, it's fun and you can get on and off practically anywhere you want.

The Philippines is a sanctuary to an amazing variety of flora and fauna that is found nowhere else in the world, such as the Philippine Eagle, the biggest eagle in the world.

It has the extraordinary Banaue Rice Terraces – a world heritage site and 'eighth wonder of the world' – carved from the high Cordilleras over 2,000 years ago.

Over two million tourists visit every year. It's a lot but is nothing like the numbers that flock to Thailand and Malaysia – countries where the tourism infrastructure is far more developed – but the numbers are growing.

These are just some of the attractions. But there is a downside: The Philippines is poor. As one American travel writer puts it: "It's a dirt poor country with many living in home-made shacks with no plumbing and crude wiring. We in the developed

FACTFILE

Capital: Manila

Population: 89 million

Area: 300,000sq. km

Language: Filipino. English is the business language and spoken widely. There are over 100 languages and dialects.

Climate: Tropical marine climate dominated by a rainy season and a dry season. The summer monsoon brings heavy rains to most of the archipelago May-Oct, whereas the winter monsoon brings cooler and drier air Dec-Feb.

Time difference: GMT +8

Entry requirements: No visas necessary for stays of 21 days but visitors must hold an onward/return ticket.

Retirement/residence visa: You need a bank deposit of $50,000-$75,000 (depending on age). [See: The rules for getting in]

Electricity: 220V/60Hz

Money Philippine peso. ATMs are available in cities but not so common in provincial areas. Credit/debit cards are accepted in major establishments throughout big cities. Travelers cheques and major foreign currency may be cashed in Manila and are accepted in most hotels, restaurants and shops. US$ notes are widely accepted. Cash is necessary when traveling in the provinces.

Public holidays 2010

Jan 1	New Year's Day	June 12	Independence Day
Feb 22	People's Power Day	June 24	Manila Day
April 2	Good Friday	Aug 31	Heroes' Day
April 4	Easter Sunday	Nov 1	All Saints' Day
Apr 9	Valour Day	Nov 30	Bonifacio Day
Apr 10	Good Friday	Dec 25	Christmas Day
May 1	Labour Day	Dec 30	Rizal Day
May 28	National Flag Day	Dec 31	New Year's Eve

Opening hours

Banks: 9am-3pm (Mon-Fri)

Offices: 8am-5pm (Mon-Fri), noon (Sat)

Shops: 9/10am-8/10pm (Mon-Sat)

Water: Boil drinking water or drink bottled. Avoid ice cubes.

Tipping: A service charge is added to bills but it is customary to leave small change.

Medical/Healthcare: Immunisation against typhoid, polio, hepatitis A and Japanese encephalitis is recommended, as well as precautions against malaria and dengue fever. Malaria is endemic in many provincial regions. Dengue fever has been on the rise in Manila and neighbouring provinces along with outbreaks of other mosquito-borne diseases. Medical facilities are adequate in major cities but limited in provincial regions. Hospitals in Metro Manila are well equipped and internationally accredited.

Pets: You must obtain an Import Permit from the Director of the Bureau of Animal Industry [www.bai.ph] and a health certificate issued by a licensed veterinarian dated within 30 days before the date of arrival certifying that the animal is free from, and has not been recently exposed to, any dangerous or communicable disease and that it has been given anti-rabies and other inoculations.

The certificate has to be authenticated by the Consulate.

countries are spoiled rotten by our standard of living.

"Most people have no idea what real poverty is until they visit a country like the Philippines. You see young kids selling bottled water at busy intersections and old women selling home-made candles on the sidewalks outside churches, earning money any way they can.

"Some woman are prostitutes simply because they have no other choice; college educated, but no jobs."

Poverty like this means the cost of living is low. You can live high on the hog for $1,500 a month. Some exist on a lot less. Many Filipinos live on less than US$1 a day.

THE RULES FOR GETTING IN

The Special Resident Retiree's Visa (SRRV) is a special resident, non-immigrant visa with multiple entry/indefinite stay privileges and comes with a number of services, privileges and benefits.

The Philippine Leisure & Retirement Authority (PLRA) describes it as "designed for those who wish to live in the Philippines on an extended or permanent basis. It is a 'lifestyle' visa for those who enjoy perks and privileges, a 'hassle-free' visa for the frequent business traveller, and a 'retirement visa' for the elderly."

The Philippine Retirement Authority [www.pra.gov.ph] is the government agency set up to help retirees to adjust.

Apart from routine medical/police checks you require bank certification of financial deposit as follows:

- 35-49 years old – US$75,000
- 50 years old and above – US$ 50,000
- Additional dependent – US$15,000 each

One-time fees are a US$1,500 processing and service fee and US$10 for the annual PRA ID card fee (waived for the first year).

Spouses must provide the ID/medical/police information and pay a reduced (US$300) processing and service fee plus US$10 for the annual PRA ID Card.

Benefits for SRRV holders include:

- Permanent, non-immigrant status with multiple entry privileges.
- Exemption from customs duties and taxes for the importation of personal effects, appliances and household furniture worth US$7,000.
- Exemption from exit clearance and re-entry permit.
- Exemption from travel tax.
- Pension, annuities remitted to the Philippines are tax-free.
- Guaranteed repatriation of invested profits, capital gains and dividends accrued from investments.
- Services of PLRA Travel Agency; the use of PLRA membership in golf clubs; membership of the PLRA Executive Club and discounts in PLRA-authorised establishments and shops.

More info: www.philembassy.se

Is it safe?

Wherever tourists rub shoulders with poverty there are pickpockets and thieves. For many Filipinos it's a matter of survival. However, the Philippines is a relatively safe place to live if you are careful and aware. Leave expensive jewellery and watches at home. Don't carry wallets in your back pocket.

In spite of their poverty most Filipinos are religious (this is a strongly Catholic country), polite and tolerant with respect for elders.

There are no-go areas: For several years, the British Government – and many others – have advised their citizens not to travel to any part of Mindanao due to terrorist and insurgent activity but recently the British Foreign and Commonwealth Office amended its travel advisory to the Philippines by lifting travel restrictions to the east side of Mindanao.

How much tax will I pay?

Retirees under the Philippines programme are exempt from income tax on their pensions and annuities. They can import household goods and personal effects up to the value US$7,000 tax free.

If you own a house or apartment there is a 1-2 per cent tax on the property's assessed fair market value.

15 bedrooms, Cebu

American inspired main house with 11 bedrooms, 8 bathrooms, library and exercise/TV room. 1.5 hours from Cebu city, 10 min from clinic, 5 min from market. Restaurants with international cuisine nearby. Approximately 1,800sq m. Auto start generator to power cuts.

Additional guest bungalow with 4 bedrooms and 4 bathrooms and 3 thatched covered picnic houses.

Property is surrounded by coconut trees, very quiet and private. Outside is a basketball court with additional land for sale for possible development or sale.

Price: $213,000

More info: seafrontcebu.blogspot.com

Email: mabuhayten@yahoo.com

Tel: Carmen +032 9162455421

Fee/Tax	% of Price	Who pays
Legal Fee	5-10%	Buyer
Local Transfer Tax	0.50% – 0.75%	Buyer
Deed of Sale	0.225-0.50%	Buyer
Capital Gains Tax	6%	Seller
Real Estate Agent's Fee	3-5%	Seller
Document Stamp Tax	1.50%	Seller
Costs paid by buyer	5.73-11.25%	
Costs paid by seller	10.50-12.50%	

Where's best to live?

Pretty well anywhere except southern Mindanao. The European Chamber in the Philippines cites Manila, Subic, Tagaytay, Cebu and Dumaguete as ideal retirement havens.

However, the choice was made on the basis of the medical facilities available to serve the needs of foreign retirees, something that might not be high on everyone's priority list.

Monthly rent on a stunning house in one of Manila's classier suburbs – Ayala Alabang is the most sought after – will be around US$1,000-2,000 [see: www.housinginteractive.com/philippines] but a good-sized house in an acceptable Manila suburb can be had for around $650-800 a month. Pay a bit more and you can have one with a pool.

Dumaguete, the choice of about 4,000 foreigners, is a lovely seaside town a stone's throw away from Cebu. It has an airport with two daily flights to Manila. The large foreign community is composed of Germans, Swiss, Americans, British, Canadians and Australians.

Near Dumaguete are the attractive towns of Valencia, Bacong, and Dauin, each about 15-20 minutes away from the city proper. Dauin and Bacong are on the sea and Valencia is an elevated town about

Is Philippines property a good investment?

Most people choose to rent. Foreign individuals are not allowed to own land. There are ways around this but they are not recommended. Foreign residents can buy a house but not the land on which it is built and they can buy an apartment or condo in developments where the foreign proportion does not exceed 40 per cent.

Many Western men buy land or property in the names of their Filipina wives or girlfriends. Unless you want to risk losing your wife and home in one go this is also not recommended.

Since rental property is cheap and readily available, this is generally the favoured option.

If you decide to buy these are the transaction costs in the Philippines, according to the very useful Global Property Guide [www.globalpropertyguide.com]

Rizal townhouse
3-storey townhouse with 4 bedrooms. One unit area is 214sq m, the other is 222sq. m
Price: $115-118,000
More info: Moveinthecity.com
Sonia Carandang   Tel: +639159324423 /+63922-8618886

Baguio City
3 storey architect-designed home with 9 bedrooms, 6 bathrooms, 3 car garage with driver's quarter. Jacuzzi in master bedroom with a large living room. Huge family room, modern kitchen with marble worktops. Price: $497,189
More info: www.besthomeclassifieds.com
Tel: Michael at (074) 442-23-87. Email robmrx@yahoo.com

PROPERTY

700-1,700-ft above sea level with views to match.

Rentals costs have increased in places such as Dumaguete because of their popularity among foreign residents. Here a typical house suitable for a Western foreigner with family is around $500 monthly.

But you can pay a lot less. 'Gellor', a contributor to the website BritishExpats.com, says: "My family and I live here in Toledo City, on the west coast of Cebu island.

"I would recommend that expats consider some of the outlying areas of Cebu province. It allows you to take advantage of the conveniences of Cebu City without paying the costs associated with actually living there.

"There are plenty of locales to investigate, such as Bogo (north), Balamban (west), and Carcar (south of Cebu City).

"The cost-of-living is quite low: I pay $90 month to rent a 2bd/2ba home. Water is $3 a month, electric is $35, cable is $5 and dinner in a Cebu City restaurant is $8. Eating out locally is a mere pittance … usually a big meal for two is around $1.50. Personally, I like to visit the local markets and cook food at home. This is even cheaper and much healthier; we had some lovely yellowfin tuna filets last night – it cost $2 a kilo."

Tagaytay, 70km south of Manila, on a 600-metre-high ridge overlooking Taal Volcano, is a popular weekend retreat from the heat of the capital. Here you can buy a 3-bedroom/2 bathroom house for around $100,000 and a palace of a place for twice that.

Better still? A 6-bedroom/5 bathroom home at the Royal Tagaytay Estates Golf & Country Club for just $312,500.

Villa, Puerto Galera
Halfway between Puerto Galera Muelle and White Beach, about 500 meters to the beach. Nice views to rice fields and Balatero Bay. 5 bedrooms, 5 bathrooms, office and workshop, staff quarters. Built in 2003 around a mature and lush garden with mangos, papaya, pineapple, guava, coconut and other fruits and vegetables, fish pond, duck pond and chicken house.
Large terrace in front of the main house, balcony in master bedroom. All rooms are tiled or carpeted and furnished.
Price: $290,000
More info: Aldanmar Real Estate
www.deanwestbury.com
Tel: (+63) 9155-619686

PHILIPPINES CONTACT DIRECTORY

Embassies/Government
Philippines' Embassy in UK
www.philemb.org.uk

The Philippine Leisure & Retirement Authority
www.pra.gov.ph

British Embassy in Manila
http://ukinthephilippines.fco.gov.uk/en

Travel & Health Advice
Foreign Office travel advice
www.fco.gov.uk/travel
www.nhs.uk/Healthcareabroad
www.masta.org

About the Philippines
www.livinginthephilippines.com
www.philippinesinsider.com
www.lakbaypilipinas.com
www.retireinphilippines.com
www.philippinedomain.com
www.philippinesinsider.com
Baguio City
www.baguio.gov.ph/
www.baguiocity.com/
www.ibaguio.net/
Tagaytay City
www.tagaytay.com/
www.tagaytayhighlands.com/home.ph...
www.thousetagaytay.com/index.htm
Cebu City
www.livingincebu.com
www.cebu.gov.ph/
www.wayblima.com/
www.cebucitytourism.com/

General & Expat
www.expatfocus.com
www.britishexpat.com
www.transitionsabroad.com

English Language Media
There are a mass of English language
publications in the Philippines
www.tribune.net.ph
www.manilastandardtoday.com
www.manilatimes.net
www.philstar.com
Radio/TV
www.abs-cbnnews.com
www.gmanews.tv
Philippine Broadcasting Services
www.pbs.gov.ph
www.radiophilippines.com
Business World Online
www.bworldonline.com

Property
real-estate-guide.philsite.net
www.bfhomes.net/
http://homes.point2.com
www.dontim.com
www.canyonwoodsretirement.com
www.megaworldcorp.com/real-estat

Travel & Tourism
www.philtourism.com
www.tourism.gov.ph
www.philippine-isles.com
www.philsite.net
www.bohol-philippines.com
www.lonelyplanet.com/philippines
www.philippinesinsider.com
www.pinoysites.org

Getting there
The cheapest option when coming from
Europe is to transit via Singapore (via Tiger
Airways), Hong Kong (via Cebu Pacific,
Philippine Airlines or Cathay) or Kuala
Lumpur (via Air Asia). Air Asia flights from
London to KL can be as low as 200 euros
off-peak season or booked well in advance.
www.philippineairlines.com
Air Philippines www.airphils.com
Cebue Pacific Airwww.cebupacificair.com
Jet Asia www.jetstar.com
South East Asian Airlineswww.flyseair.com
Malaysian Airlines
www.malaysiaairlines.com
Air Asia www.airasia.com
KLM KLM.com

Getting Around
Getting around in the Philippines is cheap
and there are many options from air-
conditioned taxis to a tricycle with a side
car. In between there are jeepneys and
buses of all kinds. Jeepneys are highly-
decorated jeeps converted to carry up to 30
people.

By air: Air Philippineswww.airphils.com
Philippine Airlines
www.philippineairlines.com
Cebue Pacific Airwww.cebupacificair.com
South East Asian Airlineswww.flyseair.com

Ferry: Travelling by is ferry to one of the
Philippines is an an adventure in itself. You
need plenty of time since some trips last
two days. It's also an economical way to
get around. Passenger ferries do not have a
good safety record so check the weather
first.
The major ports are Manila, Cebu,
Zamboanga and Davao.

Bus: There is no central bus terminal. Each
company has it's own terminal spread
throughout Manila. There are a dozen or
more bus companies operating on long-
distance routes with varying degrees of
comfort.

Train: The decrepit Philippine National
Railway system still runs from Manila to
Southeast Luzon and back. An
uncomfortable adventure for those not in a
hurry.
Manila's Mass Rail Transit system has three
lines covering the city..

Driving: Although an extensive road
network covers almost the entire nation,
the quality varies widely. Driving in Manila,
one of the world's most densely populated
automotive cities is, simply put, a
nightmare.
Drivers pay no attention to the rules of the
road and pedestrians seem hell-bent on
suicide. It is little better in the provincial
cities. Most resident expatriates have
drivers. Night driving has its own particular
hazards.
Driving is on the right (or is supposed to
be).

Retirees find a tropical paradise in the 'land of smiles'

Why Thailand?

It's only in recent years that Thailand moved much higher up the list of many people's retirement considerations. With 12 million visitors a year – 600,000 from the UK alone – it's surprising it's taken so long, especially since Thailand has been wooing foreign retirees for years and hands out 20,000-25,000 retiree visas a year.

It's particularly popular as a retirement destination among the Western European and American expatriates who have worked in the Far East and among the millions of millions who visit every year.

What is so attractive about Thailand?

The exotic nature of the country, the tropical weather and a continuous improvement of the infrastructure makes Thailand an attractive option for the more adventurous.

Marketed as the 'Land of Smiles', Thailand extends a warm welcome to visitors and has stunning beaches, exotic cities, lush landscapes, jungles, forests, beautiful mountains, waterfalls and fantastic temples. You can shop in the markets year-round for exotic fruits and vegetables.

Medical care is good and inexpensive.

Thai people are hospitable and friendly with deep-rooted traditions and culture.

The cosmopolitan culture and the wide use of English all over Thailand adds to the appeal. So too does the high standard of living available on even a relatively modest income.

Thailand's tax system is friendly to retirees and most areas have excellent standards of medical treatment. Housing is generally cheap and available along with good leisure activities. Retirees can sustain a good lifestyle at a fraction of the cost in the West.

Close to the equator and with approximately a fifth of the country's area covered in rainforest, Thailand's climate centres around the monsoon season (July to November) and is both hot and humid.

The length of the country – 1,860km north to south – means that the climate and weather can vary dramatically: the north can be cool, the east is dryer and hotter than anywhere else and the south is wetter than the rest of the country.

Cost of living

Like anywhere else the cost of living depends on your lifestyle and the location you choose. You can rent a nice two-bedroom apartment in the capital for £600-700 a month with access to facilities such as a

FACTFILE

Capital: Bangkok   **Population:** 65 million
Area: 513,115sq km
Language: Thai. English is widely spoken in tourist areas.
Climate: Tropical, with a mean annual temperature of 28°C and high humidity. Very hot in the central plains and south, cooler in the north, particularly hilly areas. Nov-March is mostly dry.
Entry requirements: No visa required for stays of less than 30 days.
Retirement/residence visa: To obtain an 'O-A' (long stay) visa you have to be aged 50 or over and with an annual income equivalent to about £14,000. [See The rules for getting in]
Electricity: 220V/50Hz
Money: Baht, plenty of ATMs. Credit/debit cards and travellers cheques are widely accepted.

Public holidays 2010

Jan 1	New Year's Day	July 1	Buddhist Lent
Feb 1	Magha Bucha Day	July 1	Bank Holiday
April 6	Chakri Day	Aug 12	Queen's Birthday
April 15	Thai New Year	Oct 23	Chulalongkorn Day
April 28	Visakha Bucha	Dec 5	King's Birthday
May 1	Labour Day	Dec 10	Constitution Day
May 5	Coronation Day	Dec 31	New Year's Eve

Opening hours
Banks: 9.30am-3.30pm, Mon-Fri (longer in shopping malls)
Offices: 8.30am-5pm (2 hr lunch break)
Shops: 10am-10pm in tourist areas
Water: Drink bottled or boil tap water.
Tipping: 10 per cent customary in restaurants and hotels.
Medical/Healthcare: No compulsory vaccinations. Precautions against malaria, hepatitis B, typhoid recommended.
Pets: An Import permit can be obtained on arrival. Documents required: export certificate from country of origin, identity and health certificate signed by a veterinary surgeon. Vaccinations for rabies (not required from countries free of rabies), Leptospirosis (at least 21 days prior to departure), distemper, hepatitis and parvovirus (at least 21 days prior to departure). Cats to be vaccinated against feline enteritis and flu.

swimming pool and gym – but a lot cheaper if you don't need those kind of facilities.

Move away from the capital – which most retirees would certainly prefer – and your cost of living takes a significant dive. In Phuket, for example, you can rent a new one-bedroom 'villa' with basic facilities [see: www.siamrealestate.com] for £250 a month. Services and utilities include cable TV, a water heater, fresh bed linen changed regularly by a maid service and a gardener. The location is quiet but close to beaches, restaurants, shopping facilities and bars.

Conversely, just down the road – at The Heights Phuket – the asking price for a two-bedroom apartment with a clubhouse, fitness centre, infinity pool, lap pool, sun deck and jacuzzi is £400,000!

If you go to up country you can rent something perfectly nice for £100 a month.

Is it safe?

Generally speaking Thailand is fairly safe although the UK's Foreign Office warns of the possibility of terrorism throughout the country, particularly in the far southern provinces of Pattani, Yala, Narathiwat and

Kokyang Estate, Phuket
Close to the beautiful Nai Harn beach, Kokyang Estate II encompasses 2 and 3 bedroom villas with private pools and gardens. Facilities include security, gym, swimming pool and internet access.
Prices: From £159,110
More info: www.experience-international.com
Tel +44 (0)207 321 5858

The Heights, Phuket
On the hillside above Kata Beach, The Heights Phuket offers 51 condominiums with large open terraces, roof gardens, water features and solar panels and views of the Andaman Sea. Facilities include a club house, fitness centre, infinity pool, lap pool, sun deck and jacuzzi.
Prices: 220sq m, 2-bedroom units from £348,200, 410sq m, 3-bedroom units from £740,000.
More info: Raimon Land
Email: steve@raimonland.com
www.theheightsphuket.com

PROPERTY

Songkhla. Since 2004 over 3,000 people have been killed and several thousand more injured. No British nationals have been involved.

Violent crime against foreigners occasionally occurs, but overall it's a safe country, the biggest problems being petty theft, scams and traffic accidents.

There have also been rare cases of visitors being drugged and robbed so offers of food or drinks from strangers should be politely declined.

Scams involving fake gemstones are fairly common in Bangkok and it's best to turn down offers from tuk-tuk and taxi drivers to take you to jewellery shops.

How much tax will I pay?

Taxpayers are classified into resident and non-resident. Resident means any person residing in Thailand for a period or periods aggregating more than 180 days in any tax (calendar) year.

A resident is liable for tax on income from any source. A non-resident is subject to tax only on income from within Thailand.

There is no capital gains tax nor inheritance tax.

Buying property

Foreigners cannot own land in Thailand and as a result, most foreigners elect to rent. However, it is possible for foreigners to purchase condominiums in Thailand and many do, especially in the tourist areas of Phuket and Pattaya. Foreign ownership is restricted to a maximum of 49 per cent of the total space of a condominium building.

This means that if, in the condominium of your choice, there are already a large number of foreigners living there and your purchase would mean foreigners would own more than 49 per cent of the total floor

THE RULES FOR GETTING IN

Thailand doesn't give its retiree visa a fancy name like others countries do. It's simply the "O-A" (Long Stay) visa which has been in existence since 2001 and has to be renewed annually. You have to be 50 or over and apply in person at Thai Embassy – ie no postal applications.

The usual rules apply: No criminal record in Thailand or your home country (you require a police clearance certificate); no medical record of contagious disease and a bank statement showing you have assets of about £14,000 and a similar annual income. The visa fee is £45 or, for multiple entry, £100. Your partner or spouse will be granted Non-Immigrant "O" in stead of "O-A"

Some documents must be certified by public notary or by "a competent authority".

More info: www.thaiembassyuk.org.uk

space, your purchase will be blocked.

Another requirement is that funds for property purchase must come from overseas. When you purchase property, you should transfer the funds from abroad in foreign currency and convert thyem into baht in Thailand. The reason for this is that the receiving bank will issue a Foreign Exchange Transaction Form which you may need in the future if you wish to repatriate funds without incurring tax penalties.

David Alexander, vice president of sales at Raimon Land [www.raimonland.com], the major player for luxury property in Thailand, with developments in Bangkok, Pattaya and Phuket, advises overseas buyers who need a mortgage, to investigate financing options in their home countries.

"Although property transactions are conducted

Phuket island
4-bedroom, 2-bathroom house with garden, pool and garage at Rawai/Nai Harn at the southern tip of Phuket island, known for great seafood and a departure point for boat day trips to surrounding islands of Bon, Coral, Phi Phi and Racha islands. With a sweeping bay and lovely island views, Rawai beach is a scenic spot for picnicking but is not noted as a swimming beach.
Price: £295,000
More info: Maya Cove Real Estate
www.mayacoverealestate.com

We live here

Nancy and Roger Lindley's path to Chiang Mai was courtesy of the US Army with which Roger had served with in Thailand. The couple retired there after senior corporate careers in America and then running a plant nursery in Michigan.

We visited Chiang Mai in late 2006 to evaluate the potential for retirement living[writes Nancy]. We found a relaxed lifestyle with many retired expatriates living there.

We attended several meetings of the Chiang Mai Expats Club, met many retirees, made some lasting friendships and returned to the US to wind down our business and to get rid of our 35-year accumulation of "stuff". We arrived in Chiang Mai in November 2008.

The people, weather, food and medical care are great and the cost of living is low. There is a vibrant community of English-speaking retirees, creating opportunities for many hobbies and pursuits.

This year we're exploring Chiang Mai, making new friends and learning the Thai language. As in Michigan, Roger is active in the local branch of Rotary International. Together, we're enjoying the learning curve of a new life, new country and new friends.

We're here on one-year retirement visas and plan to remain for 8-10 years, eventually returning to the US when we receive full social security and can utilise Medicare. Meanwhile, we're having a great adventure and enjoying a relaxed, healthy lifestyle. What better way to start retirement?

We rent a beautiful furnished two-bedroom condo of nearly 1,000 sq. ft. for which we pay less than US$450 a month.

Getting around

The Thai people are sweet, gentle and caring – until they get in the driver's seat of a vehicle. Traffic and driving practices are frightening, plus they drive on the "wrong" side of the street, like the Brits and Aussies.

Tuk-tuks are quick, but the ride is hair-raising. We prefer the song taews, or shared red taxis. You sit on a bench in the back with other passengers and see the city as the driver picks up and drops off other fares. Stand on the curb of a busy street and you will rarely wait more than a minute for one to stop. The standard fare is 20 baht per person, about 60 cents.

When we go out of Chiang Mai we can rent a very comfortable car with driver for about $25 per day, plus the cost of fuel.

Walking is our most common method of transport. Chiang Mai is compact and walking is a great way to see the sights and learn more about our new city.

The River, Bangkok
Standing on the Chao Phraya River, Bangkok's main waterway, will be the Thai capital's second tallest building. Luxury interiors feature high-quality finishes, solid timber and Italian stone flooring and fully-fitted kitchens. Offering fitness centres, riverfront infinity pool, sport courts and roof gardens.The 834 studios, 1- to 3-bedroom units and duplexes with city and river views range from 45-397sq m.
Prices: With unit prices running from £105,000 to more than £2 million. Penthouses will be available from 2011.
More info: Raimon Land
Email: sales@raimonland.com

differently than in other countries, this need not be a drawback. Borrowing in Thailand requires much larger deposits, but it can be achieved when working with an established developer with a good network of commercial banks from which to select."

Who pays what when you buy property

TAX	WHICH PARTY PAYS	AMOUNT
Transfer fee	Buyer	2% of registered value
Stamp Duty	Seller	0.5% of registered value
Withholding Tax	Seller	1% of appraised value
Business Tax	Seller	3.3% of appraised value

Is Thai property a good investment?

Thailand's resort areas have seen a steady increase in value in recent years, almost doubling in Phuket, for example, but are still relatively cheap.

Foreigners cannot own land in Thailand and most foreigners choose to rent. If you rent, what you pay depends entirely where you choose to live. A nice condo in a decent part of Bangkok or on the island of Phuket will cost US$2,000 a month, not a lot less in Pattaya, but it is possible to find a quiet three bedroom house for around US$250 a month in rural Thailand.

It is considered likely that Thai property values will slide along with international property with the next upturn in 2011.

Where's best to live

Bangkok, Pattaya, Hua Hin, Phuket and the northern capital **Chiangmai** are popular choices but buy in one of these tourist areas and you will pay more for pretty well everything, but not much more. Consider these places if you enjoy a more frenetic social scene with the ready availability of sex, drugs and rock 'n-roll.

Foreign residents in Thailand are scattered much wider than they are, for example, in Malaysia and the Philippines and there are many lesser known, and quieter, retirement destinations that we'll come to. It depends on what sort of lifestyle you're looking for.

Some retirees wouldn't be anywhere other than the capital but not if you seek the quiet life. **Bangkok** is dirty, congested, polluted, vibrant, exciting and a famed adult playground with plenty of leafy sanctuaries with condos and apartments.

Pattaya, the non-stop party town, is a popular tourist resort on the gulf of Thailand 150km southeast of Bangkok, with more bars per square mile

Near beach at Patong
3 bedrooms, 4 bathrooms, living room, dining room, big 'European' kitchen, 2 large balconies, 1,600sq m of land.
Price: £215,000
More info: Tel: (66) 81-477-5306 from outside Thailand

We live here

Briton Kevin Butters, 51, runs the website www.Visit-Chiang-Mai-Online. Originally from the UK, he settled in Thailand around three years ago following time spent living and working in China sourcing home decor products for UK retailers.

My background was in ornamental horticulture, but for the last 10 years I have been involved with the design and sourcing of home decor and accessories from Asia for multiple retailers back in the Britain.

I worked for 26 years in the family horticulture wholesale business in the East Midlands supplying garden centres and retailers throughout the UK. When the company was sold I joined another horticultural based company sourcing products from China and eventually moved there.

During this period I bought a house on Koh Samui in Thailand and, for a couple of years, split my time between China and Koh Samui.

Eventually I got bored with the travelling and decided to "retire" to Thailand. My personal passions are my lovely Thai wife Rose, baby daughter Coco, spicy Thai food and all aspects of handicrafts, so Chiang Mai is the perfect location for us to live.

Rose is originally from Isaan Province in the northeast. She is an excellent chef and a trained English teacher. We met about three years ago and now have a lovely daughter called Coco, now 18 months old.

We moved from Koh Samui to Chiang Mai about two years ago, having fallen in love with the people and the city during a visit.

We then had to consider what we could do to keep ourselves busy as well as make a little money, eventually deciding to specialise in handmade wooden items and Hill Tribe silver jewellery and rather than work as a wholesaler we decided to sell direct to the consumers through an Ebay shop.

This has been of great experience for us, making shipments to every corner of the world and sourcing suitable factories to work with. With over 500 sales in just over two years we then built our own website incorporating information about the wonderful city we live in and an online shop selling the items that we love to go out and source from the local artisans.

Chiang Mai is a great retirement option for those seeking affordable yet comfortable living, without compromising on natural beauty, entertainment and great food.

Oxygen Bay, Phuket
3 and 4 bedroom duplex apartments from an award winning developer these luxurious properties come with private pool and garden only a short distance from the beach. **Prices** start from £178,500 / THB 11,887,771 **more info:** visit www.experience-international.com or call +44 (0)207 321 5858.

PROPERTY

Other popular retirement destinations are Phuket, Pattaya, Hua Hin and Koh Samui, all coastal resorts or islands, primarily geared to tourism with costs of living accordingly. Chiang Mai, however, is completely land-locked, on a plateau in the far north of Thailand, surrounded by breathtaking mountains and beautiful scenery where the cost of living that would make most Westerners choke over their cornflakes.

This is no longer the best-kept secret in Thailand as Chiang Mai boasts thousands of foreign residents who now call Chiang Mai home. You might think you would be taking a huge risk by retiring to Chiang Mai but 20,000 people can't be wrong.

You do not have to give up any luxuries that you currently have and, along with the traditional Thai lifestyle, you will also find lots of international restaurants, fine supermarkets, cable TV, hi-speed internet and financial services all at a fraction of the cost you would pay in your home country.

Chiang Mai is served by an international airport, which has direct air services to many major destinations and daily flights to Bangkok, a major hub for flights worldwide.

My personal top 10 reasons for moving here:
- The cost of living – 35-40 per cent less than you pay back home.
- Extremely friendly people – genuinely so, not in "tourism Thai" way.
- Outstanding food – spicy Thai dishes or traditional Western fare.
- Exceptional year-round climate.
- Very low crime – safe to walk anywhere, anytime.
- Excellent food markets all around the city.
- Modern and affordable medical and dental facilities.
- A host of leisure activities to suit all.
- Excellent infrastructure, good roads, airport, shopping, local transport, schools, communications.
- A diverse range of cultural pursuits and festivals.

The chart below is based on my own living expenses, for a family of three, in a three-bedroom rented house, driving a standard SUV (4WD).

If you were going to purchase a similar sized house to mine and buy a similar car outright the cost would be in the region of 6.5m baht (approx £120,000).

My website, www.Visit-Chiang-Mai-Online, will answer many of your questions about aspects life here but if not, you are welcome to email me and I will do my best to answer them.

COST OF LIVING CHIANG MAI

Item	Monthly Costs
House	£185
Car Fuel	£73
Food & Groceries	£350
Utilities	
Electricity	£36
Water	£14
Telephone/Mobile	£18
Bottled Gas (cooking)	£6
Other Expenses	
Internet(Broadband)	£20
UBC TV (Satelite)	£30
Gardner/Cleaner	£27

Additional Annual Costs

Car (service, tax, insurance)	£815
Health(insurance & care)	£800

than any other Thai city - maybe more than anywhere else in the world. It's pretty sleezy but it's fun and you don't need to travel very far from Pattaya to be back in the 'real' Thailand.

There's restaurants from all over the world, numerous expat social and sports clubs- plus Thai boxing, rifle ranges, stylish variety and gay shows, bowling and all manner of other sports. There are 15+ golf courses.

Life in **Chiang Mai,** the northern capital, and **Hua Hin** on the north-east coast life is less frenetic but both offer great dining, entertainment, sporting and other facilities.

Chiang Mai has a significant expat community - some put the number of resident "farangs" (Westerners) at 5,000, others at over 17,000

Hua Hin has the additional benefit of being at the seaside (watch out for the poisonous jellyfish!) Here you can drop in at the Fishing Pier market on the way home to pick up fresh and cheap seafood.

Don't feel like cooking? You can dine out cheaply here at a different restaurant for a month without ever making a return visit and that doesn't include the Thai food stalls along the beachfront and in night market.

There is a huge choice - not just among Thai restaurants - but French, Italian, Indian and Japanese eateries as well as numerous bars and pubs to suit every taste.

Phuket, the largest island in Thailand, is one of the most popular tourist destinations in Asia although it is fairly easy to escape from the more touristic areas and find a beach to yourself. Hilly, forested and full of exotic tropical plants, Phuket also has many of Thailand's most beautiful beaches.

The island, the second wealthiest place in Thailand after Bangkok, was voted by Fortune Magazine as one of the top five retirement destinations in the world.

Patong, the main beach, is lined with condos, hotels, bars and restaurants.

In all of these more touristic locations you can find like-mined people from home.

That's not everyone's taste. 'David', a contributor to www.thailandqa.com, gives his vote to Buri Ram ('City of Happiness'), the capital of Buriram Province, northeast of Bangkok .

"… virtually no farangs and you can get the finest barbecued rat you'll ever taste."

The alternatives

The following are all places with far less but still fairly significant numbers of expatriate residents:

Nakhon Ratchasima (also known as Korat), one of the largest cities after Bangkok and Chiang Mai. and the premier city of the Isaan region.

Nong Khai - border town in Isaan heartlands on the Mekong River, gateway to the Laos captial Vientiane.

Nakhon Sawan - gateway between the northern central plains and the north, at the confluence of the rivers Ping, Wang, Yom and Nan, where they meet to form the Chao Praya River

Mukdahan - small city on the banks of the Mekong River, looking over to the city of Savannakhet in Laos.

Krabi, a stunning sleepy town on the Andaman Coast of southern Thailand (also the name of the province), an of outstanding beauty, unspoilt beaches, coral reefs, excellent seafood , giant limestone cliffs, the famous Phi Phi islands you will see pictured on many tourist brochures. Not recommended for those who like a busy nightlife.

Phetchburi city - Phetchaburi is a province (known by Thais as Muang Phet) about 160 km south-west of Bangkok on the western shore of the Gulf of Thailand. Phetchburi city is one of the oldest towns in Thailand whose prosperity, derived from the coastal saltpans from as early as the 12th century, can be seen in its ancient temples.

Nakhon Phanom - A quaint town on the Mekong, Kalasin in the north-east famous for its dinosaur fossils.

Chonburi, the name of the province and its capital about 100km east of Bangkok on the Gulf of Thailand, famous for its annual water buffalo festival.

Trat, the capital of Trat province on the long, narrow stretch of Thailand that borders Cambodia, is a relaxing place with a variety of attractions - beaches, waterfalls, mountains, fruit farms and a great night market.

Embassies/Government
Thai Embassy in London
www.thaiembassyuk.org.uk
British Embassy in Bangkok
www.britishembassy.gov.uk/thailand

Travel & Health Advice
Foreign Office travel advice
www.fco.gov.uk/travel
www.nhs.uk/Healthcareabroad
www.masta.org

About Thailand
www.discoverythailand.com
www.aboutthailand.info
www.trangonline.com
www.thailandguru.com
www.stickmanbangkok.com
www.thailandstories.com
www.guidetothailand.com
www.thai-blogs.com
www.thailand-free-forum.com
www.gingerasia.com

General & Expat
www.expatfocus.com
www.orientexpat.com/thailand
www.1stopbangkok.com
bangkokexpats.com
www.travelblog.org
www.thailandguru.com
www.nakedfarang.com
womenlearnthai.com
www.retirement-resort.com
Good website: www.thaivisa.com
www.expat-thai.com
www.expatinterviews.com/thailand
www.thailandroad.com
www.thailand-travelonline.com
www.chiangmaiexpatsclub.com
www.embracechiangmai.com
www.expathuahin.com
www.phuket.net
www.phuketguide.info

English Language Media
The Bangkok Postwww.bangkokpost.net
Business Day http://bday.net
The Nationwww.nationmultimedia.com
Phuket Gazette
Online English-language newspaper
www.bangkokbugle.com
Online English-language newspaper
Radio
Wave FM 88 Bangkok
Easy FM 105.5
MET 107
TV
Some Thai TV have limited English-
language programming or the facility to
change the language.
The biggest satellite TV provider is True

Visions UBC, which has a large number of
channels in English with different packages
at varying costs.

Property
These three websites allow you to click
through to dozens of property companies
throughout Thailand
www.thailandproperty.info
www.thailandproperty.info
www.thaiwebsites.com/propertieschiangmai
.asp
www.phuketrealty.net
www.ansthailandrealestate.com
www.pattayapropertyagents.com
www.hamptons.co.th
www.forbeslebrock.com
www.cbre.co.th/en
www.real-samui-properties.com
www.phuketthailandproperty.com/
www.phuketvision.com
www.tropical-homes.net

Travel & Tourism
www.tourismthailand.org
www.go-thailand.com
www.guidetothailand.com
www.discoverythailand.com
www.7thaiwonders.com
www.thaiwave.com
www.thailandtravelguide.com
www.andagraf.com
www.travelfish.org
www.beachsiam.com

Getting There
Thai Airways Internationalwww.thaiair.com
Air Asia: www.airasia.com
British Airways: www.britishairways.com
KLM: www.klm.com
Lufthansa: www.lufthansa.com
Air France: www.airfrance.fr
Bangkok Airways: www.bangkokair.com
Cathay Pacific Airways:
www.cathaypacific.com
Gulf Air: www.gulfairco.com
Malaysia Airlines: www.mas.com.my
Qantas: www.qantas.com.au
Singapore Airlines: www.singaporeair.com

Getting Around
Thailand has an extensive domestic air
service and a good road and rail system.

Air: Thai Airways International:
www.thaiair.com
Bangkok Airways: www.bangkokair.com
Orient Thai Airline: www.orient-thai.com
www.fly12go.com/en
PB Air: www.pbair.com
Nok Air: www.nokair.com
Air Asia: www.airasia.com

Train: If you prefer not to fly and see
something of the Thai countryside, there
is an efficient train network with air-
conditioned compartments offering a
more comfortable way to get around the
country than by bus. Fares are about the
same.
The line from Bangkok to Chiang Mai
also connects to the Laos capital
Vientaine. An excellent train journey is
the one from Bangkok south through
Malaysia to Singapore.
First class with air-conditioned
compartments is available (and
recommended) on many long distance
services.

Bus: Air-conditioned express buses
operate throughout Thailand operated by
private coach companies and
government services. Many have
reclining aircraft-type seating. VIP buses
are more comfortable and about 30-40
per cent more expensive
.
Boat: There are a variety of boat and
ferry services and on the Chao Phraya
river in Bangkok this is an excellent way
to avoid the perpetual traffic congestion.
Long-tail taxis and speedboats navigate
on the largest canals in the capital and
elsewhere.
Large ferries serve Koh Samui, Ko Chang
and other islands.

Driving: Not for the faint-hearted,
especially in the cities and more
especially in Bangkok where all forms of
politeness go out of the window. You
should know that when a driver flashes
his headlights at you it's not a curtesy
signal for you to go through but a
warning to get out of the way.
Most highway traffic signs are English as
well as Thai. An international driving
licence is required.
Driving is on the left

There's room for you in the world's largest island

Why Australia?

Thinking of retiring to a land of sun, friendly people and relaxed lifestyle? Then think of the unique environment in the land down under: from tropical rainforest in Far North Queensland and crystal clear waters, to vast inland deserts with scorching temperatures, to the popular coastal communities of eastern Australia and the lush natural vegetation of Tasmania.

Australia offers something to please everyone and there's room for everyone. Twenty times larger than the UK and more than twice the size of Europe, Australia is blessed with a formidable variety of desirable retirement locations.

It is a land of contrasts: from the garden atmosphere and warmth of inland Toowoomba in Queensland (a stone's throw away from the Gold Coast and its beaches), to the village atmosphere of Noosa, a small distance north on the Sunshine Coast, or the 'must consider' towns in Victoria and New South Wales.

Then there's bustling Echuca on the Murray River, with its paddle steamer heritage, or historic Queenscliff on Port Phillip Bay with a charm of its own and views across the bay.

Port Macquarie, famous for its koala hospital and laid-back way of life off the Pacific Highway is also proving very attractive for retirees. For those who treasure the lifestyle of the 1960s, living on the northern New South Wales coast may prove to be tantalising and may find that towns such as Byron Bay are just the thing.

Don't forget the irresistible areas south of Perth. Mandurah is a short distance from Perth and for those with a love of surfing and vineyards, the Mediterranean climate of Margaret River proves attractive to many retirees from overseas.

You're welcome mate!

Australia has been welcoming people from around the world since 1788 when the first British ships arrived in Port Jackson, as Sydney was then known.

With a population that exceeds 21 million, Australia has embraced many people from different lands and is a tolerant and diverse country. The arrival of millions of immigrants from Italy and Greece in the 1950s to the Vietnamese arrivals in the 1970s and many other countries since; all have made a significant contribution to present day Australia.

Coming from different lands and determined to get ahead has meant that over years Australians have developed a 'get up and go' attitude. Don't be fooled by the 'no worries mate' attitude – Australians have a strong sense of achievement and entrepreneurial spirit and excel in many fields including business, the arts, food and wine and, of course, sports.

They don't take themselves too seriously (losing the Ashes is an exception!) and are warm and friendly, liking people for 'who they are', not where they went to school or who their parents were. In other words, Australians like people who 'have a go'.

About the writers: Jill and Owen Weeks are authors and seminar speakers on the subject of Australian retirement. For their book, **Where to Retire in Australia**, the couple have visited over 200 locations to gather detailed information on medical services, security, cost of living, transport, real estate, leisure and much more. Their website, www.where2now.net, offers a mass of information to help guide retirees to their ideal location.

FACTFILE

Capital: Canberra

Population: 21 million

Area: 7,617,930 sqkm

Language: English

Climate: Australia is generally temperate, most of the country receiving more than 3,000 hours of sunshine a year. The climate varies from hot and tropical in the far north to cool and sometimes snowy in the south. Spring: Sept-Nov; summer: Dec-Feb; autumn: March-May; winter: June-Aug.

Entry requirements: All visitors require a visa and a return ticket and, if asked, need to show they have sufficient funds to support themselves. You can apply online for an Electronic Travel Authority Visa (ETA) that allows you to stay for up to three months.

Retirement/residence visa: Retirees need to be over 55 and have fairly substantial assets and income.
[See: The Rules for Getting In]

Electricity: 240 V/50 Hertz

Money: Australian $. ATMs are widely available.
Credit cards: Most cards and travelers cheques are accepted.

Public holidays 2010

Jan 1	New Year's Day	Apr 25/6	ANZAC Day
Jan 26	Australia Day	June 7	Foundation Day
March 1	Labour Day	Sept 27	Queens's birthday
April 2	Good Friday	Dec 25	Christmas Day
April 2-5	Easter	Dec 26	Boxing Day

Opening hours

Banks: 9/9.30am-4/4.30pm (Mon-Thurs); 9am-5pm (Fri). Some banks open on Saturday mornings.

Offices: 9am to 5.30pm, Mon through Fri

Shops: 9am-6pm (Mon-Sat)

Water: Tap water is universally safe to drink.

Tipping: For the most part tipping in hotels and other service industries is discouraged. Gratuities are not included in restaurant bills and tipping is supposedly not considered standard practice but 10 per cent is appreciated in posher dineries.

Medical/Healthcare

No vaccinations necessary unless you have come from a yellow fever infected country. There is an emergency reciprocal health agreement with the UK which allows UK visitors free hospital treatment but you will normally have to pay for treatment and medication at a doctor's surgery. Medical insurance for illness and accidents is recommended.

There's a useful advisory at: www.heathrowmedical.com

Pets: The Pet Travel Scheme (PETS) does not apply to Australia. All cats and dogs must meet the AQIS import conditions.
[See: www.daff.gov.au/aqis/about]

Is it safe?

On the whole Australia is a relatively safe country. There are known trouble spots in most Australian capital cities and you should heed local advice. Neighbourhood Watch operates in many areas and the police are willing to offer advice and suggestions and in some regions have established specific programmes for older residents.

Is Australian property a good investment?

Across Australia, the last few years have witnessed an explosion in real estate prices. Australia does not have an oversupply of houses so prices are rising. This varies from state to state and state capitals dominate the real estate market with the exception of Queensland (where more people live outside Brisbane).

If you are not a permanent resident of Australia you need prior approval from the Australian Government to buy property. You do not need prior approval if you hold a permanent resident visa. The policy was designed to avoid a speculative property market.

Non-resident foreigners can normally get approval to buy units, townhouses, and house/land packages in a new development but not pre-owned property.

How much tax will I pay?

In most cases there are tax benefits in transferring pensions to Australia, which, in 2007, gave pension or superannuation funds major tax-free benefits on retirement. However, this is a risky area and you need to take professional advice. Any transfer of UK benefits to an overseas scheme is only permitted if the transfer is going to a scheme registered with HM Revenue & Customs in the UK – a QROPS Scheme.

Transfer to non-QROPS can result in a 40-55 per cent tax charge on the transfer from your UK fund.

Forster, NSW
2-3 bedroom home within walking distance of beaches, golf club, shopping centre, tennis and squash courts, parks and churches.
Price: A$270,000
More info: www.noblerealty.com.au

PROPERTY

THE RULES FOR GETTING IN

If you are over 45 but under 55, there are various ways you can retire to Australia, including classes of business visa that will allow permanent residence.

Alternatively, if you have adult children in Australia it's pretty straightforward.

If you have significant assets you can apply for an Investor Retirement (subclass 405) Visa. Note that "This is not a visa that leads to permanent residence or citizenship in Australia." However, it does if the strict financial and health criteria continue to be met. This visa initially permits you to stay four years and can be extended every two years if those criteria are met.

As the holder of a temporary retirement visa, you will not be covered by Medicare (Australia's national health cover) system or be eligible for any social security benefits so you must take out private medical and hospital health care insurance cover.

To live in one of Australia's high-growth urban areas, you'll need to take £425,000 in assets and have an income of about £37,000 a year.

If you opt for a low-growth, regional area, those figures come down to about £283,000 and £28,000 respectively.

More info
www.immi.gov.au/allforms/booklets/books3.htm
www.immi.gov.au/visitors/special-activity/405/index.htm
Parents visa
www.immi.gov.au/migrants/family/family-visas-parent.htm
Investment visa
www.immi.gov.au/skilled/business/162/
There's much discussion on visa and related issues at:
www.britishpensions.org.au
www.britzinoz.co

When you reach pensionable age (60) you can receive 100 per cent of what you transferred tax-free.

From July 1,2009 limits on the amount that can be transferred tax-free were raised to £101,000 a year or £302,000 initially but with no further contributions for two years.

Remember that your UK state pension will be frozen at the rate in force at the date of entitlement, or the date you leave the UK. If you return to live in the UK, you'll receive the state pension with all of the indexation increases.

If you are eligible for the Australian pension, it may be reduced when your UK pension is taken into account.

More info

For current information on tax rates visit the Australian Taxation Office website www.ato.gov.au For information regarding social security payments, visit Centrelink website: www.centrelink.gov.au

Where's best to live?

New South Wales: Australia's most populous and highly urbanised state covering 802,000sq km. Sydney, the capital, is the largest city in Australia with just under four million residents. It is also the financial capital and home to the head offices of many of Australia's largest companies and has one of the most beautiful natural harbours in the world.

NSW has some of the best retirement destinations in Australia, many of them close to or in a major regional city. Outside Sydney, NSW's best medical facilities are in cities such as Newcastle, Wollongong,

Fairway homes
Pacific Dunes, a residential golfing community 20 minutes from Nelson Bay, 25 minutes from Newcastle and a 2-hour drive to Sydney. On 135 hectares, will eventually have 450 mixed residential units. Recreational facilities include a bar, restaurant, a practice range and putting green. It will have a swimming pool, tennis courts, barbecue facilities, nature trails, parkland and a clubhouse. Prices: Home sites from £186,000; fairway homes from £412,000
More info: www.pacificdunes.com.au Tel: +(0)2 4981 8100
Email: info@pacificdunes.com.au

Dennes Point, Tasmania
3 bedroom, purpose built home designed for retirement living or active lifestyle on Bruny island, 45 minutes from Hobart by ferry and car. Full deck on 3 sides with stunning 180-degree views. Landscaped gardens and undercover parking for 2 cars. Veggie garden and chicken pens. Price: £360,000
More info: www.wainuibandb.com
Email: courthob@clearmail.com.au Tel: +(0)3 62606220

An insider's guide

When my family and I first arrived in Oz, we had a certain amount of knowledge that we were armed with, most of it was absolutely vital to get by in the first few weeks. For instance: we knew which documents were required to rent a house and buy a car; how to get registered in the healthcare system; where to go to claim child benefit, even how to make sure we weren't going to pay a bundle in emergency tax.

However, it was only after the first few months that I realised that there were a few more minor trivialities that would creep into day-to-day life that caused me utter confusion and endless embarrassment. Trivialities that I had never encountered before when I was merely traveling the country.

Below is a list for anyone wanting to move to Australia – which, may I suggest you memorise!

■ Learn (or at least recognise) your Aussie celebrities, no matter how minor. This will save you from having awkward moments when you a) have no idea who your new friends are talking about; and b) reverse your car into the car of the newsreader from 'Channel 7' in the car park.

■ When you are invited round for a coffee (or morning tea, as its known) NEVER go empty-handed. If you are incapable of baking anything even half edible (like me) then buy something from the bakers – it's just not worth the looks you get if you don't.

■ It's ok to kill a cane toad.

■ Make sure your kids can swim; your-eight-year old does not want to be wearing arm-bands at a friend's house when you are invited round for a barbie and a swim, when their three-year-old is free-styling up and down the pool at a rate of knots.

■ Buy a car with tinted windows – you will thank me in the height of summer (air-con can only take so much!)

■ If shopping for a new quilt cover in the department store, don't look dumbfounded if the sales assistant directs you to 'Manchester'. This is the collective name given for bed linen, towels etc.

■ If you are invited to a barbie and you are asked to 'bring a plate' – it doesn't mean the host has fallen on hard times and has no crockery; it is a suggestion that you bring a plate of food to contribute to the party.

■ If you feel you really want to blend in, simply grow a long and grotesque beard – (not recommended if you are a woman.)

■ Even if you don't want to kill a cane toad – pretend you have.

"What you really need to know about life in Australia... if you only read one guide, make sure it's this one!" Toni Somers-Hargis, author, 'Russe, Britannia'

Didgeridoos & Didgeridon'ts
a Brit's guide to moving your life Down Under

Vicky Gray

australiauncovered.com

All photos:
Annie Jones
(www.funkyphoto graphy.com.au)

About the writer: After travelling extensively in her early 20s **Vicky Gray** emigrated to Australia in 2006 with her husband and three children and began writing about the many bizarre and often unnerving encounters faced by newcomers to Australia. This is an extract from her book, **Didgeridoos and Didgeridon'ts**.
She writes for magazines in Australia and New Zealand magazine and runs a blog at **www.australiauncovered.com**.

Mudgee District: Mudgee because of its airport, community and choice of wineries and restaurants.

Hunter Valley To Port Stephens because of its good medical facilities, proximity to Newcastle, freeway to Sydney and the Hunter Valley lifestyle: vineyards, restaurants, sporting and cultural events.

North Coast: Port Macquaire because of its airport, range of shops, good security and medical facilities.

South Coast: Merimbula because of its airport with regular services to Melbourne, Sydney and Canberra, direct road link to Canberra, golf and bowls facilities.

Northern Rivers District: Ballina because of its range of shops, proximity to a major (domestic and international) airport at Coolangatta.

Albury, Port Macquarie, Coffs Harbour, Lismore and Orange.

South-west of Sydney lie the Southern Highlands and the towns of Mittagong, Bowral and Moss Vale. South-east from the Southern Highlands is the Illawarra Coast and the towns of Kiama and Gerringong with some of the best scenery in Australia and most expensive real estate outside the capital cities.

Southern Highlands to Illawarra Coast because of its proximity to Sydney, its country charm, rail links, shops, good medical facilities and cultural events.

Victoria: Victoria covers 227,600 sq km, around the same size as England and has a population over 4,500,000, more than 3,000,000 in the capital city, Melbourne.

Regions that are worthy of consideration include: the Murray River in the north of Victoria, the

Brisbane river views
Mid level, 2 bedroom, 2 bathroom, 126 sq m fully-furnished apartment with panoramic views of Brisbane and botanic gardens. All city living facilities including diverse shopping, medical, banking and entertainment.
Full security, restaurant and bar on ground floor, pool with deck, spa and gymnasium under cover car parking Price: POA
More info: 360 Real Estate
www.360realestate.net.au Tel: (07) 3 852 5422

Warrnambool, Victoria
Double-fronted sandstone period residence. Full width veranda with timber floor, 3 large bedrooms, central hallway, sitting room, dining room, study/den, kitchen, bathroom, laundry. Open fire in most rooms. Double garage and workshop. Block area: 1,220sq m. Near botanical gardens, pool and city centre.
More info: John Ryan Real Estate
www.johnryanrealestate.com.au Tel: +(0)3 55628800

Goldfields and Spa country, north-west of Melbourne, the Surf Coast between Torquay and Apollo Bay, the Bellarine Peninsula east of Geelong, the Mornington Peninsula between Port Phillip and Westernport, the Bass Coast from Phillip Island to Inverloch and the Gippsland Lakes.

If you leave Melbourne at 9am you can reach any of these regions in time for lunch.

Murray River: Echuca is our preferred retirement location on the Murray River because of its weather, good medical facilities and restaurants and security.

Goldfields and Spa Country: Castlemaine because of its active arts scene, diverse range of medical facilities, relaxed village feel and above-average security.

Surf Coast And Great Ocean Road: Torquay because of its proximity to Geelong and Melbourne, wide choice of real estate and weather.

Bellarine Peninsula with its old-world charm, excellent dining, sense of community and cultural attractions.

Mornington Peninsula: Rosebud because of its central policing location, library, its position as home to the main office of the council and hospital.

Bass Coast: Phillip Island because of its natural habitat, hospital, motor racing track and ferry service.

Gippsland Lakes: Paynesville because of its flat land, closeness to Bairnsdale, its facilities, choice of accommodation and good weather.

South Australia: South Australia covers 984,377sq km and shares its borders with Western Australia, Victoria and the Northern Territory. Over 1,500,000 people live in South Australia, about 73 per cent of them in the capital city, Adelaide.

South Australia is the driest of all Australian states and territories and the Murray is the only major river. However, 42 per cent of Australia's land under vineyard cultivation is found in South Australia. To many Australians South Australia is synonymous with the very best red wines. There are four main wine-producing districts close to Adelaide.

Retirees in South Australia tend to move to an area that is within easy drive of Adelaide as the city is the cultural, medical and economic hub of the state.

Fleurieu Peninsula: Victor Harbour because of its large number of community groups and clubs, medical services and proximity to Adelaide.

Adelaide Hills: Mount Baker because of its choice of shops and retirement villages.

Copper Coast: Wallaroo because of its hospital and medical facilities, canal housing developments, closeness to services at Kadina.

Limestone Coast: Robe because of its sense of

community, range of housing choices, generally good standard of living.

Queensland: Queensland is the second largest state in Australia, covering 1,722,000sq km. With over 3,700,00 inhabitants, it is the third most populous. Brisbane, the capital, is in the south-east corner and has a population of around 1.6 million.

Over half the inhabitants live outside the capital city which is not the case in any other state or territory. The Gold Coast, south of Brisbane, has been the fastest growing region in Australia for 25 years. In excess of 500,000 people live there.

Over the next 20 years Brisbane and the Gold Coast are expected to become one combined metropolis,

Bundaberg, Queensland
Chamferboard home on a brick base in a quiet street in Svensson Heights. The 3-bedroom home has an enclosed sunroom and an oversize front patio. Price: A$265,000
More info: Wide Bay Real Estate
www.widebay.com.au Tel: (07) 4 153 1011

rivalling Melbourne in size.

The rapid population growth in Queensland is causing concern among residents as the infrastructure is stretched to the limit in many towns.

Darling Downs: Toowoomba because of its easy access to Brisbane, the Gold Coast and the Sunshine Coast, its medical services and hospitals; recreation, cultural and adult education facilities, lower humidity than coastal Queensland, ideal conditions for gardeners.

Tropical North Queensland: Cairns because of its established medical services, the international airport, adult education facilities and good infrastructure.

Sunshine Coast: Bribie Island because of its proximity to Brisbane, development limits, above-average security, lower cost of living and affordable housing options.

Tasmania: Tasmania lies approximately 240km off the south-east corners of the Australian mainland. The state includes a number of smaller islands and is 68,102sq km in area, less than one per cent of the total area of Australia.

The population is less than half a million people, around 200,000 of whom live in and around Hobart, while 100,000 live in and around Launceston.

Tasmania is largely undiscovered by mainland Australia retirees but has some of the cheapest real estate in Australia and in the north and on the east coast the climate rivals that of many mainland towns and cities and in terms of days of sunshine and lack of humidity.

Hobart, on the banks of the Derwent River and east of Mount Wellington, is the capital.

Tamar Valley: Hillwood, near Launceston, because of its quietness, proximity to Launceston, good restaurants and scenic views.

East Coast: St Helens on the East Coast because of its weather, airport, hospital, police presence and relatively low crime level and good community feeling.

Kingborough: Blackmans Bay near Kingston because of its scenic location, closeness to Hobart's medical facilities and to Kingston's facilities, ideal location for water-based activities

Western Australia: Western Australia, covering more than 2,500,00sq km, is Australia's largest state but accounts for less than 10 percent of the population – around of 1,433,000. Perth, the capital city, is the most remote city of its size in the world and is home to more millionaires than any other capital city in Australia.

On the banks of the Swan River, it is arguably the best capital city in Australia. Access to the city from all directions is made easy by a well-planned system of freeways and it has a modern suburban rail network.

Peel Region: Mandurah in the Peel district because of its good medical facilities, waterside dining, closeness to Perth's medical facilities, proactive council and Development Commission and its active community.

South West: Margaret River because of its lifestyle, art and culture, medical facilities, sea and forests.

Great Southern: Denmark because of its arts and culture, restaurants, natural environment and sense of community.

Coral Coast: because of its medical facilities, closeness to Geraldton, lack of traffic lights and relative affordability.

Rockingham Beachfront, Perth
Rockingham, an eco-tourism mecca just south of Perth, is home to a riot of bird and marine life. Cost of this 2-bedroom apartment includes all fixtures and fittings. Facilities include pool, gym, patio area, access to beachfront cafes, lawn terrace and white sandy beach. 2 car-bays and store. Price: A\$630,000
More info: glenwayrealty.com.au Tel: +(0)8 9527 5111

Andergrove, Queensland
Situated in a quiet area of Andergrove, near the city of Mackay, with council-zoned open land opposite. 3 bedrooms, en suite and walk-in wardrobe in the master bedroom. Comfortable open plan living area with well appointed kitchen, dining and lounge area.
Price: A\$425,000
More info: Mackay Regional Real Estate
mrre.com.au Tel: +(0)4 38803575

AUSTRALIA CONTACT DIRECTORY

Embassies/Government

Australia High Commission in London
www.uk.embassy.gov.au

UK High Commission in Canberra

http://ukinaustralia.fco.gov.uk
www.australia.gov.au

State governments

Australian Capital Territorywww.act.gov.au
New South Waleswww.nsw.gov.au
Northern Territorywww.nt.gov.au
Queensland   www.qld.gov.au
South Australia   www.sa.gov.au
Tasmania   www.tas.gov.au
Victoria   www.vic.gov.au
Western Australiawww.wa.gov.au

Travel & Health Advice

Foreign Office travel advice
www.fco.gov.uk/travel
www.nhs.uk/Healthcareabroad
www.masta.org

About Australia

www.australia.com
www.newcomersnetwork.com
For those who have moved or are planning to
move to Australia
www.about-australia.com/facts
www.aussie-retirement.com.au
www.livinginaustralia.org
www.retiregrand.com
www.retirementlivingaustralia.com.au

Visas, immigration & citizenship

http://www.immi.gov.au
http://www.citizenship.gov.au
http://www.passports.gov.au

State government portals

www.fed.gov.au
www.nsw.gov.au
www.vic.gov.au
www.qld.gov.au
www.sa.gov.au
www.wa.gov.au
www.tas.gov.au
www.act.gov.au
www.nt.gov.au

General & Expat

www.expatfocus.com
www.britishexpat.com
www.yobromofo.com
www.embraceaustralia.com
www.britishpensions.org.au

Retirement

www.australia.gov.au/life-events/retiring
www.healthinsite.gov.au
www.centrelink.gov.au
www.seniors.gov.au

Property

www.realestate.com.au
www.firstnational.com.au
www.ingrealestate.com.au
www.real-estate-australia.com
www.run.com.au
www.wentworthholdings.com.au
www.coldwellbankeraustralia.com.au
www.joneslanglasalle.com.a
www.bresicwhitney.com.a
www.mcgrath.com.au

Travel & Tourism

www.australia.com
www.tourism.australia.com
www.regionaltourism.com

Getting There

All the major airlines fly to Australia. This is
not an exclusive list.
Emirates Airlinewww.emirates.com
British Airwayswww.britishairways.com
Quantas
www.qantas.com.au
Cathay Pacificwww.cathaypacific.com
Singapore Airlineswww.singaporeair.com
Malaysian Airlines
www.malaysiaairlines.com
Virgin Blue Airlineswww.virginblue.com.au

Getting Around

Flying is the best way to cover large
distances in a short time. Australia's
domestic airlines – Qantas, Jetstar, Virgin
Blue, Rex and their subsidiaries - serve all
state capital cities and regional centres.
Bus/Coach: Coach and bus travel in
Australia is comfortable, easy and
economical. Coaches generally have air-
conditioning, adjustable seats and videos.
Services are frequent, affordable and
efficient.
Rail: Australia's distances are daunting for
drivers and the alternative is the extensive
rail network. Options range from budget to
luxury.
Public Transport: All of Australia's capital
cities are served by a wide variety of public
transport, including trains, buses, ferries,
monorail, light rail and trams. Taxis charge
according to their meter.
Ferries: Ferries connect suburbs in some
capital cities – they criss-cross Sydney
Harbour, the Swan River in Perth and the
Brisbane River in Brisbane.
Driving: Australia has a vast network of
well-maintained roads.
Driving is on the left.

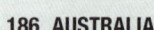

A perfect place to grow up in and retire to

Why New Zealand?

Uncrowded and unspoilt and often likened to Tunbridge Wells in the 1950s, New Zealand has a reputation as an ideal place to grow up in and to retire to. And with a tiny population of just over four million, passable weather – a bit like the UK – and easy access to beaches, ski slopes and glorious countryside, this is still true.

Other pluses? Everyone speaks English, housing is affordable and New Zealand scores well in the international surveys on cost of living and quality of life.

In its 2009 Worldwide Quality of Living Survey Mercer Human Resource Consulting rated Auckland as the fourth best place in the world to live and the highest ranked city in the Asia-Pacific region.

Wellington was in 12th place.

The analysis is based on an evaluation of 39 quality of living criteria, including political, social, economic and environmental factors, personal safety and health, education, transport and other public services.

The only cities to beat Auckland were Vienna, Zurich and Geneva. Vancouver tied for fourth place with Auckland.

In another recent survey of more than 2,000 British immigrants living in 12 countries, New Zealand received the highest ratings in all areas and topped the list of best places to live.

According to respondents to the NatWest International Bank survey, New Zealand has one of the lowest average property prices in the developed world, a better quality of life and a favourable tax regime.

Immigrants' favourite

Where once there were only Maoris, today immigrants from almost 150 different countries call New Zealand home. Not surprising for a country that has a lot going for it: fantastic scenery, cosmopolitan cities, a high standard of living, great wines and more golf courses per capita than anywhere else in the world.

Slightly bigger than the UK and located in the South Pacific Ocean, New Zealand is made up of two large islands and dozens of smaller scattered islands including Stewart Island, the Chatham Islands and Great Barrier Islands.

The country is divided into 25 geographical regions, each with distinct physical attributes, diverse culture and history, and unique points of interest.

From the sub-tropical far north, where you can stand on the tip of the North Island to witness the

About the writers: Blessed with a Kiwi wife, **Margaret** – making immigration a formality – retired publishing executive **Gordon Penny** didn't have to think long when she suggested they move from suburban London to Auckland. A bonus was that it would bring him closer to his grown-up sons in Australia.

FACTFILE

Capital: Wellington   **Population:** 4.2 million

Area: 268,680 sq km

Language: English (official) and Maori.

Climate: Varies from warm sub-tropical in the far north to cool temperate climates in the far south, with severe alpine conditions in the mountainous areas.

Time difference: GMT +12

Entry requirements: British passport holders can enter New Zealand as a visitor for up to six months without a visa. Visitors must have an onward ticket and may be asked for proof of adequate funds.

Retirement/residence visa: New Zealand has no such thing as a retirement visa. You can get in if you have a close family living there or via a business or investor category visa. [See: The Rules for Getting In]

Electricity: 230V/50Hz

Money: NZ$. ATMs are widely available. Credit cards/debit cars/travellers cheques accepted throughout New Zealand.

Public holidays 2010

Jan 1-2	New Year
Feb 6	Waitangi Day
April 2-5	Easter)
April 25	Anzac Day
June 7	Queen's Birthday
Oct 27	Labour Day
Dec 25	Christmas Day
Dec 26	Boxing Day

Opening hours:

Banks: 9.30am-4.30pm (Mon-Fri)
Some city branches open on Saturday mornings.
Shops: 9am-5pm (Mon-Fri), 9am-12pm (Sat)
Offices: 9am-5pm or 9.30am-5.30pm

Water: Tap water is OK

Tipping: Only for exemplary service in restaurants. Taxi drivers do not expect a tip but it is usual to round up change to the nearest dollar.

Medical/Healthcare

Medical facilities are excellent and standards of hospital, medical and dental treatment are comparable to those in the UK. There is a reciprocal agreement (subject to certain conditions) between Britain and New Zealand to enable citizens of either country to enjoy the benefits of the National Health Services of the other country if permanently or temporarily resident.

Pets: Only domesticated dogs and cats may be imported. Birds, rabbits, ferrets, hamsters and guinea pigs are a no-go. There is no quarantine for dogs and cats arriving from the UK but otherwise New Zealand is tough on the import of pets which all need to be microchipped. Cats require vaccinations for rabies, panleukopenia, rhinotrachetis and calicivirus. Dogs require vaccinations for canine distemper, infectious hepatitis, canine parvovirus and parainflueneza.
You can find a full list of requirements at:
www.jamescargo.com/livestock

merging of two oceans, to the deep south of the South Island, the last landmass before the ice shelves of Antarctica, each region has individual character and stories to tell.

Few countries in the world can boast New Zealand's range of natural features – from high peaks in vast mountain ranges to sub-tropical rainforests, lush rolling farmland to geothermal activity, white and black sand beaches to desert-like plains and unpopulated islands – all within one compact land.

The great outdoors

New Zealand's popularity is not surprising in a country where, for most of the year, the weather is good and outdoor pursuits are easy to find with clubs catering for most interests.

Popular activities range from the more sedate: walking – there are 14 national parks and reserves – to picnics on the beach and lawn bowls. Close to 100,000 people play bowls in NZ with many clubs offering not only a warm welcome but regular days when a bar and meal service is available.

Petanque is a sport which is gathering pace and many clubs are associated with bowling clubs.

For the more energetic there is challenging skiing and snowboarding. Most Kiwis live within half an hour's drive of the coast, so swimming, boating, diving and fishing are also popular pastimes.

New Zealand has the highest number of golf courses per capita in the world – 419 at the last count.

For the less energetic, eating out is a popular pastime with a wide range of cafes, bars and

THE RULES FOR GETTING IN

New Zealand has no such thing as a retirement visa. The government pledged to introduce such a visa in 2008 but, so far, nothing further has been heard of the proposal. There are two visas which allow those over 55 to emigrate to New Zealand – Investor Visas and the Family Visas.

Investor Migrant Category

If you have about NZ$1.2 million to invest you can obtain an investor migrant visa which has an upper age limit of 65.

The investor plus category requires funds of NZ$ 8 million to invest and has no upper age limit. You will still have to meet health and character requirements.

Family Visas

Under the Family Category, permanent residents of New Zealand (they must have been here for at least three years) can sponsor their siblings, parents and adult children.

The sponsored family members have to meet health and character requirements and the sponsor needs to meet a fairly low minimum income requirement.

There is also a "centre of gravity" test – so, for example, if you are the parents of a New Zealand permanent resident who is applying to sponsor you, New Zealand Immigration will look at how many children you have living outside NZ to determine your family's centre of gravity.

If you have two children, and one of them is living permanently in New Zealand, you can still apply under this category. But if you have three children, and two of them are still living in the UK, your family's centre of gravity will be the UK.

More info

New Zealand Immigration Service
www.immigration.govt.nz

---

restaurants. Fine dining is expensive but still cheaper than the UK. Most pubs will offer simple meals such as steak and chips with salad for about £8. The same meal in a posher establishment would cost £10-14. There is a huge number of Asian restaurants most of which are very reasonably priced.

Is it safe?

Yes. But – as with any other large city in the world - there are areas of poverty where it is unwise to flaunt wealth and areas you should avoid at night. On the whole, New Zealand is a safe country.

How much tax will I pay?

You become a tax resident in if you are in New Zealand for more than 183 days in any 12-month period, or have an "enduring relationship" with New Zealand which means anyone having a "permanent

place of abode" here.

A generous tax exemption is available to migrants to New Zealand for the first four years of their residency.

Anyone arriving in New Zealand who qualifies as a "Transitional Resident" will be exempt from NZ Income Tax for four years on all foreign sourced income other than employment income and income from the supply of services.

This means that investments held overseas that generate income, including dividends and interest, will not have this income taxed under NZ tax laws. This would also apply to certain types of pension funds held overseas.

'Transitional' resident includes immigrants who have a permanent place of abode in New Zealand and have not been resident in NZ for a continuous period of 10 years prior to moving to New Zealand.

Glendowie
Large character home with 4 bedrooms and 2 bathrooms in one of Glendowie's best streets. Glendowie is a premium seaside suburb 15 minute drive along the sea from Auckland City. Amenities include safe beach swimming, sailing, tennis and lawn bowls.   Price: POA
More info: http://cjsold.co.nz Cherilyn Jansen
Tel: ++575 9079 Email: cj@cjsold.co.nz

New home in Haswell
Halswell is a pretty suburb of Christchurch, well known for its wide tree-lined streets. This 2-storey, 4-bedroom home, with 732sq m of land, makes the most of the sunny northerly aspect and views of the hills.
Price: NZ$455,00
More info: he Key Team http://thekeyteam.co.nz

We Live Here

Gordon and Margaret Penny moved from London to Auckland seven years with their son Richard. Margaret is a New Zealander but had spent the past 30 years working and bringing up a family in London.

Gordon writes: Over the years we had made fairly regular trips from the UK to Australia to visit our sons in Perth and Sydney and to New Zealand to visit friends and family. We had a wide group of friends in the UK so the decision to sell up and move here was not an easy one to make. However, seven years down the line we have no regrets.

We live in a classic New Zealand villa built in about 1890, have built up a new circle of friends and enjoy a busy and sometimes hectic social life.

Our UK pensions both private and state provide a good standard of living enabling us to run two cars and make regular trips to Australia to see the boys and the Pacific Islands for holidays.

Margaret writes: Much to my surprise my OE (overseas experience) lasted 29 years. The surprise came when we agreed that it should end as I had naturally assumed that having established a life in England I would spend the rest of my days there.

I had left New Zealand in 1973. Not long after I arrived in London I met my husband so the actual travelling and exploring was cut short rather abruptly as he was a widower with three children and a large mortgage to service – no more overseas travelling for me at that time.

However, we did do some travelling and exploring together rather later on and in more comfortable circumstances than it would have been in the early '70s.

Around 2000 I told Gordon I wanted us to have a holiday in New Zealand to visit my aging aunts and uncles.

Standing on Marine Parade in Napier Gordon remarked: "Blue sky, blue sea, it is just like the Med". "But much cleaner," I replied. It was from that moment that we both began to think seriously of leaving England and living in New Zealand.

Since I was a Kiwi we didn't think it would be a problem from the immigration point of view. And it wasn't. As to finances, we did the figures and realised that if we sold our house 10 miles from central London, we could buy one in NZ for a lot less and live comfortably on our savings until our pensions were triggered. It took us the best part of a year to sell the house in the UK, move to NZ and find and move into our new home.

Seven years on, do we have any regrets? No way. Of course there are things we miss about Europe: the galleries, the choice of theatre, the museums, our friends, family, public transport, and the old buildings.

Do we miss the traffic congestion? The dirt? The difficulty of driving across London? Working? No way.

We lead different lives now. Gordon plays golf three times a week. We both play petanque twice a week at least. I go tramping once a week and do some voluntary work. We have a large group of friends.

Veg from the garden

My vegetable garden is at the back of the house and less than half a mile away on the local allotments. I enjoy gardening here more than in the UK because with no frosts, let alone snow, things grow much easily.

Friends urged us to take out health insurance when we came here because waiting lists are at least as long as those in the UK. Private health care is necessary for elective surgery. Just as well that we did because Gordon has had two major surgical operations in the last two years that would have cost us over NZ$40,000 without insurance. Happily he is fully recovered. How would that compare with England?

We have found that life begins with retirement. Settling into a new country is not always easy and you have to work at it. But if you join clubs and take up new ventures you will find that you have settled in before you know it.

The hardest part is learning to live far away from friend and relatives you have left behind. If you can afford to travel backwards and forwards that helps.

New technology also eases the pain as telephone calls are becoming cheaper, emails are free and so are some web cams. All these bring your friends and family that much closer.

If you hold investments in the UK and other overseas countries, the Transitional Resident rules can result in significant tax savings in your first four years in New Zealand.

There are also considerable tax advantages in New Zealand pension transfers from the UK, where funds can be accessed tax-free at retirement, providing this is outside of the reporting period of the Qualifying Recognised Overseas Pension Scheme (QROPS) into which they must first be transferred.

Is New Zealand property a good investment?

The price of property is a common topic of conversation at any gathering of New Zealanders.

Property has been a great investment over the past six years but prices have now flattened.

However, even with the lower exchange rates on offer, typical retirees would arrive in NZ able to pay cash for a property and not be bothered with a mortgage.

House prices are considerably cheaper than in the UK. For example, a four-bedroom detached house in a good city area with maybe 800sq.m of land will sell for between NZ$500,000-1 million. If the house is clifftop with fabulous views, the price will be NZ$1.6 million-NZ$3.4 million.

Houses in the country can be 40 per cent cheaper dependent on the amount of land that comes with the house. All the main estate agents have on-line listings where you can input areas, style of house wanted and price range.

Where's best to live?

While about half of all migrants to New Zealand settle in the Auckland area, census figures from StatisticsNZ

reveal the four places New Zealanders themselves would most like to move to are Canterbury (Christchurch), Bay of Plenty, (Tauranga), Waikato and Otago.

The Bay of Plenty, and especially its main town of Tauranga, have become popular retirement areas owing to their warm, sunny climate.

Canterbury is now home to more than half of the South Island's population.

Waikato has a number of pleasant, small towns close to the city of Hamilton and Otago offers very affordable housing close to or in the university city of Dunedin.

Auckland is the most populous city and also the most expensive in terms of house prices and the hardest to get around in rush hour.

Canterbury Region includes a large central portion of the east coast of the South Island, centred around the city of Christchurch, the largest city in the South Island.

From the silvery beaches of the east coast to the jagged peaks of the Southern Alps, big scenery is the

Waterfront home
Overlooking Kaipara's, Pahi Bay, this 2-storey home of 270sq m with 3/4 bedrooms and 2 bathrooms is just metres from the waterfront with mooring available. 2 reception rooms, fitted country kitchen, laundry and an upstairs veranda. Outside, a covered courtyard is surrounded by tropical plants and a Morton Bay fig tree, the largest, reportedly, in New Zealand. Price: Negotiable
More info: www.goodground.com
Tel: +09 432 1077   Email: info@goodground.com

Fruit farm
Historic home on the Waiari river with over 2 hectares in green kiwifruit and approximately 3 hectares in avocados. Some grazing with trout stream on boundary. A plant nursery also provides an extra income.
Price: POA
More info: www.ruralrealty.co.nz Tel: 07 573 6997
hprotzman@xtra.co.nz

order of the day – huge panoramas of ocean or mountains, great sweeps of pastureland, massive amounts of sky.

The highest point of the region is also the highest point of New Zealand; the spectacular Aoraki/Mount Cook stands at 3,754 metres (Aoraki is Maori for Cloud Piercer).

The Bay of Plenty lies east of the Kaimai-Mamaku Ranges and south of the Coromandel peninsula. It is a place of beautiful harbours, long white surf beaches and an easy-going lifestyle.

Located at the entrance to a beautiful natural harbour, Tauranga is a thriving commercial centre with a passion for good food, wine and stylish shopping.

Two large marinas in Tauranga hold over a thousand yachts and launches. The city offers a cosmopolitan lifestyle city, first-rate cuisine and local wines in its many cafés and restaurants.

Waikato is the first region south of Greater Auckland. It has two spectacular landscapes dominated by the serenity of the Waikato River and the rich rolling green of productive farmland. The main centre is Hamilton – a city that serves the thriving farming and university community.

Hamilton, New Zealand's fourth largest city, is famous for its themed gardens and the local zoo which has the largest free flight aviary in the Southern Hemisphere. The southern end of Hamilton's main street offers an excellent choice of restaurants, cafes and bars.

Otago is located in the centre of the South Island, inland from Dunedin. Central Otago comprises a series of river basins and deep river gorges. It has the hottest summers and coldest winters in New Zealand.

Old trails that provided access for thousands of

miners in the gold rush of the 1860s can still be seen winding over the hills, along with stone cottages, cleverly engineered water channels, mines and machinery associated with the gold rush.

Alexandra, the main town on the Clutha River, is the centre for stone fruit, particularly golden apricots. Hydro electric dams along the Clutha River have formed Lake Roxburgh and Lake Dunstan which now offer a range of recreational opportunities, from power boating and fishing to windsurfing and sailing.

Greensboro Mews
A modern development of 16 units recently completed on the campus of the University of Waikato, Hamilton. Each unit is 205sq m and has 5 bedrooms, a large living room, 2 bathrooms, 3 toilets and spacious deck. Price: £186,754
More info: greensboromews.cameron.co.nz
Email: martin@cameron.co.nz

St Lukes, Auckland
Executive style, solid construction brick and concrete apartments ideal for present or prospective retirement. Views over and direct access to extensive parklands, 8 minutes to central business district and walking distance to shopping mall. Extensive landscaped plazas,

swimming pool, tennis court, spa, sauna, gym and recreation room.
More info: Sage Realty Ltd www.sagerealty.co.nz
Tel: 649 815 1130

NEW ZEALAND CONTACT DIRECTORY

Embassies/Government
NZ High Commission in London
www.nzembassy.com/home.cfm?c=14
Visa information
New Zealand Immigration Service
www.immigration.govt.nz

British High Commission in NZ
http://ukinnewzealand.fco.gov.uk/en/

Travel & Health Advice
Foreign Office travel advice
www.fco.gov.uk/travel
www.nhs.uk/Healthcareabroad
www.masta.org

About NZ
www.portaloceania.com/nz-region-index-ing.htm
www.travbuddy.com/New-Zealand
(These two sites allow you to click through to major cities/regional websites)
www.newzealandwebsites.com
www.beautifulnewzealand.com
http://move2nz.com/

General & Expat
www.expatfocus.com
www.britishexpat.com
www.transitionsabroad.com
www.britishexpats.com

Media
www.mondonewspapers.com/world/newzealand.htm Allows you to click through to the websites of all major print media in New Zealand.
This website does the same for TV and radio
www.finda.co.nz/business/c/broadcasting-radio-tv

www.stuff.co.nz

Property
realestate.co.nz
bayleys.co.nz
raywhite.co.nz
harcourts.co.nz
ljhooker.co.nz
firstnational.co.nz

Travel & Tourism
www.newzealand.com
www.tourism.net.nz
www.nz.com
www.docgovt.nz

Getting There
Most major European airlines fly into Auckland. Air New Zealand has daily flights from London going via San Francisco, Los Angeles or Hong Kong.
Because of the distance involved a stopover is recommended. Most popular destinations are Singapore, Kuala Lumpur, Bangkok and Hong Kong.
www.airnewzealand.co.uk
www.britishairways.com
www.qantas.co.uk
www.continental.com
www.airfrance.co.uk
www.emirates.com/uk
www.singaporeair.co.uk
www.cathaypacific.com
www.malaysiaairlines.com/uk
www.thaiairways.co.uk
www.koreanair.com
www.bruneiair.com/uk

Getting Around
Air: There are regular flights between the major New Zealand cities and smaller towns. Flights are operated by:
Air New Zealand:
www.airnewzealand.co.uk
Pacific Blue: www.flypacificblue.com
Jet Star: www.jetstar.com

Train: Both Auckland and Wellington have major commuter networks. Other train services are for tourists such as the Trans Alpine in the South Island. On the North Island the Overlander runs once a day both ways between Auckland and Wellington. The journey takes 12 hours.

Bus: The major cities have local bus services with connections to other towns and villages. It is possible to travel the length of both islands on regular bus services.

Boat: Regular ferry services operate between the North and South islands. Other services cover coastal New Zealand and the larger lakes. One of the main operators is Fullers
www.fullers.co.nz

Driving: Roads are very busy especially in the major cities. Watch out for traffic turning in front of you from the right. This applies on roundabouts and in particular where an oncoming vehicle wants to turn right, you must give way to it.
If you hold an overseas licence or international driving permit you can drive for a maximum of 12 months.
Driving is on the left.

Waipu Cove Resort
A range of properties - from 1 to 4 bedrooms – is available at the Waipu Cove Resort which has a restaurant, swimming pool and is only a very short walk to Waipu Cove beach and reserve.
Prices: Various
More info:
www.coastlinerealestate.co.nz
Tel: 09 432-1003 Email
sandy@coastlinerealestate.co.nz

Nine people per square mile in a million square miles of prairies and mountains

(compared to 1,000 in the UK)

Why Canada?

Towering mountain ranges, wide expanses of prairies, warm humid summers, cold, snowy winters, quiet pastoral settings and bustling cosmopolitan cities…

It brings to mind that old song:

In that mountain greenery
Where God paints the scenery…

It might have been written about Canada.

Canada is a country that offers something for everyone.

If you have ever flown over Canada you will have got a feeling for the vast size of this, the world's second largest country. If you haven't, you simply need to look at the figures: almost a million square miles of mountains, prairies, lakes, fiords and rivers. And in among these features, huge natural resources.

Large in both size and spirit, Canada is a known for its immense natural beauty and as a place where big dreams come true. It's also pretty empty – just 3.3 people per sq. km compared to the United States (29.1), the UK (242) and Japan (335.3).

Almost every year in the last decade Canada has been top, or near the top, in the United Nations' annual Human Development Index which combines factors such as the cost of living, adult literacy, job opportunities, life expectancy and school enrolment.

That's the good news.

The bad news is that Canada doesn't want you. It has quite enough of its own 'seniors' (as it classes the over-65s) thank you very much.

While Canada accepts more immigrants from around the world than any other Western nation on a per capita basis it decidedly does not put out the welcome mat for retirees from other countries.

One of the reasons may be that because of all that fresh air and mountain scenery Canada has a growing and – for some, worrying – proportion of seniors. Over-65s represented eight per cent of the population in 1950. By 1990 it was 12 per cent. By 2008 almost one out of seven Canadian (13.7 per cent) was aged 65 and over and, if current trends continue, there will be more people in Canada in 2017 over the age of 65 than under the age of 15.

No wonder then that oldies from other countries are not made very welcome.

For retirees getting in doesn't come easy, or cheap.

Another problem? Britons who move to Canada – along with other Commonwealth countries – have their state pension frozen at the level it was when they left and do not receive the periodic increases paid to pensioners in the UK; 150,000 Britons living there are affected.

The regions

Canada consists of 10 provinces and three territories in five main regions: the Atlantic region, Central Canada, the Prairies, the West Coast and the North.

The major difference between a Canadian province and a territory is that a province receives powers directly from the Constitution Act, 1867, giving them greater competences and rights than a territory, which is delegated powers by the federal government.

The culture and population are different in each region.

The Atlantic region consists of the provinces of Nova Scotia, New Brunswick, Prince Edward Island, Newfoundland and Labrador. Activities such as fishing, farming, forestry, tourism and mining are important to the Atlantic economy.

Central Canada consists of the provinces of Ontario

and Quebec. This is the most populated region.

The Prairies include the provinces of Manitoba, Saskatchewan and Alberta. Much of the land is flat and fertile, excellent for farming and rich in energy resources.

In western Alberta the Prairies end and the Rocky Mountains begin. The Canadian Rockies include some of the largest peaks in North America.

On the West Coast the province of British Columbia is famous for its mountain ranges and forests, natural resources, fruit farming and tourism.

The North consists of Canada's three territories: Yukon, the Northwest Territories and Nunavut. Together, they make up over one-third of Canada's land mass. Northern resources include oil, natural gas, gold, lead and zinc.

Cost of living

Not one Canadian city features in the top 50 of Mercer Consulting's 2009 annual cost of living report. Canada's highest ranking city, Toronto, slipped down 31 places from 2008 to 85th. Ottawa dropped 36 places to 121st and Montreal was in 103rd place, down from 72nd in 2008.

There's good cost of living info at: www.canadaimmigrants.com

About half of all immigrants to Canada head for either Ontario (mainly Toronto) or to British Columbia (mainly Vancouver).

Is Canadian property a good investment?

The average price of a detached bungalow in Canada rose almost 11 per cent from last year to C$329,209 in the first three months of 2010.

Two-storey home prices rose 10.3 per cent to C$365,141 and condo prices rose 10.9 per cent to C$228,963. Average prices rose more than 10 per cent on a national basis in the first quarter of 2010, with prices in Vancouver and Toronto climbing at a dramatic pace, according to a Royal-Lepage House Price Survey.

The survey found that the average price of detached bungalows in Toronto was C$459,107 in the first quarter of this year, up 13.3 per cent from a year ago. Condominium prices rose 10 per cent to C$317,579.

In Vancouver, the housing market rose even more dramatically. The average price of a detached bungalow skyrocketed 21.8 per cent to C$906,045 and condo prices were up 15.7 per cent from last year at C$470,000.

Not all major Canadian cities have seen the same growth in housing prices.

Average housing prices in Montreal rose about seven per cent.

Property purchase tax is 1-3 per cent of the price, with agent's fees generally about 6 per cent and legal fees between C$800 and C$1,200.

A survey might cost C$300-500 and local property taxes (paid annually or monthly) will be about one per cent of the value assessed annually by the local council.

You can find a step-by-step guide to home-buying and other useful information at: www.cmhc-schl.gc.ca/en/co/buho/index.cfm, the website of the Canada Mortgage & Housing Corp.

How much tax will I pay?

There are no death duties and capital gains taxes are lower than in the UK but Canada's tax system does not recognise the UK entitlement to take 25 per cent ➤

Alpine home, Alberta
Beautiful riverside home in the mountain paradise of Canmore, Alberta with 178 feet of river frontage. 6 bedrooms, 5 bathrooms. All laundry and kitchen appliances are made by Miele. Windows and doors tilt & turn, swing or slide allowing the air to flow and the sunlight to bathe the rooms.
Price: C$1.89m

More info:
www.canmoreriverfront.ca
Tel: +1 403 609 1317

FACTFILE

Capital: Ottawa   **Population:** 33.2m

Area: 9,984,670sq km

Language: English and French (predominantly in Quebec). There are also over 53 native languages.

Climate: Canada has four very distinct seasons and due to the country's size the climate varies considerably from region to region. The warmest areas are on the US border (where most people live) and where summers are longer and winters are shorter. In winter, temperatures fall below freezing point throughout most of Canada. But the south-western coast has a relatively mild climate and during the summer months the southern provinces experience high levels of humidity and temperatures that can surpass 30°C. Vancouver is the city with the fewest days below freezing (51); Yellowknife is the city with the coldest winters and the sunniest summers.

Time difference: GMT -3/8

Entry requirements: No visa required for stays of up to six months.

Retirement/residence visa: Since there's no retiree visa as such, the only options are through family unification or investment. Adult children in Canada can sponsor parents, or you can sign up to the Immigrant Investor Programme. This is for those with business experience, and requires a deposit of £187,000, returned after about five years – with no interest.
This is not designed as a retiree visa, and applicants must also have an individual net worth of at least £374,000.
[See The rules for getting in]

Electricity: 110-120V/60Hz

Money: Canadian $. ATMs are widely available. Credit cards/debit cards/travellers' cheques are all widely accepted.

Public holidays 2010

Jan 1	New Year's Day
April 2-5	Easter
May 24	Victoria Day
July 1	Canada Day
Sept 6	Labour Day
Oct 11	Thanksgiving Day
Nov 11	Remembrance Day
Dec 25-26	Christmas

Opening hours

Banks: 10am-3pm, Mon-Fri
Offices: 9am-5pm
Shops: 9am-5.30pm or 9pm in larger towns and cities.

Water: Tap water is OK

Tipping: Gratuities are not normally included on restaurant bills. If not 15 per cent should be added. Tips of around 10 per cent are expected by all service personnel and taxi drivers.

Medical/Healthcare: No specific vaccinations are required. It is essential to take out full medical insurance.
See: www.hc-sc.gc.ca/hcs-sss/medi-assur/res/faq-eng.php

Pets: Dogs and cats over three months old must have signed and dated certificates from a veterinarian verifying that they have been vaccinated against rabies within the last three years. For dogs under three months old you do not need a rabies certificate but animals must be in good health.

of your pension fund as tax-free cash. To retain this benefit you will need to have started drawing your pension before becoming a Canadian resident.

Occupational Pension plans can be transferred to a Canadian Registered Retirement Savings Plan (RRSP). No tax is deducted in the UK and while the monies remain in the RRSP, no tax is payable in Canada.

Anyone resident in Canada for over 183 days in a tax year will be liable to pay income tax.

Income tax is charged at a federal level and by each of the 12 provinces and there are substantial variations in how much you pay depending on where you live. Income Tax is significantly higher than in the UK. Given retirement income of £50,000 a year, a couple retired in Ontario would pay would pay about 30 per cent tax and in Alberta about 26 per cent.

Sales tax: Sales tax also comes in two layers: A Government of Canada tax of five per cent is added to the price of goods and services plus a Provincial Sales Tax (PST) which ranges from 7-10 per cent. (There is no PST in Alberta, Nunavut, Northwest Territories and the Yukon).

Capital Gains Tax rates vary between 7.5 and 23 per cent, a lot less than the 40 per cent levied in the UK.

Where's best to live?

According to Canada's MoneySense magazine [www.canadianbusiness.com], which devised a scoring system based on climate, healthcare, taxes, low crime, easy walking and affordable homes, the top three places to retire to are Victoria (British Colombia), Kingston (Ontario) and Ottawa (Ontario).

Five of the top ten were in British Columbia, four in Ontario and one in Quebec.
The full list:

Victoria, BC	Kingston, ON
Ottawa, ON	Vancouver, BC
London, ON	Courtenay, BC
Vernon, BC	Cobourg, ON
Joliette, QC	Salmon Arm, BC

According to The Economist magazine, Vancouver is not only the best place to live in Canada but is actually the best city in the world to live in.

Here's a flavour of Canada's provinces and territories

Alberta

Named after Queen Victoria's fourth daughter, Alberta, located where the Rocky Mountains meet the prairie, was settled by pioneering farmers in the late 19th and early 20th centuries.

Memories of that era remain and are celebrated every summer when Calgarians don cowboy boots and hats and attend rodeos and chuckwagon races during

the city's internationally renowned Stampede.

But though still proud of being a part of the Canadian Wild West, many Albertans have left their farms and ranches and 80 per cent of the province's population is urban with more than half living in the provincial capital, Edmonton, and in Calgary.

British Columbia

Canada's westernmost province with its capital city, Victoria, located on Vancouver Island, BC is surrounded by the Pacific Ocean and the Rocky Mountains. The temperate climate and plentiful salmon fishing areas around the coast, hugely popular ski hills in the mountains and rich orchards in the interior have made BC a leading destination.

Every year BC welcomes about 35,000 immigrants from around the world and, with four million people, is the country's third-largest province in terms of population, nearly half of them

Wetlands home

3-bedroom house on 155 acres in the British Columbia Valley Wetlands with over 265 species of birds and home to an incredible assembly of natural habitats.
The main crop is hay (50 acres) and the balance of the land is available for pasture grazing which can be leased out to local farmers. Outdoor cookhouse with water and power. Pen for horse training. Spring-fed winter ponds for ducks · Potential for eco tourism business, either camping, bird watching, cross-country skiing etc.
Price: C$2.5m.
More info:
(Owners) Tel: 250-346-3294
www.housemaxx.ca

THE RULES FOR GETTING IN

If you are a parent or grandparent waiting to get into Canada under the family reunification category you may well die waiting!

The backlog of all immigration applications is expected to grow to 1.6 million by 2012, and the waiting time to increase from six to 10 years. The backlog includes 100,000 parents and grandparents.

Family Class

Canadian citizens and permanent residents aged 18 or older can sponsor parents from abroad. Your sponsor must sign an undertaking that they will support you for a period of three to ten years so you will not need to apply for social assistance.

The process and all forms are available online at www.cic.gc.ca. The rules are specific:

Sponsors may have to meet certain income requirements and if they have previously sponsored relatives who have received social assistance, they may not be allowed to sponsor another person.

Since immigrants do not immediately qualify for provincial health plans they must have medical insurance until they are covered

This is normally three months but each province administers its own program and there may be some variations in eligibility from province to province.

Business or Investment Visas

An alternative is the classes of investment visa Canada offers which are similar to America's EB-5 business visa. Both require you to have considerable funds at your disposal.

Note that Quebec administers its own programme and is slightly different.

The **Immigrant Investor Program** requires candidates to have a net worth of at least C$800,000 and be willing and able to make an interest-free loan of half of this amount to the Canadian government.

The investment is managed – and guaranteed – by Citizenship and Immigration Canada (CIC) and used for job creation in Canada's provinces.

CIC returns your C$400,000 investment, without interest, "about five years and two months after payment".

To qualify candidates must have at least two years of business experience and meet medical and security requirements that includes a medical examination and security and criminal checks.

The **Entrepreneur Program** is similar but aimed at those who want a more active role acquiring and running their own business. Entrepreneurs must have at least two years of business experience, a net worth of at least C$300,000 and go through the same medical and security checks.

More info

Go to www.cic.gc.ca and (under immigration) you can click through for more information on these programmes.

Quebec operates its own business immigration program: www.immigration-quebec.gouv.qc.ca

living in Vancouver.

With its breathtaking scenery and landscapes, British Columbia is visited by over 20 million tourists a year.

Manitoba

Twice the size of the UK, Manitoba – which means "where the spirit lives" – attracted waves of European immigrants in the 19th century. Its terrain includes prairie grassland, lakes, forest and Arctic tundra stretching from the 49th to the 60th parallel.

The capital, Winnipeg, where the majority of the province's over 1.1 million residents live, is a major cultural centre and home to the country's ethnic German and Ukrainian communities.

New Brunswick

The largest of Canada's three Maritime provinces, New Brunswick is also Canada's only official bilingual province. About 35 per cent of its residents are French-speaking.

Newfoundland and Labrador

Canada's most easterly province is more than three times the total area of all three neighbouring Maritime provinces. Cape Spear, the easternmost point, is closer to Ireland, than Winnipeg, 3,100km to its west.

More than five centuries after Viking explorers from Iceland and Greenland visited Labrador and Newfoundland, Basque, French and Portuguese fishermen settled there to exploit the rich supply of cod, halibut, mackerel and herring found at the Grand Banks, in the south-eastern corner of the province.

Northwest Territories

Stretching north of Saskatchewan to British Columbia, the Northwest Territories remain a mighty northern presence in Canada, occupying over 1.1m sq km. A wilderness paradise consisting of a blend of tundra and mountainous highlands, the NWT has an economy built on tourism and mining.

It has only has one city, Yellowknife, the capital, and its population is just over 42,000.

Nova Scotia

Canada's ocean playground, Nova Scotia has a centuries-old relationship with the sea, which has attracted immigrants to this province – the most easterly point on the North American mainland – since 1604, when the first European settlements were established.

In addition to its vibrant resource-based industries in fishing, mining and forestry, the province has over 3,800 coastal islands.

Nunavut

Compared to Canada's other territories and provinces, Nunavut has the smallest population, with only about 28,000 residents, 85 per cent of who are Inuit and in whose language, Inuktitut, Nunavut means "our land."

What the new territory lacks in numbers of people it more than makes up for in geographic size. Nunavut's 26 communities are spread across nearly 2m sq km, almost one-fifth of Canada's total land mass.

Ontario

The economic engine that powers the Canadian economy, Ontario contributes about 41 per cent of Canada's gross domestic product and the more than 67,000 farms in the province generate almost one-quarter of all farm revenue in Canada.

Canada's largest province, Ontario is home to about one in three Canadians. Eighty per cent of Ontario's 10 million residents live in urban centres, five million reside in the Greater Toronto Area and half of those live in the city of Toronto proper, Canada's largest municipality where more than 100 languages can be heard on the streets every day.

The province's 250,000 lakes (including much of the Great Lakes, shared with the United States), and numerous rivers and streams hold about one-third of the world's fresh water.

Home up the hill
One-Level home is located "up the hill" in the Heights neighbourhood of Vancouver. Large kitchen with oak cabinets.
Price: C$149,900 .
More info:
(Owners) Tel: 250-346-3294 www.housemaxx.ca

Bungalow, Melita
Large bungalow on over 9 acres with several outbuildings in the Souris River valley town of Melita in the province of Manitoba. 4 bedrooms and 1 1/2 bathrooms. Price: C$69,000
More info:
www.cameronagencies.ca Don Cameron Realty
Tel: +204-522-3285

Prince Edward Island

Prince Edward Island at just over 5,600sq km represents 0.1 per cent of Canada's total mass and is Canada's most densely populated province or territory, with almost 25 people per square kilometre. The island is one of Canada's most popular tourist destinations.

Québec

Occupying over 1.5m sq km of land – more than 15 per cent of Canada's total territory – Québec is Canada's largest province. About six million of Québec's total population of over seven million are French-speaking, making the province home to one of the largest French-speaking communities outside France.

Despite living in a province that is three times the size of France, almost half of Québecers inhabit less than one per cent of the province's total land area. Most prefer city life, choosing to reside in major metropolitan areas such as Montréal, which has a population of over 3.3 million and the province's capital, Québec City, with nearly 700,000 residents.

Saskatchewan

Renowned for its prairie sunsets in the summer, Saskatchewan also scores top marks as Canada's sunniest province, averaging 2,000-2,500 hours of sunshine annually. The clear skies have undoubtedly helped Saskatchewan become the country's breadbasket, producing 54 per cent of the wheat grown in Canada.

More than one in three of the province's over one million residents live in two cities, Saskatoon and the capital, Regina,.

Yukon

In 1898, two years after the start of the Klondike Gold Rush, which brought a stampede of about 100,000 fortune seekers to within its borders, the Yukon became Canada's second northern territory.

The site of an Indian fishing camp in 1896, Dawson City emerged as Canada's largest urban centre west of Winnipeg.

Lakefront home
This waterfront home with 310ft of lake front on Kemptback Lake a few miles from Kemptville, Nova Scotia is perfect for boating or fishing. In a cove on 2.48 acres of land with views of the lake. 3 bedrooms, 3 bathrooms, laundry room, mudroom and small office area. Appliances and furnishings are included. Price: C$439,000

Cambridge, Ontario
Detached executive home of 2,800sq ft in Cambridge, Ontario. 4 bedrooms, 3 bathrooms, landscaped garden with pool and hot-tub. House has hardwood floors, a spiral staircase.
Price: C$469,900
More info: www.homegroove.ca Tel: + 519-623-6200
Email: daniel@remaxcentre.ca

PROPERTY

CANADA CONTACT DIRECTORY

Embassies/Government
Canada High Commission in London
www.canadainternational.gc.ca

British Consulates in Canada
http://ukincanada.fco.gov.uk/en
You can click through to regional offices

Travel & Health Advice
Foreign Office travel advice
www.fco.gov.uk/travel
www.nhs.uk/Healthcareabroad
www.masta.org

About Canada
http://canada.gc.ca
www.onestopimmigration-canada.com

About Canada (provinces)
The following links provide detailed
information about each of Canada's regional
capitals.
Ottawa
www.city.ottawa.on.ca
www.ottawaweb.com
www.ottawakiosk.com/Ottawajgpg.html
www.tourottawa.org/index.html-ssi
St. John's, Newfoundland
www.stjohns.ca
www.infonet.st-johns.nf.ca
www.gov.nf.ca
www.capitalcoast.nf.ca
Halifax, Nova Scotia
www.region.halifax.ns.ca
www.gov.ns.ca
Charlottetown, Prince Edward Island
www.charlottetown.worldweb.com
www.city.charlottetown.pe.ca
www.peisland.com/virtualtour3/v-tour20.htm
www.charlottetownpei.com
Fredericton, New Brunswick
www.fredericton.ca
www.capnb.ca
www.tourismfredericton.ca
www.teamfredericton.com
Quebec
www.quebecregion.com
www.ville.quebec.qc.ca
www.capitale.gouv.qc.ca
www.quebecweb.com/tourisme/quebec/villequebec/
Toronto, Ontario
www.city.toronto.on.ca
www.toronto.com
www.torinfo.com
www.showmetoronto.com
www.torontotourism.com
Winnipeg, Manitoba
www.winnipeg.ca
www.winnipeg.worldweb.com
www.tourism.winnipeg.mb.ca
www.eyeonwinnipeg.com
Regina, Saskatchewan
www.regina.ca
www.tourismregina.com

Edmonton, Alberta
www.gov.edmonton.ab.ca
www.infoedmonton.com
www.cuug.ab.ca:8001/VT/edmonton.html
www.discoveredmonton.com
Victoria, British Columbia
www.city.victoria.bc.ca
www.bcpcc.com
www.tourismvictoria.com
www.attractionsvictoria.com
Whitehorse, Yukon
www.city.whitehorse.yk.ca
www.yukoninfo.com/whitehorse/index.htm
www.whitehorse.worldweb.com
Yellowknife, Northwest Territories
www.city.yellowknife.nt.ca
www.northernfrontier.com
Iqaluit, Nunavut
www.city.iqaluit.nu.ca
www.relocatecanada.com/nunavut/commune.html
www.iqaluit.worldweb.com

General & Expat
www.livingabroadincanada.com
Canadian Alliance of British Pensioners
(CABP)www.britishpensions.com
British Pensioners Association of Western
Canadawww.britishpensioners.com

Media
Go to this website to click through to any
regional Canadian newspaper which will, for
example, allow you to browse classified
advertising for property, etc.
www.cna-acj.ca/en/aboutnewspapers/media/canadian-dailies
www.canada.com (online news)
There's a similar list of radio and TV
channels at: www.ostamyy.com/TV-radio-channels/Canada.htm

Property
This is a good starting point:
www.mls.ca/splash.aspx It is part of the
website of the the Canadian Real Estate
Association (CREA) and allows you to access
property for sale across Canada. There is
also a useful buyers' guide.
Similar information can be found at:
www.remax.ca
www.earth-house.com
http://listingsca.com
www.snapuprealestate.ca

Travel & Tourism
http://uscw.canada.travel
www.canadatourism.ca
The following site allows you to click
through to provincial tourism websites
http://canajun.com/canada/tourism/index.htm
Getting There
British Airways: www.BritishAirways.com
Thomas Cook Airlines:

www.thomascookairlines.co.uk/
Air Canada: AirCanada.com
BMI: flybmi.com
Air France: www.airfrance.co.uk
Continental: continental.com
FlyGlobeSpan.com

Getting Around
Canada is huge so flying is the main option
but land travel is generally cheaper and
there are some spectacular road and train
journeys.
Air: Several low-cost operators compete
with Air Canada's large network:
Jazz: www.flyjazz.ca
CanJet: www.canjet.com
Air Canada: AirCanada.com
West Jet: www.westjet.com
Porter Airlines: www.flyporter.com
Air North: www.flyairnorth.com
Pacific Coastal: www.pacific-coastal.com
FlyGlobeSpan: FlyGlobeSpan.com
Train: With 48,000kms of track, Canada
has one of the largest rail networks in the
world and train travel is a real pleasure.
The national rail service, Via Rail, operates
rapid services between main cities.
Bus: The Greyhound bus network covers
more than 1,000 destinations in Canada
with links to many cities in the USA.
Bus services are reasonable and efficient
within towns and cities. Many cities have a
cheap subway, metro or light rapid transit
service: the SkyTrain in Vancouver, the
CTrain in Calgary and the LTR in Edmonton,
the O-Train in Ottawa.
Boat: One of the neatest ways of getting
around Canada's coastal regions is by
ferry. Ferries are fast, comfortable and
good value. There are year-round services
to nearby islands and coastal regions and
Canada also has massive inland waterways
which are well-served by ferries.
Driving: Canada has one of the best road
safety records in the world. Roads are
generally excellent but winter driving
conditions can be extreme and distance
are long (the Trans-Canada Highway runs
across the country for 8,000km from
British Columbia to Newfoundland}.
You must have minimum insurance cover
of $200,000 and you cannot rent a car if
you are under 25.
Driving is on the right.
Pets: If coming from rabies-free countries
dogs and cats can enter Canada for
without vaccination, quarantine, or
certification.Dogs can enter Canada for any
period of time (permanent stays, temporary
visits, or in transit visits) without
quarantine from any country. Canada's
import requirements take into
consideration the rabies status of the
country of export
More info: www.inspection.gc.ca

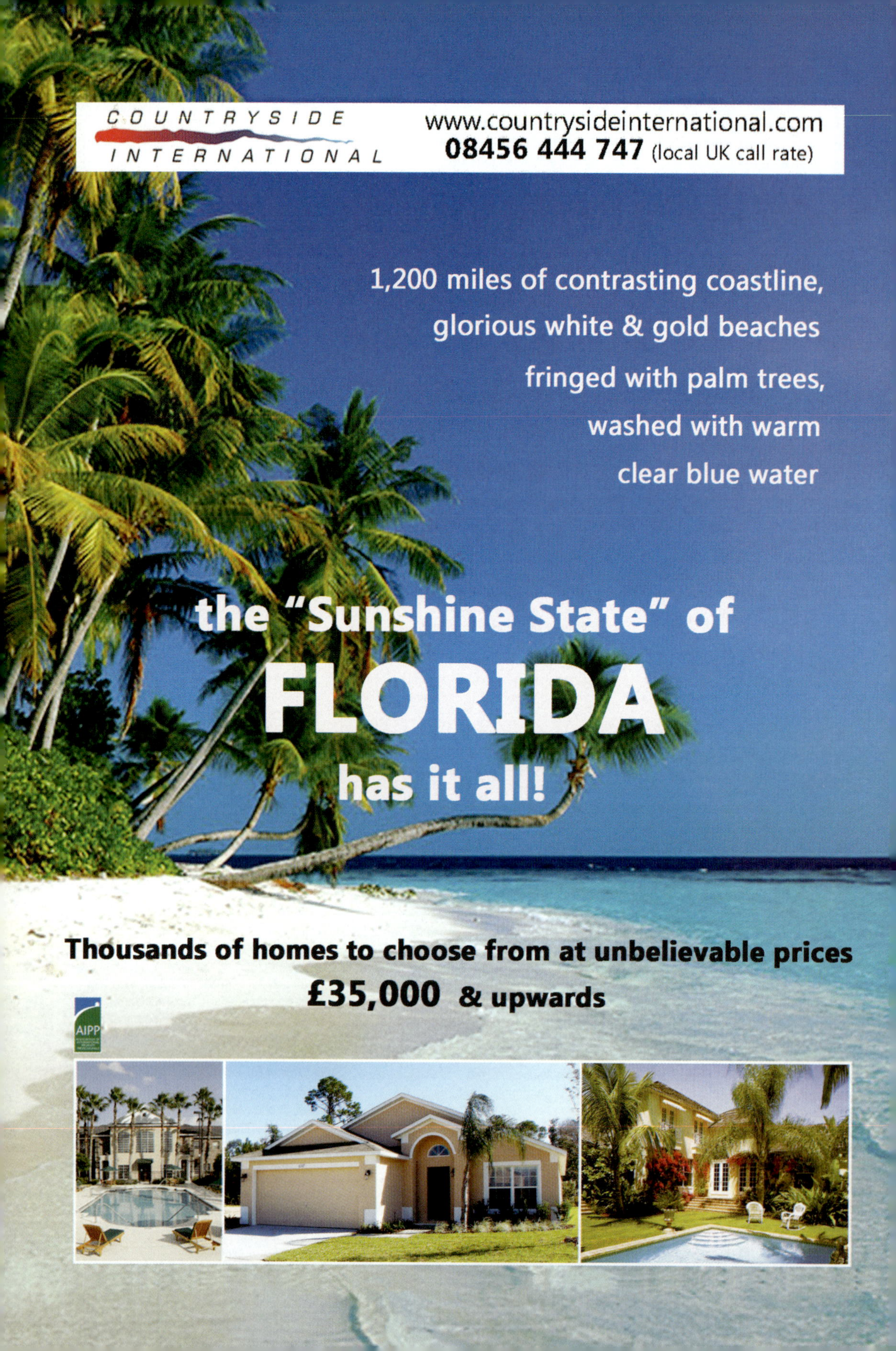
COUNTRYSIDE
INTERNATIONAL
www.countrysideinternational.com
08456 444 747 (local UK call rate)
1,200 miles of contrasting coastline,
glorious white & gold beaches
fringed with palm trees,
washed with warm
clear blue water
the "Sunshine State" of
FLORIDA
has it all!
Thousands of homes to choose from at unbelievable prices
£35,000 & upwards
AIPP

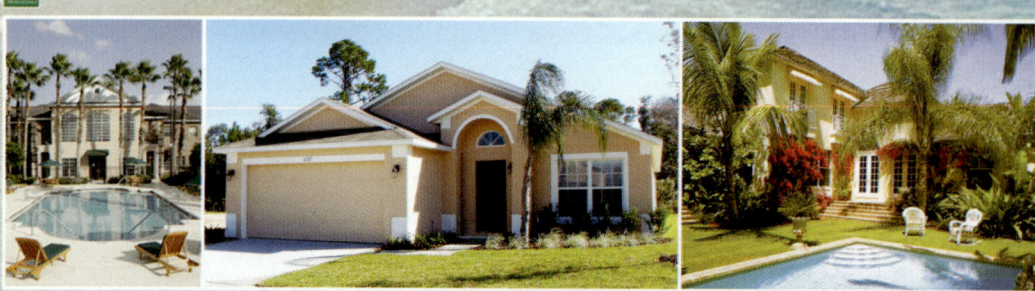

The 'snowbird' visa will give you six months a year but by far the best bet is the EB-5

Why the USA?

America is a land of stunning natural beauty and great extremes – wild coasts, beautiful beaches, granite peaks, searing deserts, emerald green forests, thundering waterfalls, the Grand Canyon, Yosemite and Yellowstone National Parks and endless grassy plains.

Side by side with these natural wonders are man-made ones: iconic public landmarks, giant shopping malls, extraordinary theme parks and stunning cities, from Los Angeles, San Francisco and Las Vegas to New York whose Times Square is the most visited place in America seen by almost 40 million people a year.

Then there are the Americans themselves – a people of immense ethnic diversity, warm, generous and welcoming, open minded and polite.

A common criticism of Americans is their national dream: They want to be rich and happy.

So what's wrong with that?

Standard of living

The current international recession means that Americans are currently experiencing the most severe blow to their living standards since the 1930s with home foreclosures and the highest unemployment rate for 25 years.

Even so, the standard of living is one of the highest in the world by almost any measure, always in the top 10 in surveys such as the UN's Human Development Index.

Although America's gross domestic product (GDP) ranks only 16th in the world, adjusted for cost of living, the US leads the rest of the world for the standard of living.

The average American family enjoys nearly twice as much living space as the British, Germans or French. And amazingly, the average American household has to spend just 5.7 per cent of its income on food.

But while the cost of living may be low, health care is another story, and this should be high on the list of concerns of those contemplating retirement to the US.

Health insurance premiums have risen 73 per cent since 2000 and insurance for a retired couple can cost about $6,000 a year.

Consider this: Over 60 per cent of all US family bankruptcies result from medical expenses, according to a study by the American Journal of Medicine.

"Unless you're Warren Buffett, your family is just one serious illness away from bankruptcy," said the study's author, David Himmelstein, associate professor of medicine at Harvard Medical School.

Americans spend more on medicine than any other

About the writer: This section – including the extensive information on the EB-5 investor visa – was put together with the help of Andrew Bartlett who provides independent advice and briefings to British clients on relocation and retirement to the USA .
More info: www.AndrewBartlettFlorida.co.uk

FACTFILE

Capital: Washington, DC   **Population**: 293m

Area: 9.6m sq km   **Language**: English

Climate: Mostly temperate, but semiarid in the great plains west of the Mississippi River, and arid in the Great Basin of the southwest; tropical in Hawaii and Florida, arctic in Alaska. Low winter temperatures in the northwest are ameliorated occasionally in January and February by warm chinook winds from the eastern slopes of the Rocky Mountains

Time difference: GMT -5/9 hours

Entry requirements: No visas required for British travellers but passports must be valid for at least 90 days from date of entry and must be machine-readable.

Retiremen/residence visa: A close relative, spouse, parent, sister or brother will usually allow you obtain permanent residence but not your first cousin twice removed! Under the visa waiver pro-gramme you can visit for up to 90 days but you cannot extend your visit. Options for longer stays are the B-2 'snowbird' visa, which allows a six-month stay, or the EB-5 investor visa, which requires a minimum investment of $500,000 in a 'Regional Center'.
[See: The rules for getting in] and The EB5 investor route to USA retirement (page xx)

Electricity: 110V/60Hz. Plugs are of the flat two-pin type.

Money: US$. ATMs widely available. Major credit cards/debit cards are accepted pretty well everywhere, but travellers' cheques should be in US$.

Public holidays 2010

Jan 1	New Year's Day.
Jan 18	Martin Luther King Day.
Feb 15	Presidents' Day.
May	31 Memorial Day.
July 4	Independence Day.
Sept 6	Labor Day.
Oct 11	Columbus Day.
Nov 11	Veterans' Day.
Nov 25	Thanksgiving Day.
Dec 25	Christmas Day

Opening hours

Banks: 9am-3pm

Offices: 9am-5pm (Mon-Fri)

Shops: (major cities) 10am-9pm (Mon-Sat); 12 noon- 5pm (Sun)

Water: Tap water is generally OK to drink.

Tipping: 10-20% is customary throughout the US in restaurants, bars and pubs, taxis and hairdressers.

Medical/Healthcare: Medical treatment is more expensive in the USA than anywhere else and insurance needs to be adequate to cover illnesses and serious injuries. The UK Consumers' Association recommends that you should have $1.6million of medical cover in Europe and $3.2million in the USA.

Pets: Those coming from rabies-free countries do not have to be vaccinated but are subject to inspection at ports of entry. Some states require vaccination of cats for rabies.
A certificate of health is not required for dogs although some airlines or states may require them. Within 10 days of departure your vet will need to issue an International Health Certificate as required by all airlines. This certificate states that your pet is in good health and OK to fly.

country but an estimated 40 million have no health insurance in a nation that has an average healthcare expense of $7,400 per person per year.

The cost of healthcare insurance in America is exorbitant and sometimes difficult to obtain, especially if you have a pre-existing medical problem. Some US-based insurers will not take on those over a certain age. You can keep premiums down by having a large excess but this can, of course, backfire on you if you need to claim.

What's not to like?

A contributor to the USA section of ExpatFocus [www.expatfocus.com] – an American married to a Brit – summarised her views on life in Florida thus:

"We lived in Britain till 2002, then moved to the US. (Here) you spend at least two hours a day in your car. Unless you are an outdoorsy person, it can be bland and boring because everything is so vast and homogenised. You can drive 500 miles and still appear to be in the same place – with WalMArt, McDonalds, Barnes & Noble, etc.

"We miss the pubs, we miss being able to walk outside and actually go somewhere. For example in the UK I could just pop to the corner store. Here you have to get in your car, drive a couple miles, and walk all the way to the back of a HUGE store. You end up wasting 30 to 45 minutes just to get milk.

… also when we were in the UK I had my daughter on the NHS with no hassles, and for free. Here in the US, two years later I had my son on private health insurance and was $10,000 out of pocket.

… the quality of life is better in America when you think in terms of the luxuries afforded to you – big house, big car, all the amenities in the home, huge portions of food, etc. However, these things do not necessarily define a good quality of life. We are going back to the UK to get the things that US dollars can't buy... like pubs, art, history and culture".

Is it safe?

America has is consistently rated as among the most dangerous countries in the world. Personal safety should be a concern in any large US city, particularly one you are not familiar with.

If you feel uncomfortable in a certain area you should leave, particularly if you are in a slum area of a large city.

Crime levels are high in black slums and after dark in the commercial areas of large cities such as Los Angeles and New York. New York's Central Park is fine in daylight but don't go near it at night.

UNITED STATES
LOW / HILLS / MOUNTAINS

Canada

Glacier Nat. Park
Seattle
Columbia River
Salem
Boise
Salt Lake City
San Francisco
Las Vegas
Mt. Whitney
Los Angeles
Death Valley
San Diego
Phoenix
Grand Canyon
Santa Fe

Rocky Mountains

Helena
Fargo
Minneapolis
Milwaukee
Yellowstone Nat. Park
Missouri
Lincoln River
Denver

Great Plains

United States of America

Oklahoma City
Dallas
Mississippi River
Houston
Rio Grande

Mexico

Brownsville

Gulf of Mexico

Chicago
St. Louis
Memphis
Atlanta

Great Lakes
Niagara Falls
Detroit
Cleveland
Indianapolis
Ohio River

Appalachian Mts.

New York City
Boston
Augusta
Philadelphia
Washington DC
Raleigh
Charleston
Savannah

Coastal Plain

New Orleans
Orlando
Everglades Nat. Park
Miami
Key West

Pacific Ocean

Atlantic Ocean

600 mi
600 km

TROPIC OF CANCER
© GraphicMaps.com

Caribbean

Avoid washrooms in train or subway stations; find a department store or a McDonald's instead.

Avoid venturing away from the tourist areas especially after dark. Valuables should be kept out of sight or left in a hotel safe but not in your hotel room.

How much tax will I pay?

The US has a bewildering array of taxes: sales taxes, excise taxes, licence taxes, income taxes, intangible taxes, property taxes, estate taxes and inheritance taxes. In some states you will pay all of these.

States that don't collect income tax include Florida, Texas, Washington, South Dakota, Alaska, Nevada and Wyoming. Of course, they obtain the revenue in other ways such as gambling taxes in Nevada.

Another half-a-dozen states (Indiana, Illinois, Colorado, Massachusetts, Pennsylvania and

THE RULES FOR GETTING IN

There is no such thing as a retirement visa that allows permanent residence in the US. Britons can legally spend up to 90 days per visit without a visa or up to 180 days with a B-2 visa.

The B-2 'snowbird' visa, usually issued for 10 years, but sometimes less, allows a stay of six months at a time. You may be required to show proof of binding ties in your home country – property, family or a job.

You may have to show a return ticket or that you have sufficient funds for your stay.

The starting point for a B-2 visa is an interview with a consular officer at the US Embassy in your home country but it is the immigration official at your point of entry (POE) who ultimately decides how long you can stay.

Many thousands of Britons hold B-2 visas, spending the UK winters in US sunspots and returning to the UK in spring.

The E-2

This is the visa class that enables investors (only from certain countries, including the UK) to purchase a business and live in the USA. The level of investment is flexible but needs to be around $150,000-$400,000.

The downside of the E-2 is that it has a 'non-immigrant' status, that children are not included once they reach the age of 21 and that renewal cannot be taken for granted – if the business is sold or ceases trading the visa will not be renewed

This is what the US Embassy has to say: "… a non immigrant (E2) visa is not a good option for someone who intends to reside permanently in the United States.

"If the investor retires or sells their investment, his or her visa status lapses and he or she must leave the US. Only single dependent children under 21 are eligible for visas to accompany their investor parent, and when these children turn 21 they lose their status as a dependent and their visa.

"Prospective investors should be cautious about claims from agents or salespeople that an investment will assure their qualification for an E-2 visa, particularly if the other party has a vested interest in the sale. Only a consular officer may approve a visa."

EB5 investor visa

The more secure option for those that have the necessary capital is the permanent resident (Green Card EB5) investor visa [see following section].

Michigan) have a flat rate of 3.5 per cent on all income.

Local property taxes vary from state to state. If you're a Snowbird and let your property while you are away you can pay up to 30 per cent withholding tax. However, you can claim interest relief and the cost of inspection flights.

There is an estate transfer tax of 1-5 per cent charged on the assessed value of the property, usually about 75 per cent of the market value.

Capital gains tax also varies but if the property is owned for more than a year, the rates will normally be 8-15 per cent.

In most states sales tax is not imposed on the purchase of property. However in 36 states a real estate transfer tax of between 1-5 per cent is charged on the assessed value of the property.

Estate and gift taxes deal with the transfer of property, either while you are alive or upon your death. Both federal and state taxes apply, with great differences between states in how your estate is taxed upon your death.

Local Tax: Local property taxes are paid in the state or county in which your property is located. The tax amount is on the assessed value of the property (which is likely to be about 75 per cent of the market value).

The following information is abridged from www.globalpropertyguide.com and readers are recommended to visit the site to get the full picture.

Individual taxation: If you move to the US permanently you become liable for income tax on your worldwide income. However, non-resident individuals are liable only on their US-sourced income.

Income Tax: Income is taxed at the federal level and at the state level although seven states (Alaska, Florida,

24th Ave, San Francisco.
3 bedroom, 1 bathroom 1,370sq ft family home in San Francisco.
Price: $762,900
More info:
http://realestate.aol.com/foreclosures

PROPERTY

Nevada, South Dakota, Texas, Washington State and Wyoming) do not impose taxes on income.

Rental income: Non-residents with rental income are taxed at the federal and, generally, at the state levels.

Federal Capital Gains Tax: When a non-resident alien sells a property, the buyer is required to withhold 10 per cent of the selling amount as tax. The withholding tax is later credited as advance payment for capital gains tax.

State Capital Gains Tax: Most states tax capital gains as part of income. State income tax rates apply.

Is US property a good investment?

As in Britain, home ownership has always been the American dream. Today it is more of a nightmare. Prices have plunged and so, for buyers, property represents a huge bargain. Prices across the country are expected to remain flat for the foreseeable future.

Quoting analysts, the influential international property news service, PropertyWire [www.propertywire.com] reports: "The latest predictions now indicate that the bottom of the market has not been reached and prices are set to keep falling in 2010."

In Florida you can buy a formerly $1 million home for $400,000.

Jane Araguel, a realtor based in Destin, Florida, says: "Real estate is an amazing investment right now. The values are 60 per cent lower than in 2004"

It is the same in California. Randy Solakian of Coldwell Banker Residential Brokerage in Santa Barbara reports that challenging market conditions provide outstanding opportunities for buyers.

Properties are standing empty; even classy Malibu is not immune to global economic forces. Dozens of properties there are unoccupied.

Where's best to live?

So diverse are the possibilities it is possible to touch on only the most popular areas. Most retirees want mild climates and warm temperatures year-round and so it is the sunbelt meccas of Florida, Nevada, Arizona and California that have traditionally been the choice of both American and European retirees. It is in these states too that house prices have been tumbling and bargains abound.

According to a recent study, Texas has leapfrogged over California and Arizona to claim the number two retirement destination state with Florida retaining the number one position.

For Brits, Florida is still the unchallenged choice with an estimated 400,000 living there permanently or temporarily although recent trends suggest that

Golf course home
4 bedroom, 3 bathroom home of 346sq m with office and 3-car garage at Laurel Oak Country Club, Sarasota with 2 golf courses, 12 tennis courts, heated pool and clubhouse. 24-hour gated community.
Price: $749,000
More info: www.sarasotabestproperties.com

We Live Here

Qualified by virtue of his sister's status as a naturalised American – she had been a GI war bride – it was relatively plain sailing for Mike Holmes and his wife Lucia when they decided to move to Florida.

There is a quota list for this category of application and the American Embassy told us we should expect to wait for at least 10 years until our number came to the top of the pile.

Bang on 10 years later and we got a letter from the embassy together with all the forms to fill in.

We couldn't start anything in earnest until we knew for sure that we had got the visa, so then it became a bit of a scramble to get it all finished in time.

The first thing was to get the house on the market. We had a good old clear out – the charity shops didn't know what had hit them – and a lot of stuff went to auction. Friends and relatives took other bits and pieces.

We had visited Florida a few times so we had a good idea of the area we would prefer, but we didn't have a detailed knowledge of anywhere in particular so we decided to take a two week trip to see things first hand.

We flew into Tampa and went south to Naples where we spent a week just looking at houses in the area.

We then worked our way up the coast, looking at places like Punta Gorda, Fort Myers etc., until we got to Sarasota where we spent another week looking at loads of houses.

We preferred Sarasota because of the more accessible beaches, the "culture" and the shopping. A big plus is that it is 184km closer to Tampa, so getting to the airport is a lot easier.

A couple of months later, when we knew we had got our visas, we had another trip over to concentrate on the Sarasota area. We had previously made contact with Andrew Bartlett [www.andrewbartlettflorida.co.uk], having seen his articles in Going USA at the US Embassy. Andrew spent a lot of time showing us houses and advising us on a lot of issues.

Within a few days we had chosen a house and – with Andrew's help – the purchase was completed in about three weeks. It was a new house, in our preferred area, plenty of space, close to the beaches, overlooking water – just right.

When we finally made the move we bought a couple of beach chairs, a breakfast table and a bed, moved in and waited for the furniture. The container arrived a couple of weeks later – right on schedule and amazingly not one item was broken or damaged.

We hired a car for a month and set about getting a Florida driving licence. I would be lying if I said that it was difficult; we were only on the road for about 50 yards, didn't go through traffic lights, and didn't cross lanes of traffic. It was all done in the car park of the licence centre – three point turns, reversing, emergency stop, etc. We both passed first time.

PROPERTY

Florida beachfront
Condo in Marathon, Florida with direct access to a sandy beach. Complex has an oceanfront pool, tennis court and covered parking. Nicely updated with a new kitchen and is being sold fully furnished. Marathon is 160km south of Miami.   Price: $690,000
More info: Coco Plum Realtors www.mymiddlekeys.com
Email: jim@MyCocoPlum.com

Saltwater canal home
This impeccable saltwater canal home at Flagler Beach has been completely remodelled with porcelain floor tiles, solid maple cabinets and granite counter tops in kitchen and all baths. Remote controlled gas fireplace, recessed lighting throughout, dock with boat lift. 2 blocks from the beach
More info: The Katsikos Group, Inc. http://tkgi.homesandland.com

Getting Social Security numbers and cards was just as straightforward. We filled out the forms and had our cards within two weeks. Meanwhile our Green Card applications were being processed by the INS and duly turned up in the post about a month after we arrived.

When we were planning our permanent move to Florida, our tax consultant advised us to sell our unit trusts, Peps, Isas, Premium Bonds, etc., as these are relatively unheard of by the average American tax accountant. So we did as advised and arrived in sunny Sarasota Florida with nowhere to live, but a healthy bank balance.

The house is sold

Our house sale in England finally happened about two weeks after we got here. We used a specialist foreign exchange company to buy the dollars and transfer the money over. By now we had set up a bank account and had a cheque card.

Credit cards were not so easy. The credit card companies will not take into account any credit history you may have in the UK so you have to build up an American credit history by, for instance, having an HP agreement on your new car, or having a mortgage. After about six months you will be able to get a credit card, probably with some insulting credit limit, but as you pay it off each month you build up a credit rating.

Car insurance was expensive but here again they won't take into account the fact that you have been driving in the UK for 40 years. You start off again as if you were 18 and have just passed your test, so the premium is high.

Florida's dominance as the number one retirement destination is slowly slipping.

If year-round warm weather is not high on your list of priorities there are dozens of other locations that score higher in the numerous quality of life surveys that are carried out on the subject.

An AARP magazine investigation examined retirement sites based on income, property and sales tax, weather and recreational opportunities. Its top five places to retire to in the U.S. were Atlanta, Georgia; Portland, Oregon; Chandler, Arizona; Boston, Massachusetts; and Milwaukee, Wisconsin – not destinations that, for Brits at least, would quickly come to mind.

The magazine's website, www.aarpmagazine.org, offers a tool called Location Scout, which asks a series of questions about your retirement preferences for climate, housing, work and money, arts, culture and lifestyle, recreation, transportation, health and education. Questions range from how important is having Internet access, to having a hockey team in the area.

Florida: The ultimate holiday destination – sunshine, exceptional beaches, vibrant cities with fantastic shopping and world class attractions, a tropical climate, friendly people, fabulous cuisine, some of the world's best fishing and diving.

Miami, Orlando, Fort Lauderdale, Florida Keys, Tampa and Sarasota, Fort Myers – these are the places known to millions of UK holidaymakers and property owners. Statewide, home prices have fallen about 20 per cent in the past year but because Florida is a favoured retirement destination prices are expected to recover during 2010.

Immigration and property adviser Andrew Bartlett

One of a kind
Dramatic views of the Monterey Bay, Pajaro Valley, hills and city lights from this unique beachfront property in Pajaro Dunes, Monterey Bay, California.
This 3 bedroom, 2 bath home, recently updated, has a wrap-around deck with views of the valley and bay beyond.
Price: $1,695,000
More info: Daw Properties
www.oceanfrontproperties.com
Email: dawrlty@cruzio.com

says, "For many years the most popular areas used to be in Central Florida, particularly Orlando and Kissimmee, but recently the benefits of other areas seem to have become more evident – the Gulf Coast in particular has attracted many Brits."

California: A land of incredible sights and diversity, from sunny beaches and rugged coastlines, ski resorts, national parks to the gateway cities of Los Angeles and San Francisco – California really does have it all, whether dining at over 78,000 restaurants or enjoying countless beaches along more than 1,264 miles of coastline.

California is also home to some of the world's best wine and cuisine and small-town gems with a never-ending parade of activities.

In the year to August 2009 California property prices declined by 12.9 per cent

Nevada: Everyone knows Las Vegas, but there's a lot more to Nevada: the largest concentration of ski resorts in North America, Lake Tahoe is a winter paradise with 15 world-class alpine ski resorts with runs from 2,300-3,300m, more than 24,000 skiable acres and blue alpine lake views – all surrounded by resort villages that offer dining, shopping, ice skating, sledding and tubing.

For sheer scenic beauty, Lake Tahoe rivals any place on earth. And nearby is Reno, home to a dazzling array of casinos, entertainment, arts, and outdoor activities.

Arizona: The weather: 330 days of sunshine a year. You need to love the heat. Winter temps range from the 70s to the 90s but in Arizona you can ski all day and be home in time to put a steak on the BBQ. Humidity is usually less than 30 per cent. Arizona has beautiful desert and mountain scenery.

It is within easy distance of Las Vegas, San Diego,

Puerto Penasco, Mexico, the Grand Canyon and Los Angeles.

Lovers of the outdoors have Camelback mountain, South Mountain Park, Sedona with its mini Grand Canyon, Oak Creek Canyon with camping, mountain climbing and the town of Flagstaff.

The Phoenix area has great nightlife centred on Mill Avenue in Tempe with its bars, clubs and great shops.

Tucson, the second largest city in the state of Arizona, boasts a combination of natural beauty and modern living from outdoor activities to shopping, art, and exciting events.

Lakeside home
1,596sq ft home with 2 bedrooms and 2 bathrooms on Shawano Lake in north-eastern Wisconsin.
Price: $384,900
More info:
Coldwell Banker Hilgenberg Realtors
Email: jwickman@hilgenbergrealty.com
www.hilgenbergrealtors.com

Blue Ridge Mountains
2 bedroom, 2 bathroom home with full basement on 3.86 acres in Fannin County in the North Georgia Blue Ridge Mountains.
Price: $154,900
More info:
www.move2northgeorgia.ne
www.hilgenbergrealtors.com

PROPERTY

USA CONTACT DIRECTORY

Embassies/Government
USA Embassy, London
www.usembassy.org.uk
British Embassyhttp://ukinusa.fco.gov.uk
www.usa.gov
Access to state government, state
travel/tourism websites
www.fco.gov.uk/en/travel

Travel & Health Advice
Foreign Office travel advice
www.fco.gov.uk/travel
www.nhs.uk/Healthcareabroad
www.masta.org

About the USA
US states
www.usa.gov/Agencies/State_and_Territori
es.shtmlwww.globalcomputing.com
www.50states.com
These sites allow you to click through for
information on all US states, cities,
counties, newspapers, etc.
CIA - The World Factbookwww.cia.gov
www.weatherusa.net

General & Expat
www.britishhomesgroup.com
www.expatfocus.com
www.britishexpat.com
http://britishexpats.com
www.britsinthestates.com
www.bigapplebrits.com
www.britsabroad.com
www.floridabritsclub.com
www.britishflorida.com
www.rovingpress.co.uk

Media
www.globalcomputing.com/NewsContent.h
tm
You can click through for info on TV and
media in every state.

Property
With almost 70,000 real estate agents in
Florida alone, arriving at a useful and
practical list for agents across the country
is next to impossible. The National
Association of Realtors [www.realtor.org]
has almost a million members and
companies specialising in particular states.
There are many big chains and companies
that specialise in individual States that
include the following:
www.countrysideinternational.com
Coldwell Banker: www.coldwellbanker.com
Long & Foster: www.longandfoster.com
Michael Saunders & Co:
www.michaelsaunders.com
Keller Williams: www.kw.com
Re/Max Properties: www.remax.com
NRT Incorporated: www.nrtllc.com
Browse those sites or narrow your search
down through multi-listing sites like the

following which allow you to click through to
realtors and agents in your targeted areas.
www.therealestatedirectory.net
www.realestatebig.com
www.usrealtorsregistry.com

Travel & Tourism
www.usa.gov
http://us.makemytrip.com
www.lonelyplanet.com
www.toptravelsites.net/america

Getting There
British Airways: www.ba.com
Virgin Atlantic: www.virgin-atlantic.com
Air France: www.AirFrance.com
BMI: www.flybmi.com
American Airlines:
www.americanairlines.co.uk
Continental Airlines: www.continental.com
Delta Air Lines: delta.com
United Airlines: www.united.com
Trailfinders: www.trailfinders.com
Expedia: www.expedia.co.uk
Thomson: www.thomson.co.uk
Thomas Cook: www.flythomascook.com
Monarch: www.monarch.co.uk

Getting Around
"It's almost impossible even to get to the
shops without a car in the USA "wailed one
website contributor. Every family has at least
one; some have several so while road
conditions are usually excellent there are
often lengthy traffic jams and congestion
around cities.

Air: If you plan to travel within the US you
can often obtain heavily discounted tickets if
you buy them along with your international
flight. Such tickets are not available once
you get there.
The lowest fares are normally offered on
advance-purchase, round-trip tickets that
include a Saturday night stay.
Several airlines serve the domestic market
and prices are competitive so you need to
shop around. You will find clickable lists of
domestic carriers at:
www.nationsonline.org
www.historycentral.com
In recent years several low-cost carriers
have appeared on the scene to challenge
the major airlines. They include Southwest
and JetBlue offering budget fares and
flexible tickets.

Train: A National rail pass gives access to
Amtrak's entire network for around $285.
Other passes give you 15 or 30 days in
regions such as the east or the far west
from $175.
Amtrak's network takes in most states,
giving a choice of 500 destinations. The
trains themselves are like mobile hotels,

with gleaming twin-decked coaches, air-
conditioning and uniformed attendants
who make you feel you have stepped
back in time into a 1930s Hollywood
movie.
Classic journeys are the daily Crescent
from New York to New Orleans or
Amtrak's Silver Service from New York to
Miami.
More info: www.usa-by-rail.com
www.amtrak.com

Bus: Long-haul bus services represent
the cheapest means of transportation
across the USA but be ready for long
trips, some lasting several days, during
which you must provide your own meals
and lodging.
Greyhound dominates long-haul services
but there are others including
Megabus.com, owned by the British
Stagecoach Group. Companies offer
increasingly sophisticated services such
as Wi-Fi access and power outlets in
every row.
Within towns and cities there are
numerous public transport options.
Underground trains operate in New York,
Washington DC, Boston, Chicago and San
Francisco and more are in the planning
stage.

Driving: You can drive for three months
on your UK licence but should obtain an
International Driving Permit if you are
going to live in the US as it may take
several months to get a US licence. This
is obtained from the state in which you
live not from the federal government. The
residency requirement for obtaining a US
driver's license varies with each state.
Driving laws can also vary from state to
state and speed limits are strictly
enforced in some but not in others. In the
western states, enforcement is generally
more lax.
Both speed and drink driving limits are
lower than in the UK.
Driving is on the right.

The International Railway

The EB5 investor route to USA retirement

Since 2003 an increasing number of British and Irish citizens have been emigrating via the EB5 investor visa attracted by the following features.

- A direct route to a Green Card*.
- Permanent residency via the Green Card for the family including children under 21.
- Freedom to live and work or retire anywhere in the USA.

The EB-5 immigrant investor visa attracts foreign capital into the USA.

It requires a minimum investment of $500,000 in a 'Regional Center' and must create full-time employment for at least 10 American workers.

Five thousand visas are specifically set aside for those wanting to invest in an EB-5 'Regional Center' - an area which has been approved for immigrant investor capital by the US Citizenship and Immigration Service as a targeted employment area of high unemployment or qualifying rural areas.

History
The first EB5 UK applicants for US visas (under new rules) were approved over four years ago. Importantly, there is now a track record of immigrants who were processed through this specific programme, have subsequently lived in America for two years, and are coming up to the time when they can determine how their investment can be recouped. .

For those looking for freedom to work or retire to the USA, the EB5 investor visa is the immigration route of choice.

Green Card
As long as certain conditions are met, a Green Card* can provide legal permanent residency for the applicant, his or her spouse, and any offspring under the age of 21. Indeed, it is a path to US citizenship if that is your objective.

The EB5 investment visa route to a Green Card avoids the usual requirement of having family connections, securing a job or running an active business - making it a viable route to retirement.

Different programmes
The programmes are a mixed bag with different track records and include, amongst others, those offering commercial properties, resort development, managed farm investments and a business loan service, etc.

It is up to each visa applicant to select a programme and professional investment and legal advice should be sought. To date, the majority of UK

---

*Green Card iis the popular name for an Alien Registration Receipt Card. Green cards (which were green many years ago but are now pink) are credit card sized plastic photographic identification cards issued to lawful permanent residents of the United States. They allow the holder to live and work in America and to re-enter the United States after travelling abroad. .

investors have shown a preference for freehold commercial properties or property-secured options and schemes which can be financed in a number of ways including the applicant's pension funds.

Application and timing

The total time from application to approval takes approximately 9-15 months and at the time of writing every EB5 Regional Center investor has received a conditional Green Card.

(Under the regulations an investor who is approved for the EB-5 immigrant visa receives a "conditional" Green Card, which must be reissued after two years; otherwise, the two cards offer the same rights and privileges).

Once an applicant has invested in an approved programme their attorney files Form I-526, (Immigrant Petition by Alien Entrepreneur) with the appropriate regional USCIS Service Center including the fees and the evidence in support of the application.

Regulations require that the investor proves his investment funds were obtained through lawful business, salary, investments, property sales, inheritance, gift, loan, or other lawful means.

Processing by the USCIS for Form I-526 is currently running between two and eight months.

The first requirement of any investor after they receive the visa at the United States overseas consulate office is to enter into the United States within 180 days of visa issuance. Evidence of intent to reside

includes opening bank accounts, obtaining a driver's licence and/or social security number, paying state and federal income taxes, renting or buying a home.

The investment must be held for a further two years, bringing the total investment time to approximately three years. At that stage an application is made to the Immigration Service office for 'Removal of Conditions', which takes a further two or three months.

Once the conditions have been removed the investment may be sold, although there are important points to bear in mind regarding this. This is a particularly critical stage and unfortunately far too little attention seems to be given to an exit strategy by some of the programmes, so this is an area the investor should examine thoroughly.

Why E2 holders are also looking at the EB5 option

Many are familiar with the E2 visa programme which has been the traditional route for emigration to the USA. However, for those who have resided in America for a number of years, there has been a degree of anxiety as well as expense at renewal periods. Indeed, it is increasingly clear that renewal of this visa cannot be taken for granted however long you have lived in the States.

New E2 applicants are finding a lengthy waiting period, the possibility of rejection, and the need to inject an increasingly higher level of funding to find a

American Life Inc.

Your Direct Route to a Green Card
and the Best Regional Center Investment

If you have researched the numerous visa categories, you will know that the EB-5 visa is the most desirable and quite possibly the only option, if you want:-

- *Security of US Residency (a green card).*
- *Residency for all your immediate family (children under 21).*
- *Flexibility to work, run a business and even retire.*
- *Access to dual citizenship for you, your spouse and children.*

Obtaining a green card has a value, but we don't see that as any reason to keep the income on your investment, which is why we are so unusual among Regional Centers. US citizens and EB-5 applicants invest on identical terms which is why American Life has the only REAL investment for EB-5 applicants. Why? Because we have:

- *Over 800 investors – more than any other Regional Center*
- *Over 300 US investors who have no need for a green card and are free to invest anywhere they choose. No other RC attracts American investors.*
- *A record of generating income and capital appreciation since 1996.*
- *Dividends from rents and cash deposits sent to you every month.*
- *A record of generating capital appreciation through tightly managed commercial property developments.*
- *Property occupancy levels maintained at close to 90 percent, even in 2009.*
- *No debt, ensuring your asset is protected, no matter what.*

We know, from the hundreds of EB-5 investors we have looked after since 1996, that after the green card itself, the overriding priorities are protection of capital and income on investment.

Emigrating is all about a better quality of life
We help you to achieve that with a better quality investment.

Contact Richard Robinson,
18 Hanover Square, London W1S 1HX.
Tel: 0203 008 2490 or email: richard@eb5-visa.net

Better investments for a Better life

Our top priorities are job creation and return of the investment

The EB-5 Visa for Immigrant Investors is a United States visa that provides a method of obtaining a green card for foreign nationals who invest money in the United States. The EB5 visa is unusual in that it provides investors with a green card at the outset. When investors emigrate they do so knowing that they and their immediate family have Permanent Residency and may apply for citizenship after five years.

The U.S. immigrant investor program is the most flexible in the world. There are no requirements as to age, business training and experience, or language skills. Permanent residents need not be continuously and physically present in the United States, and they can maintain business and professional relations in their country of origin.

EB-5 Benefits

★ **A direct route to Permanent residency in the United States for you, your spouse and any children under the age of 21.**

★ **Freedom to live, work and retire anywhere in the United States**

★ **U.S. citizenship route after 5 years of being a Green Card holder**

★ **Children may attend college /university at U.S. resident costs.**

★ **You can develop and run your own business.**

★ **You do not need a family member or employer to sponsor you.**

★ **You can sponsor Green Cards for your relatives.**

★ **Travel outside of the United States and return to the United States without a visa**

no better time than now to invest in Chicago

Why invest with CFIG?

★ **Clearly defined exit strategy**
Each project specifies a realistic exit strategy from the beginning. The investment periods will typically be five years and every investment is backed by real estate collateral.

★ **Conservative job creation estimates**
Each industry has been chosen due to its ability to create jobs in our region. Furthermore, we calculate job estimates based on direct jobs, the most accurate way to prove the requirements have been met after two years. We also make sure each project creates more than ten jobs per investor.

★ **Variety of industries and projects available**
With a wide variety of industries available for investment, and multiple projects open at any given time, we provide several options so the investor can choose an investment they feel comfortable with.

★ **Loan structure reduces risk of investment**
Most of our projects are designed as loans to the project company. Since you are not directly investing in the project, should any problems arise you will have the greatest chance of recouping your investment.

★ **Projects kept small and protected**
Project sizes remain small to allow faster

processing and more accurate monitoring for each individual investor. In additions, investor groups are kept separate so the risks from one project will not carry over into another.

★ **Option to pay in installments**
Because $500,000 (US) is a large amount of money, we provide investors the option to pay in installments so they can feel comfortable and safe investing with us.

★ **Direct involvement with each project**
CFIG is directly involved with every project and reserves the right to intervene should the actions of the company deviate from the original plan. This ensures that meeting the EB5 requirements remains the number one goal for every project.

Contact:
Chicagoland Foreign Investment Group
111 E. Wacker Drive, Suite 555
Chicago, Illinois, USA 60601
Tel (001) 312 427 0910
Email: info@ChicagoEB5.com
www.ChicagoEB5.com

qualifying business.

There are particular concerns
- If you wish to retire
- Have children approaching their 21st birthday
- If you want to remain legally in the USA

Another downside is the E-2 has 'non-immigrant' status, which has serious implications. There are thousands of E2 visa holders living in the US, but sooner or later they have to confront their status and sort it out for the long term, for if they sell their business or it ceases trading their visa won't be renewed.

Also, their children at 21 will need their own visas or be forced to leave. Such a lack of security may not suit everyone looking to reside in the US.

Who has gone down the EB5 route and why

Living costs are often lower in the US. Even after taking account additional healthcare insurance many have discovered significant financial advantage living Stateside. British parents paying fees for private schools in the UK have found areas of Florida that have state schools equivalent to the best grammar schools in the UK.

Interest in the visa has been increasing and looks likely to continue as the desire to emigrate gains momentum, stimulated by increased awareness of the advantages offered by the year-round outdoor lifestyle in Florida and Southern California.

Approximately 130 British/Irish citizens have taken the EB-5 (pilot programme) route. Outside the UK and Ireland there have been many more EB-5 (pilot programme) visa applications.

What is the EB-5?

The EB5 Immigrant Investor programme was created to attract and invest foreign capital into dilapidated inner cities and employment-starved rural areas across the US.

Under the programme foreign investors and their families obtain permanent US residency through a Green Card.

Their collective investment is pumping millions of dollars into a growing list of enterprises - in agriculture, tourism, renewable energy, education and transportation.

For a $500,000 investment in a distressed area, a foreigner and his immediate family become eligible for conditional Green Cards which are made permanent a few years later if the investment has created at least 10 jobs for US workers.

Under the programme, administered by US Immigration & Citizenship Services, 5,000 immigrant visas can be issued annually.

When is the best time to apply under the EB5 pilot programme?

Any time can be a 'good time' to apply for an EB-5 as the visa rules are changing periodically and there is a waiting list for some programmes.

Downside of the E2

Non-immigrant (E2) visas are not a good option for those who hope to reside permanently in the United States. If the investor retires or sells their investment the visa status lapses and the investor must leave. Only single dependent children under 21 are eligible for visas to accompany their investor parent and when these children turn 21 they lose their status as a dependent - and their visa.

The more secure option for those that have the necessary capital is the permanent resident (Green Card EB5) investor visa.

The different programmes - pros & cons

It is up to each visa applicant to select a programme that suits them. Some prospectuses paint a rose-tinted picture; some companies and attorneys focus on a single Regional Center, where they may have an interest, and not provide a balanced view of the pros and cons.

It is also important to bear in mind that although a Regional Center may have offered a particularly attractive programme in the past, the next one it offers can be very different.

How to avoid problems

It is important to seek independent advice before taking accepting all the claims relating to the programmes.

There are a number of areas potential EB5 investors need to be aware of from legal, investment and practical perspectives that are not readily apparent from the various programme details.

British applicants, in particular, have often focused on the investment potential, at the expense of the visa implications, which may cause them problems when it is too late.

One of the criteria for the conditions to be removed after two years relates to the job creation criterion of the EB5. However good the return on investment may be, if a particular project fails to create the required number of jobs, there is the real risk that the conditional visa could be revoked.

It is evident from site visits to the programmes that there are points that applicants are not being made fully aware of prior to investment. It is interesting to note that investors from other countries have focused

on schemes that monitor closely employment criteria.

Another problem is that British visa applicants have little opportunity to verify all the information they are given in some very convincing brochures and documents. There are significant implications relating to key political considerations behind individual programmes that may not become evident until the time comes for the conditions to be removed

Dangers of information

Naturally enough, brochures and web sites promoting particular programmes focus on the positives, however it is important to obtain an independent perspective to ascertain the negatives. Implications can be far reaching but not readily apparent. Don't expect the Regional Centers to verify points if you do not know what questions to ask!

Few attorneys specialise in the EB5 and many have not visited all the schemes; some work closely with particular schemes so a degree of bias is a possibility.

Some self-help web sites aim to be useful but can potentially be dangerous. One self-help blog site has over 20 pages of opinions contributed by those looking at the EB5, or who have done some research, but the contributor fails to identify the circumstances which could cause problems.

EB-5 INVESTMENT VISA

Benefits of permanent residency through an EB-5 investment visa

The benefits for permanent residency in the United States go far beyond economic and political stability.

- Foreign nationals who obtain a permanent visa can enjoy all the benefits of any other United States resident.
- The visa creates ease of access to the United States for trade, business or retirement.
- The visa holder and his/her qualified family members are entitled to attend public schools including enrollment in colleges and universities with an in-state cost savings.
- The health programs of the United State Government are also available including Social Security.
- Once the permanent visa (green card) is obtained there is no renewal or re-application required. The new immigrant may locate anywhere within the United States without restrictions.

What is an EB-5?

If a foreign national invests $500,000 into a regional center that qualifies as a high unemployment area and this investment results in ten new American jobs the investor and his entire family (wife, children under 21) can receive a permanent visa (green card).

How long does the process take?

Our experience has been about one year for clients to receive the conditional visa.

How safe is the investment?

The law requires the funds to be at risk. At CMB we understand that there are levels of risk from foolish to very secure. We believe our investment with the government reuse agencies and master base redevelopers are the safest EB-5 investment available today and still meets the at risk requirement.

LIVE THE AMERICAN DREAM

The United States and its territories with its natural geographic and cultural diversity provide broad opportunities for a superior standard of living, variety of climates and a safe harbor for both the investor and his/her family.

CMB EXPORT LLC

One of the oldest and most experienced Federally-Designated Regional Centers.

Midwest Executive Offices
4507 49th Avenue
Moline, IL USA 61265
Telephone: 309-797-1550 Facsimile: 309-797-1655
Email: info@cmbeb5visa.com
Web: http://www.cmbeb5visa.com

Patrick Hogan
President, CEO and Managing Member

William F. Hurley
Vice President of Business Development

Kraig A. Schwigen
Executive Director

The CMB Regional Center (an acronym for "California Military Base") was established in the State of California in 1997 to assist communities that experienced increased unemployment and economic stagnation resulting form the Federal Base Realignment and Closure Commission that ordered the closing or realigning of military bases throughout the United States.

CMB and the government reuse Agency (FVDA) invested into infrastructure - roads, bridges, water, sewer, communications and as a result of this infrastructure investment the Stater Bro. $295 Million facility was built on this former military base.

The aerial view shows the magnitude of the Stater Bros. facility. The office building (above right) is only a fraction of the entire project.

The CMB plan is simple and straight forward.

We know our clients want three things:
1) A permanent visa (green card).
2) Return of their original investment.
3) A profit on the investment if they can get it.

To accomplish the above CMB has built a solid structured investment such that all CMB investments have the same describable attributes.

Recently, the U.S. President and Congress have endorsed infrastructure investments as the way to create jobs and revitalize the economy of a specific region.

CMB has been using this job creating model for years.

- Funds are invested with government reuse agencies which have the ability to receive tax revenues, federal and state grants, and have assets that generate income or can be sold. Additionally any funds invested with former military base master developers will require community development bond backing.
- The exit strategy is simple. The term of the investment is six years. To exit the partnership once the investment is paid back the investors vote to liquidate the partnership. There is nothing to sell. Our investors are not dependant on the real estate market or subject to the pitfalls within various markets.
- The investment results in infrastructure building the very basis for job creation. This assures we meet the ten new American job requirement of the USCIS.
- The investment is transparent. The investors have the right to look at the financial statements of the partnership and the financial statements of the government agency are open to the public.
- CMB, the government agencies and private capital are combined for these infrastructure initiatives thus creating a huge pool of investment capital to ensure job creation.
- The investment ($500,000) qualifies as a high unemployment area because of the job loss when the military base closed.
- CMB has the cooperation of all levels of government including Federal, State and local.
- The day to day expenses of the partnership are limited.
- The formation of the limited partnership allows the investor to meet the requirement of activity within the partnership but not to be burdened with the day to day management.

The strength of the CMB Investment is it's very basic structure.
A simple, proven and secure investment that qualifies under the EB-5 law.

http://www.cmbeb5visa.com   www.uscis.gov

EB-5 CASE HISTORIES

The Greens

One of the British couples making an investment in return for a Green Card was Michael and Pamela Green.

Among the first dozen Britons to immigrate to America following amendments to the visa system, the Greens bought into a retail project. They receive an annual return and did not have to live in the area where they had invested.

For the first two years, their Green Cards had conditions related to maintaining the investment which can then be reviewed and removed. After five years, they can seek citizenship.

They left to move permanently into the golf course home they bought in Lakeland, Florida, 12 years ago and sold their UK property.

"There is a swimming pool, a fitness centre and the same amount of land," said Michael. "I don't have to cut the grass or clean the pool - other people take care of it.

"We now enjoy a comfortable lifestyle, a very nice climate with English-speaking people and a low cost of living. The investment is a small amount to pay for that benefit."

The couple have a son, a grandchild, and another grandchild on the way.

Michael, a 12-handicap golfer, and former managing director of a car dealership, added: "The comparison in the cost of living is incredible. Petrol is $2 a gallon, or just over £1. Cigarettes, if you have that nasty habit as we do, are £14 a carton as opposed to £42. There is no television licence. It costs £50 to license our two cars in America as opposed to £300 in the UK."

The Hodgkinsons

David and Fran Hodgkinson retired from senior local government consultancy posts in Britain before moving to the US last year via the investment visa option.

They spent several months thoroughly researching the various options and emigrated via a Green Card route, feeling that after stressful high pressure jobs, relaxation in the sun with their dogs was the key consideration rather than having to set up and maintain a business in Florida which was a requirement of the other visa options.

Fran had retained great memories of America after student days as a camp councillor with BUNAC and the thrill was reawakened on holidays to Florida including Disney.

Having looked at a shortlist of options in Florida they chose a ranch style home with six acres of land in Myakka several miles outside Sarasota as the ideal move from their home in a small Sussex village.

They feel their Florida lifestyle has given them even more than they expected.

This tropical paradise is one for your shortlist

Why Belize?

A low cost of living, a tropical climate, no tax on any income from outside Belize, the official language is English – four good reasons for considering Belize. There are others: nestled between Mexico and Guatemala, Belize has forests rich with wildlife, mountains, Maya temples, diving and fishing in its clear waters.

A house on the beach can be had for $300,000 and to sweeten the pot Belize offers a package of incentives to lure retirees. Incentives are needed since so far only about 500 foreign retirees – American, Canadian and British – have been licensed under the programme.

Previously British Honduras, Belize lies on the east coast of Central America and in the heart of the Caribbean Basin. It is bordered by Mexico to the North, Guatemala to the West and South and the Caribbean Sea to the East.

The cayes, or islands, the offshore atolls, and the barrier reef are the main attractions to Belize. The barrier reef, the longest in the western hemisphere, is 296km long. The cayes and atolls provide great opportunity for diving, snorkelling, fishing, boating, sailing and kayaking and also serve as a habitat for both nesting birds and turtles.

In the central part of Belize the land is higher – 465-1,140m above sea level in the Mountain Pine Ridge Area and the Maya Mountains. Breathtaking waterfalls, historic Mayan cities and majestic mountains are but a few of the attractions that can be enjoyed in this area.

The population of approximately 250,000 people consists of a mixture of Creoles, Garifunas, Mestizos, Mayas, Caucasians, Mennonites, Lebanese, Chinese, and East Indians.

Is it safe?

Burglaries and thefts are a serious problem, with well over 1,000 cases of each reported annually. There was a record 95 murders in 2008.

Britain's Foreign Office warns: "…you should be on your guard and exercise caution." The US State Department's travel advisory is harsher: "Crime can be a serious problem, particularly in Belize City and remote areas."

How much tax will I pay?

Belize is an offshore tax haven. While working residents can be taxed on their worldwide income, those on retiree visas are exempt and pay no tax on income from outside Belize.

There are no capital gains or inheritance taxes.

Is Belize property a good investment?

Property prices rose by about 15 per cent annually from 2003-2007, even higher in coastal and tourist

FACTFILE

Capital: Belmopan
Population: 301,022
Area: 22,800sq km
Language: English (official), Spanish, Mayan, Garifuna (Carib), Creole
Climate: Sub-tropical with high annual temperatures and humidity with a brisk prevailing wind from the Caribbean Sea. Rainy season mid-May-Nov; dry season Jan-April. Hurricane season June-end Nov.
Time difference: GMT -6
Entry requirements: Visa not required for stays of up to 30 days.
Retirement/residence visa: You need to be aged 45-plus with a guaranteed income of $2,000 a month.
[See: The Rules for getting in]
Electricity: 110V/60 Hertz
Money: Belize dollar. There are ATMs in Belize City, less available elsewhere.

Credit/debit cards/travellers' cheques are accepted in tourist resorts, hotels and large restaurants.

Public holidays 2010
Jan 1	New Year's Day
Mar 9	Baron Bliss Day
Apr 2-5	Easter
May 1	Labour Day
May 24	Commonwealth Day
Sept 10	St George's Caye Day
Sept 21	Independence Day
Oct 11	Columbus Day
Nov 19	Garifuna Settlement Day
Dec 25	Christmas Day
Dec 26	Boxing Day

Opening hours
Banks: 8am-2.30pm (Mon-Thurs), 8am-4.30pm (Fri)
Offices: 8/8.30am-12pm, 1.30pm-4.30 (Mon-Fri)

Shops: 8am-12pm/1-8pm
Water: Best to drink bottled
Tipping: Small gratuity if a service charge has already been added.
Medical/Healthcare: Recommended: Prophylaxis for malaria and vaccinations for hepatitis A, typhoid, yellow fever and rabies if spending time outdoors. Hospital and clinics are basically very well equipped, with modern technology and trained staff. Medicines, health check-ups, surgery and dental work and pharmaceutical products are all considerably cheaper than in Europe and North America,
Pets: No quarantine but pets must have a certificate, issued by a government-approved veterinarian not more than 48 hours prior to arrival stating they are free from infection/contagious disease and have been vaccinated against rabies.

BELIZE CONTACT DIRECTORY

Embassies/Government
Belize High Commission in UK
www.belizehighcommission.com
British High Commission in Belize
http://ukinbelize.fco.gov.uk/en
Belize Migration Department
www.governmentofbelize.gov.bz

Travel & Health Advice
Foreign Office travel advice
www.fco.gov.uk/travel
www.nhs.uk/Healthcareabroad
www.masta.org

About Belize
www.belizefirst.com
www.belize.com
www.belize.net
www.belizeit.com
www.mostlymaya.com
www.chatboutbelize.com
www.corozal.com
www.belizemall.com
http://belize-guide.info
www.frommers.com/destinations/belize

General & Expat
www.expatfocus.com
www.belizenorth.com
www.expatbelize.com
www.expatintelligence.com/expat-belize
www.britishexpat.com
www.transitionsabroad.com

English Language Media
The Belize Timeswww.belizetimes.bz.
The San Pedro Sunwww.sanpedrosun.net

Estate agents
Orchid Baywww.orchidbaybelize.com
Coral Beach Realty
www.coralbeachrealty.net
W. Ford Young Real Estate Ltd.
www.belizerealestate.com
Sunrise Realtywww.sunrisebelize.com
Regent Realty, Ltd.
www.regentrealtybelize.com
Ambergris Seaside Real Estate
www.ambergrisrealestate.com
Corozal Real Estate
www.corozal.com/realestate
Vilma's Real Estatewww.realestatebz.com
www.belizejewelrealtors.com
Belize Property Auctions
www.belizepropertyauctions.com
Belize Property Agents Ltd.
www.belizepropertyagent.com

Travel & Tourism
www.travelbelize.org
www.lonelyplanet.com/belize
www.worldtravelguide.net
www.belizex.com
www.belizediscover.com

Getting There
Often the easiest way is via the US gateway cities: Miami, Dallas, Houston and Atlanta. Otherwise:
British Airways: www.britishairways.com
KLM

Virgin: www.virgin-atlantic.com
American Airlines:
www.americanairlines.co.uk
United Airlines: www.unitedairlines.co.uk
Continental Airlines: continental.com
Delta: www.Delta.com
Air Canada: AirCanada.com

Getting Around
Belize is only 113km by 403km.
Air: Maya Island Air (www.mayaairways.com) and Tropic Air (www.tropicair.com) serve all the main towns in Belize.
Bus: Local buses are dilapidated and overcrowded and not recommended. Long-distance buses: These are a better bet. Express buses offer air-conditioning and greater comfort for which you pay extra.
Taxis: Cheap and quick, taxis are the best way of getting around. They don't have meters so negotiate the fare before you get in.
Ferries: and water taxis are available to a number of places hard to reach by land.
Driving: Major highways are OK although 'sleeping policemen' (speed bumps) are a major irritation. Smaller roads are narrow and poor. Heavy rains frequently create hazards.
Driving is on the right.

THE RULES FOR GETTING IN

Anyone 45 years and older from anywhere in the world can qualify under the Qualified Retired Persons Incentive Law. To qualify applicants must receive a certified monthly income of not less than $2,000 through a pension or annuity generated from outside Belize and meet certain other requirements.

The incentives to attract retirees are among the most generous. Qualified persons are permitted to import household goods, a vehicle, boat and even an airplane free of import duties.

QRPs are not supposed to work for pay in Belize but they can own rental property and be "silent investors" in Belize businesses.

Qualified applicants can include their dependants – spouse and children under the age of 18 (and under 23 if enrolled in a university).

You can qualify if you are 45 or over. There is an application fee of $150, a programme fee of $1,000 once you have been accepted and $200 for your residency card.

Each dependant costs an extra $750.

Applications must be submitted to the Belize Tourism Board with the usual documentation and applicants are required to undergo a complete medical examination including an AIDS test.

More info: http://belizeretirement.org

---

areas, according to local real estate agents, but fell flat in line with the rest of the world in 2008.

Expect to pay upwards of $300,000 for a 3-bedroom beachfront property and up to $500,000 for something really spectacular with a private beach.

A beachfront condo will set you back around $250,000. However, you can buy a very nice (but small) house near the beach for as little as $80,000.

There is stamp duty of 5 per cent and a 1.5 per cent transfer tax when you sell. Legal fees are 2-3 per cent.

Where's best to live?
Placencia: Sixteen miles of natural sandy beach, a virgin mangrove-fringed lagoon, coral-studded cayes, nearby jungle rivers and pristine rainforest.

The Placencia peninsula is fast becoming Belize's next major visitor and vacation home destination helped by the paving of the main road from the Southern Highway.

Not to be missed is the annual lobster fest held

every June.

Ambergris Caye: The largest island in Belize and the main destination for travellers, retirees and other expats and for divers and eco-tourists. San Pedro is

Belize reserve
The Belize reserve is a 100 per cent carbon neutral eco-resort in the Cayo tropical rainforest of western Belize, 15 minutes from San Ignacio and 25 from the capital. The site will include a 20-30 unit hotel as well as 350 1/2 acre development plots. Land plots cost $40,950. The developer has offered interest free 50 per cent finance over five years on a limited number of properties.
More info: www.propertyfrontiers.com

Right on the beach
Older style 2-bedroom beach house home with 30 metres of beach front less than 1km from the town centre. in Ambergris Caye.
Price: $1.25m.

the only town on the island and offers the biggest selection of restaurants and nightlife.

Fishing and coconuts were the historic means of islanders' support. Today more than two dozen development projects are under way, including the first phase of South Beach Belize, a project of nearly 600 new homes.

Caye Caulker: Ambergris Caye's sister island remains a small village with a distinct cultural flavour and is relatively inexpensive compared to other tourist destinations.

Corozal: Traditionally the heart of the country's sugar growing and processing industry, Corozal, located between two scenic rivers on the Bay of Corozal, has Maya ruins, snorkelling, swimming and fly fishing attractions.

Belize's fourth largest populated district and home to a growing community of retirees, it has the lowest property prices. You can buy a Belizean-style home for $30,000 or a beachfront lot for around $50,000.

Cayo: Geographically the largest and most fertile district in Belize, Cayo spans more than 5,000sq km across diverse terrain from rolling hills and sweeping farmland devoted to citrus orchards and cattle farming, to lush river valleys and rugged mountain ridges covered in sub-tropical jungle.

Over 60 per cent of Cayo District has been set aside as either a wildlife sanctuary, national park, or forest reserve.

Punta Gorda: Punta Gorda, known locally as PG, is the southernmost town in Belize and the capital of the Toledo District. With its cool sea breezes and friendly people, Punta Gorda is a pleasant and interesting town. The waterfront is great for strolling with light breezes blowing in from the Bay of Honduras.

Almost 336km by road from Belize City, it is the last sizeable settlement in Southern Belize. Mango trees line the streets. Most small homes are made of wood on stilts.

Rainy, beautiful and remote, Punta Gorda in far southern Belize is the jumping-off point for unspoiled Maya villages and for onward travel to Guatemala and Honduras. Over the next few years as paving of the Southern Highway to Punta Gorda is completed and the road is extended into Guatemala, this area is expected to take off, both in terms of tourism and as a place for expatriate living.

Popeye's Beach Resort
What's better than simply a home? An entire resort development with a beach bar and restaurant. Popeye's Beach Resort has 20 rooms – cabanas, deluxe rooms or suites.
Price: $1.6m.
More info: www.belizeshoresrealty.com

Condo in Caye Caulker
What's better than simply a Luxury 2-bedroom beachfront apartment of 90sq m at 'Seaside Villas' in the central area of Caye Caulker. Fully furnished with 2 bathrooms and a rooftop jacuzzi with stunning views of Caye Caulker.
Price: $430,000
.**More info:** www.cayerealestate.com

I live here

After working for an airline for 20 years as a buyer and then losing her husband, in 2001, Canadian Pamela Dayka, then aged 44, came across the retirement programme offered by the Belize Tourism Board. Via the school of hard knocks Pamela has learned how to live happily in Belize and now offers practical advice to newcomers. Email her at: caribbeangem_4sale@hotmail.com

I had a friend who had lived in Belize for several years. I got most of my info from him. I planned the move to Belize for two years. I applied for the retirement programme. The process was efficient and relatively quick – about three months. My daughter and granddaughter came with me.

I had bought land in the Progresso Heights development, a gated community in the Corozal district, with the intention of building a home. After two years I found living in an American development didn't suit me and sold at a nice profit. I wanted to live among the locals where my heart was.

I now rent a nice home in San Ignacio, Cayo district and recently purchased an acre on the Mopan River. I found Corozal was suited more to mature retirees. San Ignacio offers more entertainment and variety.

Although I love Belize, it is not without its challenges for foreigners. My advice is to accept more than to reject or try to change the ways this country functions. I now assist many to relocate.

Only once you have lived here awhile – maybe a year is enough – then you understand what it takes to live happily in harmony. So much is different, from the seasons to simple things like shopping. There are no malls where you get everything but you soon get to know where to go for what you need.

I am by no means wealthy. I'm on a budget that I expect will last until I am of age to collect my old age pension. I hope by then I will be proficient in growing a garden for food, raising a few chickens, have my fruit trees mature and simplify my needs even more than I have. This is a work in progress.

So much to do

Daily life is basically whatever you want it to be. I get up and go out when I feel like it. I meet people anywhere to have food or drink, (some openly enjoy a little cannabis – yes, in public!) chat, gossip some, play a game of pool, dominos, cards or see a movie.

I volunteer at the seniors' homes and the women's shelter, do some work with the Red Cross and Rotary Club. We collected 10,000 books from our community in Canada and one of the first things to do was to distribute them to libraries, schools and churches.

I brought two huge suitcases with me from Canada filled with toys and crafts and every few months I drop off crayons and coloring books to the poorest villages.

There are many recreational things to do: tennis, golf, horseback riding, gardening, fishing or just a leisurely kayak ride down the river. For $30 I can take a flight over to the island for the day on the beach or take a water taxi for $15.

I have two small poodles, a puppy rottweiler, a cat and a parrot. They keep me busy, they all cuddle together and all but the cat come with me to my favourite watering holes. They have buddies they like to visit and socialise with as well.

I also dabble in real estate, but in a different way to the realtors. What I do is to match foreigners with locals. Someone tells me what they are looking for and I enquire around to see what's available.

Vets and doctors

Veterinary care here is very good. If only the human medical care was as reliable! I suffered an attack a few months after I moved to my home in Corozal. I was examined briefly at the hospital (being 2am there was limited staff). My head and eye were stitched but the doctors failed to diagnose a problem with my eye and I subsequently permanently lost the sight in it.

It is very important to maintain your medical insurance from your home country and add travel insurance to treat life-threatening injuries and other eventualities that are not immediately covered.

I was in a car accident. I rolled my vehicle. Ambulances cannot reach all areas of the country and one must rely on friends or the kindness of strangers which thankfully is in abundance. I was carried to hospital but not all services, such as MRIs, CT scans, etc, are readily available in the northern towns.

I traveled two hours to Belize City and had all the tests that were available. However my broken neck and back were not diagnosed and I was then sent back to Corozal hospital for whiplash injuries. The hospital does not offer any personal care – no personal hygiene assistance, no pillow or clean clothes. One must have a friend tend to all one's needs.

After four days they discharged me against my will. At my insistence I was taken home by ambulance and gladly paid. After 10 days I called my insurance company who handled everything. I was flown to Tampa where I had emergency surgery for a broken neck and had months of physiotherapy.

After six months I returned home to Belize. Vince, a French expat, gave me the desire to live. Now Belize and Vince have jointly given me passion for life.

When I see the simple beauty of the people here, I am ashamed for feeling sorry for myself in the past … to see local folks living in a broken down wooden shack enjoy a wonderful meal, with music, laughter, genuine caring.

Cost of living

The cost of living varies from district to district. Near the border with Mexico (Corozal district) or Guatemala (Cayo district) certain things obtained over the border are relatively inexpensive including medicine, household items, electronics, even "bucket gas" (petrol).

We call it bucket gas because they fill our tank with a bucket and a hose. Most villages get gas this way as there are no stations nearby.

Groceries have gone up considerably but expats can still live comfortably on US$600 a month. Rent for a nice 700sq. ft. fenced home averages $250 a month. A more American type home of, say 900-1,400sq. ft., can cost $300-1,000 a month. The home I now rent for $350 is beautiful, large, fairly new with modern interior.

You will get a better deal buying direct from a local rather than from a realtor or an expat trying to get rich on one sale.

Banking is modern and safe. Mortgages and personal loans can be obtained once a relationship has been established. They offer direct debit card and credit cards. ATMs are readily available.

Belize welcomes foreign investors and buying land is safe if you know what you're doing. Ask questions, do some research. Lawyers are not required since the Lands Department representative can perform all necessary tasks for a fraction of the fees.

Other costs

Many of us permanent residents don't use air-conditioning as it can easily add $250 a month to your electric bill. We take useful ideas from the locals such as collecting rainwater – very helpful during the frequent water shut-offs – and great for the plants and even doing the laundry.

We use propane for cooking. One large tank costs $45. Electric stoves are also available.

If you eat locally-grown fresh food, you can live for $100, but if you buy gringo – American imported, food – everything is twice the price it would be in the US. Clothes are not expensive.

Our local cable company charges $20 a month for over 100 satellite channels. Most of us use a cell phone as the landlines have a monthly cost plus a per call charge and need current which is often off.

High speed internet access in the 'core' of towns can be obtained for about $30, but for those of us who don't live in the core our choice is satellite internet, which is very expensive; the equipment and installation can run to $1,800 with monthly costs of about $80.

Auto repairs are also reasonable and, surprisingly, even the parts are cheap. American imported vehicles are expensive because of the high duty which is 62 per cent.

A housekeeper can cost $15 a day, a gardener $20. You will pay $10-15 a day for someone to clear your land.

There are things we cannot legally bring into Belize such as dairy products, bread, imported beer, anything that the Belikin cartel supplies – no Pepsi products and no other beer or soda than what Belikin produces. We only have a few brands of local cigarettes, others are purchased on the black market. A bottle of red wine averages $15.

We have to smuggle some things out of desperation, like grain breads. The bread here is terrible – white, no flavour and so dry, it goes bad in few days.

I moved to Belize to rest and found peace, happiness and contentment I couldn't find in a First World country. The way I see it, I exchanged one set of challenges for another. With freedom comes some dangers; we must be aware of and act accordingly.

Welcome to a corner of paradise

Costa Rica has become one of the world's leading tourist destinations. Despite its small size of just 51,100 square kilometres, Costa Rica is home to an astonishing 3% per cent of the planet's biodiversity and 3.5% of the world's marine life.

Costa Rica boasts a variety of fascinating creatures and remarkable lush vegetation guaranteed to leave visitors wide-eyed. Over 450 bird species, 283 species of mammals and several rare species like the tiny red frog have made Costa Rica one of the most biologically diverse countries in the world.

Its amazing biodiversity is related to its privileged geographical position. There are few countries where a visitor can enjoy true natural wonders from coast to coast. Costa Rica is comprised of seven provinces which are home to a variety of microclimates and astonishing natural wonders; mountain ranges, rainforests, active volcanoes with thermal waters, cloud forests, and the beautiful Cocos Island are just a few of the diverse landscapes for which our country is famous.

With 26% of its land officially zoned as protected territory, Costa Ricans take much pride in maintaining the natural beauty that has brought the country fame.

Many travellers may be surprised that this peaceful and progressive country is a leader in sustainable tourism practices. With a goal of achieving complete carbon neutrality by 2021, Costa Rica is at the forefront of the environmental movement.

Because today's travellers are more educated and demanding, we make constant efforts to offer the best experience possible to our visitors. Our efforts have been rewarded by the ever-increasing number of tourist arrivals.

The last two years Costa Rica has ranked first as the most competitive tourism destination by the World Economic Forum. We also rank fifth in the Environmental Performance Index 2008 developed by Yale and Columbia universities, only behind Switzerland, Finland, Sweden and Norway.

In Costa Rica we proudly take care of our wonderful nature for our children and for our visitors to enjoy. With pleasant year-round temperatures, there is always something to do outside. Top tier golf, fishing, world class scuba diving and, of course, bird watching are all readily available in different regions of the country. Life in Costa Rica is definitely best enjoyed outdoors. Costa Rica is also home to ideal waters for surfing, white water rafting and kayaking. Dozens of beautiful beaches are a given.

I hope you will soon join the two million tourists that each year come to experience the vacation of a lifetime in our corner of paradise.

Carlos Ricardo Benavidez Jiménez
Minister of Tourism

Security can be a problem in this tropical haven

Why Costa Rica?

Costa Rica has a marvellous subtropical climate. It is unbelievably green (some days it rains all day and rains very hard so if you don't mind the rain be sure to bring your umbrella and wet weather gear.)

The beaches are absolute beauties and there are lots of them with some of the best surf in the world and great deep-sea fishing. There are plenty of championship-designed golf courses with unparalleled scenery.

Gourmet cuisine is readily available but local food is simple, very cheap and tasty.

For entertainment there is a wide variety of things to do, one being a tourist: visiting the beaches, the active volcanoes and the mountains that go as high as 2700m with no snow – ever.

Here you can see monkeys, tropical birds, sloths, big cats, and brightly coloured poisonous frogs and snakes. The variety of tropical flora and fauna is a delight to see with over 100 varieties of tropical orchids.

Costa Rica has a democratic government and there is no standing army.

Many of us choose to live here to enjoy the climate, the lifestyle and the beaches. Like everywhere else in the world, there are pros and cons of

living here. If you can live with the negatives you will love the positive things you will experience.

It's important to develop a good support system rapidly: get referred to a trustworthy attorney right away, organise your healthcare, learn where to shop for bargains and be willing and flexible enough to not expect that you will have the same lifestyle as wherever it is you came from.

Cost of living

Utility costs are cheap compared to the USA. My average monthly water bill is around $3, electric around $60 (this in a house with all the modern appliances and gadgets I had in the USA). Houses do not require air-conditioning or heating. Cable TV is about the same as the USA, ditto satellite TV and high speed Internet.

Car repairs are cheap if you use local mechanics rather than go to dealerships. (The dealership was going to charge me $600 to change the timing belt in my 2002 Nissan Pathfinder. The local shop charged me just over $100 for parts and labour.)

The downside

Costa Rica was once a true tropical paradise – safe,

ABOUT THE WRITER: After a hectic and stressful career in corporate USA, **Robert Holloway**, PhD, chose Costa Rica for his retirement having vacationed there a number of years earlier. Now a resident in Costa Rica for five years, Robert has lived in various parts of the world, has travelled extensively and chose Costa Rica for the low cost of living, the climate and quality of life.

Robert, who runs two businesses in Costa Rica, CostaRicanArt.net, and LatinAmericaLanguageSchool.com, is happy to offer advice to those interested in Costa Rica and can be contacted at: robcholloway@hotmail.com

FACTFILE

Capital: San José **Population:** 4.3 million

Area: 51,100sq km **Language:** Spanish, English

Climate: Sub-tropical and tropical with a dry season from December to April. The rainy season is May-November. December is the wettest month on the Caribbean coast.

Time difference: GMT -6

Entry requirements: No visa required for stays of up to 90 days.

Retirement/residence visa: You can obtain a retiree pensionado visa if you can prove an income of $1,000 a month. (Previously it was $600). There is an additional $1,000 for a spouse and $500 for each child. A rentista visa requires you to prove an income of $2,500 a month for a minimum period of five years. [See: The rules for getting in]

Electricity: 120V/60Hz

Money: Costa Rican colon. ATMs available in larger towns. Credit/debit cards and travellers' cheques are accepted throughout Costa Rica. Banks charge a service fee for cashing travellers' cheques. US dollars are the favoured currency.

Public holidays 2010

Jan 1	New Year's Day
Apr 2-5	Easter
Apr 10	Juan Santamaría's Day
May 1	Labour Day
July 25	Guanacaste Annexation
Aug 2	Virgin of Los Angeles
Aug 15	Mothers' Day and Assumption
Sept 15	Independence Day
Oct 11	Columbus Day
Dec 25	Christmas Day

Opening hours:

Shops 9am-6pm (Mon-Sat)

Banks: 9 am to 3 pm (Mon-Fri), Sat am

Offices: 8am-4pm

Water: Better to drink bottled in rural areas.

Medical/Healthcare: Medical and dental treatment is world class. Many physicians are trained in Europe or the USA and operate with modern equipment.

No vaccinations are compulsory but polio, typhoid, tetanus, yellow fever and hepatitis A are recommended.

Malaria is common in Costa Rica, especially in areas close to banana growing areas and precautions should be taken.

AIDS is widespread on the eastern coast.

Pets: Cats and dogs are not quarantined but must arrive with a health certificate validated by the nearest Costa Rica Embassy. The examination for the certificate must be conducted within the two weeks prior to travel to Costa Rica.

Immunisations must be up to date including proof of a rabies vaccination performed at least 30 days prior to entering Costa Rica, but no more than one year old.

cheap, easygoing with people who loved contact with foreigners. Times have changed over the years and the CR I once loved has become ugly.

It is dangerous here now. Many people don't have the same love for foreigners and will try to take advantage of them since it will be obvious that they are naive and from somewhere else.

There is extensive corruption among government officials (three ex-presidents have been indicted for corruption) and police officers. Many are on the take or involved in organised crime due to their low rate of compensation (around $300 per month).

Sub-quality products are sold here since there are not the tight restrictions on quality as in other countries. The same brand names are available but they are made for this market with less safety and quality standards. Cars are the same. New cars here are built for this market and would not meet the safety standards of Europe or the USA.

THE RULES FOR GETTING IN

You can obtain a retiree Pensionado visa if you can prove an income of US$1,000 a month from a qualified retirement plan or a lifetime pension source outside Costa Rica.

There is an additional $1,000 for a spouse and $500 for each child.

A Rentista visa requires you to prove an income $2,500 a month for a minimum period of five years.

It takes about a year to gain legal residency once the applicant has provided all the necessary documentation. A good attorney may be able to speed this up a little. The problem is finding a trustworthy attorney. Local attorneys will charge around $300-500, while others may charge two to three times as much.

Residency has to be renewed annually the first year and then every two years and this is much easier under the new system. Renewals can be done at any of the 32 branches of the Banco de Costa Rica (BCR).

BCR promises that the process can be finished in 20 minutes.

Once a permanent legal resident has resided here for seven years they are eligible for citizenship. I won't go into the requirements since they are also subject to change.

Is it safe?

Home security is a huge issue. You must have a strong security system and/or guards. Twice in two months my house was burgled and all my electric tools stolen, even with a guard in front of the house.

Vehicle security is also a problem with auto jacking and stealing things from on and in your car. The Nissan emblems on my car (front and back) have had to be replaced three times in the past year.

Violent crime is out of control, matching the worse crime areas in the USA, with an average of over three violent deaths a day last year. Youth crime is as bad.

Keep your guard up and use common sense when travelling by car, walking or any other method of getting around. Use extreme caution when walking anywhere alone. Organised gangs patrol areas in San Jose. They are armed and dangerous and will take your wallets, your jewellery, cell phones and anything else that is not a permanent part of your body.

If it's any comfort, foreigners can own guns here and, if you become a permanent resident, you can have a concealed weapons permit.

How much tax will I pay?

Income tax is not currently charged on pension income. That could change in the future but right

Gated community
House on 1,425sq m of land in the hills above Hereida Costa Rica. 3 bedrooms, separate maid's house. Garage, 2 driveways, barbecue, covered terrace, wonderful views, mature gardens with avocado and orange trees and bananas. 1 hour from the beach. Completely furnished.
Price: $325,000
More info: costaricahouseforsale.howardandteresa.com
Email: howarddrew@hotmail.com

Tamarindo condo
1 bedroom condo within a gated complex in Tamarindo 5 blocks from the beach and within walking distance to everything in Tamarindo. Lush gardens and communal pool.
Price: $99,000
More info: www.costarica1realestate.com
Email: franck@coastalestates.org

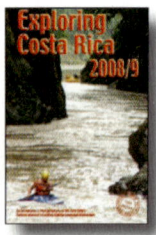

now, only income earned in Costa Rica is subject to income tax. If you are liable for tax it is important that you are up to date on payments or you may not be allowed to leave the country.

Property

Foreigners can own property here with full ownership rights and privileges. Foreigners enjoy the same ownership rights as Costa Rican citizens regardless of whether the property is placed in the name of a corporation or in the name of an individual. You can still find good deals everywhere. Be sure to have a good real estate attorney to help you with the purchasing process, the title search and arranging the financing.

Be cautious when dealing with realtors. They are not required to have any training nor a license.

Modern to Third World homes are available depending on your budget and your preferences.

Assisted care homes are popping up everywhere since Costa Rica has become increasingly popular as a retirement location. Recently I have seen ads for single

houses for sale in the north for a couple or single person for $17,000.

Like anywhere else in the world, beach property is expensive. A number of movie stars own property on the northern beaches.

Property taxes
Property taxes are low compared to North America. There are two forms of taxes, the Municipal Tax and Real Estate Tax. The Municipal Tax, paid quarterly, is 0.25 per cent of the registered value of the property. Houses with a registerd value of less than $11,000 are exempt. There is also a local community government charge. This is based on the frontage of the property and varies in each area but is limited to $10 per month per resident.

There is no capital gains tax.

Right now there is a move on to re-evaluate property values in Costa Rica. Local municipalities have been instructed by the Federal government to appraise all properties in their jurisdictions.

Most property in Costa Rica is owned within a corporate structure and thus has not been appraised for up to 50 years now so prices are really understated. Property prices have been minimal in the past and will be adjusted over the coming five years to a current appraisal which of course is being fought over already due to the stagnation of property sales. So it seems that property taxes will soon be charged more appropriately but they still will be quite low I am told.

Where's best to live?
If you prefer beach living you will find homes to fit any budget on the beautiful beaches of the Northern Province.

Again, a support system will be important in these areas since there are less shopping and medical facilities. The infrastructure in these areas does not adequately support the population growth being seen but Costa Rice is aware of these problems and in time living conditions will improve.

If you prefer a more moderate climate, then the Central Highlands will suit you well, with the average temperature ranging between 16-27°C year round. You will almost certainly find housing to suit your budget and lifestyle. It is advisable to have a good real estate attorney assist you with the process of any property purchase. You can even find farms, coffee plantations, cattle ranches and other like

Estate and farm, San Ramon
Palatial colonial-style house with breathtaking ocean views just 60km from the Juan Santamaria airport near San Jose. Currently operated as an inn/B&B, this 70-acre estate and farm is one of the most beautiful properties in Costa Rica – secluded, private, and secure. Unsurpassed hiking, biking, bird watching and horseback riding. 5 bedrooms, 5.5 bathrooms, large courtyard with two fountains, numerous terraces and porches.
More info: www.costa-rica-luxury-real-estate.com

COSTA RICA CONTACT DIRECTORY

Embassies/Government
Costa Rica Embassy in London
No apparent website
Email: costaricanembassy@btconnect.com
UK Embassy in Costa Rica
http://ukincostarica.fco.gov.uk/en

Travel & Health Advice
Foreign Office travel advice
www.fco.gov.uk/travel
www.nhs.uk/Healthcareabroad
www.masta.org

About Costa Rica
www.therealcostarica.com
www.infocostarica.com
2 sites with loads of information about Costa
Rica and living there
www.costaricanet.net
http://blog.therealcostarica.com
www.buzzle.com
ARCR.net
Site offering commercial services to those
planning to move to Costa Rica
www.costarica-discover-it.com
www.infocostarica.com
www.welovecostarica.com

General & Expat
www.abroadincostarica.com
www.expatfocus.com
www.britishexpat.com
www.transitionsabroad.com

English Language Media
The Tico Times, free biweekly for tourists.
Online newspapers
http://insidecostarica.com
www.amcostarica.com
http://thecostaricanews.com
www.whereincostarica.com

Property
www.costaricarealestatepages.com
www.costaricaretirementvacationproperties.com
www.emeraldforestproperties.com
www.ksrm.com
www.costarica1realestate.com
www.costaricatopbrokers.com
www.costa-rica-luxury-real-estate.com
www.pacificlandsales.com

Travel & Tourism
www.infocostarica.com
www.costarica.com
www.whatcostarica.com
www.trycostarica.com
http://costa-rica-guide.com
www.travelblog.org
(You need to navigate to Costa Rica)

Getting There
Most flights are via a North American hub
Air France: www.airfrance.co.uk
(via Atlanta)

Air Madrid: www.airmadrid.com
(Direct flights from Madrid)
Grupo Taca: www.taca.com
American Airlines:
www.americanairlines.com
Continental Airlines:
www.continental.com/uk/
Delta Airlines: www.delta.com
British Airways: www.bristishairways.com
Iberia Airlines: www.iberia.com
Continental Airlines: www.continental.com
Delta Airlines: www.trycostarica.com
Iberia Airlines: www.iberia.com

Getting Around
Air: Sansa Airlines: www.FlySansa.com
Nature Air: www.natureair.com
Train: There are limited services from San
Jose to the neighbouring city of Heredia
and San Pedro.
Bus: Public buses are cheap and
comfortable. Tourist minibuses are about 10
times more expensive but are air-
conditioned.
Driving: Many roads are in poor condition
with potholes and occasional landslides in
the wet season and dangerous especially at
night. Drivers are aggressive and, according
to one blogger, "driving in Costa Rica is
based on one simple concept: Get to your
destination as quickly as possible,
regardless of safety considerations, road
conditions, speed limits or anything else
that is in the way."
There is an amusing article on driving at:
www.insidecostarica.com
There are instances of car-jacking at night.
You can drive on your home country licence
for up to three months or on an
International Driving Licence.
Driving is on the right.

Los Sueños Resort
Los Sueños Resort includes a
600-acre rainforest reserve,
located on Playa Herradura
Costa Rica, just north of Jaco
Beach on the Pacific coast. Los
Sueños is Costa Rica's premier
residential resort community.
Available properties range from
1, 2 and 3 bedroom
condominiums to single-family
homes.
Los Sueños has a well-
developed infrastructure and the
surrounding area provides
shops, restaurants and services.
More info: www.ksrm.com Tel:
(Costa Rica) 011 506 26304000

South of the border is the first choice of US retirees

Why Mexico?

Mexico is a wonderful destination for the 'people person.' If you are open to their embrace, Mexicans will welcome you into their community with open arms. While solitary refuges can be created, Mexicans celebrate togetherness. Join in by being flexible and relaxed enough and you will find yourself living a new life that will let you be more yourself than ever before.

For Americans, Mexico is the No1 choice for sun-seeking retirees. The US embassy in Mexico City estimates that there are more than 600,000 Americans living in Mexico. An estimated 300,000 Canadians live there, at least part-time.

A wide variety of climates exist in Mexico, including coastal areas, deserts, high mountain regions, and tropical paradises. Many towns host large populations of expatriates from around the world – not all of them are from Canada and the United States.

If cultural sights, sounds and flavours catch your fancy, Mexico is a rewarding place to live. Informal (and sometimes more formal) musical performances happen daily in the central square of most towns and cities. All you have to do is wander downtown and grab a shady park bench. Professional

performances are available at reasonable costs. Numerous holidays are celebrated throughout the year with tons of local colour and flavour. Special foods, music, dances and activities give newcomers plenty to delight in and the pre-Hispanic aspect of Mexico enriches many aspects of daily life.

Mexico is not only a great place to live; it's a great place to travel. As a resident you can invite friends and family to take in the sights or relax on the beach together. Trips to see world-class destinations, such as Chichen Itza or the Museum of Anthropology in Mexico City, are within relatively easy reach.

While not without its difficulties, Mexico's infrastructure is well-developed. Mobile and land-based phone service, high speed internet, cable and Hollywood movies are widely available. Highways allow travel by car, or even better, via superb first-class buses. International airports connect Mexico to the rest of the world. There is easy access to services such as doctors, dentists, and banks.

Although globalisation is taking an ever-increasing bite out of the local economy and mega stores are increasingly popular, it is a pleasure to frequent locally owned businesses as you learn about your new home and the people in your new community.

Cost of living

The cost of living in Mexico has increased

ABOUT THE WRITER: Julia Taylor is the author of the book "**Mexico: The Trick is Living Here**," a guide to living, working, retiring and adjusting to the culture in Mexico. She is also the creator of www.home-sweet-mexico.com, a unique resource for all those who want to work, live, or retire in Mexico. Julia moved to Mexico in 2001 with her Mexican husband, where they lived for eight years.

FACTFILE

Capital: Mexico City   **Population**: 111,200,000

Area: 1,959,248 sq km

Language: Spanish. English is generally understood in main towns and cities.

Climate: Mexico has tropical forests, deserts, snow-capped mountains, the weather being determined by latitude and by altitude. Most of the country has two seasons: wet (June-Sept) and dry (Oct-April). Generally low rainfall in the interior and north, abundant rainfall along the east coast, in the south, and in the Yucatan Peninsula.

Entry requiorements: No visa required for stays of up to for 180 days.

Retirement/residence visa: Retirees can obtain a Rentista visitor carnet (FM3). The minimum monthly income is US$1,150 per head of family plus US$550 for each dependant (spouse and children under 18). [See: The rules for getting in]

Electricity: 110 volts AC, 60Hz. American two-pin (flat) plugs

Money: Peso. ATMs in cities and major tourist areas. US dollars widely accepted.

Credit/debit cards: Not as widely accepted as in Europe or the USA.

Public holidays 2010

Jan 1	New Year's Day	Sept 16	Independence Day
Feb 4	Constitution Day	Oct 12	Columbus Day
Mar 15	B'day of Ben. Juárez	Nov 2	Day of the Dead
April 1	Maundy Thursday	Nov 20	Revolution Day
April 2	Good Friday	Dec 12	Lady of Guadalupe
May 1	Labour Day	Dec 25	Christmas Day
May 5	An. of Battle of Puebla		

Opening hours

Banks: 9am-4pm Mon-Fri

Offices: 9am-2pm, 4pm-6pm

Shops: 10/11am-9pm (or later) Mon-Sun in large towns and cities.

Elsewhere: 9am-4pm Mon-Sat

Water: Only drink bottled or boiled and avoid ice in drinks.

Tipping: Poorly paid service industry staff all expect a tip. This includes washroom, car park and petrol pump attendants, hotel and restaurant staff and porters. Taxi drivers normally build a tip into the price they quote you.

Medical/Healthcare: Malaria is common in low-lying rural areas and outbreaks can occur throughout the year. Dengue fever is common and can occur throughout the year. Almost 100 cases were reported in Guadalajara in 2008. You should take all precautions against mosquito bites.

There is a reciprocal medical agreement between the UK and Mexico, which means British travellers can receive most treatments on the Mexican Medicare scheme. Even so, travellers should not go without comprehensive travel and medical insurance.

Pets: You will need is a certificate from a veterinarian that shows your pet has been vaccinated for rabies, hepatitis, PIP and Leptospirosis and a health certificate from a veterinarian that was issued no longer than 72 hours before arriving in Mexico.

dramatically over the last few years. I remember when we came to Mexico in 2001 we were excited to be able to buy avocados for 12 pesos a kilo! That's about a dollar for two pounds! Now they are 25 pesos per kilo and have recently been as high as 35 to 40 per kilo.

But while inflation (6.2 per cent in 2008) has pushed prices up, the Mexican peso has lost value so you get a lot more for your dollars and pounds.

To an extent the cost of living is dictated by where you choose to live. If this is an up-market neighbourhood then obviously you will pay more for pretty well everything – from rent to groceries.

The best way to save money in Mexico is to live like a Mexican; shopping at the local tianguis or market, rather than the mega-style grocery stores will save money and help support the local economy. Give up packaged foods in favour of fresh fruits and vegetables which are astoundingly delicious. Use the great public

PROPERTY

Casa Villa Chuparosa

Lovely hacienda style Home with 2 casitas located high on the hillside of La Penita, 40 miles north of Puerto Vallarta. Ocean views. Easy walk to town. Selectively planted gardens attracts hummingbirds and butterflies and Birds. Main house has 2 bedrooms, bath, kitchen

transit system; don't own a car. When eating out, eat comida corrida, rather than at touristy restaurants. When you step out of the "rat race" it costs less to live.

If you live like your Mexican friends you can get by on about $1,200 a month – rent included (the annual per capita income in Mexico is about $14,000) but your cost of living will increase significantly if you choose to live in an up-scale section of a city or in a tourist area.

Living "like a Mexican" is acceptable for some and not for others. My book, 'Mexico: the Trick is Living Here', includes a description of three "lifestyle levels" available to residents of Mexico. I created this unique way of considering the cost-of-living in Mexico because there are many hard to foresee differences between living in Mexico and living in one's country of origin and I wanted my readers to understand those differences. Retiring in Mexico doesn't mean you get the same thing for less; you get something different- and if you plan it right, it can cost you less.

Is it safe?

The great majority of places in Mexico are very safe, a few require caution, and very few should be avoided. New residents can easily find a safe place to live in which they will feel comfortable going out and about and where their homes will be safe. It is not necessary to live in a gated community to be safe.

Many expats say that they feel safer in their adopted Mexican communities than they did in their previous homes. With a little searching, prospective residents can find a town and neighborhood where they will come to know their neighbours by name, can walk freely in the evening, and feel safe and relaxed.

Car-related crime is prevalent throughout Mexico

THE RULES FOR GETTING IN

The Rentista Visa
To reside legally in Mexico, you need an FM3 visa which, according to the Mexican Embassy in London, takes just two days to issue.

A Rentista visitor is a foreign national who lives off the income from savings and investments or any legal income from abroad, such as retirement pensions.

The minimum monthly income is $1,150 per head of family plus $550 for each dependant (spouse and children under 18), for at least one year.

The Rentista Visitor Carnet (FM3) visa is valid up to one year with multiple entries and is indefinitely renewable.

Application requires proof of monthly income issued by a bank or trustee institution and has to be certified by a public notary.

More info: http://portal.sre.gob.mx/conreinounido

and study, covered veranda overlooking ocean and pool. Separate studio casita sleeps 2 with kitchen and bathroom. Second casita sleeps 5, kitchen, dining and bathroom. Raised palapa for entertaining and relaxing. Covered carport for 3-4 vehicles. Large secure storage room. Most furniture and fixtures included.
Price: $349,900
More info: http://jeaniemintzmyer.point2agent.com

Villa Alta, Chapala, Jalisco
Ideally located between Chapala and Ajijic just minutes from the main road and 35 minutes from Guadalajara International Airport. Villa with fully separate casita (guest house) on second story. Lot size: 18,000 sq. ft. House size: 3,440 sq. ft. 2 bedrooms, 2 bathrooms, dining room, living room, kitchen and den. Spectacular lake views, beautiful gardens. Solar hot water and electric Fully self-contained casita, with own balcony, kitchen and bath.
Price: $499,000
More info: www.chapalahouseforsale.com

and prospective residents must consider prevention methods when selecting a new home. Kidnapping exists and appears to be spreading. Violent crime, related to the drug trade has been making headlines, but should not cause people to avoid Mexico. Headlines generally don't reflect the norm, rather the extreme exception.

Visiting an area before moving there will give the prospective resident a feel for the safety of a town and neighbourhood and provide opportunities to ask locals if there are any dangers to be considered in the town. In eight years, despite hearing many real-life horror stories from Mexican acquaintances, I have experienced only one crime – a car stereo stolen. Even the Mexico City metro, which is reportedly dangerous, posed no problem for me and my husband.

Bottom line: To be safe be smart. Don't indulge in over consumption of alcohol, don't participate in any illegal activities, don't stay out alone late at night and make wise decisions about where you go, when you go there and what you eat.

I don't mean to imply that you should stick only to the touristy areas. Some of the best experiences in Mexico are to be had in the places frequented by Mexican tourists and in ordinary Mexican neighbourhoods. I personally feel even safer in these areas because of the community of good people.

How much tax will I pay?
Residents, defined as those spending six months a year in Mexico (consecutive or not), are subject to income tax on their worldwide income, regardless of nationality. However, many retirees stay as tourists and are taxed only on their Mexican source income.

There are one-off fees and taxes relating to property purchase. The acquisition tax is 1-2 per cent of the value of the property depending on the state in which you buy.

Capital Gains Tax Law is complex and you should understand the rules before you buy rather than when you come to sell. There two options: 34 per cent of the net profit or 25 per cent of the gross sale price. A variety of deductions are included in the first option and although the tax seems high there are tricks to lower your capital gains. However, if you are a resident and your Mexican property is your "primary residence", you pay no capital gains after two years.

There is no inheritance tax.

Is Mexican property a good investment?
Property prices in some areas have increased enormously – as much as tenfold in prime locations such as the Riviera Maya on the coast of the Yucatan peninsula, famous for diving, jungle walks, beautiful sandy beaches and archaeological sites.

Major cities and popular coastal areas have also seen

PROPERTY

a big increase in values while in smaller towns and villages prices have increased only steadily.

Where's best to live?

Popular retiree destinations include:

Guadalajara – A vibrant city, with absolutely everything and popular among expatriates. An international airport makes it easy to connect with their own country.

Ajijic – (pronounced ah-hee-HEEK) A small town that has become a favourite of expatriates, especially from Canada and the United States – almost half its population comes from the US. This town is located on Lake Chapala and is relatively near Guadalajara.

Lake Chapala Region – A number of small towns on the shores of this lake are becoming increasingly popular among expatriates looking for lower prices than can be found in Ajijic.

San Miguel de Allende – A small, beautiful colonial town. This town is favoured by many expatriates who love its authentic feel.

Los Cabos and surrounding areas – Los Cabos is growing by leaps and bounds due to its relatively small size and the wonderful beaches nearby. Air transportation to and from Los Cabos is available.

Cuernavaca – Located in the heart of Mexico, an hour south of Mexico City. Cuernavaca has a moderate climate, plenty of local traditions and celebrations, as well as modern conveniences. Cuernavaca's climate is always relatively comfortable and there are flowers in bloom all year round.

Tepoztlan – Located 45 minutes from Cuernavaca, this little town, nestled below stunning cliffs is picture-perfect.

Cancun and Mayan Riviera – There are many different towns on the stunning Mayan Riviera, including Playa del Carmen. The beaches, snorkelling and diving are reason enough to live there.

Merida – Merida has lots of character. This mid-sized city is modern and colonial at the same time and art, culture and music are quite accessible.

Morelia – A smaller city in the lovely, traditional state of Michoacan. The expatriate population in this city is quite small and loosely knit.

Veracruz – Veracruz is a port town on the Gulf of Mexico described as both modern and beautiful. It is famous for its vibrant culture and friendly people.

Mexico City – This is the central hub of Mexico. If you can handle its intense urban feel, this city has a lot to offer.

Queretaro – Approximately two hours north of Mexico City, this city has a small expatriate population and offers a good standard of living.

Guanajuato – Guanajuato is quite colonial, with

Hacienda, Guanajuato
Large house on a plot of 8,675sq m, 4 bedrooms, 3 bathrooms, beautiful gardens with fruit trees, private well, swimming pool, basketball court, large covered and open parking lot.
Built in the Mexican colonial style, this is one of the most beautiful properties in Guanajuato's planelands.
Price: $650,000
More info: Casas Eugenia www.eugeniahomes.net

2-bed condos, San Felipe
Pair of 2 bedroom, 2 bathroom condos, each of 185sq m close to beach. New split A/C heat pump & jacks to the roof for satellite TV, internet, phone, ceiling fans and much more. Great sea and mountain views.
Price: $499,000 for both units
More info: San Felipe Real Estate
www.sanfeliperealestate.com

narrow, cobblestoned streets, lively colours and rich aromas. It is one of Mexico's designated "magic" towns as well as a World Heritage city. The city's temperate climate makes it quite liveable.

Puebla – industrial city 130km from Mexico City, but offers museums, monuments, colonial architecture, local cuisine, festivals and events. It is a large city with over a million residents and truly has it all.

Puerto Vallarta – Puerto Vallarta combined with Nuevo Vallarta (the bordering resort area) is relatively large with a population of loyal expatriate residents. The international airport makes it easy to get there. This is city is located on the Pacific Ocean and boasts recreation galore including beaches, golf courses, tennis courts, Mariachi music, and tequila.

Ensenada – Hot and dry, Ensenada is always sunny. This port town on the Pacific Ocean is relatively close to Mexico's border with California and many expatriates from the U.S. make it home. Seafood and sport fishing are two of the pleasures to be enjoyed here.

San Felipe – Recently San Felipe has changed from tiny fishing town to a small retirement community with a population of only around 25,000. There are good air and other transportation connections from San Felipe to San Diego, California.

MEXICO CONTACT DIRECTORY

Embassies/Government

Mexican Embassy in London
www.sre.gob.mx/reinounido/
Email: mexuk@easynet.co.uk
British Embassy in Mexico
http://ukinmexico.fco.gov.uk/en

Travel & Health Advice

Foreign Office travel advice
www.fco.gov.uk/travel
www.nhs.uk/Healthcareabroad
www.masta.org

About

www.home-sweet-mexico.com
www.mexonline.com
www.mexonline.com
www.mexperience.com/
mexicocity.en.craigslist.com.mx
www.latinworld.com/section/mexico
http://lcweb2.loc.gov/frd/cs/mxtoc.html
www.peoplesguide.com/1pages/retire

General & Expat

www.home-sweet-mexico.com
www.expatfocus.com
www.britishexpat.com
www.expat.com.my
www.expatfinder.com/Mexican-expats
www.expatexchange.com
www.justlanded.com/english/Mexico

English Language Media

www.thenewsmexico.com
Guadalajara Reporter
www.guadalajarareporter.com
MexicoReporter.com
www.directv.com

Estate Agents

Mexico Best Buywww.mexicobestbuy.com
Casas Eugeniawww.eugeniahomes.net
San Felipe Real Estate
www.sanfeliperealestate.com
Tierra Yucatanwww.tierrayucatan.com
Merida Homes Real Estate
www.meridahomes.com
www.mls4rivieramaya.com
Real Estate Yucatan
www.realestateyucatan.com
www.propertyworld.com/_Mexico
Viviun www.viviun.com
Puerto Vallarta Mexico Real Estate
/www.puertovallartabestrealestate.com

Travel & Tourism

www.visitmexico.com
www.antor.com/members/Mexico
www.360travelguide.com/Mexico
http://gomexico.about.com
http://travel.latimes.com/destinations/mexico
http://cancuntop100.com

www.ourmexico.com
www.lonelyplanet.com/mexico
www.mexicocity.gob.mx – official tourism
website of Mexico City
http://www.solutionsabroad.com
www.allaboutmexicocity.com

Getting There

Aeromexico
www.aeromexico.com/usa/english/
British Airways
www.britishairways.com/travel/mexico
Air France www.airfrance.co.uk
Air Europa www.aireuropa.com
Thomas Cook.com
http://book.flythomascook.com
Lufthansa www.lufthansa.com
Iberia www.iberia.com/mx
KLM KLM.com

Getting Around

Mexico has an excellent bus systems with
four classes of service on the main routes.
Mexico is a big country and journeys can
be long and tedious. Competing with the
bus operators are an unusually large
number of domestic airlines.
www.virtualmex.com/mileage.htm offers
point-to-point travel information.

Air: These are the main operators:
Aeromexicowww.aeromexico.com
Mexicana Airlines Mexicana.com
Click www.clickmx.com
Aviacsa www.aviacsa.com/english
Aladia www.aladia.com
Interjet www.interjet.com
Viva Aerobus www.vivaaerobus.com
Volaris www.volaris.com

Train: Since the government discontinued
rail subsidies few services remain. The
Chihuahua Pacific Railway winds through
the sites along the Copper Canyon and
connects the Pacific coast town of Los
Mochis to the interior desert city of
Chihuahua (10 trains a week in each
direction); there is a Guadalajara-Amatitán-
Guadalajara twice a week.
There are urban rail systems (metros) in
Mexican City, Guadalajara, Jalisco,
Monterrey and Nuevo León.

Bus: Most towns have at least one main
bus terminal and it can be confusing where
there are more. Mexico City has four
different terminals. If you're not on a
budget always take the highest level of
service available. Express (non-stop) costs
around US$10 for every hour of travel and
offer spacious seating and often
complimentary soft drinks and snacks and
movies.

Driving: Cattle, pigs, people and dogs roam
at will on Mexico's rural roads and you risk
hitting at least one if you drive fast. Beware
of potholes, slow moving vehicles, vehicles
changing lane without indicating and going
through red lights. Many local drivers do
not have any form of car insurance. If you
hire a car take all extra insurance available.
At night and in the cities keep your car
doors locked at all times and the windows
shut, especially at traffic lights.
Mexico City and some other regions have
introduced restrictions on driving. Cars will
be forbidden from certain areas on
particular days based on number plates.
This applies equally to permanent,
temporary and foreign plates. These
regulations are strictly enforced and
offenders face heavy fines and temporary
confiscation of their vehicle.
Roads are fairly good but topes, Mexico's
infamous speed bumps are big and
frequently unmarked.
Driving is on the right.

Just $400 a month opens the door to the 'new' Nicaragua

Why Nicaragua?

Forget everything you thought you knew about Nicaragua, a country that has historically been dogged by disaster and despair, and discover the new Nicaragua, one that's garnering favourable comparisons to its neighbour to the south, Costa Rica.

Today's Nicaragua is a country with plentiful natural beauty framed by a coastal paradise that is being discovered by thousands of visitors each year and embraced by adventurous investors and adventure seekers alike.

Often referred to as the next Costa Rica, Nicaragua shares the same unspoiled and magnificent coastlines as its neighbour.

Property prices are still among the least expensive in the world yet as tourism climbs and the economy continues to strengthen, substantial rises in value are expected for many prime coastal locations.

Of all the countries within South and Central America, Nicaragua offers the most generous

concessions to entice retirees and requires the most modest of incomes – currently just $400 a month.

Is it safe?

Over the last two decades Nicaragua has transformed itself into one of the safest and fastest-growing countries in Latin America, with a strong and stable democratic government. As a result it now possesses one of the most dynamic economies in Central America, experiencing substantial increases in private investment and exports.

Everywhere you look there are signs of progress – new highways, re-paved roads, world-class hotels, state-of-the-art shopping plazas and international franchises.

Shortly after his election, Daniel Ortega met with dozens of the country's top business leaders and foreign investors and promised to respect property rights and support the country's Central American Free Trade Agreement with the United States. The Ortega of today is more a businessman than a revolutionary – more a deal maker than a war maker.

He reassured existing investors and threw out a welcome to new ones. "No-one is going to allow seizure of property, big or small. We need to eradicate poverty but you don't do that by getting rid of investment and those who have the needed resources."

As a result tourism, exports, and foreign investment numbers are holding up. The tourist towns of Granada and San Juan are buzzing with new hotels, restaurants and bars. A hotel room in high season in Granada is difficult to find. Property owners in certain projects are starting to get rental income for the first time.

ABOUT THE WRITER: Vinnie Apicella is a travel writer and property specialist whose website, **www.vinniesworld.com** provides a mass of information on Nicaragua and the services he offers investors: tours, business consulting and deals on Nicaragua beach properties

Honduras
Caribbean Sea
El Salvador
Coco River
75 mi
75 km
Tegucigalpa
WaWa River
Cerro Mogoton
La Rosita
Puerto Cabezas (Bilwi)
Somoto Ocotal
Siuna
Nicaragua
Gulf of Fonseca
Esteli Matagalpa
Rio Grande
Corn Islands
Lake Managua
Escondido River
Corinto
Juigalpa Rama
Leon **Managua**
Puerto Sandino Masaya Granada
Bluefields El Bluff
Monkey Pt.
Rivas
San Carlos
Caribbean Sea
Pacific Ocean
San Juan del Sur
Ometepe Island
San Juan River
San Juan del Norte
Solentiname Archipelago
Costa Rica
NICARAGUA
LOW / HILLS / MOUNTAINS
San Jose

THE RULES FOR GETTING IN

Applicants must prove a "stable, permanent income generated abroad" of not less than $400 a month and $100 for each family member. (It is believed the Nicaraguan Government is considering revising these requirements to $600/$200). The minimum age is 45.

All documents must be translated into Spanish, authenticated by a Nicaraguan consulate abroad and submitted to the General Consular Office of the Ministry of Foreign Affairs in Nicaragua, for legal validation.

In addition to the usual forms, photos, birth certificates, etc, applicants need a certificate of good conduct issued by a police authority in the applicant's home country and a certificate of good health.

The incentives

There is a package of incentives: income from abroad is free of tax and retiree visa holders can bring in $10,000 worth of household goods and a car duty/tax free.

More details:
www.consuladonicamiami.com/pdf

A land of lakes and volcanoes, Nicaragua is the largest yet most sparsely populated of the Central American nations, with a population just over 5.5 million.

Nicaragua borders Honduras to the north and Costa Rica to the south. Its topography includes a mountainous region to the west, two vast lakes, Nicaragua – the largest freshwater lake in Central America – and Lake Managua, which are connected by the Tipitapa River.

The Pacific coast is volcanic and very fertile which lends itself to an abundant supply of agricultural exports, while the marshy Caribbean coast is known as the "Mosquito Coast."

Nicaragua has some of the most spectacular beaches in Central America. It is also home to the colonial city of Granada, purportedly the oldest in the Americas, and the remarkable Crater Lake Apoyo, recommended for accreditation as a World Heritage site.

It has a tropical climate with two seasons – a wet season from May to January and a dry season from January to mid-May.

Nicaragua has always been primarily an agricultural country, but in the last 12 years tourism has grown by almost 400 per cent to become the second largest source of foreign capital.

Nicaragua remains one of the world's poorest countries. Yet, having survived governmental instability and natural calamities during the 1980s, the country is now one of the most dynamic economies in Central America due in large part to a

PROPERTY

Gran Pacifica

2 of several property options at a huge new resort development of 2,500 acres on Nicaragua's Pacific coast. Homes vary from beachfront to park and village, luxury condos, golf course villas. The development has a marina, parks, a boulevard and 5.6km of beach.
Villa prices from: $229,732
More info: www.vinniesworld.com
Email: nicaragua@vinniesworld.com

Golf condo

2nd floor condo at the Hacienda Iguana Golf and Beach Resort. 2 bedrooms, 2 bathrooms. 130sq m. Amazing view. Fully furnished.
Price: $250,000
More info: www.NicaraguaisHot.com
info@nicaraguaishot.com   Tel: +(505)-276-0309

substantial increase in private investment and exports.

A World Bank cited Nicaragua as being the country with the best conditions for business and attracting foreign investments in Central America.

Is it safe?

The crime rate in Nicaragua is lower than in Germany, France or the US and, according to the Inter-American Institute on Human Rights, Managua is the safest capital in the region and Nicaragua is the safest country in Central America.

That said, crime in the capital and other major cities is a problem: from gang violence, robbery, assault and petty crime. Pick-pocketing occurs on buses, at bus stops and at markets. The road from Managua's International Airport is notoriously dangerous.

How much tax will I pay?

There is no tax on overseas sourced pension or investment income and no inheritance tax. Capital gains tax is charged at income tax rates. Property tax is charged at one per cent of the value of the property and is paid to the Municipal Government.

Is Nicaragua property a good investment?

Nicaragua is very inexpensive, features beautiful coastal settings, exemplary topography, temperate year-round climate and a relaxed lifestyle, drawning

favourable comparisons to the Costa Rica of more than a decade ago when it too was awakening from the slumber of its own troubled past and beach properties could be had at a fraction of what they command today.

Many believe that Nicaragua, offering the more affordable alternative next door, will ultimately overtake Costa Rica as the settlement of choice along the Pacific with the thriving expatriate communities. Opportunities along Nicaragua's Pacific coast abound.

Where's best to live?

The buzz is about Nicaragua's central Pacific coast with much of the attention going to the strategically located beaches west of Managua, the capital city.

Coastal developments are moving at an accelerated pace. A number of projects are under way touting tantalising dream homes in exclusive communities only minutes from the beach. The bulk of foreign investment into real estate and tourism sectors is focused on the south-western corner of the country, which boasts a dramatic geography and comfortable climate.

Numerous developments continue to appear along the Pacific coast, offering luxurious living for expats at a fraction of the cost back home. Many find it more favourable to buy within these already established projects where property is purchased outright with no risk of ownership issue or title claims.

These are some of the more appealing projects: **Seaside Mariana Spa & Golf Resort,** near the town of San Rafael Del Sur and about an hour from the capital of Managua, has ocean-view homes, condos and golf villas, an 18-hole golf course, a spa, boutique hotel and plaza with shops, restaurants, cafes, and

performing arts venue. Home lots start at $45,000.

El Camino del Sol is a tranquil community in the foothills above the seaside village of San Juan del Sur, Nicaragua. Facilities include indoor/outdoor yoga studios, a clubhouse and a lap pool. Prices for home sites begin at $34,500.

Montecristo Beach, a new community 60km north of the capital, is large enough to be friendly, yet small enough to be personal. The Montecristo Golf Club features a par-71 course that stretches from the Pacific to high in the mountains. A beach club and equestrian centre are among the on-site amenities. Prices: Condos $209,990, lots $65,000.

Valle del Mar is set beside the equestrian centre among small private parks and only a few blocks from the shore. The village will include shopping, a clinic, a pub, a chapel, an inn, a neighbourhood centre, spa/gym/pool and tennis courts and a village green for community activities. Home sites start at $27,000 and include membership of Montecristo Golf Club. Turn-key lot/home packages from 145sqm to 200sq m are priced from $115,000.

Gran Pacifica, a five-star resort community is already home to more than 200 retirees and other overseas home-owners. The Gran Pacifica master plan consists of 2,500 acres with a variety of lots from beachfront to park and village, luxury condos, golf course villas, a marina, a colonial plaza, parks, a boulevard, plus 6km of beach. Prices: Single family home sites are priced from $69,990; casita village homes plus lot from $123,000;and new oceanfront condos are priced from $134,990. Developer financing is available.

Rancho Santana, 70km from the border with Costa Rica, is a 2,700-acre reserve with more than 3.2km of coastline and five beaches. It offers world-class surfing,

ocean-front dining, horse riding, spectacular beaches, nature trails, luxurious condominiums fronting the Pacific, a hotel and the new Santana Beach Club and Spa.

The newest phase of development, The Seagate Condominiums, features spectacular views of the Pacific Ocean and offer buyers a choice from two luxury models from 120-150sq m

Priced from $289,000 with financing available.

Eco resort villa
Villa at Norome Ecological Resort in the beautiful laguna de apoyo. Clubhouse, swimming pool, beach access, restaurant. 1 bedroom, 2 bathrooms in 200sq m. Rental management Price: $65,000
More info: www.localtreasureinternational.com
Email: info@localtreasureinternational.com

Fully furnished
1st floor condo of 121sq m. Beautiful finish with 2 bedrooms, and 2 bathrooms. Fully furnished.
Price: $229,000
More info: www.NicaraguaisHot.com
info@nicaraguaishot.com
Tel: +(505)-276-0309

FACTFILE

Capital: Managua **Population:** 5.7 million
Area: 120,254sq km **Language**: Spanish
(official) and some indigenous languages.
English is spoken within business locations
in Managua and in coastal resort areas.
Climate: Nicaragua has a tropical climate
with two seasons – a wet season from May
to January and a dry season from January
to mid-May. Average annual rainfall in the
capital, Managua, is 90cm and average
temperature ranges are 20-44°C.
Time difference: GMT -5 hours
Entry requirements: British nationals can
visit Nicaragua for up to 90 days without a
visa. This is renewable.
Retirement/residence visa: You need to
over 45 with a monthly income of at least
US$400. [See: The Rules for Getting In
Electricity: 110 V/60Hz.

Money: The cordoba. ATM machines are
available at banks and some shopping
centres in most towns and tourist areas.
Major credit/debit cards are accepted in
main cities. If you use travelers cheques
those denominated in US$ are more
acceptable.
Public holidays 2010
Jan 1   New Year's Day
April 1/2 Easter
May 1   Labour Day
July 19   Liberation Day
Sept 14   Battle of San Jacinto
Sept 15   Independence Day
Nov 2   All Souls' Day
Dec 8   Immaculate Conception
Dec 25   Christmas Day
Opening hours
Banks: 8am-3/4pm (Mon-Fri); 8.30am-

12pm (Sat)
Offices: 9am-5pm
Shops: 8am to 4pm
Water: Drink bottled or boiled.
Tipping: 10 per cent (usually added to bills).
Taxi drivers do not expect a tip.
Medical/Healthcare: Private healthcare
insurance is essential. There are no required
vaccinations but precautions against the
following are recommended: Hepatitis A and
B, anti-malarial drugs, rabies, typhoid and
yellow fever. Medical care is very limited,
particularly outside of Managua. Doctors and
hospital personnel are unlikely to speak
English. Medical notes and reports will be
written in Spanish.
Pets: Make sure your animals are up-to-date
on all vaccinations, including rabies, and
obtain a health certificate from your vet.

NICARAGUA CONTACT DIRECTORY

Embassies/Government
Nicaraguan Embassy in UK
36 Upper Brook Street, London, W1Y 1PE
Tel: 020 7409 2536
No website
There is no British Embassy in Nicaragua.
The British Embassy in Costa Rica has
overall responsibility for Nicaragua.
http://ukincostarica.fco.gov.uk/en/nicaragua/

Travel & Health Advice
Foreign Office travel advice
www.fco.gov.uk/travel
www.nhs.uk/Healthcareabroad
www.masta.org
http://travel.state.gov/travel

About Nicaragua
www.visitanicaragua.com/ingles
www.vinniesworld.com
www.nicaliving.com
www.nuwireinvestor.com
www.aurorabeachfront.com
www.nicaragua.com
http://gotonicaragua.com
www.thenicaraguagringo.com

General & Expat
www.expatfocus.com
www.britishexpat.com
www.transitionsabroad.com

English Language Media
www.nicaraguanpost.com
Free Bi-weekly English language newspaper
serving Nicaragua
www.topix.com/world/nicaragua
www.wavesnicaragua.com
Free quarterly magazine distributed to
airports, hotels, restaurants, travel agencies
and embassies.

Property
www.primenicaraguaproperty.com
www.nicaland.com
www.nicaPlaza.com
www.nicaraguaishot.com
www.aurorabeachfront.com
nicaraguarealestateinvestment.org
www.serenity21.com
www.nicaraguaproperty.com

Travel & Tourism
www.visitanicaragua.com/ingles
www.nicaragua.com/tourism/
www.nicaraguatrip.com
www.lonelyplanet.com/nicaragua
www.centralamerica.com/nicaragua
www.gotonicaragua.com
www.vinniesworld.com

Getting There
There are no direct flights from the UK. You
can get there via Madrid, Miami or Houston.
Iberia: www.iberia.com
South American Experience:

www.southamericanexperience.co.uk
British Airways: www.britishairways.com
American Airlines:
www.americanairlines.co.uk
Spirit Airlines

Getting Around
By air: Taca Regional is the local carrier and
for flights to neighbouring countries.
www.tacaregional.com/costena/index.html
Train: There are no railway services.
Bus: Most buses on short or long-distance
trips are former American school buses.
Fares are very cheap and, because of the
roads, pretty uncomfortable.
Taxis: Authorised taxis have red plates.
Most have no meters so fares must be
negotiated before you set off.
Driving: Not highly recommended. Outside
of the cities road conditions are poor and
sometimes dangerous particularly in the wet
season and at night. Car doors should be
kept locked and, if stopped at traffic lights,
windows should be closed.
Car hire is available at Managua
International Airport, as well as major hotel
locations within the city but since the roads
are bad outside of the main cities, a 4-
wheel drive vehicle is preferred which
makes it quite expensive.
Driving is on the right.

1,518 islands, perfect weather and the best retirement programme in the world

Why Panama?

With 30 per cent of its land set aside for conservation, 940 bird species, 12 national parks and 1,518 islands, Panama is bordered by both the Pacific and Caribbean oceans and offers beach, mountain or city life and an open door policy to investors and retirees alike.

If you want to retire abroad Panama could well be that place you are looking for.

Here you can have your own private beach, enjoy the many plants and animals that fill this country with beauty or even buy your own farm for a few hundred thousand dollars.

The fishing, bird watching, golfing and surfing are second to none.

The rain forests are magnificent, with a large variety of birds, monkeys, waterfalls, gorgeous trees and vegetation of all kinds. Pick your own bananas and other fruits and go swimming under the waterfalls on your hike or go kayaking through the many picturesque streams running through Panama.

Many are discovering the beautiful panoramic mountain region of Boquete, with its year-round spring weather, clean air and home grown coffee.

Panama has warm weather all year round, mountains, beaches, a cosmopolitan capital, a stable government, a huge number of benefits for retirees, low cost of living, great food (not good, great), affordable health care and friendly people, a large percentage of whom speak English.

America's Modern Maturity magazine rated Boquete in Panama as the fourth best destination in the world. International Living rates Panama at No.1. Panama was also rated as the No.1 place in the world to retire to in 'Smart Money' magazine

Panama's Pensionado programme is considered one of the best in the world and is not age related. Residents do not pay tax on foreign earned income and can buy and own property with the same rights and protections as Panamanian citizens. There are numerous incentives and tax breaks.

Panama has a reliable and modern communication system with fibre optic telephone lines and ADSL internet in much of the country.

These are just a few of the reasons why 50,000 Americans live here already and more are on the way.

Panama has no standing military. Why? The people felt that the military was being used to suppress them not defend against invading armies so they got rid of it. This relieves the country of an enormous tax burden.

At a time when many economies around the world

ABOUT THE WRITER: Originally from Cambridge, **Helen Owen** is a 'been-there-done-that' kind of girl who worked in Paris for six years, moved to Istanbul, married a Turk, moved to Bodrum where she stayed for 13 years and ran a restaurant called the Secret Garden and a real estate agency. Next stop was Panama where she fell in love with an American. She now lives in the USA.

"…not that my life has been about new adventures or anything," she says!

FACTFILE

Capital: Panama City
Population: 3,232,000
Area: 75,517sq km
Language: Spanish, English
Climate: Days are warm to hot, nights much cooler; temperatures range from 32°C during the daytime to 21°C in the evening practically year-round. Humidity is always high at about 80 per cent. Rainy season Oct-Nov.

Temperatures vary according to geography. The climate is less tropical at higher elevations. In mountain areas the average annual temperature ranges from 10°C-19°C at various mountain elevations.
Time difference: GMT -5 hours
Entry requirements: No visa required for stays of up to 90 days.
Retirement/residence visa: The main requirement is proof of a minimum income of $1,000 a month plus $250 for each dependant.

[See: The rules for getting in]
Electricity: 120V/60Hz
Money: The Balboa. US$ is accepted everywhere. Credit/debit cards and traveller's cheques are widely accepted.
Public holidays 2010

Jan 1	New Year's Day
Jan 9	National Martyrs' Day
Apr 2	Good Friday
May 1	Labour Day
Aug 15	Old Panama City Day
Nov 3	Independence Day (from Colombia)
Nov 10	First Call for Independence from Spain
Nov 28	Independence Day
Dec 8	Mothers' Day
Dec 25	Christmas Day

Opening hours:
Banks 8am-3pm (Mon-Fri) and Sat morning.
Offices: 8/9an-4/5pm and Sat morning
Shops: 9am-6pm Mon-Sat

Water: Tap water is claimed to be perfectly safe to drink.
Medical/Healthcare: There are no compulsory vaccinations when visiting Panama. Malaria is a risk only in jungle areas. Medical care is inexpensive and of a high quality. Modern hospitals are available throughout the country. Many Panamanian doctors are US-trained, and hospital standards are on par with what you would find in North America or Europe.
Pets: You need to complete a form, Quarantine for Domestic Animals (available from dcontreras@minsa.gob.pa) which should be accompanied by a health certificate, signed by a vet. The form and a rabies vaccination certificate must be faxed (507) 238-4234 or emailed to the Ministry of Health in Panama – dcontreras@minsa.gob.pa.

PANAMA CONTACT DIRECTORY

Embassies/Government
National Directorate of Immigration and Naturalization
http://www.migracion.gob.pa/
British Embassy in Panama
http://ukinpanama.fco.gov.uk
Panama Consulate General in UK
www.panamaconsul.co.uk

Travel & Health Advice
Foreign Office travel advice
www.fco.gov.uk/travel
www.nhs.uk/Healthcareabroad
www.masta.org

About Panama
www.everything-panama.com
www.businesspanama.com
www.panama-guide.com
www.panarail.com
www.panamalaw.org

General & Expat
www.expatfocus.com
www.britishexpat.com
www.transitionsabroad.com

English Language Media
www.thepanamanews.com
www.topix.com/world/panama
www.thebocasbreeze.com

Property
www.allpropertiespanam.com
www.properties-in-panama.com

www.realestatepanama.net
www.panamarealtor.co
www.panamarealestate.com
www.sunsetpointbocas.com

Travel & Tourism
www.atp.gob.pa
www.odyssei.com
www.visitpanama.com
www.panamaride.co
www.panamainfo.com
www.explorepanama.com
www.panama-guide.com
www.bocas.co
www.panamatravel.com

Getting There
There are no direct flights from the UK but options via Madrid, Amsterdam or the US.
Iberia: www.iberia.com
KLM: www.klm.com
American Airlines:
www.americanairlines.co.uk
Continental: www.continental.com
Delta Air Lines: www.delta.com

Getting Around
Air: Several domestic/regional services are available.
Copa Airlines: www.copaair.com
AirPanama: www.flyairpanama.com/
Aeroperlas Regional:
www.aeroperlas.com/eng
Train: The Panama Canal Railway Company has a scenic train route between Panama

City and Colon.
Bus: Air-conditioned buses are available from Panama City to most other parts of the country and are very cheap. Within cities there are extensive bus and minibus services. They are crowded and mostly not air-conditioned.
Taxis: Plentiful, safe and cheap. Best form of inner-city travel.
Boat: Several islands off the coast are reachable by boat. Services operate between Bocas del Toro and San Blas archipelagos and between Puerto Obaldía and Colón along the San Blas coast.
Driving: Traffic in Panama City is chaotic and a challenge for newcomers with long traffic jams at rush hours. Driving is erratic with no respect for traffic laws. On the highways driving conditions are relatively normal.

The Pan-American Highway from west to east and the Trans-Isthman Highway between Panama City and Colon are in good condition. Potholes are a problem on most other roads.

This might put you off: motor insurance is not compulsory in Panama, even for third party damage and injury, and many Panamanians drive without it.
Driving is on the right.

THE RULES FOR GETTING IN

Applicants require a proven income of at least $1,000 a month and $250 for each dependent. The programme covers applicant, spouse and children under the age of 18.

Requirements: You must apply in Panama, must be aged at least 18 years old, produce a health certificate and a certificate of good conduct (police record check) issued by the authorities at the place of residence during the last five years.

More info: www.embassyofpanama.org/cms/retire
Benefits: Tax exemption to import a new car every two years and reduced rate mortgages for homes used for personal residence.

Other discounts are offered on: Utility bills (25%), airline tickets (30%), transport (1%), doctor's bills (20%), hospital services (15%), dental and eye exams (15%), medicines (10%), professional services (10%) restaurant meals (25%), films, concerts, cultural and sporting events (50%) hotels Mon-Thurs (50%), on weekends (30%).

are in a downward spiral, especially real estate, Panama's real estate and investments are still on the up.

Panama has an annual income of two billion dollars just from the Panama Canal – imagine that much money spread amongst 3.3 million people. Tourism in 2007 brought in US$1.1 billion and will increase over the next few years. Panama also generates income from trade, mining and other raw materials.

Is it safe?

Panama ranks 48th in the Global Peace Index published by Britain's Economist Intelligence Unit – one place ahead of the United Kingdom.

It has an extremely low crime rate (the lowest in Latin America) but you need to observe the basics: Travel in groups rather than alone; refrain from carrying large bags; be aware of your surroundings; surrender your valuables if confronted by thieves; and be extra careful when using public transport.

How much tax will I pay?

Panama does not tax offshore income: pensions, social security, investment derived income, etc. You can even operate a Panama corporation that has customers outside Panama and still have no tax liability and you can obtain a 20-year tax exemption on an enterprise that promotes tourism, such as a dive business or a bed and breakfast.

Is Panama property a good investment?

When buying and selling real estate, foreigners – whether residents or non-residents – enjoy the same rights and privileges as Panamanian citizens

Prices for real estate have doubled and in many cases tripled in the last three years but still a three-bedroom

apartment in an older building somewhere central like El Congrejo can be bought for $180,000, a lot of land to build your own house in beautiful Bocas del Toro islands for $35,000 or a 60-acre farm on the mainland with ocean access for $250,000.

Panama City currently still has an undervalued real estate market; however, prices have been rising as more people discover Panama's advantages.

The writer offers a mass of information and advice on property purchase on her website [www.everything-panama.com]. These are some of the important points:

- Get an honest, reliable English-speaking real estate agent, preferably a referral.
- Don't pay any money directly to a real estate agent. Let the lawyer do that at the right time.
- If buying in a planned community or off plan check the developer's finances carefully .
- Don't rely on promised amenities being built.
- Don't buy off-plan with stage payments. Pay only on completion.

It has happened everywhere and will no doubt happen in Panama. The condo bubble will burst! Be very careful when buying a condo with the hope of flipping it for a profit on completion.

Panama is the place where that dream house on the beach can become reality. There are some things you should know about it, however. One of them is that in Panama, as in most countries, all water and beaches are public and cannot be bought or sold.

Under the law, you need a "concession" to build within this setback zone.

Where's best to live?

There are many residential districts in and around Panama City. Beautiful condos with fantastic ocean views are available in price ranges to suit all pockets. Many have the use of a pool, spa, gym and children's play area.

Beautiful condominium towers like "Megapolis" and

"Yacht Club" are being constructed on Balboa Avenue right on the ocean. Beneath Balboa avenue there is another high class condominium area called **Marbella** overlooking Panama Bay and near cinemas, restaurants and shopping.

Bordering Marbella is a residential and commercial district called **Obarrio** with trendy restaurants, clothing shops and high-end boutiques. This is a favoured embassy area.

In most areas of Panama City you can still find apartments for around $150,000, but be sure to check out the location before you buy, as in all big cities some areas have advantages or disadvantages that are not immediately apparent to a newcomer.

The district of **San Francisco** is more middle-class and offers excellent housing value. This district is perhaps 3-5km from the city centre and is considerably quieter. A newer three-bedroom condo with say 135sq m, with a modest ocean view, can be purchased here in the $150,000-250,000 range.

There are many other quality residential districts in and around Panama City. One US style development called **Costa del Este** has hundreds of homes and ocean view condos in the $300,000-950,000 range.

Casco Viejo is a charming colonial style town facing Panama City that, as it gets bought up and restored, is becoming one of the most sought after parts of the city.

Declared by UNESCO as a site of world interest, due to its historical location, it is located at the Panama Canal, just minutes outside Panama City and is a true cultural gem reminiscent of the French Quarter of New Orleans or perhaps Havana.

After the US military departed Panama at the end of 1999, they left behind a vast amount of land,

hillsides gourmet coffee is grown and the aroma of roasting coffee wafts through the town. You can buy a picturesque 270sqm home for $65,000.

The Chiriquí Gulf: The 'Lost Coast' on the Pacific Ocean in the Chiriquí Lowlands near the city of David is accessible by land, sea and air, perfect for both retirement and investment in real estate.

This gulf is famous for dozens of little islands and for three huge national parks, world-class fishing, scuba diving and boating. It is among the most picturesque regions of Panama.

Anton Valley: This picturesque town sits in the crater of an extinct volcano. At 1,000m above sea level its cool, spring-like climate makes it an excellent resort area, a long-time favourite retreat with the Panama City elite.

El Valle, with a colourful mix of locals, Panamanian tourist and foreign retirees, is approximately two hours from Panama City by good roads. There are many exciting things to do in El Valle such as biking, hiking or horseback riding in the mountains, viewing waterfalls or taking a dip in a mountain pool.

Dozens of Americans live in the new Valle Escondido development, an enclosed residential area that has a nine-hole golf course, convenience store, high speed internet, and many other amenities.

Down the mountain from El Valle, just 30 minutes drive away, you can enjoy the beach during the day and retreat to the cool mountains for a refreshing night's sleep. You can buy five hectares of land here (for development) for around $160,000.

If you prefer uncommercialised beaches, mountains and nature there is no place on earth like the **Azuero Peninsula,** characterised by rolling hills,

buildings and residential structures at the Old Panama Canal Zone.

Here, sharp developers have snapped up these properties and have begun transforming them into residential and commercial developments. The residential area of Albrook (formally Albrook Air force Base) is home to some of Panama's most beautiful suburban homes. Although it is very near the city it is an oasis of green gardens, winding roads and parks.

The archipelago of Bocas Del Toro is stunning: palm-fringed islands, white sandy beaches – everything you ever imagined for the picture perfect tropical retreat to hang your hammock.

You can buy whole islands, teak plantations and island hideaways, huge tracts of ocean-front land for development as well as small lots on which to build your home in paradise.

Beachfront lots start as low as $32,000.

Boquete has a perfect spring-like climate at an elevation of a little over 970m, with clean air, clear water and a friendly community. On the lush green

Trump Ocean Club

Being built on a waterfront lot with views of the Pacific Ocean and the Panama Bay in the premier and upmarket district of Punta Pacifica, the Trump Ocean Club International Hotel & Tower will give buyers the choice of 7 restaurants, 6 pools, a casino, boutique shops, a spa and gym and access to a private beach club.

The 5-star project has 600 private condominium residences set for completion in 2010.

Prices: condominiums, $530,000; lofts, $420,000; penthouses (410sq m): POA.

More info: Hot Properties Worldwide
www.hotpropertiesworldwide.com
Tel: +44 (0)20 7095 8701
Email: info@hotpropertiesworldwide.com

stunning beaches and a rugged coastline. Offshore you can find some of the most pristine islands in the country.

The Azuero Peninsula is about 300km southwest of Panama City and protrudes south into the Pacific Ocean between the Gulf of Panama and the Gulf of Montijo. It is about 100km from east to west and 90km from north to south.

There are two seasons, one golden and dry, the other green and lush. This area is one of the most physically stunning in Panama. Because it is remote there is little development and large, pristine acreages are still available at very reasonable prices: a 1,000m beach front lot for $80,000 or a one-bedroom 'do-er-upper'

just half a block from the sea for $35,000.

One-and-a-half hours from Panama City on the Pacific coast is **Coronado**, Panama's first gated community. Well-established homes set in their own gardens, they range from nine-bedroom mansions on the beach for $3m to very pleasant three and four bedroom homes on one or two levels for $300,000. New condo high-rises are currently being built on the beach here for around $350,000 for a three-bedroom unit with mountain and sea views.

Just after Coronado is **Punto Barko** which is an area of mostly very up-market private homes on large lots. It is wonderfully quiet and beautiful here.

A few kilometres further on is **Costa Esmeralda,** another gated community with privately built low-rise homes mostly on large lots. As an example of price there is a large Mexican villa for sale here for $850,000. It has a main house with three bedrooms and three guesthouses with one or two bedrooms each as well as a staff house.

One bay further down the coast is the fabulous new development **Rio del Mar,** a high-rise resort in a beautiful location.

Pearl Islands is unspoiled, its waters abound with sea turtles, whales, dolphins and game fish and in its jungles you'll see parrots, toucans, deer, iguanas, monkeys, agouties and anteaters.

Bocas del Toro on Colon Island, the province's capital city, has seen the beginnings of a tourist boom in recent years with numerous restaurants offering fabulous seafood.

Pedasi, a small quite town in the peninsula de Azuero, known as the 'cradle' of Panamanian folklore, is the ideal place for a retiree seeking to experience the pleasures of small town Panama.

PROPERTY

Blue skies and swaying palms – everyone's dream of island life

Why the Caribbean?

As a retirement destination the Caribbean has a lot going for it. The list of its attractions is well known: sun, sea, great beaches, wonderful fresh fruits and seafood, exotic islands and coral reefs and hospitable and friendly people.

No. 1 on the list has to be the climate – year-round balmy weather (apart from the occasional hurricane) and no winter as we know it.

If you are among those who like strong seasonal variations – the Caribbean may not be for you, for

In this section **James Henderson** and **Feona Gray** share their experience of 20-plus years living in the Caribbean. Their website, **definitiveCaribbean.com** answers pretty well every question you might have about living there.

while weather patterns vary from island to island there is very little seasonal variation.

The barometer in the Caribbean – situated almost entirely within the tropics – is usually stuck in the mid to late 20°C. Temperatures range from around 28°C in the hotter months (July-August) to around 24°C in the cooler months (January-February).

The warmest temperatures are found in the more southern islands including Aruba, Curaçao, Trinidad and Tobago.

Remember, however, the Bahamas and Bermuda are not in the Caribbean (although we have included them in this section) and temperatures can sometime be too cool for swimming in the winter months.

Then there's the hurricane season to consider. This runs from the beginning of June to the end of November. The south-eastern islands have the least number of hurricanes and the south-western and the north-east region has the most.

With all the attractions listed above, it's no surprise that the European powers fought wars over these islands. The legacy – and it adds to the appeal – is a cultural melting pot formed by influences from Africa, Arabia, Spain, China, Polynesia, East Indian, Cajun, and indigenous Amerindian as well as most of the European nations.

This melting pot extends to the cuisine of the Caribbean, a fusion of all these influences.

Is it safe?

Crime is the number one social issue for much of the Caribbean. "High rates of crime and violence in the Caribbean are undermining growth, threatening

human welfare and impeding social development," according to a report by the World Bank and the United Nations Office on Drugs and Crime (UNODC).

The report, "Crime, Violence, and Development: Trends, Costs, and Policy Options in the Caribbean," found that murder rates in the Caribbean are higher than in any other region in the world.

According to a World Bank report, the murder rate in the Caribbean is four times that in North America and 15 times the average for Western and Central Europe.

Jamaica experienced 1,547 murders last year and in Trinidad & Tobago the rate has quadrupled in the past decade.

The cause: high unemployment and a lack of economic development, along with narcotics trafficking.

Countries with the lowest threat to tourists and foreign residents are considered to be Anguilla, Aruba, Montserrat, The Cayman Islands, St. Barts, British Virgin Islands, Bonaire and Dominica, St. Vincent and the Grenadines

At the other end of the scale are the Bahamas, Belize, Honduras, Jamaica, St. Maarten, St. Lucia, and Trinidad and Tobago.

How much tax will I pay?

See individual country sections.

Where's best to live?

See individual country sections.

FACTFILE

The Caribbean region comprises more than 7,000 islands, islets, reefs and cays.

Country	Capital	Population '000	Size (sq. km)	Language
Anguilla	The Valley	10.3	102	English
Antigua	St. Johns	64.3	280	English
Aruba	Oranjestad	81.5	180	Dutch, Eng, Spa
Bahamas	Nassau	283.7	11,826	English
Barbados	Bridgetown	259.2	440	Engish
BVI	Road Town	19.2	174	English
Cayman Is.	George Town	39.3	241	English
Dominica	Roseau	64.9	790	English, French
D. Republic	Santo Domingo	8,129.7	48,730	Spanish
Grenada	St. George's	97.0	345	English
Guadeloupe	Basse-Terre	420.9	1,702	French, Creole
Jamaica	Kingston	2,652.4	11,424	English
Martinique	Port-de-France	411.6	1,090	French, Creole
Montserrat	Plymouth	12.8	84	English
St Martin/ St Maarten		70		Fr, Dutch, Eng
Puerto Rico	San Juan	3,887.7	8,897	
St. Kitts	Basseterre	42.8	176	English
St. Lucia	Castries	154.0	603	English, French
St. Vincent	Kingstown	120.5	389	English
Tobago	Scarborough	50	300	English
Trinidad	Port-of-Spain	1,102.1	4,828	English
Turks & Caicos	Cockburn Town	16.9	430	English
U.S. Virgin Isl	Charlotte Amalie	119.8		English

Climate: The Caribbean is situated almost entirely within the tropics with a temperatures range of 24-28°C.

Entry requirements: You normally need a passport valid for the period of travel and for six months after your return. You should not need a visa but rules can change and you should check with the high commission/embassy of the country you are travelling to.

Residence/retirement visa Different rules apply to most of the Caribbean island nations. The key that opens the door to most is money – in fees, investment and/or property ownership.

[See: The rules under 'Permanent Residence' in each country section]

Electricity: Most American-made electrical appliances work at 110 volts while most of the world uses 220-240 volts. Caribbean countries use voltages between 100 and 125.

For a complete list of voltage requirements by country, visit Current Solutions [www.currentsolutions.com]

Money: Dollars and Euros are accepted throughout the Caribbean. ATMs are widely available.

Credit cards: Most American and European credit cards are accepted throughout the islands.

Water: Considered fairly safe throughout the Caribbean.

Tipping: Because it's such a holiday area, everyone expects tips. Hotels and restaurants usually add 10-15 per cent so a few extra coins are discretionary. Taxi fares are best negotiated in advance.

Health & Healthcare: Most Caribbean nations have generally good health care systems in place. However, serious problems might mean a trip to the USA so comprehensive medical insurance is essential.

Vaccinations: Hepatitis A vaccination is recommended for visits to all Caribbean countries. Typhoid, rabies and yellow fever come under the 'sometimes recommended' classification. Malaria is not a risk in most islands but is not unheard of and outbreaks of dengue fever, a mosquito borne viral disease, have been increasing. There are country specific advisories at:
www.masta-travel-health.com
www.surgerydoor.co.uk

Pets: If you are coming from a rabies free country such as the UK, all you should need is a pet passport and to have your pet microchipped. To be sure you should obtain a "health certificate" signed by a vet and, since rules can change, you should check with the high commission/embassy.

CARIBBEAN CONTACT DIRECTORY

Embassies/Government
The website: www.embassiesabroad.com allows you to click through to the high commission/embassy you want to reach.

Travel & Health Advice
Foreign Office travel advice
www.fco.gov.uk/travel
www.nhs.uk/Healthcareabroad
www.masta.org

About the Caribbean
http://definitivecaribbean.com
www.lonelyplanet.com
www.selectcaribbean.com
www.gettingaway.com
www.caricom.org
(Official site of the Caribbean Community and Common Market)

General & Expat
www.expatfocus.com
www.britishexpat.com
www.transitionsabroad.com
www.expat-blog.com
www.expatwebdirectory.com/caribbean
http://expatcaribbean.meetup.com
www.expatriates.com

Media
www.caribbeannewspapers.com
(links to Caribbean newspapers)

Travel & Tourism
www.caribbeanconsulting.com
(Allows you to click through to individual tourist boards)
www.caribbeantravel.com
www.bestcaribbean.info
www.itzcaribbean.com
www.nationalgeographic.com
www.frommers.com
www.lonelyplanet.com
www.caribbeantravelforums.com

Getting There
British Airways: www.britishairways.com
Flies to: Antigua, Bahamas, Barbados, Bermuda, Cayman Islands, Dominican Republic, Grenada, Jamaica, St Kitts and Nevis, St Lucia, Trinidad & Tobago, Turks & Caicos Islands
Virgin: www.virginholidays.co.uk
Flies to: Barbados, Antigua, St Lucia, Tobago, Grenada (via Tobago), Jamaica

Other carriers
Monarch: www.monarch.co.uk
First Choice Airways:www.firstchoice.co.uk
Thomsonfly: www.thomson.co.uk
Thomas Cook Airlines:
www.thomascookairlines.co.uk
Air Jamaica: www.airjamaica.com

Antigua & Barbuda

FACTFILE

Capital: St John's
Population: 68,000
Area: Antigua 281sq km
Barbuda 161sq km
Language: English
Getting in: Passport valid for six months after date of entry.
Permanent residence: You need to own a property and reside in Antigua and Barbuda for not less than 30 days a year. In addition you need to obtain an alien landholding licence costing five per cent of the property value, pay stamp duty of 2.5 per cent and an annual levy of $20,000. Expensive but for this you don't have to pay tax on income from any source.
Money: East Caribbean $.
Golf: There are two golf courses on Antigua, none on Barbuda.

Antigua and Barbuda are like two sisters – visibly from the same stock but unlike in so many ways. Antigua is a gregarious, populous island, with a highly developed tourism industry while Barbuda, just under 50km to its north, is much quieter, laid back even to the point of doziness.

What they share is their appearance and setting in a stunning blue sea in the north-eastern Caribbean. Their beaches are supreme and there are always deserted stretches of sand where you can get away on your own. Barbuda's beaches are even finer – miles and miles of perfect sand with barely any development.

Inland the plantation history of the island is clearly visible; stone windmills, standing every few hundred yards on the high ground run through the island like a leitmotif.

Antigua is one of the main hubs for arrival into the Caribbean from Europe and one of the heartlands of Caribbean sailing, home to the region's most famous sailing regatta, Antigua Race Week. Nowadays waterfront hotels have replaced the coastal forts and the bars are just as busy with modern-day sailors.

Antigua has a large number of places to stay in all sorts of styles, from private villas overlooking the island's secluded bays, to guest houses and apartments, large, mid-price resorts and then to a small clutch of hotels that measure among the finest in the Caribbean.

The island's traditional tourist hot spot is Dickenson Bay, just north of the capital, St John's, which is backed along its length by large hotels, apartment complexes and beach bars.

The other major gravitational centre of tourism is the southeast, around English Harbour. This has a completely different feel from Dickenson Bay. Life there is centred more on yachting and private villas.

Barbuda

Barbuda is almost completely undeveloped by comparison and, though hard to imagine, has even better beaches than its larger sister. There is just one town (more of a village really), Codrington, on the lagoon, a huge stretch of inland water that is home to the largest colony of frigate birds in the Caribbean. The best beaches are along the southern shore, where there are a couple of hotels, and in the west, which is relatively remote.

There are just a couple of very smart hotels with nothing between them and the very simple West Indian guesthouses.

More info
www.antigua-barbuda.org
www.antigua-barbuda.com
http://definitivecaribbean.com
www.ab.gov.ag
www.lonelyplanet.com/antigua-and-barbuda
www.antiguanice.com
www.turq.com/antiguaandbarbuda
www.antiguamarineguide.com
www.myantigua.org

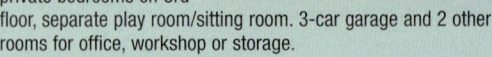

The map shows Antigua with locations including:

Barbuda (26 miles)

Atlantic Ocean

Beggar's Point, Long Island, Guiana Island, Crump Island, Nonsuch Bay, North Sound, Runaway Bay, Cedar Grove, Ft. James, Potters Village, Parham, Willikies, Green Island, Five Islands, St. John, Golden Grove, All Saints, Potworks Dam, Jennings, Bethseda, Freetown, Bolands, Jolly Harbour, Liberta, Half Moon Bay, Crab Hill, Boggy Peak, Falmouth, English Harbour, Johnson's Point, Willoughby Bay, Old Road, Rendezvous Bay, Nelson's Dockyard

ANTIGUA
LOW - HILLS - MTS.

WorldAtlas.Com

Hodges Bay, Antigua

2 bedrooms 1 bathroom furnished with great view and AC.
To let: $1,500 p.m.
More info: ABI Realty www.abirealtors.com
Tel: (268) 460-9707

Casa Akwaba, Dom Republic

Beautiful house situated on the top of a hill with ocean view. 3 bedrooms, 2 bathrooms with wc , fully-equipped kitchen, living room with view of the swimming pool
More info: www.cblasterrenas.com
Phone: 809 240 5656 / 809 240 6411
Email: info@cblasterrenas.com

Property and taxes

There are many development projects, the largest of which is at Jolly Harbour, the 'Venice of the Caribbean', where there are 501 townhouses and assorted custom homes among the marina, golf course and casino.

Others include the very smart La Perla Living development in Nonsuch Bay, The Peninsula, the James' Club and Emerald Cove in the north-east. Set on its own island, Jumby Bay is an exclusive development of about 30 homes.

Besides the ongoing developments there is plenty of land on which houses can be built. Prices for undeveloped parcels (between a half and one acre in the south-east) range from under $100,000 to $800,000 on the waterfront. A good quality three-bedroom house can vary from $350,000 to well over $1 million.

Property tax is levied in Antigua, but not in Barbuda. There is no capital gains or inheritance tax.

Estate agents

If you go to www.antiguanice.com you can click through to dozens of estate agents
Others include:
www.remax-antigua.com
www.tradewindrealty.com
http://antigua-and-
barbuda.r24e.com/ENG/
http://stanleysestates.com
www.elysianpropertysales.com
www.jhr-caribbean.com
www.laperlainternationalliving.com

Anguilla
FACTFILE

Capital: The Valley
Population: 10,000
Area: 102sq km
Language: English
Getting in: Passport valid for six months after date of entry.
Permanent residence: Retired persons who own property in Anguilla qualify for residence status, as do those who have lived there for at least seven years. Otherwise… "the Governor may grant to a person not belonging to Anguilla a permit of permanent residence subject to such conditions as he may think fit."
Money: East Caribbean $
Golf: There is one championship course on Anguilla surrounded by the spectacular villas of Temenos estates.

Anguilla is fashionable but low key, with ice-cool islanders and an unhurried pace of life; generally expensive; not that easily accessible (but this keeps the crowds away); truly magnificent white sand beaches, some with beach bars, others barely developed.

The island has excellent restaurants, a small crop of luxurious hotels.

The island is not as stylish (nor as pretentious, some might say) as nearby St Barths nor the depth of Barbados. In fact there isn't so much to do there. But it offers an easy Caribbean life that many visitors come to love. It is expensive and a touch exclusive.

The most northerly of the Leeward Islands, Anguilla lies around 320km east of Puerto Rico, just a few kilometers north of the French side of St Martin. The island is made of coral limestone which explains Anguilla's fabulous white sand and it has a number of offshore cays which make an excellent day out on a sailing trip.

More info

http://definitivecaribbean.com/guide/Anguilla
www.anguilla-vacation.com
www.caribbeantravel.com/anguilla/
www.gov.ai
www.caribseek.com/Anguilla

Property and taxes

Villas for sale are few and far between and so prices continue to rise. A three-bedroom house in a not particularly prestigious location has been on sale for $365,000 recently and in more prestigious areas for $2,500,000. The highest price recorded so far for a private villa sale is $8 million.

There is no income or capital gains tax but there is a transfer duty of five per cent.

Estate agents

www.anguillaproperties-sothebysrealty.ai
www.islanddreamproperties.com
www.seaislandrealties

Aruba
FACTFILE

Capital: Oranjestad
Population: 103,500
Area: 180sq km
Language: Dutch (official). Papiamento,

Spanish, and English also are spoken.
Getting in: Passport and return ticket. (Visas required for stays longer than six months).
Permanent residence: Proof of adequate funds, a medical certificate, a police certificate and a 'why you want to live in Aruba' testament.
Money: The Aruban florin
Golf: Aruba has one 18-hole championship golf course and a couple of 9-hole courses.

A lively mid-size island, quite developed (particularly in the west) off the coast of Venezuela in the southern Caribbean, Aruba is an autonomous territory attached to the Netherlands.

Languages are Dutch, Papiamento Creole, some English (mainly in the tourism industry) and some Spanish. Gracious and welcoming islanders have a strong local culture.

There are two spectacular main beaches, backed by hotels, some with casinos and entertainment, just a few smaller independent inns and guest houses.

There are plenty of activities, many restaurants, casinos, some natural life, horse-riding, golf, sailing, scuba, good windsurfing, and considerable cruise tourism.

More info

http://definitivecaribbean.com/guide/Aruba
www.aruba.com

www.caribbeantravel.com/aruba

Property and taxes

There is a good selection of apartments and condominiums in Aruba. Property prices have flattened out for a year or more and are not expected to make significant gains until late 2010.

Property owners pay annual rates amounting to 0.4 per cent of the value of the property and buyers pay three per cent capital transfer tax. Rental income is taxed but there is no capital gains tax.

Estate agents

http://aruba-sunshine.com
www.keyrealtyaruba.com
www.coldwellbanker.aw
www.vecchiaestates.com/
www.arubarealestate.com

Ocean View, St. Peter, Barbados
2 bedroom, 2 bathroom furnished 150sq. m apartment with views across Mullins Bay. Secure environment with gated access. 2 parking spaces, communal pool and easy walking access to the famed Mullins Beach.
Price: US$595,000
More info: www.aaaltman.com Email: anna.croney@aaaltman.com

Ginn Sur Mer, Grand Bahamas
Luxurious bespoke villas on the island of the Grand Bahamas. Facilities include two golf courses and a marina.
Prices: $495,000-1.2 million
More info: Barton Wyatt www.bw-international.com
Tel: 44 (0) 1344 843000

Bahamas

FACTFILE

Capital: Nassau (New Providence Island)
Population: 306,000
Area: 13,940sq km
Language: English
Getting in: No visa required for stays of up to eight months but you need proof of funds and a return ticket.
Permanent residence: If you are a "fit and proper person", residence can be achieved through the purchase of a home valued at $500,000-plus or through evidence of adequate funds. Bank and character references are required. For an annual residence permit, a head-of-household pays $1,000 and each dependent, $25. Non-Bahamians can obtain an annual homeowner's residence card, cost $250, renewable annually, which entitles the owner, spouse and any minor children to enter and remain in the Bahamas.
Money: BH$
Golf: Golfers are spoiled for choice. There is a range of courses on the main islands and a course each in Abaco and Eleuthera.

There are 700 islands and cays in 15 main groups, scattered to the south-east of Florida. The capital, Nassau, on New Providence, is easily accessed from US cities (mainly Miami) with some access from Europe. Grand Bahama, Bimini, Abaco, Exuma and Eleuthera have direct access from Florida, others via Nassau.

There is extensive tourism in all prices and categories.

More info

http://definitivecaribbean.com/guide/Bahamas
www.bahamas.com
www.caribbeantravel.com/bahamas
www.thebahamasguide.com
www.thebahamasinvestor.com
www.bahamashandbook.com

Property and taxes

Under the International Persons Landholding Act, approval is granted automatically for non-Bahamians to purchase residential property of less than five acres on any single island in the Bahamas.

There is no income tax, capital gains tax, VAT, sales or use tax or wealth tax. There are no income taxes but stamp duties are imposed when leasing Bahamian real property.

Stamp duty (shared by buyer and seller) is six per cent on properties valued at $100,000-250,000 and eight per cent on properties over that.

You will find a useful article about the islands themselves and real estate under the heading 'Investing in Bahamas Real Estate' at www.bahamasb2b.com/financial/investment_real_estate.htm

William Wong, president of the Bahamas Real Estate Association, recently described the market as "pretty slow," although demand for in the $350,000-650,000 price range is the least affected.

Estate agents

www.bahamasb2b.com
www.coldwellbankerbahamas.com
www.bahamasproperty.com
www.hgchristie.com
www.bellchannelclub.com
www.bahamasnet.com
www.bahamasrealty.bs
www.lyfordcayhomes.com
www.emeraldbayresort.com
www.viviun.com

Barbados

FACTFILE

Capital: Bridgetown
Population: 280,000
Area: 431sq km
Language: English and Bajan dialect.
Getting in: Passport and return ticket.
Permanent residence: This is fairly informal but you can't apply for permanent residence until you've lived there for five years.
Money: Bds$
Golf: There are seven golf courses.

Barbados, set on its own to the east of the Windward Islands in the south-eastern Caribbean, has the greatest depth of tourism of any 'small' Caribbean island, with a full range of accommodation options.

Easily accessible from Europe, the US and Canada, it has a good variety of excellent beaches and is a busy, developed island with gracious and approachable islanders and a strong island culture.

There are excellent hotels, including some of the Caribbean's best known, as well as some all-inclusives, superb villas, excellent restaurants, a large cruise industry and shopping.

For its size it has more to offer than any other island in the region.

The west coast, along its stretches of sand and equally pretty cliffs, has a string of the Caribbean's finest hotels and restaurants with a regular clientele of millionaires. The south coast has a completely different feel – younger and more active – and it is considerably less expensive.

The island is also more sophisticated than many travellers expect of the Caribbean. There is excellent windsurfing, kitesurfing and golf. Polo, cricket, horse racing and the annual motor rally are other attractions.

The music is fun too. There are excellent calypsonians and bands to be heard in the lively clubs. There

BARBADOS

Retirement, although often viewed as a time to exit the workforce and to outlive one's pension, really is an opportunity when you can savour the true meaning of life: enjoy quality time with your spouse and grand children, engage in your favourite past time, and savour a few more of life's luxuries.

The desire will be extremely high to take that tropical holiday you've always fantasized about and having worked so hard and made many sacrifices for your pension, you have every right to be discerning.

Barbados, recently rated by the United Nations as the world's No. 1 developing country, often tops the shortlist for retirees. Our relaxed and friendly island life attracts numerous repeat visitors. Actually, according to the Caribbean Tourism Organisation, Barbados stands out as being the most revisited destination in the Caribbean.

Our relaxed and friendly island life attracts numerous repeat visitors. Actually, according to the Caribbean Tourism Organisation, Barbados stands out as being the most revisited destination in the Caribbean.

Should you decide to make our paradise your home, you would soon discover that Barbados has a sophisticated infrastructure: the water, which is some of the purest in the world, can be drunk straight from the tap; the road network is modern with frequent signage; and our healthcare, education and telecommunications facilities are among the best in the western hemisphere.

If you are fortunate to have a chat with our expatriate retirees they are sure to fascinate you with their memorable stories about our heart-warming citizens, affectionately known as Bajans.

Whether they were lost on their way to Harrison's Cave, a popular visitor attraction, or seeking advice on whether to try one of our local dishes washed down with a glass of mauby or a shot of the world's oldest rum, which is home to the island, visitors are always awed by the genuine helpfulness and friendliness of Barbadians.

They marvel also at the pleasantly paradoxical nature of our coastline - the inviting therapeutic waters of our west and south coast beaches and the contrasting vistas and sights of the rugged east coast.

Thanks to the Barbados Tourism Authority, they can now leverage the Zagat Survey - Best of Barbados, an independent customer review - the only one of its kind in the Caribbean, which would afford the opportunity to enjoy the diverse network of quality restaurants, nightlife, attractions and golf facilities available on the island.

Above all, Barbados, with its quaint, old-British charm, continues to enjoy a very stable and peaceful socio-political climate.

So, if you are seeking a relaxing Caribbean escape with the modern conveniences of the United Kingdom, a stable government, world class accommodation and excellent facilities to suit your budget, then Barbados is unquestionably the destination for you.

Property and taxes

While the current worldwide downturn has caused prices to stall, in recent years the island has seen an extended building boom. According to Cluttons Barbados, property price inflation has been 10-15 per cent annually over the past few years. There is no capital gains tax or inheritance tax but there is a transfer tax of 2.5 per cent.

Estate agents

These are four real estate agents on Barbados that are recommended:
www.bajanservices.com
www.aaaltman.com
www.realtorslimited.com
www.royal-westmoreland.com
There are many more and you can find clickable websites at:
www.barbadospropertynews.com

be heard in the lively clubs. There is even opera in Barbados from time to time. The island has an extraordinary history, much of which is still visible in the plantation houses.

There are some fantastic homes and the west coast has some of the most valuable real estate in the Caribbean although there are more affordable homes in lovely locations inland and on the south coast.

More info

http://definitivecaribbean.com
www.visitbarbados.org
www.caribbeantravel.com
www.barbados.org
www.accessbarbados.com
www.allinfoaboutbarbados.com
www.visitbarbados.org
www.funbarbados.com

Bermuda

FACTFILE

Capital: Hamilton
Population: 62,000
Area: 53.3sq km
Language: English
Getting in: No visa required for stays of up to 180 days.
Permanent residence: The Bermuda Government website is bereft of useful information on this score but there's information at: www.bermuda-online.org/citizenship.htm
Money: The Bermudan dollar is tied to the US Dollar ($1=BD$1)
Golf: Bermuda has nine golf courses, the highest concentration per square mile in the world, many designed by famous names. Strict dress codes are enforced at all clubs. Shorts can be worn but, obviously, must be of Bermuda length (to the knee).

A British Overseas Territory, Bermuda is English speaking, very genteel and well organised but not actually in the Caribbean – in fact it is 2,400km to the north-east.

There is a very large, primarily American-directed tourism industry, but top of the range, with excellent hotels and condos, some inns and guesthouses. Excellent (often pink sand) beaches, fine restaurants, extensive cruise tourism and shopping. Good scuba diving and snorkelling. Spectacular parks, nature reserves and underground cave formations .

While people tend to visit the Caribbean during the wintertime, Bermuda's season is more in the summer, when the weather and the sea are warmer.

More info

www.bermuda.com
www.bermudatourism.com
www.definitivecaribbean.com
www.bermudatourism.com
www.gov.bm
www.bermuda-online.org
www.experiencebermuda.com
www.bermuda4u.com

Property and taxes

Bermuda is a tax haven with no income, capital gains or inheritance tax. However, purchase of properties by non-Bermudians requires a licence from the Minister and payment of a fee of 25 per cent of the value of the property (increased from 22 per cent in the 2009 budget).

There are strict regulations on the sale of property to non-citizens. In general, single-family dwellings with price tags of less than $5.5 million may be sold to Bermudians only. Properties in this range include those over 280sq m on more than 0.25 acres of land with a protected mooring and nice views. Condominiums are exempt. There's a useful overview of the rules at: www.mouraandassociates.com

Certain transactions are subject to stamp duties and fees when properties are transferred or conveyed. The duty rate is levied on the property value at progressive rates from 2.5 per cent on properties up to $100,000 to six per cent on properties over $1,500,000.

Land tax is assessed on the annual rental value of the property.

Estate agents

www.bermudarealty.com
www.mouraandassociates.com
www.kitson.bm/realestate
www.bermudarealtor.com
www.joylusher.com
www.beckyparis.com
www.regorealtors.bm
www.knightfrank.com/caribbean/Bermuda

Bonaire

FACTFILE

Capital: Kralendijk
Population: 15,000
Area: 294sq km
Language: Dutch (official) Papiamentu, English and Spanish.
Getting in: Passport and return ticket.
Permanent residence: At the discretion of the Immigration Department but you may be required to provide proof that you have adequate financial resources.
Money: Netherlands Antillean guilder
Golf: None

Bonaire is a quiet, relatively undeveloped island off the coast of Venezuela in the south-western Caribbean, with reasonable connections to USA and Holland.

Local culture is a mix of Dutch and Spanish, with polite, slightly reserved islanders.

There are a few reasonable beaches, some small and remote, barely any large hotels, but many small, independent inns and guesthouses and self-catering apartments. Activities include magnificent scuba diving, some nice restaurants, a couple of small casinos, horse-riding, sailing and windsurfing.

More info

www.infobonaire.com
www.tourismbonaire.com
www.geographia.com/bonaire
www.bonaire-travelguide.com
www.bonairetalk.com

Property and taxes

Bonaire is expensive with the best ocean view villas priced at $3 million plus. However, it is possible to find a small, two bedroom, family house with a garden for $100,000-150,000.

An annual real estate tax on Bonaire, called ground tax, is in the range $800-1,500. There is no capital gains or inheritance tax. Transfer tax is approximately four per cent of the purchase price or the registered value (whichever is the higher).

Estate agents

www.bonaireproperties.com/janga
www.elpueblobonaire.com
www.bonairehomes.com
More info:
http://definitivecaribbean.com
www.tourismbonaire.com
www.caribbeantravel.com/bonaire

British Virgin Islands

FACTFILE

Capital: Road Town (Tortola)
Population: 22,000
Area: 153 sq km
Language: Spanish (official). English is widely spoken.
Getting in: Passport and return ticket
Permanent residence: Purchase of a property is the starting point and to do this you need an Alien Land Holding License. This leads to an identification card which allows the holder to remain in the BVI for up to six months. Finally, a certificate of residence, entitling the holder to remain for an indefinite period.
Money: US$
Golf: None. Golfers need to cross to St Thomas.

The BVI are 60 small but stunningly beautiful islands in the north-eastern Caribbean. Some are extremely dozy, others contain nothing but a luxury hotel. Tortola, the main island, is quite developed. One of the unique qualities of the BVI is the many small and even private islands where seclusion is pretty much guaranteed.

The BVI has superb beaches on the main islands and on offshore cays and a beach bar in virtually every cove. There are a small number of first-rate hotels with a few inns and some excellent villas.

Having spent most of its history as a group of poor outcrops whose main export was its people, the BVI is currently more prosperous than it has ever been. In addition to its successful tourism industry it now has a considerable offshore finance sector.

More info:

www.bvitourism.com
http://definitivecaribbean.com
www.bvitourism.com
www.britishvirginislands.com
www.bviwelcome.com
www.caribbeantravel.com/britishvirginislands
www.b-v-i.com
www.bvi.gov.vg

Property and taxes

The BVI has seen a huge amount of development over the past 20 years, much of it in Tortola, which has the by far the largest population.

There are quite a few restrictions on property ownership. 'Non-belongers' (those not born in the BVI or with naturalisation) require a land holding licence and it can take up to two years to get one.

Prices vary enormously.

Heron Court, St. James, Barbados
Pair of townhouses (available individually) well located at the northern end of the Heron Court development on a slight rise. Each has 3 bedrooms and 2 bathrooms, 210sq m of living space and 550-650sq m garden.
Each priced: $650,000
More info: www.aaaltman.com Email: anna.croney@aaaltman.com

Pavilion Grove, St. James, Barbados
4 bedroom, 2 storey with a plunge pool and wooden deck off living area. Pavilion Grove is a well maintained community of 6 detached homes across from the Royal Pavilion Hotel. Close to amenities in Holetown and great restaurants and shops along the west coast.
Price: $850,000 furnished
More info: www.aaaltman.com Email: anna.croney@aaaltman.com

Undeveloped plots in the Ridge Road area overlooking Road Town sell for around $50,000 for half an acre while a relatively simple three bedroom cottage on Cooper Island has been on the market for $914,000.

Some of the more spectacular villas go for over $2 million.

Tortola: The island is fairly developed but there are still some areas that have barely been touched. Land in the Sage Mountain area is currently for sale at around $100,000 for a building plot and a good quality villa in the Belmont Estate will set you back $1,500,000.

Virgin Gorda has more of a tradition of villas and holiday homes than Tortola. They have been built all over the island and include some architecturally striking buildings. The few stand-alone villas can go for as much as $2-3 million for a five-bedroom house with pool and tennis court.

Jost Van Dyke, owned largely by BV islanders, has been laid out in plots for a long time, but building has hardly begun. There is not much infrastructure and there are just a few houses, which come onto the market at prices ranging from $400,00 for two bedrooms to plots at $500,000 per acre for a prime beachfront location.

Other islands: Islands do occasionally come up for sale. Recently Mosquito Island and Ginger Island have been available, the latter for $6m.

New developments include:
n Nail Bay Luxury Villa ResortVirgin Gorda
A 147-acre luxury villa resort on a historic waterfront sugar plantation below Gorda Peak.
n Oil Nut Bay, Virgin Gorda
Residential community on the untouched eastern end of Virgin Gorda. Beachfront and cliffside homes from one to 10 acres.
n Raffles Tortola
Opening 2011 and set on 50 acres of pristine beachfront property at the north-eastern end of Tortola, it will offer 250 luxury villas, casitas, condominiums and estate lots.

More info
www.nailbay.com
www.oilnutbaybvi.com
www.rafflestortola.com

There is no capital gains tax, wealth tax, inheritance or gift taxes, sales tax or VAT. Stamp duty is 12 per cent of the cost of the property for non-citizens. Annual property taxes are very low.

Estate agents
www.caribbeanrealtybvi.com
www.coldwellbankerbvi.com
www.islandrealestatebvi.com
www.smithsgore.com
www.trudebvi.com
www.propertyforge.com

Cayman Islands

FACTFILE

Capital: George Town
Population: 70,000
Area: 260sq km
Language: English
Getting in: Passport valid for six months after date of return.
Permanent residence: To be eligible for a Residency Certificate for Persons of Independent Means in Grand Cayman you need to go through health and criminal checks and have "a continuous source of annual income in the amount of $185,000 in addition to investing $935,000 in Grand Cayman of which at least $295,000 must be in property. These sums are halved for those opting to live in Cayman Brac or Little Cayman.
Money: The CI$.
Golf: One 18-hole course and two nine-hole courses.

Three small islands in the Western Caribbean, to the south of Cuba and west of Jamaica. Low-lying and coral based, which gives them excellent diving and beaches.

Grand Cayman is highly and

CAYMAN ISLANDS GOVERNMENT OFFICE
IN THE UNITED KINGDOM

Welcome to the Cayman Islands! Here you will find the perfect retirement home, as this British Overseas Territory offers a blend of peace and tranquillity with all the conveniences and luxuries of those accustomed to a very high standard of living. With a strong British connection, friendly people and a low crime rate, it is easy to feel comfortable.

The Cayman Islands compromise three tropical islands situated in the pristine waters of the Caribbean, 500 miles south of Miami. These attractive islands cover a total of 100 square miles, the largest being Grand Cayman, followed by Cayman Brac and Little Cayman. They are well located for easy access to US destinations with frequent daily flights, as well as direct flights to London four times a week. The Cayman Islands have an average temperature of 80° and a relaxed lifestyle; they also possess a modern well-developed healthcare system, excellent infrastructure and telecommunications. There is a wide choice of restaurants and a range of outdoor activities including watersports and golf. The islands are rated as one of the top diving destinations in the world and also offer and abundance of flora and fauna to enjoy and explore.

The Cayman Islands is a tax free country and is renowned as a thriving offshore financial centre with many opportunities for investment. If you are considering purchasing a property, there are numerous beach-front homes and condominiums, many overlooking the water, all built to the highest standards and generally set in colourful gardens, with pools and other facilities.

We welcome those wishing to retire to the Cayman Islands and, as a retiree you can apply to the Immigration Board for a 'Residency Certificate for Persons of Independent Means'. Once you have satisfied the criteria and your application is successful, you will be granted a Certificate which is valid for 25 years and is renewable thereafter at the discretion of the Chief Immigration Officer. This entitles you to reside, without the right to work.

We hope you will consider retiring to the Cayman Islands and wish you well in your retirement years!

Sincerely,

Jennifer P Dilbert

Jennifer P Dilbert

Representative in the United Kingdom: Jennifer P. Dilbert MBE JP
Deputy Representative: Mary R. Chandler-Allen
6 Arlington Street, London SW1A 1RE   Telephone: 020 7491 7772   Facsimile: 020 7491 7944
e-mail: info@cigo.co.uk   website: www.gov.ky

successfully developed – more than 70,000 companies are registered there, including 446 banks and trust companies. Air access is good from the USA and the UK and locally from Jamaica. It is quite American in feel and relatively expensive.

Cayman islanders are charming and quite reserved. There are large expatriate communities of Britons, Americans, Canadians (involved in offshore finance and tourism) Hondurans and Jamaicans (mainly in construction and tourism).

The main beach, Seven Mile Beach, is excellent with large hotels, some inns, many apartments, condominiums and private villas, very good restaurants and good water sportsg.

Little Cayman and Cayman Brac

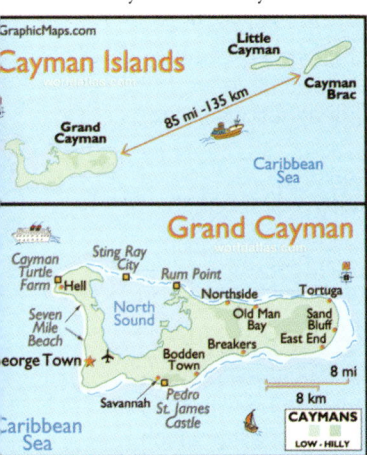

are much quieter and accessed mainly via Grand Cayman. They have a few inns and private villas.

More info
http://definitivecaribbean.com/guide/Cayman
www.caymanislands.ky
www.caymanislands.com
www.caribbeantravel.com/aruba
www.caymanislands.ky
http://cayman.com.ky

Property and taxes
There are no restrictions on foreign ownership. According to Coldwell Banker [hpci.coldwellbanker.com] the average property price in 2009 was $526,250.

There are no annual property taxes, no income tax, no capital gains tax and no inheritance tax.

The title to most property is freehold although there are some leasehold properties.

Estate agents
www.century21cayman.com
www.coldwellbankerbvi.com
www.viviun.com/Real_Estate/Cayman_Islands
www.caymanluxuryproperty.com
www.oceanfrontproperties.com/property/cayman
www.caribpro.com/Cayman_Islands
www.SIRCaymanIslands.com

Dominica
FACTFILE
Capital: Roseau **Population:** 85,000
Area: 290 sq. mi. (753sq km)
Language: English + Creole
Getting in: No visa required for visits of 21 days or less.
Permanent residence: Residence permit will be granted on proof that you have sufficient funds to maintain yourself and your family. Residence permits are valid for a year and can be renewed annually for five years after which you can apply for permanent residency. After two years as a permanent resident you can apply for citizenship.
There is a grace period of three months during which you import household and personal effects and a vehicle duty free.
More info: http://investdominica.dm
Dominica second passport
Dominica also has a programme offering a passport and citizenship to foreigners, which involves a donation to the government of $100,000 for the 'family' option or $75,000 for the 'single'.
Once granted, there are no additional residence requirements.
Fees on top of the donation are $25,000 for a family and $15,000 for a single applicant.
According to the official website of the granting authority, CCP Inc. [www.goccp.com] applicants have to attend an interview with the Prime Minister. Benefits include no capital gains, gift, wealth and inheritance taxes.
Money: Eastern Caribbean $
Golf: Hotel courses only

Arlington Estate, Cayman Islands
Substantial property of 4 bedrooms, 4 bathrooms on 90 acres with botanical gardens, hiking trails, two private residences and four 2-bed/2.5 bath townhouses along with a pool, spa area and a pool house. Price: $2,500,000
More info: www.westindiesbrokers.com

Westland Heights, St. James, Barbados
5 bedrooms, 5 bathrooms, pool, 1 minute from Royal Westmoreland Golf Resort and 2 minutes from the Sugar Hill Tennis Community. A development of 9 house and land lots. Infinity pools and spacious patio areas, exceptional craftsmanship and finishes with marble and coral stone service. Lot Size 4,000sq m house area 630sq m.
Price: $3m
More info: www.aaaltman.com UK 0808 234 1774
Email: realestate@aaaltman.com

THE NATURE ISLAND OF
Dominica

Welcome to Dominica, the Nature Island of the Caribbean; an island of soaring mountain peaks, rushing rivers and waterfalls, pristine rainforest, secluded beaches and endless natural beauty.

Nestled in the Eastern Caribbean, with Guadeloupe to the north and Martinique to the south, Dominica is an English speaking island with a unique culture, blending influences of European, African, Caribbean and indigenous Kalinago traditions.

As a retirement destination, Dominica offers a pleasant year-round climate averaging 27-31°C; numerous outdoor and leisure pursuits; and the perfect natural resources to pursue a healthy lifestyle. Scenic hiking trails can be found all over the island, while the waters in natural hot springs are said to have restorative properties. In addition, Dominica is one of the best destinations in the Caribbean for scuba diving, snorkelling and whale watching.

Whilst tourism is a strong industry and the island welcomes many visitors each year from around the world, Dominica remains unspoiled, a fact that has helped to preserve the island's authentic appeal. The two airports are served by regional flights from Antigua, St Lucia, Barbados, Trinidad, Puerto Rico and St Maarten, with Guadeloupe and Martinique accessible by ferry.

Those choosing a retirement destination may also want to take into consideration Dominica's stable economy and industrial climate; low crime rates; international banking services; welcoming locals and efficient telecommunications; all of which add to the benefits of building a new life on the island. Retirees will not be taxed on income from foreign sources and health care facilities are good, with three main hospitals and several community health centres. Dominica's transport links also provide access to specialist medical centres elsewhere in the Caribbean.

The application for residency is a relatively straight-forward process, details of which can be found on the website www.dominica.gov.dm.

To find out more, why not visit Dominica, where nature, adventure and new opportunities await your arrival.

The Dominica Ministry of Tourism
www.discoverdominica.com

Mountainous and immensely green and fertile, Dominica is the least developed of the Windward Islands and not that easy to reach. Access is via Puerto Rico, Antigua, Martinique or Guadeloupe.

It has a strong local life with lively English and French Creole speakers, the last survivors of the original Caribbean inhabitants, the Caribs.

With just a few white sand beaches in the north-east, but mostly grey volcanic sand on the northern leeward (western) coastline, Dominica offers limited watersports but excellent hiking, rainforest trails and waterfalls. Superb natural and marine life for good scuba diving.

There are just a few inexpensive hotels and inns, inland as well as on the shore and near Roseau, and local restaurants in town.

More info:
www.dominica.gov
www.dominica.dm
www.newsdominica.com
http://definitivecaribbean.co
www.avirtualdominica.com
www.caribbean-on-line.com
www.visit-dominica.com
http://dominicayp.com
www.dominica.dm
www.can-offshore.com

Property and taxes
"Economic citizens" are not liable for tax except on income earned in Dominica. No capital gains tax nor inheritance tax.

Property transfer fees, calculated on the market value of the land or property being sold, payable by the purchaser, are stamp duty (4%), judicial fees (2.5%), assurance fund (1%) and legal fees (3%). The vendor pays 2.5% stamp duty.

You need an Alien Landholding Licence to own more than one acre of land for residential purposes.

Estate agents
www.dominicadreams.com
www.safehavenrealestate.com
www.dominicasrealestate.com
www.acecaribbeanrealestate.com
www.viviun.com
www.caribpro.com
www.fusedworld.com
http://homes.point2.com/Dominica

Dominican Republic

FACTFILE

Capital: Santo Domingo
Population: 9.6m
Area: 48,442sq km
Language: Spanish (official). English is widely spoken.
Getting in: Passport and return ticket.
Permanent residence: Long-winded three-stage process: First a residence visa, then (within two months) applicants must apply for 'provisional residence' which takes about four months and is granted for a year, at the end of which the applicant must apply for residency. You also need to have financial solvency – which means having about $20,000 in the bank.
Money: Peso
Golf: With 23 courses this is an extremely popular golfing destination.

The Dominican Republic is a large independent country in the

western Caribbean that shares an island (Hispaniola) with Haiti, with a huge variety of terrain from near desert to jungle and the Caribbean's highest mountain.

It is well connected to mainland US (Miami and New York) and regionally to Puerto Rico. Spanish is spoken with some English in tourist areas, together with German, French, Italian.

Santo Domingo has a very strong Latin culture, music (merengue, bachata), food and old Spanish colonial architecture. There is a variety of beaches, several resort towns, many resort hotels (generally mid-range) some gated resorts and excellent palacio hotels in Santo Domingo and a sprinkling of good beach inns and guest-houses.

There are numerous activities, restaurants and bars, many casinos, good natural life, horse-riding, hiking, extensive golf, some scuba-diving, whale-watching, windsurfing and considerable cruise tourism.

The countryside is beautiful, tropical on the coasts but the mountainous interior is cool and fertile enough to grow strawberries and apples.

Along the south coast, at the famous Casa de Campo, there are thousands of acres of neatly tended grassland with smart villas, a hotel

and four golf courses. This is where the Dominican wealthy and a few Americans keep their weekend retreats.

More info:
http://definitivecaribbean.com
www.godominicanrepublic.com
www.caribbeantravel.com/dominicanrepublic
www.lonelyplanet.com/dominican-republic
www.domrep.org

Property and taxes
The Dominican Republic, the second largest island in the Caribbean, is currently undergoing huge investment in infrastructure.

Existing US investments of $1.5 billion are expected to double within three years. Currently the biggest development in the Caribbean, Cap Cana, on the southeast coast is a 30,000-acre resort community of hotels, golf courses, residences and a marina. Thousands of property options include villas, bungalows, estate homes and beachfront condos.

There are no restrictions on

foreign ownership. For tax purposes, any person residing in the Dominican Republic for more than 182 days in a year is considered a resident and is liable to income tax from all sources.

Taxes: Annual property tax (1%), property transfer tax (3%), mortgage tax (2%), capital gains tax (25%) and inheritance tax (3%).

Estate agents
www.selectcaribbean.com
www.juanperdomo.com
www.sea-horse-ranch.com
www.oromontique.com
www.coldwellbanker.com.do

The Grenadines

FACTFILE
Capital: St. George's **Population:** 95,000
Area: 344sq km **Language:** English
Getting in: Passport and return or onward ticket.
Permanent residence: Pretty routine after the usual checks. Property purchasers need to apply for an Aliens Land Holding Permit (cost is 10 per cent of the value of the property.) Permanent residence status can be obtained after five years.
Money: Eastern Caribbean $ (EC$)
Golf: Nine-hole course near Grand Anse.

Grenada, Carriacou and Petite Martinique – three very different islands stretched over 60 miles of aquamarine and azure sea, make up the most southerly country in the Windward Islands.

Tall, volcanic and immensely green, Grenada is the southern anchor of the Grenadines, which run north-east to St Vincent in a scattering of pretty islands and cays. Carriacou and Petite Martinique are two of the Grenadines, much smaller than their sister island.

Grenada has white sand beaches on which you will find the island's

hotels and some of the best sailing in the Caribbean. It is typical of the other Windward Islands – green and beautiful, immensely fertile and famed for its spices.

St George's, the capital, is well known as one of the prettiest towns in the Caribbean. It is also extremely lively. Elsewhere the pace of life is less frenetic. Getting out and about in Grenada is fun and is bound to bring a strong West Indian experience, whether you are in a rum shop or on a plantation tour.

The Grenadians themselves are typical of the Windward Islanders, welcoming and easy-going, and they make exploration of the island a real pleasure. The vast majority of the 95,000 islanders live on Grenada itself.

Not that developed a tourist destination, Grenada has a reasonable crop of restaurants, beaches and beach bars but is also ideal for lazy days spent at a beach bar in a secluded cove.

Carriacou and Petite Martinique, the two northern islands politically attached to Grenada, are completely different in character from the larger island. Here you will find classic Caribbean small island life, Grenadines style – quiet, sleepy and enchanting with a visit to one of the bars and restaurants in Tyrell

Bay, which occasionally sees a lively crowd in season.

Petite Martinique (petty martnik), with a population of around 800, is even smaller and quieter. Basically it is a mountain that rises in a pyramid just east of the northern tip of Carriacou.

Just 8km by 13km, Carriacou (pronounced carrikoo) feels quite mountainous, though the highest point is only 305m above sea level.

More info
www.grenadines.net
www.definitivecaribbean.com
www.gov.vc/govt
www.grenadaexplorer.com
www.grenadagrenadines.com
www.lonelyplanet.com/grenada
www.DiscoverSVG.com
www.grenadakiosk.com
www.mygrenada.org
http://svgblog.blogspot.com

Property and taxes
Although it has seen a steady increase in building, Grenada is still relatively undeveloped. Prices have never reached the heights of say, Barbados or Anguilla, and are of comparatively good value.

The most developed area is the south-west, around St George's and south of there, but most particularly on the Point Salines Peninsular and at L'Anse aux Epines. Gradually development has crept east and there are now villa developments at Westerhall and Fort Jeudy.

Grenada has attracted major investment and prices are rising fast as top-notch villa developments come on line at the new Four Seasons. A 740sq m villa will cost $8 million or more but there are cheaper options.

British developer Peter de Savary is investing heavily and there are new developments at Prickly Bay and Bacolet Bay.

Carriacou has a few villas in the west of the island. Three bedroom

villas have been on the market for around $500,000.

Property is taxed at variable rates. There is no capital gains tax or inheritance tax but non-resident individuals must pay an annual license fee to hold land in the islands at a flat rate of $926.

Estate agents
www.simplycaribbean.com
http://grenadaegmont.com
www.remax-grenada.com
www.villasofgrenada.com
www.viviun.com
www.grenadaexplorer.com
www.simplycaribbean.com
www.landoreefvillas.com

Guadeloupe
FACTFILE
Capital: Basse-Terre
Population: 452,776 **Area:** 1,628sq km
Language: French (official) and Creole.
Getting in: You need a valid 10-year passport and return or onward ticket.
Permanent residence: Guadeloupe is a Department of France and, as such, immigration is relatively simple for those from EU member states.
Money: Euro
Golf: Saint François Golf Course (18 holes) in the east of Grande Terre.

Guadeloupe, another of the overseas departments of France and thus part of the European Union, is an archipelago with smaller offshore islands, easily accessible from France, OK from USA (Miami or San Juan), but there are no direct flights from the UK. It has a metropolitan French infrastructure overlaid on a lively French Creole culture. There is a good variety of beaches, many with white coral sand, particularly Grande-Terre, some with water sports, others secluded and several with beach bars and restaurants.

Guadeloupe has many large, mainly mid-range hotels, with a small clutch of more stylish inns,

particularly in Basse-Terre; a variety of restaurants, French and Creole, old plantations, excellent rainforest and hiking, sugar/rum factories, good sailing, casinos and cruises.

Offshore islands

The Saints are pretty islands south of Basse-Terre with a less developed, simpler French Caribbean life, a few inns and nice beaches.

Marie Galante, accessed from Point à Pitre, has a strong traditional culture with a simple French West Indian life. It is low-key with a tradition of sugar cane and rum. La Désirade, accessed via St François, has an extremely simple life, just a few guesthouses and goats.

More info

www.in-west-indies.com/guadeloupe
www.definitivecaribbean.com
www.tripbase.com/Guadeloupe-Tourism-Guadeloupe.html
www.lonelyplanet.com/guadeloupe
www.guadeloupevacations.mobi/

Property and taxes

The Global Property Guide [www.globalpropertyguide.com] cites apartment prices in Grande-Terre and Basse-Terre as around $2,100-3,400 per sq m and the average price of a 120-sq m

apartment as around $260,000.

There is a transfer tax of 4.89 per cent. Rental income earned by non-residents is taxed at a flat rate of 20 per cent. Capital gains is 16 per cent on the net gain (higher for non-EU residents), after allowable deductions.

Estate agents

http://homes.point2.com
www.belgimmo.be/uk/agence-513.html
www.caribbeanlandandproperty.com

Jamaica

FACTFILE

Capital: Kingston
Population: 2.7 million
Area: 10,991sq km
Language: English, Patois
Getting in: British nationals do not require a visa for stays of up to 90 days.
Permanent residence: Granted at the discretion of the Minister of National Security and Justice. Requires evidence of adequate funds and a police certificate.
Money: Jamaican $
Golf: Around a dozen golf courses, the best centred on Montego Bay in the north-west. Others in Negril, Rio Bueno, Runaway Bay, Ocho Rios and Port Antonio (nine holes).

A large, busy, beautiful, lively island with extensive air access and a full range of beaches. Good golf, superb music, strong local life and vibrant culture. There are endless things to do, not just on the beaches, but inland in the mountains and rivers as well, and Jamaica has a lively cultural life, with excellent music. The Jamaicans are funny, charming and eccentric, exasperating at times, but always engaging.

Located in the Greater Antilles, Jamaica is the third largest island in the Caribbean after Cuba and Hispaniola (home of Haiti and the Dominican Republic).

Extremely rough and mountainous and immensely fertile, Jamaica comes in a million

fantastically beautiful shades of green. On the flanks of the Blue Mountain Peak, which rises to 2,290m, you will find pine forest, cloud forest and rainforest, with orchids and enormous ferns. Yet within 160km there is drier, savannah-like grassland and the extraordinary 'Cockpit Country', an area of subterranean rivers and karst limestone peaks.

All over the island there are tight valleys that explode with greenery and run with stunningly beautiful rivers. Down on the coast you will find mangroves, meandering shorelines, cliffs with nesting seabirds and an incredible variety of beaches.

Jamaica also has thousands of flowering plants, a very varied wildlife – over 250 species of birds, reptiles such as iguanas and tree frogs and curiosities such as manatees and the hutia, a guinea-pig like creature.

Jamaica is the largest English-speaking island in the Caribbean and, with a population of around 2,710,000, the fourth most populous.

There are botanical gardens, art galleries and museums. You can even watch polo. And of course, this is not to forget that Jamaica is the home of reggae to be found in the bars and clubs around the island.

More info

www.visitjamaica.com
www.jamaicans.com
www.definitivecaribbean.com
www.my-island-jamaica.com
www.discoverjamaica.com
www.my-island-jamaica.com

Property and tax

Famous names are linked with Jamaica, Hollywood stars such as Errol Flynn, Bette Davis and politicians such as Winston Churchill.

By the end of the 20th Century the two most important towns were

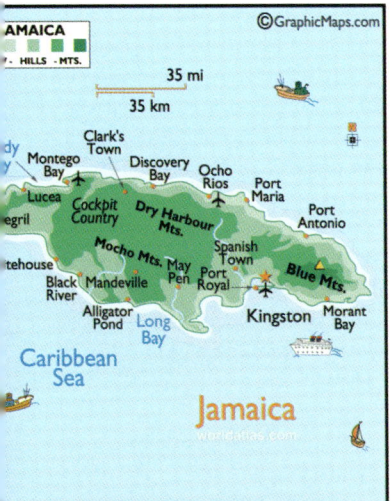

Ocho Rios, where there were less formal communities of villas (more like private estates) above the town, and Montego Bay, where there are estates on the shorelines and hillsides on both sides of the town.

Villa 'resorts' (villas communities with some central hotel-type facilities) in this area include Tryall and Half Moon. And the development is continuing with newer estates at Rose Hall being built around golf courses.

In the towns and along the coast you will also find a few condominium complexes with apartments. Scattered in between the main resorts you will find smaller clusters of villas set on a good beach or in another spectacular setting.

The south coast is completely different from the north and barely developed by comparison.

Prices range enormously across Jamaica and offer good value. A four or five bedroom home set in an acre of gardens in an established villa resort such as Tryall will cost upwards of $1.5 million but there are many cheaper options.

Apartments in Ocho Rios come onto the market from $55,000 and in Negril and other tourist areas you might find homes for as little as $50,000.

If the romantic dream of two centuries ago catches you, and you want to live in a plantation great house, you can find one with four or five bedrooms, a swimming pool and 15-20 acres of land for $500,000-900,000.

Estate agents

www.realtorsjamaica.com
www.vlarealtors.com
www.cbjamaica.com
www.vmpropertyservices.com
www.mbellrealtors.com
www.langford-brown.com
www.sagicorproperties.com
www.hjrealtors.com

Martinique

FACTFILE

Capital: Fort-de-France
Population: 432,990   **Area:** 1,100sq km
Language: French, Creole
Getting in: No visa required but you must hold a return ticket.
Permanent residence: Extended stays are at the discretion of the Immigration Department.
Money: Euro
Golf: One 18-hole course located just south of Trois-Ilets.

Another Département of France, Martinique is a mountainous and highly developed French Caribbean island with an excellent Creole life.

Easily accessible from France, Martinique is a mix of metro-politan French and French Creole – French infrastructure, zouk music, Creole style and food, a good variety of beaches with beach bars and restaurants.

There are many large, mid-range hotels, some smaller, friendlier inns and gîtes and a good variety of restaurants and varied attractions include museums, themed plantations (rum, bananas etc), botanical gardens, rainforest and hiking, mountain biking,

some sailing, casinos and cruises.

More info
www.martinique.org
www.lonelyplanet.com/martinique
www.martinique.org
www.definitivecaribbean.com
www.carriacoupetitemartinique.com
www.martinique.com.au

Property and tax
Global Property Guide
[www.globalpropertyguide.com]
puts coastal property prices at
around $4,650 per sq m with
apartments in Fort-de-France less
expensive, with 120sq m apartments
averaging $3,200 per sq m.

After deduction of acquisition
and improvement costs, capital
gains tax is 16 per cent but
discounts of 10 per cent a year are
allowed after the fifth year of
ownership, with the effect that after
15 years no gain is chargeable to tax.

Properties, which have been used
as a principal residence from the
date of purchase, or for a minimum
of five years, are exempt from
capital gains tax. Pensioners, even if
non-resident, are exempt from
CGT. However, owners who are
not residents of an EU country pay
CGT at a rate of 33.3 per cent,
subject to discounts for the period
the property has been owned.

French laws on inheritance tax
apply. There are annual property
taxes but there are exemptions for
over 60s.

Estate agents
www.caribbeanlandandproperty.com
www.offplanpropertyexchange.com
www.propertyworld.com
A number of agents are listed on
the Global Property Guide website:
www.globalpropertyguide.com

Montserrat

FACTFILE
Capital: Was Plymouth but it was abandoned in 1997. Interim government buildings have been built at Brades Estate.
Population: 5,000
Area: 102sq km
Language: English
Getting in: No visa required.
Permanent residence: Property investment or a deposit at a commercial bank equal to $152,000.
Golf: None

Montserrat is small, quiet and
delightful but severe volcanic
activity in 1995 destroyed the main
town of Plymouth and all the
houses in the south and another
catastrophic eruption in 1997
closed the airports and seaports.
Many inhabitants fled.

While it certainly encourages

visitors, Montserrat does not have
much infrastructure but is still a
lovely island and you can expect to
be welcomed graciously. There are a
few beaches, mainly in the north-
west, just a couple of hotels and
inexpensive guesthouses, a few
restaurants, bars and a couple of
beach bars, all very low key.

More info
www.visitmontserrat.com
www.definitivecaribbean.com
www.gov.ms
http://giu.gov.ms
www.montserratreporter.org
montserratyp.com
www.themontserratreporter.com

Property and tax
Foreigners can buy property
without restrictions and the
government welcomes expatriate
investment so buying or building
property is a straightforward
process for a non-national.

The total cost of the landholder
licence, land transfer, stamp duty,
tax and legal fees is approximately
10 per cent of the property price.

Estate agents
www.montserratenterprises.com
www.montserratvillas.com
www.tradewindsmontserrat.com
www.sunislandrealestate.com

Puerto Rico

FACTFILE

Capital: San Juan
Population: 4,000,000
Area: 13,790sq km
Language: Spanish and English.
Getting in: 10-year passport and return ticket. (Visas required for stays longer than six months).
Permanent residence: Puerto Rico is a US territory and permanent residence rules are the same as for the United States.
Money: US$
Golf: There are more golf courses in Puerto Rico than anywhere else in the Caribbean.

A relatively large and mountainous island, 160km by 56km with three smaller islands and many cays,

Puerto Rico is easily accessible from the US (less so from Europe), mainly Spanish-speaking but English is understood everywhere.

It is highly developed and quite modern compared to the rest of the Caribbean, with a strong and lively Latin culture.

Old San Juan, with a rich history and culture, is the best-preserved colonial district in the Caribbean and has evolved into a charming residential and commercial neighbourhood with more than 400 carefully restored 16th and 17th Century Spanish colonial buildings, painted in a rainbow of pastel colours.

The beaches are varied, some excellent, particularly on Vieques and Culebra; inland there is excellent countryside including rainforest.

There is an extremely broad range of tourism at all price levels, beach resorts and country retreats, some smaller hotels with charm in town and country. There is huge cruise ship traffic into San Juan, shopping, extensive sports, golf, national parks, hiking and sailing.

Vieques and Culebra, off the east coast towards the Virgin Islands, are smaller, much less developed and lower key, with better beaches.

More info
www.topuertorico.org
www.gotopuertorico.com
www.lonelyplanet.com/puerto-rico
www.definitivecaribbean.com

Property and tax

According to the Global Property Guide [www.globalpropertyguide.com] Puerto Rico's housing market has been stagnant for the past 18 months, after enormous price increases in the early 2000s.

The average price of four-bedroom houses in San Juan was $329,750 in 2008, down from $357,500 in 2007.

There are no restrictions on foreigners buying property in Puerto Rico. Long-term capital gains are taxed at a flat rate of 20 per cent and property is subject on an annual real property tax based on value.

Estate agents

www.puertoricorealestateguide.com
www.activerealtypr.com
www.baezrealestate.com
www.callcoll.com
www.delhome.net
www.extrarealtypr.com
www.find-a-house.com
www.piramide.com
www.alrtech.com

Las Canas, Dominican Rep

Las Canas Beach Resort on the north coast is a 500-acre development with studios, 1 and 2 bedroom apartments and 1 to 4 bedroom villas. 10 minutes from Cabarete, rich in lush jungle forests, mountains, blue waters and pristine beaches with water sports, restaurants, bars, shopping and golf. Fully furnished.
Prices: Studios from $120,000
One bedroom apartment from $200,000
Two bedroom apartment from $240,000 Villas $360,000-630,000
More info: www.brooksfeller.com Tel (UK): 01392 459501
Email: info@brooksfeller.com

Cowers Isle, Jamaica

5 bedrooms, 3 bathrooms. Pool. Short drive to local beaches. Ocean view from the villa. There are two condos that are rented and 3 apartments included on grounds.
Price: $1,500,000
More info: www.caribmove.com

St Barts

FACTFILE

Capital: Gustavia **Population:** 6,850
Area: 25sq km **Language:** French and
English are widely spoken
Getting in: Passport and return ticket
Permanent residence: Proof of adequate
funds.
Money: Euro, but US$ are accepted
Golf: None

St Barts, the most chic and sexiest island in the Caribbean, is very French (rather than French Créole/Caribbean), exclusive and well developed, with excellent beaches, hotels and expensive real estate as well as superb restaurants, people-watching and plenty of activities.

A favourite with the jet set, St Barts is the uncontested crème de la crème destination of the Caribbean. Nut-brown beauties can be seen daily in bars, zipping by on motorbikes, in open-topped Smart cars or strolling the beaches in a mere nuance of a bathing suit.

This island is a getaway for movie stars and the winter home to millionaires. It is the most fashionable island in the Caribbean, expensive and exclusive with immense style and atmosphere.

The food is excellent, life is stylish, the island is completely safe and the shopping is the best in the Caribbean. All that France does so well has been transported across the Atlantic to a blip in the Caribbean.

St Barts lies about 24km southeast of St Maarten/St Martin, the main access point from the US or mainland Europe – British visitors tend to travel via Antigua. The island is just 10km by 3-4km in size, extremely rough and mountainous but surprisingly beautiful. The beaches, some developed and some completely undeveloped, are excellent.

Officially the island is called St Barthélemy, but it is usually known by familiar abbreviations – St Barth in French and St Barts in English.

The islanders, the Barthéleminois, are predominantly white, descendants of a few poor and hardy settlers, and they own the majority of the business.

There is a large constituency of home-owners of all nationalities and a working population of mainly French.

St Barts is quite exclusive (expensive). The yachts in the harbour over Christmas are a sight to behold, massive hardware that teeters between magnificence and supreme vulgarity.

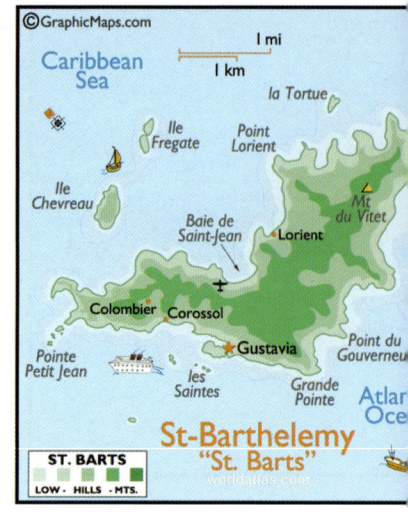

The millionaires may park their jets in St Maarten but in St Barts they go barefoot. You probably won't recognise them in their bathing suits anyway.

More info
www.saint-barths.com
www.sbhonline.com
www.definitivecaribbean.com
www.gotostbarths.com
www.caribbean-on-line.com/st-barts

Property and tax
With an estimated 500 foreign-owned homes on the island, there is plenty of opportunity to buy desirable houses in spectacular settings.

Although not that many villas

are on the beach, the island's terrain is so rough and steep that there is a different spectacular location, with another magnificent view, every 90m. As you would expect, with all these wealthy home-owners, there are some truly fantastic houses.

The most fashionable area to live has always been around St Jean because of its restaurants and excellent beaches. Other areas have specific reasons for their popularity, Gustavia for its proximity to the shops and the very pretty harbour.

Undeveloped land is extremely hard to come by and so most purchases are resales. House prices are usually quoted in euros and average prices for a two bedroom house with no view might be €1 million, while in St Jean, a nice three-bedroom house could fetch €5 million, or €8 million for something brand new.

A recommended real estate agent is Sibarth Real Estate [www.sibarthrealestate.com], which is affiliated to Christies Great Estates, and is the longest established agent on the island. Other estate agents www.caribbeanbestrealestate.com www.stbarth.com/sales/realestate

There is a property transfer tax of 8-10 per cent of the value of the property but no annual property taxes. Capital gains tax is levied at 16-33 per cent depending on citizenship and status of the owner.

St Eustatius

FACTFILE

Capital: Oranjestad
Population: 3,000
Area: 21sq km
Language: English and Dutch (official). Papiamento (a mixture of African, Dutch, English, Portuguese and Spanish) is the commonly used lingua franca.
Getting in: No visa required for stays of up to 90 days.
Permanent residence: Proof of adequate means of support, plus good conduct and medical certificates.
Money: Netherlands Antilles florin
Golf: None

St Eustatius, pronounced sint-u-stay-shus and generally known as Statia, is a very small and quiet, English and Dutch-speaking island that is barely known and quite hard to get to (via St Maarten).

Sandwiched between St. Kitts and Saba and a 20-minute flight from St. Martin, it has retained its old Caribbean charm. There are just a couple of grey sand beaches, some hiking and a very strong

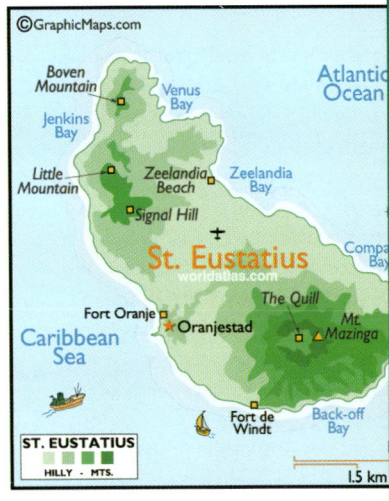

history that is visible in a few attractive old buildings in town. Rated as one of the top 10 dive destinations in the world, St Eustatius has a handful of small hotels and guesthouses and a few mainly local restaurants and bars.

More info
www.statiagovernment.com
www.statiatourism.com
www.definitivecaribbean.com
www.lonelyplanet.com/sint-eustatius
www.steustatiushistory.org
www.caribbeantravel.com/steustatius

Property and taxes
A tiny island with little development, properties for sale are few and far between. Land

Duhaney Park, Jamaica
4 bedroom 3 bathroom house of 300sq m with 2 car garage. Unfinished 2 bedroom flat at rear. Roof balcony.
Price: $118,913
More info: www.mceachron-clarke.com
Email: mceachron-clarke@cwjamaica.com

Le Francois, Martinique
Luxury villa on the windward side of the island. Sea view. 4 bedrooms, 3 bathrooms, large living room. Kitchen opening onto terrace. Pool.
Land: 2,788sq m.
Price: $1,055,360
More info: www.caribmove.com Email: support@caribmove.com

and property is relatively cheap. A 4-bedroom villa can be had for around $350,000, while condos start at about $250,000.

At the time of writing you could have a choice between one of two, two-bedroom wooden houses, one priced at $110,000, the other at $70,000 [see: www.statia.info]

There are no capital gains taxes and no property taxes but non-residents inheriting property are liable for property transfer tax of eight per cent of the property value.

Residents are taxed on their worldwide income.

Estate agents
Norako Real Estate & Mortgages
SMD Architects & Consultants
www.viviun.com
www.islandrealestate.com

St Kitts & Nevis

St Kitts and Nevis have been united politically since 1882 and became independent from Britain as the Federation of St Kitts and Nevis in 1983.

Set in the north of the Leeward Islands in the Eastern Caribbean, the islands lie near the tip of the diminishing arc of vast volcanic islands that starts in the south with Grenada. These two beautiful islands face each other across 'the Narrows', but despite their proximity the two are in fact quite different in atmosphere.

St Kitts
FACTFILE
Capital: Basseterre **Population:** 31,880
Area: 176.1sq km **Language:** English
Getting in: Passport and return ticket.
Permanent residence: 'Economic citizenship' is obtained via two components – real estate purchase for not less than $250,000 and a fee of $35,000 for a single applicant, with an additional $15,000 per dependent.
Money: Eastern Caribbean $
Golf: Currently one, the Royal St Kitts Golf Club, Frigate Bay, but at least two others are planned or under construction.

St Kitts is relatively small, just 8km by 29km, but it soars to over 1,000m. The views of St Kitts from its sister island are some of the loveliest in the Caribbean. St Kitts offers a lively West Indian life on an attractive island which is not that developed. The Kittitians are a demonstrative people (unlike their cousins in Nevis, who are generally quieter) and so life in downtown Basseterre is lively.

Air access is quite good and there are a few beaches, some secluded.

There are two halves to the island, which are distinct in geography and in atmosphere. The north is lush and green, with a patchwork of steep green slopes. The coastline is dotted with traditional West Indian villages, churches, agricultural plots and the occasional windmill or brick chimney from an old sugar estate.

All the flatlands in this section of St Kitts were once carpeted with sugar cane but the industry came to an end in 2005.

Life is typical of the Caribbean, a fairly simple agricultural and light industrial existence. The capital, Basseterre, which lies in the lee of the mountains, is a small, busy town of stone buildings set on the waterfront.

If you head for the south of the island, over the hill from Basseterre, the atmosphere changes completely. You arrive first in Frigate Bay, the island's tourist heartland. Hotel complexes line the beaches on both coasts (Atlantic and Caribbean side). There is golf and water sports.

Beyond here, the whole south-eastern peninsular is lower-lying and drier and consequently less green, but with the best beaches.

St Kitts has a couple of excellent plantation house hotels set in

restored historic buildings, some of the most atmospheric and delightful in the Caribbean.

More info
www.definitivecaribbean.com
www.stkittstourism.kn
www.stkittsnevis.org
www.stkittsnevis.com
www.lonelyplanet.com
www.thestkittsnevisobserver.com
www.turq.com/stkittsandnevis

Property and taxes
The real estate market in St Kitts has seen an extraordinary upswing over the past few years. For a long time the island was in the doldrums but it has suddenly seen an explosion of building – and a rise in the price of land, though

much of it is still considerably less expensive than most islands.

The upswing can be dated to 2004, pretty much to the opening of the Marriot hotel on the Atlantic side of Frigate Bay, which is by far the most popular area for property.

Although a road was built along the south-eastern peninsular in the early 1990s interest in that area is just taking off. Particularly at the far south-eastern tip of the island where 185 villas in the Ocean's Edge Resort at nearby Frigate Bay have been built along with a new marina.

The marina will occupy over 300 acres of water surface with 40-60 yacht slips and a heliport. There will also be a Tom Fazio golf course, marina village, restaurants, retail and residential villas.

Ocean's Edge overlooks the crescent beach of Cable Bay below. Buyers qualify for the 'Citizenship by Investment' programme, which means they get Kittitian passports and tax advantages, including no income or inheritance tax.

Two-bedroom, two-bathroom hillside apartments, complete with their own plunge pools, start at $575,000.

In the arid southern peninsula, previously occupied mainly by wild

goats, work has just begun on the Christophe Harbour project, another golf course and a super-yacht marina plus villas where starting prices are rumoured to be in the region of $1 million per bedroom.

Estate agents (common to both)
www.coldwellbankerstkittsnevis.com
www.oualierealty.com
www.sknvibes.com
www.eliteislandresorts.com
www.century21islandrealty.com
www.eliteislandresorts.com
www.stkittsrealty.com
www.ilovestkittsnevis.com
www.nelsonsprings.com
www.stkittsnevisrealestate.com
www.buschhillvillas.com
www.nevisvillas.com
www.nevishouses.com
www.parexcellencerealtors.com

Nevis
FACTFILE
Capital: Charlestown
Population: 11,245
Area: 93.2sq km **Language:** English
Getting in: No visa but you must hold a return ticket.
Permanent residence: An investment of at least $350,000 in an "approved investment project" or a minimum contribution into the Sugar Industry Diversification Foundation of $200,000 (spouse and two children below the age of 18, $250,000;

Ocean's Edge, St Kitts
A development of apartments, cottages and individual villas - 1 to 4 bedrooms - spread around the beachfront location of Frigate Bay in St Kitts.
Covering almost 40 acres, and adjacent to the Royal St. Kitts Golf Course, Ocean's Edge will have a beachfront bar and restaurant, clubhouse with restaurant, a recreation centre, seven swimming pools and two tennis courts.
Owners are offered a comprehensive property management programme and may choose to participate in a rental programme.
More info: www.aaaltman.com

Village Home, St Kitts
5 bedrooms, 2 bathrooms, 2-storey house of 1,710sq ft
Price: $116,000
More info: www.edenvalue.com
Tel: (869) 466-5744
Email: service@edenvalue.com

The island of Nevis extends a warm welcome to visitors and future residents.

Choosing a location to retire to is an important decision. One must consider standard of living, weather, surroundings and social opportunities. The charming island of Nevis, reminiscent of the way the Caribbean used to be, is situation in the Leeward Islands and offers lush natural surroundings, friendly, welcoming people and an array of activities to satisfy those who like to stay active.

With a strong tourism industry, as well as a vibrant financial services sector, Nevis' economy remains stable. There is no income tax on Nevis and the British pound is currently exchanged at a rate of four Eastern Caribbean (EC) dollars. The popularity of tourism, sophisticated financial services and the recently opened medical school has attracted many expats looking to live, work, invest and retire on Nevis

Tropical weather, with warm year-round sun and cool breezes, makes the island an ideal destination for Britons interested in relocating for retirement. Whether looking for a beachfront condo, a cottage at the edge of the rainforest or a majestic villa overlooking the Caribbean Sea, there are a number of residential options.

Charlestown is the charming capital of Nevis. Here you will find shops, restaurants and the port from which you can take a ferry to the neighbouring island of St Kitts. Charlestown is also home to quaint museums and galleries, including Alexander Hamilton's birthplace and the Horatio Nelson Museum of Nevis, currently hosting the largest collection of Nelson memorabilia in the western hemisphere.

Outdoor enthusiasts can stay active in a number of ways on Nevis. For the sports-lover the island offers excellent golf and tennis facilities. Those looking for more adventure can arrange for guided hikes at varying degrees of difficulty up the steep slopes of Mount Nevis Peak. There are windsurfing and sailing opportunities, snorkelling and diving excursions, mountain bike trails and horseback riding. Of course, there's always the option to sit back on one of the beautiful golden beaches with a good book and enjoy the breeze swaying in the coconut palms.

I welcome you to enjoy life in Nevis where you're only a stranger once.

Best Regards

Garcia Thompson-Hendrickson
CEO Nevis Tourism Authority

five dependants; $300,000; six or more dependants, $400,000).

Money: Eastern Caribbean $

Golf: 18 hole course at the Four Seasons Hotel on the west of the island. 9-hole pitch and putt in Newcastle.

Nevis is a small and delightful volcanic island, not that easy to get to (usually via Antigua or St Kitts) but consequently uncrowded and largely unspoiled. It is an unhurried island with a gracious, old West Indian air and a handful of the Caribbean's most enchanting plantation house hotels, many lovely villas, some good restaurants; excellent golf, biking, hiking and some water sports.

Nevis is immensely fertile and overwhelmingly green. And, with its lovely old buildings and plantation houses, it hints at the grace and finery of past times. Just 9km by 13km, the island is dominated by a massive volcanic cone, the Nevis Peak. Its slopes sweep down in graceful concave curves, rising momentarily and then tumbling to the flatlands, beaches and the sea.

Charlestown is a pretty town and all around the island you will see the beautiful blackened stonework of the past in the walls, bridges and churches. There is excellent walking in the island's rain-forested flanks. Everything is on quite a small scale but if you don't need round-the-clock entertainment Nevis can fill your days and evenings.

A good part of the historic enchantment of Nevis comes from its plantation house hotels, which are the loveliest in the Caribbean.

Property and taxes

Nevis was a late developer in the Caribbean real estate market but since the late 1980s the island has had a band of faithful visitors who came here in spite of the

difficulties. They built their houses, often in the hills, and lived quietly, enjoying the peace and simplicity of this beautiful island.

It was only with the arrival of the Four Seasons Resort in the early '90s that the market began to open up.

There are some stunning new private houses in the hills of the south-east side of the island. Occasionally there is even the opportunity to purchase an old estate house or a sugar mill for restoration.

St Lucia

FACTFILE

Capital: Castries **Population:** 173,000
Area: 616sq km
Language: English (official), Creole, French
Getting in: Passport valid for at least six months from the date of entry plus onward or return ticket.
Permanent residence: Considered to be relatively simple and can be applied for at the Ministry of Foreign Affairs. Visitors receive a 42-day visa on arrival and extensions must be obtained for periods of six months. For longer stays, "special arrangements may be made on a case-by-case basis". Citizenship can be applied for after seven years.
Money: Eastern Caribbean $ (EC$)
Golf: St Lucia Golf and Country Club. A second championship course is under construction nearby, part of a villa development on 350 acres. There is a nine-hole par 3 at Sandals St Lucia Golf Resort & Spa.

St. Lucia is a strikingly beautiful island in the heart of the Windward chain in the Eastern Caribbean, between St Vincent and Martinique. The largest and most developed of the Windward Islands, St. Lucia is easily reached from Europe, a little less easy from the USA.

It stands with massive green bulk, a network of forested peaks that soar and ridges and valleys that tumble to the coastlines.

The island has classic white sand beaches and many pretty, steep-sided, hidden coves, most with beach bars. There are all-inclusive hotels but also an excellent crop of smaller, more individual hotels, good, lively restaurants, good sailing and a growing golf scene.

St Lucia has been quite successful at projecting itself as a romantic destination. It has a large number of visitors including a considerable wedding business.

The St Lucians are charming and have a mixed heritage that results from the island's complex historical past, passed backwards and forwards many times in treaties between the French and the British.

The result is a population that largely speaks both English and French Creole.

St Lucia's most famous landmarks are the Pitons, twin pointed volcanic peaks that rise side by side midway down the Caribbean coast like massive eye teeth. The island is attractive for many reasons. Lively and

We Live Here

Island hopping retirees pick St Lucia as their place in the sun

Peter and Pat (2nd and 3rd from left) with their four children. Julie (extreme left) and Susan (4th from left)

Retired oil industry executive Peter Norey and his wife Pat didn't want to rush things when it came to choosing their perfect retirement haven. So they took their time. Plenty of it.

Peter's career had taken them to many parts of the world and when he left the oil business the couple took over a hotel in Guernsey that they ran for 10 years.

As retirement beckoned the couple decided it was time to get serious about finding the perfect retirement spot and their search began in Queensland, Australia where they spent several months looking around.

Next stop was Puerto Rico where the search took even longer – so long that Peter, now aged 65, and Pat, 62, and their two daughters, Julie and Susan, put down roots, staying there for five years.

Then the Caribbean beckoned and since the couple were experienced sailors – Peter had taken part in a transatlantic race from Gran Canaria to St Lucia in 2006 – they short-listed islands with marina developments and took a two-month cruise to take a closer look. This odyssey started in the southern Caribbean, in Grenada, before they slowly worked their way north looking at properties in St Kitts, Nevis, Barbados and the British Virgin Islands, before finally deciding on St Lucia.

The five-star marina development that caught their attention was The Landings on 245m of pristine beachfront overlooking Rodney Bay. Built on reclaimed land, it offered a rare opportunity to buy a freehold beachfront property.

The Landings facilities include a beachfront restaurant, a private yacht harbour for 80 boats, white sand beaches with an array of water sports and a 650 sq. m spa and gym. It had been named 'Best Caribbean Development' and 'Best Marina Development Worldwide' in the Bentley International Property Awards.

"We loved the style of architecture and North American standards of building quality," said Peter.

"The apartment would have cost three times that amount in Barbados, or even Grenada, for the equivalent floor space."

Not to be left out of the plans, the couple's daughters each snapped up a three-bedroom apartment there, sight unseen.

Now fully retired, Pat and Peter spend their winters in St Lucia and their summers in Guernsey. Daughter Julie has already moved her big yacht to Rodney Bay.

More info:
The Landings
Tel (UK): 0845 217 7851
Email: info@thelandingsstlucia.com
www.thelandingsstlucia.com

accessible, it has a strong Creole aspect and weekly events that are fun to join in, fish fries in local villages and, of course, Friday night at Gros Islet.

Property and taxes

There is a considerable development of private villas but also of larger projects from the likes of Raffles, Ritz-Carlton and Westin. With affordable land and this development, St Lucia is a good prospect in terms of real estate for second homes as well as an investment.

Traditionally development has been concentrated in the north of the island, mainly north of the capital Castries, but new build is gradually spreading farther afield. The smartest area is still in the Cap Estate at the far northern tip of St Lucia.

The Jack Nicklaus Golf Course at Raffles St Lucia and the 5-star resort, The Landings, are pulling in developers and investors quicker than they can get round the 18 holes.

Rodney Bay is also very popular and, as demand increases in that area, plots and houses are coming up for sale further and further east.

South of Castries there is also some development with plenty more on the way. The pretty Marigot Bay has a big project and there are some lovely individual plots in the hills above the bay.

There is no capital gains tax and no inheritance tax. Non-residents owning residential property pay tax at five per cent of the annual rental value.

Estate agents

www.tropicalvillas.net
www.cap-estate.com
www.sugarbeachvillas.com
www.capmaison.com

St Martin/ Sint Maarten

FACTFILE

Capital: Marigot (St. Martin) Philipsburg (Sint Maarten)

Population: 44,600 (St. Martin); 40,100 (Sint Maarten)

Area: 52sq km (St. Martin); 33sq km (Sint Maarten)

Language: English is spoken everywhere, but Dutch is the official language of St.Maarten and French the official language of Saint Martin.

Getting in: Tourist visa for 90 days issued on arrival (Sint Maarten); Dutch citizens can stay without a residency permit for up to six months;

Permanent residence: Since St. Martin is part of France and Sint Maarten part of the Netherlands, the formalities are fairly straightforward for EU passport holders.

Money: Euro (St. Martin); Netherlands Antilles florin (Sint Maarten). US$ widely accepted.

Golf: There is only one course, the Mullet Bay Resort on the Dutch side of the island.

A single island divided between French (Saint Martin) and Dutch (Sint Maarten). Excellent access from Europe and the US.

The Landings, St Lucia

5-star development of waterfront homes on Rodney Bay in the northwest of St Lucia. Built around a private yacht harbour overlooking harbour or beach. Extensive facilities include a 650sq m spa, yacht mooring and slips, beach club, watersports, beach and gourmet restaurants, fitness club, hair salon, swimming pools, boutique and tennis club. Owners have membership at the St. Lucia Golf and Country Club close by. Prices: 1, 2 and 3 bedroom 'grande residences' and 4 bedroom duplexes range from $610,000-3 million.
More info: www.thelandingsstlucia.com Tel (UK): 0845 217 7851
Email: info@thelandingsstlucia.com

Pelican Key, St Maarten

2-bedroom cottage on 1,100sq m of tropical landscaped grounds perched on top of the hills in Pelican Key consists of a 2-bedroom home with a pool and with rental property income apartments. Price $1.5 million
More info: www.keyrealtysxm.com

French and mainly English spoken with a very mixed population with over 140 different nationalities among its residents.

There are excellent white sand beaches, some offshore islands, good sailing (yachting hub for the area). Cruise ships visit both sides. There is extensive duty-free shopping, casinos (Dutch side), a large number of hotels on both sides, many restaurants, excellent on the French side (particularly Grand Case), very lively nightlife, day sails and golf.

More info
www.stmartin.com
www.sint-maarten.net
http://stmartin-guide.info
www.stmaarten-info.com
www.geographia.com/st-martin
www.definitivecaribbean.com
www.geographia.com/st-maarte
www.caribbean-on-line.com/sm
www.caribbeanedge.com/st_maarten
www.experiencestmaarten.com
www.beststmartin.com

Property and taxes
Property in Saint Martin is expensive: $1 million-plus for a 3-bedroom house, up to $700,000 for a luxury 3-bedroom apartment but there's a wide choice of cheaper apartments.

One island, two different tax structures explained in detail by the Global Property Guide [www.globalpropertyguide.com].

On the French side pensioners, even if non-resident, are exempt from capital gains tax. However, owners who are not EU residents pay CGT at a rate of 33.3 per cent. There are no capital gains taxes on Dutch St. Maarten.

Just as confusing is that on Dutch St. Maarten there are no annual property taxes while there is on the French side.

Estate agents
www.portocupecoy.com

www.sunshine-properties.com
www.stmaartenproperties.com
www.romacsothebysrealty.com
www.remaxislandproperties.com
www.caribbeanedge.com
www.islandrealestate.com
www.holprop.com
http://gobeach.com

Trinidad & Tobago

FACTFILE

Capital (Trinidad): Port-of-Spain; (Tobago) (Scarborough)
Population: 1.4 million (Trinidad); 50,000 (Tobago): **Area:** 4,830sq km (Trinidad); 300sq km (Tobago): **Language:** English
Getting in: You can stay for 90 days without a visa
Permanent residence: Owning property is not a qualification but individuals may apply to the Minister of National Security who has the power to grant residence to any person he thinks fit. 90-day visas are said to be easily renewable.
More info: www.immigration.gov.tt
Money: Trinidad & Tobago $
Golf: There are nine courses.

Trinidad
Trinidad is a large, busy and populous island in the southern Caribbean, with easy access from Europe and the USA. It is developed (and part industrial), English-speaking, a cultural leader in the region with an extraordinary racial mix.

There is not much traditional beach-based tourism but there is an excellent range of restaurants and cuisine, superb natural life, the finest bird-watching in the Caribbean by far, magnificent rainforest, interesting city life, art, music and carnival, the biggest in the Caribbean.

Tobago
Tiny Tobago – a low key, relatively undeveloped and friendly island with superb natural life above and below the waterline, is a late

developer by Caribbean tourism standards and still quite unspoiled.

There are very pretty beaches, remote coves forested down to the shore; a few nice hotels, villa resorts and good restaurants.

Some of the best scuba diving in the Caribbean is to be found here. Other water sports include windsurfing and game fishing; on land magnificent nature and birdlife, turtle-watching, good golf and hiking.

There are two distinct halves to Tobago. The western end, with its stretches of coral sand beaches, has the bulk of the tourism, with sports, hotels and restaurants.

As you head east, beyond the main town of Scarborough the land crumples and rises into hills and mountains, with incredibly lush greenery.

Inland there are caymans (a species of alligator), iguanas, opossum or manicous and armadillos, called tattoos. Turtles nest on the beaches. The scuba diving is among the finest in the Caribbean.

More info
www.gotrinidadandtobago.com
www.tdc.co.tt
www.definitivecaribbean.com
www.newsday.co.tt
www.trinidadexpress.com
http://guardian.co.tt

www.tobagotoday.com
www.simplytobago.com
www.visittobago.gov.tt
www.thetobagonews.com

Property and taxes

After enormous price increases
from 1991 to 2006, Trinidad and
Tobago's property market suddenly
cooled and has been falling for the
past two years, according to the
Global Property Guide
[www.globalpropertyguide.com].
Quoting the Central Bank of
Trinidad and Tobago (CBTT), it
says that in 2008 the median house
price dropped by nine per cent to
about $164,474 from a year earlier.

In Trinidad foreigners can buy
up to one acre for residential
purposes but in Tobago must
obtain a licence to acquire land.

Residents are taxed on worldwide
income. There is no capital gains tax
except on properties sold within one
year of acquisition. There is no
inheritance tax but controversially

the Government is proposing to
introduce a new property tax
regime based on the market values.

Estate agents

www.sabrinacasas.com
century21cycb.com
www.remax-caribbeanislands.com
www.tuckerrealestate.com
www.mondinion.com
www.seajadeinvestments.com
www.mwms.de/residential.htm
www.eqlrealestate.com/

Turks & Caicos Isles

FACTFILE

Capital: Cockburn Town, Grand Turk
Population: 14,000 **Area:** 308sq km
Language: English
Getting in: Visa not required. A 30-day temporary residence permit can be extended
for a further 30 days. A residence permits
entitles the holder to reside in the islands
for one year (cost $1,000).
The retirement category permit requires one
of the following:
1. An investment of not less than $500,000
in a home, business or approved enterprise
in Providenciales.
2. An investment of not less than $125,000
in a home, business or approved enterprise
on Grand Turk, Salt Cay, South Middle or
North Caicos.
3. An investment of $50,000 in an autho-
rised investment on Grand Turk, Salt
Cay, South Middle or North Caicos.
Money: US$
Golf: The 18-hold Provo Golf & Country
Club and a par 3 course on Grand Turk.

There are two groups of islands
and cays (five main islands in
all) at the south-eastern corner
of the Bahamas. Easily accessed
from the USA and UK this is a
British Overseas Territory
(known familiarly as TCI).

English-speaking, with
extensive tourism, quite
American in style, many mid-
size hotels and condominiums,

some small and smart hotels on
remote islands with an increasing
numbers of villas and some cruise
ships. The islands have superb
sand, vivid blue sea and excellent
scuba diving.

Providenciales is the most
developed of the islands in the
west. It has the most hotels and
condominiums. North and
Grand Caicos have some small
development. East Caicos is
undeveloped. Other smaller
islands with habitation are Parrot
Cay and Pine Cay, each of which
has a smart hotel.

The two Turk Islands lie 20
miles to the east. Grand Turk, the
capital of TCI, has a strong local
community and cruise tourism.
Salt Cay is very small and
undeveloped.

More info

www.turksandcaicostourism.com
www.definitivecaribbean.com
www.turksandcaicos.tc
www.geographia.com/turks-caicos
http://turksandcaicos-guide.info

Property and taxes

There is no restriction on
property ownership, no income
tax, inheritance tax, capital gains
tax or annual property tax.

Estate agents

www.coldwellbankertci.com

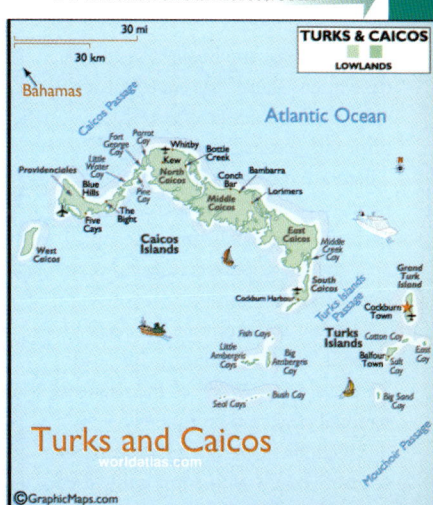

Turks and Caicos

www.gracebayrealty.com
www.hortonrealty.tc
www.islandvillatci.com
www.marketplacevillas.com
www.tcvillas.com
www.tcsafari.tc

USA Virgin Islands

FACTFILE

Capital: Charlotte Amalie (St Thomas)
Population: 110,000 Area: 347.1sq km
Language: English (official). Spanish, Creole and some French are also spoken.
Getting in: No visa required for stays of less than 90 days but you must have a return or onward ticket and a machine-readable passport.
Permanent residence: Entry requirements are the same as for the USA.
Money: US$
Golf: Three 18-hole courses, one nine-hole. No golf on St John.

There are three mid-size islands (and 70 small ones) in the Virgin Islands archipelago, each with a very different character; easy access from the USA, harder from Europe. A territory of the United States, it is very American in style, English-speaking, with some Spanish. There is extensive tourism, generally excellent beaches, cruise ship traffic and good service.

St Thomas, the busiest and most developed island, has excellent air services, is an active cruise ship port with extensive shopping. There are many resort hotels, a handful of small, independent places to stay, villas, self-catering apartments, good restaurants, very lively nightlife and golf.

St John, a 20-minute ferry ride from St Thomas, is far quieter and less developed. Much of the island is national park and completely untouched. There is a small number of resort hotels with some mid-price properties. There are some nice restaurants in Cruz Bay, good bars, sailing and nice remote beaches.

Less built up, St Croix is usually accessed direct by air (independently of St Thomas, though there is a ferry link). There is considerable cruise ship business, casinos (one of just a few islands that have them), resort hotels and several inns, visible history in the towns and plantations and golf.

More info
www.caribbean.co.uk/usvirginislands
www.usvi.net
http://ltg.gov.vi
www.usvitourism.vi
www.usviguide.com
www.vinow.com
www.here.vi/islands

Property and taxes
Foreigners can freely buy property. The market showed strong increases from 1997 to 2007. In 2008, the average home price in St John was $1.5 million while the average condominium unit was $634,923.

Property taxes are 1.25 per cent

of the property's assessed value, generally 60 per cent of the property's fair market value. Capital gains taxes are imposed at a maximum rate of 15 per cent for properties held for over a year.

There is no inheritance tax.

Estate agents
www.chrishanley.com
www.coldwellbankervi.com
www.davidjones.vi
www.americanparadise.com
http://listingsus.com/US-Virgin-Islands

The land of fire and ice offers the best of all worlds

Why Argentina?

Warm, hospitable people, low cost of living and cheap property, fine wines and wonderful food, breathtaking scenery ranging from forests and deserts to icebergs and glaciers in the Andes, vast fertile plains in the Pampas, 50 country parks, wine producing regions, world class ski resorts, excellent golf courses.

Argentina's cosmopolitan cities offer diverse culture, fashionable shopping in elegant boulevards with stylish restaurants and old-time cafes.

In the regions people throng to carnivals, concerts and festivals of all kinds. There are 500 museums. Argentina's gift to the world? The tango.

Is it safe?

Street crime is fairly common in major cities. The most frequent crimes involve distraction theft, bag snatching and armed robberies in the street, in taxis and in restaurants.

How much tax will I pay?

Foreigners on permanent visas are considered residents as far as tax is concerned and pay tax on their worldwide income. Rates range from 9-35 per cent.

There is no capital gains tax. Inheritance tax is three per cent and there is a property transfer tax of 1.5 per cent of the property value on property owned by individuals whether residents or not.

Stamp tax in Buenos Aires is 1.25 per cent for both the buyer and seller and varies in the various provinces. This tax is waived for a first property purchase. There is also an annual "asset tax" on property of one per cent of the value.

Is property a good investment?

After the 2001/2002 economic crisis, values dropped by 30-40 per cent but recovered fairly quickly. Following the financial crisis mortgages fell into disuse but have gradually become available. Property values have increased at an average of over 10 per cent a year for several years – a trend that is expected to continue.

There are substantial differences to the buying process in other countries. Transactions are 100 per cent in cash, paid in US$. However, the purchase price stated in the deed is rarely the actual purchasing price as sellers try to avoid paying tax on the full amount.

Estate agents are unregulated which makes property purchase somewhat of a minefield although protection is provided since purchases go through a special attorney called an escribano publico whose role is to check that the seller is registered as the owner, all taxes and duties have been paid, there is no lien on the property and that there are no existing mortgages.

He prepares the boleto (binding pre-contract) and the deed and, unlike a realtor, he is fully responsible for his advice and actions.

Where's best to live?

Many foreign residents would not consider living outside Buenos Aires, the cultural Mecca of Latin America, with a wide choice of theatres, cinemas, museums, shows, exhibitions and plenty of joie de vivre.

In the capital the popular areas for foreigners include the **Barrio Norte, Palermo** and **Belgrano** and **Recoleta** where you can buy a two-bedroom apartment for $40,000. Around the city there are extensive developments of gated communities with golf and country clubs. Provinces such as **Santa Cruz, Rio Negro, Neuquen, Santa Fe, Mendoza** and **Cordoba** have attracted foreign buyers and retirees.

Mendoza, the wine capital of South America and an important commercial, industrial and cultural centre, has wonderful restaurants and shopping centres, and wide, tree-lined streets and squares.

The centre of tourism, Mendoza faces the Andean mountain range and Mount Aconcagua – the highest peak in the American continent.

Cordoba, founded in 1573, today presents a modern face to the tourists who throng there and is also a business and tourist centre, famed too for shopping, cultural and recreational activities.

Bariloche on the shores of the Nahuel Huapi lake in the province of Río Negro is surrounded by mountains, lakes, woods and glaciers and is a perfect playground for outdoor activities and winter sports.

Salta, with its white colonial buildings and red tiled roofs, 16km from San Rafael, is near shopping, schools, hotels, restaurants, golf and a riding school.

Mansion near Buenos Aires
Renovated mansion in approx 1,000 acres of parkland, 98km fom Buenos Aires, recently run as a hotel. 9 bedrooms 7 bathrooms, lounge, huge dining area in separate building, pool, small spa, 2 staff houses, 4 barns, various other buildings.Possible uses: farm/ranch venture, rural resort, and gentleman-style estate.
Price: $3.2 million
More info: Peer Voss Tel (Germany) 040 - 457 121,
Email: pvoss@pvoss.de

Eldorado Misiones
New house, 2 bedrooms, one bathroom, gallery. Ceramic floors.
Price: $36,000
More info:www.cimeldorado.com.ar +54 (03751) 425705
Email: crisinmob@yahoo.com.ar

FACTFILE

Capital: Buenos Aires
Population: 39.9 million **Area:** 2.7 sq km
Language: Spanish. English in main cities.
Climate: Temperate except for a small tropical area in the NE and a sub-tropical region in the north. Sub-Antarctic in S. Patagonia, mild/humid in the Pampas plains.
Time difference: GMT -3 hours.
Entry requirements: No visa required for stays of up to 90 days.
Retirement/residence visa
Assets of $16,000 and a minimum monthly income equivalent to $800.
[See: The rules for getting in]
Electricity: 220V, AC 50 Hz.
Money: Peso. ATMs are available in the larger towns and cities. Credit/debit cards

andtraveller's cheques are accepted in hotels, larger restaurants and stores in major towns and cities.

Public holidays 2010

Jan 1	New Year's Day
March 24	Truth and Justice Day
April 2	Good Friday
April 2	Veterans' Day (Malvinas)
May 1	Labour Day
May 25	National Day
June 14	National Flag Day
July 9	Independence Day
Aug 17	Anniv. death of Gen San Martín
Oct 12	Columbus Day
Dec 8	Immaculate Conception Day
Dec 25	Christmas Day

Opening hours
Banks: 10am-3pm Mon-Fri
Offices: 9am-12pm, 2pm-7pm
Shops: 9am-8pm
Water: Considered safe in main cities.
Tipping: 10 per cent in bars and restaurants. Doormen, porters and cinema/theatre ushers are generally tipped.
Medical/Healthcare: No immunisations are compulsory but vaccinations for Hepatitis A and Typhoid are recommended. Malaria is confined to rural areas along the borders with Bolivia and Paraguay.
Pets: A health certificate must be provided declaring that the animal was examined

CONTACT DIRECTORY

Embassies/Government
Argentine Embassy in UK
www.argentine-embassy-uk.org
British Embassy in Argentina
http://ukinargentina.fco.gov.uk
Argentina Migration Department
www.migraciones.gov.ar

Travel & Health Advice
Foreign Office www.fco.gov.uk/travel
www.nhs.uk/Healthcareabroad
www.masta.org

About Argentina
www.buenosaires.gov.ar
www.cia.gov/library/publications/the-world-factbook/print/ar.html
www.bue.gov.ar
www.frommers.com
http://exposebuenosaires.com
www.welcomeargentina.com

General & Expat
www.expatfocus.com
www.britishexpat.com
www.transitionsabroad.com
www.expatinterviews.com

English Language Media
Buenos Aires Herald
www.buenosairesherald.com
Argentina's only English-language daily .

Property
www.andeslandproperties.com
www.gatewaytosouthamerica.com
www.northside.com
www.patagonias.net
www.argentinahomes.com

Travel & Tourism
www.turismo.gov.ar
www.argentina.ar
www.allaboutar.com
Latin American Travel Association
www.lata.org/
www.vivatravelguides.com
Hotel and tourism directory
www.argentinacontact.com
www.easybuenosairescity.com
www.bue.gov.ar
www.visitbue.com
www.cordoba.gov.ar

Getting There
Airlines flying to Argentina arrive mainly at Ezeiza International Airport, 37km from Buenos Aires.
British Airways: www.british-airways.com
Aerolíneas Argentinas:
www.aerolineas.com.ar
Air France: www.airfrance.com
Emirates: www.ekgroup.com
Lufthansa: www.lufthansa.com
KLM: www.klm.com
Return fare range from UK: $800-1120

Getting Around
Air: Argentina is a very large country – 2,300 miles from top to bottom – which makes flying the favoured form of internal travel over long distances. Aerolineas Argentinas [www.aerolineas. com.ar] has the largest network. The main airport for domestic flights is Jorge Newbery.
LAN [www.lan.com] has daily flights from Buenos Aires to the regions as well as to neighbouring countries.
A 'Visit Argentina' or 'Discover Argentina'

package offers reduced internal travel.
Train: Many longhaul services have been discontinued and trains are mostly crowded and uncomfortable. Coche de cama is the best and most comfortable of the four classes available. Avoid 'tourist' class.
Bus: Local buses are cheap and reasonably comfortable. Short-distance buses (Omnibus) run in urban areas or connect several districts. Mini-buses provide inter-urban services. Overnight long-distance buses are cheap and comfortable and, in coche cama (first class) you get a fully reclining seat.
Taxis: In towns and cities you can find taxis on every street corner or flag them down in the street. Otherwise there are remises , or minicab radio taxis, that you must book by phone or at their central booking booth. Urban taxis have meters. Shared taxis, colectivos, also run on fixed routes.
Driving: Road conditions are OK throughout Argentina and major towns and cities are well connected by main highways, but drivers are aggressive, especially in the capital.
Car hire is readily available but can be expensive as rental companies often charge by the km. A UK driving licence is sufficient but some car hire companies may ask for an international licence.
Driving is on the right.

Latin America's 'secret' haven for retirees

Why Bolivia?

With its breathtaking vistas, unblemished swathes of Amazon rainforest and isolated location high in the Andes, Bolivia possesses a physical beauty that still manages to go largely unnoticed.

Tucked in the middle of South America, historians, archaeologists, naturalists and adventure travellers have long been drawn by its riches – atmospheric cities, pristine forests, sparkling rivers and streams and Native American culture.

But most expats (and mainstream tourists, for that matter) have overlooked its rugged terrain for the more familiar Latin landscapes of Mexico, Costa Rica and Panama. The reasons are simple: There are no direct flights from Europe and only two a day from North America, meaning relatively few Brits and Americans pop in to enjoy its charms and it's not the sort of place you stumble upon on your way to somewhere.

Bolivia has a relatively small population – 8.9 million in a country twice the size of France – leaving plenty of room for wildlife, notably llamas, which number three million. And although the poorest nation in South America, it's also one of the richest in terms of affordable real estate, a low cost of living, natural beauty, friendly people and a range of climates to suit almost every taste.

Bolivia has something for everyone except beaches. This landlocked country's soaring peaks, steamy jungles, wildlife-rich grasslands, colonial cities and ancient civilizations attracting 300,000 foreign visitors a year.

Cost of living

You can stay in a clean, comfortable hotel in the city centre for $16 a night. A typical restaurant meal for two costs less than $12. A pint in a local pub? 60c. The cost of a taxi back to your place after having one too many: 30c. Groceries are up to 70 per cent cheaper than back home. A routine trip to a good English-speaking doctor will set you back no more than $25. You can see first-run American movies for only $3. Need domestic help? A housekeeper can be hired for under $80 a month.

The climate is another plus. Temperatures are in the 18-28°C range with the average being in the mid-20s. Even the most sweltering days are usually

ABOUT THE WRITER: Shannon Roxborough, an American, is a widely-published writer and international consultant on international lifestyles. For 20-plus years he has advised on foreign relocation and managing personal, financial and business affairs . He is editor and publisher of BorderlessLiving.com, an online magazine for global lifestyles.

FACTFILE

Capital: La Paz   **Population**: 9.1 million
Area: 1.08million sq km   **Language**:
Spanish, Quechua, Aymara, Guarani
Climate: Vary widely from tropical in the
lowlands to polar in the highest parts of the
Andes. Temperatures depend primarily on
elevation and show little seasonal variation.
Northern lowland areas have a tropical wet
climate with year-round high temperatures,
high humidity, and heavy rainfall. La Paz is
usually bright and sunny all year round with
showers most afternoons.
Time difference: GMT -4 hours
Entry requirements: A visa is not required
for stays of up to 30 days.
Retirement/residence visa
You need to own property or show you have
adequate funds.
[See: The rules for getting in]

Electricity: 220V/50Hz (La Paz 110 & 220V)
Money: Boliviano (BOB) = 100 centavos.
ATMs are available in larger towns and
cities. Credit/debit cards are accepted in
bigger hotels, restaurants and shops. US$
travellers cheques are best.
Public holidays 2010
Jan 1   New Year's Day
Feb 16   Carnival
Apr 2   Good Friday
May 1   Labour Day
Jun 3   Corpus Christi
Aug 6   Independence Day
Nov 1   All Saints' Day
Dec 25   Christmas Day
Opening hours
Banks: 8.30am-6pm Mon-Fri
Offices: 8.30am-6pm Mon-Fri
Shops: 9am-12.30pm, 2.30pm-6.30/8pm

Water: Drink bottled water and avoid ice
cubes.
Tipping: Restaurant and hotel staff expect
10 per cent in addition to the service charge
added to bills. Taxi drivers don't expect a
tip.
Medical/Healthcare: Bolivia hadthe worst
outbreak of dengue fever, the mosquito-
transmitted infection, for 20 years in 2009.
Travellers entering the country from areas
affected by yellow fever are required to hold
a certificate of immunisation. Malaria
affects rural areas below 2,500m. Cholera
is endemic around La Paz.
Pets: You need a letter from your vet
(translated into Spanish) stating your pet is
in good health, has no contagious diseases
and that vaccinations are all up to date.

BOLIVIA CONTACT DIRECTORY

About Bolivia
www.boliviaweb.com
www.travel-bolivia.com
http://bolivia.rica24.com
www.sharingbolivia.com
www.boliviaweb.com/
www.realestateinbolivia.com
www.boliviabella.com
www.mcentellas.com

English Language Media
www.boliviatimes.com

Property
www.boliviaproperty.com
www.realestateinbolivia.com/working-
bolivia.html
www.4321.co.il/property/bolivia
www.latinlistings.com/en/Bolivia

Travel & Tourism
www.enjoybolivia.com/
www.boliviacontact.com

Getting There
There are no direct flights from Europe and
only two a day from the USA. Flights from
Europe are usually via Buenos Aires, Rio or
São Paulo. Carriers are:
United Airlineswww.unitedairlines.co.uk
Iberia www.iberia.com
Continental Airlineswww.continental.com/uk
Lufthansa www.lufthansa.com
KLM www.klm.com

Getting Around
By Air: Regularly scheduled air service is
available between the major airports: La
Paz, Cochabamba and Santa Cruz. Domestic
flights are reasonably priced.
The national airline is Lloyd Aéreo
Bolivian.www.labairlines.co.uk
Other carriers are:
www.aerosur.com/
which connects most major cities.
Aerocon www.aerocon.bo/
Flies from Trinidad to Cobija, Guayaramerin,
Riberalta and Santa Ana (La Paz region La

Paz, Cochabamba and Santa Cruz.
Amaszonaswww.amaszonas.com
Flies to Rurrenabaque, Trinidad,
Guayaramerin, Riberalta, Cobija, San Borja,
Cochabamba and Santa Cruz.
GOL www.voegol.co
Train: There are two major train lines: The
Red Occidental serves the western cities of
Oruro, La Paz, Cochabamba, Sucre and
Potosi. The Red Oriental serves the eastern
cities of Santa Cruz, Quijarro and Yacuiba.
From Santa Cruz there also is a train to
Yacuiba on the Argentine border.
Trains are cheap and comfortable but
delays are common. Book in advance.
Bus: In Bolivia long-distance buses are
called flotas, then there are buses, micros
and minibuses as well as fixed route taxi
trufi and trufibus. Long-distance bus travel
is very cheap and relatively comfortable.
Beware of travelling on the "World's Most
Dangerous Road" from La Paz to Yungas.
Apart from the dangers, it takes 20 hours.
Taxis: Very cheap but agree a price first. On
longer trips shared taxis are common.
Driving: Traffic in La Paz is chaotic and
difficult to negotiate if you don't know your
way around. Driving outside is worse. Less
than five per cent of Bolivia's roads are
paved. Many winding stretches of road
through mountain areas are unlit and
without guardrails or traffic signs.
Pedestrians, cyclists and moped riders all
appear to have a death wish and present a
constant hazard to car drivers.
Car hire is available but expensive as rental
companies often charge by the mile/km.
Driving is on the right.

tempered by cooling breezes. Best of all, perhaps, is Bolivia's status as a constitutional democracy that respects individual rights and freedoms.

Is Bolivian property a good investment?
Good looks and personality are not all Bolivia has going for it. Real estate options provide something for almost every taste and budget. And its diverse terrain extends to its housing stock – providing opportunities for city, suburban and country living with prices that are half those of comparable dwellings in neighbouring Argentina or Chile.

If your idea of paradise is a flat in a vibrant old-world colonial town, a house in a quiet middle-class neighbourhood or a cottage in slow-paced rural development where hunting, gathering and fishing are a way of life, this South American Andean nation may have your name on it.

Whichever you choose, you'll take advantage of cheap property, with three-bedroom houses costingas little as $45,000 and apartments at half that amount. Currently, a two-story four-bedroom detached house with large front yard and rear gardens in La Paz's Achumani district can be rented for $250 a month.

Is it safe?
Bolivia enjoys a low crime rate, with violent crime being virtually unknown and theft rare.

How much tax will I pay?
Real estate taxes in Bolivia are very affordable. The highest rate is 0.75 per cent of the property's assessed value. The smaller the property, the lower the rate. There is no tax on capital gains, stock market transactions and other intermittent dividends but there is inheritance tax.

THE RULES FOR GETTING IN
Permanent residence is available for foreigners and their dependents who own property or invest and to retirees and their families showing adequate means of support from whatever source. Residence visas must be renewed every two years. Permanent residents are eligible for naturalisation after five years.

Bolivia has a programme under which foreign "donors" can obtain citizenship via a donation of $10,000-$25,000, the larger sum covering the main applicant, spouse and dependent children under 18.

Where's best to live?
La Paz: Altitude sickness will almost certainly greet you in the thin air of the world's loftiest capital. This two-mile-high enclave is Bolivia's largest city (1.5 million), its seat of government and home to a thriving community of expatriates.

Santa Cruz: This dusty boomtown in eastern Bolivia still feels more like a small-town with its low-rise buildings and relaxed tropical atmosphere but it is Bolivia's business centre and most affluent city. Here, American and British expats, Argentine businessmen, trendy cruceños (Santa Cruz locals), Japanese and Cuban immigrants, German and Russian Mennonites, Brazilian labourers and descendants of formers Nazis all live in an exotic melting pot.

Sucre: Set in a valley surrounded by low mountains, genteel Sucre is arguably Bolivia's most picturesque city and a place of beautiful colonial architecture.

Cochabamba: Situated in the foothills of the Andes, a fertile landscape of fields and low hills, its avenues lined with restaurants and bars jam-packed with students and young professionals. Despite its exuberance and popularity, Cochabamba remains an affordable place to live.

20-bedroom hotel
Not far from city of Santa Cruz, this 20-bed hotel is on offer at $450,000. It is the only 3-star hotel within 320km. It has tropical gardens and a swimming pool.
More info: www.4321.co.il/

Country house with pool
Only 30km from the city of Santa Cruz on a 7.5 acre site with a pool, this country house, built 5 years ago has a price tag of $250,000. It has 3 bedrooms, 2 bathrooms, office and laundry.
More info: www.4321.co.il/property/Bolivia_property.asp

A tropical paradise and the world's most famous beach

Why Brazil?

Brazilians believe they live in the greatest and most beautiful country in the world. Most of the nine million tourists who visit every year and the tens of thousands of overseas retirees and property buyers probably agree with them.

Brazil has names to conjure with: Ipanema, Copacabana, Joaquina. Are they girls or are they places. Doesn't matter – they're bound to be beautiful.

To match this beauty Brazil has an incredible joie de vivre and a cocktail of attractions: 6,400km of beaches for a start – more than California, Florida, Blackpool and Brighton put together. It has the amazing Amazon and the Amazonia National Park, covering seven of Brazil's 27 states .

There's the Iguassu Falls, with 275 cataracts, one of the seven natural Wonders of the World and the Pantanal, one of the world's great wildlife reserves.

But Brazil does have a dark side: the vast gulf between the haves and the have-nots, those who

survive in threadbare shantytown homes clinging to hillsides in Rio, Sao Paulo and elsewhere. For this reason, crime is a problem.

Foreign property buyers and retirees are moving here in large numbers and buying all over the country from Fortaleza in the north-east to Porto Alegre in the south.

Is it safe?

Brazil has a very high crime rate and robberies involving tourists are common, even during the day. Rural and resort areas are safer than the big cities.

How much tax will I pay?

Tax is charged on worldwide income for residents of Brazil at 15 per cent. Capital gains are also taxed at 15 per cent but are tax-exempt if gains are from the sale

PROPERTY

House on the beach
Renovated 3-bedroom house (2 en suite) 50m from beach in a quiet part of the fishing village of Taiba in the north east Brazilian state of Ceara and 40 miles from the lively city of Fortaleza.

Large kitchen, living and dining area, all opening onto a wide veranda. Large private garden with room for a pool and off street undercover parking for 3 cars. Taiba has plenty of shops and restaurants to cater for the various nationalities that now live in the area.
Price: $82,500
More info:
www.homesgofast.com

of an individual property, provided you have not sold another property in the previous five years and the total value of the sale does not exceed $210,000. Brazil has no inheritance or wealth taxes.

Is Brazilian property a good investment?

By international standards, property is dirt cheap. You can buy a dog kennel of a place in resorts in the sun and beach destinations in the northeast for as little a $32,000. Places such as Angra dos Reis, Buzios and Ilha Grande are up-and-coming. Even so a decent beachfront property can be had for $80,000.

Ipanema and Leblon are pretty exclusive resorts but $210,000 will get you a spacious three-bedroom apartment in a concierge building on the beach.

However, while property is still relatively cheap, the cost of living – presently about 20 per cent less than the UK – is rising. City life particularly is becoming increasingly expensive with Mercer Consulting listing both Rio and São Paulo among the 35 cities with the highest cost of living in the world for foreigners in 2008. São Paulo occupies the 25th position (62nd in 2007) and Rio 31st (64th in 2007).

Cars, electronics and all imported goods are expensive and residents complain that the cost of utilities has risen rapidly. Even food is starting to get expensive. Car hire is more expensive than Spain and while beer is about the same, wine is very expensive.

Where's best to live?

The popular tourist resorts in the northeast are the areas of most international attention for the obvious reasons: the near perfect climate and the beaches. But it doesn't suit everyone. If you thought sex-on-the-beach was a cocktail served up in tacky bars in Spain, you'll see the real thing here.

But travel down the coast for a couple of hours to somewhere like Joao Pessoa and you'll find somewhere far more sedate. The centre of this city is a large lagoon surrounded by shops and restaurants.

Natal, 'The city of the Sun' also has a lot to recommend it. Stylish and safe and only seven or eight hours from Europe, it is said to have the second highest pure air quality in the world.

Here, a two-bedroom apartment at the 5-star Natal Ocean Club will set you back about $480,000, but you get a lot for your money: direct access to a private beach, gourmet dining, fitness centre, water sports facilities, golf and a marina.

If your budget doesn't stretch that far, the Elegance Natal Golf Resort, a half-hour drive from the city centre and 15 minutes from the new airport, is a beachfront site on 400 acres and with Natal's first golf course.

The first phase – called Elegance Natal Miltonia – is part of a 2,000 home low-rise development among

Trancoso
Large farmhouse with 3 bedrooms, 2 suites and 2 bathrooms (total of 5 bedrooms and 4 bathrooms). Large kitchen, living room and dining rooms, laundry and storage room. Floors are made with dark green androsia tiles. Price: $200,000
More info: www.worldwide-realestate.com/
www.experience-international.com

Praia Bonita, Brazil
Beachside 1 and 2 bed apartments and duplexes adjacent to a fresh water lagoon and only 2 minutes from the popular destination of Natal. Properties start from $72,000.
More info: AB Property Marketing Ltd
www.experience-international.com
Tel: 44 (0)207 321

FACTFILE

Capital: Brasilia

Population: 186 million

Area: 8.5m sq km. **Language:** Portuguese (with various regional dialects). Spanish, English, Italian, French and German are also commonly spoken in cities.

Climate: Tropical or subtropical climate, except in the temperate south, especially in the mountains, where it can get very cold. The rainy season is in the summer months, though in the northeast there are desert areas that suffer from regular drought.

In winter, June to August, temperatures in the south range between 13°C and 18°C. In the summer, December to February, temperatures in the south are in the upper 30°Cs, sometimes higher, with high humidity. Spring and autumn have temperatures of around 25°C. In the northern Amazonian region, humidity is high with average temperatures of 27°C.

Time difference: Mostly GMT -3 hours but there are four time zones.

Entry requirements: A visa is not required for stays of up to 90 days.

Retirement/residence visa: You require proof of income of at least $2,000 a month and an additional $1,000 per dependent. [See: The rules for getting in]

Electricity: Generally 110/220 V/60Hz but Brazil has a variety of electrical voltages, sometimes within the same city. Plugs are mainly of the two-pin type.

Money: Real (pronounced rey-al, plural rey-eyes). 100 centavos to the real. There is an extensive network of ATMs. Credit/debit cards are accepted at most shops, hotels and restaurants. Travellers cheques are less acceptable and you may be charged a hefty commission when you cash them.

Public holidays 2010

Jan 1	New Year's Day	June 3	Corpus Christi
Jan 20*	Founding of Rio	Sep 7	Independence Day
Jan 25*	Founding São Paulo	Oct 12	Lady Aparecida Day
Feb 12-17	Carnival	Nov 2	All Souls' Day
Apr 2	Good Friday	Nov 15	Republic Day
Apr 13	Easter Day	Dec 24	Christmas Eve
Apr 21	Tiradentes	Dec 25	Christmas Day
May 1	Labour Day	Dec 31	New Year's Eve

*Regional

Opening hours

Banks: 10am-4pm Mon-Fri

Offices: 8/9am-6pm Mon-Fri

Shops: 8am-7pm/9pm

Major shopping centres 10am-10pm

Water: Tap water is considered safe for drinking in cities and major towns. Elsewhere drink bottled.

Tipping: 10 per cent added to most restaurant bills. Taxi drivers do not expect a tip.

Medical/Healthcare Risks are dengue fever in urban areas and malaria and yellow fever in the Amazon and central western regions. Rabies and cholera are not uncommon. Typhoid vaccinations are recommended, and polio vaccination certificates are required for children under six. Brazil has a first class medical infrastructure but healthcare varies in quality in remote areas.

Pets: Dogs or cats must have a certificate legalised by the Brazilian Consulate where the certificate was issued.

palm trees, where two bedroom apartments with sea views are available from $92,000. Owners will have use of all facilities which include eight hotels, an equestrian centre, tennis courts and beach clubs.

This is only an eight-hour direct flight from the UK with Thomson.

Two hours from Rio de Janeiro and half an hour from trendy Buzios, **Arraial do Cabo** is an oceanfront city with stunning beaches, great restaurants and facilities. A beachfront house can be had for about $160,000, one needing refurbishing for half that.

Foreign retirees tend to favour the coastal resorts such as **Fortaleza**, the state capital of Ceara in the northeast, or **Florianopolis**, further south on the coast is also hugely popular – and safer. Smaller coastal areas of Bahia are also attractive to overseas buyers, places like **Praia do Forte, Porto Seguro** and **Itacimirim**.

Brazil's cities are the choice of many retirees: Rio, chaotic, brash and sexy on the one hand; sophisticated and cultured on the other with Brazil's leading universities, museums and galleries … and, of course, the famous carnival.

The second choice for city-loving foreigners is usually the vast sprawling city of **São Paulo**, said to be the New York of South America. In both cities most expatriates live in gated communities with 24-hour security.

It gets cheaper when you move to the provincial areas of the big cities. Smaller towns popular with expatriates include **Alphaville** and **Tambore**, around 20km outside Sao Paulo.

Embassies/Government
Brazil Embassy and Tourist Office
www.brazil.org.uk
Consulate General
www.consbraslondres.com
British Embassy in Brazil
http://ukinbrazil.fco.gov.uk/pt

Travel & Health Advice
Foreign Office travel advice
www.fco.gov.uk/travel
www.nhs.uk/Healthcareabroad
www.masta.org

About Brazil
www.brasil.gov.br/ingles
www.brazilmax.com
http://brazilplaces.com
www.deltatranslator.com/brazil
www.gringoes.com/articles
www.brazzil.com/articles
www.v-brazil.com

General & Expat
www.expatfocus.com
www.britishexpat.com
www.transitionsabroad.com

English Language Media
www.einnews.com/brazil
online news
Brazil Herald
The Rio Visitor
Both available in Rio

Property
www.planetaimovel.com
www.colliers.com
www.beachfront.brazil.net
www.propertyfrontiers.com
www.brazilianpropertyshop.com
www.brazilbahiaproperty.com
www.judicearaujo.com.br
http://brazil.propertyhaven.com
www.ireypg.com
www.investmentsonthebeach.com
www.alexanderrichards.co.uk
www.propertyinbrasil.com
www.offplanworld.tv
www.paraibaproperty.co.uk
www.brazilpropertycentre.co.uk
www.nuwireinvestor.com
www.brazil-real-estate.co.uk
For free 'e-books' on Brazil property
purchase
www.essentialww.com/
Very useful website on property purchase
procedures

Travel & Tourism
www.brazil.org.uk
www.braziltour.com
www.justbrazil.org
www.virtually-brazil.com
www.travel-brazil.info/
www.paradisepath.com/brazil
http://braziltravelnews.com
Latin American Travel Association
www.lata.org/
www.vivatravelguides.com
www.brazil-travel-guide.com
www.contactchile.cl

Getting There
British Airways (Direct flights)
www.britishairways.com
Thomson flies to Natal in the north of Brazil
www.thomson.co.uk
TAM (Direct flights)www.tam.com.br
www.dialaflight.com
Air Portugal www.flytap.com/UK
Iberia www.iberia.com/gb
KLM www.klm.com
Air France www.airfrance.co.uk
Lufthansa www.lufthansa.com
Return fare range from UK: £450-600+
Most international flights arrive at São
Paulo, Rio de Janeiro, Recife or Salvador.

Getting Around
Air: The size of Brazil makes internal flights
the best way of getting around although
flights are relatively expensive. São Paulo
and Rio de Janeiro are the main hubs.
If you're going to Brazil and planning several
internal trips, perhaps to look at properties,
you should consider a Brazilian Airpass
which has to be bought outside of the
country by non-residents with a return air
ticket. The cost is about $400 for up to four
internal flights. The main operators are:
www.oceanair.com.br
www.flybrasil.com.br
www.voegol.com.br

Train: There's not much in the way of
railway services. The Curitiba to
Paranaguá service is a scenic 150km
route linking the capital of Paraná to the
coastal cities of Morretes and Paranaguá,
through Serra do Mar mountains. It takes
about three hours.
A steam train operates from São João del
Rei to Tiradentes.
There is no train service at all between
Rio de Janeiro and Sao Paulo.
More info:
www.antt.gov.br/destaques/TrensDePassa
geiros.asp.

Bus: Long-distance buses:
Brazil has a very good bus transport
system. Major cities linked by frequent
services and long-distance buses are
comfortable (buy the best tickets),
convenient and economical.
Brazil has two kinds of bus services: the
lotação is for public transport within a
municipality or small region. A bus that
connects several cities is called an ônibus
intermunicipal.
There are extensive bus services in all
the main centres, often with air-
conditioned express executive coaches
running at premium fares.
Rio and São Paulo have metros, local rail
lines and trolleybuses.

Taxi: Fares are inexpensive and metered
but passengers should insist that the
meter is turned on. Taxi drivers do not
expect a tip.

Driving: The standard of driving is poor
and accidents frequent. Avoid night-time
driving if possible, otherwise you will
quickly get used to some of the driving
curiosities. The driver ahead of you
flashing a left signal may mean he's
turning left but also means 'don't
overtake'. Conversely, if he wants to show
you that it is safe to pass he will flash the
right signal.
Flashing headlights from the incoming
cars may mean the driver is warning you
of danger ahead or a speed trap.
You can drive on your home licence or an
international driving licence, but the rules
say you must have this translated into
Portuguese.
Car hire is readily available but can be
expensive as rental companies often
charge by the mile.
Driving is on the right.

From tropical Arica to fjords and glaciers, Chile is just spectacular!

Why Chile?

Chile is one of the world's most geographically diverse and beautiful countries. It stretches the distance from Norway to Nigeria and contains some of the most breathtaking scenery imaginable: from desert, lush valleys, volcanoes, the incomparable Patagonia, the Andes and Pacific Ocean.

The cost of living is 25-40 per cent lower than in the USA or Europe. There are excellent restaurants and world class wines.

Chile has a respected legal system and highly respected financial institutions backed by a competent, democratic government. The police are honest, unbribeable and widely respected.

Chile boasts a stable and growing economy without the boom and bust cycles of other countries in the region and one of the world's most open and investment friendly economies.

Is it safe?

Crime levels are lower than in any other South American country.

How much tax will I pay?

During the first three years of residence in Chile foreigners are subject to tax only on their Chilean-source income and thereafter on all income. Residents are defined as those who reside in Chile for more than six months in one calendar year, or for more than six months within two consecutive assessment years.

Capital gains on sales of personal property are exempt from taxation. Property Tax is levied on the valuation of property. The tax rate is 1.2 per cent of the valuation plus 0.025 per cent.

Is property a good investment?

Real estate is still excellent value and significantly cheaper than in Europe and the USA.

The capital offers some excellent investment opportunities. Rental returns on apartments range from 6-9 per cent.

Where's best to live?

The **Central Region** is home to Chile's best sporting facilities. You can play golf, football, rugby, tennis, go hiking in the mountains or rafting down the rivers. Mountaineering and climbing are popular pastimes and **Portillo** and **Valle Nevado**, two of South America's premier ski resorts, are just a short drive away.

Santiago, a bustling, pulsing city, is

ABOUT THE WRITER: A graduate of the University of Leeds Business School, Briton **Matt Ridgway** has lived and worked in Chile since 2003. With his Chilean partners he runs **Chile Investments** [www.chileinvestments.com] which offers consultancy services in all aspects of investment and property acquisition in Chile. A fluent Spanish speaker, Matt divides his time between the UNESCO World Heritage port city of Valparaiso and Santa Cruz.

home to almost one third of the population. It houses the country's best museums, theatres, bars and restaurants.

If you're not the big city type then just a one and a half hour drive away is **Valparaiso**, one of South America's most original and spectacular cities and declared a UNESCO World Heritage Site in 2003.

Here, new boutique hotels are springing up and some of Chile's best and most innovative restaurants are to be found in 'Valpo', as the city is commonly known. Old mansions are being converted into loft apartments and investment is pouring in.

Foreigners are also moving in and it's easy to understand why: The city is an incredible, multicolour jumble of Victorian mansions and 19th Century architecture with stunning views of the Pacific Ocean at almost every turn and the potential is obvious. It has a small town atmosphere but with excellent amenities.

A 15-minute drive up the coast is **Viña del Mar**, Valparaiso´s smarter, more grown up sister city and home to high class restaurants, bars, clubs, a huge casino and a large shopping mall. Viña is a modern, high rise seaside city that becomes packed during the summer holidays (January and February) but is relaxed and sleepy outside of those months.

Heading further north up the coast there are many small towns and villages. The first really desirable beach town north of Viña is **Maitencillo**, about an hour's drive away. In the summer many chefs and bar owners from Santiago move to the town and the place fills up. Outside of the summer months, the town is quiet, peaceful and spectacularly pretty.

A little further north are the elite towns of **Cachagua** and **Zapallar** where mansions overlooking the bay cost in excess of a million dollars. The beaches on this part of the coast are beautiful and the seafood incredible.

South of Valparaiso has traditionally seen less investment but this is rapidly changing. There are many small towns and fishing villages that are now receiving substantial investment and the price of raw land is considerably cheaper than to the north.

Go to the bottom of Chile and you think you're in Bavaria or Switzerland. You'll find popular resorts in breathtaking landscapes of towering forests, emerald green lakes, snowcapped mountains, fjords and lagoons, fast-flowing rivers, hot springs and icefields.

House on the ocean
House of 800sq near Pichilemu, 259km from Santiago, with 500m of ocean front, 150 hectares of eucalyptus trees and 60 hectares of pine trees. Caretaker's house of 120sq m.
Price: $1 million Ref: ZEA-P101005
More info: www.chile-real-estate.com
Email: alfredoromero@chile-real-estate.com

Santiago area
Living room, dining room, wooden floor, roof terrace, garden with swimming pool. 4 bedrooms, 3 bathrooms
Price: $260,896
Ref: 1156088
More info: www.engelvoelkers.com

FACTFILE

Capital: Santiago **Population:** 16.6m **Area:** 756,950sq km
Language: Spanish (Castellano in Chile). Other common languages are Mapudungun, German and English.
Climate: Mediterranean in parts, with hot, dry summers and mild, moist winters. Chile's odd shape – 4,200km long but only 160-320km wide – accounts for its odd weather: The mountainous east with a climate of snow and glaciers, the north is one of the world's driest regions, while the south is wet all year round with as much as 500cm of rain a year. Santiago's temperatures range from 14°C in June to 29°C in January.
Time difference: GMT -4 hours
Entry requirements: A visa is not required for stays of up to 90 days. This period may be extended only once.
Retirement/residence visa: Immigration is simple. You can only apply for legal residency after you have held temporary residency for a year. [See: The rules for getting in]
Electricity: 220V/50Hz. Outlets use three round pins in a line.
Money: Peso. ATMs are found everywhere except in small villages. Credit/debit cards and traveller's cheques are widely used and accepted in towns but cash is king in rural areas.

Public holidays 2010

Jan 1	New Year's Day	Aug 15	Assumption
Apr 2	Good Friday	Sept 11	Reconciliation Day
Apr 3	Holy Saturday	Sept 18	Independence Day
May 1	Labour Day	Sept 19	Army Day
May 21	Navy Day	Oct 12	Columbus Day
June 11	Corpus Christi	Nov 1	All Saints' Day
June 29	St Peter and St Paul	Dec 8	Immac Conception
Dec 25	Christmas Day		

Opening hours
Banks: 9am-2pm (Mon-Fri) Offices: 9am-7pm Shops: 10am-8pm
Water: The tap water is safe to drink in most parts of the country. Tipping:10 per cent in restaurants. Taxi drivers don't expect a tip.
Medical/Healthcare: No vaccines are required, but several are recommended. Outbreaks of hepatitis, typhoid, dengue fever and rabies occur from time to time. Good health facilities are available in Santiago and major cities but far less so in rural areas.
Pets: Must arrive with a certificate issued by a veterinarian and have been vaccinated against rabies 1-12 months before arriving.

CHILE CONTACT DIRECTORY

Embassies/Government
Chilean Embassy in UK
www.echileuk.co.uk
British Embassy in Chile
http://ukinperu.fco.gov.uk/en/

Travel & Health Advice
www.fco.gov.uk/travel
www.nhs.uk/Healthcareabroad
www.masta.org

About Chile
www.enjoy-chile.org
www.chile.cl/tpl/english
www.allsouthernchile.com
www.santiago.cl
www.chile.cl/tpl/english
Chilean Government (English)
www.chileangovernment.cl

General & Expat
www.expatfocus.com
www.britishexpat.com
www.pacificfive.co.uk

English Language Media
www.chilejournal.com
www.santiagotimes.cl
www.valparaisotimes.clcl

Property
www.allsouthernchile.com
http://realestatevalparaiso.com
chileinvestments.com
www.easier.com/ads
www.viviun.com/Real_Estate/Chile
www.nubricks.com
www.movewithusinternational.com

Travel & Tourism
Government Tourist Agency
(English option)
www.sernatur.cl/internacional/?lang=2
www.visitchile.cl/index2.html
www.gochile.cl
www.turismochile.cl/isla_de_pascua/en
www.chile-travel.com

Getting There
There are no direct flights to Chile from the UK. You need to go via Madrid or Brazil. International flights arrive at Santiago.
Among the carriers are:
www.iberia.com
www13.lanchile.com/english/cl
Flies from Madrid and Frankfurt

www.britishairways.com
www.airfrance.com
www.lufthansa.com

Getting Around
Air: There are frequent services between the main towns. LAN Express (www.lan.com) and Sky Airline (www.skyairline.cl) are the main carriers.
Train: The Chilean train system, in decline for a century, is gradually improving. There is a daily train between Santiago and Temuco in the south with air-conditioned berths. Santiago has an excellent Metro.
Bus: Santiago's transport system is fairly modern with buses, minibuses and shared taxibus services. Intercity buses are relatively cheap, comfortable and reliable.
Taxis: Should have meters but for long journeys, fares should be negotiated.
Driving: Major roads are generally in good condition but some secondary roads are poorly maintained. Fog can also be a hazard. You can drive on your UK licence although in theory an international licence is required. Santiago is confusing for drivers since traffic flows can change direction depending on rush hour traffic. Driving is on the right.

Forget the past, today this is a country that oozes charm

Why Colombia?

Stunning landscapes, warm and friendly people, the magic of the old Cartagena, the beautiful tiny colonial streets of Villa de Leyva and Giron, a unique cuisine. These are just some of the attractions.

Facts you might not know about Colombia: It has the world's largest number of bird, butterfly and orchid species and the longest established democracy in South America.

A French travel writer summed up Colombia's allure neatly like this: "If you want to know the Caribbean, go to Cuba or the Dominican Republic; if you want to know the Pacific Ocean, go to Chile; if you want to know the Andean Mountains, go to Ecuador; if you want to know the Amazon Jungle, go to Brazil; if you want to know pre-columbian cultures, go to Mexico or Peru; but if you want to know all of those in just one place, go to Colombia!"

Colombia offers great geographic diversity; a single car journey means you can move from Andean snowscapes to the soft warm breeze of a colonial town. Even on the Caribbean coast you can find a snowy mountain right next to the sea!

The cost of living is low. Large supermarket chains such as the giant French retailer Carrefour are well established in most Colombian cities.

Colombia has an advanced technology infrastructure with high Internet access and the third-highest telephone density in Latin America.

Blessed with tropical and sub-tropical regions, Colombia produces all kind of fruits and vegetables in abundance.

There is an extensive modern private healthcare infrastructure and health insurance costs half of that in the USA. Hospitals and clinics have well-trained doctors, up-to-date technology and equipment.

Is it safe?

Once famed for its gun-toting guerrillas and drug cartel shoot-outs, today's Colombia is a shadow of its former self. Some remote parts of the south and east are controlled by rebels and are thus no-go areas. The usual rules apply to towns and cities: don't carry large amounts of cash, avoid exposing cameras, wallets, purses and jewellery.

The British Foreign & Commonwealth Office urges visitors to avoid unnecessary travel to deprived areas of all Colombian cities.

How much tax will I pay?

Resident individuals are taxed on worldwide income. Non-residents are taxed on Colombian-source income only. An individual is considered resident for a tax year if staying in Colombia for more than six months in the tax year.

There is a property tax of 0.1-1.6 per cent on the appraised value of a property (it varies between municipalities). Property values are automatically readjusted each year for inflation.

Capital gains on property are taxed at a flat rate of 34 per cent after the deduction of the price paid, legal fees and improvement costs.

ABOUT THE WRITER: Mauricio Jaimes, a 35-year-old Colombian, runs the website www.buycolombiarealty.com. Mauricio, a father of three, has a master's degree in international business from the Graduate School of Business in Grenoble, France and has worked as an industrial engineer, property investor and realtor.

FACTFILE

Capital: Bogotá

Area: 1.14m sq km

Climate: Tropical along the coast and the eastern plains, cooler in the highlands. Bogotá is a city high in the Andes Mountains and the weather is generally cool and variable. It is hot and humid in Cartagena. Cali is hot all year round and Medellín has the most agreeable weather of the major cities.

Population: 44.5 million

Language: Spanish. On the islands of San Andres and Old Providence, English is also spoken. There are numerous Indian dialects.

Time difference: GMT -5 hours

Entry requirements: A visa is not required for stays of up to 90 days.

Retirement/residence visa: You must prove an income of about $1,800 a month. [See: The Rules for Getting In]

Electricity: 110 V/60 Hz

Getting in: A visa is not required for stays of up to 90 days.

Electricity: 110 V, 60 Hz

Money: Peso (Col$). ATMs are available in larger towns and cities. Credit/debit cards: Visa and MasterCard are widely accepted, less so American Express and Diners Club. Use of traveller's cheques generally limited to banks, hotels or bureaux de change.

Public holidays:

Jan 1	New Year's Day	July 5	St Peter and St Paul
Jan 11	Epiphany	July 20	Independence Day
Mar 22	St Joseph's Day	Aug 7	Battle of Boyacá
Apr 9	Maundy Thursday	Aug 16	Assumption
Apr 10	Good Friday	Oct 18	Columbus Day
May 1	Labour Day	Nov 1	All Saints' Day
May 17	Ascension	Nov 15	Cartagena City Ind.
June 7	Corpus Christi	Dec 8	Imm. Conception
June 14	Sagrado Corazon	Dec 25	Christmas Day

Opening hours

Banks: 9am-3 pm Mon-Fri (Bogotá), 2-4.30pm in other cities.

Offices: 9am-6pm Mon-Fri   Shops: 9am-8pm

Water: Drink bottled water outside of the main cities.

Tipping: 10 per cent is usual for any service

Medical/Healthcare: No particular vaccinations are required for Colombia. For tourists visiting jungle regions in the Amazon, vaccination against yellow fever and tetanus is recommended. Most doctors and dentists have a good working knowledge of English. Access to medical treatment is limited in more rural areas.

Pets: A notarised health certificate from a veterinarian is required as well as vaccination certificates for rabies, distemper, hepatitis and parpovirosis. Quarantine is not required for dogs and cats.

Is Colombian property a good investment?

House prices have risen consistently for five years or more – eight per cent in 2007, almost seven per cent in 2006 and almost nine per cent in 2005.

Where's best to live?

The capital, **Bogotá**, flanked by mountains to the east, has a lot to offer and for this reason it has become the prime destination for foreigners. The best areas for foreigners are the north and north-east side of the city

PROPERTY

Country club condo

2 stories and an attic, total of 300sq m. 4 bedrooms, 4 bathrooms. High quality finish in wood, marble and quartz stone. Hot tub, spa and laundry room. Double garage.

Price: $325,000

More info: www.buycolombiarealty.com

with better restaurants, bars, fashionable stores and other commercial services along with medical, religious, recreational and educational services.

There is a great network of biking routes, parks that connects with other areas of the city. This is also the location of the Country Club with tennis, polo and two golf courses and, in Santa Barbara, elegant houses and apartments look down on a tiny central park where, over lunch at any of the restaurants, you will feel the peace and quiet of country town.

Outside of the capital, **Cartagena** is the hottest real estate market. Romantic and glamorous, it is by far the best colonial city in America. Declared a World Heritage location by UNESCO, the "Walled City" is an extraordinary place to live: a colonial city enclosed within stone fortifications, modern and luxurious

hotels, beautiful beaches and restaurants for all tastes.

People from all over the world especially Europeans are starting to buy properties here.

Medellin, surrounded by green mountains, has all-year-round spring weather with an average temperature of 24°C. Well known for its beautiful women, it is also known as "The Capital of the Flowers".

Bucaramanga is what Colombians call "Un buen vividero" – a great place to live. Surrounded by forest and mountains, it's close to several types of landscapes and is the kind of town where everything is nearby.

Santa Marta is the most visited Colombian tourist destination. Great beaches, white sand, good hotel infrastructure and outstanding landscapes.

Cali, in the south western region, is Colombia's third largest city and is famous as the world salsa capital. **Villa de Leyva** is a picturesque colonial-era town with cobble-stoned streets, red-tiled roofs, balconies and private courtyards.

THE RULES FOR GETTING IN

A permanent visa can be obtained after you have held a temporary visa for five continuous years. This is a one year multiple entry visa.

To obtain a permanent visa as a retiree you need a monthly guaranteed income of 10 times the Colombian minimum monthly wage of 408,000 pesos (about $210). In other words you have to provide evidence of an annual income of about $25,000 with original documentation (translated into Spanish), plus the usual criminal checks.

An alternative is the **Investor's Visa.** The fee is $475 and you need a minimum deposit of $100,000 with the Banco de la Republica.

Bello Horizonte beach
Beautiful villa on the outskirts of Santa Marta, with a spectacular view of the sea of Bello Horizonte beach. Land area of 2,900sq m, property, 230sq m. 3 large bedrooms, 1 small bedroom, 3 bathrooms, large living room, dining room, modern kitchen, library, balcony with terrace. BBQ area and swimming pool. House for guard with kitchen. Price: $210,000
More info:
www.buycolombiarealty.com

COLOMBIA CONTACT DIRECTORY

Embassies/Government
British Embassy in Colombia
http://ukincolombia.fco.gov.uk
Colombian Embassy in UK
www.consuladodecolombia.co.uk
www.colombianconsulate.co.uk

Travel & Health Advice
Foreign Office travel advice
www.fco.gov.uk/travel
www.nhs.uk/Healthcareabroad
www.masta.org

About Colombia
www.colombiareports.com/
www.colombianblog.com
welovebogota.com
www.cartagenainfo.net
http://medellintraveler.com
www.colombiacrawler.com

General & Expat
www.expatfocus.com
www.britishexpat.com
www.transitionsabroad.com
www.welovebogota.com

English Language Media
The Colombia Times and The Bogotá Daily.

Property
www.buycolombiarealty.com
http://homes.point2.com/Colombia
www.inmobiliarialafortaleza.com/ingles
www.luquemedina.com/home.htm
www.vivareal.net/colombia
www.viviun.com/Real_Estate/Colombia

Travel & Tourism
www.colombia.travel/en
(Tourism Ministry website)
www.ecotet.com/visitcolombia/
www.worldtravelguide.net

www.virtualtourist.com
www.colombiacontact.com
www.webtourist.net/colombia
www.lonelyplanet.com/colombia
www.world66.com

Getting There
There are no direct flights from the UK.
Avianca (via Madrid) www.avianca.com
American Airlines (via JFK)
www.americanairlines.co.uk
Air France (via Paris) www.airfrance.co.uk
Delta (via JFK)   www.delta.com
Iberia (via Madrid)www.iberia.com
Fares range: $740-1100

Getting Around
Bogotá has a modern mass transit system
Transmilenio. Medellín has a metro system.
Colombian cities have efficient public
transport systems and there are good links
between major cities.
Air: If you want to avoid hours on long
distance buses flying is the only option. The
three carriers are Aerorepublica, Avianca

and Easyfly. This will get you there quicker
but you will miss out on the amazing
scenery that Colombia has to offer.
Train: The passenger rail system is very
poor. There is no national train service but
special tourist trains between some cities
Bus: Long-distance buses arrive and depart
at the Terminal de Transportes in the heart
of Bogotá,. There are buses, busetas and
micro buses. Generally speaking, the longer
the trip, the more comfortable the service is.
Taxis: Taxis are cheap even for long
distance journeys. Taxis must display a
price list showing the fares between cities.
Driving: There is a well-maintained
network of roads but landslides are
common during the rainy season (Nov-Feb).
It's safer to drive during the day since when
travelling to rural tourist destinations there
is a risk of violence, kidnapping and being
caught in road blocks set up by illegal
armed groups. Foreigners require an
international driving licence.
Driving is on the right.

Cheap property, low taxes and a scenic wonderland

Why Ecuador?

A country of great beauty and biodiversity, very low cost of living, hospitable and friendly people, varied and exotic landscapes with startling contrasts of scenery from steaming tropical rainforests, windswept highlands, ice-capped volcanoes and miles of empty palm-fringed beaches.

Ecuador has the Galapagos Islands, beautiful Pacific Coast beaches, the Andes Mountains and a portion of the world's largest rainforest, the Amazon Basin.

Property is cheap and taxes are low (the average annual property tax is 0.2 per cent of the value). There are generous incentives for the over-65s – 50 per cent off public transport, electric and water bills, half-price tickets for cultural and sporting events, including the cinema, and a free domestic phone service.

Ecuador has about 95,000 American and 30,000 European Union expatriates. There are 112,000 German speakers, mainly descendants of immigrants

who arrived in the late 1800s.

The downside: A high crime rate. Ecuador is one of the poorest nations in Latin America, ranking 99th in the world.

Is it safe?

No. Crime is a serious problem, particularly in areas of high levels of unemployment. The UK's Foreign Office warns that crime is a constant hazard throughout the country; muggings and pick pocketing are common.

Travellers in resort areas along the coast and in Quito and Guayaquil have sometimes been victims of violent robbery.

How much tax will I pay?

Resident individuals (those living in Ecuador for at least six months a year) are subject to tax on their worldwide income with a credit for foreign tax paid.

Dividends and other profit distributions received, and interest on savings deposits, are tax-exempt.

There is no capital gains tax on the occasional (non-business) transfer of property, shares, etc.

If you buy property and let it, say prior to your retirement, it will be subject to a flat tax of 25 per cent on the gross income.

Inheritance tax is paid not per estate but per person inheriting and begins at $50,000. For example, if your estate is worth $150,000 and you have three children they will pay nothing.

Above the threshold, the bands are:

$50,000-100,000	5%
$100,000-200,000	10%
$200,000-300,000	15%

There is a Property Appreciation Tax of one per cent of the market value of the property, reduced to 0.5 per cent for the first transfer of any property.

Is Ecuadorian property a good investment?

Yes and no. Yes in that property values have

FACTFILE

Capital: Quito **Population:** 13.9 million
Area: 256,370sq km
Language: Spanish and Quichua. English, German and Chinese are other languages used.
Climate: The name gives a clue – Ecuador is on the equator so it gets plenty of sun. However, because of its geography – a narrow coastal plain, a high mountainous central region including the main Andean mountain ranges and a forested lowland (part of the Amazon basin) – Ecuador has a variety of microclimates.
The coast is hot throughout the year, with a humid rainy season between December and May. It's cool in the mountains depending on altitude. The Amazon region is hot and wet while the Galapagos Islands are dry with a steady year-round average temperature of 25°C.
Time difference: GMT -5 hours.
Entry requirements: A visa is not required for stays of up to 90 days.
Retirement/residence visa: Foreign pensioner must have a guaanteed income of $800 a month plus $100 for each depen-dant.
[See: The rules for getting in]
Electricity: 120V/60Hz American-style plug with two parallel flat blades above a circular grounding pin.
Money: US$. ATMs are available at most banks in urban areas. Credit/debit cards and traveller's cheques are generally accepted.
Public holidays 2010

Jan 1	New Year's Day
Feb 12	Amazon and Galapagos Day
Feb 27	National Unity Day
April 2	Good Friday
May 1	Labour Day
May 24	Battle of Pichincha
July 24	irthday of Simón Bolivar
Aug 10	Independence Day
Oct 9	Guayaquil Independence
Nov 2	All Souls' Day
Nov 3	Cuenca Independence
Dec 25	Christmas Day
Dec 31	New Year's Eve

Opening hours
   Banks: 8.30am-4/5pm Mon-Fri. Sat mornings.
   Offices: 9am-5/6pm Mon-Fri
   Shops: 9am-6pm Mon-Sat
Water: Drinking tap water is not advisable anywhere.
Tipping: Restaurants will normally add a 10 per cent service charge (along with 12 per cent tax). It is not customary to tip taxi drivers.
Medical/Healthcare: Good quality medical care is available in major cities but scarce in rural areas. No immunisations are compulsory, but vaccinations for hepatitis A and B and typhoid are recommended. Cholera and rabies are minor risks. Avoid street food and peel fruits and vegetables.
Pets: Must have up-to-date vaccinations plus a health certificate signed by a vet.

increased by around 12 per cent a year for about five years. The downside is the corruption among local officialdom that can cause problems with property rights. However, this and the crime problem, has not discouraged many Europeans and Americans from moving to Ecuador.

Where's best to live?

Ecuador has three main geographical regions, La Costa, La Sierra, and El Oriente – the region made up of the Amazon rain forest – plus the insular region of the Galapagos Islands in the Pacific.

The popular choice of foreign retirees includes **Baños** which boasts an active volcano and hot spring mineral baths; **Guayaquil**, Ecuador's largest city and largest port city; **Manta**, another important seaport, and **Cuenca**, the third largest city and listed as a UNESCO World Heritage Trust site.

One of the most attractive cities in South America, Cuenca's attractions include its beautiful architecture and its culture, with easy access to ballet, concerts, art exhibitions, cinema and shopping as well as good clinics and excellent doctors.

Montanita, a small village on the southern coast, which started as a settlement with a few rustic houses of native fishermen, is now known far beyond the borders of Ecuador as a fantastic surfing beach, popular with local and international surfers. Here there are holiday homes, small hotels and great seafood.

Unfortunately, it's also popular with stingrays that lurk close to the water's edge. Have no fear, there's is a

One and half hours north of Quito there's a small expatriate community in the delightful town of **Cotacachi**, located between two towering volcanoes. At 2,400m, the climate is cooler than most of Ecuador.

Then there's the capital itself. Nestling high in the Andes Mountains and the centre of Ecuador's political and cultural activity, Quito is a modern, bustling city with dozens of museums, parks, cafes and restaurants.

All this in the heart of the Andes at over 9,000 feet, at the base of the Volcano Pichincha and with an all-year temperate climate.

The Old City – Centro Historico – is a magnificent example of Spanish colonial architecture, with narrow cobblestone streets, beautiful plazas and a cathedral.

small hospital in Manglaralto that is experienced with such emergencies.

International retirees in Montanita share this idyllic place with tourists from all over the world, together enjoying the surf, seafood, music and nightlife.

Also popular is **Riobamba**, the starting point of the famous train ride down the Nariz del Diablo and gateway to Mount Chimborazo, Ecuador's highest peak, and, for beach resorts, there's **Esmeraldas** and **Bahía de Caraquez**.

THE RULES FOR GETTING IN

The Pensioner, 10-I Visa is available for those who receive a guaranteed monthly income of $800, plus $100 for each dependent.

A simpler alternative may be the Ecuador Investment Visa, under which the applicant has to purchase real estate worth $25,000 ($500 more for each dependant).

In addition to a certificate of income the usual documents are required. The visa fee is equivalent to US$200.

This summarises information is from the website of the Ecuador embassy in Washington.

[www.ecuador.org/immigrantvisas.htm]
UK applicants must apply via the UK embassy.

One for footballers!

Situated in the exclusive Cuenca suburb of Challuabamba (pronounce it ch-wa-bamba) on over an acre of land, with a

river behind, mountain views in the front and 15 minutes from downtown Cuenca that is the principal city in the southern highlands of Ecuador. Over 550sq m of living area with 150sq m of covered patio. 5 bedrooms and 6 bathrooms in the main house. 4 more bathrooms in the workout room, sauna and steam room, guest room and maid's quarters, 3 sitting areas, office, 2 dining rooms. Large yard with soccer field and avocado trees in front.
Price: $360,000 or rent for $1,500/mo
More info: www.ecuadorhomesonline.com
Email: info@EcuadorHomesOnline.com

Olon beach house

Less than 50-ft from the beach in a gated community in Olon near Montanita, the surfing capital of Ecuador. Main house has 2 bedrooms and 2 baths, master bedroom with a private balcony. Guest house has 2 bedrooms, 1 bath, and storage area. There is an outdoor kitchen/BBQ area and covered parking.
Price: $140,000

More info: www.ecuadorhomesonline.com
Email: info@EcuadorHomesOnline.com

ECUADOR CONTACT DIRECTORY

Embassies/Government
Ecuador Embassy in UK
www.consuladoecuador.org.uk

British Embassy in Ecuador
http://ukinecuador.fco.gov.uk

Ecuador Government
http://www.mmrree.gov.ec/mre/documentos/
pol_internacional/migratoria%20consular/leg
alizaciones.htm
(Spanish only)

Travel & Health Advice
Foreign Office travel advice
www.fco.gov.uk/travel
www.nhs.uk/Healthcareabroad
www.masta.org

About Ecuador
www.garyascott.com
www.pro-ecuador.com
www.ecuador-travel-guide.org
http://ecuador.org/country_information.htm
www.ecuador.com
www.thebestofecuador.com
www.ecuador-travel-guide.org
http://ezinearticles.com
www.globalaging.org
http://blog.pro-ecuador.com

General & Expat
www.pro-ecuador.com
www.retireecuador.com/visa.htm
www.hipecuador.com

English Language Media
www.ecuadorreporter.com
Online newspaper with Ecuador news, travel
and sport stories, reviews of clubs, bars and
restaurants.

Property
www.ecuador-properties.com
www.viviun.com/Real_Estate/Ecuador/
http://mandatolpm.com
www.coldwellbanker.com.ec
www.ecuainternet.com
www.colonialecuador.co
www.mancasas.com
www.ecuadorhomesonline.com
www.housesunderfiftythousand.com/ecuador
www.cuencarealestate.com
http://ecuador.world-estate.com
www.inbienes.com
www.bienesraices.ec
www.realtymandato.com
www.property-ecuador.com.ar

Travel & Tourism
www.ecuadortouristboard.com
www.vivecuador.com
www.ecuadorial.com
www.ecuador-travel.net
Latin American Travel Association
www.lata.org
www.ecuadorline.com
www.worldtravelguide.net
www.thebestofecuador.com
www.ecuador-travel-guide.org

Getting There
The international airports are in Quito and
Guayaquil. There is also a smaller airport in
Cuenca. Quito Airport is five miles (8km)
from the city centre. Flying time: London to
Quito - 17 hours. Guayaquil is 3 miles (5km)
from the city.

Airlines Serving Ecuador
British Airways: www.british-airways.com
TAME: www.tame.com.ec
Air France: www.airfrance.com
Emirates: www.ekgroup.com
Lufthansa: www.lufthansa.com
KLM Airlines: www.klm.com

Getting Around
Air and bus are the best bets for travel
within Uruguay. Carry your passport when
travelling as there are frequent checkpoints.

By Air: Considering the relatively short
distances involved, flying Ecuador is not
cheap. A flight from Quito to Guayaquil
takes about 35 minutes and costs $99
return, compared to $24 by bus which takes
about 10 hours.
Internal flights are with:
Aerogal: www.aerogal.com.ec
Club VIP: www.vipec.com
Icaro: www.icaro.com.ec
www.getquitoecuador.com
For more info on domestic flights.

Train: Lack of funding and frequent rock
falls have combined to make Ecuador's rail
system pretty useless. The famous Nariz del
Diablo (Devil's Nose) route makes a
spectacular mountain descent between
Riobamba and Sibambe.
Passengers are permitted to ride on top of
some of the cars (some have been killed
doing this), an experience you need cool
nerves and warm clothes for.
Foreigners pay more to travel by train than
locals.

Bus: Local buses are slow, crowded and
cheap. Ecuador is a small country so you
can reach almost anywhere in under a day.
However, since many roads are rough, bus
travel can be uncomfortable. Busetas (22-
seat buses) cover long distances quickly in
reasonable comfort.
Bus travel out of Quito is from the Terminal
Terrestre de Cumandá in the old town, close
to Plaza Santo Domingo. Journeys to
neighbouring countries also begin here.
Travel after dark, either by long-distance or
international coaches, should be avoided.

Taxis: Plentiful and efficient. Meters usually
work but set a price before starting. It's
safer to use a radio taxi at night. There's no
extra charge. Legal taxis have a four-digit
number on the side door and in the front
window.

Driving: Driving is hazardous and
unpredictable. If you drive a hire car you will
be one of the few people on the road who
has any type of insurance. Rural roads are
unpaved and during rainy periods can
become impassable. Emergency services
are extremely limited away from the main
cities and tourist destinations.
Car Hire: Not recommended for the faint-
hearted because of the above conditions.
However you pay you need a credit card to
reserve a car and you will be responsible
for at least the first $1,000 of any damage.
An International Driving Permit is required.
Driving is on the right.

Cheapest country in the world will tempt only the bravest

Why Paraguay?

Dirt poor with well over half the population living at or below the poverty level, Paraguay is a country of extremes – not just those of wealth and poverty but also of geography: criss-crossed by navigable rivers and divided by the Río Paraguay into strikingly different eastern (Paraneña) and western (Chaco) regions.

The Paraneña, home to 95 per cent of the population, ranges from lowlands to mountains, while Chaco's vast low plain, more than 60 per cent of the total land area, is alternately flooded and parched.

Paraguay is among the most sparsely populated countries in the world. It is the cheapest, according to the annual cost of living survey conducted by the research company Mercer.

But, after nearly two centuries of political instability,

Paraguay boasts a fully democratic government and a growing economy. Less comforting is the fact that it is also the criminal capital of South America. According to Paraguayan police, over half the cars on the road are stolen (mostly by crooks who trade them for drugs which are then exported to Europe and America.) Ciudad del Este is the largest city with a population of 240,000.

The centre of criminality. it is also an interesting place to live. Anything can be bought here (guns, drugs, electronic goods, cameras, counterfeit CDs, watches and booze) and bandits, smugglers and money launderers rule.

While Ciudad del Este may be a den of thieves it is also the jumping-off point to the famous Itaipú Dam and Iguazú Falls in neighbouring Brazil and Argentina.

Other parts of the country offer a more relaxed way of life, friendly people and natural beauty – rain forest, ranches, sub-tropical farmland, marshland and savannah. The vast and empty Chaco region is great for trekking, nature lovers, anglers and bird-watchers.

However, most foreign residents agree that the only place realistically worth considering is Asuncion, the sleepy, laid back, elegant capital where you can rent a nice apartment for $300 a month.

Is it safe?

Armed robbery, car-jackings, and home invasions occur in all areas. Low level street crime, including pick-pocketing and mugging, is prevalent in cities although instances of serious violent crime, including kidnapping, have decreased lately.

How much tax will I pay?

There is no taxation on foreign-source income

Explore, discover, feel..... *PARAGUAY*

Paraguay is an emerging tourist destination located in the center of South America, offering a unique combination of authenticity, strong cultural identity, natural resources with great diversity of flora and fauna, a captivating history, modern cities with accordant installations, and its kind and friendly people.

Why visit Paraguay?

1. **Geographic Location:** The very natural location, in the heart of South America, makes it easier to include it in tourism circuits with the countries in the region. Its capital, Asunción, is located just a short time by plane of the major cities of the region.

2. **Natural, Historical and Cultural Attractions:** Paraguay is not for massive tourism, but for the discerning traveler that enjoys authenticity in nature and culture

   - **Jesuit Missions:** to the south of Asunción, we find the different Jesuit Reductions. The Trinidad Jesuit Reduction is a part of the Cultural Heritage of Humanity and the best restored.
   - **Artisanal Towns:** around Asunción we will find towns where its people make handicrafs of all kind.
   - **Paraguayan Chaco:** A region that combines dry forests and wetlands, with mennonites and indigineous cultures, regarded as the second lung of South America. Its main atraction is its distinctive flora and fauna.

3. **Prices:** Nowhere else in South America and probably in the world will you be ofered such competitive prices like in Paraguay; a fact that was recently published in the international press.

This luminous region showing bright colors and blessed by God, this green heart of the continent, is now resolutely opening to tourism, inviting the world to come and experience it in order to understand it, because it can not be explained; Paraguay is just as our tourism slogan says... *"You have to feel it"*

Liz Rosanna Cramer Campos
Minister Secretary Executive
National Ministry of Tourism
www.paraguay.gov.py

including pensions and retirement benefits. Real Estate Tax is levied annually at one per cent of the value of property. Assessed property values increase annually according to a consumer price index.

There is a 30 per cent capital gains tax on the sale of property after the deduction of the purchase price paid.

There is no inheritance tax.

Is Paraguayan property a good investment?

Property has appreciated in value by four to five per cent per year for several years.

Paraguay guarantees equal treatment to foreign investors. However, due to widespread judicial corruption, protection of property ownership is extremely weak. Acquiring title documents for land can take two years or more.

Because of the above, property purchase has to be done by the book. This involves a complex procedure with the Notary Public obtaining the certificates necessary for the transfer of ownership, ensuring there are no encumbrances on the property and paying a Municipal Tax of 0.2-0.3 per cent

Foreigners may not purchase land within 50km of the borders.

Where's best to live?

Most foreign residents live in **Asuncion**, the capital and largest city, or its wider suburbs. Asuncion is laid out on hills above the east bank of the Rio Paraguay. It has colonial architecture, museums and peaceful parks. Home hunters can view colonial mansions, beaux-art buildings and modern apartment blocks, all incredibly cheap.

Surprisingly, **Ciudad del Este** (see above) is the second choice of foreign residents.

The following cities have a thin sprinkling of foreign residents: **Encarnacion, Pedro Juan Caballero,**

THE RULES FOR GETTING IN

Applicants for permanent residence must apply at the Paraguayan Embassy/Consulate in their country of residence.

In addition to all the usual documents they must produce a health certificate and an 'economic solvency statement' showing a deposit in a bank in Paraguay of at least $5,000 in the name of the applicant or/and a property deed of a property located in Paraguay.

You also need a certificate of good conduct from your local police station in the UK.

More info: www.paraguayembassy.co.uk

Coronel Oviedo and **Concepción**, a river port on the River Paraguay 300 km upstream from Asunción.

Then there's **San Bernardino**, a resort town, 35 km from Asunción on Lake Ypacaraí, surrounded by tropical vegetation and a favourite retreat for wealthy city dwellers and overseas residents.

There are about 12,000 German-speaking Mennonites in Paraguay, descendants of the evangelical Christians who fled religious and linguistic persecution in the Soviet Union in the late 1920s.

The men wear black and the women are clothed from head to toe. They speak in Platdeutsch (low German).

The Mennonites have established several communities in **Chaco**, the largest of which is Filadelfia, home to about 2,500 Mennonites.

Here, a five-hour drive from the capital, you will find orderly rows of German-looking bungalows, complete with satellite dishes. No Alps in the background but large cooperative farms with cattle in neat pastures which provide a large part of the dairy products consumed across the country.

Central Paraguay
Detached house of 540 sqm in Lambaré, a small city in Paraguay's central region. 4 bedrooms, 4 baths Price: $90,000
More info: January First Real Estate
www.jfestate.com   sales@jfestate.com

Chaco, Rio Paraguay
3 bedrooms, bathroom, lounge, dining room, kitchen, laundry room. Garden/land patio 100 x 50m.
Price: $95,000
More info: http://paraguay.homesgofast.com/properties

FACTFILE

Capital: Asunción
Population: 6.8 million
Area: 406,750 sq km
Language: Guarani and Spanish (both official), both spoken by most people. There are communities of Brazilians, Argentines, Germans, Arabs, Koreans, Chinese and Japanese.
Climate: Two distinct seasons: summer (subtropical to temperate) from Oct-March and winter (mild pleasant) from May-Aug. Rainy season Dec-April. Substantial rainfall in the eastern parts of the country, becoming semi-arid in the far west.
Time difference: GMT -3 or -4 hours
Entry requirements: A visa is not required for stays of up to 90 days.
Retirement/residence visa: You need to deposit a minimum of $5,000 in a bank and/or produce proof of property purchase. [See: The rules for getting in]

Electricity: 220V AC 50Hz. Plug has two round pins.
Money: Guarani (plural guaranies), usually written as a G with a stroke through it. ATMs are readily available in the larger towns. Credit/debit cards: Credit cards and traveller's cheques are generally accepted as are reals, pesos and US$.
Public holidays 2010

Jan 1	New Year's Day
March 1	Heroes' Day
April 2	Good Friday
April 4	Easter Sunday
April 5	Easter Monday
May 1	Labour Day
May 15	Independence Day
June 12	Peace of Chaco
Aug 15	Founding of Asunción
Sep 29	Battle of Boquerón
Dec 8	Immaculate Conception
Dec 25	Christmas Day

Opening hours
Banks: 9am-3pm Mon-Fri
Offices: 8am-12pm & 3pm-7pm; 7am-1pm (public offices)
Shops: 9am-12pm , 3pm-9pm Mon-Fri 8am-4pm Sat
Water: Use bottled.
Tipping: Restaurants normally add a 10-15 per cent service charge. If not, tip that amount. Taxi drivers don't expect a tip.
Medical/Healthcare: No immunisations are compulsory but vaccinations for yellow fever are recommended. Some medical authorities recommend polio and typhoid vaccinations. Medical facilities and supplies are very limited outside the capital.
Pets: Cats and dogs require a veterinarian's health certificate.

PARAGUAY CONTACT DIRECTORY

Embassies/Government
Paraguay Embassy in UK
www.paraguayembassy.co.uk/
There is no British Embassy in Paraguay. There is a consular office for emergency assistance only:
British Honorary Consulate in Asunción:
Email: guillermo.peroni@pstbn.com.py
Paraguay Government
www.mre.gov.py/en/

Travel & Health Advice
Foreign Office travel advice
www.fco.gov.uk/travel
www.nhs.uk/Healthcareabroad
www.masta.org

About Paraguay
http://lanic.utexas.edu/la/sa/paraguay/
www.cia.gov/library/publications/the-world-factbook/geos/pa.html
http://en.wikipedia.org/wiki/Paraguay
www.state.gov/r/pa/ei/bgn/1841.htm

General & Expat
www.expatfocus.com
www.britishexpat.com
www.transitionsabroad.com

English Language Media
www.einnews.com/paraguay/
www.topix.net/world/paraguay/

Property
Some of these estate agents give information in Spanish only.

www.alquiler.com.py/
http://www.paraguay-homepage.de/englisch/immobilien.htm
www.alquiler.com.py/
www.360terra.com
www.paraguayinmuebles.com
www.inmobiliariarolon.com
www.queenpropiedades.com

Travel & Tourism
There is no tourist office in the UK but there is information at:
www.senatur.gov.py
www.turismo.com.py
www.paraguay.com
Tourism office (in Paraguay)
www.lonelyplanet.com/paraguay

Getting There
Paraguay's only international airport, Aeropuerto Internacional Silvio Pettirossi, is 20km East of Asunción. International flights are via Buenos Aires, Argentina; La Paz and Santa Cruz, Bolivia; São Paulo and Rio be Janeiro, Brazil; Iquique and Santiago, Chile.

Airlines Serving Paraguay
British Airways: www.british-airways.com
TAM: www.tam.com.py
Air France: www.airfrance.com
Emirates: www.ekgroup.com
Lufthansa   www.lufthansa.com
KLM: www.klm.com
www.southamericanexperience.com
Varig: www.varig.co.uk
Return fare range from UK: $1,100-1,450.

Getting Around
Air: TAM Airlines offers domestic services and flights to neighbouring countries. Regional Paraguaya which began operations in July 2008 is the new flag carrier.
www.tam.com.py
www.regionalparaguaya.com.py
Train: Not worth bothering with. There is a 438km line from Asunción to Encarnación which is used mainly by tourists but very little of it is open.
Bus: Bus and minibus services are cheap and fairly efficient. Most buses are old and rickety except the faster deluxe ejecutivo.
Taxis: Radio-taxis are the most reliable and can be ordered by phone or recognised in the street by the phone number displayed on the door of the vehicle.
Driving: Driving in Asunción is a nerve-racking experience. Finding your way around is difficult and many roads in the capital and other cities are unsurfaced, cobbled or under repair.
Rural roads are largely unpaved and during rainy periods can become impassable. The main road from Asuncion to Ciudad del Este is OK.
Police may pull you over on country roads and demand bribes. Do it like the locals and offer a small banknote while shaking hands.
Car hire is expensive. A national licence or International Driving Permit is required Driving is on the right.

Land of the Incas with 3,000 species of orchid

Why Peru?

Peru is a stunningly beautiful country with a capital, Lima, crammed with culture and and history. It's cheap. You can rent a very nice house for $400 a month and have a good restaurant meal for $4 (you can pay less than half that and still eat well).

In its jungles Peru has 3,000 species of orchids and the country is home to about 10 per cent of all mammals and reptiles living on the planet.

It has the incredible lost Inca city of Machu Picchu, 2,500m above sea level in the middle of a tropical mountain forest, one of the seven 'new' wonders of the world and declared a world heritage site by UNESCO in 1983.

Peruvians of European descent make up about 17 per cent of the population and there are smaller numbers of people of African, Japanese and Chinese descent.

Founded in 1532 by the conquistador Francisco Pizarro, Peru was ruled by Spanish viceroys for almost 300 years and, in Lima, they created one of the richest and most prosperous cities in Latin America. Many of the structures from the 17th and 18th centuries have been restored or rebuilt.

Peru's history spans several millennia and it is blessed with numerous attractions, from Machu Picchu to Lake Titicaca, the world's highest navigable lake. It has snow-capped mountains, the Colca's canyon – the world's deepest; and Cusco, the capital of the Incan Empire.

There has to be a down side. There is: crime [See: Is it safe]. Another: parts of the capital and cities are dirty and down at heel.

Is it safe?

No. Crime is a hazard, particularly in Lima. Street crime is rampant and visitors need to be on constant guard against pickpockets. Rural areas are safer but crime is also a problem in the provincial cities of Cusco and Puno on the shores of Lake Titicaca. Unfortunately, both are 'must-see' places.

Foreigners are vulnerable in crowded areas such as train and bus stations and markets. In Lima, the area around the International Airport is especially dangerous and visitors should only take official taxis. Women should not travel alone. Road conditions are poor and it's safer to travel in convoys because of highway bandits in remote areas.

How much tax will I pay?

Foreigners domiciled in Peru must pay tax on income created both in and outside the country. Foreigners are considered to be resident if they have lived in Peru for two years without being abroad

FACTFILE

Capital: Lima   **Population:** 28.2 million
Area: 1.3million sq km   **Language:** Spanish and Quechua (both official) Aymara and a number of minority Amazonian languages.
Climate: Tropical in the east to dry desert in the west, freezing in the Andes. Although only 1,200km south of the equator, Lima never has temperatures above 35°C. Average summer temperature (mid-Dec-mid-March) is 25/28°C. Winter, 10-16°C. 20°C on the coast.
Time difference: GMT -5 hours
Entry requirements: A visa is not required for stays of up to 90 days.
Retirement/residence visa
The 'Rentista' visa requires evidence of a income from outside Peru of at least $1,000 a month and $500 for each dependent. [See: The rules for getting in]

Electricity: 220V/60Hz 2 pin round or flat.
Money: Nuevo sol = 100 centimos. ATM machines are available even in small, remote towns. Credit/Debit cards and traveller's cheques are OK in Lima and Cusco but not in smaller towns.
Public holidays 2010

Jan 1	New Year's Day
April 1	Maundy Thursday
April 2	Good Friday
May 1	Labour Day
June 29	St Peter's and St Paul's Day
July 28-29	Independence Anniversary
Aug 30	St Rosa of Lima Day
Oct 8	Angamos Battle
Nov 1	All Saints' Day
Dec 8	Immaculate Conception
Dec 24	Christmas Eve (half day)
Dec 25	Christmas Day

Opening hours
Banks: 10am-6pm Mon-Fri, 9.30am-12.30pm Sat
Offices: 9am-5.30 Mon-Fri & 9am-1pm Sat
Shops: 9am-6pm (7pm Sat).
Water: Drink bottled.
Tipping: Most restaurants add 10 per cent and a few more coins are appreciated.
Medical/Healthcare: No vaccinations are required but tetanus, diphtheria, typhoid and hepatitis A are recommended. Travel to the Amazon requires malaria and yellow fever vaccinations. Malaria precautions are essential in low-lying rural areas. Altitude sickness troubles many in Cusco (3,000m) and Lake Titicaca (4,000m).
Pets: Must have up-to-date vaccinations and a health certificate signed by a vet within two weeks prior to arrival.

PERU CONTACT DIRECTORY

Embassies/Government
Peruvian Embassy in UK
www.peruembassy-uk.com
or www.conperlondres.com

British Embassy in Peru
http://ukinperu.fco.gov.uk/en/

Travel & Health Advice
Foreign Office travel advice
www.fco.gov.uk/travel
www.nhs.uk/Healthcareabroad
www.masta.org

About Peru
www.peru.info/perueng.asp
www.theperuguide.com
http://wikitravel.org/en/Peru
http://en.wikipedia.org/wiki/Wikiproject_Peru
theultimateperulist.blogspot.com
www.therealperu.co.uk
www.perutourist.info/

General & Expat
www.expatperu.com
www.livinginperu.com
www.expatfocus.com
www.britishexpat.com
www.transitionsabroad.com

English Language Media
www.peruviantimes.com
www.einnews.com/peru

Property
(Mostly in Spanish)
www.alfredograf.com
www.cuscoproperties.com
http://casascasella.com/english
www.villaran.com
www.perucorretaje.com
www.cmi-peru.com
www.inmuebleperu.com

Travel & Tourism
www.perutourist.info
www.peru-explorer.com
www.travel-budget.com/peru
www.enjoyperu.com
www.virtualperu.net
Latin American Travel Association
www.lata.org/
www.enjoyperu.com/peru

Getting There
There are no direct flights to Peru from London. British Airways flies via Miami
www.british-airways.com
Iberia flies via Madrid www.iberia.com
KLM via Amsterdam www.klm.com

Getting Around
Air: Flying is the only practical way around due to the long distances and poor roads. Internal flights are relatively inexpensive. LAN has an air pass programme for its international passengers.
Domestic carriers include:
AeroCondor www.aerocondor.com.pe
LAN www.lan.com
LC Busre www.lcbusre.com.pe

StarPerú www.starperu.com
Taca Peru www.taca.com
Train: This is the most spectacular way travel in Peru. Rail journeys take you through scenery of outstanding beauty and to places almost inaccessible otherwise. Main routes are between either historic Cusco or the Sacred Valley and the legendary Machu Picchu and between Cusco and Lake Titicaca. 3 rail companies offer comfortable first class services.
Bus: By far the cheapest way to travel. Omnibuses, minibuses (or micros) and minivans operate in the cities and services are generally cheap and efficient. Long-distance buses run by private companies cost around $1.50 per hour on the fast coastal Pan-American Highway.
Taxis: Most are unregulated which means you negotiate the fare before you set off.
Driving: Avoid driving. Peru registers 30 deaths per 100,000 vehicles (by comparison to one in the USA and six in the UK.) The roads are bad, poorly designed and maintained and pitted with potholes. Rockslides are frequent. Drivers ignore traffic lights and stop signs where they do exist, hardly surprising since there's no driving test of any kind in Peru. Road crashes are common on winding mountain roads, often with steep cliffs and no lighting.
Car hire: Bad roads, high rental costs, hidden charges, poorly-maintained cars, incomprehensible road signs, long distances – you decide.
Driving is on the right.

during each calendar year for 90 days or more.

There is a property tax, Alcabala, amounting to three per cent of the value of the property.

Capital gains are regarded as income and taxed as such (up to 30 per cent). There is no inheritance tax.

Is Peruvian property a good investment?

Property values have flattened out recently after increasing rapidly in the mid and late 1990s. But demand is steady due to easier access to mortgage funds.

Where's best to live?

The capital. With a population of nine million – about a third of the population – Lima stretches along the Pacific coast for more than 50 miles and is divided into six districts where most foreign residents find their homes.

Lima has a temperate climate, a lively nightlife and a wonderful seafood cuisine. Less pleasant is the pollution and the misty coastal fog which hangs around for much of the year. The best period is December to April.

Miraflores, a fun beach neighbourhood with good restaurants and clubs, stylish shopping and cultural opportunities, has high priced apartments with magnificent sea views but there are cheaper options.

San Isidro is the business and diplomatic district of Lima but also has parks, golf courses, luxury apartments, shopping, restaurants, cinemas and theatres.

Barranco, south of Miraflore with stylish apartments atop of the cliffs, is the bohemian district of Lima and, with its bars, clubs and restaurants, is the city's late night party heart.

Surco, the universities district and home to some of

the city's largest shopping centres, has handsome houses, parks and up-market apartment blocks. And within Surco, pleasant neighbourhoods include Las Casuarinas, Chacarilla del Estanque, San Jorge and Santa Teresa.

Other districts popular among foreign residents are **La Molina**, set on a hilltop, with broad avenues, green spaces, lakes and fine homes, and **La Encantada de Villa**, with properties built directly on the beach.

Peru's second biggest city and one of the most beautiful is **Arequipa**, called "Ciudad Blanca" – the white city – because the historic centre and the Santa Catalina Monastery there are built from white, volcanic stone from the volcano Misti nearby.

A popular tourist resort, Arequipa is well supplied with restaurants, bars, clubs and places to stay.

Cusco, which has a large foreign population, is in the eastern part of the country near Bolivia and is the gateway to Machu Pichu.

The problem here is that Cusco's height, at about 4,200m above sea level, leads to many visitors suffering from altitude sickness.

Resort/eco-Lodge

Currently a lodge and alternative healing centre in Iquitos. Property is 10km from the international airport of and 14 km south of the Amazonian city of Iquitos, 30 minute by bus down the all weather road from Iquitos to Nauta and overlooking the rainforest.
It is situated on a secure and protected land and consists of 4 buldings – 4 single rooms, 4 double rooms & 1 triple rooms with, 3 bathrooms, and a garage
Price: $88,000
More info: www.mondinion.com

Chacarilla
3-bedroom house of 230sq m with 2 1/2 bathrooms.
More info: Email: vgiraldo@terra.com.pe
Ref: CD 5029

*Ministerio de Turismo y Deporte
de la República Oriental del Uruguay*

Uruguay welcomes you to the safest country in South America!

Uruguay offers endless natural scenery and a wide variety of historical sites in a small area which makes it a natural destination in which to reside.

The preservation and care of the environment have positioned Uruguay among the countries with the best sustainability indicators - something that has been recognized by numerous international organizations. With the highest level of quality of life, literacy and cultural awareness Uruguay has become the highlight of South America.

From the late 19th century up to the second half of the 20th century Uruguay received its most important migratory flows with Spaniards and Italians strengthening the current cultural stratification.

During the last few years Uruguay has become the second home to many people from around the world who have chosen this small country to enjoy the benefits that it offers. You can take advantage of its economic and political stability and find a good variety of excellent properties in which to live, at reasonable prices.

Uruguay has a total population of 3.5 million half of them in Montevideo, a city that combines the benefits of being the capital - such as modernity, good services, historical centres, entertainment, shopping and much more - with the bonus of being a safe place to live.

Only a few hours from the capital you can be surrounded by the marvellous beauty of the thermal springs with relaxing and healing benefits, or - in Colonia del Sacremento - a magnificent historical patrimony of the world, or enjoy the spectacular beaches such as Punta del Este which is renowned around the globe as the most stunning beach in Latin America, not only because of its beauty but also its charming people.

If you are looking for beauty with the added spice of living in a Latin country then you will not find a better place than here.

Hoping to see you soon

Best Regards

Sra. LILIAM KECHICHIAN
Subsecretaria
Uruguay *Natural* Ministerio de Turismo y Deporte
Ministerio de Turismo y Deporte

Tiny Uruguay is South America's Switzerland

Why Uruguay?

It may not have the dramatic landscapes of some of its neighbours but Uruguay's rich past – fought over between Britain, Spain and Argentina – along with diverse immigration, has given it a wonderful legacy of culture, arts and literary traditions.

Sandwiched between Argentina and Brazil, Uruguay is the Switzerland of South America: prosperous, cosmopolitan, efficient, peaceful and safe. It is also essentially a European country, since most of its people are descended from Spanish and Italian immigrants.

Crime is not a serious problem as it is with some of its neighbours. The standard of living is high, the cost of living low. The rent of a furnished two-bedroom house in a good area of Montevideo will set you back no more than £300 a month – considerably less than

this away from the capital.

Small (the second smallest country in South America), it has a lot to offer: white sandy beaches along the Atlantic Ocean east of Montevideo; pricey Punta del Este, the so-called Hamptons of Latin America and playground for the wealthy and, in the country, a gaucho experience on numerous working ranches.

Then there's cosmopolitan Montevideo itself, charming and spacious with broad boulevards and one of Latin America's most vibrant cities.

A big attraction is the old inner city, known as the Ciudad Vieja on a small peninsula surrounded by the sea near the metropolitan port. There, a vast wrought-iron structure is home to some of the city's finest seafood restaurants and steakhouses.

The clincher: The people are charming and friendly, although reserved.

Uruguay's coastline stretches to the Brazilian border and holds some of the most impressive seaside resorts in South America. Colonia del Sacramento is a coastal town just west of Montevideo and across the Rio de la Plata from Buenos Aires, Argentina. Colonia is an amazing historical site from the 17th century, a legacy of the Portuguese colony.

Is it safe?

Uruguay is considered one of the safest countries in South America. Except for petty stealing crime is rare outside the capital. However, non-violent street crime is prevalent in Montevideo. Victims are usually foreign tourists and motorists in unlocked vehicles stopped at busy intersections, particularly on Montevideo's riverfront road known as the Rambla. Drivers should keep all car doors locked.

FACTFILE

Capital: Montevideo **Population:** 3.5 million
Area: 176,220sq km, the second smallest country in South America.
Language: Spanish, Portunol or Brazilero. Almost 90 per cent are descended from colonial-era settlers (mainly Spanish).
Climate: Warm, temperate with pronounced seasonal variations but without extremes in temperature. Spring damp, cool, and windy; summers warm; autumns mild; winters are chilly and damp. High humidity and fog are common. The absence of mountains makes all locations vulnerable to high winds.
Time difference: GMT -2/3 hours
Entry requirements: No visa required for stays of up to 90 days.
Retirement/residence visa: Retirees need a minimum monthly income of US$1,500. [see: The rules for getting in]
Electricity: 220V AC/50Hz. (Various types of plugs are in use.)
Money: Uruguayan peso. There is a large ATM network. Credit/debit cards ar e accepted in better hotels, restaurants and shops. US$ travellers cheques are more acceptable.

Public holidays

Jan 1	New Year's Day	May 18	Battle of Las Piedras
Jan 6	Epiphany	June 19	Birth of Gen. Artigas
Feb 19/20	Carnival	July 18	Constitution Day
April 9	Maundy Thursday	Aug 25	Independence Day
April 10	Good Friday	Oct 12	Día de la Raza
April 20	Landing of the Patriots	Nov 12	All Souls' Day
May 1	Labour Day	Dec 25	Christmas Day

Opening hours
Banks: 1pm-5pm, Mon-Fri Offices: 9am-6/7pm
Shops: 9am-7pm (sometimes later), Mon-Fri, 9am-1pm, Sat.
Water: Use bottled.
Tipping: 10 per cent in restaurants. Taxi drivers don't expect a tip but appreciate the odd coins.
Medical/Healthcare: Medical facilities are adequate with 24-hour emergency care available at the British Hospital in Montevideo. A Hepatitis A vaccination is recommended and precautions should be taken against mosquito bites because of dengue fever. Most drugs and medications are available without a prescription.
Pets: Must have a veterinary good health certificate.

Burglars target foreign residents in the better parts of Montevideo and homes should be fitted with alarms and windows with grills. Many residents use guard dogs and/or use security serv-ces.

How much tax will I pay?

Income from outside Uruguay is not subject to tax. Interest on foreign currency deposits is taxed at 12 per cent and deposits in local currency at 3-5 per cent.

If you sell property, capital gains of 12 per cent is charged on the difference in sale price and the original purchase price (adjusted for inflation and improvements on the property).

There is no inheritance tax.

Is Uruguayan property a good investment?

Property prices offer exceptional value when compared to Europe. Homes in the capital and coastal resorts cost $500- $800 per sq m. Montevideo and Punta Del Este have the most expensive real estate.

Punta del Este
24 units of 2 and 3 bedrooms, 6 penthouses of 2 and 3 bedrooms, all en suite, with private terraces and in 3,600sq m of landscaped gardens. Amenities include 24 hour security, swimming pool, solarium, fully equipped spa and fitness centre, large sun terrace, broadband

Farmhouse, Chacra
Colonial style farmhouse on 16.2 ha, 15 km from Montevideo. 4 bedrooms, 3 bathrooms, large living room. House is surrounded by a parkland and eucalyptus trees and is ideal for fruit growing.
Price: $180,000
More info: www.privatepropertyforsale.net

6-bed mansion
New house of 1,800sq m on 5,900sq m in a quiet residential area near golf and tennis. Gallery, gym, separate guest wing, en suite bathrooms in all bedrooms. Servants' quarters, jacuzzi, pool and solarium.
Price: $5,500,000
More info: www.real-estates-network.com

Where's best to live?

The three most popular destinations are the culturally vibrant capital **Montevideo**, with its historic quarter, Barrío Historico, on a small peninsula jutting out into the river; the picturesque 17th-century port of **Colonia**; and the trendy coastal resort **Punta del Este** with its 30km of pristine sandy beaches, fine restaurants and party-till-you-drop nightclubs.

With the Atlantic on one side and the River Plate on the other, Punta is a jet set centre for nightlife lovers with classy restaurants, casinos and discos. There are over 100 hotels, 80 restaurants and numerous clubs and live music on the beaches.

Half an hour away there's **José Ignacio**, a small village on the southern coast, which has evolved into the capital of South American chic, an exclusive retreat where celebrities and the rich have their summer residences overlooking the sea.

On the east coast **Colonia Suisa** is more German than Spanish because there was a large influx of Germans during WWII. The west of the country along the Rio Negro is more agricultural and hilly. The city of Salto has a beautiful city centre with a big social life. Paysandu is smaller and more rural.

THE RULES FOR GETTING IN

Any foreigner with temporary immigration status can apply for permanent residence.

Change in status must be by written request to the immigration authority, Dirección Nacional de Migración (DNM) and presented at the main immigration department in Montevideo or at its branches around the country.

After the DNM has authorised the change, applicants must present the usual variety of documents, the critical one being evidence of the monthly income. The minimum is $1,500.

There's no website for the Uruguay Embassy in London but you can find full details of the retiree visa at: www.uruwashi.org/Consular.htm

---

URUGUAY CONTACT DIRECTORY

Embassies/Government
Uruguay Embassy in UK (no website)
Email: emburuguay@emburuguay.org.uy
Tel: (0207) 589 88 35
Fax: (0207) 581 95 85
British Embassy in Uruguay
http://www.ukinuruguay.fco.gov.uk
Uruguay Migration Department
www.dnm.minterior.gub.uy (in Spanish)

Travel & Health Advice
Foreign Office travel advice
www.fco.gov.uk/travel
www.nhs.uk/Healthcareabroad
www.masta.org

About Uruguay
www.uruguayliving.com
www.uruguayconnection.com/
http://globaledge.msu.edu/countryInsights
http://fita.org/countries/uruguay.html
http://directory.totaluruguay.com

General & Expat
www.expatfocus.com
http://britishexpats.com
www.transitionsabroad.com
http://board.classifieds1000.com
www.expatexchange.com

English Language Media
www.uruguaydailynews.com/

Property
www.criterio.com.uy/
www.puntacolorada.com.uy/english.htm
www.verdemar.com.uy
www.riodelaplatainmobiliaria.com/
www.buscandocasa.com
www.miramar.com.uy/
www.ventas.com.uy
www.promocionesyservicios.com.uy
www.Casasweb.com/default_es.aspx

Travel & Tourism
Ministry of Tourism
www.uruguaynatural.com
Latin American Travel Association
www.lata.org/
www.vivatravelguides.com

Getting There
Carrasco (Montevideo) is the main airport and there are other international airports in Punta del Este (Maldonado) and in Colonia. International flights arrive mainly via Buenos Aires.
Pluna is the national airline with flights to Spain, Paraguay, Chile, Brazil, Argentina. Iberian has flights from London, Edinburgh, Glasgow and Dublin.
www.pluna.com.uy
www.iberia.com
www.lufthansa.com
www.tam.com

Getting Around
Air: Domestic flights are cheap but limited. PLUNA flies to Punta del Este.
Train: Almost non-existent.
Bus: Regional and international buses leave from the Tres Cruces station. There are fast, comfortable and inexpensive intercity buses within Uruguay and beyond to the Brazialian cities of Porto Alegre, Sao Paulo and Rio.
Boat: There is a ferry service between Buenos Aires, Colonia and Montevideo and Punta del Este. There are daily services of hydrofoil and car ferries between Buenos Aires and Colonia or Montevideo
Taxis: Plentiful, efficient, safe and cheap. Taxis are metered in towns and cities and there are set fares for long journeys. The city's black-and-yellow taxis can be hailed on the street or called by phone.
Driving: Driving in Montevideo is not easy; streets are unmarked, traffic lights ignored or not working. Traveling by car poses few problems once outside the capital although winding roads and hills require some care. Roads are generally good. There is a universally ignored speed limit of 90km/hour. The main highway is from Montevideo to Punta Del Este.
Car Hire: Readily available but can be expensive as rental companies often charge by the mile.
Driving is on the right.

This Latin American beauty has a dark side

Why Venezuela?

A country of striking natural beauty and dramatic contrasts, Venezuela is the size of France and Germany put together and ranges from tropical Caribbean beaches to snowy Andean mountain peaks. It has 40 national parks, enormous rivers, forests, jungle, the highest waterfall in the world, the longest cable car ride and the largest lake in South America.

Except for the Andes the weather is balmy (average 27°C) and varies little year round.

There is no problem for foreigners to own property in Venezuela.

The clincher: Venezuela has amassed more Miss World and Miss Universe titles than any other country.

Is it safe?

This is a pretty dangerous country. The incidence of street crime is high, both in the capital, Caracas, and in the interior. Most sections of large cities are not safe to walk at night.

Armed muggings and kidnappings are a regular occurrence and can take place in broad daylight throughout the city including areas generally presumed safe and frequented by tourists. Armed gangs often set up fake police checkpoints. Investigation of all crime is haphazard and ineffective.

The road to and from Caracas International Airport (Maiquetia) is particularly dangerous. Corruption at the airport itself is rampant and travellers have been victims of personal property theft as well as mugging and "express kidnapping" in which they are forced to withdraw money from ATMs, often at gunpoint. Some travellers have been kidnapped and held captive for ransom in roadside huts.

It is also important to be wary of all strangers, even

those in official uniform or carrying official identification.

Incidents of taxi drivers in Caracas overcharging, robbing and injuring passengers are common.

How much tax will I pay?

Rental income from property owned by non-residents is taxed at 34 per cent after deductions for administrative expenses, repairs and maintenance, insurance, real estate tax and municipal tax.

Capital gains earned by non-residents are also taxed at 34 per cent.

Individuals resident in Venezuela are taxed on their income from any source. Residents are defined as those who spend more than 183 days in the country in one calendar year. Residents are allowed personal deductions and allowances.

Those whose annual net income is greater than $23,505 are subject to income tax. Deductible allowances include medical, dental and hospitalisation payments.

Is Venezuelan property a good investment?

There are no restrictions on the purchase of residential property by foreign nationals.

Local red tape is a cumbersome problem. So too is corruption and the expropriation of land and businesses deemed "essential to the public" by the Venezuelan government.

However, the concensus of opinion is that the right to own private property in the country will remain safe.

Where's best to live?

Groups of foreigners are rediscovering once feted resorts such as **Miranda**, with its inland waterways and Caribbean coast.

Margarita Island, also in the Caribbean, and the Paraguana peninsula on the north-west coast near Colombia are both designated as tax-free zones which means there is no VAT.

Margarita Island, hugely popular with tourists and less crime-ridden than the rest of the country, is likened to a mini Miami. Because of Venezuela's bad relations with the USA it is more popular with European visitors than those from the US.

Here you can buy a reasonable apartment for $62,000 and a modest house for double that amount.

Miranda, on Venezuela's Caribbean coast – said to be the most beautiful stretch of coastline in the country – vies for top spot with Margarita Island.

Then there's **Isla de Oro**, built by a former

PROPERTY

Caracola Beach and Spa

The Caracola Beach & Spa Resort comprises 1,244 apartments and duplex apartments spread over 15 floors, overlooking Caracola Beach on the eastern fringes of Margarita Island.
Apartments come with fully-fitted kitchens, air-conditioning systems and other aminities. There is a furniture option.
Prices range from $79,000.
More info: Bradleys International   www.thecaracolaresort.com
Tel: +44 (0) 1395 227700   Email: international@beagroup.co.uk

Margarita Island

1, 2 and 3-bed villas close to the beach on the Last Wind five-star resort estate on Margarita Island are on offer on a 10-year scheme with rental income of eight per cent guaranteed for the first two years.
Owners are guaranteed four weeks a year for their own use during the 10-year repayment period.
Price range: $105,000 (1 bed, semi-d)-$200,000 (3 bed, det)
More info: http://venezuela.homesgofast.com

FACTFILE

Capital: Caracas
Area: 912,050sq km
Population: 26.8 million
Language: Spanish with numerous dialects (the population is composed of Spanish, Italian, Portuguese, Arab, German, African and indigenous people)
Climate: Caracas has a tropical climate, tempered by its relatively high altitude position and proximity to the sea. Temperatures are comfortably warm (average 27°C) and vary little year round except in the Andes. There are really only two seasons: the dry season from October to April and the wet season from May to November. Some coastal areas go without rain for weeks.
Time difference: GMT -4.30 hours
Entry requirements: No visa is required for stays of up to 90 days.
Retirement/residence visa: Proof of a permanent source of income generated abroad of $1,200+ a month, plus $500 for each accompanying family member.
[See: The rules for getting in]
Electricity: 120V/60Hz (American two-pin plugs are generally used).
Money: Bolivar Fuerte (VEF). ATMs are widely available. Credit/debit cards and travellers cheques are generally accepted.
Public holidays 2010

Jan 1	New Year's Day
Feb 13-16	Carnival
April 1	Holy Thursday
April 2	Good Friday
April 19	Declaration of Independence
May 1	Labour Day
June 24	Battle of Carabobo
July 5	Independence Day
July 24	Birth of Simón Bolívar
Oct 12	Day of Indigenous Resistance
Dec 25	Christmas Day

Note: There are some additional regional holidays.
Opening hours
Banks: 8am-3.30pm Mon-Fri
Offices: 8am-5pm Mon-Fri
Shops: 8am-7pm on weekdays, later in shopping malls. In rural areas shops close from 12noon or 12.30pm until 2-3pm but stay open late.
Water: Use bottled.
Tipping: 10 per cent in restaurants and hotels, loose change for taxi drivers. Petrol pump attendants expect a tip.
Medical/Healthcare: No vaccination are required but those travelling in rural areas should be immunised against yellow fever, hepatitis A and typhoid. Some airlines may insist on a yellow fever certificate. There is a risk of malaria in jungle areas.
If you use regular medication it is advisable to take a supply with you. Medical services and supplies are limited in remote areas. Good private hospitals and clinics can be found in Caracas and other major cities but are expensive and will usually request up-front cash payment.
Pets: Dogs and cats require good health and rabies certificates. Dogs also require distemper certificate.

president of Venezuela 30 years ago as a playground for the rich, and now being restored after years of neglect. Many foreigners are buying here.

A two-hour drive from Caracas is **Los Canales**, a 100km network of canals (natural and man-made) in the state of Miranda. Popular among foreign buyers, it includes the towns of **San Jose** and **Rio Chico** and is famous for sport fishing and water sports of every kind.

Los Canales, whose banks are lined with houses and apartments, has a year-round sunny climate and is popular with Caracas's second homes owners.

There is a handy 18-hole golf course and in Rio Chico there are plenty of restaurants, bars and shops and services of every kind.

At the opposite end of the geographic scale is **Mérida**, the town of the 'never-ending spring', at an altitude of 1600m in the Andes. Here you can hike, climb or stroll in lush green mountains, camp in the national park at Mucuy, bathe in the icy streams and fish for trout.

You can also take the longest cable car lift in the world – to the top of Bolivar mountain.

After Margarita Island, Mérida is the second largest tourist destination in Venezuela and, although more suitable for outdoor types, offers a busy nightlife with restaurants where you can dine well for less than $5.

A city of culture, Mérida has a treasure-trove of period architecture dating from the 1500s and many ancient buildings that have been restored as galleries and museums.

Then there's **Gran Sabana** with sweeping landscapes of mountains, forests and rivers; **Paria** with lush green landscapes of small hills, farms and villages; and, washed by the Caribbean, the beautiful **Paraguana Peninsula** in the state of Falcon with picturesque scenery and endless golden beaches.

VENEZUELA CONTACT DIRECTORY

Embassies/Government
Venezuela Embassy in UK
www.venezlon.co.uk/visa_eng.htm
British Embassy in Caracas
http://ukinvenezuela.fco.gov.uk

Travel & Health Advice
Foreign Office travel advice
www.fco.gov.uk/travel
www.nhs.uk/Healthcareabroad
www.masta.org

About Venezuela
www.venezlon.co.uk/travellers.htm
http://think-venezuela.net
www.margarita-island.com
http://www.embavenez-us.org/
http://www.lonelyplanet.com/destinations/south_america/venezuela/
http://lcweb2.loc.gov/frd/cs/vetoc.html
http://www.cia.gov/cia/publications/factbook/geos/ve.html
www.casatrudel.com/living.htm

General & Expat
www.expats-welcome.com/en/venezuela
http://venezuelaexpats.net
www.expatfocus.com
www.britishexpat.com
www.transitionsabroad.com

English Language Media
www.thedailyjournalonline.com
(pretty feeble) English language newspaper

Property
(mostly in Spanish)
Caracas Real Estate
www.caracasinmuebles.com
www.bestrentals.org
Coldwell Banker Moviliza EL Rosal
www.coldwellbanker.com.ve
www.immomargarita.eu

www.margarita-real-estate.com
www.immomargarita.com
www.margaritadreamhomes.com
www.margaritabiz.com

Travel & Tourism
http://www.venezlon.co.uk/jewel.htm
www.think-venezuela.net
www.geodyssey.co.uk/venezuela
www.travel-amazing-southamerica.com/venezuela.html
Latin American Travel Association
www.lata.org/
www.vivatravelguides.com
Latin American Travel Association
www.lata.org

Getting There
British Airways offers direct flights to
Caracas www.british-airways.com
Air Europa   www.aireuropa.com
Air France   www.airfrance.com
Alitalia   www.alitalia.com
Iberia   www.iberia.com
Lufthansa   www.lufthansa.com
TAP   www.flytap.com
Continental Airlines
www.continental.com/uk
Aerolineas Argentinas
www.aerolineas.com.ar
Return fare range from UK: £450-600+.

Holiday charters, flights plus hotel, are
available for Margarita Island for about
£700 from:
www.firstchoice.co.uk
www.westernair.co.uk

Getting Around
Air: Since distances are relatively long
flying is usually the best option and
Venezuela has half-a-dozen provincial
airlines covering a network of regional and
remote routes and tourist destinations:
Laser www.laser.com.ve/laserweb_2008
Aeropostal
www.aeropostal.com/aero2004/home.html
Conviasa www.conviasa.aero/ or
Aserca www.ascercaairlines.com/
Avior www.avior.com.ve
Train: Limited to the Caracas subway and
a suburban light rail line.
Taxi: Because of the high levels of crime
visitors should always use a 24-hour
radio-dispatched taxi service.
Buses: Long-distance bus routes connect
most towns and cities with varying
degrees of comfort depending on what you
pay. Popular routes are serviced by
expreso (express), ejecutivo (executive) or
de lujo (luxury) buses. Buses are cheap –
around $4 for a two-hour journey and $15-
20 for a day-long trip.
Ferries: Venezuela has a number of
islands but the only ferry service is to
Margarita Island from the mainland at
Puerto La Cruz and Cumaná (two hours).
Weekly passenger boats operate between
Venezuela and Trinidad.
Driving: The roads are variable in standard
but the main roads in Caracas and to the
interior are good. Some of the top tourist
destinations, such as Angel Falls, Los
Roques and Canaima, are inaccessible by
car. The maximum speed on most roads is
55mph (80kph) but is generally ignored
and rarely enforced.
Car hire: Drivers are aggressive so self-
drive is not recommended. However, it's
tempting since petrol costs about 2p a litre
– 54 times cheaper than the UK (soft
drinks are 20 times more expensive).
Car hire can be expensive as rental
companies often charge by the mile.
Driving is on the right.

How to buy safely abroad

Avoid the potential pitfalls of purchasing abroad. Here's advice from the Association of International Property Professionals.

When buying abroad you will be operating in a culture and under the jurisdiction of a legal system that you will be unfamiliar with. Often language will be another barrier, and certainly if problems arise you will be at a major disadvantage if you end up trying to get justice in a faraway country.

Reduce the risks

The best advice is simply not to take unnecessary risks. Just because American buyers don't always use a lawyer when buying in Florida, it doesn't mean that you shouldn't. And even though most Greeks don't bother to get a survey done before buying their dream home in Skiathos, it doesn't mean that you should follow suit. Instead, load your purchase with safety features.

Know your limits

From the start, consider how risk-averse you are. Though there is much you can do to make a purchase safe, some countries are more regulated than others. In general, the areas that offer the most legal protection are also the most expensive.

There are breathtakingly beautiful parts of Afghanistan that offer extremely reasonably priced property, but would you feel safer buying in Florida even though the property is 100 times more expensive?

Between those two extremes there are nations with a history of British interest and therefore an English-speaking legal infrastructure; but perhaps you would prefer to buy in an area where there are relatively few British buyers. The choice is yours, but adjust your level of awareness and take extra care accordingly.

Check the small print

Politics and local government overseas can be a murkier business than in the UK so you need to know that any planning permissions are in order and have been approved officially. Working with government departments abroad can also be a frustrating business – many of us buy overseas for the relaxed pace of life, but aren't so keen when that lack of speed extends to our property purchase!

Estate agents are often unregulated, and almost everyone you deal with has a vested interest in your property purchase going ahead, so don't expect many of them to counsel caution.

Finding a reputable agent

Once you have chosen the country you wish to buy in, your first point of contact is likely to be an estate agent. You will probable find the agent in the pages of a magazine or via the internet. It is important to check that they are reputable and trained for the job.

Many countries have a register of qualified and accredited agents and some, such as the USA, have indemnity insurance to cover you

in case an agent's mistakes cost you money.

Membership of the AIPP is a good benchmark of quality, too – becoming a member requires relevant experience and voluntary agreement to a code of conduct, so it is a sign that an agent is committed to professional standards.

Word-of-mouth recommendation is highly valuable, so try to get in touch with people who have previously used the same estate agency, or speak to other professionals in the business, such as lawyers and surveyors, to see if they know of a good agent that they can recommend to you.

Dealing with developers

For those buying off-plan, being able to trust the developer is all-important. Sometimes the developer will be acting as an estate agent too, but usually they will be simply building the property.

When buying off-plan you need to be extra careful because you are buying the promise of a building rather than bricks and mortar. However, that is reflected in the price, which is usually lower than for a finished property.

There are various safeguards you can use to minimise risk. Firstly, is the developer reputable? Many are Members of AIPP, and as with agents, checking the list of members is a good starting point. There are also several industry awards for quality of development, and the AIPP has its own awards that focus on customer service.

A winning team

Even the best developer and agent will have a vested interest in you buying as much property for as high a price as possible, so it is vital to get a team together that is batting just for you.

The team should also include a lawyer, a surveyor and a currency broker at the very least. Get a lawyer on board as soon as possible, as they may be able to save you money from the start by structuring the purchase, the ownership and dealing with any inheritance issues.

AIPP Members have to recommend the use of an independent lawyer. 'Independent' means that the lawyer represents you and only you in the transaction. Your lawyer should also be experienced in property law in the country in which you plan to buy.

Essential viewing

Such was the mania for buying property before the credit crunch that some buyers bought without even seeing the property.

Travelling to a country and viewing the property is really a no-brainer, even for investment property, and many agents will even pay for your flight and accommodation. The alternative is to use a property finder.

When viewing a property, remember that building practices and descriptions are not the same in other parts of the world. In some places kitchens are treated like furniture; something that the owners brings with them. In others, 'finished' might not mean habitable. Take nothing for granted; no question is too obvious

for you to ask your agent.

If you are viewing a property built by a developer, ask to see another of their projects while you are in the country. This way you can assess the quality and style of the finish and the standard of the fixtures and fittings. Pay attention to the upkeep of the development. If it looks shoddy or unkempt, chances are that your development will end up the same way.

With resale properties it is vital that you understand exactly where the boundaries of your property are, and that can only be done by being there. And, as previously mentioned, having a survey done before you buy is vital.

Don't lose your head

When it comes to buying the property, don't sign anything unless your lawyer has approved it first. In the excitement of finding the perfect property, it is all too easy to over-commit yourself to a purchase.

You have a responsibility to inform and protect yourself when buying property overseas just as you would when you buy in your own country. Ask a lot of questions and be sure that you are fully informed about the process, and financial commitment you are undertaking.

By following these basic rules, you should ensure that your purchase runs safely and smoothly. After this stage it is largely up to your lawyer. Most British buyers have purchased perfectly safely and happily.

Let's keep it that way.

AIPP – The Association of International Property Professionals – is a non-profit organisation whose aim is to improve the standards of professionalism in the international property market. AIPP members sign a code of conduct requiring them to "act with honesty, transparency and integrity in all the dealings with the public and with the industry".
The AIPP website [www.aipp.org.uk] has a list of members or you can search by company name.

Top 10 mistakes when buying overseas

1. Losing your deposit

When choosing a property, perhaps at an exhibition or an inspection trip, you will often be asked to pay a small holding deposit of around £2,000, and to sign a reservation contract.

Generally, this is a perfectly reasonable request as a statement of your serious intent to buy a property and for it to be taken off the market. However, you need to check if the deposit will be refunded should you change your mind.

2. Signing contacts too early

When paying a holding deposit you should only sign a reservation contract which does not bind you into buying the property. You may be asked to sign a preliminary contract, which is a much more serious document and commits you to buying the property or to possibly losing your deposit and opening you up to the risk of damages if you pull out. It is essential that you sign this only after your lawyer has read it.

3. Overstretching your finances

Many buyers have been convinced that if they buy, for example, three off-plan properties, they can sell two on completion and use the profit to pay for the third. This is a high-risk strategy: ask yourself what you will do if you cannot find a buyer.

4. Over-leveraging investment

If you buy a £100,000 investment property with £20,000 cash (equity) and £80,000 mortgage, and property values increase by 20 per cent, then your property is worth £120,000 and your equity has doubled. This is called leveraging. But if property prices drop by 30 per cent, your investment is wiped out and you are into negative equity. It is a great investment strategy in a rising market, but beware of the risks.

5. Whose house is it?

Many of the countries in which we are now buying have seen wars and political changes that may make it difficult to pin down exactly who is the rightful owner of a property. Other countries may have complex inheritance laws where assets must be split several ways. Either way, it is essential to get a good lawyer with local knowledge.

6. Developers going to bust

There are two kinds of guarantee: 'Extrinsic' guarantees are where a bank has accepted joint liability with the developer, meaning that if the developer goes bankrupt, the project will still be finished. 'Intrinsic' guarantees simply promise that the developer will refund your money if they are unable to complete the project. All guarantees will have conditions – get your lawyer to check these carefully.

7. Expensive renovations

We have all seen those beautiful, dilapidated houses that could be lovely if only they were done up. Beware! Unless you are on site to supervise, are au fait with building processes and have builders you can trust, renovating abroad can be hard work and more expensive than buying new.

8. Planning permission

Some buyers seem to believe that local planning laws are barely enforced at all and that if they are caught breaching them they can plead that as a British buyer they just did not understand the rules. This may have worked 20 years ago, but not now.

9. Changing airline routes

Do not rely on airline routes staying in place forever. Many airlines chop and change routes at very short notice. Ensure you have an alternative route worked out.

10. Poor neighbourhood

Agents and developers are in the business of selling property. They may only show you the best of an area; so make sure that you take a good look around the neighbourhood before committing yourself to a purchase. Check it out at different times of the day, too.

You may not know this, but you should

You can never have too much information when buying abroad. Here are some things to consider

You don't know the cost of your property until you have funds in the local currency. With volatile currencies, the price of your property will fluctuate according to exchange rates. For added certainty speak to a foreign exchange (FX) company about 'forward buying' currency. Alternatively, pay for the property with a mortgage in the local currency.

Pension values fluctuate with exchange rates

When planning to retire abroad, your UK-paid income will be subject to fluctuations that are entirely out of your control. The way round this is to forward buy currency. Speak to a foreign exchange company.

Building site blues

Buying in 'phase one' means there will be more building once your property is finished. Be absolutely clear about where the next phase of the development will be, when building will take place and whether it continues through the holiday season. If pools,

clubhouses and sports facilities are part of the deal, pin down when they will be completed.

Freezing pensions

In all of the EU and many other countries, pensions paid to expatriate Britons rise each year, just as they do in the UK. However, in many countries, including much of the Commonwealth including Canada, Australia and South Africa, they are frozen at the level when you moved abroad.

In many countries the buyer pays the estate agent's fees

Buying costs can be higher in some countries where the agent fees are split between buyer and seller, rather than paid by the seller alone. In France you might pay as much as 4-8 per cent to the agent. In Italy each side will sometimes pay 3 per cent.

Make a will

A valid English will is accepted in most major European countries but should its terms conflict with the laws of the country, it may only have a partial effect. Solicitors with expertise in UK and foreign property law will be able to advise on any restrictions and inheritance

tax implications under the laws of both countries.

Furniture packages

If furniture packages provided by the developers seem expensive, before rushing out to buy your own furniture, consider the full costs. You may need to hire a large van, spend several days choosing the furniture, transport it, carry it up several flights of stairs and then assemble it. Plus, you may pay more, because the developer will have been buying in bulk.

Cheats rarely prosper

It has long been a tradition in some parts of the world to understate the purchase price of a property to cut down on taxes and notary fees. However, not only is this illegal, but when you come to sell, unless you can persuade the new buyer to try the same trick, you may be liable for higher Capital Gains Tax.

Rental guarantees

Often an off-plan property comes with a guarantee that the developer will let the property for you for a certain number of weeks per year. Check if the purchase price of the property is higher to pay for the guarantee.

Trading places
Here's a way to have a quick look first

Friends might think you mad if you moved to another country to retire without taking a look first. There's a way of doing so which allows you to save money, live like a native, meet the neighbours, shop in local stores, and eat in neighbourhood restaurants. Welcome to the world of home exchange as described by www.homeexchange.com

If you're willing to allow someone else to live in your home and you don't mind living in someone else's house or apartment, this is a way for you to explore some of the options.

Home exchangers trade their homes at a time that is convenient to both parties. Such arrangements are not restricted to conventional properties. For example, one exchanger traded his home for a 40-foot yacht. Another couple swapped their villa in Italy for a motor caravan in Oregon. Often, home exchangers will include their cars as part of the package.

There are also hospitality exchangers where couples or families host each other in their homes at designated times. Your home exchange partners stay with you as guests and then you go and stay with them as their guests. There is a social aspect to this kind of exchange that some exchangers particularly enjoy. With this mode of exchange you also get a built-in tour guide.

A bistro too

If the idea of home exchange is unfamiliar to you, or even a bit frightening, rest assured – there are 250,000-plus successful home exchanges every year. Swapping homes can bring many unexpected rewards. You get a much closer look at other cultures and a better "feel" for the places you visit and the connections you make with your home exchange partners can turn into lifelong friendships.

Every exchange is unique and the whole concept of home exchange relies on building a relationship of mutual trust and goodwill. As with all things, there are risks involved. It's natural to have reservations about giving up your home to strangers.

What if they are not as tidy as you? Will they be able to work your DVD without breaking it? How can you be sure you're not getting a bungalow instead of the villa they described? Most of these risks can be minimised to alleviate your fears. And don't forget, the people you're exchanging with face the same risks.

Who are home exchangers? They come from all walks of life. Most are fairly well educated, adventurous, reliable, and have an interest in learning more about different places and cultures. Home exchange is ideal for retirees who wants to consider their options.

The world is your oyster and there are unlimited opportunities. Do you long for a mountain setting? A seaside resort? Do you want to have a quick look at Mexico or Malaysia, Australia or the Azores, Cyprus or Colombia?

Make a list of all the places you'd like to visit, then nail down some dates of when you want to go and how long you'd like to stay. Keep your options open until you see what's available. Don't hesitate to add a place to your list that you may not have given a lot of thought about. It takes time to complete arrangements for an exchange, so allow plenty of lead time. Figure on four to six months.

Home exchanges have been around for some time. In the past, they've been done through word-of-mouth. Now, via the Internet, exchanges are at your fingertips, literally. Each year, more and more people are getting into home exchange as a way to see the world. Why not give it a try?

Log on to HomeExchange and look around. You may discover a whole new world!

More info
www.homeexchange.com
www.homelink.org.uk
www.yourhomeformine.com
www.yourhomeformine.com
www.1sthomeexchange.com
www.HomeExchangeNow.co.uk
www.christianhomeswap.com/
www.easyhomeexchange.com/
www.exchangeholidayhomes.com
www.exchangehomes.com
www.holswap.com/default.htm
homeexchange50plus.com

Tor FX helps you get the best exchange rate

UK based foreign currency provider Tor FX offers a variety of services that can ensure you obtain a fair and preferential exchange rate when moving your money overseas, while also helping to manage the risks associated with volatile currency markets.

The worst recession in a generation has caused the Pound to depreciate 26% against the U.S Dollar over the past year, and 23% versus the Euro, so it's even more important to choose the best course of action to prevent your purchase becoming any more expensive, and maximise your buying power.

Banks simply do not offer this service

On contacting Tor FX, you will be allocated a personal currency account manager who can help you effectively manage your exposure and develop a strategy to ensure that you plan the timing of your purchase to your benefit. A major benefit of dealing with an independent broker is the ability to talk to currency experts throughout the course of your transaction. The banks simply do not offer this service.

Opening a private trading account couldn't be simpler through our website, and usually takes a couple of minutes. Tor FX is a regulated company and we are bound by law to identify every client that trades with us as part of our anti-money laundering regulations.

Once you are registered, your dedicated account manager will contact you and begin plotting the best

Tor FX doesn't charge any commission

course of action for you to purchase your currency. We offer a range of services including daily market updates by email, forward contracts and the use of stop and limit orders.

Forward buying means that our clients can reserve their currency for a date up to two years in the future

if the current rate of exchange is attractive for them to do so. We will only require 5-10% deposit on forward purchases with the remaining balance on the due date specified by the client.

If you have a view on where the market is likely to go, you can place a limit order at your desired rate. The order will be closely monitored by our dealing desk and we will guarantee you that rate if the trading rate reaches the specified level (day or night).

A limit order can be used if the client believes that the rate is likely to improve. However, what if the rate of exchange seems to deteriorating? Your account manager can recommend price levels for a 'stop order', characterized as your 'worst case scenario'. If there is a particular rate that you deem to be your worst acceptable level, then Tor FX can work an automatic buy order that is triggered if the rate reaches that level. This mechanism protects you against a sudden adverse movement in the market. Many clients use "stop and limit" orders in combination. This allows the possibility of obtaining a better rate, with the added protection against unforeseen events that can cause unexpected volatility.

Your step by step guide to get the best exchange rate

Step 1

Set up your account
We need to register you as a client in order to open a trading facility, enabling you to instruct a dealer to purchase or sell currency over the telephone. We will also send you regular market updates allowing you to keep up to speed on currency movements.

Step 2

Discuss your foreign exchange requirements
Your dealer will provide you with up-to-date views on market trends, and suggest strategies to meet your objectives and optimise your potential savings. The strategy you agree with your dealer will depend on your time frame and your risk profile. This may, for example, involve trying to achieve a target exchange rate (Market Order) or simply transacting at the current market rate.

It is important that you understand that the currency markets can be volatile. If, for example, the market improves, you cannot amend the agreed contract. Any decision to proceed is yours alone. Tor FX can only act upon your specific instructions.

Step 3

Buy and transfer your currency
Having discussed your requirements the dealer will offer you an exchange rate. If you are happy with the rate offered, you should instruct your dealer to proceed with the transaction. All our phone calls are digitally recorded to ensure that your verbal instruction has been accurately executed. Please note that your verbal instruction to buy currency is a legally binding contract between you and Tor FX. The Contract Note we send you is simply a confirmation of your transaction.

Step 4

When you receive your Contract Note
In part 2 of your Contract Note you will have details of Tor FX segregated accounts held within BARCLAYS, you initiate the transfer from your end and return the contract note back to your dealer with part 3 completed showing the deposit account of your purchased currency. Tor FX accounts will inform you by e-mail when your funds arrive and when they send your currency out.

Buying and Selling Currency - Your Options
Whatever your situation, it is important to identify and minimise the risk that the market may move against you. Unlike your high street bank, Tor FX gives you access to a number of currency options to ensure you stay on budget and firmly in control.

Get to know the terminology

Base Currency
The currency against which other currencies are quoted. Example, the primary base currency is the US dollar.

Bear Market
A market in which prices decline sharply against a background of widespread pessimism (opposite of Bull Market). Bear Markets are generally shorter in duration than Bull Markets.

Bid
The rate at which a dealer is willing to buy the base currency.

Bull Market
A market characterized by rising prices.

Broker
An agent who handles investors' orders to buy and sell currency.

Counterparty
The customer or bank with which a foreign exchange deal is executed.

Cross Rate
An exchange rate between two currencies, usually constructed from the individual exchange rates of the two currencies, measured against the United States dollar.

Day Trading
Refers to opening and closing the same position or positions before the close of that day's trading (3:00p.m. EST).

Flat/Square
Where a Client has not traded in that currency or where an earlier deal is reversed thereby creating a neutral (flat) position. Example: bought $100,000 then sold $100,000 = FLAT.

Forex
An abbreviation of foreign exchange.

Fundamental Analysis
Analysis based on economic factors.

GTC
"Good Till Cancelled." An order left with a Dealer to buy or sell at a fixed price. The order remains in place until it is cancelled by the client.

Interbank Rates
The FX rates large international banks

Tor FX also offers a regular overseas payment facility for smaller amounts of money ideal for pension transfers and mortgage payments. This service is available on a monthly or bi-monthly basis for transfers ranging between £250 and £5000 per month. It also cuts out the hassle of having to arrange individual transfers each month. All you need to do is set up a standing order, and Tor FX will do the rest. You can elect to receive the prevailing spot rate for each payment, or you can fix your exchange rate so you know exactly how much currency will reach your account each month.

As well as providing highly competitive exchange rates on regular overseas payments, Tor FX also charge 0% commission, providing a saving on average of 3% over the exchange rates offered by high street banks. Your funds are held in a segregated client account to provide that extra bit of security and Tor FX will guarantee same day delivery of your currency.

The table below outlines the typical minimum savings achieved by using Tor FX rather than the bank.

Regular Overseas Payments - ideal for pension transfers

Foreign exchange

	Commission		Transfer Fee		Total Per Year
	Monthly	Annual	Monthly	Annual	
Tor FX	£0	£0	£0	£0	£0
Bank	£30	£360	£30	£360	£720

SAVING OVER 12 MONTHS = £720

Based on a monthly transfer of £1,000

Contact us now

**Call free from the UK: 0800 612 6896
Outside the UK: 00 44 1736 335292,
Email: currency@torfx.com**

If you would like to speak to a Tor FX account manager and discuss your requirements and/or seek advice please contact:

**Tor FX New Business Team. Call free from the UK: 0800 612 6896
Outside the UK: 00 44 1736 335292, Email: currency@torfx.com**

quote other large international banks. Normally the public and other businesses do not have access to these rates. Global Forex is one of the few companies able to provide clients with rates provided by multiple global banks.

Limit Order
An order given which has restrictions upon its execution, where the client may specify a price and the order can be executed only if the market reaches that price.

Long
A market position where the Client has bought a currency he previously did not own. Normally expressed in base currency terms. For example: long Dollars (short Japanese Yen).

Margin
Margin is a cash deposit provided by

clients as collateral to cover possible future losses that may result from the clients Foreign Exchange trades.

Margin Call
A demand for additional funds. A requirement by a clearing house that a clearing member (or by a brokerage firm that a client) brings margin deposits up to a required minimum level to cover an adverse movement in price in the market.

Offer
The rate at which a Dealer is willing to sell the base currency.

Open Position
Any deal which has not been offset or reversed by an equal and opposite deal.

Pip or Points
Depending on context, normally one basis point, i.e. 0.0001.

Short
A market position where the Client has sold a currency he does not already own. Normally expressed in base currency terms, example, short Dollars (long Japanese Yen).

Spread
The difference in prices between bid and offer rates.

Stop Loss Order
An order to buy or sell at the market when a particular price is reached, either above or below the price that prevailed when the order was given.

Technical Analysis
Based on market action through chart study, moving averages, volume, open interest, formations, and other technical indicators.

Volatility: A measure of price fluctuations.

Successfully Financing Your Overseas Property Purchase

The first priority is obviously to find the finance for your overseas property purchase.

You will need the services of a company that specialises in sourcing mortgages for overseas property purchases worldwide, whether this is via an overseas mortgage or by releasing equity from your main residence.

So how do overseas mortgages work?
Behind all of the hype and scaremongering surrounding the credit crunch the most fundamental and important elements of borrowing remain the same. If you get good experienced help and take advantage of what's available you'll be in good shape.

When should you get advice?
The answer's simple - as early as possible in the buying process.

If you arrange the finance first then you'll end up with the peace of mind of knowing that a property is within your budget, that you qualify for a mortgage, and that you may find that you can actually afford a better property than you originally thought.

So how do overseas lenders calculate what you can borrow?
Overseas lenders calculate what you can borrow based upon affordability. Each lender has its own set of terms but in general they all work to similar guidelines.

These guidelines hinge in the main on two questions
- Can the clients prove their income?
- What is the clients' debt to income ratio (DTI)?

If they cannot prove their income then the mortgage will be declined. Even when overseas banks were keen to lend they still didn't embrace self certified mortgages. This is probably why a number of them have weathered the credit crunch better than their counterparts. Proof of income, if employed, will be via payslips and end of year tax figures; if self-employed then by providing two years accounts.

Most lenders work on what they call a debt to income ratio. This ratio differs from country to country and from lender to lender. In Egypt for example the DTI tends to be 40%.

For example, a client has net income per month of £4000. Therefore £1600 has to cover the clients' new overseas mortgage payment plus their existing monthly debt payments including any existing mortgage, loans or credit card payments.

Let us assume they have a mortgage payment of £700, a monthly credit card bill of £100 and their new overseas mortgage will be £700 - then, in this instance, they would be approved by the overseas bank.

However, if their monthly debt payments were £1000 then this would exceed this ratio because the total would be £1700 and the lender would decline the case.

So "How do I propose to finance my overseas property purchase?" should be the first question you should ask yourself before signing anything.

Armed with that information you already have an idea as to how you will be viewed by an overseas bank and how successful your mortgage application is likely to be.

Frequently asked questions

How do you propose to finance your purchase?
I intend to pay cash. Have you considered the tax implications of paying cash for your property? If you are planning on renting out your property then mortgage interest is a tax deductible item. Therefore, it may be more advantageous for you to keep your savings and use mortgage finance. If you are planning on living in your property then there may be tax advantages of having a mortgage.

I'm selling my house. If your house doesn't sell quickly how long are you prepared to put your life on hold? Had you considered the benefits of letting your main residence property? You need to evaluate how you can make the move abroad before you've sold your home, and how it needn't cost you more than your existing mortgage payments. You also need to

review the pros and cons of letting your property and the tax benefits.

I don't own a property in the UK - can I get a mortgage? Yes, you can get an overseas mortgage providing you have a sufficient deposit.

I'm self employed - can I get a mortgage? Yes, providing you can provide business accounts or recent tax returns.

I'm on a pension can I get a mortgage? Yes, as a retired person you cannot be made unemployed and your income isn't reliant on whether you're healthy enough to work. Therefore, your advisor should research the whole of the market and have links with lenders that will not discriminate because of your age.

My bank said no - so why would anyone else lend me the money? Every lender has a different set of criteria for each client. Your bank can only offer its own products whereas independent advisors research the whole market to find a lender that meets your needs. Your advisor should have a strong relationship with lenders and underwriters who will judge each case on its merits.

I want to keep my home and rent it out - is it possible? Yes, your advisor should recommend the best buy to let deal for your property and discuss the pros and cons of letting your property and the tax benefits.

My existing mortgage deal has penalties if I move away - can these be avoided? You need to discuss with your advisor the options of a further advance with your existing lender or a secured loan.

I already have a financial advisor. Does he specialise in overseas mortgage finance? Is there any reason why you wouldn't value a second opinion - some advisors have access to exclusive deals that are not available to other brokers.

Surely going straight to a bank would be better and cheaper? Not necessarily - a good advisor will provide independent advice researching the whole of the mortgage market ensuring you get the best deals.

I have had credit problems - can I get a mortgage? It will depend upon your individual circumstances. An advisor will ensure you get the best deal by finding a lender that will take your circumstances into consideration.

How quickly can I arrange the finance? Your advisor will discuss your requirements and will then complete a fact-find which will determine whether you qualify. If you do he should then confirm what deals are available and the associated fees in writing. Once you are happy to proceed then he will submit your application and get a decision from the bank. As your advisor should already know the bank's criteria then he should only be sending applications that are likely to be agreed. Typically it takes around 8 weeks from initial contact to when you receive your mortgage offer.

I intend to do the research for finance myself. Are you qualified? Products change on a daily basis so advisors keep up-to-date and will have details of new products. Some deals are only available through intermediaries.

What will it cost me? Your advisor should always look to obtain the best rate with the lowest fees depending upon your requirements and circumstances. Before you agree to proceed you will be able to make an informed decision based upon written details of the proposed deal

Happy property hunting!

Overseas
Mortgage Broker

*This section was compiled by **Overseas Mortgage Broker Ltd** - a specialist company that provides advice on funding overseas purchases via a mortgage or equity release. Their contact details are as follows:*
www.overseasmortgagebroker.co.uk Freephone 0800 783 0459.
Quote IDR as a reference when calling

Planning your move

Moving home internationally is one of the biggest decisions you will make. However, with effective planning even a complex international move can be handled efficiently, economically and with the least possible disruption.

'Moving Checklist'
Your first steps towards a trouble free move:

1. 3/4 weeks before moving day
- Confirm dates with your removal company
- Sign, complete and return your agreement along with all supporting documentation
- Book insurance at the declared value
- Make arrangements to sell anything you are not taking with you: cars, furniture, etc
- Book flights and check luggage allowance with travel agent/airline
- Make arrangements for pets: inoculations, pet passport, kennelling, and flights
- Contact: doctor, dentist, optician. Get copies of your medical history and prescription details
- Copy all personal papers: educational certificates, birth/marriage certificates, insurance policies, legal documentation, etc
- Transfer and/or set up new bank accounts
- Notify credit card companies
- Cancel any store cards
- Advise the relevant authorities that you are leaving: NHS, HM Customs and Revenue, DVLC
- Notify all policy companies: insurance, assurance, investments, etc
- Notify all service providers:
  - Bank
  - Doctors
  - Dentist
  - Optician
  - Vet
  - Telephone
  - Water
  - Gas
  - Electricity
  - TV Licence
  - Passport Office
- Send change of address cards to family and friends
- Ask Post Office to re-route mail
- Clear the loft
- Put items you are not selling or disposing of into storage
- Confirm the Pre-Move Survey inventory completed by your removal company to ensure the correct allocation for you shipment

2. One week before moving day
- Cancel milk/newspaper deliveries

- Start running down contents of fridge/freezer
- Find and label keys
- Separate jewellery, trinkets and other small items
- Sort out linen and clothes
- Clean all outdoor items

3. One day before moving day

- Take down curtains and/or blinds
- Defrost fridge and freezer
- Pack your travel luggage
- Identify and isolate items not to be part of your shipment

4. Moving day

- Check meter readings and advise the relevant suppliers
- Pack essential items into your hand luggage
- After removal team has emptied the property check through to ensure that everything has been removed
- Switch off power and water
- Hand keys to estate agent

Packing for export

Packing is a specialist skill so most removal companies have experienced and professionally trained staff to provide this service for you. They will decide what type of packing and wrapping is necessary during the pre-move survey.

They should use modern, environmentally friendly, purpose-made materials to pack all your possessions ready for moving. China and glassware should be wrapped in special paper and then packed in double-thickness cartons, and furniture wrapped in bubble-blanket for extra protection. Items ren uiring special care such as antin ues should be packed in made-to-measure wooden crates, if appropriate.

Air Freight and LCL (Less than a Container Load) cargo should be over-cased in purpose-built, tri-wall board cases for optimum protection.

The 'Moving Checklist' is provided by White & Company - one of the founder members of the prestigious British Association of Removers (BAR). With over 130 years experience in the removal industry, a fleet of more than 200 vehicles each fitted with state-of-the-art tracking devices, it offers a complete door-to-door service to wherever in the world you are moving to. White & Company can also provide storage in one of their bonded storage facilities if you haven't already found your ideal property.

Put your toe in the water before you jump in!

Visit the country of your choice if you have never been there and at different times of the year. If you have been to the country as a tourist you may need to see it out of season as well and, if the climate is a reason for moving, find out what to expect in all seasons.

Your needs as a resident will be different from your needs as a holiday visitor. Find out the advantages and potential pitfalls. Living in another country on a trial basis may help you to gain a better understanding of the lifestyle without giving up your home in the UK.

Consider your normal daily life and how this may change, for example if you use public transport, are there good transport links in your chosen area and if you had to give up driving, would you still be able to get around easily?

Are there any different rights or responsibilities you may face, in law or socially? In regions where there are a high proportion of expatriates, voluntary associations may have been formed to assist new and existing non-nationals to settle.

Is moving abroad the right choice?

Before planning a move abroad it is important to consider whether it is the right decision for you. Why are you going? What do you hope to get out of it? Are you being realistic?

Although living abroad is an exciting new experience, no matter where you go you cannot escape all the realities and problems of daily life. It is important to find out as much as possible about the country you plan to live in to ensure that the culture and lifestyle will suit you. Research what life in your chosen country is like and talk to others who have made the move, perhaps through local expatriate or returning residents' groups.

If you are considering moving to a non-English-speaking country, mastering the language can be vital in helping you to settle in. Paying bills, maintaining

your property, going to the doctor and socialising will be extremely difficult if you cannot communicate.

Choosing your home

Often the most exciting aspect of beginning a new life abroad is purchasing the perfect home; the type of home you choose and its location can be crucial in ensuring that your life abroad is a long-term success.

If you decide to buy a property it is important to engage the services of an independent legal adviser. It is also important to be aware of local inheritance laws and any additional land or service charges you may be subject to.

If the property you are buying is somewhere you intend to stay for many years, consider how suitable it would be if your circumstances change. For example, if you were reliant on a car to reach local amenities, what would happen if you or your partner were no longer able to drive?

To summarise: before buying a property abroad consider the following:

- Are there local amenities (shops, medical facilities) within easy walking distance?
- Are there good public transport links nearby?
- Will the property be easy to maintain or adapt should your needs and abilities change?
- Do properties in the area sell quickly and easily?

* Age UK is the organisation combining Age Concern and Help the Aged.
This article is a summary of more detailed advice you can find at: www.ageconcern.org.uk

Receiving your state pension abroad

Advice from the Department for Work and Pensions

You can claim your state pension if you live outside the UK. However, you will only receive the yearly index-linked increases if you live in the European Economic Area (EEA) or Switzerland or in a country with which the UK has a social security agreement that includes state pensions (see below).

If you live outside those areas you will not be entitled to the yearly index-linked increases.

If you live abroad your state pension can be paid electronically into a bank or building society in the UK or into a bank in most countries.

Payment will be made in the local currency of the country in which the bank account is held. No charges are made for this service.

If you live in a country that is not listed, payment can be made directly into any UK bank account or by a sterling cheque to your home address. Cheques can be sent every four or 13 weeks.

For small amounts of pension, under £5 per week, annual payments may be made, usually at Christmas.

If you only spend part of the year abroad

If you divide your time between the UK and abroad you will have to choose which country you want your state pension paid into. You cannot choose to have it paid in one country for part of the year, and a different country for the rest of the year.

Paying tax on your state pension

Your tax position will depend on whether you are classed as 'non-UK resident' for tax purposes and the country in which you're living

If you spend part of your time in the UK and part abroad you are likely to be classed as a UK resident. If you move abroad permanently you are likely to be classed as a non-UK resident.

If you are a non-resident your tax position depends on whether you live in a country with a double taxation agreement with the UK. This means you won't have to pay UK tax on your state pension, but it will be taxable in the country where you live.

If you live in a country without a double taxation agreement, you will have to pay UK tax and may be taxed again abroad.

It's a good idea to get advice about paying tax on your state pension if you live abroad. You can contact HMRC Residency. You can view a list of countries with double taxation agreements with the UK at: www.hmrc.gov.uk/si/double.htm

Who to contact before you move abroad

If you're moving abroad to live, you'll need to tell:

- The Pension Service
- HM Revenue & Customs' National Insurance Contributions Office
- Your Tax Office

You will also need to give them your change of address.

Countries with social security agreements with the UK:

Barbados	Mauritius
Bermuda	New Zealand
Canada	Philippines
Israel	Former Yugoslavia
Jamaica	Switzerland
Jersey (CI)	Turkey
Guernsey (CI)	USA

This article summarises more detailed advice to be found at:
www.direct.gov.uk/en/Pensionsandretirementplanning/StatePension/index.htm

Staying healthy abroad
Nanny knows best

The government gets a lot of stick for telling us how to run our lives but – to be fair – does dish out some sensible advice. Here's a checklist of things to remember when planning your trip, covering steps to take before you go and while you're away.

Before you go

Before you go look at the potential health risks for the country you're going to. Your doctor can give you advice and arrange any immunisations and anti-malaria medication you need or you can go to a specialist travel clinic. Try to go at least two months before you leave.

For certain countries you may also need to start taking anti-malaria medication before you go.

You can also get information about health risks from the embassy or high commission of the country you're going to, or online from the National Travel Health Network and Centre (Nathnac) [http://www.nathnac.org] and the Foreign and Commonwealth Office (FCO) [www.fco.gov.uk]

Immunisations

Make sure you've got all the immunisations you need for the country you're going to by checking the NHS immunisation website [http://www.immunisation.nhs.uk] or by asking your GP.

Prescription medicines

If you are taking prescription medicines find out whether you will be able to get them where you are going.

You will also need to find out if there are any restrictions on taking your medicines in and out of the UK or the country you are going to – some medicines available over the counter in the UK may be controlled in other countries, and vice versa. Ask the relevant embassy or high commission, contact the Home Office Drugs Branch on 020 7035 0472 or check the Home Office website.

You might need a letter from your doctor giving details about your medication. Always carry medicines in a correctly labelled container.

Existing medical conditions

Take a written record of any medical conditions you have and the proper names – not just the trade names

– of any medication you are taking. Keep the record with you.

First-aid and travel kits

A basic first-aid kit, with some plasters, insect repellent, antiseptic cream and water sterilisation tablets, won't take up much space and could be extremely useful. You can buy them in pharmacies and specialist travel clinics.

Health insurance

Making sure you've got adequate health insurance is essential. Even if you are going to a country that has a reciprocal healthcare agreement with the UK, you may still need to pay for medical treatment. [See separate article]

Food and drink

Lots of travellers get diarrhoea from eating or drinking something contaminated. You can also get diseases like cholera, typhoid and hepatitis A from contaminated food and water. You can reduce the risk by:

- Washing your hands after going to the toilet and before handling food or eating.
- Boiling or sterilising water with purification tablets or using bottled water and using clean water for washing food and cleaning your teeth.
- Avoiding ice unless you're sure it's made from treated, chlorinated water.
- Making sure food has been thoroughly cooked.
- Avoiding uncooked food or food that is likely to have been exposed to flies.
- Fish and shellfish can be suspect in some countries. Uncooked shellfish is especially risky.

Insect and animal bites

Use an insect repellent, and keep your arms and legs covered if there's a chance of being bitten. Remember, you can catch tick-borne diseases in cooler countries, not just in the tropics. Animal bites can lead to serious – and even fatal – infections.

Lack of cover could cost you

Medical cover is arguably the most important element of any travel insurance policy, if only because of the cost if something should happen without it.

The Consumers' Association recommends that you should have £1m of medical cover in Europe and £2m in the USA and the rest of the world.

You may think this seems like a huge amount but when you consider the cost of medical care outside the UK it begins to make sense. For example, the Foreign and Commonwealth Office notes the following costs:

- Returning you to the UK in an air ambulance from the east coast of the USA can cost up to £35,000 and emergency medical treatments such as surgery can cost even more.
- A flight, stretcher and doctor escort from Australia could cost £15-20,000.

What's covered?

A large number of things are covered under the term "medical expenses" in your policy. Some include:

- Emergency medical treatment or surgery.
- Returning your ashes to the UK, or the cost of a funeral in the country where you die.
- Accommodation and travel expenses if a medical condition makes you unable to return home.
- Extra accommodation and travel expenses for someone to accompany you on the journey home.
- Expenses for someone to travel from the UK to stay and return home with you, if this is deemed absolutely necessary under medical advice.

Each policy will offer different levels of cover, but one thing is common to all; they will not pay for extra accommodation and travel expenses unless it has been deemed absolutely medically necessary.

It is important to know what kind of healthcare is on offer in your destination before purchasing travel insurance as some countries have healthcare agreements with the UK. This may reduce the cost of the insurance you need.

Useful contacts:
www.travelinsuranceguide.org.uk
www.travmed.com
www.masta-travel-health.com
http://treehouse.ofb.net/go/en/vaccinations
www.hobotraveler.com/water.php

Avoiding health hiccups in the EU
Don't forget your EHIC

The European Health Insurance Card (EHIC) allows you to access state-provided healthcare in all European Economic Area (EEA) countries and Switzerland at a reduced cost or sometimes free of charge.

Everyone who is resident in the UK should have one and carry it with them when travelling abroad. Remember to check your EHIC is still valid before you travel. Applying for the card is free and it's valid for up to five years.

Presenting the EHIC entitles you to treatment that may become necessary during your trip, but doesn't allow you to go abroad specifically to receive medical care. However, maternity care, renal dialysis and managing the symptoms of pre-existing or chronic conditions that arise while abroad are all covered by the EHIC.

Your EHIC will allow you access to the same state-provided healthcare as a resident of the country you are visiting. However, many countries expect the patient to pay towards their treatment, and even with an EHIC you might be expected to do the same. You may be able to seek reimbursement for this cost when you are back in the UK if you are not able to do so in the other country.

The EHIC is NOT an alternative to travel insurance. It will not cover any private medical healthcare or the cost of things such as mountain rescue in ski resorts, repatriation to the UK or lost or stolen property.

For these reasons and others, it is important to have both an EHIC and a valid private travel insurance policy. Some insurers now insist you hold an EHIC and many will waive the excess if you have one.

Applying for an EHIC is easy. Even if you don't have any plans to travel in the near future, it is always a good idea to get one.

More info:
www.nhs.uk/NHSEngland/Healthcareabroad

Don't be a fish out of water

Culture shock is feeling lost or uncomfortable in a new country. Symptoms can include homesickness, disorientation, even fear. Culture shock will hit you hardest when you move to a country that is completely different from your own, often a Third World country if you are moving from a developed country in the West.

You can cushion yourself against the effects of culture shock by learning as much as you can about your new country before setting foot there.

Finnish-Canadian anthropologist Kalvero Oberg coined the term 'culture shock' and described the various stages you may go through when moving to another country.

Oberg believed all those travelling abroad were affected by culture shock, with some experiencing much stronger reactions than others.

Oberg identified five such stages; other experts believe it is a six or even a seven-stage process. Not everyone goes through all these stages but most experience the highs and lows of living in a new culture.

Oberg found that the human experience of living in a new country was almost like a disease – with a cause, symptoms and a cure. Those moving abroad were like a fish out of water, he said, unfamiliar with the cues of interpersonal communication in the new culture – body language, words, facial expressions, tone of voice, idioms and slang.

Oberg's five phases:

1. The honeymoon phase
During the first few days everything usually goes fairly smoothly. The newcomer, excited about being in a new place with new sights and sounds, new smells and tastes, accepts problems as just part of the newness.

Often the red carpet has been rolled out and the newcomer is cushioned against practical difficulties.

2. The rejection phase
As the support diminishes, the newcomer has to deal with the practical problems of day-to-day life: transport, shopping, accommodation and communication and notices only the bad things about the new environment.

3. The regression phase
Homesickness kicks in. You spend most of this time complaining about your new country and culture and thinking about your home country and wondering why you ever left. The problems you had there are forgotten.

4. The recovery phase
You begin to feel more comfortable with the language, customs and food and may even find yourself preferring some things in the host country to things at home.

5. Reverse culture shock:
This occurs when you return home after a considerable period away. You have become so used to the habits and customs of the new country you may find that you are no longer completely comfortable in your home country and it takes a while to readapt.

... how to go with the flow

Culture shock is simply a form of learning and will almost certainly affect you, but it wears off quickly. There are ways that the effects of culture shock can be lessened.

- Studying the culture and language before you go helps.
- Become involved socially as soon as possible by joining a group, club, gym, etc.
- Once you have arrived – and before you have had the chance to establish social contacts – don't sit around being negative and critical which prolongs your gloom.
- Keep busy – learn ten new foreign phrases a day, for example.
- Look for the best, not the worst, in your situation.

Here's the quick answer

For easy reference all amounts in this section are quoted in £sterling

This is a 'snapshot' view of entry requirements for all the countries covered in the International Retirement Directory. You will find fuller details in each country section. All the figures have been converted into sterling to enable easy comparison.

ARGENTINA
A monthly income of £500.

AUSTRALIA
No family there? You need a minimum annual income of £28,000 – and a lump sum of 10 times that amount.

AZORES
No problem – the Azores are an autonomous region of Portugal.

BALEARICS
No problem. The islands are a province of Spain.

BELIZE
£1,250 a month gets you in under the Qualified Retired Persons Incentive law. You need to be 45 years or older.

BOLIVIA
Permanent residence available to retirees and their families with unspecified but "adequate" means of support. Citizenship can be obtained by donation of £6,250-15,500, the larger sum covering the main applicant, spouse and dependent children under 18.

BRAZIL
The minimum required for a Permanent Resident Visa is a monthly income of £1,250 for the applicant and two legal dependants.

CANADA
There's a 10-year waiting list for parents and grandparents under the family reunification visa classification. You can jump the queue if you're worth £444,000 and be willing to lend half of it to the Canadian Government – interest free! Options: Investor/ Entrepreneur programmes which require candidates to commit £166,000-444,000.

CANARY ISLANDS
Straightforward. It's another autonomous region of Spain.

CAPE VERDE
To obtain residency you need evidence of a monthly pension or income of 130,000 Cape Verdean escudos (about $1,500).

CARIBBEAN
It's all to do with money – and plenty of it, in fees, investment or property ownership – which opens the door to most Caribbean islands but different rules apply to most of the islands. See country sections.

CHILE
One of the easiest countries in which to obtain residency with various classes of permanent residence. A Temporary Residence Visa takes about two months to obtain and costs £220. An application for a Rentista or Retiree Visa can be made by post once you arrive and requires you to prove unspecified but adequate funds.

COLOMBIA
To obtain a permanent visa as a retiree you need a monthly guaranteed income of 10 times the Colombian minimum monthly wage. The bottom line is that you need about £14,000 a year to qualify. An alternative is the Investor's Visa for which there is a requirement for a minimum deposit of £66,000 with the Banco de la Republica.

COSTA RICA
One of the cheapest. You can obtain a retiree Pensionado Visa if you can prove an income of £625 a month from a source outside Costa Rica.

CROATIA
No visa is required for a stay of up to 90 days but red tape is worst here than most places. First a Temporary Residence Permit and loads of documents are required, all translated into Croatian by certified translator and legalised at the Croatian Embassy at £11 for the first page, and £5 per page for all other pages. An 'apostille'* must be attached to each relevant document.

CYPRUS
Cyprus does not require EU citizens to have residence permits. Residential status is established after living there for 185 days a year.

ECUADOR
The Pensioner 10-I Visa is available for those who receive a guaranteed monthly income of £500, plus £66 for each dependant. An alternative is the Investment Visa, under which the applicant has to purchase real estate worth £15,625 (£330 more for each dependant).

EGYPT
Three-month tourist visa on arrival, then you must apply for either a three-year Temporary Residence Permit or a five-year Residence Permit, a formality if you own property in Egypt.

FRANCE
Few formalities for EU citizens.

GREECE
The Residence Permit has been replaced by the Registration Certificate but a new document available to EU nationals is the Permanent Residence Certificate (Engrafo Monimis Diamonis) which is optional.

INDIA (GOA)
A visa for a six-month stay is relatively easy to obtain but there are tough laws on foreigners buying property and a five-year residential visa is notoriously difficult to obtain and renew.

INDONESIA
To obtain a Temporary Stay Permit, renewable annually, you must be at least 55 years old and be able to prove an income of at least £940 a month. After five years you can apply for a permanent permit (KITAP).

ITALY
Few formalities for EU citizens.

* An 'apostille certificate' authenticates the signature of the public official who has signed a document and deems it to be a legal entity.

MALAYSIA

Applicants aged 50 and above must have a pension income of £2,000 a month and £100,000 in liquid assets. Other requirements include a medical report and medical insurance but exemptions may be given in the case of age or medical condition.

MALTA

'Economically self-sufficient' EU nationals can move to Malta providing they have sufficient resources not to become a burden on the state. Current requirements are capital of at least £12,000 or a weekly income of £77 or, in the case of a married couple, capital of £20,000 or a weekly income of £80.

MEXICO

The Rentista Visa (FM3 visa) is for foreign nationals who live off the income from savings and investments or any legal income from abroad. The minimum monthly income is £720 per head of family plus £340 for each dependant.

NEW ZEALAND

New Zealand has no such thing as a retirement visa. There are two visas which allow in those over 55: the Investor Visa – you need £608,000 to invest and there is an upper age limit of 65 – or the Family Visa but candidates must still meet health, character and (fairly low) minimum income requirements.

NICARAGUA

Nicaragua offers a package of incentives to encourage foreign retirees. The minimum age is 45. Applicants must prove a "stable, permanent income generated abroad" of not less than £250 a month and £66 for each family member.

PANAMA

Panama offers a mass of incentives and discounts on everything from travel to restaurant meals, doctors' bills and cinema tickets. You need an income of at least £625 a month and £155 for each dependent.

PARAGUAY

You need a health certificate, an 'economic solvency statement' showing a deposit in a bank in Paraguay of at least £3,125 and a deed showing you have bought a property in Paraguay.

PERU

£625 a month will get you permanent residence plus £310 for each dependent.

PHILIPPINES

The Special Resident Retiree's Visa (SRRV) is a non-immigrant visa with multiple entry/indefinite stay privileges and comes with a number of services, privileges and benefits.
The visa requires financial deposts of £50,000 for those aged 35-49 years old and £33,000 for those aged 50 years and over.

PORTUGAL

EU nationals can stay in Portugal for up to three months without having to comply with any formalities. To remain longer you must apply for a Registration Certificate which is valid for five years and requires you to show you have sufficient funds to support yourself.

SOUTH AFRICA

You need to prove a monthly income of at least about £1,500 from a pension, an annuity or other assets. Initially you apply for a Temporary Residence Permit which allows multiple re-entry.
You can then apply for a Retired Person Permit which has to be renewed every four years.

SPAIN

The same as in Portugal. After three months EU citizens must register in person at the Foreigners' Office (Oficina de Extranjeros) in their province of residence or at designated police and obtain a Registration Certificate.

THAILAND

You need the "O-A" (Long Stay) visa which has to be renewed annually. You have to be 50 or over and apply inperson at Thai Embassy. You need a bank statement showing you have assets of £14,000 and an annually income equivalent to about £14,000.

TUNISIA

Big on bureaucracy and it's a long-winded process to get a Carte de Sejour. Some foreign residents don't bother and simply leave the country every three months. The police issue a Temporary Carte de

Sejour and you may have to make several return visits and wait several weeks (or even months). Loads of documents required and everything has to be translated into Arabic or French – or both. You also need evidence of adequate means of support.

TURKEY

You get a 30-day visitor visa on entry and can then apply for a residence permits at the Alien's Branch of local police (you can apply from abroad – it takes up to eight weeks). You will also need evidence to prove adequate (unspecified) retirement income.

UAE

A 30-day visitor visa is granted on arrival. Property purchase normally entitles the buyer and immediate family to residence visas, normally issued for three years. Applicants for residency visas must pass medical and security checks.

URUGUAY

Any foreigner with temporary immigration status can apply for permanent residence. Change in status must be by written request to the immigration authority and you need evidence of a monthly income of £940.

USA

There's no retirement visa that allows permanent residence but you can legally spend up to 90 days per visit without a visa or up to 180 days with a B-2 'snowbird' visa. Then there's the (non-immigrant) E-2 visa that enables investors to live in the USA. The investment level is £95,000-250,000. The downside of the E-2 is that it has a 'non-immigrant' status and lapses if you dispose of the investment.
Best bet is the EB5 which requires an investment of £310,000 and, although not a retirement visa as such, is as good as since it leads to a Green Card.

VENEZUELA

A monthly (attested) income of £750 (plus £330 for each accompanying family member) will get you a 'Visitors with Fixed Income' visa.

CRUISING
FOR RETIREMENT

By Simon Veness, Editor
World of Cruising Magazine

Finding the right region in which to consider that all-important retirement home, holiday hideaway or new start can be hard enough, let alone finding that one property that is exactly what you need when you get there.

But there is one handy solution in getting to grips with a large area in a short period of time – by sea.

Cruising has become the big (in every sense!) attraction for holiday-goers in recent years, with some of the most luxurious facilities, high-tech amenities, eye-catching styles – and rewarding opportunities.

The sheer value for money provided by a sea-going sojourn are now well documented, along with the huge variety of choice – from headline-grabbing mega-liners to small-scale deluxe boutique vessels.

But one element which many still overlook – and which is of particular note to those looking for that new home – is the way in which you can cover a large area in quite a short space of time (and in great style).

In each case you will get a full day to get the feel for places as varied as Palma and Palermo; Constantza and Cartagena; and Livorno and Limassol. You can compare Portugal with Spain, Sicily with Sardinia or Malta with Tunisia in terms of the general lifestyle and ambience.

And, while a typical Med cruise will showcase the widest range of countries and cultures, there are similar opportunities when you look a little further afield. Northern Europe and the Baltic is another regular cruise route in the summer, with typical itineraries taking in much of Scandinavia, Latvia, Germany and Poland.

Or how about the Caribbean? Here you can combine the perfect holiday rest-cure with house-hunting in places such as Florida, Grand Cayman, Jamaica, the Turks and Caicos islands, the Virgin Islands, Barbados, St Kitts, Trinidad and Martinique.

> *"The important thing to bear in mind when sampling this ocean-going idyll for the first time is to ensure you consult a specialist cruise agent"*

You can even think more exotic and consider the likes of Aruba, Curacao, Belize, Honduras, Costa Rica and Colombia. The permutations are seemingly endless, but in each case there is a genuine opportunity to 'test the water' in a variety of places that would be difficult (and certainly more expensive) to combine in any other manner.

CRUISING
FOR RETIREMENT

For instance, on a two-week Western Mediterranean cruise your moving holiday vehicle will call at places like southern Spain, the Balearic isles, the Cote D'Azur in France, the Neapolitan Riviera in Italy, Sardinia, Corsica, Malta and North Africa.

Take the Eastern Med voyage and you will sample the Venetian Riviera, Croatia, Greece, the sparkling Aegean islands, Cyprus, Turkey and even, in some instances, the countries of the Black Sea – Bulgaria, Romania and Ukraine.

But you also don't need to limit your thinking to cruising's mainstream (good as it is). The Far East is increasingly an enticing destination for the cruise lines, and you will now find voyages that will showcase countries like Malaysia, Thailand and Indonesia in the space of little more than seven days. There are both specific cruises within that region or sectors of World Cruises which take in a large slice of 'Down Under,' with Sydney to Singapore being a regular route.

The important thing to bear in mind when sampling this ocean-going idyll for the first time is to ensure you consult a specialist cruise agent, as there is a lot to consider when booking this kind of holiday. There is a truly mind-boggling array of choice these days, and you need to make sure the one you pick is the one that most suits your needs and style.

At the last count, there were some 40 mainstream cruise lines from which to choose, offering more than 200 ships sailing to areas as diverse as Alaska and the Amazon, New England and New Zealand.

"There is a truly mind-boggling array of choice these days, and you need to make sure the one you pick is the one that most suits your needs and style"

The Association of Cruise Experts (ACE or www.cruiseexperts.org) is a body geared towards training and representing the best cruise agents in the country, and you can be confident of finding the right expertise in consulting one of their members. Sussex-based The Cruise Line Ltd (www.cruiseline.co.uk) is a good example of an ACE agent, and their expert consultants are exceedingly well trained in ensuring the right passenger is on the right ship and destination.

But beware! Once you have sampled a cruise, there is a very good chance you will want to try another, and another. Put simply, this is an addictive business and it's easy to get hooked on holidaying on the high seas. But what a way to go!

Embassies and High Commissions in London

Where available we have included contact details for consular/visa sections. Website addresses can be found in each country's Contact Directory

High Commission for Antigua & Barbuda
2nd Floor, 45 Crawford Place, W1H 4LP
020 7258 0070
enquiries@antigua-barbuda.com

Embassy of the Argentine Republic
65 Brook Street, W1K 4AH
020 7318 1300
info@argentine-embassy-uk.org
Consulate General
27 Three Kings Yard, W1K 4DF
020 7318 1340

Australian High Commission
Australia House, Strand, WC2B 4LA
020 7379 4334

High Commission of the Commonwealth of the Bahamas
10 Chesterfield Street, W1J 5JL
020 7408 4488
Information@bahamashclondon.net

Barbados High Commission
1 Great Russell Street, WC1B 3ND
020 7631 4975
london@foreign.gov.bb

Belize High Commission
Third Floor, 45 Crawford Place, W1H 4LP
020 7723 3603
020 7723 9637
bzhc-lon@btconnect.com

Bolivian Embassy
106 Eaton Square, SW1W 9AD
020 7235 4255/2257
bolivianembassy@yahoo.co.uk
Consular Section
020 7235 4248/4255
Consulado@boembassy-london.com

Embassy of Brazil
32 Green Street, WlK 7AT
020 7499 0877/020 7399 9000/020 7399 9004
infolondres@brazil.org.uk
Consular Section
3-4 Vere Street, W1G ODH
020 7659 1554

Canadian High Commission
Macdonald House, 1 Grosvenor Square, W1K 4AB
020 7258 6600
General Enquiries 020 7258 6600
ldn@international.gc.ca
Immigration & Visa Section
38 Grosvenor Street, W1K 4AA
Immigration & Visa Information 020 7258 6699

Embassy of the Republic of Cape Verde
Avenue Jeane 2, 1050 Brussels
0032 2 643 6270

Embassy of Chile
12 Devonshire Street, W1G 7DS
020 7580 6392
embachile@embachile.co.uk
Consulate General
12 Devonshire Street, W1G 7DS
020 7580 1023

Embassy of Colombia
3 Hans Crescent, SW1X 0LN
020 7589 9177/5037
mail@colombianembassy.co.uk
Consulate General
3rd Floor, Westcott House, 35 Portland Place, W1B 1AE
020 7637 9893 or 020 7927 7121
info@colombianconsulate.co.uk

Embassy of Costa Rica
14 Lancaster Gate, W2 3LH
020 7706 8844
Costarica@btconnect.com
Consulate General
12 Devonshire Street, W1G 7DS
020 7580 1023

Embassy of the Republic of Croatia
21 Conway Street, W1T 6BN
020 7387 2022
croemb.london@mvp.hr

High Commission for the Republic of Cyprus
13 St James's Square, SW1Y 4LB
020 7321 4100
cyphclondon@dial.pipex.com
Consular Section
020 7321 4101/3/6

Office of the High Commissioner for the Commonwealth of Dominica
1 Collingham Gardens, SW5 0HW
Fax 020 7373 8743
dominicahighcom@btconnect.com

Embassy of the Dominican Republic
139 Inverness Terrace, W2 6JF
020 7727 7091
info@dominicanembassy.org.uk
Consular Section 020 7727 6285

Embassy of Ecuador
Flat 3B
3 Hans Crescent, SW1X 0LS
020 7584 8084/2648/1367
eecugranbretania@mmrree.gov.ec
Consular Section
1st Floor, Uganda House, 58/59 Trafalgar Square
London WC2N 5DX
Ceculondres@mmrree.gov.ec

Embassies and High Commissions in London

Embassy of the Arab Republic of Egypt
26 South Street,
W1K 1DW
020 7499 3304/2401
Consulate General
2 Lowndes Street,
SW1X 9ET
020 7235 9719
info@egyptianconsulate.co.uk

Embassy of France
58 Knightsbridge,
SW1X 7JT
020 7073 1000
Fax 020-7073 1004
www.ambafrance-uk.org
Consular Section
21 Cromwell Road,
SW7 2EN
020 7073 1200

Embassy of Greece
1A Holland Park,
W11 3TP
020 7229 3850
political@greekembassy.org.uk
Consulate General
020 7221 6467
0906 5540 744 (Visas only)
consulategeneral@greekembassy.org.uk

High Commissioner for India
India House, Aldwych,
WC2B 4NA.
020 7836 8484
administrativewing@hcilondon.in

Embassy of the Republic of Indonesia
38 Grosvenor Square,
W1K 2HW
020 7499 7661
Fax 020 7491 4993
www.indonesianembassy.org.uk
Consular Department & Visa Section
38A Adam's Row,
W1K 2HW

Italian Embassy
14 Three Kings Yard, Davies Street,
W1K 4EH
020 7312 2200
Embasciata.london@esteri.it
Consular Section
38 Eaton Place,
SW1X 8AN
020 7235 9371
consolato.londra@esteri.it
(Visa Office: visti.londra@esteri.it)

Jamaican High Commission
1-2 Prince Consort Road,
SW7 2BZ
020 7823 9911
jamhigh@jhcuk,com

Malaysian High Commission
45 Belgrave Square,
SW1X 8QT
020 7235 8033
mwlon@btconnect.com
Consular Section
020 7919 0210

Malta High Commission
Malta House,
36-38 Piccadilly,
W1J OLE
020 7292 4800
maltahighcommission.london@gov.mt
visa.london@gov.mt

Embassy of Mexico
16 St. George Street,
W1S 1FD
020 7499 8586
Embgbretana@sre.gob.mx
Consular Section
16a St George Street,
W1S 1FD
Consulmexuk@sre.gob.mx

New Zealand High Commission
2nd Floor, New Zealand House,
80 Haymarket,
SW1Y 4TQ

NZ Immigration Service
General Enquiries 09069 100 100

Embassy of Nicaragua
Suite 31, Vicarage House,
58-60 Kensington Church Street,
W8 4DP
020 7938 2373
Embaniclondon@btconnect.com

Embassy of Panama
40 Hertford Street,
W1J 7SH
020 7493 4646
panama1@btconnect.com
Consulate General
40 Hertford Street,
W1 7SH
020 7409 2255
legalizations@panamaconsul.co.uk

Embassy of the Republic of Paraguay
Chancery Division 3rd Floor,
344 Kensington High Street,
W14 8NS
020 7610 4180
Consular Section
020 7610 4180
embapar@btconnect.com

Embassy of Peru
52 Sloane Street,
SW1X 9SP
020 7235 1917/8340/3802
postmaster@peruembassy-uk.com
Consulate General
52 Sloane Street, Basement,
SW1X 9SP
020 7838 9223/9224
peruconsulate-uk@btconnect.

Embassy of the Republic of the Philippines
6-8 Suffolk Street,
SW1Y 4HG
020 7451 1800
embassy@philemb.co.uk

Consular Section
Passport Information 020 7451 1818
visaofficer@philemb.co.uk

Embassy of Portugal
11 Belgrave Square,
SW1X 8PP
020 7235 5331
london@portembassy.co.uk
Consular Section
3 Portland Place,
W1B 1HR.
020 7291 3770
mail@cglon.dgaccp.pt

High Commission for Saint Christopher & Nevis
10 Kensington Court,
W8 5DL
020 7937 9718
sknhighcomm@btconnect.com

High Commission for Saint Lucia
1 Collingham Gardens,
SW5 0HW
020 7370 7123
hcslu@btconnect.com

High Commission for Saint Vincent & the Grenadines
10 Kensington Court,
W8 5DL
020 7565 2874
Info@svghighcom.co.uk

South African High Commission
South Africa House,
Trafalgar Square,
WC2N 5DP
020 7451 7299

Embassy of Spain
39 Chesham Place,
SW1X 8SB
020 7235 5555
emb.londres@maec.es
Consular Section
20 Draycott Place, SW3 2RZ
020 7589 8989

0906 550 8970 (Visa Information)
020 7594 4905 (Schengen Visa)
conspalon@mail.mae.es

Royal Thai Embassy
29-30 Queen's Gate,
SW7 5JB
020 7589 2944
thaiduto@btinternet.com
www.thaiembassyuk.org.uk
Consular Section
Basement, 29-30 Queen's Gate,
SW7 5JB
020 7589 2944 ext 5505

High Commissioner of the Republic of Trinidad & Tobago
42 Belgrave Square,
SW1X 8NT
020 7245 9351
tthc@btconnect.com

Embassy of Tunisia
29 Prince's Gate,
SW7 1QG
020 7584 8117

Embassy of the Republic of Turkey
43 Belgrave Square,
SW1X 8PA
020 7393 0202 (Switchboard)
turkish.emb@btclick.com

Embassy of the United Arab Emirates
30 Princes Gate, SW7 1PT
020 7581 1281
information@uaeembassyuk.net
Consular Section
48 Princes Gate,
SW7 2QA
020 7581 1281

American Embassy
24 Grosvenor Square,
W1A 1AE
020 7499 9000

Embassy of Uruguay
125 Kensington High Street, W8 5SF
020 7937 4170
emburuguay@emburuguay.org.uk

Embassy of the Bolivarian Republic of Venezuela
1 Cromwell Road,
SW7 2HW
020 7584 4206 or 020 7581 2776
info@venezlon.co.uk

REPRESENTATIVES OF BRITISH OVERSEAS TERRITORIES
Anguilla
c/o 78 Plumer Road, High Wycombe,
Bucks, HP11 2SR
01494 447 033
rjewilliams@sky.com

British Virgin Islands
BVI House,
15 Upper Grosvenor Street,
W1K 7PJ
020 7355 9570
dsmith@bvi.org.uk

Cayman Islands
Cayman Islands Government Office
6 Arlington Street,
SW1A 1RE
020 7491 7772
jpdilbert@cigo.co.uk

Montserrat
Government of Montserrat
180-186 Kings Cross Road,
WC1X 9DE
020 7520 2622
j.panton@montserratgov.co.uk

Turks and Caicos Islands
Turks and Caicos Islands Government
Office
42 Westminster Palace Gardens, 1-7
Artillery Row,
SW1P 1RR
020 7222 9024

Country index